Study Guide

to accompany

Greenberg and Page

STRUGGLE FOR DEMOCRACY

Fifth Edition

James Lance Taylor
University of San Francisco

Longman

New York • San Francisco • Boston
London • Toronto • Sydney • Tokyo • Singapore • Madrid
Mexico City • Munich • Paris • Cape Town • Hong Kong • Montreal

Study Guide to accompany Greenberg/Page, *Struggle for Democracy, 5/e*

Please visit our website at http://www.awlonline.com

ISBN: 0-321-05266-8

12345678910 - VG- 03020100

CONTENTS

Chapter 1
DEMOCRACY AND AMERICAN POLITICS

Key Concepts and Objectives

The Key Concepts and Objectives highlight the fundamental goals and main points of this chapter. This section serves as a guide to a basic understanding of the objectives of your textbook.

After reading this chapter, you should be able to:
- Explain how the organizing framework of *The Struggle for Democracy* may be used to understand and evaluate the American political process.
- Think critically about how democracy can be used as a standard to evaluate American government and politics.
- Understand the relationship of the citizenry to the laws and government of the United States.
- Develop both supporting and opposing views of the concept of majority rule, compared to other forms of government, as the key component of a democratic process.
- Explain the contrasting theories of direct democracy and representative democracy, and determine the circumstances in which they could operate.
- Describe the fundamental principles of representative democracy, including popular sovereignty, political equality, political liberty, and majority rule.
- Identify the social and political issues that led to the passage of the first comprehensive Civil Rights Act in 1964.
- Describe how the Civil Rights Act of 1964 and the Voting Rights Act of 1965 were enacted into law and how the legislation changed American society.
- Identify key terms and concepts used in Chapter 1.

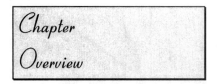

This section provides a brief overview of the chapter contents. Read this section as a preview **before** *reading your textbook. Then use this material as a review to help you retain information from your reading.*

➔INTRODUCTION TO PART ONE: MAIN THEMES

American political life has always involved a struggle among individuals, groups, classes, and institutions over the meaning, extent, and practice of democracy. The goal of the authors of the textbook is to help students critically analyze and evaluate how American government and politics work together to enhance or limit democratic processes in the United States and other parts of the world. **Part One** of the text explains the overall plan of the book, describes the main themes of the book, and explains why it is important to understand the topics that are explored.

The authors introduce the major theme that ties the book together—*the struggle for democracy*. This suggests that despite the tremendous progress that has been made in areas ranging from voting rights to the creation nondiscriminatory public policies such as "Jim Crow" segregation, democracy is still incomplete in the United States; the continuing struggle for democracy is a major feature of American political history.

➔ROBERT MOSES AND THE STRUGGLE FOR AFRICAN-AMERICAN VOTING RIGHTS

The right to vote in periodic elections is one of the essential features of democracy. Different citizens groups such as property-less men (during the "Jacksonian Revolution") African American men (15th Amendment in 1870), women (19th Amendment in 1920), and young people 18-20 years old (25th Amendment in 1971), secured the right to vote only after major social upheavals and political movements. The struggle of individuals such as **Robert Moses** (founder of the "freedom schools") influenced the passage of fundamental civil rights legislation.

The **Civil Rights Acts** of 1957 and 1960 were intended to guarantee that African-Americans living in the southern states be allowed to vote. These laws had little effect in rigidly segregated states in the early 1960s, due largely to discriminatory voting registration rules (such as the "poll tax" and literacy tests), economic pressures, and physical intimidation and violence. The **Student Non-Violent Coordinating Committee (SNCC)** launched its **Voter Education Project** in 1961, with the goal of ending black political isolation and powerlessness in the Deep

South states. Nevertheless, African-American voting registration in Mississippi barely increased in the early 1960s. The Voter Education Project became one of the key building blocks of a powerful citizenship rights movement, but a significant increase in voter registration did not occur until after the enactment of the **1965 Voting Rights Act**. Still, even with its shortcomings, the gains that different citizens groups have secured in the United States have encouraged similar democratic efforts in other parts of the world such as South Africa, Eastern Europe and Latin America.

→DEMOCRACY

The advantage of using **democracy** as the *main standard of evaluation* in this text stems from the relevance of democracy for judging the adequacy of the political process and from its exalted position among the values held by most Americans. Except for some **anarchist** intellectuals, who generally reject organized government because of the ways it may stifle individuals' natural sense of mutuality and altruism, most people in the modern world see government as necessary and inevitable. Since governments develop in organized society, the question "who is to govern?" is answered by, the common, **ordinary citizens** who are not necessarily the wealthiest, most sophisticated, or best trained. Democracy is increasingly regarded as the best form of government because a majority of the common people have input in what is best for society. The **legitimacy** of the laws and governments in a democratic society rests on the belief that it best protects individual civil and human rights, provides an opportunity for economic growth, and personal freedom.

→THE DEMOCRATIC IDEA

The *demos* (or common people majority) was accustomed to being ruled by smaller groups of individuals who inherited their status as part of the aristocratic classes (the *few*), or by a king or monarchy (*the one*). As a form of rule, democracy was very unpopular during the eighteenth century because ordinary people were viewed negatively. Still rule by an aristocracy or monarchy is contrary to democracy because they often lead to **tyranny** where leaders abuse their power. Thus this chapter places the democratic ideal at the center of the American political system as an evaluative approach for understanding American politics.

→DIRECT VERSUS REPRESENTATIVE DEMOCRACY

The work of women and slaves in Athenian society made it possible for adult male citizens to engage directly in the decision making process of the city. Thus **direct, participatory democracy** requires that all citizens be able to participate directly in the political process. However, the large population **size** and the restraints of **time** make the Athenian idea of direct, participatory democracy incompatible with large societies such as the United States where elected *representatives* do the public business on behalf of the people in a **representative or (indirect) democracy**. Under this form of government, the people rule indirectly through elected representatives.

➜FUNDAMENTALS OF REPRESENTATIVE DEMOCRACY

The text focuses on three *fundamental attributes of democracy*: **popular sovereignty**, which requires that the ultimate source of authority rests with the people and that government functions in the interest and "deliberative will" of a majority of citizens who are active and *participate* in the political process armed with *accurate political information*; **political equality**, which refers to decision making where each person carries the same weight in voting and other political decision making, is coded in the **"equal protection" clause of the 14th Amendment** to the U.S. Constitution; and **political liberty**, under which certain basic freedoms such as those listed in the **1st Amendment** including the freedom of speech, of conscience, of religion, and of the press, are essential to form the popular will and translate it into policy.

➜OBJECTIONS TO MAJORITARIAN REPRESENTATIVE DEMOCRACY

There are also some possible objections to democracy, each of which is refuted by the authors of the textbook. Criticisms of democracy include the following:

Democracy Leads to Bad Decisions-A majority can be unwise, cruel, and/or uncaring, and can be misled by unscrupulous or incompetent leaders. In response, the textbook refers to democratic theorist **Robert Dahl**, who maintains that no other form of decision making can be shown to lead consistently to better and wiser decisions than democracy.

"Majority Tyranny" Threatens Liberty-Many of the Founders of the American republic such as James Madison feared that majority rule would undermine freedom and threaten individual rights. Atheists and communists are two recent groups that have had their rights infringed upon by the majority in American society. However, the text notes that there is no evidence that the *many* consistently threaten liberty more than the *few* or the *one*. Violations of freedom seem as likely to come from powerful individuals and groups or from government officials as from the majority. Such was the case in the 1790s when criticism of public officials was a violation of the *Alien and Sedition Acts;* during the first "Red Scare" after WWI; and during the second "Red Scare" of the 1940s and 1950s when anticommunist *McCarthyism* reigned. Still majority rule does not uniquely or inevitably threaten basic political liberties.

The People Are Irrational and Incompetent-Scholars have argued that most Americans are politically apathetic, poorly informed, and unstable in their political views. The authors, however, view the political rationality of the American public more optimistically than these other scholars.

Majoritarian Democracy Threatens Minorities-Because the individuals who make up the "losing" minority on one issue such as welfare reform, can potentially be part of the majority in other issues, the authors reject the idea that majoritarian democracy necessarily threatens minority rights. Different groups such as Native Americans, African Americans, the Irish, Eastern European, Asian, and Latin American immigrants, Jews, gays and lesbians certainly have been subjected to majority intolerance and violence. Nevertheless, the authors cite Robert Dahl's findings that there is no evidence to support the belief that the rights of minorities are better protected under other forms of government, whether rule by *the few* or by *the one*. Equal citizenship rights (such as the right to vote, hold public office, jury service, to be protected from violence) coupled with a full range of civil liberties (such as freedom of speech and so forth) best preserve minority rights in a majoritarian democracy.

➜DEMOCRACY AS AN EVALUATIVE STANDARD: HOW DEMOCRATIC ARE WE?

A number of questions related to **popular sovereignty, political equality,** and **political liberty** emerge from the foregoing discussion concerning just how democratic America society and government are. Even though these ideals are probably unattainable in perfect form, they represent important standards and ideals against which we can understand American society and government.

➜A FRAMEWORK FOR UNDERSTANDING HOW AMERICAN POLITICS WORKS

The authors proposes a simple way to organize information and to think about how the American political system works; the authors set out the basic guidelines that enable us to understand government and politics in the United States. Passage of the **1965 Voting Rights Act** is used to illustrate how the main factors of political life are interconnected. To understand why things happen in government and politics, we begin with the actors and institutions most immediately involved in an event or decision, but a full explanation of why events such as the 1965 Voting rights Act happened requires that we move beyond a narrow focus on government officials and daily political affairs.

Organizing the Main Factors of Political Life-The authors use a simple organizing framework or *taxonomy* to help students comprehend the complexities of politics. The framework visualizes the world of American politics as a set of interrelated actors and influences (institutions, groups, and individuals) that operate in four interconnected categories: *structure, political linkage*, and *government and government action*.

The **Structure** category includes more fundamental and enduring factors (such as the U.S. economy, American society, the constitutional rules, the political culture, and the international system) that influence government and politics. Structural factors largely determine what issues become important in American politics (the **political agenda**); shape the distribution of resources and power in American society; and influence the wants, needs, and perceptions of the American people. Constitutional rules structure how political conflict takes place and how government behaves. Your authors consider structural level factors to be particularly important.

The **Political linkage** category includes political actors, institutions, and processes (such as public opinion, political parties, interest groups, the mass media, and elections) that are involved in transmitting the wants and demands of individuals and groups to government officials, and in effecting the policies that the government pursues.

The **Governmental** category includes all public officials and institutions (such as Congress, the president, the executive branch, and the Supreme Court) that have formal, legal responsibilities for making public policy.

The **Government** category looks at government action such as passing laws, issuing rules and regulations that govern society, waging war and providing national defense, settling civil disputes, and providing order and so forth. The *struggle for democracy* has played an important role in American history and remains an important theme in our country today. Democracy holds a special place in Americans' values; it is particularly relevant to judging political processes and is a standard used throughout this text to evaluate the quality of our politics and government. The materials about politics and government are organized in this text in a way that will allow us to understand the confusing details of everyday events and see *why* things happen the way they do. Thus the chapters in **Part Two** of the text focus on the *structure* category. The chapters in **Part Three** focus on the *political linkage* processes and institutions. **Part Four** focuses on *governmental* institutions and leaders, while **Part Five** examines what *government* does.

→CONNECTING THE MAIN FACTORS OF POLITICAL LIFE

The most effective way to understand the relationships between the main analytical categories of this text, the authors demonstrate how they came together in the passage of the historic **1965 Voting Rights Act**. This way, it becomes clearer how governmental, political linkage and structural factors interact to bring about significant change in American politics (government action).

Chapter Outline

This section gives you a comprehensive review of the chapter. Use this outline in combination with your textbook to look for key concepts and objectives, to identify essential terms and names, and to gain a basic understanding of political practices and principles from this chapter.

I. **INTRODUCTION TO PART ONE: MAIN THEMES (p. 1)**
    A. The goal of the authors of the textbook is to help students *understand* how American government and politics work.

B. Part One of the text explains the overall plan of the book, describes the main themes of   the book, and explains why it is important to understand the topics that are explored.

   1. Chapter 1 introduces the central thread that ties the book together: *the struggle for democracy.*
   2. The authors explain how the book will make the point that American political life has always involved a struggle among individuals, groups, classes, and institutions over the meaning, extent, and practice of democracy.
      a) This section of the text suggests that democracy has made great progress over the course of United States history, but also that democracy is still incomplete and "imperfectly realized."
      b) The materials about politics and government are organized in a way that will allow us to understand the perplexing details of everyday events and see *why* things happen as they do.

II. ROBERT MOSES AND THE STRUGGLE FOR AFRICAN-AMERICAN VOTING RIGHTS (pp. 3-4)

   A. The right to vote in meaningful elections is fundamental to democracy.
   B. Many Americans won the right to vote only after long struggles, including people without property, women and minorities, and young people.
   C. The **Civil Rights Acts** of 1957 and 1960 were intended to guarantee that African-Americans living in the southern states be allowed to vote.
      1. These laws had little effect in rigidly segregated states in the early 1960s, due largely to biased voting registration rules, economic pressures, and physical intimidation and violence.
      2. The **Student Non-Violent Coordinating Committee (SNCC)** launched its **Voter Education Project** in 1961, with the goal of ending black political isolation and powerlessness in the Deep South.
         a) SNCC wanted to increase black voter registration, challenge exclusionary rules like the **poll tax** and the **literacy test**, and enter African-American candidates in local elections.
         b) SNCC's first step was to create **"freedom schools"** (founded by **Robert Parris Moses**) in some of the most segregated counties in Mississippi, Alabama, and Georgia to educate black citizens about their rights and encourage them to register to vote.
      3. The **Voter Education Project** became one of the key building blocks of a powerful civil rights movement, but a significant increase in voter registration did not occur until after the enactment of the **1965 Voting Rights Act.**
   D. We live in an age of democratic aspiration and upsurge.
      1. People around the globe are demanding the right to govern themselves, and many of them have been successful in places like South Africa and Eastern Europe.
      2. American political ideas and institutions often have provided inspiration for democratic movements elsewhere, but *the struggle for democracy still continues*

in our own society.

III. DEMOCRACY (pp. 5-8)

  A. The goal of the textbook is to help students think analytically about the quality and progress of democracy in the United States; considerable clarification is needed before democracy can be used as a standard of evaluation; we need to be clear about the *meaning* of democracy.

  B. **The democratic idea**

    1. Many of our ideas about democracy originated with the ancient Greeks—the Greek roots of the word *democracy* are *demos* ("the people") and *kratein* ("to rule").

    2. The central meaning of democracy is *rule by ordinary people,* self-government by the *many* as opposed to rule by an aristocracy (*the few*) or a monarch (*the one*).

        a) Democracy involves faith in the capacity of ordinary people to govern themselves wisely.

        b) The purpose of a government is to serve *all* of its people.

    3. None but the people themselves can be relied upon to know and to act in accord with their own values and interests. *Tyranny* results from the abuse of power.

  C. **Direct versus representative Democracy**

    1. **Direct participatory democracy**—to the ancient Greeks, democracy meant;

        a) Rule by the people exercised *directly* in *open assemblies*.

        b) People actively and directly ruling themselves.

        c) That citizens be able to regularly meet to debate and make decisions.

        d) Only "free" male citizens participated in Athenian direct democracy

        e) New England town meetings are one form of direct participatory democracy that exists in the United States.

    2. **Representative democracy**—rule by the people, exercised *indirectly* through representatives selected by the people.

    3. Representative (indirect) democracy seems to be the only form of democracy that is feasible in large-scale societies.

    4. Millions of citizens cannot practically meet in open assemblies.

    5. The Internet has great potential for more direct involvement of the citizenry.

IV. FUNDAMENTAL PRINCIPLES OF REPRESENTATIVE DEMOCRACY (pp. 8-14)

  A. **Popular sovereignty**

    1. Popular sovereignty exists when the ultimate source of public authority rests with the people.

    2. Government *policies reflect what the people want.*

    3. Democracy is incompatible with aristocracy (rule by the *few*) and monarchy (rule by the *one*)

    4. *People participate* in the political process.

5. High-quality information and debate are available
6. The *majority rules*.
    a) Majority rule is the only way to make decisions to be consistent with political equality; the alternative is minority rule, which would unacceptably elevate the few over the many.
    b) Majority rule maximizes the number of people involved in decision making; this enhances participation (important to popular sovereignty).
    c) Majority rule benefits from the "pooled judgments" that take into account a broader range of information, opinions, and expertise than any other way of making decisions.

B. **Political equality**
    1. Each person's decision making carries the same weight in voting and other political situations
    2. People deliberate about their common problems and concerns *as equals*. Without political equality, we would not be able to accurately measure or enforce the popular will.
    3. The "equal protection" clause of the 14th Amendment to the US Constitution guarantees political equality to all citizens.
    4. Some thinkers believe that economic equality reinforces political equality.

C. **Political liberty**
    1. Certain basic freedoms are essential to form the popular will and translate it into policy.
    2. Without these liberties (many of which are embodied in the First Amendment to the U.S. Constitution), the other fundamental principles of democracy could not exist; popular sovereignty cannot be guaranteed if people are prevented from participating in politics or if opposition to the government is crushed.
    3. For most people, democracy and liberty are inseparable; this is the concept of *self-government*.
    4. Some thinkers have suggested that democracy threatens, rather than enhances liberty.

D. **Objections to majoritarian representative democracy**
    1. Democracy leads to bad decisions.
    2. A majority can be unwise, cruel, and/or uncaring; it can be misled by unscrupulous or incompetent leaders.
    3. Despite these problems, democratic theorist **Robert Dahl** maintains that no other form of decision making can be shown to lead consistently to better and wiser decisions.
    4. **Majority tyranny** threatens liberty.
        a) The Founders of the American Republic feared that majority rule would undermine freedom and threaten individual rights.
        b) Majority rule constitutes a potential threat to minorities and to liberties; popular "passions" have sometimes stifled the freedoms of groups and

individuals.

    c) Despite instances of majority tyranny in which a majority violated the rights of a minority, there is no evidence that majority rule is a special or unique threat; the majority was not the major culprit in periods of U.S. history when liberty was most endangered, such as the "Red scare" after World War I and the era of McCarthyism in the late 1940s and early 1950s.

5. The people are irrational and incompetent.

    a) Evidence shows that individual Americans do not care a great deal about politics and are rather poorly informed, unstable in their views, and not very interested in the political process.

    b) The authors of your textbook note that this evidence about *individuals* has often been misinterpreted and that the American public taken as an *aggregate* is more informed, sophisticated, and stable in its views than is generally given credit for (see Chapter 5).

    c) Majoritarian democracy threatens minorities. Critics of democracy believe that the majority can be unwise and tyrannical.

        (1) In rebuttal, the authors of the textbook note that the composition of the majority and the minority is always shifting; in most cases, the minority on the losing side of an issue is protected from majority tyranny because the minority is likely to be on the winning side in future decisions.

        (2) More permanent concerns are raised in cases that involve race, ethnicity, or religion, where minority status is fixed; this worry has some historical foundations, based on numerous instances where majorities have trampled on the rights of minorities.

    d) In practice, the threat of majority tyranny may be exaggerated; Robert Dahl points out that there is no evidence to support the belief that minority rights are better protected under alternative forms of political decision making such as fascism, communism, authoritarian dictatorship, or theocracy.

6. Democracy, as defined by your authors, *requires the protection of crucial minority rights*; society falls short of the democratic ideal when a majority violates the citizenship rights and liberties of minorities.

V. DEMOCRACY AS AN EVALUATIVE STANDARD: HOW DEMOCRATIC ARE WE? (pp. 14-15)

    A. This chapter shows how and why the democratic ideal can be used as a measuring rod to evaluate American politics.

    B. Each of the fundamental attributes of democracy (popular sovereignty, political equality, political liberty) suggests a set of questions that will be used throughout this book to think critically about American political life.

    C. How does the political system of the United States measure up to the elements or principles of democracy described in this chapter?

VI. A FRAMEWORK FOR UNDERSTANDING HOW AMERICAN POLITICS WORKS (pp. 15-17)

A. American politics display regular tendencies and patterns.

    1. These patterns can seem random and disconnected without an organized framework through which they can be understood.

    2. The authors use a *taxonomy* or way of categorizing things and ideas in order to make them clearer.

    3. Groups, institutions, laws, and individuals all factor into the workings of the American political system. The authors set out the basic guidelines that enable us to talk about and understand government and politics in the United States.

    4. The main factors of political life are interconnected (illustrated in the text by the passage of the 1965 Voting Rights Act). To understand why things happen in government and politics, we begin with the actors and institutions most immediately involved in an event or decision.

        a) A full explanation of why policies such as the 1965 Voting Rights Act come about requires that we move beyond a narrow focus on government officials and daily political affairs.

        b) For example, economic changes in the nation over the course of many decades triggered the **great migration** of African-Americans from the rural South to the urban North; over the long run, this population shift to states with large blocks of **Electoral College** votes increased the political power of African-Americans.

B. The main factors of political life are organized into four interrelated categories:

    1. **Structure**—includes more fundamental and enduring factors (such as the U.S. economy, American society, the constitutional rules, the political culture, and the international system) that influence government and politics.

        a) *Structural level factors* are particularly important.

        b) Structural factors largely determine what issues become important in American politics (the **political agenda**), shape the distribution of resources and power in American society, and influence the wants, needs, and perceptions of the American people.

        c) Constitutional rules structure how political conflict takes place and how government behaves.

    2. **Political linkage**—includes political actors, institutions, and processes (such as public opinion, political parties, interest groups, the mass media, and elections) that are involved in transmitting the wants and demands of individuals and groups to government officials, and in effecting the policies that the government pursues

    3. **Governmental**—includes all public officials and institutions (such as Congress, the president, the executive branch, and the Supreme Court) that

have formal, legal responsibilities for making public policy
    4. **Government action**—includes what government does such as making laws, waging wars, issuing rules and regulations, providing national defense, and so forth.
  C. The textbook is organized around these four categories—chapters in **Part Two** focus on the structural level; chapters in **Part Three** deal with political linkage processes and institutions; and chapters in **Part Four** are concerned with government institutions and leaders. **Part Five** focuses on what actions government takes on behalf of the nation.

VII. CONNECTING THE MAIN FACTORS OF POLITICAL LIFE (pp. 17-18)
  A. Understanding American politics holistically.
    1. American political life must be understood as an *integrated, ordered whole of what* goes on in government can only be understood by considering all four categories of analysis.
    2. Actions by public officials are not simply the product of the personal desires of such officials, but of the influences and pressures brought to bear by other governmental institutions and by individuals, groups, and classes within the political linkage sphere.
  B. Political linkage institutions and processes can often be understood only when we see how they are shaped by the larger structural context, including factors such as the economy and the political culture.

VIII. SUMMARY (p. 20)
  A. The struggle for democracy has played an important role in American history and remains an important theme in our country today.
  B. Democracy holds a special place in Americans' values; it is particularly relevant to judging political processes and is a standard used throughout this text to evaluate the   quality of our politics and government.
  C. The materials about politics and government are organized in this text in a way that will allow us to understand the confusing details of everyday events and see *why* things happen the way they do.
  D. The framework visualizes the world of American politics as a set of interrelated actors and influences (institutions, groups, and individuals) that operate in three interconnected sectors (structural, political linkage, and governmental).

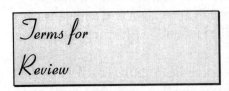

Terms for Review

Use this list to review essential principles, functions, and concepts from this chapter. Refer to your textbook for help in identifying and defining terms on this list. When you study, do not merely memorize terms; ask questions about the material you are reviewing, and look for the importance or significance of each item.

anarchist

civil rights

Civil Rights Acts of 1957 and 1960

civil rights movement

Cold War

democracy

direct democracy

electoral college

freedom schools

governmental level

Jim Crow

linkage institutions

literacy tests

majority rule

majority tyranny

political agenda

political equality

political liberty

political linkage level

poll tax

popular sovereignty

representative democracy

segregation

structural level

Student Non-Violent Coordinating Committee (SNCC)

taxonomy

tyranny

Voter Education Project

voting rights

Voting Rights Act of 1965

Research Topics: Applying What You Have Learned

*You will derive more benefit from your reading if you try to apply what you have learned. Some of the suggested research topics can be answered exclusively from your text, while others require you to conduct some basic research on your own. The references suggested under **Internet Sources** will help you in your search.*

- The Internet can be a powerful tool for conducting research. The **WEB EXPLORATIONS** cover each major section of the chapter and enable you to evaluate issues and questions by exploring Internet sites that serve as general gateways to the World Wide Web. Locate each of the sources listed in Chapter 1, and write a brief description of the type of information that can be found and of what you have learned. Pay particular attention to the site that your text lists for *Internet Sources*.

- Does democracy require equality of income and wealth? Does majority rule undermine freedom and threaten individual rights? What was James Madison's view, and what is your reaction?

- If American political life must be understood as an integrated, ordered whole, how do the constitutional rules structure the structural, political linkage, and governmental sectors?

Internet Sources

A number of sites on the World Wide Web serve as "gateways" to vast collections of material on American government and politics. The following Internet sources are recommended for students who would like to do additional research in areas covered by this chapter. These references would also be helpful in expanding on the questions suggested under Research Topics.

Weblinks: A Guide to Internet Resources in Political Science
www.abacon.com/internetguides/pol/weblinks.html

The Jefferson Project www.capweb.net/classic/jefferson/

Internet Public Library http://ipi.org/ref/RR/static/gov0000.html

Yahoo/Government http://www.yahoo.com/Government/

New York Times, Political Points
www.nytimes.com/library/politics/polpoints.html

Self-Evaluation

Circle the correct answer for each question. Questions are listed in the same order in which the information appears in the text. Use the Answer Key in the back of the Study Guide *to check your responses.*

1. To the ancient Greeks, democracy meant

    a.   Rule by the people, exercised directly in open assemblies.

    b.   Rule by the people, exercised indirectly through elected representatives.

    c.   Rule by the people, exercised by a select few.

    d.   Rule by the people, exercised on their behalf by hereditary positions.

2. According to both Aristotle and Jefferson, the ideal society for the practice of democracy
   a. Is one with a large middle class built on a wide dispersion of private property.
   b. Would be based on a large upper-class elite to make decisions for the smaller middle-class and lower-class populace.
   c. Would have a large middle class of wage earners, but private property would be held by the landed elite.
   d. Is one with a large lower class who would provide the necessary support for large merchants and plantation owners.

3. The central idea of **democracy** is that
   a. Minorities have full power of decision making over all matters that directly or indirectly affect them.
   b. Rule by the majority must prevail, even if majority tyranny is the result.
   c. Ordinary people want to rule themselves and are capable of doing so.
   d. Tyranny by the majority is impossible because a democratic system is based on consent by a rational majority.

4. James Madison and other Founders of the American republic feared that
   a. Minority tyranny would impede democracy by interfering with majority rule.
   b. Democracy would be undermined because the majority of the population would be unwilling to participate in decision making.
   c. Democracy would not develop in the new republic because inadequate educational facilities could not provide adequate training for leadership.
   d. Majority rule would undermine freedom and threaten the rights of the individual.

5. A significant increase in voter registration did not occur until after the enactment of the
   a. 1798 Alien and Sedition Acts.
   b. 1957 Civil Rights Act.
   c. 1961 Voter Education Project.
   d. 1965 Voting Rights Act.

6. Robert Parris Morris was
   a. Founder of the "freedom schools."
   b. The first African-American appointed as a federal judge.
   c. A leading opponent of the Civil Rights Acts of the 1950s and 1960s.
   d. One of the signers of the Declaration of Independence.

7. **Political equality** means that

a. The opinions and preferences of citizens are combined into a binding decision through the principle of majority rule.
b. Each person carries the same weight in voting and other political decision making.
c. Protection will be provided for basic freedom essential to the formation and expression of the popular will and its translation into policy.
d. The will of the majority should not be the ultimate determinant of what government does.

8. The authors of your textbook believe that popular sovereignty, political equality, and political liberty are
    a. Attainable in perfect and absolute form.
    b. Unrealistic standards with little meaning for the American public.
    c. Important only to politicians and historians.
    d. Standards against which we can measure reality.

9. The framework of this textbook is used to
    a   Help us understand why political events occur.
    b. Show how individual rights have been extended.
    c. Understand how the Constitution is interpreted.
    d. Evaluate short-term principles and procedures of politics.

10. Laws that required separation and segregation of the races were commonly known as
    a. Egalitarian laws.
    b. Reapportionment laws.
    c. Jim Crow laws.
    d. Martin Luther King laws.

11. According to the principle of **popular sovereignty**,
    a. Power should be exercised by an educated elite.
    b. The final or ultimate source of authority rests with the people.
    c. A democratic system is based on the concept of material equality.
    d. Majority rule is unacceptable because it may be tyrannical.

12. Which of these statements best reflects the conclusion of your authors concerning democracy as a form of government?
    a. Majority rule constitutes a threat to freedom because majority tyranny often threatens the citizenship rights of a minority.
    b. Citizens are ill-equipped for the responsibility of self-governance and democratic decision making.
    c. Liberty is essential to self-government, and rule by the majority does not seem to be a special or unique threat to liberty.
    d. The American public is too irrational and incompetent for a democratic system to prevail.

13. (T/F) The **political linkage sector** includes political actors, institutions, and processes that are involved in transmitting the wants and demands of individuals and groups to government officials, and in effecting the policies that the government pursues.

14. (T/F) Democracy is the main standard of evaluation used throughout your text, in part because it is a standard based on widely shared values.

15. (T/F) People around the world are demanding the right to governed by military regimes.

16. (T/F) James Madison and other Founders of the American republic believed that majority rule was the only effective way to protect freedom and individual rights.

17. (T/F) **Political liberty** refers to basic freedoms essential to the formation and expression of the popular will and its translation into policy.

18. (T/F) The **governmental sector** of the political system includes fundamental and enduring factors that influence government.

Chapter 2
THE CONSTITUTION

Key Concepts and Objectives

The Key Concepts and Objectives provide a look at the fundamental goals and ideas of this chapter. This section serves as a guide to a basic understanding of the objectives of your textbook.

After reading this chapter, you should be able to:

- Recognize the legacies of the Declaration of Independence and the American Revolution.
- Explain why the Articles of Confederation failed as a governing document.
- Describe the political environment that led to the Constitutional Convention, and explain what the Founders intended to accomplish.
- Identify democratic and undemocratic aspects of the Constitutional Convention.
- Understand the disagreement between proponents of liberty and democracy, and explain the role that the debate played in the formulation of the Constitution.
- Identify the fundamental principles of the U.S. Constitution.
- Describe the major compromises that were adopted at the Constitutional Convention.
- Assess the positions of the Federalists and the Anti-Federalists, and explain why the fight over ratification of the Constitution was so impassioned.
- Explain why the Framers of the Constitution feared certain democratizing and egalitarian tendencies.
- Explain how some democratic practices such as majority rule can lead to majority tyranny.
- Understand the important position of Constitutional rules as part of the structural context of American political life.
- Identify key terms and concepts used in Chapter 2.

```
┌─────────────────────────┐
│  Chapter Overview       │
└─────────────────────────┘
```

This section provides a brief overview of the chapter contents. Read this section as a preview before reading your textbook. Then use this material as a review to help you retain information from your reading.

➔ INTRODUCTION TO PART TWO: STRUCTURE

The chapters in Part Two serve to show the *structural underpinnings* of American politics and government. Structural influences play a substantial role in determining the importance of issues, the distribution of political power, the perceptions that guide the behavior of citizens and public officials, and the ways in which political and governmental institutions operate. Constitutional rules are a particularly important part of the structural context of American political life. The first two chapters explore the *relationship of the constitutional rules and the practice of democracy* in the United States.

The *struggle for democracy* has always been a feature of political life in the United States. Chapter 2 examines the founding of the United States and the formulation of the constitutional rules that shape its politics today. This chapter reviews the heritage of the Declaration of Independence and the Revolution, reveals problems with the Articles of Confederation, explores both democratic and undemocratic facets of the Constitutional Convention, and describes the philosophical and political debates that surrounded the battle over ratification.

The constitutional *rules of the game* are examined as fundamental structural factors that influence American political life. Chapter 3 looks at **federalism** and explores what the framers intended and how federalism has changed over the years.

The basic characteristics of American society influence the working of our political and governmental institutions, as well as the attitudes and behaviors of our citizens and public officials. Chapter 4 looks at this country's place in the world and examines the American economy, society, and political culture, showing how they structure much of what goes on in our political life.

➔ SHAYS'S REBELLION (1786)

The end of the Revolutionary War brought widespread economic problems among farmers, precipitated by the collapse of prices for agricultural products. Several states loaned money to farmers (in the form of **scrip**, or paper money) to pay their taxes and debts and some states passed **stay laws** to postpone taxes and mortgage payments. However, the Massachusetts state legislature—dominated by financial and merchant interests—blocked relief measures for poor farmers. Nonpayment of taxes and debts in Massachusetts led to foreclosure proceedings and imprisonment for debt.

Desperate for relief, farmers in western Massachusetts took up arms to prevent courts from meeting. **Artemas Ward** and other judges were prevented from holding legal proceedings to seize farms for nonpayment of taxes. When Governor **James Bowdoin** issued a proclamation against unlawful assembly and called out the militia to enforce it, the soldiers he sent to Springfield were met with armed farmers led by a former Revolutionary War officer, Captain **Daniel Shays**. The militia withdrew after a long standoff, leaving the rebels in charge and the courts unable to meet. Although the rebellion was quickly put down by armed forces sent from Boston, Shays's Rebellion reinforced the fears of national leaders about the dangers of ineffective state governments and popular democracy out of control.

→THE POLITICAL THEORY OF THE REVOLUTIONARY ERA

Initially, the Revolution was fought *to preserve an existing way of life*—existing rights seemed to be threatened by British policies on trade and taxation. The Revolution was inspired by a concern for **liberty** (which was understood as the *preservation of traditional rights* against the intrusions of government) and accompanied by the development of sentiments for **popular sovereignty** (which assumes that ultimate political authority belongs to the people) and **political equality**.

→THE DECLARATION OF INDEPENDENCE

Delegates to the **Second Continental Congress** did not originally desire independence, but with the publication of Thomas Paine's *Common Sense* they concluded by the spring of 1776 that separation and independence were inescapable. A special committee was appointed to draft a declaration of independence. **Thomas Jefferson** was chosen to draft the document, and the **Declaration of Independence** (primarily the work of Jefferson) was adopted by the Second Continental Congress on July 4, 1776. **South Carolina** was the first state to declare independence from Britain.

Key Ideas in the Declaration of Independence- The philosophy in the Declaration reflected the political culture of the era in which it was written. Prior to the Declaration, the idea of the rule of kings based on a divine right was the dominate view of government. The writing of the Declaration closely follows John Locke's *The Second Treatise of Government*, as it argues that legitimate government can only be established with the consent of the governed. It remains a part of American political culture—particularly the philosophy that human beings possess rights that cannot be legitimately given away or taken from them, that people create government to protect these rights, and that people can withdraw their consent from government and create a new one if government fails to protect rights or if government itself becomes a threat to them. Many revolutions have been influenced by its sentiments including the French Revolution of 1789 and the "velvet revolution" in Czechoslovakia. The main arguments of the Declaration of Independence go as follows:

- *Human beings possess rights that cannot be given away or take from them*: "We hold these truths to be self-evident, that all men are created equal, that they are endowed by their Creator with certain unalienable Rights, that among these are Life, Liberty, and the Pursuit of Happiness."
- *People create government to protect these rights*: "That to secure these rights, Governments are instituted among Men, deriving their just powers from the consent of the governed."
- *If government fails to protect people's rights or itself becomes a threat to them, people can withdraw their consent from that government and create a new one*: "That whenever any Form of Government becomes destructive to these ends, it is the Right of the People to alter or to abolish it, and to institute new Government, laying its foundation on such principles, and organizing its powers in such form, as to them shall seem most likely to effect their Safety and Happiness."

Omissions in the Declaration-American slavery was one of the major subjects that the Declaration carefully avoided although Jefferson's initial draft denounced the British Crown for violating human rights by "captivating and carrying Africans into slavery." The institution of slavery and the ideas of the Declaration of Independence were as contradictory to many citizens then, as it is to us today. Jefferson himself owned slaves and fathered several children with his slave Sally Hemmings. The Declaration was also silent on the political status of women, Native Americans and (free) African-Americans. The signers of the Declaration did not have any of these groups in mind when they called for a new political society based on its principles.

Early State Constitutions-11 of the 13 colonies wrote their constitutions during the Revolutionary War. They shared the following:

- *Bill of rights*. These protected free speech, conscience, and association. *Restrictions on the powers of the executive*. Many states limited governors' terms in office, powers of appointment, and use of veto out of fear of tyranny.
- *Legislative supremacy*. Most state constitutions made the **legislative branch** superior to the **executive branch**.
- *Frequent elections*. The states held annual elections to prevent the emergence of a permanent governing class.

- *Restrictions on the right to vote and hold elective office.* The ownership of property qualified citizens to vote and hold public office. Between thirty and forty percent of white males were excluded from the political life of the states because they did not own land, couldn't afford to pay poll taxes. Women, African slaves, and free Blacks were also excluded. Native Americans had no rights at all.

→THE ARTICLES OF CONFEDERATION: THE FIRST CONSTITUTION

The Articles of Confederation were introduced in the Continental Congress in July 1776 and adopted in 1781. Leaders envisioned a loose **confederation** among largely sovereign states; little power was intended for the central government. The structure was intended to assure that central government did not infringe on the *liberty of the people* and the *power of the states*.

Provisions of the Articles-The Articles of Confederation created a loose confederation of independent sovereign states where state legislatures make most important decisions. The United Nations is an example of a confederation. The central government had no power to levy taxes, to regulate interstate commerce, to deny the states the right to collect customs duties, or national court to settle disputes between the states. All national laws required the approval of 9 of the 13 states.

Shortcomings of the Articles-The objective of the Articles was to preserve the power, independence, and sovereignty of the states. The central government could not finance its own activities without the ability to force states to pay annual taxes. The central government was unable to maintain a standing army to fight external threats. States like New York and New Jersey imposed high tariffs on goods that crossed their borders from other states, thus exposing the central government's inability to prevent commercial warfare between the states.

→ CONVENING THE CONSTITUTIONAL CONVENTION

Failures of the Articles of Confederation and growing concern by influential citizens about the passions of democracy and equality *among the common people* led most of the leading citizens to favor a new constitution. In an attempt to obtain popular support for the American Revolution, leaders had appealed to the people for the *defense of freedom* and for the spread of the *blessings of liberty*. The common people were convinced that success in the American Revolution would bring substantial improvements in their lives, but this desire for popular participation and greater equality is not what most of the leaders of the Revolution had in mind.

The Republican Beliefs of the Founders-The Framers favored **republicanism** as opposed to **democracy**. Republicans (not the political party) were most concerned with preventing tyranny by the rulers and the destruction of the liberty of their subjects. Under republicanism, government is insulated against the tyranny of the improper rule of the *one*, the *few*, or the *many*.

23

Any form of government had the potential to become tyrannical, therefore Eighteenth-century republicans believed that the only way to gain the consent of the governed *and* to simultaneously prevent tyranny was to elect government leaders and limit the power of government. Although eighteenth-century republicans believed in representative government, they were unsympathetic to popular democracy; they felt that public affairs should be left to the "better" parts of society. Those with social standing, substantial financial resources and property, and highly educated individuals should rule society. Eighteenth century republicans, did not believe in democracy.

Why the Founders Were Worried-The Framers were concerned with the threat of an excess of democracy in the states. The Revolution took on a more democratic character than the leaders of the Revolution intended as increasing numbers of common people became involved. In the mid-1780s, popular conventions were established to monitor and control the actions of state legislators; conventions issued instructions to representatives on how they were to vote on issues. The constitution replaced the property qualification to vote with smaller tax, created a unicameral or single-house legislative body whose members were elected in annual elections, mandated that legislative deliberations be open the public.

The Differences Between Republicanism and Democracy-Under **republicanism**, government is based on popular consent; indirect rule by the people through representatives; the term *people* is narrowly defined (by education, property holding, social standing); elected representatives act as "trustees" (act on their own to discover the public good); barriers to majority rule exist; government is strictly limited in function; government safeguards rights and liberties, with a special emphasis on property rights.

Under **democracy**, government is based on popular consent; rule by the people may be direct or indirect, the term people is broadly defined; elected representatives act as "delegates" (act as instructed by the people, accurately reflect their wishes). Majority rule prevails, government does what the people want it to do; government safeguards rights and liberties with no special emphasis on property rights

The Threat to Property Rights in the States-Republican governments was concerned with protecting private property from tyrannical government. During the 1770s and 1780s popular culture grew hostile toward privilege of any kind. Laws favored debtors over creditors in states such as Rhode Island and North Carolina where cheap money was produced to settle debts. **Stay acts** which forbade farm foreclosures for nonpayment of debts. **Shay's Rebellion** was the clearest example of how the interests between creditors and debtors came into conflict.

→ THE CONSTITUTIONAL CONVENTION

Leaders in the thirteen states selected 73 delegates to attend the Constitutional Convention in Philadelphia in May of 1787; 55 actually attended. George Washington presided over the secret meetings that lasted for four months that produced a constitutional framework which is a major **structural foundation** of American government and politics.

Who Were the Founders?-The 55 delegates were not common people. There were no common laborers, skilled craftspeople, small farmers, women, Black or Native Americans in attendance. The delegates were wealthy, propertied, and well educated individuals averaging about forty years old. Charles Beard's *An Economic Interpretation of the Constitution* (1913) claims that the framers were engaged in a conspiracy to protect their immediate and personal economic interests. Beard argued that the Founders were owners of public securities who were interested in a government that could pay its debts, merchants interested in protections of commerce, and land speculators interested in the protection of property rights.

Controversies over Beard's book prevail. The authors of *The Struggle for Democracy* argue that a simple self-interest analysis such as Beard's is not supportable. Still they agree that his work was on the mark in suggesting the broad economic and social-class motives were at work in shaping the actions of the Framers. The Framers were equally concerned with the strengthening the economic condition of the nation.

Consensus and Conflict at the Convention-The results of *consensus and conflict at the Convention* are developed in this chapter. There was strong support for a substantially *strengthened national government* with a reduction in the power and sovereignty of the states (combined with concern that a strong national government is potentially tyrannical) and belief in a *republican form* of government (based on popular consent but not unduly swayed by public opinion). Conflict at the convention often centered around *disagreements between large and small states*, involving issues such as representation of the states in the legislature and the method of selecting a president. The delegates were in agreement on the need to substitute a new constitution for the Articles of Confederation. Alexander Hamilton and Ben Franklin were major proponents of this position.

The most intense debate concerned representation in Congress and the relative power of large and small states in the newly formed nation. Proposals for representation of the states centered around the **Virginia Plan** (designed to create a strong central government controlled by the wealthiest and most populous states) and the **New Jersey Plan** (which envisioned a slightly more powerful national government than under the Articles of Confederation and was favored by the small states). The debates eventually culminated in the **Great Compromise** (sometimes known as the **Connecticut Plan** or **Connecticut Compromise**), which called for a **bicameral (two house)** national legislature with representation in the lower house based on population (favoring the large states) and equal representation for each of the states in the upper house (favoring the small states).

Slavery-The word "slavery" does not appear in the Constitution, but the Founders did condone slavery in the new nation. The legal standing of "involuntary servitude" is affirmed with the "three-fifths" formula used to count slaves as "three-fifths of all other Persons" in the calculation of how many representatives a state was entitled to in the House of Representatives (Article I, Section 2, paragraph 3). The Constitution also forbade laws and enactments against the slave trade until 1808 (Article I, Section 9). Third, it required nonslave states to return runaway slaves to their owners in slave states (Article IV, Section 2, paragraph 3).

The Presidency-The Virginia Plan called for a single executive, while the New Jersey Plan called for a plural executive. Both sides of the debate on the executive rejected direct election by the people. The **electoral college** was agreed upon as the method of selection of the chief executive. In the electoral college, each state would have a total of votes equal to its total number of representatives and senators in Congress. Members of the electoral college would then cast their votes for president. If the electoral college fails to select an executive, the House of Representatives would choose the president, with each state having one vote (Article II, Section 1, paragraphs 2 and 3).

➔WHAT THE FRAMERS CREATED

The Constitution of the United States is the cornerstone of American politics. It has been amended 27 times, but the major outlines of our present-day government are expressed in and substantially determined by the Constitution that was written in Philadelphia in 1787. The constitution is one of the major structural factors that has influenced the direction of American government and continues to shape politics today.

A Republican Form of Government-The republican doctrine advocated a form of government that, while based on popular consent and some popular participation, places obstacles in the path of majoritarian democracy and limits the purposes and powers of the government in order to prevent tyranny.

Federalism-Unlike the Articles of Confederation, the Constitution created a federal system in which some powers are left to the states, some powers are shared by the component units and the central government, and some powers are granted to the central government alone. The **supremacy clause** (Article VI, Section 2,) notes that "this Constitution and Laws of the United States which shall be made in Pursuance thereof; and all Treaties made, or which shall be made, under the Authority of the United States, shall be the Supreme Law of the Land; and the Judges in every State shall be bound thereby, any Thing in the Constitution or Laws of any State to the Contrary notwithstanding."

Under the federal arrangement, the national government has the power to regulate interstate commerce, to provide a uniform currency, to provide uniform laws on bankruptcy, to raise and support an army and a navy, to declare war, to collect taxes and customs duties, to provide for the common defense of the United States and so forth. Article I, Section 8 of the Constitution contains the "necessary and proper clause" which grants Congress the power to "make all laws which shall be necessary and proper" to carry out its specific powers and responsibilities. This clause is also known as the **elastic clause**.

Limited government-The Constitution limits governmental power by listing what powers are permissible and what powers are impermissible. The Bill of Rights is an example of how governmental power is limited in the Constitution.

Checks on Majority Rule-The House of Representatives is the only branch of government that is selected by the direct vote of the people (Article I, Section 2, paragraph 1). The president is elected by the electoral college; the members of the Senate are elected by the state legislatures; and judges appointed by the president and confirmed by the Senate: Representatives, senators, and presidents are elected for different terms (two years for representatives, four years for presidents, and six years for senators), from different constituencies, and (often) at different times.
The framers also made the amendment process extremely difficult. Popular will is considered, but it is very limited.

Separation of Powers, Checks and Balances-The Framers were also concerned that executive, legislative, and judicial powers were limited by a balanced government. Balanced government is based on the notion that concentrated power of any kind is dangerous and that the way to prevent tyranny is first to fragment governmental power into its constituent parts—executive, legislative, and judicial—then place each into a separate and independent branch. **Article I** of the Constitution focuses on legislative power, **Article II** on executive power, and **Article III** on judicial power. Separation of powers requires that each branch has specific powers and responsibilities. The idea behind **checks and balances** is based on the framers belief that "ambition...be made to check ambition." No branch of government is able to act entirely on its own in the most important areas of governing. Each branch has a way of blocking the actions of others.

The Foundations for a National Free Enterprise Economy-Property rights were thought to be fundamental and inalienable rights that governments were instituted to defend. **Article I, Section 10**, of the Constitution forbids the states to impair the obligation of contracts, to coin money, or to make anything but gold and silver coin a tender in payment of debts. States could no longer help debtors by printing inflated money, forgiving debts, or otherwise infringing on the rights of creditors, as happened in Rhode Island and North Carolina under the Articles of Confederation. **Article IV, Section 1**, guarantees contracts by establishing that the states must give "full faith and credit" to the public acts, records, and judicial proceedings of every other state. The Constitution guaranteed that the U.S. government would pay all debts contracted under the Articles of Confederation (**Article VI, Section 1**). **Article IV, Section 2, paragraph 3**, protected private property in slaves by requiring states to deliver escaped slaves back to their legal owners.

Article I, Section 8, grants Congress the power to regulate interstate commerce , to coin money and regulate its value, to establish uniform bankruptcy, and to protect the financial fruits of invention by establishing patent and copyright laws. Finally, Article I, Section 9 and 10, broke down barriers to trade by forbidding the states to impose taxes or duties on other states' exports, to enter into foreign treaties, to coin money, or to lay any imposts or duties on imports or exports.

→THE STRUGGLE TO RATIFY THE CONSTITUTION

Under the Articles of Confederation, alterations required the unanimous consent of all 13 states before changes could be made. Rhode Island was one of the states that were hostile to the proceedings at Philadelphia. The Framers ratified the new Constitution based on guidelines specified in Article VII of the unratified document they had just written, namely, the approval by 9 states meeting in special constitutional conventions. The battle over ratification sided the **Federalists** (those who favored a strong centralized government and supported the Constitution) against the **Anti-Federalists** (those who favored a loose confederation of states and opposed the Constitution). The Federalists were simply better organized than the Anti-Federalists. The Federalists wrote 85 articles in defense of the Constitution for New York newspapers under the name **"Publius,"** by Alexander Hamilton (who wrote the most), James Madison (who wrote the best), and John Jay (who only wrote three). These articles would later become known as *The Federalist Papers*. The Federalist Papers strongly influenced the debate over ratification and remain the most impressive commentaries ever written about the U.S. Constitution (Numbers 10 and 51, written by Madison, are reprinted in the Appendix of *The Struggle for Democracy*).

The Federalists represented the wealthy and town interests, which favored ratification, against the less wealthy and rural interests, which opposed ratification. It also pitted advocated of small-scale, decentralized republican government against advocates of a more centralized republican system.
The Anti-Federalists were very concerned that the new Constitution did not include a bill of rights. The Federalists were content that each of the thirteen states already had bills of rights in their constitutions before the ratification of the US Constitution. Ratification of the new Constitution was less likely without the Federalist's promise to include a bill of rights. The 1st Congress passed a bill of rights in the form of ten amendments to the Constitution. Ratification in the different states such as Rhode Island, North Carolina, New York, Virginia, and Massachusetts was very intense. George Washington, James Madison, John Marshall, and Edmund Randolph. George Mason, Richard Henry Lee, and Patrick Henry sided with the Anti-Federalists. Virginia and New York were key states to ratification because of their population sizes, but New Hampshire was the ninth of thirteen states to vote in favor of ratification.

→THE CHANGING CONSTITUTION, DEMOCRACY, AND AMERICAN POLITICS

The theme of this text is *the struggle for democracy*, and Chapter 2 examines the question of *how the constitution relates to democracy*. The authors of your textbook refer to the Constitution as *the basic rulebook* for the game of American politics. It is a fundamental *structural factor* influencing all of American political life. Constitutional rules apportion power and responsibility among governmental branches, define the fundamental nature of relationships between governmental institutions, specify how individuals are to be selected for office, and tell how the rules themselves may be changed. Major outlines of our present-day government that continue to fashion our politics are expressed in the document written in 1787.

Constitutional rules can and do change over time. The Constitution has been formally amended only 27 times, the first ten of which (the Bill of Rights) were added within three years of ratification. That the Constitution has changed only 17 times over the past 200 years by means of *formal amendments, judicial interpretations* of the Supreme Court, and through changing *political practices* reveals how difficult changes to the Constitution can be. The tendency of the Constitution to change with the times is why we sometimes refer to the outcome of the 1787 Philadelphia Convention as the "living Constitution."

The Constitution may be formally amended by use of the procedures outlined in **Article V**. The Framers' contribution to the advance of democracy is mixed. They tried to control popular sovereignty and political equality; at the same time, they promoted the cause of democracy by strengthening and protecting political liberty. Political life has become more democratic than the framers imagined or wanted. The *framers especially valued liberty*; instituting democratic government was *not* one of their aims. They believed that liberty and popular sovereignty were contradictory. They did not fully appreciate the extent to which liberty, popular sovereignty, and political equality are compatible; by contrast, most people today include political liberty as a basic attribute of democracy.

In *Marbury v. Madison* (1803) the Supreme Court claimed the power of **judicial review**—the right to declare the actions of the other branches of government null and void or unconstitutional—even though judicial review is not specifically written or enumerated in the Constitution. In *Griswold v. Connecticut* (1965) and later in *Roe v. Wade* (1973), the Court supported a fundamental right of privacy even though such a right is nowhere explicitly mentioned in the Constitution. So much has changed because of how political parties function in modern American politics, and the Framers would most likely not recognize the modern presidency.

→SUMMARY

The Articles of Confederation was the first constitution of the United States. Under its terms, the states were organized into a loose confederation in which the states retained full sovereignty and the central government had little power. The many defects or weaknesses that the Articles contained and fears among many American leaders that democratic and egalitarian tendencies were spinning out of control, led to the 1787 Philadelphia convention out of which the

Constitution of the United States was created. The new Constitution is based on the principles of republicanism (federalism, limited government, the separation of powers, checks and balances, and limitations on majority rule). The 1787 Philadelphia Convention was very contentious, with Federalists on one side and Anti-Federalists. The Federalists were supported primarily by the economically better-off, urban interests, and believers in a more centralized republicanism; the Anti-Federalists were supported primarily by small and poor farmers, rural interests, and believers in small-scale republicanism.

> *Chapter Outline*

This section gives you a comprehensive review of the chapter. Use this outline in combination with your textbook to look for key concepts and objectives, to identify essential terms and names, and to gain a basic understanding of political practices and principles from this chapter.

I. INTRODUCTION TO PART TWO: STRUCTURE (p. 23)
   A. The chapters in Part Two show the *structural underpinnings* of American politics and government; information in these chapters sets the stage for the chapters that follow.
      1. Structural influences are enduring features of American society that play a substantial role in determining the importance of issues, the distribution of political power, the perceptions that guide the behavior of citizens and public officials, and the ways in which political and governmental institutions operate.
      2. Constitutional rules are a particularly important part of the structural context of American political life.
         a) Chapter 2 examines the founding of the United States and the formulation of the constitutional rules that structure American politics today—why a constitutional convention was convened, what the Founders intended to accomplish, and how specific provisions of the Constitution have shaped our political life.
         b) Chapter 3 looks at **federalism** and asks what the framers intended and how federalism has changed over the years.
   B. The basic characteristics of American society influence the workings of our political and governmental institutions, as well as the attitudes and behaviors of citizens and public officials.
      1. Chapter 4 examines the American economy, society, and political culture.
      2. Particular attention is paid to the global economy and its impact.
   C. This chapter is about the founding of the United States and the formulation of the constitutional rules that structure American politics to this day; the authors point out

that the *struggle for democracy* has been a feature of political life in the United States from the very beginning.

    1. Chapter 2 examines why particular constitutional rules were selected and how they influence what happens at all levels of government and politics in the United States.

    2. The authors pay significant attention to conflicts over the meaning of democracy and its place in the Constitution.

II.   SHAYS'S REBELLION, 1786 (p. 25)

    A. The end of the Revolutionary War brought *widespread economic problems* among farmers, precipitated by the collapse of prices for agricultural products; in desperation, farmers sought economic assistance from state governments.

        1. For the most part, political leaders responded to farmers' requests for help.

            a) Several states loaned money to farmers (in the form of **scrip**, or paper money) to pay their taxes and debts.

            b) Some states passed **stay laws**, which postponed taxes and mortgage payments for farmers.

        2. By contrast, the Massachusetts state legislature and governor blocked relief measures and decided that all state debts were to be paid in full in order to establish the creditworthiness of the state.

            a) State debt had accumulated to pay the costs of the Revolutionary War (owed primarily to a handful of the wealthiest citizens of the state who had bought outstanding notes for pennies on the dollar).

            b) To make good on the debt, the Legislature levied heavy taxes that fell disproportionately on farmers in the western part of the state.

    B. Nonpayment of taxes and debts in Massachusetts led to foreclosure proceedings and imprisonment for debt.

        1. Farmers in western Massachusetts took up arms to prevent courts from meeting.

        2. State judge **Artemas Ward** was denied access to the courthouse in Worcester, thus preventing him from presiding over farm foreclosure proceedings (September 1786); other judges were equally unsuccessful.

        3. Governor **James Bowdoin** issued a proclamation against unlawful assembly and called out the militia to enforce it.

        4. Armed farmers in Springfield led by Captain **Daniel Shays** forced the militia to withdraw, but special armed forces recruited from the Boston area defeated the rebels in battles at Springfield and Petersham.

    C. Aftermath of **Shays's Rebellion**

        1. Although the insurrection was put down quickly, most of the nation's leading citizens were alarmed by the apparent inability of state governments under the **Articles of Confederation** (our first constitution, in effect from 1781 to 1788) to maintain public order.

2. In this climate of crisis, a call was issued to meet in Philadelphia to correct defects in the Articles of Confederation.
    a) The national government was virtually powerless under the Articles.
    b) Responsibility for civil order was mainly in the hands of the states.

III. **THE POLITICAL THEORY OF THE REVOLUTIONARY ERA (pp.26-27)**
   A. Conflicts over the meaning of democracy and liberty in the new nation
      1. Initially, the Revolution was fought *to preserve an existing way of life*—traditional rights of life, liberty, and property seemed to be threatened by British policies on trade and taxation.
      2. The Revolution was inspired by a concern for **liberty**, which was understood as the *preservation of traditional rights* against the intrusions of government and accompanied by the development of sentiments for **popular sovereignty** (which assumes that ultimate political authority belongs to the people) and **political equality** (which refers to each person's decision making carrying the same weight in voting and other political situations).
   B. **The Declaration of Independence**
      1. The **Second Continental Congress** opened its session on May 10, 1775; the delegates did not originally have independence in mind, but they concluded by the spring of 1776 that separation and independence were inescapable.
         a) South Carolina and Virginia adopted written constitutions and declared themselves free from British control.
         b) Movement toward separation and independence was influenced by **Thomas Paine**, author of *Common Sense*, who favored independence and self-government, opposed the institution of a monarchy, and appealed to the common person.
      2. A special committee was appointed (composed of Thomas Jefferson, John Adams, and Benjamin Franklin) to draft a declaration of independence; the **Declaration of Independence** (primarily the work of Jefferson) was unanimously adopted by the Second Continental Congress on July 4, 1776.
   C. **Key ideas in the Declaration of Independence**
      1. Jefferson was heavily influenced by the writings of **John Locke**, especially his *Second Treatise on Government*.
      2. Jefferson's ideas are so familiar to us today that it is easy to miss their revolutionary importance.
         a) In the late eighteenth century when most societies were ruled by divine right of kings, Jefferson posed the seemingly outrageous argument that *legitimate government could only be established by the people and governed with their consent.*
         b) These ideas sparked a responsive chord among peoples everywhere when they were first presented, and they remain very popular all over the world.

(1) Human beings possess rights that cannot be legitimately given away or taken from them.

(2) People create government to protect these rights.

(3) If government fails to protect rights or itself becomes a threat to the people, then people can withdraw their consent from government and create a new one.

D. **Omissions in the Declaration of Independence**

1. Did not deal with the issue of what to do about *slavery*, a glaring omission in light of its defense of inalienable rights and the claim that *"all men are created equal"*

2. Did not consider the question of whether the colonies were declaring their independence as a *single new nation* or as *thirteen separate nations*

3. Did not say anything about the *political status of women, Native Americans, or African-Americans who were not slaves*

E. **Early state constitutions**

1. By the end of the war in 1783, eleven of the colonies had created their own governments, free from royal control; each state began with a *written constitution*.

2. Provisions of the new constitutions

a) **Bills of Rights**—rights that could not be violated *by governments*, even governments based on popular consent (such as freedom of speech)

b) **Restrictions on the powers of executives**—states took various steps to limit the power of the executive branch (including election of the executive by the legislature, limitations on terms of office, limited powers of appointment, and no veto power over legislation); constitution makers wanted their chief executives to be administrators rather than rulers

c) **Legislative supremacy**—sought to make the legislative branch supreme and protect it from intrusions by the executive branch; most state constitutions gave a broad range of powers to the legislative branch

d) **Frequent elections**—most required annual legislative elections; there were fears that long terms of office could lead to tyranny

e) **Restrictions on the right to vote and hold elective office**—although the new state constitutions were more democratic than any others existing at that time, they implied a much narrower conception of *people* and *popular consent* than we hold today; requirements for **suffrage** continued to include property qualifications, poll tax, and property tax; women, slaves, and most free blacks were excluded

IV. **THE ARTICLES OF CONFEDERATION: THE FIRST CONSTITUTION (pp. 30-31)**

A. Leaders of the American Revolution envisioned a loose **confederation** in which the states were to be virtually independent and hold most governmental powers.

B. Provisions of the Articles of Confederation

1. The first constitution, passed by the Second Continental Congress during the Revolutionary War in 1777 but not ratified by the required number of states until 1787)
2. A loose confederation of independent states
   a) Most important decisions took place in state legislatures.
   b) States retained veto power over constitutional change; defects in the constitution were almost impossible to remedy because amending the Articles required unanimous consent of the states.
   c) States held independent power over commerce and the militia.
3. Weak central government
   a) No independent chief executive to ensure that laws were enforced
   b) No national judiciary to settle disputes between states
   c) Weak Congress with no power to levy taxes or to regulate interstate commerce
   d) The few areas of responsibility assigned to the central government were almost impossible to legislate because congressional legislation had to be approved by 9 of the 13 states.

C. **Shortcomings of the Articles**
   1. Indebtedness and inability to finance its activities—bonds and notes of the confederate government had no value because the central government could not compel states to pay tax assessments
   2. Inability to defend American interests in foreign affairs—without a chief executive, with veto power in the hands of the states, and without a standing military, the confederation lacked the capacity to reach binding agreements with other nations or to deal with a wide range of problems
   3. Commercial warfare among the states—states became the commercial rivals of their neighbors, and some states imposed high tariffs on goods that crossed their borders

V. **THE CONVENING OF THE CONSTITUTIONAL CONVENTION (PP. 31-34)**
   A. *Growing concern* by influential citizens about *democratizing and egalitarian tendencies*
      1. In an attempt to obtain popular support for the American Revolution, *leaders had appealed to the people* for the *defense of freedom* and for the spread of the *blessings of liberty*; the common people believed that success would bring substantial improvements in their lives, but their desire for popular participation and greater equality is not what most of the leaders of the Revolution had in mind.
      2. Failures of the Articles of Confederation led most of the leading citizens to favor a new constitution.
   B. **The republican beliefs of the Founders**
      1. The Framers favored **republicanism**, not democracy
      2. Republicanism is a theory of *how nontyrannical governments might be constructed.*

3. Objectives of eighteenth-century republicans
   a) A form of government based on popular consent, but with limits on office holding and the right to vote
   b) Placed obstacles in the path of popular democracy and limited the purposes and powers of the government
       (1) Although republican doctrine held that legitimate government must be based on the *consent of the governed*, a fear of **tyranny** (the abuse of power by the ruler and the destruction of the liberty of the ruler's subjects) caused republican doctrine to limit the role of the common people; republicans believed that tyranny can be imposed by the *one*, the *few*, or the *many*.
       (2) Eighteenth-century republicans believed that the only way to gain the consent of the governed *and* to simultaneously prevent tyranny was to elect government leaders and limit the power of government.
4. The Founders did not favor a society with substantial popular participation.
5. Although eighteenth-century republicans *believed in representative government*, they *did not favor democracy* as defined in Chapter 1.
   a) Eighteenth-century republicans envisioned a political order in which a natural elite rules.
   b) Elected representatives were to exercise independent judgment once in office, taking into account the needs and interests of the entire community rather than the opinions of the people.
   c) Eighteenth-century republican doctrine allowed the common people a larger role in public life than existed in other political systems of the day, but the role of the people was expected to be far more limited than we expect today.
6. **Why the Founders were worried**.
   a) The Founders were concerned with the threat of too much democracy in the states.
   b) The American Revolution took on a more democratic character than the leaders of the Revolution intended, as increasing numbers of common people became involved.
7. The Differences between republicanism and democracy.
   a) Under **republicanism**, government is based on popular consent; indirect rule by the people through representatives; the term *people* is narrowly defined by education, property holding, and social standing; elected representatives as "trustees"; barriers to majority rule exist; government is strictly limited in function; government safeguards rights and liberties, with a special emphasis on property rights.
   b) Under **democracy**, government is based on popular consent; rule by the people may be direct or indirect; the term people is broadly defined; elected

representatives act as "delegates"; majority rule prevails; government safeguards rights and liberties with no special emphasis on property rights.
8. The threat to property rights in the states.
   a) Republican governments were concerned with protecting private property from tyrannical government.
   c) During the 1770s and 1780s popular culture grew hostile toward privilege of any kind. Laws favored debtors over creditors in states such as Rhode Island and North Carolina where cheap money was produced to settle debts.
   d) Other states enacted **stay acts** which forbade farm foreclosures for nonpayment of debts.
9. **Shay's Rebellion** was the clearest example of how the interests between creditors and debtors came into conflict.

VI. THE CONSTITUTIONAL CONVENTION (pp. 35-44)
A. By 1787, most of America's economic, social, and political leaders were convinced that the new nation—and the experiment in self-government—were in great danger of failing. Leaders in the thirteen states selected 73 delegates to attend the Constitutional Convention in Philadelphia in May of 1787; 55 delegates actually attended. George Washington presided over the secret meetings that lasted for four months that produced a constitutional framework which is a major **structural foundation** of American government and politics.
B. **Who were the Founders?**
   1. There were no common laborers, skilled craftspeople, small farmers, women, Black or Native Americans in attendance.
   2. Charles Beard's *An Economic Interpretation of the Constitution* (1913) claims that the Framers were engaged in a conspiracy to protect their immediate and personal economic interests.
   3. The authors of *The Struggle for Democracy* argue that Beard's theory is not totally accurate. They contend that the Framers were concerned with strengthening the economic condition of the nation.
C. **Consensus and conflict at the Convention**
   1. Agreed on the need to substitute a new constitution for the Articles of Confederation; in so doing, the delegates far exceeded their instructions from Congress in deciding to write a new constitution
   2. Support for a substantially *strengthened national government* with a reduction in the power and sovereignty of the states, combined with concern that a strong national government is potentially tyrannical
   3. Conviction that government should not be allowed to fall into the hands of any particular interest or set of interests (particularly what Madison referred to as *the majority faction,* by which he meant the majority of the people)

4. Belief in a *republican form* of government—based on popular consent but not unduly swayed by public opinion

D. **Compromises**

1. Proposals for representation centered on the relative power of large and small states.

   a) **Virginia Plan**—designed to create a strong central government controlled by the wealthiest and most populous states (Virginia, Massachusetts, and Pennsylvania); drafted by **James Madison**

      (1) Seats for both houses apportioned to the states on the basis of population; popularly elected **bicameral** (two-house) national legislature with power to veto state laws and to appoint the executive and the judiciary

      (2) National sovereignty was expected to be superior to state authority.

   b) **New Jersey Plan**—envisioned a slightly more powerful national government than under the Articles of Confederation; favored by the small states; drafted by **William Patterson**

      (1) **Unicameral** (one-house) legislature with one member from each state

      (2) Organized on representational lines similar to the Articles of Confederation

      (3) Each of the states remained sovereign.

   c) **The Great Compromise** (sometimes called the **Connecticut Compromise** because it was drafted by **Roger Sherman** of Connecticut)—compromise between opposing views of supporters of large states and small states

      (1) Representation in the lower house was to be based on population (favoring the large states), with direct popular election of representatives.

      (2) The upper house was to have equal representation for each of the states (favoring the small states); senators were to be selected by state legislatures.

      (3) Provisions of the Great Compromise are included in Article I, Sections 2 and 3, of the Constitution.

2. **Slavery**

   a) The word slavery was omitted from the Constitution, but the Founders did condone slavery in the new nation.

   b) The "three-fifths" formula was used to count slaves as "three-fifths of all other Persons" in the calculation of how many representatives a state was entitled to in the House of Representatives (Article I, Section 2, paragraph 3).

   c) The Constitution forbade laws and enactments against the slave trade until 1808 (Article I, Section 9).

   d) The Constitution required nonslave states to return runaway slaves to their owners in slave states (Article IV, Section 2, paragraph 3).

3. **The presidency**

a) The delegates quickly decided on a single executive, but the method of selection was a matter of intense debate and disagreement.

b) The eventual compromise called for *indirect election* of the president by an **electoral college** (Article II, Section 1, paragraphs 2 and 3).

   (1) Each state would have a total of electoral votes equal to the total number of representatives and senators from each state in Congress.

   (2) The House of Representatives would choose a president if no one received a majority of electoral votes (an event the framers assumed would usually occur).

   (3) The *system of presidential election* did not work out as expected and *became far more democratic* over the course of our history.

E. **What the Framers created**

   1. The broad outlines of our present-day government are expressed in the document written in 1787; only 27 formal amendments have been added in more than 200 years.

   2. **Republican form of government**

      a) Based on popular consent and some popular participation

      b) Limits officeholding and the right to vote

      c) Places barriers in the path of majoritarian democracy

      d) Limits the purposes and powers of government in order to prevent tyranny

   3. **Federalism**

      a) Division of powers—some powers are left to the states, some are shared by the component units and the central government, and some are granted to the central government alone

      b) The framers created a federal system with a relatively strong central government.

      c) Nationalized power was heightened by exclusively assigning important powers to the national government.

         (1) Powers to tax, regulate interstate commerce, provide a uniform national currency

         (2) Powers to raise an army and navy, call state militias to national service, declare war

         (3) **Elastic clause** (Article I, Section 8)—Congress granted power to "make all laws which shall be necessary and proper" for carrying out its listed (enumerated) powers

      d) The powers in the Constitution tilt slightly toward the center, but the states remain important components within the federal system.

   4. **Limited government**

      a) The Constitution lists specific powers of the national government (Article I, Section 8) and specifically denies others (Article I, Section 9).

b) The Bill of Rights imposes restraints on the national government by protecting fundamental rights of citizens.

5. **Checks on majority rule**
   a) Created a system in which the people rule only indirectly
      (1) Only the House of Representatives was to be directly elected (Article I, Section 2).
      (2) The president (Article II, Section 1) and Senate (Article I, Section 3) were indirectly elected; direct election of senators was provided for in Amendment XVII.
      (3) Judges were to be appointed by the president and confirmed by the Senate (Article II, Section 2).
   b) Different terms of office and different constituencies were intended to ensure that popular majorities would be unlikely to overwhelm those who govern, at least in the short run.
   c) Amendment process is cumbersome and difficult

6. **Separation of powers** and **checks and balances**
   a) To deal with the danger of legislative tyranny, the framers turned to the idea of mixed or **balanced government**, which had been popularized by the French philosopher **Montesquieu**.
      (1) The central idea of balanced government is that *concentrated power of any kind is dangerous*; the solution is to fragment government executive, legislative, and judicial powers, and to place them into different branches (the basis for the U.S. constitutional principle of separation of powers).
      (2) Balanced government designates spheres of responsibility and enumerates specific powers attached to these responsibilities; no branch could control all powers or dominate the other branches
   b) The framers also ensured that no branch of the national government would be able to act entirely on its own without the cooperation of the others; each branch has powers, but none is able to exercise all of its powers on its own (the concept of checks and balances).

7. Foundations for a national **free enterprise economy**
   a) Following the lead of John Locke, the Founders believed that the right to accumulate, use, and transfer property was one of the fundamental, inalienable rights.
   b) *Property rights are protected* in several sections of the Constitution.
      (1) States are prohibited from impairing the obligation of contracts, coining money, or making anything but gold and silver coin a tender in payment of debts (Article I, Section 10).
      (2) States must give **full faith and credit** to public acts, records, and judicial proceedings of every other state (Article IV, Section 1).

      (3) The U.S. government is obligated to pay all debts contracted under the Articles of Confederation (Article VI, Section 1).

      (4) States were required to deliver escaped slaves back to their owners (Article IV, Section 2).

   c) The Framers took steps to *encourage the emergence of a national free enterprise economy.*

      (1) Congress was granted power to regulate interstate and foreign commerce, coin money, establish uniform laws of bankruptcy, and establish patent and copyright laws (Article I, Section 8).

      (2) States are prohibited from imposing taxes or duties on other states' exports, entering into foreign treaties, coining money, and laying imposts or duties on imports or exports (Article I, Sections 9 and 10).

VII. THE STRUGGLE TO RATIFY THE CONSTITUTION (pp. 44-46)

   A. Debate over ratification centered around positions of the **Federalists** (who favored ratification) and the **Anti-Federalists** (who opposed ratification).

   B. **Federalists**

      1. Federalists enjoyed intellectual advantages in the dispute, as illustrated by ***The Federalist Papers*** (85 essays in defense of the proposed Constitution, written by Alexander Hamilton, James Madison, and John Jay), originally published in New York newspapers as a series of articles under the name **Publius.**

      2. Although the Federalists believed that a bill of rights was not necessary because of the protection of rights that was provided in state constitutions and safeguards already included in the proposed Constitution, they promised to add a bill of rights during the first session of Congress.

   C. **Anti-Federalists**

      1. Anti-Federalists believed that the new Constitution threatened people's liberty; they were particularly concerned about the absence of a bill of rights.

      2. Patrick Henry charged that the constitution "squints towards monarchy."

   D. During the debate over ratification, Federalists promised to add a bill of rights during the first session of Congress.

      a) Twelve amendments were proposed during the first session.

      b) Ten amendments (the Bill of Rights) were ratified by December 15, 1791.

   E. Most of the small states quickly approved, but the battle over ratification was intense (and the vote was close) in the larger states; New Hampshire became the ninth state to approve (June 21, 1788).

VIII. THE CHANGING CONSTITUTION, DEMOCRACY, AND AMERICAN POLITICS (pp. 47-49)

A. The Constitution is *the basic rule book* for the game of American politics.
B. Constitutional rules
    1. Apportion power and responsibility among governmental branches
    2. Define the fundamental nature of relationships between governmental institutions
    3. Specify how individuals are to be selected for office
    4. Tell how the rules themselves may be changed
C. How the Constitution relates to **democracy**
    1. The *framers especially valued liberty*; instituting democratic government was *not* the aim of the framers.
        a) They *believed that liberty and popular sovereignty were contradictory.*
        b) They did not fully appreciate the extent to which liberty, popular sovereignty, and political equality are compatible; by contrast, most people today include political liberty as a basic *attribute of democracy.*
    2. The Framers' *contribution to the advance of democracy* is *mixed.*
        a) Because they especially valued liberty, the framers tried in a number of ways to *control* the place of popular democracy in American political life (using constitutional mechanisms to do so).
        b) At the same time, they *promoted* the cause of democracy by strengthening and protecting political liberty.
    3. Political life has become more democratic than the Framers imagined or wanted.
D. **How the Constitution changes**
    1. Constitutional rules can and do change over time.
    2. The tendency of the Constitution to change with the times is why we sometimes use the term **the living Constitution.**
        a) *Formal amendment*—the Constitution has been formally amended 27 times (with the first ten amendments added within three years of ratification)
        b) Judicial interpretation—the Constitution is changed through decisions and interpretations of the Supreme Court (as seen in the shaping of judicial review in the classic 1803 case of *Marbury* v. *Madison*)
        c) *Political practices*—the meaning of the Constitution changes through changing political practices (such as the development of political parties and nominating conventions)

IX. SUMMARY (p. 49)

A. The Articles of Confederation was the first constitution of the United States. Under its terms, the states were organized into a loose confederation in which the states retained full sovereignty and the central government had little power.
B. The many defects or weaknesses that the Articles contained and fears among many American leaders that democratic and egalitarian tendencies were spinning out of control, led to the 1787 Philadelphia convention out of which the Constitution of the United States was created.

C. The new Constitution is based on the principles of republicanism (federalism, limited government, the separation of powers, checks and balances, and limitations on majority rule.
D. The Federalists won the debate against the Anti-Federalists. The Federalists were supported by the economically better off. The Anti-Federalists were supported by small and poor farmers, rural interests, and believers in small-scale republicanism.

Terms for Review

Use this list to review essential principles, functions, and concepts from this chapter. Refer to your textbook for help in identifying and defining terms on this list. When you study, do not merely memorize terms; ask questions about the material you are reviewing, and look for the importance or significance of each item.

veto

Articles of Confederation

Federalist Papers

legislative branch

executive branch

confederation

republicanism

Common Sense

stay acts

Virginia Plan

New Jersey Plan

Connecticut Compromise

electoral college

federalism

supremacy clause
elastic clause

Bill of Rights

checks and balances

Federalists

Anti-Federalists

judicial review

suffrage

tyranny

Marbury v. Madison (1803)

Publius

ratification

Shay's Rebellion

separation of powers

Research Topics: Applying What You Have Learned

You will derive more benefit from your reading if you try to apply what you have learned. Some of the suggested research topics can be answered exclusively from your text, while others require

*you to conduct some basic research on your own. The references suggested under **Internet Sources** will help you in your search.*

- Although eighteenth-century republican doctrine allowed the common people a larger role in public life than existed in other political systems of the day, the role of the people was to be far more limited than we expect today. Write a brief essay in which you expand on this theme.

- Following is a quotation from the text: "Popular democracy proved to be an idea of such power that our political life has become considerably more democratic than the Framers imagined or wanted." Use this quotation to distinguish between republicanism and democracy, in a brief essay.

- How have the constitutional "rules of the game" changed in the past 200 years? What structural factors have been significant in leading to changes in constitutional rules? Have these changes contributed to a more democratic form of government, or have they increased the dangers of majority tyranny?

Internet Sources

A number of sites on the World Wide Web serve as "gateways" to vast collections of material on American government and politics. The following Internet sources are recommended for students who would like to do additional research in areas covered by this chapter. These references would also be helpful in expanding on the questions suggested under Research Topics.

Annotated Constitution www.access.gpo.gov/congress/senate/constitution
An annotation of the Constitution in which each clause is tied to Supreme Court decisions concerning its meaning; done by the Library of Congress.

Bibliographical Sketches of the Delegates to the Constitutional Convention
http://www.nara.gov/exhall/charters/constitution/confath.html
Profiles of the delegates to the Constitutional Convention.

The U.S. Constitution On-Line www.usconstitution.net
A very rich site that presents material on every aspect of the history and development of the Constitution.

Cornell University Law School http://www.psr.keele.ac.uk/
A vast collection of documents on democracy, liberty, and constitutionalism.

> *Self-Evaluation*

Circle the correct answer for each question. Questions are listed in the same order in which the information appears in the text. Use the Answer Key in the back of the Study Guide *to check your responses.*

1. The author of *Common Sense* was
    a. John Locke.
    b. James Madison.
    c. Alexander Hamilton.
    d. Thomas Paine.

2. The Constitution
    a. Still reflects the basic intentions of the framers with regard to democracy and popular sovereignty.
    b. Became far more democratic over the years than was originally intended by the framers.
    c. Has become less democratic and more republican than the framers intended.
    d. Has been amended so often that there is little of substance that remains from the original document.

3. The constitutional provision often referred to as **extradition**
    a. Requires states to grant full faith and credit to public acts, records, and judicial proceedings of other states.
    b. Means that citizens of other states are entitled to all the privileges and immunities of citizens that a state grants to its own citizens.
    c. Provides that a fugitive from justice shall be returned to the state that has jurisdiction.
    d. Guarantees a republican form of government to the states.

4. The **electoral college** provides for
    a. Presidential election by political parties.
    b. Election of the president by proportionate representation.

    c.   Direct popular election of the president.

    d.   An indirect election of the president.

5.   A **federal system** of government is one in which
    a.   Powers are divided between states and a central government.
    b.   Powers are divided between state and local governments.
    c.   Powers are concentrated in a central government.
    d.   Powers are concentrated in state or regional governments.

6.   Which of the following was NOT one of the features of the Articles of Confederation?
    a.   Sovereign states had a veto power over constitutional change.
    b.   The legislature had no power to regulate commerce between the states.
    c.   There was no chief executive or national judiciary.
    d.   The states had no power to control the militia or interstate commerce.

7.   Which of the following is NOT one of the provisions of the U.S. Constitution?
    a.   The national government has powers to tax, regulate interstate commerce, and provide a uniform national currency.
    b.   The states have electoral votes in presidential elections and have power to ratify constitutional amendments.
    c.   The local governments have control over police protection, education, and the interstate highway system.
    d.   The national government has powers to raise an army and a navy and to call state militias to national service.

8.   The **republican form of government** that was favored by the Founders included the belief that
    a.   Rule by the majority must be absolutely guaranteed.
    b.   Limitations must be placed on government powers.
    c.   A democracy must be instituted as soon as possible.
    d.   Suffrage must be extended to all white adult males.

9.   Of the various national officeholders, which was made directly accountable to the people by the original Constitution?
    a.   Supreme Court
    b.   Senate
    c.   House of Representatives
    d.   President

10. In the climate of crisis following Shays's Rebellion,

a. Leading citizens demonstrated their growing concern with the welfare of minority factions.

b. The rebellion reinforced fears about the dangers of majority rule.

c. Prominent citizens were pleased with the ability of the government to respond quickly to a crisis.

d. Public demands for a bill of rights resulted in the adoption of the first ten amendments to the Constitution.

11. Initially, the American Revolution was fought primarily to
    a. Establish a basis for popular sovereignty.
    b. Create a democracy.
    c. Preserve an existing way of life.
    d. Eliminate unfair laws.

12. The **Virginia Plan**
    a. Was a compromise between the New Jersey Plan and the Connecticut Plan.
    b. Called for a single-house legislature in which each state would have one vote.
    c. Was designed to create a strong central government controlled by the most populous states.
    d. Counted three-fifths of a state's slave population to determine taxation and representation in the House of Representatives.

13. (T/F) The decision to convene a Constitutional Convention reflected a growing concern felt by many of the most influential people about the failure to democratize the nation following the American Revolution.

14. (T/F) The system of **checks and balances** was designed to give each branch of government specialized functions to perform.

15. (T/F) The basic characteristics of American society influence the working of our political and governmental institutions, as well as the attitudes and behaviors of our citizens and public officials.

16. (T/F) The framers of the Constitution believed that **liberty** and **popular sovereignty** were contradictory principles.

17. (T/F) The **supremacy clause** of the Constitution creates the basis for a more centralized federal system.

18. (T/F) Montesquieu's views are incorporated in the doctrine of popular sovereignty.

Chapter 3
FEDERALISM: STATES AND NATION

Key Concepts and Objectives

The Key Concepts and Objectives provide a look at the fundamental goals and ideas of this chapter. This section serves as a guide to a basic understanding of the objectives of your textbook.

After reading this chapter, you should be able to:

- Explain what federalism is and compare different forms or types of federalism.
- Distinguish between federalism and other forms of government, such as confederation and unitary systems.
- Describe how today's federal system emerged out of the conflicts between those who advocated a stronger national government and those who wanted to retain power for the states.
- Evaluate advantages and disadvantages of federalism, and examine how the American federal system differs from those of other countries.
- Examine how the interplay between national and state governments illustrates the dispersion of power in our federal system.
- Identify provisions of the Constitution that form the foundation for federalism.
- Explain how the Supreme Court solidified its power within the federal system over the course of American history.
- Identify the major forms of grant-in-aid programs and describe how state policies are influenced by national mandates and conditional aid.
- Analyze the consequences and implications of federalism for a democratic system.
- Identify key terms and concepts used in Chapter 3.

This section provides a brief overview of the chapter contents. Read this section as a preview before reading your textbook. Then use this material as a review to help you retain information from your reading.

→ WELFARE REFORM AND THE STATES

The opening story demonstrates the dispersion of power in our federal system through the interplay between national and state governments. Under the **Social Security Act** of 1935, the U.S. government established **Aid to Families with Dependent Children (AFDC)** as an **entitlement program** for children in poor, mostly female-headed, families. The national government—which provided most of the money—guaranteed that any eligible family in the country was entitled to benefits; it made the rules about who was eligible, for how long, and under what circumstances. The program was administered by the states, a process that resulted in different levels of benefits from one state to another. The system began to change around the beginning of the 1990s. The shift in responsibility from the national government to the state governments on welfare may signify a change in the long history of enhancing the power of government at the national level.

President **Bill Clinton** and many members of Congress from both political parties promised to "end welfare as we know it" when they took office. New (mostly Republican) state governors and legislatures promised to reform welfare by encouraging work and parental responsibility. The **Bush** and Clinton administrations granted many waivers (exceptions to the national rules) so that states could experiment with these ideas. By 1995, 32 states had been given waivers, affecting about one-half of the nation's 14 million recipients. Some of the results were impressive.

In 1996, the **Personal Responsibility and Work Opportunity** Act made public welfare a state responsibility with federal financial support. The new law *ended welfare as an entitlement program*, limited recipients to *no more than five years of benefits*, and imposed *work and/or work-training requirements*. Within these general guidelines, *states are allowed wide latitude* in creating their own welfare programs; this has led to considerable diversity of benefits, with some states more generous than others.

→ FEDERALISM AS A SYSTEM OF GOVERNMENT

Federalism refers to the **division of power** between the national government and the states. It is a system under which significant government powers are divided between the central government and smaller governmental units, such as state, county, and city governments; neither one completely controls the other, and each has some room for independent action.

The Nature of Federalism-Most countries or governmental bodies in the world are based on unitary rather than federal systems. Yet many large and diverse countries employ federal systems, often modeling them on the U.S. system. American **federalism** involves a multiplicity of governing levels and units. All these governments are organized and related to each other in a particular way; together, they form the federal system. In our federal system, policy is made by the states as well as by the national government. By contrast, a **confederation** is a political system in which constituent *units or states retain ultimate authority* and can veto major actions of the central government. In a **unitary** system, the *central government exercises all governmental powers* and can change its constituent units.

There is no single model of federalism; there are major differences between the 21 nations in the world which claim to have federal systems. For example, German *Lander* and Mexican states do not have exactly the same independent powers that American states do. Countries with unitary systems (such as the United Kingdom and Italy) have subunits with a certain amount of autonomy, while others (such as France and Japan) are more completely dominated by the central government. There are no neat boundaries; scholars have suggested that there is a continuum from "unitary" to "formally federal," "quasi-federal," "federal," and "confederal" (or confederation) polities. See Table 3.1.

Countries have also been known to change their systems periodically, especially when ethnic minorities demand self-rule. Old Soviet republic states such as Ukraine, Kazakhstan, broke away from the larger Soviet Union. Yugoslavia also disintegrated into a number of different countries such as Yugoslavia (now only Serbia and Montenegro), Slovenia, Croatia, Bosnia, and Macedonia. Great Britain agreed to grant increased autonomy to Scotland and Wales where significant nationalist movements have been seeking independence. Quebec remained part of Canada in 1995 by less than one percent of the vote on a national referendum for its autonomy. In Western Europe, just the opposite appears to be happening as more countries have moved toward a single currency and European Union.

The Roots of Federalism-Modern federalism is largely an American invention, but there is evidence of some elements of federalism at least as far as the Union of Utrecht in the Netherlands in 1579.

Historical Origins-American federalism grew out of the American Revolution against Britain as the 13 Colonies first became independent and then joined together to form a confederation and finally, a single nation.

Role of Size and Diversity-Federal systems tend to be found in countries that are *geographically large and ethnically, economically, religiously and linguistically diverse.* Germany's Catholic and Protestant regions are very different from one another; as are the farmers of the central plains of Canada, the fishers of Nova Scotia, and French-speaking (Catholic) Quebec different from the mostly English-speaking Protestants of the rest of the country. Switzerland has three dominant languages—German, French, and Italian—spread throughout its borders. India consists of many different ethnic and religious groups that speak various languages and reside in very different climates. The United States is also very large and diverse ethnically, economically, regionally, and politically. *The Federalist Papers* argued that federalism best suited the size and diversity of the United States.

U.S. Federalism: Pro and Con-The debate that raged over federalism during the Constitutional Convention has persisted to the present day. Strong arguments for and against federalism, in contrast to a more unitary system are listed below:

Pro: Diversity of Needs-Because of the variety of needs that exist in large and diverse countries, national standards may not take into consideration specific policies that distinct majorities in different states may prefer.

Con: The Importance of National Standards-The needs or desires that different states pursue may not be worthy ones. The manner in which white majorities in southern states enslaved and then discriminated against African-Americans, without interference from the North is a good example of how national standards my be preferable to local standards.

Pro: Closeness to the People-Because state governments are closer to their citizens, it is sometimes claimed that government will be more responsive to their needs and demands.

Con: Low Visibility and Lack of Popular Control-Since many Americans are more informed about the national government than they are about state governments, and more people participate in national versus local elections, geographic proximity is not as important. Therefore, responsiveness to ordinary citizens may actually be greater in national government.

Pro: Innovation and Experimentation-Wisconsin and Michigan experimented with their welfare systems in the 1990s. Other states have influenced national standards concerning issues such as voting rights for women and 18 to 20 year-olds, and air and water pollution. States can be "laboratories" for more creative public policy programs. As well, if one party, say the Republicans, rules the national government, then the citizens of majority Democratic states can still enact policies that they prefer. Multiple governments reduce the risks of bad policy or the blockage of the popular will; if things go wrong at one governmental level, they may go right at another.

Con: Spillover Effects and Competition-The innovation by state governments may result in bad policies which spill over from one state to another. Poverty is typically viewed as a national problem. If a city raises taxes to pay for poverty-related social programs, businesses and the wealthy may move out of town, and the poor may move in, resulting in the impoverishment of the city.

Pro: Training Ground for Women and Racial Minorities-A number of women and racial groups have been able to launch noteworthy political careers, women such as the late Texas Congresswoman Barbara Jordan, former U.S. Senator from Illinois, Carol Moseley Braun, California Congresswoman Loretta Sanchez and Black Republican J.C. Watts of Oklahoma have all demonstrated how state and local offices can catapult underrepresented groups to national office.

What Sort of Federalism?-Federalism is likely to be a permanent feature of the American political system. What may vary is *what sort* of federalism will exist in the United States; how much power the state and national governments retain in this relationship. The political parties have had very different views of the balance of power between the state and federal governments. The Republicans have tended to favor state power, while the Democrats have tended to favor retention of national and government programs and standards. The Clinton administration and Republicans in Congress changed the course of federalism with the passage of two important pieces of legislation. The first restricted "unfunded mandates" and the second changed the welfare system. The **Supreme Court** has interpreted the Tenth Amendment in a way that shifts power to the states. In 1997, the Court rejected a portion of the Brady gun control law, saying that the national government could not force states to do background checks on gun buyers. The Court recently reinforced the autonomy of the states when it introduced the idea of "state sovereign immunity" where states could not be sued for violating federal rules and laws. Opinions about federalism depend on their interests, their ideologies, and the kinds of things they want government to do.

→THE CONSTITUTION AND SHARED POWERS

The Constitution embodies federalism in two main ways: power is expressly given to the states, as well as to the national government; and the states have important roles in shaping the national government and in choosing officials for the national government. The Constitution makes the national government supreme in certain matters, but it also makes clear that *state governments have independent powers*—the **supremacy clause** declares that the Constitution, laws, and treaties of the United States shall be the "supreme law of the land" (Article VI); the kinds of laws that Congress has the power to pass are **enumerated** in the Constitution (Article I, Section 8); and the **Tenth Amendment** declares that the powers not delegated to the United States by the Constitution, nor prohibited by it to the states, are "reserved to the states respectively, or to the people" (the **reservation clause**). The reservation clause is unique to the United States. Other federal systems, such as Germany, reserve functions *to the national government* that are not explicitly given to the states. The Constitution's provisions about the formation of the national government also recognize a special position for the states.

The States' Roles in National Government-Article VII of the Constitution declares that it was "done in Convention by the unanimous consent of the states present" and provides that the Constitution would go into effect when the conventions of nine *states*, ratified it. Article V provides that the Constitution can be amended only when conventions in or the legislatures of three-quarters of the states ratify an amendment. Article IV, Section 3, gives states final say in determining its boundaries. The Constitution also allows the states to decide who can vote for members of the U.S. House of Representatives by deciding who votes for their own legislatures (Article I, Section 2). Each state has equal representation in the U.S. Senate (Article V). Until the passage of the 17th amendment in 1913, Senators were chosen by the state legislatures rather than by the voters (Article I, Section 3). The electoral college also reveals the special role that states play in selection of the president of the United States (Article II, Section I).

Relations Among the States-Relations among states are regulated by Article IV of the Constitution. Article IV provides that each state is required to give **"full faith and credit"** to the public acts, records, and judicial proceedings of every other state; citizens in each state are entitled to all the **"privileges and immunities"** of citizens in the several states; and fugitives from justice must be delivered up to a state demanding their return. Same-sex marriage has gain increasing attention since the 1990s. If same-sex marriages became legal in one state, the Article IV clauses would obligate the other states to recognize them. Twenty-eight states passed laws to immunize themselves from such a marriage law.

→THE EVOLUTION OF FEDERALISM

Federalism as we know it emerged slowly. There were *variations over time in the relative power of the states and the federal government.* The *national government gradually gained ground*, reflecting factors such as industrialization and economic growth, increased foreign policy involvement, and bitter conflicts over a series of divisive issues such as race, slavery, and regional economic interests.

Federalism Before the Civil War-During the 1790s, the Federalist administration of John Adams created bitter resentment among the Jefferson–led Anti-Federalists (now called Republicans) when it passed the Alien and Sedition Acts. The Virginia and Kentucky Resolutions (secretly authored by Jefferson and Madison) declared that the states did not have to obey unconstitutional national laws, leaving it up to the states to decide what was unconstitutional. The Republicans were advocating **states' rights** against the national government. During the War of 1812 against Britain, New England political and business leaders

53

resolved that unconstitutional actions by the national government (namely an embargo against Britain that hurt their merchant-related businesses) could be declared null and void by the states. These attempts by states to nullify national laws (a reference to the theory that state could declare U.S. laws "null and void" within its own borders), preceded the Civil War that was fought over the question of whether southern states had the right to secede from the Union of the United States. Advocates of states' rights have come from all regions of the country, from different parties, and from different philosophies (depending upon exactly who would gain or lose).

Nullification-The theory of nullification has presented great challenges to the philosophy and system of federalism. "Nullification," is usually associated with powerful southern Senator John C. Calhoun who championed the doctrine that since the states created the federal government, they could disregard its laws and policies. This was in response to adverse and high tariffs being imposed by the federal government in 1833. But nullification has never gained much support in the states or the nation.

The Marshall Court-One crucial question about federalism in the early years of the United States concerned who, if anyone, would *enforce the supremacy clause*. The answer turned out to be that the U.S. Supreme Court would do it, but this answer emerged haltingly as the *Supreme Court gradually solidified its power* within the federal system. Under the leadership of Chief Justice **John Marshall**, the Court established the doctrine of **judicial review** (*Marbury* v. *Madison*, 1803). In 1810, the Supreme Court for the first time clearly exercised the power to find *state* laws unconstitutional (*Fletcher* v. *Peck*). In 1816, the Court solidified its position in relation to the states by upholding Section 25 of the Judiciary Act of 1789.

Struggles over federalism in the nineteenth and twentieth centuries resulted in gradual increases of national government power. *McCulloch* v. *Maryland* (1819) upheld the constitutionality of the incorporation of the Bank of the United States and its immunity from taxation by the state of Maryland where it was located. Chief Justice Marshall argued that "the power to tax involves the power to destroy," thus making the states supreme; a clear violation of the *supremacy clause*. Marshall justified national authority with his declaration that the Constitution emanated from the sovereign people. Justice Marshall's broad interpretation of the **necessary and proper clause** (also known as the *elastic clause*) laid the foundation for national dominance in the federalist system of the United States.

Limiting and Preempting the States-In 1824, the Court ruled that provisions of the U.S. Constitution may exclude states from acting in certain areas (*Gibbons* v. *Ogden*). **The contract clause** of Article I, Section 10 and the **commerce clause** of Article I, Section 8 have been interpreted by the Court to limit the states while strengthening the national government through the doctrine of **preemption**—which precludes state action when the national government has already acted on a certain subject—based on the principle that federal laws take precedence over state laws (the **supremacy clause**).

The Slavery Issue-The shape of federalism was strongly affected by the Supreme Court and by events surrounding the Civil War. The issue of slavery in the western territories began to dominate disputes about the nature of federalism; as new, nonslave states were settled and sought to join the Union, white southerners feared that their political power was eroding. The Missouri Compromise of 1820 established an equal number of free and slave states and banned slavery in territories above a line (36'30 parallel) running westward to the Rockies from Missouri's southern border. Land acquired through the Mexican American War reopened the question of whether the new states would be slave or free. California was admitted to the Union as a free state as a result of the 1850 Compromise. The Fugitive Slave Act of 1850 (part of the Compromise) required that private citizens in the North return runaway slaves to their owners. In 1854, the Kansas-Nebraska Act nullified the 1820 Missouri Compromise entirely by allowing states to decide for themselves whether they would be slave or free regardless of the Missouri Compromise line. The result was violence in the state of Kansas that many scholars call "bleeding Kansas." In 1860, the Northern and Southern wings of the Democratic party split apart over the slavery issue, and the newly formed Republican party nominated **Abraham Lincoln** (who opposed slavery in the western territories) as president in 1860. South Carolina seceded from the Union and was soon followed by the other six states of the Deep South; these states formed the Confederate States of America.

→THE CIVIL WAR and the EXPANSION OF NATIONAL POWER

The Civil War or "war between the states" had profound effects on the relationship between the states and the national government.

Indissoluble Union-Northern victory established that the Union was indissoluble—that is, states could not withdraw or secede. Though the Union of the United States is a given in modern American society, many Americans today support the right of new countries such as Croatia and Bosnia to secede from existing countries (such as Yugoslavia).

Constitutional Amendments-The war resulted in constitutional changes that *subordinated states to new kinds of national standards*. The most notable changes came through implementation of the **Thirteenth, Fourteenth, and Fifteenth Amendments**. The Thirteenth Amendment abolished slavery while the Fifteenth Amendment granted former male slaves a constitutional right to vote; a right which was largely ignored until the passage of the 1965 Voting Rights Act).

The Fourteenth Amendment included broad language going well beyond the slave issue with the declaration that no *state* shall "deprive any person of life, liberty, or property, without due process of law; nor deny to any person within its jurisdiction the equal protection of the laws." The **due process** and **equal protection** clauses eventually became important vehicles for the protection of many civil liberties. Prior to adoption of the Fourteenth Amendment, protections in the Bill of Rights had been applied only against the national government. Precedents were established for expansion of the federal government's powers, especially in wartime. President Lincoln exerted **emergency powers**, such as spending money without congressional authorization, suspending the writ of *habeas corpus* in war zones, and issuing the **Emancipation Proclamation** to free slaves in occupied southern territories. The huge military and industrial effort of waging the war established patterns for future government action of many sorts.

Expanded National Activity Since the Civil War-Activities of the national government have expanded greatly since the Civil War. The national government was increasingly active in the late nineteenth century. These activities gave the national government increasing weight in relation to the states, which was greatly accentuated in the twentieth century with Woodrow Wilson's **New Freedom** domestic programs in 1913 and 1914, and with World War I.

The New Deal and World War II-In response to the *Great Depression* of the 1930s, the New Deal of President Franklin D. Roosevelt created many new national regulatory agencies to supervise the various aspects of business, including the Federal Communication Commission (FCC), Civil Aeronautics Board (CAB), the Securities Exchange Commission (SEC), and the National Labor Relations Board (NLRB). Welfare and Social Security programs were also established during the New Deal. Through the 1960s, national government spending on domestic programs continued to grow, particularly during and after Lyndon Johnson's Great Society. Since World Wars I and II the federal government's spending has dwarfed that of the state governments.

The Supreme Court's Role-The Supreme Court initially resisted the growth of national government power to regulate business .It permitted monopolies in manufacturing during the end of the nineteenth century, struck down national child labor laws as unconstitutional, and ruled against measures of the New Deal such as the National Recovery Act and the Agricultural Adjustment Act. After Roosevelt attempted to expand the number of justices of the Supreme Court (from 9 to 13), the Supreme Court became more supportive of FDR's domestic policies. The Supreme Court has since upheld virtually all national legislation that has come before it such as the **1964 Civil Rights Act** which rests on a very broad interpretation of the **commerce clause**. More recently however, the Court has signaled a reluctance to continue to support a broad interpretation of that clause.

"Marble Cake"-The metaphors of layer cake and marble cake federalism have often been used to illustrate the changing relationships between the national government and the states. **Layer cake** federalism is an *outdated metaphor* that describes a system of federalism in which *state and national powers are distinct and separate* from each other. It is based on the assumption that states and the national government are equal and separate entities. **Marble cake** federalism is a *more accurate metaphor for today's federalism* in which elements of national and state influence swirl around each other, *without any clear boundaries*. Marble cake federalism (often called cooperative federalism) is based on the theory that states and the national government share power and cooperate to solve problems. Grant-in-aid programs that involve a complicated mixture of national, state, and local government activity and control illustrate this cooperation. State and national government powers and activities have become deeply intertwined. The national government is dominant in many policy areas; only very recently has some of this dominance been challenged.

→THE RISE OF NATIONAL GRANTS-IN-AID TO THE STATES

The growth and decline of national **grants-in-aid** to the states define some of the pragmatic complexities of federalism in action. Grants-in-aid are federal funds allocated to states and local governments. Grants involve a complicated mixture of national and local government activity and control. Grant funds are often used by administrations to increase national government influence over what state and local governments can do.

Origin and Growth of Grants-National government grants to the states began with the 1787 Northwest Ordinance which provided land for government buildings, schools, and colleges in the Northwest Territory. Land grants to the states for roads, canals, and railroads have been important features of federalism throughout the nation's history. The biggest growth in federal grants occurred during the 1950s, 1960s, and 1970s under both Republican and Democratic administrations. Programs are largely shaped or regulated by the national government.

Reasons for Grants-Congress increasingly used federal grant money in order to deal with nationwide problems—especially interstate highways, poverty, crime, and pollution—by setting policy at the national level and providing money from federal tax revenues while having states carry out the policies. There were three main reasons for this:

Externalities: States seldom took responsibility for the "externalities" or "spillover effects" that state policies and practices had on other states and their citizens. States had no interest in spending money on problems such as toxic clean up if it didn't benefit them.

Abundant National Government Resources: In the 1960s, the federal government used the federal income tax (a progressive tax wherein those with more were taxed at higher percentages than lower income individuals) to administer grants. The federal income tax was a major source of funds aimed at federal poverty programs.

Local Provisions: Many of the programs that were created required management at the state and local levels. Many of the clinics and facilities that were constructed in order to carry out the objectives of the federal programs were most effective when administered locally.

Categorical Grants-Categorical grants allocate money to states for *clearly defined categories of activity*, while **block grants** provide money to states for *broad, general purposes*. Grants often come with strings attached that involve detailed rules and regulations. When these stipulations conflict with state objectives, they often complain of "red tape" and bureaucracy. When federal stipulations harmonize with state objectives, we often here of "cooperative" federalism.

The New Federalism: Block Grants and Revenue Sharing-Under **general revenue sharing—** in which federal money was shared with other levels of government—money was granted to states and localities, with *virtually no federal controls*. This program was implemented in 1972 during the Nixon administration but was eliminated in 1986 under the Reagan administration. These programs often provided money under an automatic formula related to statistical characteristics such as the number of needy residents, the total size of the population, or the average income level. However, the use of formulas affects the politics of national grants. Census counts become the subjects of political conflict because statistical counts affect how much money states and localities will receive. Disputes frequently arise when these formulas benefit one state or region rather than another.

The Slowdown in National Money-The flow of federal money to the states had begun to slow by the end of the 1970s. The reasons for the slowdown in federal money to states and localities—which continues today—include certain *structural factors* (such as the general decline in the growth rate of the U.S. economy and increasing pressure on national tax revenues) together with major *political factors* (such as increased interest group pressure to cut domestic spending, which contributed to more conservative political leadership in the 1980s and 1990s).

- Economic problems in the late 1970s and early 1980s contributed to lower-than-expected tax receipts and greater-than-expected government outlays.
- Business-oriented conservative interest groups and think tanks were successful in building and publicizing the case against big government in Washington. Some state governments—with tax rates already too high—face great difficulty in finding new revenue to match their new responsibilities.
- The failure of **policy implementation** between national policies and state use or objectives were very complicated, and were often administered by uncoordinated agencies. It was difficult to attain the objectives of national legislation.
- The conservative shift in national mood and policy reached which ushered in the Reagan administrations also resulted in the major cut backs in federal aid to the states.

Though federal grants-in-aid rebounded in the 1990s, federal government grants were unable to keep pace with the growth in the states. The federal government satisfied many state governors when it turned power over the states in the areas of welfare, Medicaid, and child nutrition.

➔**THE BALANCE OF POWER AND CONTROL**

Many contemporary facets of federalism involve *questions of control* rather than money because the national government exerts control over many state-administered programs, particularly through mandates and conditions on aid.

Mandates-The federal government, through mandates, requires the states to carry out certain policies, even when little or no national government aid is involved (these are also known as "unfunded" mandates). Such mandates often are found in regulations involving *civil rights* and the *environmen*t and are enforced by the federal courts. States often complain bitterly about federal mandates that require state expenditures without providing federal funds. Courts have also mandated expensive reforms of overcrowded state prisons, most notably in Texas. Republicans have strongly opposed "unfunded mandates" and targeted them in the 1994 *Contract with America.*

Conditions on Aid-Conditions are characteristic of categorical grant-in-aid programs and are increasingly included in general block grants. In theory, these conditions are voluntary because the states could refuse to accept the aid; but the states usually have to accept the conditions because they generally cannot afford to give up federal money. The national government uses its money to influence to influence many diverse kinds of policies.

Resurgence of the States-There are a number of indicators that demonstrate that the states are becoming more important in the American federal system. With reduced federal assistance during the 1980s and early 1990s, many states increased their own commitments to social and environmental issues; New York and California are good examples of this. Some state innovations require substantial government spending. By contrast, some state-level innovations have simply required shifting existing funds to new purposes. Some states took the lead in requiring that women be paid according to "comparable worth" of their jobs. After the U.S. Supreme Court's *Webster v. Reproductive Health Services* (1989) decision, which gave states more leeway to regulate abortion, several states, including Washington and Oregon, liberalized their abortion laws, while Louisiana made them more restrictive. Some have called these developments the "new New Federalism" or "New Federalism II." The emerging consensus favoring **devolution** (policymaking responsibilities transferred to the states) is also evident in the words and actions of America's political leaders, including recent Supreme Court decisions, support by President Clinton, and support from the Republican majority in the 104th Congress.

→THE CONSEQUENCES OF FEDERALISM

Federalism entails a high degree of complexity in policymaking and policy implementation, but it also permits diversity of responses to different situations and allows experimentation at state and local levels. Multi-level government agencies in the same policy areas means possible inefficiency and confusion about who is responsible. Our federal system leads to substantial inequality of certain kinds, such as occurs when individual states set their own levels of benefits under welfare programs that are partially funded by the national government. Certain kinds of policies may be difficult or impossible to implement at state or local levels, including redistributive programs (that transfer resources from the rich to the poor) and protections that cross local and state lines (such as environmental issues or voting rights for 18-year-olds). Some states such as Idaho and Wyoming have done nothing at all with the increased federal dollars.

→SUMMARY

Federalism is a system under which political powers are divided between state, local, and national governments. Federalism is an important *structural factor* of American politics; modern federalism is an American invention. Federalism is most commonly found in large, diverse countries. There are many *pros* and *cons* concerning federalism. Federalism enables local and state governments to address the particular needs of the citizens in their communities, while it also enables the federal government to address areas that states may neglect such as civil rights and the environment.

The U.S. Constitution enumerates the powers of the national government and reserves most other powers to the states. The states in the United States are given greater latitude in dealing with the powers of the national governments than in most countries. The balance of power between the state and central governments continues to evolve over time; the Supreme Court has acknowledged the Constitutional supremacy of the national government over the states. The national government has often dictated its policies to the states through grant-in aid programs. Federalism has mixed implications for democracy.

Chapter Outline

This section gives you a comprehensive review of the chapter. Use this outline in combination with your textbook to look for key concepts and objectives, to identify essential terms and names, and to gain a basic understanding of political practices and principles from this chapter.

I.   **WELFARE REFORM AND THE STATES (p. 53)**
      A. The opening vignette shows the interplay between the national and state governments.
      B. Under the **Social Security Act** of 1935, the U.S. government established **Aid to Families with Dependent Children (AFDC)** as an **entitlement program** for children in poor, mostly female-headed, families.

1. The national government (which provided most of the money) guaranteed that any eligible family in the country was entitled to benefits; it made the rules about who was eligible, for how long, and under what circumstances.
2. The program was administered by the states, a process that resulted in different levels of benefits from one state to another.

C. The system began to change around the beginning of the 1990s.
1. President **Bill Clinton** and many members of Congress from both political parties promised to "end welfare as we know it" when they took office.
   a) Many state governments took the lead in trying out their own welfare reforms.
   b) New (mostly Republican) state governors and legislatures promised to reform welfare by encouraging work and parental responsibility.
2. This *interplay between national and state governments* illustrates the dispersion of power in our federal system.
   a) The mixture of state and national action on this issue, the state experimentation that affected policymaking in the nation as a whole, and the conflict between national standards and local flexibility are all characteristic of American federalism.
   b) The shift in responsibility from the national government to the state governments on welfare may signify a change in our long history of enhancing the power of government at the national level.

II. FEDERALISM AS A SYSTEM OF GOVERNMENT (pp. 54-62)
A. **The nature of federalism**
1. **Federalism** is a system under which significant government powers are divided between the central government and smaller governmental units; neither one completely controls the other, and each has some room for independent action.
2. **Forms of government**
   a) **Federalism**—significant government powers are *divided between the central government and smaller governmental units*
   b) **Confederation**—constituent *units or states retain ultimate authority* and can veto major actions of the central government; illustrated by the United Nations or the revolutionary government under the Articles of Confederation
   c) **Unitary**—*central government exercises all governmental powers* and can change its constituent units; this is the most common form of government today.
3. **National systems compared**
   a) Federalism is not a common way of organizing governments around the world; in the mid-1990s, 88 percent of United Nations members had unitary rather than federal governments.

b) In the years since the founding of the United States, a number of important countries have established federal systems, often modeling them on the U.S. system.

c) There are no neat boundaries among different forms of government; scholars have suggested that there is a continuum from unitary, to formally federal, quasi-federal, federal, and confederate systems, but we can *observe patterns in the types of countries* that have had federal systems.

B. **The roots of federalism**

1. Modern federalism is largely an American invention that is best understood as the historical process by which the colonies became independent states and then formed a confederation as its first governing system.

2. The role of size and diversity

   a) The Founders argued in *The Federalist Papers* that the rather large size and diversity of the new nation made federalism especially appropriate.

   b) Most federal systems around the world are found in countries that are geographically large and have regions that differ in economic activity, religion, ethnicity, and language.

C. **U.S. federalism: pro and con**

1. Federalism is one of the key *structural characteristics* of American government.

   a) Tends to prevent the emergence of fully unified or disciplined political parties

   b) Limits what Congress and the president can do by reserving some powers to the states

   c) Allows for a diversity of different policies to be pursued in different states and regions

2. **Advantages of federalism**

   a) Diversity of needs—different states can enact different public policies to meet their own needs

   b) Closeness to the people—state and local governments may be more responsive to the people than the federal government, which is more distant from ordinary citizens

   c) Innovation and experimentation—individual states can try out new ideas and may act as "laboratories" for the nation, as illustrated by California laws designed to fight air pollution, New York laws to deal with water pollution, various states that allowed women and 18-year-olds to vote before the nation did as a whole, and health care policies of several states

   d) Training ground for women and racial minorities—a number of people from historically underrepresented groups have been catapulted from local and state leadership positions to national leadership.

3. **Disadvantages of federalism**

   a) Lack of national standards—localized needs may not be worthy ones, as illustrated by historical patterns of discrimination against minorities

b) Low visibility and lack of popular control—more Americans are actually better informed about the national government than about state and local governments, so responsiveness to ordinary citizens is probably greater through the national government

c) Lack of uniformity in rules and programs—certain kinds of government policies do not work well without uniform national rules

    (1) Divergent regulations can cause confusion or bad effects that spill over from one state to another.

    (2) Some problems are too large for individual states to handle effectively, such as poverty and some social problems.

    (3) **Spillover effects**—Problems such as air pollution do not stop at state boundaries.

    (4) Innovation by local governments can be undercut by competition among communities for wealth and resources.

4. **What sort of federalism?**

a) The *balance of power between states and nation* has become a hot political issue in recent years, particularly after Republican congressional candidates campaigned in 1994 on the **Contract with America**, which emphasized reducing the role of the national government.

    (1) President Clinton (a former governor of Arkansas) agreed that federalism needed to be reoriented.

    (2) The president and congressional republicans joined to pass legislation that significantly changed the course of federalism. The outcome included the restriction of "unfunded mandates" and dramatic welfare reform.

    (3) The U.S. Supreme Court under Chief Justice **William Rehnquist** also showed signs of shifting power from the national to the state governments by giving new force to the **Tenth Amendment**.

b) Decisions about federalism often affect who wins and who loses valuable benefits; people's opinions about federalism often depend upon their ideologies, on what kinds of things they want government to do, and upon who controls the national government at the moment.

III. THE CONSTITUTION AND SHARED POWERS (pp. 62-65)

A. **The Constitution embodies federalism in two main ways**:

1. Power is expressly given to the states, as well as to the national government.
2. The states have important roles in shaping the national government and in choosing officials for the national government.

B. **How federalism is depicted in the Constitution**

1. **Independent state powers**

a) The Constitution makes the central government supreme in certain matters, but it also makes clear that *state governments have independent powers*.

(1) The **supremacy clause** declares that the Constitution, laws, and treaties of the United States shall be the "supreme law of the land" (Article VI).

(2) The kinds of laws that Congress has the power to pass are **enumerated** in the Constitution (Article I, Section 8).

(3) The **Tenth Amendment** declares that the powers not delegated to the United States by the Constitution, nor prohibited by it to the states, are "reserved to the states respectively, or to the people" (the provision known as the **reservation clause**, which establishes the **reserved powers** of the states).

  b) The reservation clause is unique to the United States; other federal systems (such as Canada and Germany) reserve to the national government all functions not explicitly given to the states.

  2. **The states' roles in national government**

    a) The Constitution's provisions about the formation of the national government recognize a special position for the states.

    b) State governments play a central part in amending the Constitution—states cannot be combined or divided into new states without the consent of the state legislatures concerned (Article IV, Section 3).

    c) The Constitution provides special roles for the states in the selection of national government officials.

    d) Each state has equal representation in the U.S. Senate

    e) States play a central role in the Constitutional amendment processes.

    f) Article II, Section I explains the states' role in the **Electoral College**.

  3. Relations among the states (national provisions are established in Article IV of the U.S. Constitution)

    a) Each state is required to give **full faith and credit** to the public acts, records, and judicial proceedings of every other state.

    b) Citizens in each state are entitled to all the **privileges and immunities** of citizens in the several states.

    c) Fugitives from justice must be delivered up to a state demanding their return.

IV. THE EVOLUTION OF FEDERALISM (pp. 65-69)

  A. **Federalism before the Civil War**

    1. When the Federalist party passed the Alien and Sedition Acts which prohibited criticism of the federal government, James Madison and Thomas Jefferson secretly wrote the Virginian and Kentucky Resolutions which contended that the states were not obligated to obey unconstitutional national laws, leaving it up to the states to decide what was unconstitutional.

    2. During the War of 1812, the merchant interests of the Northeast whose trade relations with Britain were negatively affected, resolved that unconstitutional

actions by the national government (namely an embargo against Britain) could be declared null and void.

B. **Nullification**

    1. The political doctrine known as nullification emerged during the 1830s as some southern states protested burdensome tariffs imposed by the federal government. Under the leadership of powerful Senator John C. Calhoun, opponents to the federal intrusion maintained that the states could disregard the laws and policies of the national government.

    2. Nullification has never gained much support in the states or the nation.

C. **The Marshall Court**

    1.One crucial question about federalism in the early years of the United States concerned who, if anyone, would *enforce the supremacy clause.*

        a) The answer turned out to be that the U.S. Supreme Court would do it, but this answer emerged haltingly as the *Supreme Court gradually solidified its power* within the federal system.

        b) Under the leadership of Chief Justice **John Marshall**, the Court established the its authority to declare *national* laws *unconstitutional* (the doctrine of **judicial review**), in the 1803 case of *Marbury* v. *Madison*.

D. **Judicial review of state action**

    1. *Fletcher* v. *Peck* (1810)—for the first time, the Supreme Court clearly exercised the power to find *state* laws unconstitutional; Chief Justice Marshall simply took the power for granted and used it, without any explicit discussion of the Court's power

        a) Although the Supreme Court clearly established its power to declare state laws unconstitutional, the Court rarely used this power until after the Civil War.

        b) Struggles over federalism in the nineteenth and twentieth centuries resulted in gradual increases of national government power.

        (1) *McCulloch* v. *Maryland* (1819)—upheld the constitutionality of the incorporation of the Bank of the United States and its immunity from taxation

           (a) Chief Justice Marshall's broad reading of the **necessary and proper clause** (often referred to as the **elastic clause**) laid the foundation for expansion of what the national government could do.

           (b) In a major statement justifying national authority, Chief Justice Marshall declared that the Constitution emanated from the sovereign people.

           (c) Congress had the power to incorporate the bank under its authorization to make all laws "necessary and proper" for carrying out its named powers (Article I, Section 8).

   (d) Maryland's tax on the national bank was invalid because "the power to tax involves the power to destroy," which would defeat the national government's supremacy within its sphere of powers.

c) **Limiting and preempting the states**

   (1) In 1824 the Supreme Court ruled that provisions of the U.S. Constitution may exclude states from acting in certain areas (*Gibbons v. Ogden*). The **contract clause** of Article I, Section 10, and the **commerce clause** of Article I, Section 8 have been interpreted by the Court to limit the states while strengthening the national government.

   (2) At other times, the Court used the doctrine of **preemption** in ruling that provisions of the U.S. Constitution may *exclude* states from acting in certain areas where they might interfere with federal legislation; this doctrine of preemption precludes state action when the national government has already acted on a certain subject, based on the principle that federal laws take precedence over the state laws (the **supremacy clause**).

E. **The slavery issue**

   1. The issue of slavery in the western territories began to dominate disputes about the nature of federalism; as new, nonslave states were settled and sought to join the Union, white Southerners feared that their political power was eroding.

      a) **Missouri Compromise of 1820**—established an equal number of slave and free states and banned slavery in the territories above a line running westward to the Rockies from Missouri's Southern border, but the acquisition of vast new territories in the Southwest after the Mexican War reopened the question as to whether new states would be slave or free

      b) **Compromise of 1850**—admitted California as a free state and temporarily balanced matters in white Southerners' eyes by enacting the **Fugitive Slave Act**, that required citizens in the North to help return runaway slaves (an act that was bitterly resented by many Northerners and helped lead to the Civil War)

      c) **"Bleeding Kansas"**—violence between proslavery and antislavery forces resulted from the decision in 1854 to organize Kansas and Nebraska as territories and then let them decide for themselves whether to become slave or free states (even though they were above the Missouri Compromise line and, therefore, were supposed to be free)

   2. In 1860, the Northern and Southern wings of the **Democratic party split apart** over the slavery issue, and the newly formed **Republican party** nominated **Abraham Lincoln** (who opposed slavery in the western territories) for president in 1860.

a) South Carolina seceded from the Union and was soon followed by the other six states of the Deep South; these states formed the Confederate States of America.

b) The Civil War began at Fort Sumter, South Carolina.

V. THE CIVIL WAR AND THE EXPANSION OF NATIONAL POWER (pp. 69-72)

A. The shape of federalism was strongly affected by the Supreme Court and by events surrounding the Civil War. The national government gradually gained ground, reflecting factors such as increased industrialization, economic growth, and increased foreign policy involvement.

B. The profound effects of the Civil War on the relationship between the states and the national government.

1. Indissoluble union

   a) Northern victory established that the *Union was indissoluble*.

   b) The Civil War decisively meant that states could not withdraw or secede.

2. **Constitutional amendments**

   a) Constitutional changes were established that *subordinated states to new kinds of national standards*; protections in the Bill of Rights had previously been applied only against the national government.

      (1) **Thirteenth Amendment**—abolished slavery

      (2) **Fourteenth Amendment**—guarantees due process of law and equal protection of law

      (3) **Fifteenth Amendment**—gave former male slaves a constitutional right to vote (enforced by the national government for a short time after the Civil War but then widely ignored until passage of the 1965 Voting Rights Act)

   b) The most notable changes came through implementation of the **Fourteenth Amendment** (1868), which included broad language going well beyond the slave issue with the declaration that no *state* shall "deprive any person of life, liberty, or property, without due process of law; nor deny to any person within its jurisdiction the equal protection of the laws."

      (1) **Due process clause**—the vehicle by which the Supreme Court ruled that essential civil liberties of the Bill of Rights were protected against the *states*

      (2) **Equal protection clause**—became the foundation for protecting rights of minorities against discrimination by state or local governments

3. Emergency powers—*precedents were established* for the expansion of the federal government's powers, especially in wartime.

   a) Extraordinary **emergency powers** were exerted by President Lincoln, such as spending money without congressional authorization, suspending the writ of *habeas corpus* in war zones, and issuing the **Emancipation Proclamation** to free slaves in occupied Southern territories.

    b) The huge military and industrial effort of waging the war established patterns for future government action of many sorts.

C. **Expanded national activity since the Civil War**

    1. Activities of the national government have expanded greatly since the Civil War.
        a) They now touch on almost every aspect of daily life.
        b) They are thoroughly entangled with state government activities.

    2. The national government was increasingly active in the late nineteenth century with activities that gave the national government increasing weight in relation to the states.

    3. The national government became still more active with **Woodrow Wilson's New Freedom** domestic legislation in 1913-14 and with the economic and military efforts of World War I.

    4. **The New Deal and World War II**
        a) **Franklin Roosevelt's New Deal** of the 1930s—created in response to the Great Depression—was much more important in creating the foundation for increased government activity.
            (1) Created many new national regulatory agencies to supervise various aspects of business
            (2) Brought national government spending in such areas as welfare and relief (which had previously been reserved almost entirely to the states) and established the Social Security pension system
        b) **Lyndon Johnson's Great Society** program of the 1960s launched new federal programs to solve social and economic problems.
        c) Wars were crucial in the expansion of national government power.
            (1) Ever since World War II, the federal government has spent nearly twice as much per year as the states and localities put together (with much of the money going to direct payments to individuals).
            (2) Increasingly, the states, and especially local governments, have had many more civilian employees.

D. **The Supreme Court's role**

    1. The Court *initially resisted the growth in the power of the national government to regulate business.*
        a) In 1895, the court ruled that the Sherman Antitrust Act could not forbid monopolies in manufacturing because manufacturing only indirectly affected interstate commerce.
        b) The Court declared important New Deal measures unconstitutional in the 1930s, including the National Recovery Act and the Agricultural Adjustment Act.

    2. After 1937, the Court became *a nationalizing force.*
        a) The Court has approved almost all pieces of national legislation since President Roosevelt's **court-packing plan** in 1937.

b) The Court upheld the **Civil Rights Act of 1964**, a law that rests partially on a broad interpretation of the **commerce clause**.

E. Two metaphors based on images of baked goods have been used to illustrate the changing role of federalism.

1. **Layer cake federalism**—old, simple *metaphor that describes a system of federalism in which state and national powers are distinct and separate* from each other; seen as a system in which state and national powers are neatly divided, like layers of pastry; often referred to as **dual federalism**

2. **Marble cake federalism**—a *more accurate metaphor for today's federalism* in which elements of national and state influence swirl around each other, *without any clear boundaries*; often called **cooperative federalism**

VI. THE RISE OF NATIONAL GRANTS-IN-AID TO THE STATES (pp. 72-76)

A. Origins and growth of grants

1. National government grants to the states began with the 1787 Northwest Ordinance.
2. The federal government has provided land grants to the states for roads, canals, and railroads.
3. The biggest growth in federal grants occurred during the 1950s, 1960s, and 1970s under both Republican and Democratic administrations.

B. Reasons for grants

1. Congress increasingly used federal grant money in order to deal with nationwide problems such as interstate highways, poverty, crime, and pollution.
a) Spillover effects are seldom addressed by states that adopt policies which negatively impact bordering states. Environmental policies are an example.
b) Federal tax revenues provide an abundant resource for the national government in carrying out its policy objectives on issues such as poverty.
c) State and local governments are probably more capable of efficiently managing and administering federal grants than the central government in Washington, DC.

C. The new federalism: Block grants and revenue sharing

1. **Categorical grants**—money granted to states for *clearly defined categories of activity* that specify precisely how the program has to work.
2. **Block grants**—money is granted to states for *broad, general purposes* and involves fewer rules than categorical grants
3. **General Revenue Sharing**—money was granted to states and localities, with *virtually no federal controls*; federal money was "shared" with other levels of government in a program that was implemented in 1972 during the Nixon administration but was eliminated in 1986 under the Reagan administration (in the wake of the "budget crunch" of the 1980s)
4. Slowdown of the national money
a) Economic problems in the 1970s and 1980s contributed to lower-than-expected tax receipts and greater-than-expected government outlays.

b) Some states with high taxes face great difficulty in finding new revenue to match their new responsibilities.

c) Some scholars and journalists complained about failures of **policy implementation**; they believed that there was no hope of attaining the stated objectives due to the complicated relationships between state and national governments involving many different and uncoordinated agencies with rigid rules and questionable competence.

d) The conservative shift in national mood and policy reached which ushered in the Reagan administrations also resulted in the major cut backs in federal aid to the states.

e) Congressional Republicans (delivering on a provision in their **Contract with America** to cut federal spending) made many state governors happy by trying to turn power over to the states, but they also cut the overall amount of spending directed to the states.

VII. THE BALANCE OF POWER AND CONTROL (pp. 76-80)

A. Many contemporary facets of federalism involve **questions of control** rather than money because the national government exerts control over many state-administered programs, particularly through mandates and conditions on aid.

B. Federal controls

1. **Mandates** require the states to carry out certain policies, even when little or no national government aid is involved; such mandates often are found in regulations involving *civil rights* and the *environment* and are enforced by the federal courts.

   a) Mandates have been especially important in the areas of civil rights and the environment.

   b) States often complain bitterly about federal mandates that require state expenditures without providing federal funds (**unfunded mandates**), and cutting back on unfunded mandates was one of the main promises in the Republicans' 1994 *Contract with America.*

2. **Conditions on aid** require states to spend grant money in certain ways if they want to receive federal funding; conditions are characteristic of categorical grant-in-aid programs and are increasingly included in general block grants.

   a) The national government uses its money to influence many diverse kinds of policies.

      (1) During the energy crisis of the 1970s, highway assistance funds were based on requirements that states impose a 55 mph speed limit (a requirement that was repealed in 1995).

      (2) In 1984, states were required to set a minimum drinking age of 21 or lose 15 percent of their highway aid.

   b) Because states cannot generally afford to give up federal money, they have to accept the conditions.

c) The national government often preempts state action concerning some policy area, but relies on state enforcement of the national standards; examples include clean air standards, occupational health and safety rules, and environmental restrictions on surface mining.

C. **Resurgence of the states**

1. With reduced federal assistance during the 1980s and early 1990s, many states increased their own commitments to social and environmental issues.

   a) Many states increased their Medicaid programs to help the poor with medical expenses.

   b) Some states took the lead in requiring that women be paid according to the comparable worth of their jobs.

   c) Several states liberalized their abortion laws, while others made them more restrictive.

2. There are a number of indicators that demonstrate that the states are becoming more important in the American federal system.

   a) The states account for an ever-increasing share of public spending in the United States; state governments are beginning to capture a rising share of the talented people who enter government service, both in elected office and in state bureaucracies; the states are becoming more important as jurisdictions where women and racial minorities can make their marks; and the states are becoming more active as independent actors in the global economy.

   b) The emerging consensus favoring **devolution** (policymaking responsibilities transferred to the states) is also evident in the words and actions of America's political leaders, including recent Supreme Court decisions, support by President Clinton, and support from the Republican majority in the 104th Congress.

VIII. SUMMARY (pp. 80-81)

A. Federalism is a system under which political powers are divided between state, local, and national governments.

1. Federalism is an important *structural factor* of American politics; modern federalism is an American invention.

2. Federalism is most commonly found in large, diverse countries. There are many *pros* and *cons* concerning federalism.

3. Federalism enables local and state governments to address the particular needs of the citizens in their communities, while it also enables the federal government to address areas that states may neglect such as civil rights and the environment.

B. The U.S. Constitution enumerates the powers of the national government and reserves most other powers to the states.

1. The states in the United States are given greater latitude in dealing with the powers of the national governments than in most countries.

2. The balance of power between the state and central governments continues to

evolve over time; the Supreme Court has acknowledged the Constitutional supremacy of the national government over the states.

C. The national government has often dictated its policies to the states through grant-in aid programs. Federalism has mixed implications for democracy.

Terms for Review

Use this list to review essential principles, functions, and concepts from this chapter. Refer to your textbook for help in identifying and defining terms on this list. When you study, do not merely memorize terms; ask questions about the material you are reviewing, and look for the importance or significance of each item.

federalism

confederation

unitary system

supremacy clause

reservation clause

nullification

judicial review

necessary and proper clause

contract clause

commerce clause

preemption

due process clause

equal protection clause

dual federalism

cooperative federalism

spillover effects
progressive tax

categorical grants

block grants

general revenue sharing

policy implementation

mandate

conditions

devolution

Research Topics: Applying What You Have Learned

You will derive more benefit from your reading if you try to apply what you have learned. Some of the suggested research topics can be answered exclusively from your text, while others require you to conduct some basic research on your own. The references suggested under **Internet Sources** *will help you in your search.*

- Although there are no neat boundaries that separate federalism from other systems such as unitary systems and confederations, there are observable patterns in the types of countries that have had federal systems. As an exercise in critical thinking, write a concise essay that would help another student understand the patterns or differences that distinguish basically federal systems from those that are essentially unitary.

- Make a list of all state and local programs that you think include some involvement of federal money. Look through the front pages of your local newspaper for ideas on local programs, and review a major newspaper from a large city in your state to get ideas on state projects. Make your list as extensive as possible, then compare it to the lists compiled by two or three other students in your class. What similarities and differences do you find?
- Why do the authors of your textbook refer to the federal system as a structural feature of American politics? What is the significance or importance of federalism within the framework of the U.S. Constitution, and how does this relate to the first part of this question?

Internet Sources

A number of sites on the World Wide Web serve as "gateways" to vast collections of material on American government and politics. The following Internet sources are recommended for students who would like to do additional research in areas covered by this chapter. These references would also be helpful in expanding on the questions suggested under Research Topics.

Assessing the New Federalism http://newfedralism.urban.org/
-News, essays and research on the New Federalism and devolution.

National Center for State Courts www.ncsl.org/
-Links to the home pages of the court systems of each of the states.

National Conference of State Legislature http://www.ncsl.org/
-Information about state governments and federal relations, including the distribution of federal revenues and expenditures in the states.

Publius http://www.lafayette.edu/publius/annual.html
-Home page of the leading academic journal of federalism.

State Constitutions www.findlaw.com/
-A site where the constitutions of all the states may be found.

U.S. Federalism Site www.min.net/~kala/fed/
-As complete a site as one might wish for on the history, philosophy, law and operation of federalism in the United States.

Self-Evaluation

Circle the correct answer for each question. Questions are listed in the same order in which the information appears in the text. Use the Answer Key in the back of the Study Guide *to check your responses.*

1. The appropriateness of the **marble cake** metaphor for federalism
    a. Relates particularly to programs that are designed to deal with local problems of only very limited significance.
    b. Has been questioned as a significant departure from the constitutional principle of separation of powers.
    c. Reflects eighteenth-century philosophies and principles concerning the role of local governments within the federal system.
    d. Is especially evident in programs in which the national government grants money for use by the states within programs largely shaped or regulated by the national government.

2. **Layer cake federalism** involves the theory that
    a. Federal grants to the states should be used within programs largely shaped or regulated by the national government.
    b. The national government should be dominant in most important policy areas.
    c. State and national government powers are neatly divided and occupy separate spheres.
    d. Elements of national and state influence swirl around each other, without any clear boundaries.

3. The doctrine of **preemption**
    a. Proposes that governors may interpose their authority between the national government and the citizens of the state.
    b. Provides that federal law should take precedence over state actions only when one of the enumerated powers of Congress is involved.
    c. Excludes the states from acting on certain subjects when the national government has already acted.
    d. Permits the Supreme Court to override an action of the executive or legislative branch.

4. **Categorical grants** are federal grants awarded to the states for
    a. Clearly specified activities with rules that define how the program is to work, such as the Clean Air Act.

    b.   General purposes and with fewer rules than many other programs, such as community development.

    c.   Programs established by the states, with no federal rules or strings attached.

    d.   Activities for which an automatic formula is used to define eligibility, with no restrictions on expenditures.

5.   An important theme in President Nixon's program of **new federalism** was that

    a.   There should be more funding for grants that involved agreements by the states to implement specific policies outlined in the grant agreement.

    b.   There should be less emphasis on categorical grants and more emphasis on block grants and general revenue sharing.

    c.   General revenue sharing should be gradually phased out over a period of years, and would be replaced by block grants and categorical grants.

    d.   A constitutional convention should be convened to modernize the provisions on federalism and intergovernmental relations.

6.   What is the central meaning of the **supremacy clause**?

    a.   Powers not delegated to the national government are reserved to the states.

    b.   Powers enumerated in the constitution list functions that are delegated exclusively to Congress.

    c.   States are obligated to recognize the validity of public acts and judicial proceedings of the other states.

    d.   Federal law has precedence over conflicting state laws when the two levels are operating within their spheres of authority.

7.   **Federalism** is a system in which

    a.   Powers are divided between the central government and smaller governmental units.

    b.   The constituent units or states retain ultimate authority and can veto major actions.

    c.   The central government retains all governmental power and can change its constituent units.

    d.   The smaller units or states retain most power, but must submit essential legislation for approval by the public.

8.   Which of the following illustrates a **mandate** imposed by the federal government?

    a.   Education policies that establish state-by-state criteria for certification of public school teachers

    b.   Policies that use money for leverage, such as the requirements that states had to impose a 55 mph speed limit or lose part of their highway assistance funds

    c.   Federal policies that would cut off money that goes to universities to help with teaching and research if universities discriminated in admissions or hiring

    d.   Civil rights policies that restrict state action and impose uniform national standards

9. Which of these statements is NOT correct?
    a. Federalism tends to prevent the emergence of fully unified or disciplined political parties.
    b. Federalism limits what Congress and the president can do by reserving some powers to the states.
    c. Federalism allows different states to enact different public policies to meet their own needs.
    d. Federalism provides for uniformity in rules and programs among the states.

10. The **reservation clause** of the Constitution
    a. Is a feature that is common to most federal constitutions.
    b. Reflects a political environment that feared involvement of the states in national policies.
    c. Is unique to the United States.
    d. Contains a specific list of powers that are to be retained by the states.

11. (T/F) National and state authority often overlap in our federal system, with complex combinations of policy made at the national, state, and local levels.

12. (T/F) Federalism permits diversity and experimentation by the states, but it also entails substantial inequality and can interfere with democratic processes.

13. (T/F) **General revenue sharing** provided money for innovative new state programs, but it was costly to implement because of the multiplicity of rules and regulations that it entailed.

14. (T/F) Most civil rights policies flow from the equal protection clause of the Fourteenth Amendment or from national legislation that imposes uniform national standards.

15. (T/F) **Redistributive programs** are tax policies that place a heavier tax burden on those with limited incomes than on those with high incomes.

16. (T/F) **Implied powers** are derived from interpretation of the full faith and credit clause.

17. (T/F) The Fourteenth Amendment included important guarantees relating to due process of law.

18. (T/F) Federalism is a system which divides power between "the one", "the few", and "the many".

Chapter 4
THE STRUCTURAL FOUNDATIONS OF AMERICAN GOVERNMENT AND POLITICS

The Key Concepts and Objectives provide a look at the fundamental goals and ideas of this chapter. This section serves as a guide to a basic understanding of the objectives of your textbook.

After reading this chapter, you should be able to:

- Explain how structural factors affect the American political agenda.
- Explain why ethnic, racial, and religious diversity seems to be an important factor in the relatively low level of class-consciousness in the United States.
- Examine the political and social consequences of the aging of the American population.
- Explain how developments that occur in society and the economy affect the issues that become part of the American political agenda and the distribution of political power.
- Determine how inequalities of income and distribution of wealth may have an impact on political equality.
- Understand the demographic characteristics of the American population (race, ethnicity, geographical location, occupation, income, and education), the U.S. economy, and how it is evolving and changing, and the American political culture.
- Discuss the evolution from America's superpower status within a bipolar world to the growth of a multipower world.
- Show how beliefs about democracy and liberty also help to explain our political culture.
- Identify key terms and concepts used in Chapter 4.

This section provides a brief overview of the chapter contents. Read this section as a preview before reading your textbook. Then use this material as a review to help you retain information from your reading.

➔ "B-1 BOB" LEARNS ABOUT HIS DISTRICT

As a nine-term member of Congress (from Orange County, California's 46th district), Republican incumbent Bob Dornan along with the political establishment was stunned at his defeat by political newcomer Democrat Loretta Sanchez. Sanchez's victory highlighted the demographic changes that had occurred throughout the state of California. Dornan was simply out of touch with the newly emerged Latino, Asian, and working-class white populations in his formerly white middle class majority district. In fact, Dornan and other Republican leaders in the state and nation underestimated how the various anti-affirmative action, anti-immigrant initiatives which they sponsored would galvanize the Hispanic vote in 1996 and again in 1998. By the end of the decade, Hispanics representation in the California legislature had increased by 40 percent, and Hispanic political leaders filled a number of important positions in the state and nation. The demographic changes in this story reveal how economic and social changes are shaping American politics and what government does.

➔ AMERICAN SOCIETY: HOW IT HAS CHANGED AND WHY IT MATTERS

In terms of demographics, the American public has changed dramatically since the first census was taken in 1790. Neighborhoods, jobs, ethnicity, and our average age and standard of living have all changed substantially. These changes have influenced our political life.

Growing Diversity-The United States has tremendous diversity. European Protestants, African slaves, and Native Americans who made up the bulk of the U.S. population when the first census was taken in 1790 were joined by Catholic immigrants from Ireland and Germany in the 1840s and 1850s. In the 1870s, waves of Chinese migrated to the United States in pursuit of railroad construction work. Immigration patterns have continued as many eastern, central, and southern European groups have come to the United States. Today, Asian and Latin American groups are the largest shares of immigrants to the United States. The percentage of foreign-born people resident in the United States has more than doubled since 1970, reaching about 26 million in the year 2000; over 10 percent of the total population. Immigration is concentrated in the Big Five immigration states: New York, California, Texas, Florida, and New Jersey.

Immigration has had many positive cultural, linguistic, and religious effects on American society. But it has also generated significant **Nativist** (anti-foreign) reactions. Irish, Chinese, and Catholic immigrant groups have all been the targets of the anti-immigrant reactions. In the early 1920s Congress responded to anti-immigration agitation by enacting laws that closed U.S. borders for thirty years.

California's 1994 ballot *Proposition 187* attempted to bar welfare, education, and health benefits to illegal immigrants; the initiative has since been declared unconstitutional. In 1998, California voters approved another proposition that banned bi-lingual education. The University of California Board of Regents eliminated affirmative action programs at its institutions that same year.

Americans oppose "illegal" immigration, not "legal" immigration per se. Polls show that they fear that "illegals" burden the welfare, health, and education systems; none of this is certain. Substantial majorities report that they are comfortable with the changing racial and ethnic composition of the United States. Politicians, like Pete Wilson of California, have not been able to gain widespread national support for their political aspirations while using the "anti-immigrant card." Hispanic voters in California contributed to a new Democratic majority in the state legislature and a Democratic governor. Candidates for state-wide and national office in California now avoid Wilson's mistake of agitating specific immigrant groups. Prominent Republicans have since urged their party to embrace Hispanic immigrants. In the race for the 2000 GOP presidential nomination, George W. Bush openly courted immigrant groups and racial minorities. Arch-conservative Pat Buchanan consequently left the Republican Party for the Reform Party.

Changing Location-The United States began with most people living on rural farms and small towns. By 1910, nearly 50 cities had populations of more than 100,000 and New York, Philadelphia, and Chicago had more than one million. Urbanization, caused mainly by industrialization—the rise of large manufacturing firms required many industrial workers, while technology made farm worker less necessary—continued until the mid-1940s. After World War II, the United States became an overwhelmingly suburban nation. As people moved from the rural areas for the cities and suburbs, rural communities lost power and influence in the political realm. Many cities are faced with public service problems that are too burdensome for them to handle without federal assistance. City residents have typically favored them Democratic Party because of its association with activist government. People in suburban communities have become less willing to support programs for central-city populations and more friendly to politicians with proposals to deal with traffic congestion and "sprawl."

As many corporations moved south and west for lower taxes and favorable labor laws, major population shifts occurred in these regions. Over the past 50 years (1950-2000), states in the East and Midwest have lost congressional seats and presidential electoral votes. The western and southern **Sun Belt** states gained congressional seats at the expense of the other regions.

Changing Jobs and Occupations-Though the United States began with a large agriculture based workforce, with smaller numbers working in various trades and transportation, related to agriculture, the American occupational structure was radically transformed by the **Industrial Revolution** of the late 19th century. The American labor force shifted increasingly to wage and salary earners who were skilled, semiskilled, or unskilled **blue-collar workers** in manufacturing based industries. In 1950, the United States became the first nation in the world where **white-collar workers** (in clerical, technical, professional, managerial, services, and sales jobs) were in the majority.

Technological change, corporate downsizing, and the declining power of labor unions have contributed to large numbers of Americans working on a part-time basis, working from their homes for themselves or for companies, or working as independent consultants. Displaced workers often make great demands on government to expand welfare and unemployment benefits, job retraining, and programs that encourage economic development. Another way that occupational change impacts politics can be seen where the decline in heavy industry has resulted in the decline of the number of people who belong to labor unions by more than half (from 33 percent in the 1950s to 16 percent today). Because labor has been a strong voice for liberal social and political policies, liberal demands on government have grown weaker.

Female workers have been a substantial part of the "white-collar" work force. The participation of women in the workforce has passed 75 percent and is rapidly approaching the participation rate of men. Women working outside the home have improved the overall earning power of women, and increased their influence in politics. The women's movement of the late 1960s and 1970s was a likely outcome of these occupational changes in American society. With the fact that 63 percent of married women with children are in the paid workforce, increased demands on government-funded child care programs and early education are likely.

The Aging of the American Population-America is getting older. In 1800, the median age of the American population was just under 16; today it is 35. By 2030, it will be nearly 38. The proportion of the population over age 65 has been growing, while the proportion between the ages of 18 and 64. Today 12.7 percent of Americans are elderly; by 2030, this segment is expected to reach 20 percent. The very old—those age 85 and older—is the fastest-growing age segment of all. This aging of American society is likely to affect public services and public policy.

Income, Wealth and Poverty- Although the United States leads the world in per capita **gross domestic product** (GDP, the usual measure of standard of living), there is mounting evidence that Americans are not entirely happy about their living standards. The United Nation's Human Development Index—which takes into account education and life expectancy as well as GDP— reveals that the United States in 1999 was among the five nations (also Canada, France, Norway and Iceland) with the highest standard of living.

 The median household income of American families had barely improved in real dollar terms between 1973 and 1994, but things improved with the long economic boom of the mid and late 1990s. The different racial and ethnic groups in the United States experienced very different economic trends. Black and Hispanic households have the lowest incomes, while Asian Americans and Non-Hispanic Whites have the highest. All groups suffered declines in the late 1980s and 1990s and when they began to recover, African American household incomes recovered first, even as Hispanic households continued to decline. The White and Asian American household incomes began to grow. All groups benefited from the long economic boom of the late 1990s.

The tendency toward stagnation in living standards is politically important. Discontent generated among the "angry middle class" by unmet expectations probably plays an important part in rising hostility toward taxes, new immigrants, and welfare recipients. Middle class anger was undoubtedly a factor in the defeat of incumbent President **George Bush** in the 1992 election. Similar middle-class anger was aimed at congressional Democrats in 1994 and gave the Republicans control of Congress for the first time in 40 years.

Talk of "middle class anger" had largely disappeared by the late 1990s. It is not certain how permanent the confidence that American's currently have in the nation's future is. It would probably not take much of an economic reversal to rekindle anger. While even traditionally high unemployment groups such as young Black men are enjoying job growth, some groups have benefited far more than others.

Poverty-Though there had been a steady decline in official poverty rates from 1955 to 1973, the percentage of Americans classified as poor began to move upward. It declined in the mid-1980s and moved upward again in the mid-1990s, reaching 14.5 percent in 1994. By the end of the century, the poverty rate declined significantly. The United States' poverty rate is still high in raw numbers (34.5 million) and is substantially higher than poverty rates in the other rich democracies. The percentage of Americans who are poor remains higher than it was in 1973.

Poverty is not random in the United States. It is concentrated among racial minorities, and single-parent, female-headed households and their children. More than one-fourth of African-American and Hispanic Americans live in poverty (though a sizable middle class has emerged in both communities). Over one-third of the poor live in single-parent, female-headed households, and one in five is a child.

Inequality-Inequality increased between the 1980s and 1990, reaching its all time high in 1995 when the top 20 percent of the population took home 48.5 percent of the national income (the highest proportion ever recorded—it has remained unchanged since then. Despite the economic boom of the 1990s, the gap between the wealthy and those without wealth in the United States did not dwindle. Most of the income and wealth gains from economic growth between 1973 and 1995 went mainly to upper income groups, rather than being evenly distributed across the entire population.

Income inequality is greater in the United States than in any other Western democratic nation. In the United States, wealth is more unequally distributed than income. Inequality of wealth today seems similar to that of the 1920s, and is more unequally distributed in the United States than any other Western democratic nation. Extensive *material inequality* may undermine the possibilities for *political equality*, an important aspect of democracy. The wealthy are able to use their financial resources to enhance their political voice and their ease of access to public officials. Poorer Americans are less likely to participate in politics. Jefferson feared that democracy would be ar risk in a highly unequal society.

→ THE AMERICAN ECONOMY

The U.S. economic system is based on **capitalism**, sometimes called a **market economy** or a **free enterprise** system. A capitalist economy has two defining features: private ownership of the means of production, and markets to coordinate economic activity. American capitalism has two distinctive features: private ownership of economic factors such as factories, machinery, office buildings, land, and intellectual property and the existence of markets to coordinate most economic activity.

The Industrial Revolution and the Rise of the Corporation-As with other structural factors, the economy was transformed over a period of time. The economy was characterized by numerous small enterprises before the Civil War, originally linked to agriculture. The Civil War helped spur the Industrial Revolution, and the economy became increasingly industrialized after the war. Industrial enterprises grew to unprecedented size in the late nineteenth and early twentieth centuries, accompanied by transformations in technology, corporate law, and industrial organization.

The Post-World War II Boom-During the first two-thirds of the twentieth century the American economy and American corporations grew. Despite the Great Depression, Word War II, and the Cold War, technology and research contributed to a high standard of living and burgeoning middle class for citizens of the United States. After World War II, American corporations revived the early twentieth century oil companies' practice of looking abroad for sources of raw materials and markets for their finished products.

Steady growth in the size, health, and economic importance of corporations continued (except for the period of the Great Depression) until the early 1970s. Corporations were consolidated into massive units and played increasingly important roles in the economy. The largest American corporations gradually dominated global markets after World War II. The transformation in the relative position of the United States in the world economy—and what to do about it—have become important issues in American politics. Globalization affected U.S. foreign policy, with economic interests placing American political leaders under great pressure to pay attention to developments and events in other areas of the world.

The Temporary Fall from Grace-Although the U.S. economy continued to grow in the 1970s and 1980s, its rate of growth began to fall behind that of Western Europe and Japan. American corporations began to face intense competition from foreign corporations. Between the early 1970s and the late 1980s, the U.S. share of world manufacturing declined; a large part of the reason was the lower share of its GDP that the United States devoted to fixed investment in plant, equipment, and research and development as compared to the percentage spent by major competitors. The United States lost its position as the world's preeminent and unchallenged economic power. The relative decline of the United States in the international economy had important political consequences. These consequences included a devastating impact on workers' wages, increasing protectionist sentiments accompanied by proposals to shield American industry from foreign competition, and influences on public policies, including federal taxes, education, social welfare, national defense, and business regulation. The fierce political debates between business, labor and government over the North American Free Trade Agreement (NAFTA) and the General Agreement on Tariffs and Trade (GATT) highlight America's changing economic position in the world and how it has generated a set of important issues in American politics.

Globalization and the American Economy-The American economy rebounded in the 1990s. The economies that were once seen as the principal threats to America's position began to lose ground, and American corporations were better positioned to succeed in the new global economy. The most important characteristic of this new global economy is the integration of most of the world *into a single market and production system.*

Corporations are able to operate globally because of three revolutions. The revolution in telecommunications and computers has enabled corporate managers to coordinate the activities of scores of manufacturing plants, subcontractors, shippers, sales representatives, and retail outlets all over the world; the revolution in transportation has allowed corporations to assemble parts for manufacturing from multiple locations and to ship final products from almost anywhere in the world; and the revolution in the formation of global financial markets has encompassed stocks, bonds, insurance, and a range of credit instruments, where billions of dollars are moved instantaneously to where they are needed. Private and institutional investors, not governments, almost entirely make the determination of where dollars are needed. Global corporations no longer depend on their home country citizens or governments to generate the investment capital they need. American corporations are proving to be the dominant actors in the new global economy, and the new dynamism of the U.S. economy has several effects that are politically consequential.

Globalization, with its national borders-spanning web of interconnected finance, trade and information, means the national governments have lost or will soon lose a substantial part of their power to control what goes on within their own countries. The new global economy is one where certain skills are sought after and rewarded, and others are not. Globalization ties the fates of nations together as never before.

→ THE UNITED STATES IN THE INTERNATIONAL SYSTEM

The United States emerged as the world's last remaining superpower after American leaders from the nineteenth century shifted their focus from dominance on the North American continent, to the world. America's foreign policy before World War I was *isolationist*. It was World War II that propelled the United States into its position as the world's most important power.

The United States as a Superpower I-World War II propelled the United States into a position of leadership. The United States emerged from the war as the economic, political, and military power among the Western nations. For the first time, the United States was willing and able to exercise leadership on the world level. At the same time, the Soviet Union entered the postwar era with the world's largest land army, superpower ambitions of its own, and a strong desire to keep border nations of Western and Southern Europe in hands it considered friendly. The **Cold War**, which began in the late 1940s and lasted for four decades, characterized that era of tensions between the United States and Soviet Union. The United States and the Soviet Union became adversaries in conflicting political, economic, and ideological policies. Superpower status and the struggle with the Soviet Union contributed to a climate of secrecy in the name of "national security," with unfortunate consequences for the practice of democracy.

The United States as a Superpower II-Dramatic changes occurred in the world political, military, and economic systems in the 1980s and 1990s, centering on the collapse of Communism in Eastern Europe and the break-up of the Soviet Union into independent republics. As well, China switched to a market economy. The U.S. military and economic dominance of the world, however, has given way to a world with multiple centers of power as the United States has found it increasingly difficult to lead Europe and Japan on economic, trade, and military matters. U.S. influence in China, (human rights and protection of intellectual property), Russia (nuclear, proliferation) and the Middle East (Palestine, Syria, and Israel) all pose challenges to American influence in the world.

Most Americans reject "isolationism" as the best foreign policy strategy for the U.S. Some feel that the U.S. should approach most world problems on a cooperative basis; economic disputes should be settled through organizations such as the United Nations and the America's NATO allies. Others feel that the U.S. is sufficiently strong enough that it can act unilaterally where U.S. vital interests are at stake. The 1999 debate surrounding the U.S. Senate's rejection of the Nuclear Test Ban Treaty highlights this division.

→ THE FOUNDATION BELIEFS OF AMERICAN POLITICAL CULTURE

There is a great deal of evidence that *Americans share a political culture* based on certain *foundational beliefs* that shape how people classify, think about, and resolve particular issues that arise. The American political culture is interrelated with the market, competitive individualism, and private property.

Competitive Individualism-The popularity of Horatio Alger stories in American literature helps explain the American belief that an individual's fate is (and ought to be) tied to his or her own efforts. Those with talents, grit, and the willingness to work hard are more likely than not to be successful. The belief in competitive individualism among Americans influences their widespread support of "equality of opportunity" as opposed to equality of rewards. As long as the process is fair, Americans find inequality of income and wealth acceptable. Competitive individualism is not popular in countries such as Japan and Sweden which are concerned about cooperation and community.

Limited Government-Too powerful of a government is a threat to individual rights and economic efficiency.

Free Enterprise-The basic precepts of free enterprise such as the primacy of private property, and the efficiencies of the free market are supported by most Americans. John Locke's beliefs concerning humans and their relationship to property have been very influential in framing Americans' views of free enterprise. Adam Smith's *The Wealth of Nations* emphasized his belief that government should refrain from regulating a nation's economy since it is efficient and capable of managing its own operations. Americans hold the business system in high regards even though it dislikes large corporations. *Classical liberalism* (individualism, limited government, and the free market) influences public policy in the United States.

Citizenship and the Nature of the Political Order-There are three main American beliefs about political order that your authors explore:

Democracy: Americans cherish the idea of democracy. Yet Americans have not always behaved democratically with regard to groups such as African Americans who were denied the right to vote and other citizenship rights until the 1960s.

Freedom and Liberty: Freedom (or liberty) is a bedrock of American political beliefs and culture. The promise of freedom in the New World has been very attractive to people all over the world.

Populism: The hostility that common people have toward power and the powerful is *populism*. From the early periods of the nation's history, there have been different movements or waves of hostility toward concentrated power including Andrew Jackson's war against the United States Bank (1830s); the Populist movement (1890s); the Great Depression (1930s) and during the economic crisis of the 1970s. Populism is also hostile to the concentration of power in government. One manifestation of modern day populism was the election of Jesse Ventura as governor of Minnesota. American writer **Walt Whitman** was such a strong supporter of the principles of democracy that he considered by many to be "the poet of Democracy."

➜STRUCTURAL INFLUENCES ON AMERICAN POLITICS

This chapter deals with the main features of American society, the economy, the political culture, and the international system, and how each influences important aspects of politics and government in the United States. These structural factors are interrelated, and each helps define the others.

➜SUMMARY

The various structural factors such as the nature of society, the economy, the nation's place in the world, and the political culture shape American politics and government. The American political agenda is affected by changes in diversity, regional economies, and its gradual aging. Although Americans have a high standard of living, there is also substantial poverty and inequality.

The American economy is a market economy which has changed over the years from a highly competitive, small-enterprise form to a corporate-dominated one with a global reach. Economic change has had important reverberations in American politics. The emergence of the United States as a super power in the twentieth century changed the content of foreign policy, the balance of power between the president and Congress, the size of the federal government, and the priorities of the government's budget. The collapse of socialism in Eastern Europe affirmed the position of the United States as the world's most important military power.

Americans believe strongly in individualism, limited government, and free enterprise. Beliefs about democracy, liberty, and the primacy of the common people also help define the political culture. The political culture shapes American ideas about what the good society should look like, the appropriate role for government, and the possibilities for self-government.

Chapter Outline

This section gives you a comprehensive review of the chapter. Use this outline in combination with your textbook to look for key concepts and objectives, to identify essential terms and names, and to gain a basic understanding of political practices and principles from this chapter.

I. **"B-1 BOB" LEARNS ABOUT HIS DISTRICT (p. 85)**
    A. The opening vignette points to several of the *structural factors* that provide the context or environment for politics and governing, including influences that are found in society, the economy, the political culture, and the international system. The authors discuss the particular demographic changes in Orange County California's 46th Congressional district which resulted in incumbent Bob Dornan's electoral defeat by Loretta Sanchez in 1996 and again in 1998.
        1. Sanchez's victory highlighted the demographic changes that had occurred throughout the state of California. Dornan was simply out of touch with the newly emerged Latino, Asian, and working-class white populations in his formerly white middle class majority district.
            a) In fact, Dornan and other Republican leaders in the state and nation underestimated how the various anti-affirmative action, anti-immigrant initiatives which they sponsored would galvanize the Hispanic vote in 1996 and again in 1998.
            b) By the end of the decade, Hispanics representation in the California legislature had increased by 40 percent, and Hispanic political leaders filled a number of important positions in the state and nation. The demographic changes in this story reveal how economic and social changes are shaping American politics and what government does.
        2. This section examines how the American people have changed and why the change is important.
        3. The authors complete their examination of the structural factors that affect the American political agenda, the distribution of power in American politics, and the perceptions and outlooks of the American people.

II. AMERICAN SOCIETY: HOW IT HAS CHANGED AND WHY IT MATTERS (pp. 86-100)

A. Growing diversity

1. The United States is a racially diverse society and is becoming more so every year.
   a) Steady population growth from 1790 to 1990
   b) High birth rates and successive waves of immigration.
2. Changing patterns of immigration
   a) Nineteenth-century immigration was primarily from Europe.
   b) Immigration today is primarily from Latin America and Asia.
   c) Anti-immigration agitation accompanied the arrival of immigrants from different backgrounds.
   d) The rate of migration to the United States has accelerated in recent years, but it should also be noted that the number of immigrants who have been coming to the United States *relative to the total population* is fairly low in a historical sense.
   e) The result is substantial diversity in the American population.
3. Effects of ethnic, religious, and racial diversity
   a) Rich language and cultural diversity
   b) Some periods were marked by anti-immigration agitation and demands on public officials to curb the flow of immigrants.
      (1) The arrival of immigrants who are different from the majority population has often sparked **nativist (anti-foreign)** reactions and demands that public officials reduce the inflow of immigrants.
         (a) Many Americans are more concerned with "illegal" immigration than with "legal" immigration.
         (b) A majority of Americans feel that "illegals" are a burden on the welfare, education, and health care systems of the United States, even though there is no solid evidence to support this view.
      (2) The current wave of Spanish-speaking immigration has led to similar unease.
         (a) Legislation has been passed in several states to make English the official language.
         (b) In 1994, Californians approved **Proposition 187**, which barred welfare, health, and education benefits to illegal immigrants; the Proposition has since been declared unconstitutional by a Federal District Court.
         (c) Politicians pay attention to immigrant groups as more of their number become citizens and voters. California governor Pete Wilson's use of the anti-immigrant card backfired during his attempt to win the 1996 Republican presidential nomination.

(d) Candidates for state-wide and national office in California today try to avoid Wilson's mistake.

B. **Changing location**
  1. Movement from **urbanization** to **suburbanization**
     a) The United States was originally a nation of rural and small-town people.
     b) **Industrialization** led to rapid **urbanization**, which continued until after the mid-1940s.
     c) The United States became **suburbanized** after World War II; movement to the suburbs followed unprecedented levels of government spending on highways and mortgage loan guarantees for veterans.
  2. Political effects of **population movement** from rural areas to cities and from cities to suburbs
     a) Diminished power of rural areas and small towns in national politics
     b) Shrinking tax base for central cities makes it difficult to provide public services
     c) Central cities are heavily dependent on federal assistance—consistently vote Democratic
     d) Suburbs consist primarily of middle-class and working-class homeowners—more conservative politics, base of support for Republican party
  3. U.S. population has steadily moved West and South as employment opportunities have shifted.
     a) Heavy manufacturing, traditionally located in the East and upper Midwest, has suffered serious setbacks.
     b) Following each census from 1950 to 2000, states in the East and the upper Midwest lost congressional seats and presidential electoral votes.
     c) Many companies have shifted their activities to the nonunion and low-tax **Sun Belt** states (states of the lower South, Southwest, and West, where sunny weather prevails; because a majority of Sun Belt states are more conservative than other states, their increasing importance in national politics may have contributed to Republican gains in Congress in the 1990s.

C. **Changing jobs and occupations**
  1. Changes in American *occupational structure*
     a) Almost three-quarters of the population was engaged in agriculture at the time of the first census in 1790.
     b) The **Industrial Revolution** transformed the occupational structure: large mass production industries were characterized by the assembly line and semiskilled labor.
     c) The "typical" American by 1940 wore a **blue collar** and worked in manufacturing as a skilled, semiskilled, or unskilled worker; **white-collar workers** (clerical, technical, professional, managerial, services, and sales) were in the majority by 1950.

90

2. Political implications flow from changes in the American occupational structure.
   a) Changes in the types of demands that are placed on government by displaced workers
      (1) Demands for expanded welfare benefits and job retraining programs
      (2) Demands for policies to encourage economic development
   b) Reduction in the proportion of Americans who belong to labor unions as heavy industry has become less important.
      (1) Decline in union strength has reduced support for the Democratic party in national elections.
      (2) Diminished support for liberal economic and social policies
   c) Substantial expansion in the number of female workers
      (1) Sixty percent of all new jobs in the 1980s went to women, mostly in the white-collar and service sectors.
      (2) The participation of women in the paid work force has passed 75 percent and is rapidly approaching the participation rate for men.
      (3) Entry of women in the work force has political consequences:
         (a) Paid work has improved women's income (though women still earn only about three-quarters of what men earn).
         (b) Contributed to the formation of the women's movement in the late 1960s and early 1970s
         (c) Pressures for government-funded child care and early education, and for extension of the school day

D. **The aging of the American population**
   1. The proportion of the population over age 65 has been growing and will continue to grow; the proportion of the population between the ages of 18 and 64 has been shrinking and will continue to shrink; the number of the very old (those over 85) is growing at an especially fast rate.
   2. The **aging** of the population is one of the most significant trends in the United States and in other industrialized countries.
      a) A growing proportion of the population is likely to be dependent and in need of services, and a shrinking proportion is likely to be taxpaying wage or salary earners; the tax load on those still in the workforce may feel increasingly burdensome.
      b) Because the elderly require more medical care than the young, the question of the appropriate role of government will become an increasingly important part of the national debate over health care.

E. **Income, wealth, and poverty**
   1. The United States has one of the highest standards of living in the world, but there is mounting evidence that Americans are not entirely happy about their living standards. Even though the United States was named by the UN's Human Development Index as one of the five nations with the highest standard of living, the high standard of living is not shared by all.

2. Income
   a) Although the United States leads the world in per capita **gross domestic product** (GDP), the usual measure of standard of living), there is mounting evidence that Americans are not entirely happy about their living standards—a feeling that sometimes spills over into politics.
   b) In 1994 the median household income of American families began to rise for the first time in real dollar terms since 1973 as a result of the economic boom of the mid and late 1990s.
   c) African and Hispanic Americans are much worse off economically than White and Asian Americans. African and Hispanic households have the lowest incomes, while Asian and Non-Hispanic Whites have the highest.
   d) Although median household incomes have declined in the late 1980s and early 1990s, all groups benefited from the long economic boom of the late 1990s.
   e) The long stagnation produced an "angry middle class."
   f) The **decline of the middle class** is likely to have *long-range political implications* for American politics.
      (1) Middle class anger was undoubtedly a factor in the defeat of incumbent President **George Bush** in the 1992 election. A similar middle-class anger was aimed at congressional Democrats in 1994 and gave the Republicans control of Congress for the first time in 40 years.
      (2) Talk of "middle class anger" largely disappeared in the late 1990s as a result of the economic boom.

3. **Poverty**
   a) The distribution of poverty is concentrated among racial minorities, female-headed households, and children.
   b) The federal government's official **poverty line** has steadily declined between 1955 and the early 1970s. Though poverty has declined over the years in the United States in the mid to late 1990s, the poverty rate in the United States remains high in absolute terms and when compared to other rich democracies.
   c) Political implications of material inequality and poverty:
      (1) Social problems (crime, drug use, family disintegration) are tied to economic distress.
      (2) Societies with large concentrations of the poor are susceptible to disruption and social turmoil.
      (3) Policing and social welfare programs are two of several possible public policy responses.

4. **Inequality**
   a) Income and wealth are distributed in a highly unequal fashion in the United States. The economic boom of the late 1990s has done little to close the gap between those with high income and wealth and those with less.
   b) Income inequality increased dramatically during the 1980s and the early 1990s.

(1) It reached its all time high in 1995.

(2) It has remained unchanged since 1995.

(3) The recent economic good times have not managed to redistribute income downwards from the top.

c) Among Americans, wealth is even more unequally distributed than income.

d) Inequality is important in determining how democracy works: extensive material *inequality* may undermine the possibilities *for political equality* (one of the foundations of democracy).

(1) Those with financial resources can use their resources to enhance their political voice and their ease of access to public officials.

(2) Those with fewer financial resources vote less often and are unlikely to be politically active.

III. THE AMERICAN ECONOMY (pp. 100-103)

A. The American economic system is based on **capitalism**, sometimes called a **market economy** or a **free enterprise** system.

B. A capitalist economy has two defining features:

 1. *Private ownership of the means of production.*
 2. *Markets to coordinate economic activity.*

C. The Industrial Revolution and the rise of the corporation

 1. There were numerous small enterprises before the Civil War, originally linked to agriculture.
 2. The economy became increasingly industrialized after the Civil War; concentrated in giant enterprises.
 3. The Civil War helped spur the Industrial Revolution and allowed the North to enact government policies that favored free enterprise.
 4. The South was temporarily eliminated as a significant political power.
 5. Industrial enterprises grew to unprecedented size in the late nineteenth and early twentieth centuries, accompanied by transformations in technology, corporate law, and industrial organization.

D. **The post-World War II boom**

 1. Steady growth in the size, health, and economic importance of corporations continued (except for the period of the Great Depression) until the early 1970s.
 a) Consolidation of corporations into massive units
 b) Increasing importance of large corporations in the economy.
 2. The largest American corporations became overwhelmingly global after World War II.
 a) American corporations dominated world markets during this period.
 (1) As late as 1975, 11 of the largest 15 corporations in the world were American.

(2) As recently as 1981, 40 percent of the world's total foreign direct investment was still accounted for by the United States.

  b) The global reach of American corporations affected U.S. foreign policy, with economic interests placing American political leaders under great pressure to pay attention to developments and events in other areas of the world.

3. The temporary fall from grace
  a) Although the U.S. economy continued to grow in the 1970s and 1980s, its rate of growth began to fall behind that of Western Europe and Japan.
    (1) Between the early 1970s and the late 1980s, the U.S. share of world manufacturing declined; a large part of the reason was the lower share of its GDP that the United States devoted to fixed investment in plant, equipment, and research and development as compared to the percentage spent by major competitors.
    (2) The United States lost its position as the world's preeminent and unchallenged economic power. The United States lost ground in steel, autos, machine tools, electronics, computer chips, and finance.
  b) Consequences of the relative decline of the United States in the world economy
    (1) A devastating impact on workers' wages
    (2) Raised protectionist sentiments and spurred proposals to shield American industry from foreign competition
    (3) Affected public policies, including federal taxes, education, social welfare, national defense, and business regulation
    (4) The intensity of the fight over the North American Free Trade Agreement (NAFTA) and the General Agreement of Tariffs and Trade (GATT) reveals America's changing economic position in the world.

4. Globalization and the American economy
  a) The American economy rebounded in the 1990s.
    (1) The economies once seen as the principal threats to America's position began to lose ground.
    (2) American corporations were better positioned to succeed in the new global economy.
  b) The most important characteristic of this new global economy is the integration of most of the world *into a single market and production system.*
  c) Corporations are able to operate globally because of three revolutions.
    (1) The revolution in telecommunications and computers
    (2) The revolution in transportation
    (3) The revolution in the formation of global financial markets
  d) The determination of where dollars are needed is made almost entirely by private and institutional investors, not governments.
    (1) Global corporations no longer depend on their home country citizens or governments to generate the investment capital they need.

    (2) U.S. corporations are proving to be the dominant actors in the new global economy.

  e) The new dynamism of the American economy has several effects that are politically consequential.

    (1) The steady economic growth, low inflation, and heady stock market performance in the mid- and late-1990s has helped fuel an impressive rate of job creation, low levels of unemployment, and heightened consumer confidence.

    (2) The *new global economy* is one where certain skills are highly sought after and rewarded, while others are not; the result is rising inequality in income and wealth across all the developed nations, especially the United States.

IV. THE UNITED STATES IN THE INTERNATIONAL SYSTEM (pp. 103-106)

A. For most of the nineteenth century, the attention of most Americans and their leaders was focused on the North American continent.

  1. They concentrated on filling a vast, continental-scale nation-state and on building an industrial economy.

  2. Our foreign policy was **isolationist** (the policy of avoiding involvement in foreign affairs).

  3. By the late nineteenth and early twentieth centuries, American attentions began to turn abroad, and our growing economic power furnished influence with the world's most important nations.

B. **The United States as a superpower I**

  1. World War II propelled the United States into a position of leadership.

    a) The United States emerged from the war as the economic, political, and military power among the Western nations.

    b) The United States emerged from the war with a large military establishment and military superiority in most areas.

  2. Within a decade of World War II, the United States stood as the unchallenged economic, political, and military power among the Western nations.

    a) For the first time, the United States was willing and able to exercise leadership on the world level.

    b) The United States pulled the major capitalist nations together (for the first time in their history) into a *political and economic alliance.*

      (1) Provided funds for the rebuilding of Europe and for development projects in the Third World

      (2) Led the movement toward liberalization of trade by lowering tariff barriers

      (3) Provided a stable dollar to serve as the basis of the international monetary system

      (4) Organized and largely paid for joint military defenses

C. **The United States as a superpower II**

1. The **Soviet Union** entered the postwar era with the world's largest land army, superpower ambitions of its own, and a strong desire to keep border nations of Western and Southern Europe in hands it considered friendly.
2. The **Cold War** (the era of tensions between the United States and the Soviet Union) began in late 1940s and lasted for four decades.
3. The United States and the Soviet Union became adversaries in conflicting political, economic, and ideological policies.
4. Implications of America's superpower status
   a) Transformation in U.S. foreign policy required a large military establishment
   b) Government spending priorities tilted toward defense
   c) Presidential position in policymaking enhanced; congressional role diminished
   d) Growth of secrecy in the name of national security

D. A **multipower-centered** world?
   1. Dramatic changes in the world political, military, and economic systems occurred in 1980s and 1990s.
      a) Communism collapsed in Eastern Europe.
      b) The Soviet Union was broken up into independent republics.
      c) China switched to a market economy.
   2. Although the collapse of the Soviet Union left the United States as the world's only military superpower, American presidents have sometimes had difficulty translating this position into diplomatic preeminence; because of the collapse of the USSR, friends and former adversaries feel more free to go their own ways, and the **bipolar** world of the post-World War II years has given way to a **multipolar** world with multiple centers of power.

V. **THE FOUNDATION BELIEFS OF AMERICAN POLITICAL CULTURE (pp. 106-110)**
   A. Fundamental beliefs that have political consequences make up the American **political culture**.
      1. A broad consensus seems to exist among Americans on many of the fundamental beliefs that shape our political life.
      2. **Foundation beliefs** are beliefs that shape how people classify, think about, and resolve particular issues.
      3. Public policy tends to reflect the public's ideas and beliefs.
   B. **Competitive individualism**
      1. Americans tend to believe that an *individual's fate is tied to his or her own efforts*.
      2. Competitive individualism means that people are naturally competitive, always striving to better themselves in relation to others.
      3. The belief in competitive individualism affects the way we think about many political issues, including inequality.

4. Americans endorse the idea of equality of opportunity, but reject the idea that people should have equal rewards.
   a) Americans tend to look favorably on government programs that try to equalize opportunity (such as Head Start) but generally oppose programs that redistribute income from those who are seen as the hardworking middle class to those who are considered undeserving.
   b) Belief in *equality of opportunity is seen as being consistent with highly unequal outcomes*, in contrast with countries like Sweden, where more emphasis is placed on social obligations rather than on individual rights.
5. Competitive individualism is not common in most other modern capitalist nations.
   a) Japan—commitment to the work team, to the company, and to the community is more highly regarded than commitment to personal advancement
   b) Sweden—people are less likely to talk about their individual rights and more likely to talk about their social obligations

C. Limited government—the belief that government must be limited in its power and responsibilities; closely associated with the idea of individualism
   1. A powerful government is likely to threaten individual rights.
   2. Reflected in the words of the Declaration of Independence and in the ideas of Adam Smith and John Locke; an idea that still remains attractive to most Americans

D. Free enterprise
   1. Americans tend to support the basic precepts of free enterprise capitalism: private property and the efficiencies of the free market.
      a) Many of our ideas about private property stem from the philosophies of **John Locke**.
         (1) Locke argued that people turn common property into private property when they use abilities such as work and creativity; by adding their labor to the natural environment, people are justified in taking the product of their efforts as private property.
         (2) Inequality will result because people are different in their abilities and willingness to work.
      b) Locke's views have been reinforced by the experience of fairly widespread property ownership in the United States.
   2. The free market
      a) **Adam Smith** taught that the market works best if people are free to pursue their own interests, following the **law of supply and demand**.
      b) In *The Wealth of Nations* (1776), Smith wrote that the *market is efficient and effective if left alone*; therefore, government should not interfere.
      c) Most Americans today do not advocate a pure free market ideal, but they believe that the private sector is usually more effective than the public sector.

3. This set of ideas about individualism, limited government, and the free market (referred to by some as **classical liberalism**) influences many aspects of public policy in the United States.
   a) Americans favor private consumption over public provisions, and they favor private initiatives over public initiatives.
   b) By contrast, other developed nations favor more extensive public services such as mass transit and health care.

E. Citizenship and the nature of the political order
   1. The behavior of citizens and political decision makers are influenced by certain *beliefs about what kind of political order is appropriate and what role citizens should play.*
   2. **Democracy**—one of the foundations of the American belief system
      a) Not highly regarded during the early part of our history
      b) As the practice of democracy was enriched and expanded, the term became an honored one.
      c) The democratic process requires a political culture that respects ordinary people and believes in their ability to govern themselves.
      d) Poet **Walt Whitman** helped fashion the transformation of the American political culture from its aristocratic roots; his most famous work, *Leaves of Grass* (1855), celebrated the dignity of common people and the character of their everyday lives.
   3. **Freedom** and **liberty**—freedom (also called *liberty*) is at the top of the list of American beliefs and is more strongly honored here than elsewhere
      a) The promise of freedom attracted immigrants to the United States.
      b) Despite widespread belief in freedom, there have been many intrusions on basic rights.

F. **Populism**—refers to the hostility of the common person to power and the powerful
   1. Populism has always been part of the American belief system.
   2. Populists have particularly opposed concentrated economic power and those who exercise it; populism is also hostile to the concentration of power in government.
   3. The populist sentiment may be seen today in the rising discontent of portions of the middle class.

VI. **STRUCTURAL INFLUENCES ON AMERICAN POLITICS (pp. 110-112)**
   A. Chapters 2 and 3 examined the constitutional rules; this chapter dealt with the main features of American society, the economy, the political culture, and the international system.
      1. Each of these factors influences important aspects of politics and government in the United States.
      2. These *structural factors* are interrelated, and each helps define the others.

a) Constitutional rules are shaped by beliefs about the nature of the individual, society, and government that make up our political culture.

b) The political culture is interrelated with the market, competitive individualism, and private property.

B. One of the *recurring themes* that appears throughout this book is the *substantial growth in the size, reach, and responsibilities of the federal government*; much of this growth is *related to changes in the structural factors* described in this chapter.

Terms for Review

Use this list to review essential principles, functions, and concepts from this chapter. Refer to your textbook for help in identifying and defining terms on this list. When you study, do not merely memorize terms; ask questions about the material you are reviewing, and look for the importance or significance of each item.

nativist

immigration

globalization

urbanization

suburbanization

superpower

competitive individualism

Sun Belt

Industrial Revolution

blue collar worker

white collar worker

poverty line

capitalism

demographics

isolationism

Cold War

bipolar world order

multipolar world order

Research Topics: Applying What You Have Learned

You will derive more benefit from your reading if you try to apply what you have learned. Some of the suggested research topics can be answered exclusively from your text, while others require you to conduct some basic research on your own. The references suggested under **Internet Sources** *will help you in your search..*

- In California, a significant percentage of the population is foreign-born. What relationship does this fact have to anti-immigrant legislation passed in California, such as Proposition 187 (1994), which attempted to bar welfare, health, and education benefits to undocumented immigrants and their children? Create a list of five major benefits of immigration and five consequences of immigration.

- The authors of your textbook indicate that the questions of the appropriate role of government in the provision of medical care will become an increasingly important part of the national debate. For example, a growing elderly population is likely to press political decision-makers to transfer public expenditures from programs that serve the young to those that serve the old. How do you think younger working taxpayers will react to the increased burdens that they will be required to carry? Is there any solution that will be fair and equitable to both young and old?

- American corporations are becoming more closely aligned with corporations from other countries, either through outright purchase of stock or through joint ventures. Would you favor more protectionist policies to protect the interest of American businesses and consumers, or would you favor a more open market economy? Write a brief essay that explains your thoughts on this issue.

- Although there is widespread support for the concepts of freedom and liberty in America, there have been many intrusions on basic rights in American history. Can you explain why we find such discrepancies in an area where we also find almost complete public support for the general principle?

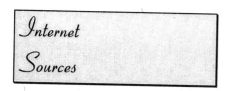

A number of sites on the World Wide Web serve as "gateways" to vast collections of material on American government and politics. The following Internet sources are recommended for students who would like to do additional research in areas covered by this chapter. These references would also be helpful in expanding on the questions suggested under Research Topics.

The Economist http://www.economist.com/
The home page of the world's leading publications on the U.S. and international economies.

Fedstats http://www.fedstats.gov/
Statistical information on the U.S. economy and society from more than 70 government agencies.

Globalization and Democracy Homepage http://www.colorado.edu/IBS/GAD/gad.html
Information on a National Science Foundation-funded graduate training and research program, directed by one of the authors of this textbook.

Statistical Abstract of the United States http://www.census.gov/statab/www/
A vast compendium of statistical information on the government, the economy, and society.

Statistical Resources on the Web www.umich.edu/libhome/Documents.center/stats.html
A vast compendium of statistical information on society, economy and culture for the United *States and other countries, organized by the University of Michigan library in a very user-friendly format.*

Yahoo/Business and Economy http://www.yahoo.com/Business_and_Economy/
A gateway to a wealth of information about business and the economy.

Yahoo/Society and Culture http://www.yahoo.com/Society_andCulture/
A gateway to a wealth of information about social and cultural issues.

Circle the correct answer for each question. Questions are listed in the same order in which the information appears in the text. Use the Answer Key in the back of the Study Guide to check your responses.

1. Because African-Americans are much worse off economically than white Americans and have suffered discrimination on many fronts, they have been
   a. Suspicious of an activist role for government in providing jobs and public services.
   b. Dependent on an activist role for religion in providing jobs and public services.
   c. Favorable toward an activist role for big business in providing jobs and public services.
   d. Supportive of an activist role for government in providing jobs and public services.

2. Foundation beliefs of the American public include .
   a. Belief in government interventionism.
   b. A strong sense of competitive individualism.
   c. Distrust of free enterprise.
   d. Hostility toward religion.

3. Fundamental beliefs that have political consequences make up the
   a. Political culture.
   b. Economic environment.
   c. Social status.
   d. Pluralistic contradictions.

4. The development of foreign competition in American markets is used in your text to illustrate

a.   Some of the ways in which political factors are used to control the American economy.

b.   How inferior products from Europe and Japan have gained a foothold in the American market despite superior American technology.

c.   The failures of U.S. constitutional principles when they come into competition with different practices of other nations.

d.   Several of the structural factors that shape American politics.

5.   Which of these ideas was not highly regarded at the time the nation was founded but has since gained widespread acceptance?
a.   Competitive individualism
b.   Limited government
c.   Democracy
d.   Freedom

6.   Competitive individualism
a.   Encompasses a belief in both equality of opportunity and equality of results.
b.   Is an essential theme of socialism.
c.   Is not common in most other modern capitalist nations.
d.   Violates the basic concept of a free enterprise system.

7.   One of the most significant trends in the United States has been
a.   Increasing equalization of income, which creates demands on government to fund programs for the middle class.
b.   Increasing levels of voter turnout in elections at all levels, which creates demands on government to pay attention to the needs of the electorate.
c.   The average age of the population is declining, which creates demands on government for programs to address the needs of youth.
d.   The population is aging, which creates demands on government for programs to deal with the problems of the elderly.

8.   Which of these is NOT one of the characteristics of the American standard of living?
a.   The proportion of American families living in poverty has increased significantly since 1980.
b.   Income inequality is high in the United States when compared to other Western democratic nations.
c.   Inequality in income and wealth is high in the United States and is becoming more pronounced.
d.   Wealth is more evenly distributed among Americans than is income.

9.   The opening vignette in Chapter 4 points out that
a.   A growing number of people in America have prospects for good jobs, increasing wages, and increased benefits packages.

b. Declining wages and shrinking benefits are reflected in low profits for American corporations and the decline of American industry in world markets.

c. The historical link between worker compensation and worker productivity has been broken, as shown by the fact that wages and benefits of American workers are declining at a time when corporations are enjoying near-record profits.

d. Workers in the 1990s are taking home a larger percentage of the nation's economic output in the form of wages than at any previous period in history.

10. The term *populism* refers to
   a. The hostility of the common person to power and the powerful.
   b. Support for majoritarian democracy and the direct election of senators.
   c. Fundamental and enduring factors that affect the American agenda.
   d. The transformation of the occupational structure brought about by the growth of labor unions.

11. According to the authors of your textbook, what is the most likely relationship of extensive **material inequality** to democracy?
   a. Extensive material inequality may undermine the possibilities for political equality because those with financial resources have greater access to public officials.
   b. Material inequality may increase the possibilities for political equality by creating incentives for political participation.
   c. Material inequality leads to public unrest, which will create a more democratic system as the majority begins to demand more protection.
   d. The degree of material inequality has no relationship to democracy.

12. (T/F) Ethnic, racial, and religious diversity seems to be an important factor in producing the relatively low level of class consciousness and unionization in the United States.

13. (T/F) America's rise to superpower status has enhanced the role of Congress in policymaking and has diminished that of the president.

14. (T/F) Public opinion polls find that the American people are generally less religious than people in other western societies.

15. (T/F) The largest American corporations are global in character in the sense that they produce and market their products all over the world.

16. (T/F) There is more poverty in the United States than in other Western democratic nations, a fact that may be attributed to the smaller role of social welfare in the United States.

17. (T/F) A capitalist economic system is characterized by private ownership of the means of production and the existence of markets to coordinate economic activity.

18. (T/F) One result of the massive entry of women into the workforce is that women now receive salaries that are approximately the equivalent of those earned by men for comparable work.

Chapter 5
PUBLIC OPINION

Key Concepts and Objectives

The Key Concepts and Objectives provide a look at the fundamental goals and ideas of this chapter. This section serves as a guide to a basic understanding of the objectives of your textbook.

After reading this chapter, you should be able to:

- Explain what public opinion is and how it plays a crucial part in democratic government.
- Establish how public opinion polls or surveys can be designed in order to avoid distorted or inaccurate results.
- Examine how much the American public knows about politics, and recognize the basic beliefs and values where American public opinion reflects a high degree of consensus.
- Identify areas where Americans' collective policy preferences have been stable over a long period of time.
- Show how opinions differ according to factors such as race, gender, age, and income.
- Understand how public opinion may be changed or manipulated by political leaders or interest groups.
- Explain why high levels of public confidence and political efficacy are essential to satisfactory government.
- Identify the agents of political socialization and summarize how the process of political socialization influences the formation of public opinion.
- Evaluate how well democracy is working in America, particularly with respect to how closely the government's policies correspond to the expressed wishes of its citizens.
- Identify key terms and concepts used in Chapter 5.

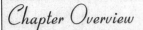

This section provides a brief overview of the chapter contents. Read this section as a preview before reading your textbook. Then use this material as a review to help you retain information from your reading.

➔INTRODUCTION TO PART THREE: POLITICAL LINKAGE

Part Two discussed a number of fundamental **structural** factors that affect how American politics works. Part Three looks at the **political linkage** sector. The chapters in Part Three discuss how institutions in the political linkage sector work, how they affect policymaking, and what part they play in helping or hindering democracy. In separate chapters, the authors discuss public opinion, the mass media, organized interest groups and social movements, political parties, and elections—all of which are not a formal part of government, but which directly influence what sorts of people are chosen to be government officials. They also affect what these officials do when they are in office and the resulting public policies.

➔THE VIETNAM WAR AND THE PUBLIC

The Tonkin Gulf incident during the **Vietnam War**—when the Defense Department announced that North Vietnamese PT boats had engaged in an "unprovoked attack" on the *U.S.S. Maddox* and two days later on the *C. Turner Joy*—is used to illustrate how government officials can sometimes manipulate public opinion, how events and circumstances affect opinion, and how public opinion impacts policymaking. People were willing to go along when their leaders told them that action was needed in order to resist communist aggression. Few questions were raised at the time of the incident, and Congress quickly passed the **Tonkin Gulf Resolution,** authorizing the president to take "all necessary measures" to repel any armed attack and to assist any ally in the region. Years later, it was revealed that the *Maddox* had steamed near the coastline, deliberately provoking North Vietnamese radar defenses; the second attack apparently never happened, but instead was imagined by an inexperienced sonar operator. Public support for the war increased.

The number of U.S. troops in Vietnam rose rapidly from 184,300 at the end of 1965 to 536,000 at the end of 1968, and casualties increased correspondingly. By 1967, Americans were divided over whether or not Vietnam had been a mistake. A large majority said they favored "Vietnamization," bringing U.S. troops home as South Vietnamese replaced them. Catastrophe struck during the January 1968 Vietnam *Tet* holidays when the North Vietnamese army launched what became known as the *Tet Offensive*: massive attacks throughout South Vietnam, including an assault on the U.S. embassy in Saigon. After Tet, criticism of the Vietnam war by politicians, newspaper editorials, television commentators led the public to withdraw it support for the war. Anger over Vietnam contributed to the election defeat of the Democrats the following November. When the Nixon administration took office, most Americans favored the reduction of U.S. soldiers in Vietnam. Most Americans also wanted to continue monthly troop withdrawals even if it meant the collapse of the South Vietnamese government. Despite Americans' dislike of a communist victory in the country, the North Vietnamese army took control of Saigon and reunified a nation that had been divided since the end of World War II. The Vietnam story, from the Gulf Tonkin incident to U.S. troop withdrawal, shows how government officials can sometimes lead or manipulate public opinion and how public opinion can have a strong impact on policymaking.

→ DEMOCRACY AND PUBLIC OPINION

Public opinion is defined as the political attitudes expressed by ordinary citizens. In a perfect democracy, based on popular sovereignty and majority rule, the government would do exactly what its citizens wanted. Many democratic theorists have doubted the political wisdom of the public. The Founders feared of the public's "passions."

Modern survey researchers have turned up evidence of public ignorance, lack of interest in politics, and reliance on group or party loyalties rather than judgments about issues. The public's relatively inconsistent views of politics have been identified as *nonattitudes*: on many issues of public policy, most Americans seemed to have no real views at all. However, authors of your textbook note that the collective public opinion of Americans is quite stable, and we can legitimately speak of a rational public. Americans' basic beliefs and values are more fundamental than opinions about specific policies. There is often a high degree of consensus about values such as freedom, democracy, capitalism, and equal opportunity.

What People Know About Politics-Conducting an opinion poll or **sample survey** can eliminate most of the guesswork that relates to public opinion. In the past, there were no scientific measures of what people thought or felt. Early attempts to determine public opinion by guesswork or from the views of personal acquaintances is defective: the views of personal acquaintances, media voices, or rally audiences are often not representative of the whole public.

Measuring What People Think-Surveys taken during the presidential elections of 1936 and 1948 illustrate how our knowledge of polling techniques evolved out of past failures. Scientific polling techniques became the standard following **Franklin Roosevelt's** landslide election in 1936 when the highly respected *Literary Digest* inaccurately predicted Roosevelt's defeat by Republican Alf Landon. An opinion poll or survey can be highly accurate if the **sample** of people interviewed—usually about 1,000 of 1,500—is representative of the whole population. A

representative sample should have the same characteristics as the population being measured. Although perfectly **random sampling** is not feasible, the samples that survey organizations use are sufficiently representative so that survey results closely reflect how the whole population would have responded.

When surveys are being interpreted, the wording of questions is also important. "Closed-ended" or "forced-choice" questions, which ask the respondents to choose among preformulated answers, do not always reveal what people are thinking on their own. "Open-ended" questions are more flexible and spontaneous.

Individuals' Ignorance-Most Americans do not know or care much about politics. Few know basic facts about the leadership or constitutional rules of the United States. During the Cold War, most Americans did not know that the Soviet Union was not a member of NATO, an alliance directed against the Soviet Union. The authors suggest that knowledge of these, while important, does not represent stupidity or laziness. People are simply busy with their families and jobs. The real surprise may be that people know as much as they do. It is unrealistic to expect everyone to have a detailed knowledge of a wide range of political matters; everyone does not have an elaborate **ideology**.

Collective Knowledge and Stability-The collective whole is greater than its individual parts. Regardless of the instability of individuals' knowledge about politics, the collective responses of thousands of people tend to average out this randomness and reveal a stable **collective public opinion**.

How People Feel About Politics-Americans have opinions about many different political matters and specific policies. They hold basic values and opinions about the political parties and government in general.

The System in General-Political **efficacy** refers to the public's feelings about whether the government pays any attention to ordinary people, and to whether involvement such as voting has any effect. Citizens' sense of efficacy has dropped noticeably; these feelings of anger, alienation, and mistrust are closely related to many people's judgments that Congress, the presidency, and the other institutions of government have not been performing well.

Government Performance-Another important aspect of public opinion involves evaluations of government's performance, including citizens' judgments of how the government is doing. The public's general **confidence**, or trust in government institutions, tends to react to how particular institutions, or the government generally, are performing. A president's **approval rating** (the percentage of people saying they approve of how the president is handling his job) is a crucial indicator of presidential popularity. A president's popularity affects his influence on Congress and his ability to persuade the public, and it is a good predictor of whether or not he will win reelection and of whether his party will win or lose congressional seats. *Evaluations of Congress* have not been surveyed as regularly as those of the president, but it appears that Congress has often been highly unpopular.

Party Loyalty-Party identification, the sense of belonging to a political party, is still an important factor. Most people identify with a political party, despite the decline in the proportion of people who identify with either of the two major parties. Opinions and party loyalties differ according to race and ethnicity, religion, region, urban or rural residence, social class, educational level, gender, and age. **Party balance** has important effects on who rules in Washington, and especially on which party controls Congress. One recent political phenomenon is a decline in the proportion of people who identify with *either* of the two major parties. There has been a rise in the number of **independents** and **leaners** from approximately one-in-five Americans in the mid-1970s to one-in-three today.

Government's Role-The foundation beliefs of Americans are identified as the American political culture. Most Americans support capitalism, and the main ideas of democracy. Public opinion surveys show solid support for concepts of democracy, including popular sovereignty, political equality, majority rule, and political liberty. An overwhelming majority of Americans say that public officials should be chosen by majority vote, that everyone is entitled to the same legal rights and protections no matter what their political beliefs are, and that people in the minority should be free to try to win majority support for their opinions. Support for majority rule and popular control of government is extremely firm; there is solid public opposition to any arrangements that are thought to dilute democracy.

Americans show strong support for **economic liberty**, such as private ownership of property, and overwhelming rejection of communism or socialism. The public also supports **equality of opportunity** but not equality of *results*. **Economic conservatives** tend to put more emphasis on economic liberty and on freedom from government interference, while **economic liberals** emphasize equality of opportunity and the need for government regulation and safety nets. **Social liberals** and **social conservatives** differ on issues such as abortion, prayer in schools, homosexuality, pornography, crime, and political dissent.

Policy Preferences-Americans prefer some policies over others. A major test of democracy is whether government does what the citizens *want* them to do.

Spending Programs-Large majorities of Americans think that there is "too little" spending on anti-crime and education programs. The public strongly supports Social Security, Medicare, and environmental programs. While large majorities of Americans support spending for research on AIDS and cancer, they believe that the U.S. is not spending too much on national defense. Except for disaster relief, foreign aid is unpopular.

Social Issues-Americans have mixed views on the issue of abortion. The 1973 *Roe v. Wade* ruling may have been the result of changes in the American public's opinions on the issue. Strong liberalizing trends have led to the support of civil rights and civil liberties, political dissent, gay rights, and gun regulations.

The conservative trends among the American public show support for organized prayer in public schools, banning pornography, preventing flag burning, penalizing drug use, punishing crimes severely, and imposing capital punishment for murder.

Foreign Policy-The American public supports the nation's active role in world affairs. Vietnam had a tremendous effect on how Americans feel about the U.S. role in foreign affairs. General support for internationalism does not mean that Americans support foreign military or financial aid. **Isolationism** is a view of a minority of Americans. There is great division over whether U.S. involvement should be **unilateralist** or **multilateralist**. Most Americans prefer a multilateralist cooperation with the UN and NATO and other international organizations.

➜ **SOURCES OF POLITICAL ATTITUDES**

Political socialization is the process by which we learn our political values, attitudes, and behavior. It plays an important role in the formation of public opinion. People acquire their political attitudes and beliefs from their families, schools, churches, peers, the mass media, and places of employment. They also respond to political events and public debate, and party loyalties are known to adjust for the perception of the parties' effectiveness. Public opinion is strongly influenced by the economic and social structure.

Family-One of the most important agents of political socialization is family. The family powerfully shapes the attitudes, values, and beliefs of individual Americans. Party identification, like religious faith, is greatly shaped by the family.

Schools-Children are influenced by teachers, peers, and the surroundings of the classroom such as flags and talk about "liberty and justice for all." As they mature, political lessons become less symbolic and more explicit. All students are taught the duty to vote. By the time most Americans reach their twenties, most Americans have a reasonably well formed set of basic values, party affiliation, and some policy preferences.

Workplace and Home-The workplace exposes many young people to the realities of taxes, unemployment insurance, pensions, and labor rights. As people establish homes, schools, property taxes, crime, sanitation they tend to become more attuned to politics.

Events-The Great Society, the Vietnam War, and the Cold War are all events that have shaped and re-shaped individuals' attitudes and beliefs. People tend to adjust their evaluations of political leaders and policy preferences to new circumstances.

Economic and Social Structure-Structural characteristics have profound effects on American public opinion and make it different from public opinion in other countries. Public opinion is a source of influence on policymaking, but public opinion is itself affected by structural factors. The economic and social structures that have shaped Americans' basic values have also affected many of our policy preferences, such as reluctance to have government interfere with the economy and support for some social welfare policies. Structural changes bring about changes in policy preferences, the end of the Cold War and the breakup of the Soviet Union, for example, led people to favor arms control and cuts in military spending.

➜ HOW PEOPLE DIFFER

Although there are group differences, millions of Americans tend to learn many of the same ideas and attitudes. The learning experience is based on a common history and shared experiences, and on particular characteristics. Dedication to democracy, political and economic liberty, and the free enterprise system are supported by the social conditions and historical experience found in the United States.

Race and Ethnicity-Public opinion consists of the political attitudes and beliefs expressed by ordinary citizens. The authors have described public opinion as a collective whole, but they also point to important distinctions among different sorts of people in different circumstances.

African-Americans: Among the biggest differences are those between black and white Americans. African-Americans became Democrats in large proportions with the New Deal of the 1930s, and today are the most solidly Democratic of any group in the population. Other ethnic groups are not as distinctive in their opinions as African-Americans. Black and white divisions are most apparent on issues related to affirmative action and the criminal justice system.

Hispanics: Hispanics or Latinos are the fastest-growing ethnic group in America, but they are also one of the least politically active groups in the United States. Cuban-Americans tend to be strongly Republican, conservative opponents of communism; we were reminded of the very strong anti-Castro feelings among many Cuban-Americans in the case of the Cuban boat child Elian Gonzalez. Americans of Mexican or Puerto Rican ancestry are strongly Democratic and quite liberal on economic matters, though they are rather traditional on social questions—reflecting their predominant Roman Catholicism.

Asian-Americans: There are many different Asian groups who come from very different backgrounds in Japan, China, Korea, Vietnam, Thailand, and elsewhere. Asian-Americans have tended to be successful educationally and economically, to participate fairly actively in politics, and to be conservative and Republican.

White Ethnics: People of Irish, Italian, Polish, and other Southern or Eastern European ancestry became strong Democrats as part of the New Deal coalition, but by the 1980s these distinctions had faded as they achieved economic success.

Religion-Ethnic differences are often interwoven with differences in religious faith and values.

Catholics: Roman Catholics have been very supportive of family values, social morality (e.g., antipornography laws) and law and order. Catholics generally oppose birth control and the right to abortion. Catholics' affiliation with the Democratic Party has declined with the rise of their income and social mobility.

Jews: American Jews have been one of the strongest and most liberal wings of the Democratic Party. They tend to support abortion rights, civil liberties, and civil rights. There have been tensions between some Jews and some Black leaders over U.S. policy toward Israel and the Palestinians and affirmative action which Jews tend to oppose. Rising incomes have tended to undercut Jews' economic liberalism.

Mormons: Members of the Church of Jesus Christ of Latter Day Saints are distinguished by their staunch conservatism and strong Republican identification.

Protestants: American Protestants represent many different perspectives and beliefs. From the more affluent Episcopalian and Presbyterian (socially liberal, economically conservative) groups to the generally liberal Unitarian-Universalists and middle-class northern Baptists to the lower-income and quite conservative Southern Baptists and evangelicals of various denominations. In the 1980s, evangelical Christians of the Christian Coalition supported the conservative movement opposing abortion, pornography, law and order, and family values that stretched from the early 1980s of the Reagan era to the Republicans' 1994 congressional election victory.

Region-Regional policy preferences influence party identification. Policy preferences have undercut southern whites' traditionally strong identification with the Democratic Party. Urban, rural, and suburban residents also tend to differ from one another. *Regional* policy preferences influence party identification.

Social Class-Class has not been a significant source of political conflict among American citizens even though they are evenly divided in identifying themselves as either "working class" or "middle class." For comparison, in Great Britain, nearly three-fourths of the population

113

identify themselves as "working class." Most of the poor, working class and union members have identified with the Democratic Party. The middle and upper classes in the United States tend to support the Republican Party.

Education-Educational level is the strongest single predictor of participation in politics. The highly educated know more about politics, what they want, and how to go about getting it. Moreover, some policy preferences are related to education—those with more education show more support for civil rights, civil liberties, and individual freedom.

Gender-Women were prevented from fully participating in politics for a large part of U.S. history. Today, women vote in approximately the same proportions as men, but a substantial office-holding gap still remains between men and women. Women tend to identify more with the Democratic Party than do men. Women tend to oppose all kind of violence, including capital punishment and military force. Women differ among themselves on issues such as abortion.

Age-The *young and old* differ on certain matters that touch their particular interests, such as the draft or the drinking age. Young people are often more attuned to the particular times in which they are growing up, illustrated by civil rights during the 1960s and environmental issues during the 1980s and 1990s. Social change often occurs by **generational replacement**—old ideas die off with old people.

➔PUBLIC OPINION AND POLICY

Issues ranging from the 1964 Civil Rights Act, 1973 *Roe v. Wade*, gun control laws, and the recent presidential impeachment all demonstrate the relationship between public opinion and public law and policy. As well, studies have shown that as Americans have moved in different ideological directions, from liberal to conservative, elected leaders in Washington have shaped their policies to fit the public mood. One scholar found that U.S. government policy corresponded with what opinion surveys said the public wanted about two-thirds of the time, and the same two-thirds correspondence has appeared when other scholars investigated how *changes* in public opinion relate to changes in federal, state, and local policy.

Opinion manipulation-Public opinion is a substantial and important *proximate* influence on policymaking (that is, "stands next to" policymaking and directly affects it). Even if public opinion is a proximate influence on policy, we still need to know what factors affect public opinion itself. This chapter discusses reasons for being skeptical of the idea that public opinion can easily be manipulated. Personal experiences, objective events, and structural realities usually have the most to do with shaping public opinion. Exceptions may be most common in foreign affairs, where the government sometimes can control what information is made available.

➔SUMMARY

The political attitudes and beliefs expressed by ordinary citizens, public opinion, can be measured accurately through polls and surveys. The democratic ideals of popular sovereignty and majority rule imply that government policy should respond to the wishes of the citizens. One important test of how well *democracy* is working is how closely government policy corresponds to the expressed wishes of its citizens. The authors relate that public opinion in the United States has meaningful effects upon what governments do at all levels, but the government's responsiveness to public opinion is not perfect. Opinions and party loyalties differ according to race, religion, region, urban or rural residence, social class, educational level, gender and age. Blacks, Jews, city dwellers, women and low-income people tend to be liberal and Democratic, while white Protestants, suburbanites, males, and the wealthy tend to be conservative and Republican.

Chapter Outline

This section gives you a comprehensive review of the chapter. Use this outline in combination with your textbook to look for key concepts and objectives, to identify essential terms and names, and to gain a basic understanding of political practices and principles from this chapter.

I. **INTRODUCTION TO PART THREE: POLITICAL LINKAGE (P. 115)**
   A. The chapters in Part Two discussed a number of fundamental **structural** factors that affect how American politics works—the Constitution, the federal system, the nature of our population and society, the economy, and the international system.
   B. The authors turn to the **political linkage** sector in this section—public opinion, the mass media, organized interest groups, political parties, elections, and social movements.
   C. These people and institutions are not a formal part of government, but they directly influence what sorts of people are chosen to be government officials.
   D. They also affect what these officials do when they are in office and the resulting public policies.
   E. Chapter 5 explores the content of public opinion, and how it is formed and what impact it has on American politics and government. **Public opinion** is defined as the political attitudes expressed by ordinary citizens.

II. THE VIETNAM WAR AND THE PUBLIC (pp. 117-118)

A. **Vietnam** and the **Gulf Tonkin incident** are used in the text to illustrate important points about public opinion.
   1. How government officials can sometimes lead or manipulate opinion
   2. How public opinion is affected by events and circumstances, as well as by reports in the mass media
   3. How public opinion can have a strong impact on policymaking

B. Chronology
   1. For more than a decade, the United States had given large-scale military aid to the French colonialists and then to the South Vietnamese government to fight nationalists and communists in Vietnam; U.S. "military advisers" occasionally engaged in combat, but the American public knew little about the guerrilla war.
   2. People were willing to go along when their leaders told them that action was needed in order to resist communist aggression.
   3. Gulf Tonkin incident and escalation of the war
      a) On August 2, 1964, the Department of Defense announced that three North Vietnamese PT boats had engaged in an "unprovoked attack" on the *U.S.S. Maddox*; two days later, the Defense Department announced a "second deliberate attack" on the *Maddox* and the *C. Turner Joy*.
      b) President **Johnson** referred to "open aggression on the high seas," and air attacks were launched against North Vietnamese PT boat bases and an oil storage depot.
      c) Congress quickly passed the **Gulf Tonkin Resolution**, authorizing the president to take "all necessary measures" to repel any armed attack and to assist any ally in the region; this resolution established a legal basis for full U.S. involvement in the Vietnam War.
         (1) At the time of the incident, few questions were raised, and public support for the war increased after the Tonkin incident.
         (2) Years later, it was revealed that the *Maddox* had steamed near the coastline, deliberately provoking North Vietnamese radar defenses; the second attack apparently never happened, but instead was imagined by an inexperienced sonar operator.

C. Escalation of antiwar sentiment
   1. The number of U.S. troops in Vietnam rose rapidly.
      a) American casualties increased, and some troops were captured or reported missing.
      b) The American public reacted bitterly to televised scenes of American casualties and to reports of soldiers being wounded or captured.

    c) Antiwar testimony was aired in Senate hearings; peace marches and demonstrations accentuated the tragedies of the war and increased pressure to end it.

    d) By the end of 1967, as many people (45 percent) agreed as disagreed with the proposition that the United States had made a mistake by sending its troops to fight; a large majority of respondents said they favored **Vietnamization** (replacing U.S. troops with South Vietnamese troops).

  2. **Tet Offensive**—the National Liberation Front (NLF) and the North Vietnamese army launched massive attacks throughout South Vietnam at the end of January 1968, during the Tet holidays; the attack on the U.S. Embassy in Saigon and televised scenes of American soldiers destroying Ben Tre village "in order to save it" led to further erosion of public support

    a) After the initial shock, criticism of the war intensified from various sources, including journalists, politicians, and campus antiwar protesters.

    b) When the Nixon administration took office in January, most Americans favored the reduction of U.S. soldiers in Vietnam; even if it meant a communist victory in the country. The proportion of Americans describing themselves as **hawks** (those who wanted to increase the military effort) declined, while the proportion of **doves** (those who wanted to reduce military efforts) grew.

  3. President **Johnson** announced that he would limit the bombing of North Vietnam, seek a negotiated settlement, and withdraw as a candidate for reelection.

D. **Richard Nixon** was elected president in 1968

  1. By the time the new administration took office, a substantial majority of the public favored monthly reductions in the number of U.S. troops in Vietnam.

  2. A peace agreement was signed in January 1973; the North Vietnamese army took control of Saigon two years later and unified Vietnam.

III. DEMOCRACY AND PUBLIC OPINION (pp. 118-119)

A. **Public opinion** can be defined as the *political attitudes and beliefs expressed by ordinary citizens.*

B. Public opinion is a crucial part of democratic government.

  1. **Abraham Lincoln** defined democracy as "government of the people, by the people, and for the people."

  2. One important test of how well democracy is working is how closely government policy corresponds to the expressed wishes of its citizens.

C. Many leading thinkers have expressed strong doubts about the quality and stability of public opinion.

  1. Many of the Founders (James Madison, Alexander Hamilton, and others) worried about the "passions" of the public.

2. French philosopher **Alexis de Tocqueville** expressed concern about dangers of a "tyranny of the majority."

3. Journalist **Walter Lippman** (an early public opinion expert) declared that most people rely on stereotypes and do not know what goes on in the world.

D. Modern survey researchers (beginning with voting studies carried out during the 1940s and 1950s) turned up evidence of public ignorance, lack of interest in politics, and reliance on group or party loyalties rather than judgments about issues.

1. **Philip Converse** coined the term **nonattitudes** to describe the fact that many Americans seemed to have no real views at all on many issues of public policy, but simply offered *doorstep opinions* to satisfy interviewers.

2. The textbook points to evidence that this assessment of public opinion is exaggerated.

IV. WHAT PEOPLE KNOW ABOUT POLITICS (pp. 119-123)

A. Early attempts to determine public opinion by guesswork or from the views of personal acquaintances is defective: the views of personal acquaintances, media voices, or rally audiences are often not representative of the whole public.

B. Measuring what people think: the development of modern surveys

1. Most of the guesswork can now be eliminated by conducting an **opinion poll** or **sample survey**.

   a) One of the most famous examples of an improper polling techniques occurred during the 1936 presidential contest between Democratic incumbent Franklin Roosevelt and Republican Alf Landon. The *Literary Digest* incorrectly predicted Roosevelt's defeat.

   b) A survey consists of systematic interviews by trained, professional interviewers, who ask a *standardized set of questions* of a rather small number of *randomly chosen* Americans.

   c) Findings from a **random sample** of 1,500 people have a 95 percent chance of being accurate within three or four percentage points.

2. A **representative** sample should have the same characteristics as the population being measured.

   a) Representativeness is achieved best when the sample being interviewed is chosen **randomly** (by chance) from the population.

   b) Because of the nature of sampling, even highly rigorous surveys can be off by several percentage points, but the samples that survey organizations use are sufficiently representative so that survey results closely reflect how the whole population would have responded.

C. Individuals' ignorance

1. Modern survey results consistently show that most Americans do not know or care a lot about politics.

2. Lack of knowledge comes from several factors:

a) People are busy with their jobs and families; time is limited.

b) There may be little reason for the public to invest much effort in politics; scholars recognize that a single voter has almost no chance of determining the outcome of an election because of the large number of votes cast.

3. Lack of detailed knowledge or ideology does not mean that public opinion is unstable or irrelevant.

a) Responses of large numbers of people tend to average out the randomness, and it is unrealistic to expect the public to possess detailed knowledge about a wide range of political matters.

b) We should not expect the average American to have an elaborately worked out **ideology**, or system of interlocking attitudes and beliefs.

D. **Collective knowledge and stability**

1. Americans' **collective public opinions** are very stable over a long period of time.

a) Some recent research has indicated that Americans' collective policy preferences react sensibly to events, changing circumstances, and new information.

b) Although not all scholars are convinced that public opinion acts rationally, the evidence is clear that the American public has real opinions and not merely nonattitudes.

2. The evidence is clear that many of the Founders' fears of capriciousness or fluctuations in public opinion are no longer justified, if they ever were.

V. HOW PEOPLE FEEL ABOUT POLITICS (pp. 123-133)

A. **The system in general**

1. The public's general **confidence**, or trust in government institutions, tends to react to how particular institutions, or the government generally, are performing.

a) At the most general level, Americans are quite proud of their country and its political system.

b) At the more specific level, trust and confidence have been low; many Americans feel angry and alienated.

2. **Political efficacy** refers to the public's feelings about whether the government pays any attention to ordinary people, and to whether involvement such as voting has any effect; citizens' sense of efficacy has dropped noticeably in recent years.

B. **Government performance**

1. Evaluations of government's performance includes citizens' judgments of how the government is doing; this is another important aspect of public opinion.

a) A president's **approval rating** (the percentage of people saying they approve of how the president is handling his job) is a crucial indicator of *presidential popularity*.

b) **Bill Clinton's** presidential approval ratings reached into the high sixties in 1998, despite Independent Prosecutor **Kenneth Starr's** investigation and other

scandals–and rose even higher during impeachment hearings in the House of Representatives.
2. Trends in presidential popularity tend to fluctuate more than party loyalties or policy preferences; the public's evaluation of the president depends on how well things are going.
   a) The state of the economy is especially important: the president tends to be popular when the country is prosperous, and unpopular during high inflation or unemployment; **George Bush** ran into this problem in 1992.
   b) International crises can lead the public to "rally around the flag" and support the president, but only for a limited time.
3. Evaluations of Congress's performance have not been surveyed as regularly as those of the president, but it appears that Congress has often been highly unpopular.
   a) The Democratic-controlled Congress of the 1980s and early 1990s was thoroughly disliked by the time the Democrats were ousted from control in 1994.
   b) The Republican-controlled 104th Congress, which took office after the 1994 elections, initially won solid public support, but this enthusiasm quickly faded.

C. **Party loyalty**
   1. **Party identification** is the sense of belonging to a party.
      a) Many Americans feel some degree of loyalty to a political party.
      b) Slightly more than one-third of Americans identify themselves as **independents** (although many tend to lean toward one of the parties).
      c) Many people begin to identify with a party at a very young age, usually adopting the same party as their parents.
      d) People use the party label to help organize their thinking about politics—for example, to guide them in voting, in judging new policy proposals.
      e) Most people remain with the same party throughout their lives, but the extent and strength of party identification seems to be slipping.
   2. **Party balance** among voters has important effects on who rules in Washington, and especially on which party controls Congress.
      a) The proportion of people who identify with *either* of the two major parties has declined.
      b) There has been a rise in the number of **independents** and **leaners** from approximately one in five Americans in the mid-1970s to one in three today.

D. Basic values and beliefs
   1. Americans' **basic beliefs and values** are more fundamental than opinions about specific policies; there is often a high degree of **consensus** (agreement) about such values as freedom, democracy, capitalism, and equal opportunity.

2. **Freedom**—the rights of individuals to speak, write, assemble and worship freely, engage in occupations and pastimes of their own choosing, and to be secure from arbitrary restraints on their conduct
   a) No other value is given a higher place.
   b) High regard for liberty *in the abstract* often falls apart when it comes to *specific cases*, such as attitudes toward extreme or threatening minorities.
3. **Economic liberty**—strong support for economic liberty, such as private ownership of property and overwhelming rejection of communism or socialism
4. **Capitalism**—strong support for free markets and private ownership of the means of production; most Americans think it is fair to tie economic rewards to work and that it is necessary in order to get people to work
5. **Equality**—Americans favor *equality of opportunity*, but not *equality of result*
   a) There is overwhelming sentiment in favor of **equality of opportunity**: most Americans think that everyone should have an equal chance to do well and that government should help make sure that they can.
   b) There is little public support for substantial redistribution of wealth or income, especially as compared with the attitudes of citizens in other advanced industrial countries; at the same time, public opinion also does not support unrestrained private enterprise.
6. **Government's role**
   a) The ideas of equal opportunity, government regulation of business, and safety nets *can come into conflict with the ideas of economic liberty and capitalism.*
   b) Questions of how to resolve these conflicts form one of the main sources of political disagreement in America, and make up a big part of the difference between **liberalism** and **conservatism.**
      (1) **Economic conservatives** tend to put more emphasis on economic liberty and on freedom from government interference.
      (2) **Economic liberals** emphasize equality of opportunity and the need for government regulation and safety nets.
      (3) **Social liberals** and **conservatives** differ on issues such as abortion, prayer in schools, homosexuality, pornography, crime, political dissent and gun control.
   c) The terms *liberalism* and *conservatism* are also used to refer to positions on various political issues.
      (1) Those who favor free choices on social issues are often said to be liberals, while those preferring government enforcement are called conservatives.
      (2) Opinions on economic issues, foreign policy, and social issues do not necessarily have much to do with each other; many people are liberal in some ways but conservative in others.
E. **Policy preferences**

1. According to democratic theory, one of the chief determinants of what those in government do should be what the citizens *want* them to do, that is, citizens' **policy preferences**.
2. Americans have favored various government policies at different times.

F. **Spending programs**
   1. Large majorities of Americans think that there is "too little" spending on anti-crime and education programs.
   2. The public strongly supports Social Security, Medicare, and environmental programs.
   3. Large majorities of Americans support spending for research on AIDS and cancer.

G. **Social issues**
   1. Americans have mixed views on the issue of abortion.
   2. The 1973 *Roe v. Wade* ruling may have been the result of changes in the American public's opinions on the issue.
   3. Americans generally support some issues with what are considered liberal leanings (such as gay rights and gun regulations) and some issues that are considered conservative (prayer in public schools, preventing flag burning, and capital punishment).

H. **Foreign policy**
   1. Even in the area of foreign affairs, public opinion is very stable as it relates to certain policies; there is general support for internationalism (but not for foreign aid), and the public has been hesitant to use U.S. troops abroad.
   2. There is division among the American citizenry over whether U.S. involvement in international affairs should be **unilateralist** or **multilateralist**. Most Americans support multilateral cooperation with the UN and NATO.

VI. **HOW PEOPLE DIFFER (pp. 133-141)**
   A. The authors have described *public opinion as a collective whole*, but they also point to *important distinctions* among different sorts of people in different circumstances.
   B. **Race and ethnicity**
      1. **African-Americans**
         a) Among the biggest differences are those between black and white Americans.
         b) African-Americans became Democrats in large proportions with the New Deal of the 1930s, and today they are the most solidly Democratic of any group in the population.
         c) Black Americans tend to be much more liberal than white Americans on economic issues, especially those involving aid to minorities or help with jobs, housing, medical care, education, and related issues.
      2. **Hispanics or Latinos**
         a) They constitute several groups that are quite different in their backgrounds and opinions

     b) Cuban-Americans tend to be conservative Republicans, strongly anticommunist, and skeptical of government social welfare programs; Americans of Mexican or Puerto Rican ancestry are mostly Democrats, quite liberal on economic matters but rather traditional on social questions (reflecting their predominant Roman Catholicism).

  3. **Asian-Americans**

     a) Asian-Americans come from diverse backgrounds in Japan, Korea, Vietnam, China, and elsewhere.

     b) As a group, they have tended to be successful educationally and economically, to participate fairly actively in politics, and to be conservative and Republican.

  4. **White ethnics**

     a) Other ethnic groups are not as distinctive in their political opinions.

     b) People of Irish, Italian, Polish, and other Southern or Eastern European ancestry became strong Democrats as part of the New Deal coalition, but by the 1980s these distinctions had faded as they achieved economic success.

C. **Religion**

  1. Ethnic differences are often interwoven with differences in religious faith and values

  2. **Catholics**

     a) Roman Catholics were heavily Democratic after the New Deal but now are similar to other Americans in their party affiliations.

     b) They have tended to be especially concerned with family issues, morality, and law and order; American Catholics disagree with many Church teachings, and they strongly support birth control and the right to have abortions in about the same proportions as do other Americans.

  3. **Jews**

     a) Next to African-Americans, they remain the most Democratic group in the United States, with 47 percent Democrat and only 23 percent Republican.

     b) Jews tend to be liberal on social issues such as civil liberties and abortion, and they are strong supporters of civil rights.

     c) They are more supportive of social welfare policies than other groups.

  4. **Mormons** (Church of Jesus Christ of Latter-Day Saints)

     a) Mormons are the most staunchly conservative and most solidly Republican of any major religious denomination.

     b) A survey taken at the beginning of the 1990s identified 51 percent as Republican and only 23 percent as Democrat.

  5. **Protestants**

     a) Protestants constitute the large majority of the U.S. population, but there are many varieties of Protestants.

     b) Episcopalians and Presbyterians are relatively high-income; they tend to be socially liberal and economically conservative.

      c) Universalist-Unitarians and middle-class Northern Baptists are generally liberal.

      d) Southern Baptists and evangelicals tend to be lower-income and conservative.

D. **Region**
1. Although regional differences have been reduced, there are still substantial differences
2. Southerners tend to be conservative on social issues, but supportive of military spending and fairly liberal on economic issues; white Southerners tend to be less supportive of civil rights than Northerners.
3. Northeasterners tend to be the most different from Southerners; Midwesterners are somewhere in the middle; Pacific Coast residents resemble Northeasterners in many respects; people from the mountain states tend to be very conservative.
4. Regional *policy preferences influence party identification*
      a) Policy preferences have undercut Southern whites' traditionally strong identification with the Democratic party.
      b) Westerners are now the most Republican of regional groups.

E. **City and country**
1. Urban, rural, and suburban residents tend to differ from one another.
2. **City dwellers**—concerned about poverty, unemployment, and urban problems; many want the federal government to help.
3. **Suburbanites**—higher incomes, less eager to fight poverty, and more resistant to high taxes; tend to be highly concerned about the environment and to be socially liberal.
4. **Country dwellers**—socially and economically conservative, favor military strength, support law and order and conventional morality, and oppose strong gun controls.

F. **Social class**
1. Compared with much of the world, there has been little political conflict in the United States among people of different incomes or occupational groupings, but there are some differences.
2. Since the New Deal, more low-income people have identified themselves as Democrats than as Republicans; more high-income people have identified themselves as Republicans than as Democrats.
3. Although income is related to some distinctive policy preferences, simple liberal-conservative distinctions cannot accurately explain all the differences in opinions.
      a) Lower-income people tend to favor more government help with jobs, education, housing, and medical care; higher-income people tend to oppose these programs.
      b) Some high-income groups tend to favor government action to protect the environment and to be very liberal on social issues involving sexual behavior, abortion rights, free speech, and civil rights.

G. **Educational level**
   1. The strongest single predictor of participation in politics
   2. People who are highly educated know more about politics, what they want, and how to go about getting it.
   3. Some policy preferences are related to education; those with more education show more support for civil rights, civil liberties, and individual freedom.
   4. The most highly educated people tend to be the most tuned in to news and commentary in the media, and they tend to change their opinions somewhat more quickly than others do.

H. **Gender**
   1. Women were prevented from participating in politics for a large part of our history
   2. Women now vote in approximately the same proportions as men, but a substantial office-holding gap still remains between men and women.
   3. A moderate and apparently growing **gender gap** exists in party loyalties.
      a) More women than men identify themselves as Democrats.
      b) Women differ somewhat from men in certain political respects, including differences in certain policy preferences.
         (1) They tend to be more opposed to violence and more supportive of protective policies for the poor, the elderly, and the disabled.
         (2) More women than men oppose capital punishment and the use of military force abroad, while favoring arms control and peace agreements.
         (3) Women have not been substantially more supportive than men of women's rights or abortion, but women working outside the home are more liberal on issues such as abortion and women's rights than are homemakers.

I. **Age**
   1. The young and old differ on certain matters that touch their particular interests, such as the draft in wartime and the minimum drinking age
   2. Young people are often more attuned to the particular times in which they are growing up—for example, civil rights during the 1960s, environmental issues during the 1980s and 1990s.
   3. Social change often occurs by **generational replacement**, where old ideas (such as the Depression-era notion that women should stay at home and not take jobs away from men) die off with old people.

VII. PUBLIC OPINION AND POLICY (pp. 141-142)

A. One *test of how democracy is working* is how closely a government's *policies correspond to the expressed wishes of its citizens*; in this section, the authors look at how close the relationship is between what American citizens want and what the U.S. government actually does.
B. **The effects of public opinion on policy**

1. Public opinion seems to have a significant influence upon government policy in the United States.
   a) The opening story about the Vietnam War suggests that public opinion does affect policymaking, at least under some circumstances.
   b) Issues ranging from the 1964 Civil Rights Act, 1973 Roe v. Wade, gun control laws, and the recent presidential impeachment all demonstrate the relationship between public opinion and public law and policy.
2. Public opinion usually influences policymaking with less drama and without such open conflict.
   a) One scholar found that U.S. government policy corresponded with what opinion surveys said the public wanted about two-thirds of the time.
   b) Another study found that policies enacted in particular *states* also correspond rather closely to the opinions of the citizens of the states, and the same two-thirds correspondence has appeared when other scholars investigated how *changes* in public opinion relate to changes in federal, state, and local policy.

C. **Opinion manipulation**
   1. Even if public opinion is a **proximate** influence on policy (that is, "stands next to" policymaking and directly affects it), we still need to know what factors affect public opinion itself; we need to know if public opinion can be manufactured by the media or easily manipulated by interest groups or political leaders, as occurred in the Tonkin Gulf incident.
   2. This chapter mentioned reasons for being skeptical of the idea that public opinion can easily be manipulated.
      a) Personal experiences, objective events, and structural realities usually have the most to do with shaping public opinion.
      b) Exceptions may be most common in foreign affairs, where the government sometimes can control what information is made available.
   3. The authors of your textbook conclude that public opinion is a substantial and important proximate influence on policymaking, but that responsiveness to public opinion is incomplete.

VIII. SUMMARY (p. 143)
   A. Public opinion has been shown to both influence and to be influenced by political decision-makers.
   B. Public opinion can be accurately measured through surveys or polls.
   C. One important test of how well *democracy* is working in the United States is how closely government policy corresponds to the expressed wishes of its citizens.
   D. Many factors influence and individual's opinions and policy preferences on a number of important social and political issues.

Terms for Review

Use this list to review essential principles, functions, and concepts from this chapter. Refer to your textbook for help in identifying and defining terms on this list. When you study, do not merely memorize terms; ask questions about the material you are reviewing, and look for the importance or significance of each item.

Abrams et al. v. *United States* (1919)

Brady Bill

capitalism

collective public opinion

confidence

conservatives

economic conservatives

economic liberals

equality of opportunity

gender gap

generational replacement

ideology

independents

isolationism

leaners

liberals

multilateralist

party identification

permissive consensus

policy preferences

political efficacy

political socialization

presidential approval rating

public opinion

random sampling

representativeness

safety net

sample

sample survey

social conservatives

social liberals

Tonkin Gulf Resolution

unilateralist

Research Topics: Applying What You Have Learned

You will derive more benefit from your reading if you try to apply what you have learned. Some of the suggested research topics can be answered exclusively from your text, while others require you to conduct some basic research on your own. The references suggested under **Internet Sources** will help you in your search..

- Write a short essay in which you respond to the following question: Do you think American policymakers should follow public opinion, or should they lead public opinion? Are there types of issues or events that would cause you to reach different conclusions on the same question?

- Modern methods of polling first won prominence in the 1936 presidential election when George Gallup, Elmo Roper, and Archibald Crossley used sophisticated sampling and interviewing techniques. Use several of the Internet sources that are listed in the textbook at the end of Chapter 5 to locate information on polling for the 1936 election. How did the techniques in 1936 differ from modern survey methods?

- Using the information gleaned from your textbook, write a brief explanation explaining how public opinion serves as a source of influence on policymaking but is also shaped by structural factors. Write as clearly and concisely as possible, with the assumption that you are explaining the subject to another student who knows nothing about public opinion.

- Do you discern any policies in our modern government that would tend to substantiate the framers' fears of a tyranny of the majority? Are there also some illustrations that would tend to show that the fears were unjustified?

A number of sites on the World Wide Web serve as "gateways" to vast collections of material on American government and politics. The following Internet sources are recommended for students who would like to do additional research in areas covered by this chapter. These references would also be helpful in expanding on the questions suggested under Research Topics.

Doonesbury www.doonesbury.com/strawpoll/index.html
A daily on-line poll on current issues.

Gallup Organization www.gallup.com/
Access to recent Gallup polls as well as to the Gallup archives.

General Social Survey www.icpsr.imich.edu/GSS99/

Online access to the National Opinion Research Center's biennial survey of American attitudes.

National Election Studies http://www.umich.edu/-nes
Biennial survey of voters, focusing on electoral issues.

Polling Report www.pollingreport.com
A compilation of surveys from a variety of sources on politics and public affairs.

Roper Center www.lib.uconn.edu/RoperCenter/
Access to the main repository in the United States of public opinion polls on government and politics.

Social Science Data Collection http://ssdc.ucsd.edu/index.html
Lists of articles and books about polling, published public opinion polls, and raw polling data.

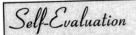

Circle the correct answer for each question. Questions are listed in the same order in which the information appears in the text. Use the Answer Key in the back of the Study Guide *to check your responses.*

1. Public opinion plays a crucial role in democratic government because
    a. The Founders designed the Constitution specifically so that office holders would be responsive to the needs of the majority of the citizens.
    b. One important test of how well democracy is working is how closely government policy corresponds to the wishes of its citizens.
    c. Public ignorance, lack of interest in politics, and reliance on group or party loyalties has resulted in an elite form of government.
    d. Organized groups counterbalance each other and lead to more representational government.

2. The sense of belonging to a political party is known as
    a. Party cohesion.
    b. Party sponsorship.
    c. Party identification.
    d. Party indoctrination.

3. The most important factor in constructing an accurate poll or survey is
    a. A large number of people must be interviewed in order to avoid skewing the sample with distorted viewpoints.
    b. The survey must be completed several weeks in advance of the election or event that is being measured.
    c. The sample of people interviewed must be representative of the population being measured.
    d. The questions must contain broad generalities in so that the person being interviewed will not be influenced.

4. Which of the following are among the biggest differences between white and black Americans?
    a. Black voters constitute a solid core of support for the Republican party.
    b. Black Americans have tended to be much more conservative than white Americans on economic issues.
    c. Black voters are more solidly identified with the Democratic party than any other group in the population.
    d. Black Americans are more liberal than whites on social issues that reflect religious values.

5. The single most important agent of **political socialization** is
    a. Church.
    b. School.
    c. Workplace.
    d. Family.

6. One thing we have learned about public information polls and surveys administered during the last five or six decades is that
    a. Most Americans can name their senators, representatives, and governors.
    b. Most Americans are unable to even name the president of the United States.
    c. Most ordinary Americans are very knowledgeable about politics.
    d. Most Americans have particular trouble with technical terms, abbreviations, and geography.

7. When comparing the ideologies of **conservatism** and **liberalism**, conservatives
    a. Emphasize government protection of the rights of individuals to participate in marches and demonstrations.
    b. Stress equality of opportunity and the need for government regulation and safety nets.
    c. Tend to put more emphasis on economic liberty and freedom from government interference.

131

d. Favor free choices and a minimum of government involvement in enforcement of law and order.

8. Social change often occurs when old ideas die off with old people, in a process known as
   a. Population development.
   b. Policy inception.
   c. Issue reinstatement.
   d. Generational replacement.

9. Citizens' sense of **political efficacy** is
   a. Their feelings about whether government pays any attention to ordinary people.
   b. Their general sense of confidence in whether government institutions are efficient and effective.
   c. Their general level of satisfaction about the state of the economy.
   d. Their feelings about whether government is capable of handling international crises.

10. The strongest single predictor of participation in politics (such as voting) is
    a. Race.
    b. Gender.
    c. Social class.
    d. Education.

11. In measuring how stable collective public opinion generally is, we find high and stable support given to
    a. Foreign aid.
    b. Environmental programs.
    c. Space program.
    d. Arms sales abroad.

12. The authors of your textbook conclude that
    a. Lack of detailed knowledge does not mean that public opinion is unstable or irrelevant.
    b. Public opinion, as a whole, is unstable and irrelevant.
    c. We cannot measure public opinion accurately enough to obtain usable information.
    d. Most people do not have opinions on major political and social issues.

13. (T/F) The collective public opinion of Americans is highly unstable and does not take available information into account in decision making.

14. (T/F) **Representativeness** in public opinion polling is achieved when the sample is chosen randomly, with each individual having an equal chance of being chosen.

15. (T/F) There is overwhelming support among Americans for equality of opportunity, but less support for equality of results.

16. (T/F) There is evidence of a high degree of **consensus** among Americans concerning basic beliefs and values.

17. (T/F) Women and men belong to the Republican and Democratic parties in nearly the same proportions and take similar voting positions on most issues.

18. (T/F) Presidential popularity tends to fluctuate more than party loyalties or policy preferences.

Chapter 6
THE MASS MEDIA

Key Concepts and Objectives

The Key Concepts and Objectives provide a look at the fundamental goals and ideas of this chapter. This section serves as a guide to a basic understanding of the objectives of your textbook.

After reading this chapter, you should be able to:

- Explain the relationship between the government and the mass media.
- Understand how the mass media in the United States is organized, how it works, and what effects it has on the quality of political life in the United States.
- Identify the various types of mass media.
- Explain the constitutionally prescribed relationship between the federal government and the mass media.
- Understand how the mass media can shape what government does.
- Identify how the mass media are influenced by technological changes and changes in government regulation.
- Assess whether the mass media promote or frustrate democracy in the United States.
- Assess whether the mass media promote popular sovereignty, political equality and liberty.
- Evaluate the advantages and disadvantages of both free enterprise journalism and government ownership of the news media.
- Assess how changes in the media are cause for concern in terms of the health of democracy in the United States.
- Identify whether the media hold a particular bias in their conventional role as "watchdog" of the government.
- Explain why government officials are key news sources.
- Identify key terms and concepts used in Chapter 6.

This section provides a brief overview of the chapter contents. Read this section as a preview before reading your textbook. Then use this material as a review to help you retain information from your reading.

→VERNON JORDAN MEETS THE PRESS

Prominent Washington, D.C. attorney and presidential confidant Vernon Jordan's experience with the American mass media highlights the manner in which "infotainment" has gained prominence in many media circles. An unsubstantiated rumor that Jordan had obstructed justice in Ken Starr's investigation of president Clinton took on a life of its own as it moved from a gossip columnist's website, to the commentary of "**pundits**" from major media outlets. Rumor was treated as fact and reporting took a back seat to investigation, research, and serious analysis.

→ROLE OF THE MASS MEDIA IN DEMOCRACY

Journalist and scholar Walter Lippman insisted that a "free press" is a "necessity" without which "the government" cannot govern. If democracy is based in part on the idea that government does what ordinary citizens want, then good information is essential to their ability to maintain their sovereignty. Most of that information must come through the mass media, whether newspapers, radio, television or, increasingly, the Internet. How well democracy works depends on how good a job the mass media are doing.

Watchdog Over the Government-The media have been regarded as the **watchdog** of the government since the founding of the nation. The First Amendment constitutional design created an adversarial relationship where the media will be able to expose officials' misbehavior without fear of censorship or prosecution. This constitutional arrangement is unusual; dictatorships, and even more democratic nations such as Great Britain, France, Israel, and Sweden all have more strict controls over the media than do American government officials.

Clarifying Electoral Choices-In a democracy the media are expected to provide clear electoral choices to the public. The public, in order to make informed and intelligent decisions in elections, must have access to information concerning what the political parties stand for and how the candidates shape up in terms of personal character, knowledge, experience, and positions on the issues.

Providing Policy Information-A third important role of the mass media is to present thorough information on the policy positions of the candidates and the parties in electoral contests. Citizens need to know how current policies are working as well as the pros and cons of alternative policies.

Other Roles-The media also act as amplifiers for speaking to citizens, as channels of communication among political and governmental institutions, helping Congress, the president, and members of the executive branch to figure out what the others are doing. The media serve as political institutions in their own right.

→ THE MEDIA LANDSCAPE

The media represent a multitude of ways for the public to gain access to political news, analysis and commentary.

Newspapers-At the founding of the nation, newspapers were largely accessible to the political elite such as the Federalists and the Democratic Republicans (Anti-Federalists) only. By the 1830s "penny-papers" such as the *New York Herald* reached mass audiences of ordinary workers. The Associated Press (AP) was organized in the 1840s by several New York newspapers in order to gather and distribute news by telegraph. John Pulitzer of the *New York World* (1883) and William Randolph Hearst of the *New York Journal* invented **yellow journalism**, where sensational news was combined with political crusades; oversized headlines, full-color illustrations and comics were prominently featured. Hearst's tactics helped provoke the Spanish American War in 1898.

Wire services such as the now defunct United Press International (UPI) and the Scripps-Howard Service, along with the AP made it possible for news to be conveyed to more people with greater speed than ever before. This process of homogenization of the news coupled with large newspaper "chains" revolutionized the news business. Today most multimedia corporations are dependent on the AP.

In addition to the chain-associated metropolitan dailies, newspapers come in three categories. First, there are the more credible, in-depth newspapers such as the *New York Times, Washington Post, Wall Street Journal*, and to a lesser extent, the *Los Angeles Times*, the *Miami Herald*, and the *Chicago Tribune*. The second category of newspapers cover specific groups such as African Americans, Jews, Hispanics, Asians, and gay and lesbians. The third category of newspapers includes supermarket tabloids such as the *National Inquirer*, the *Globe*, and the *Star*, which also do political stories that have periodically ended up in the mainstream press. Today people are relying more on electronic media such as radio, television and the Internet, and less on the print media.

Magazines-*The Nation* and the *Atlantic Monthly* were among the earliest journals of political opinion and analysis. *Time* magazine, *Newsweek, U.S. News &World Report*, are among the few weekly newsmagazines that report on current and historical events. There are also many news journals representing various political ideologies and opinions.

Radio-When radio was introduced in the 1920s, it changed American politics and society. During the Great Depression for instance, citizens were able to listen to president Roosevelt's "fireside chats." During World War II, the radio was also a key instrument in keeping the citizenry informed. Recently radio has been revived as many Americans spend hours in their cars during traffic-congested commutes. Syndicated talk show host Rush Limbaugh is the epitome of this revival.

Television-Television was invented before World War II; it entered American households in the 1950s. The three major networks—ABC, CBS, and NBC—provided most prime-time programming until the development of cable, all-news networks such as CNN, CNBC, C-SPAN, as we as BET (Black Entertainment Television). Most Americans name television as their most important source of news, and most say they trust television a great deal.

The Internet-Computers have led the most recent revolution in telecommunications. The Internet impacts many areas of life including politics, government, and the news. Many political candidates have invested in websites in order to inform the public of their policy positions.

The Internet makes it possible for two-way, interactive communication between political leaders and citizens. Commentators disagree about the democratic potential of the Internet, however. The reliability of information is one concern, while the ability of hate groups to spread their messages is another. Still the Internet gives citizens easier access to information and opinions about government. Some even suggest that the Internet ought to be thought of as a new space for participation in the political process.

➔HOW THE MEDIA WORK

The precise way in which the media are organized and function affect whether citizens get the kinds of information they need for democracy to work properly.

➔ORGANIZATION OF THE MASS MEDIA

The mass media in the United States are overwhelmingly large, privately owned conglomerates.

Corporate Ownership-Family owned local television and newspapers are on the decline. Most of the biggest stations, papers, and cable networks are corporate owned. A few firms such as Gannett, Knight-Ridder, and Newhouse dominate the newspaper business. Time Warner, Rupert

Murdoch's News Corp., and Gannett control magazine publishing. General Electric, Westinghouse, Disney and Time Warner dominate television. Six corporations dominate receive more than half of all book-publishing, and four firms dominate motion pictures.

Mergers have characterized the organization of many media outlets. One of the many examples that your authors provide is AOL's acquisition of Time Warner which consisted of Time Magazine, Warner Books, Turner Broadcasting (CNN, TNT,TBS, the Atlanta Braves baseball team, Atlanta Falcons football team), Warner Music group, Warner Bros. Pictures, Warner Bros. Television, Time Warner Cable, Home Box Office (HBO), and various newspapers and magazines. The Telecommunications Act of 1996 enabled a number of radio stations to merge. The result is that many national conglomerates will soon control radio broadcasting in every-medium sized and large market in the United States.

A major concern about these developments with regard to the working of democracy is that they add dangerously to the already strong business presence in American politics. Others worry that the consolidation of mass media outlets will undermine debate and diversity of news and opinion.

Uniformity and Diversity-Most news outlets receive their information from just a few sources for news. The practice of contracting, where news originates in fewer and fewer centralized sources, is becoming more commonplace. The AP supplies most of the national and international news in the United States. Along with the centralization and homogenization of the mass media, there are alternative media outlets such as the *Weekly Standard* or conservative *National Review, The Nation* (liberal) and *Commentary* (neoconservative), or the *New York Review* of *Books* (intellectual and critical). The World Wide Web also provides important information that is not controlled by government or corporations. There are some outlets that cater to specific groups such as African Americans, Spanish language, and gay and lesbians. Together, these media sources represent a small fraction of media outlets available to the public.

Profit Motives-Media corporations are driven by the profit motive. These corporations must therefore appeal to the public as an audience for sales, programming, advertisement, and ratings. The profit motive also forces mass media outlets to avoid controversial material that might seem "extreme" or offensive to some viewers.

→ POLITICAL NEWSMAKING

The kind of news that the media present is affected by the organization and technology of news gathering and news production. Much depends on where reporters are, what sources they talk to, and what sorts of video pictures are available.

138

The Limited Geography of Political News-The national news normally emanates from Washington, D.C., and New York. The major media companies are reluctant to have reporters in every city. The majority of newspapers print mostly wire service reports generated in other parts of the country.

Dependence on Official Sources-Most political news in the United States comes directly from what key public officials say. This poses real problems for democracy. Heavy reliance on official sources means that government officials may be able to control a great deal of what journalists report.

Beats and Routines-Most reporters have routine **beat** areas from which they seek on-going news reports. Political beats typically center on official government institutions such as a local city hall, police station, the White House or Congress. Investigative reporting of the sort that Bernstein and Woodward did on Watergate is rare. Most reporters get their news from sources such as press conferences, press releases form officials, and comments solicited from officials. One study shows for example, that government officials, foreign or domestic, were the sources of nearly three-quarters of all news in the *New York Times* and the *Washington Post*.

Military Actions-News sources are especially dependent on officials during military actions. Government officials in the Gulf War were careful to avoid the actions of military and political leaders during Vietnam where on-site news coverage eventually eroded public support for the war. During the Gulf War media reports celebrated the accuracy of "smart bombs." After the war, it was revealed that most "smart" weapons did not work and that conventional bombs did most of the damage.

Mutual Needs-A comfortable relationship tends to develop between public officials and the media: reporters want fresh stories, and they cultivate access to people who can provide stories with quotes or anonymous leaks. At the same time, officials want favorable publicity and want to avoid a counter attack of unfavorable publicity. Reliance on officials also means that when officials of both parties agree, debate tends to be restricted. This was true in the case of the Telecomunications Act of 1986 which fundamentally changed the way mass media and telecommunications do business.

The Struggle for Democracy: Covering the Watergate Scandal-The Watergate scandal revealed the unprecedented investigative work of 29-year-old *Washington Post* journalist Bob Woodward and his 28-year-old partner Carl Bernstein. When Woodward and Bernstein were done with their investigation, the president of the United States was forced to resign because of the illegal activities of the Committee to Re-elect the President (CREEP) and an unconstitutional abuse of power by Richard Nixon.

Newsworthiness-Professional judgments determine what is worth reporting or presenting to the public. Newsworthiness seems to depend on factors such as novelty (man bites dog), drama and human interest, relevance to the lives of Americans, high stakes (e.g., physical violence or conflict), and celebrity (e.g., the death of John F. Kennedy, Jr.,).

Episodic Foreign Coverage-Most newspapers cannot afford to station reporters abroad. The *New York Times*, one of the few that can, station reporter in countries of greatest interest to the United States, such as China, Japan, Great Britain, Germany, Israel, and Russia. In most countries they depend on "stringers" (local journalists who file occasional reports). Most media devote most of their attention to limited areas of the world, dropping in only occasionally on others. When an unknown place such as Rwanda makes the news, it usually disappears as quickly as it emerged, with the public never fully understanding the relevant issues. Thus they find it difficult to form judgments about U.S. foreign policy.

→INTERPRETING

Journalistic objectivity guards against news commentators offering explicit interpretations of events. Typically, when explicit interpretations are presented, they are labeled as editorials. Reporters cannot volunteer that an event is staged. So-called experts are used to offer explicit opinions and comments. These experts are usually called upon by the news media because their opinions are predictable. "Pundits" are well known for being on television a lot and are not experts on any subject at all. Media savvy scholars and commentators regularly offer opinions on news events.

Commentators from conservative **think tanks**, such as the American Enterprise Institute and the Center for Strategic and International Studied were frequently called upon to reinforce the conservative views of the Reagan and Bush administrations. Liberals and moderates have appeared frequently during the Clinton administration. Radical thinkers like Noam Chomsky have rarely penetrated the mainstream media. Representatives of racial groups appear even less frequently.

→IS THE NEWS BIASED?

There is considerable debate concerning media **bias.** All sides of the political spectrum charge the media with a certain bias, usually opposing the view to which they adhere. Liberals charge conservative biases exist and conservatives charge liberal biases exist.

Liberal Reporters-There is evidence that many reporters and journalists hold liberal biases on social issues such as abortion, the environment, and civil rights. But there is no evidence that these biases filter into news reporting. Journalists' reliance on official sources and conservative owners effectively offset any liberal biases that they may hold.

Conservative Owners-Owners tend to be very conservative. The shareholders and executives of multibillion-dollar corporations are not very interested in undermining capitalism, or to increase their own taxes, raise labor wages, or lose income from offended advertisers. That owners have a conservative bias may be evidenced by the fact that between 1968 and 1988, more newspapers endorsed the Republican over the Democratic candidate.

What Constitutes Bias?-Biases have been measured in many ways. Some have tabulated positive or negative references to issues or political leaders and candidates, others use more sophisticated concepts of bias.

➔**PREVAILING THEMES IN POLITICAL NEWS**

There are certain values and tendencies in the media that are readily identifiable, certain values that are assumed, and certain points of view that are assumed.

Nationalism-Most coverage of foreign affairs is framed in a pro-American, patriotic fashion. It is also ethnocentric, to the degree that it reports on symbols of patriotism such as the valor of American troops or hostages. But much less is covered concerning the massacres in foreign lands such as East Timor, Bosnia, Rwanda, Nigeria, Cambodia, and Indonesia. The news generally harmonizes well with U.S. foreign policy and the media usually accept the government's view of U.S. allies and enemies. For instance, when the U.S. was assisting Iraq in its war against Iran, Saddem Hussein was depicted in a positive light: with the coming of the Gulf War, media characterizations of him changed dramatically.

Approval of the American Economic System-News coverage concerning free markets, free international trade, and minimal regulation tends to be favorable. U.S. capitalism wins approval, while social democracies with comprehensive social welfare programs are depicted negatively; systems that reflect the U.S. system are depicted positively.

Negativity and Scandal-The American public is turned off by negative campaign advertisements and political scandal. Much of the Clinton presidencies were dogged by rumors of sexual impropriety. Clinton would eventually be impeached. Sexual and financial scandals would also force other prominent political leaders out of office.

Infotainment-Political reporting and news presentation has become increasingly more entertainment oriented. Cable television, the Internet and the multiplication of media outlets have all contributed to the entertainment slant of journalism. The bitter conflicts between the various political elements in society are perfect grist for the "infotainment" mill.

Limited, Fragmented, and Incoherent Political Information-Corporate ownership, prevailing technology, organization of the news and the profit motive all influence the absence of substantive news coverage in the modern era.

→EFFECTS OF THE MEDIA ON POLITICS

The media powerfully affect public opinion and policymaking in a number of ways, including setting the agenda for public debate and framing how issues are understood.

Agenda Setting-News coverage often reflects the issues that people are most concerned with in the country. This is not just based on public interest, it is also an effect of media influence. People tend to be concerned with the social problems that they come into contact with through media coverage. Publicity about crime may reflect editors' fears or a few dramatic incidents rather than a rising crime rate. One scholarly study shows that in the foreign policy area, media choices about coverage shape what presidents pay attention to.

→FRAMING AND EFFECTS ON POLICY PREFERENCES

The media also influence how society thinks about political problems. Whether citizens ascribe poverty to the individual poor person or to the economic system depends partly on whether the media run stories about poor individuals or about overall economic trends like wage stagnation and unemployment. Peoples' policy preferences are also impacted by media coverage.

→IMPACT ON POLICYMAKING

The media impact public policy indirectly by influencing what citizens think about issues and the government in turn, gauges public opinion. The media also affect who is elected to office by framing ideas about who would make a good leader. The media also have a direct impact on policymaking as they provide information about political competitors' activities.

→CYNICISM

"Attack journalism" has had a tremendous impact on the general cynicism that many citizens have expressed concerning politics and political leaders over the past twenty years. Personal behavior and the private lives of political leaders have become increasingly fair game. As well, coverage of money and special interest maneuvering has contributed to an increasing disenchantment with government and politics in the United States.

→GOVERNMENT REGULATION OF THE MEDIA

The U.S. Constitution protects freedom of press and although the U.S. government has less legal control over the mass media, it does have the authority to regulate the electronic media.

Print Media-Violation of the **Alien and Sedition Acts of 1798** resulted in the arrests and imprisonment of several Anti-Federalist newspaper editors. Since then however, the First Amendment has been interpreted to allow broad publication rights as long as they do not infringe on national security.

Prior Restraint-The Constitution prohibits government's use of pre-publication censorship or restraining techniques against material to which it objects. When president Nixon sought to use prior restraint tactics against the *New York Times* and *Washington Post* which planned on publishing secret Defense Department *Pentagon Papers* concerning U.S. involvement in Vietnam, the Supreme Court rejected the president's arguments.

Wartime Controls-Nixon's attempts might have been more successful had there been an active war at the time of the lawsuit. The government has exercised broad restraint powers in war times especially if news coverage threatens the lives of U.S. soldiers or national security.

→THE ELECTRONIC MEDIA

The government has greater regulatory powers over electronic media than print media.

Government Licensing of the Airwaves-Ever since the passage of the Radio Act of 1927 and the Communications Act of 1934—which established the FCC—the government has had the power to license radio and television stations and set the rules for licenses renewals. The FCC dictates the frequencies of television and radio stations. The Telecommunications Act of 1996 revolutionized the industry by allowing telephone companies, cable companies, and broadcasters to control, free of charge, public airwaves. The massive mergers that are discussed above in this chapter were made possible through the 1996 Act.

Public Service Broadcasting-Broadcasters, under the direction of the FCC are required to provide a minimal number of hours of news and "public service" programming. The FCC, which once imposed public service programming under the threat of license renewals, no longer enforces the public service requirement to any serious degree.

Fairness-The fairness doctrine (1949), which once required that licensees present contrasting viewpoints on controversial issues of public importance, is not enforced today.

Equal Time-The 1934 Communications Act stipulated that news outlets grant air time, equally, to candidates in pursuit of political office. The 1960 Nixon versus Kennedy debate effectively suspended the equal time provision which has since become irrelevant in political coverage and debates.

Rate Regulation-Federal and local regulations which imposed rate controls through the 1996 Act, have not yet had the intended effect of lowering prices through increased competition.

The Internet-The Internet has been much more difficult for the federal government to regulate than radio and television. Congress's and the executive branch's attempts to ban obscenity on the Internet have been considered unconstitutional.

Judging the Media-The evolution of the American media from the serious political debates of the eighteenth century to the contemporary phase of "attack journalism," and "infotainment," news does not bode well for democracy if it hinges on extensive public deliberation and discussion.

→SUMMARY

Structural factors have greatly determined the organization of the mass media in the United States. The many technological developments, changes in both the population and economy, and the development of privately owned corporate-dominated media have shaped the ways in which the American media do business. The profit motive should not be underestimated when evaluating the operations and organization of the American mass media.

The profit motive leads the major media to appeal to large audiences by limiting the quantity and depth of political news, by appealing to patriotism and other mainstream political values. Newsgathering for the nation is centered mainly in New York City and Washington, D.C. Whether the media have a ideological bias is an ongoing debate. The noted liberality of news journalists is offset by the conservatism of official news sources and share-holding owners and editors. The media have a tremendous impact on public opinion and public policy. The American government does not have as much control over the mass media as do governments in other countries, but censorship is permissible in war times and domestic crises. The Internet remains relatively free from government regulation. The mass media are essential to the workings of democracy in a large modern nation. The development of mass media in the United States has undoubtedly helped democracy, but it has also created real causes for concern.

Chapter Outline

This section gives you a comprehensive review of the chapter. Use this outline in combination with your textbook to look for key concepts and objectives, to identify essential terms and names, and to gain a basic understanding of political practices and principles from this chapter.

I.   VERNON JORDAN MEETS THE PRESS (p. 149)

A.   The goal of this chapter is to better understand the relationship between the mass media and democracy.

1.   When rumor spread that federal prosecutors in the Independent Counsel's Office were seeking obstruction of justice charges against president Bill Clinton's personal friend and confidant Vernon Jordan, the mass media ran with the story despite no corroboration from witnesses, evidence, or prosecutors.

2.   Respected news outlets throughout the nation reported on a story that was generated out of publicity for an anti-Clinton book; the story was first posted on a gossip-column website.

3.   Jordan reportedly urged witness Monica Lewinsky to lie to federal prosecutors. When the dust cleared amid the Clinton impeachment, nothing was said concerning Jordan telling Lewinsky to lie.

B.   The opening vignette highlights the evolution of the mass media in the United States in its coverage of political news. The story precedes a discussion of the ways in which the operations of the mass media have been influenced by changes in technology and business organization. With the reporting tactics used in modern journalism, rumor is often treated as fact and investigative reporting takes a back seat to argument, punditry, and "infotainment."

II.   ROLES OF THE MASS MEDIA IN DEMOCRACY (pp. 150-152)

A.   The central idea of democracy is that ordinary citizens should control what their government does.

1.   The citizenry's capacity to speak intelligently on political matters, to control officials, to choose candidates, and to embrace certain policies is contingent upon the information it receives from the various media.

2.   Since most of that information must come through the mass media, how well democracy works depends partly on how good a job the media are doing.

B.   Possible roles for the media in a democracy

1.   **Watchdog over government**-the press, acting as a protector, should dig up facts and warn the public when officials are doing something wrong.

a) The **First Amendment** of the Constitution helps to ensure that the media can expose officials' wrongdoing without fear of censorship or prosecution.

b) Though freedom of the press is not perfect in the United States, the media enjoy greater freedom than their counterparts in other countries.

2. **Clarifying electoral choices**

a) The media have an obligation to the public to make clear what electoral choices it has.

b) The public should be informed of what the political parties stand for and how the candidates shape up in terms of personal character, knowledge, experience, and positions on the issues.

3. **Providing policy information**

a) Democracy is best served when the mass media present diverse, full, and enlightening facts and ideas about public policy.

b) Citizens need to know how well current policies are working as well as the pros and cons of alternative policies. In a democracy, government should respond to public opinion, but that opinion should be well informed.

4. **Other roles**

a) The media act as amplifiers for speaking to citizens and trying to persuade them.

b) The media serve as channels of communication among political and governmental institutions, helping Congress, the presidents, and members of the executive branch to figure out what the others are doing.

c) The media may themselves be political actors, with their own goals and interests, trying to influence politics just as other interest groups do.

d) The mass media serve as a critical link among political and governmental institutions, and they also act as political institutions in their own right.

III. THE MEDIA LANDSCAPE (pp. 152-157)

A. The media have changed greatly over the history of the United States and continue to change even more rapidly. Taken together, the mass media represent, a multitude of ways for the public to gain access to political news, analysis and commentary.

1. **Newspapers**

a) **Newspapers**-At the founding of the nation, newspapers were largely accessible to the political elite such as the Federalists and the Democratic Republicans (Anti-Federalists) only.

b) By the 1830s "penny-papers" such as the *New York Herald* reached mass audiences of ordinary workers. The Associated Press (AP) was organized in the 1840s by several New York newspapers in order to gather and distribute news by telegraph.

c) John Pulitzer of the *New York World* (1883) and William Randolph Hearst of the *New York Journal* invented yellow journalism, where sensational news was combined with political crusades; oversized headlines, full-color illustrations and comics were prominently featured.

    (1) Hearst's tactics helped provoke the Spanish American War in 1898.

    (2) Wire services such as the now defunct United Press International (UPI) and the Scripps-Howard Service, along with the AP made it possible for news to be conveyed to more people with greater speed than ever before.

    (3) This process of homogenization of the news coupled with large newspaper "chains" revolutionized the news business. Today most multimedia corporations are dependent on the AP.

  d) In addition to the chain-associated metropolitan dailies, newspapers come in three categories.

    (1) First, there are the more credible, in-depth newspapers such as the *New York Times*, *Washington Post, Wall Street Journal*, and to a lesser extent, the *Los Angeles Times*, the *Miami Herald*, and the *Chicago Tribune*.

    (2) The second category of newspapers cover specific groups such as African Americans, Jews, Hispanics, Asians, and gay and lesbians.

    (3) The third category of newspapers includes supermarket tabloids such as the *National Inquirer*, the *Globe*, and the *Star*, which also do political stories that have periodically ended up in the mainstream press.

  e) Today people are relying more on electronic media such as radio, television and the Internet, and less on the print media.

2. **Magazines**

  a) *The Nation* and the *Atlantic Monthly* were among the earliest journals of political opinion and analysis. *Time* magazine, *Newsweek,* and *U.S. News &World Report* are among the few weekly newsmagazines that report on current and historical events.

  b) There are also many news journals representing various political ideologies and opinions.

3. **Radio**

  a) When radio was introduced in the 1920s, it changed American politics and society. During the Great Depression for instance, citizens were able to listen to president Roosevelt's "fireside chats."

  b) During World War II, the radio was also a key instrument in keeping the citizenry informed. Recently radio has been revived as many Americans spend hours in their cars during traffic-congested commutes. Syndicated talk show host Rush Limbaugh is the epitome of this revival.

4. **Television**

  a) Television was invented before World War II; it entered American households in the 1950s. The three major networks—ABC, CBS, and NBC—provided most prime-time programming until the development of cable, all-news networks such as CNN, CNBC, C-SPAN, as well as BET (Black Entertainment Television).

Chapter 6

b) Most Americans name television as their most important source of news, and most say they trust television a great deal.

5. **The Internet**
   a) Computers have led the most recent revolution in telecommunications. The Internet impacts many areas of life including politics, government, and the news.
   b) Many political candidates have invested in websites in order to inform the public of their policy positions.
   c) The Internet makes it possible for two-way, interactive communication between political leaders and citizens. Commentators disagree about the democratic potential of the Internet, however. The reliability of information is one concern, while the ability of hate groups to spread their messages is another.
   d) The Internet gives citizens easier access to information and opinions about government. Some even suggest that the Internet ought to be thought of as a new space for participation in the political process.

IV. **HOW THE MEDIA WORK (pp. 157-166)**
   A. **Organization of the mass media**
      1. Most of the media in the United States are privately owned, usually by very large businesses.
      2. Corporate ownership: concentration of ownership has been increasing.
         a) Most of the media in the United States are privately owned, usually by very large businesses, and the concentration of media ownership in the hands of a few companies has been rapidly increasing.
         b) Although some of the smaller television stations and newspapers are locally owned by families or groups of investors, the television networks and many of the largest stations and papers are owned by large media corporations which are subsidiaries of large conglomerates.
         c) There has been a strong tendency for newspapers to merge; in most towns and cities that have a newspaper, there is only one.
   B. **Uniformity and diversity**
      1. Most newspapers and television stations depend largely on the same sources for news.
      2. The Associated Press (AP) supplies most of the major national and international news stories. Many news outlets are contracting where much of what comes to us over a multitude of media avenues originate in fewer and fewer centralized sources.
      3. The AP wire influences most of what appears on network and cable television news.
      4. Along with centralization and homogenization of the mass media, there is also quite a lot of diversity, with a variety of special interest publications with political

148

commentary; however, the audiences for these news sources represent only a small fraction of the number of people who depend on the mass media for their news.

C. **Profit motives**
   1. Media corporations, like other corporations, are in business primarily to make a profit. This means that the major mass media must appeal to large audiences and get many people to buy their publications or the products they advertise.
   2. "Infotainment" news is characteristically short, snappy, and sensational.
   3. The profit motive means that the biggest mass media avoid controversial material that might seem "extreme" or offensive to many groups.

D. **Political newsmaking**
   1. The organization and technology of news gathering and news production affect the kind of news that the media present.
   2. Much depends on where reporters are, what sources they talk to, and what sorts of video pictures are available.
   3. The **limited geography of political news** is evidenced by the fact that most reporters are located in Washington, D.C. and New York City, the center of most media operations.
      a) The national news has a strong Washington-New York orientation. The networks usually add Chicago, Los Angeles, Miami, Houston, and Dallas.
      b) Most television news stories are assigned to predictable events such as news conferences. Spontaneous news such as riots, accidents, and natural disasters are typically covered by special video camera crews that are rushed to the location.
      c) **CNN** (Cable News Network) broadcasts 24 hours a day and has a near-monopoly on fast-breaking news.

E. **Dependence on official sources**
   1. Most political news is dependent on what public officials say. This fact has important consequences for how well the media serve democracy.
   2. *Beats and routines*: A newspaper or television reporter's work is usually organized around a particular beat; most political beats center on some official government institution that regularly produces news, such as a local police station, city hall, or the White House.
   3. Investigative reporting, such as that done by Carl Bernstein and Bob Woodward in the Watergate scandal is rare in today's "infotainment" news.

F. **Military actions**
   1. News sources are especially dependent on officials during military actions. Government officials in the Gulf War were careful to avoid the actions of military and political leaders during Vietnam where on-site news coverage eventually eroded public support for the war.
   2. During the Gulf War media reports celebrated the accuracy of "smart bombs." After the war, it was revealed that most "smart" weapons did not work and that

conventional bombs did most of the damage.

G. **Mutual needs**

1. A comfortable relationship tends to develop between public officials and the media: reporters want fresh stories, and they cultivate access to people who can provide stories with quotes or anonymous leaks. At the same time, officials want favorable publicity and want to avoid a counter attack of unfavorable publicity.

2. Reliance on officials also means that when officials of both parties agree, debate tends to be restricted. This was true in the case of the Tele- communications Act of 1986 that fundamentally changed the way mass media and telecommunications corporations do business.

H. **Newsworthiness**

1. Professional judgments determine what is worth reporting or presenting to the public.

2. Newsworthiness seems to depend on factors such as novelty (man bites dog), drama and human interest, relevance to the lives of Americans, high stakes (e.g., physical violence or conflict), and celebrity (e.g., the death of John F. Kennedy, Jr.).

3. Pressure by advertisers, media owners, and high government officials is usually exercised quietly and inconspicuously, through editors and producers who are hired and fired by media owners.

I. **Episodic foreign coverage**

1. Most newspapers cannot afford to station reporters abroad. The *New York Times*, one of the few that can, stations reporter in countries of greatest interest to the United States, such as China, Japan, Great Britain, Germany, Israel, and Russia.

2. In most countries they depend on "stringers" (local journalists who file occasional reports).

   a) Most media devote most of their attention to limited areas of the world, dropping in only occasionally on others.

   b) When an unknown place such as Rwanda makes the news, it usually disappears as quickly as it emerged, with the public never fully understanding the relevant issues. Thus they find it difficult to form judgments about U.S. foreign policy.

V. **INTERPRETING**

A. **Objectivity**

1. Journalistic objectivity guards against news commentators offering explicit interpretations of events. Typically, when explicit interpretations are presented, they are labeled as editorials. Reporters cannot volunteer that an event is staged.

2. So-called experts are used to offering explicit opinions and comments. These experts are usually called upon by the news media because their opinions are predictable. "Pundits" are well known for being on television a lot and are not experts on any subject at all. Media savvy scholars and commentators regularly offer opinions on news events.

3. Commentators from conservative **think tanks**, such as the American Enterprise

Institute and the Center for Strategic and International Studied were frequently called upon to reinforce the conservative views of the Reagan and Bush administrations. Liberals and moderates have appeared frequently during the Clinton administration. Radical thinkers like Noam Chomsky have rarely penetrated the mainstream media. Representatives of racial groups appear even less frequently.

B. **Is the news biased?**
1. There is considerable debate concerning media **bias.** All sides of the political spectrum charge the media with a certain bias, usually opposing the view to which they adhere. Liberals charge conservative biases exist and conservatives charge liberal biases exist.
2. **Liberal Reporters**
   a) There is evidence that many reporters and journalists hold liberal biases on social issues such as abortion, the environment, and civil rights.
   b) But there is no evidence that these biases filter into news reporting. Journalists' reliance on official sources and conservative owners effectively offset any liberal biases that they may hold.
3. **Conservative Owners**
   a) Owners and top managers tend to be very conservative.
   b) The shareholders and executives of multibillion-dollar corporations are not very interested in undermining capitalism, or to increase their own taxes, raise labor wages, or lose income from offended advertisers.
   c) Newspapers' endorsements of presidential candidates are decided primarily by owners and publishers.
   d) That owners have a conservative bias may be evidenced by the fact that between 1968 and 1988, more newspapers endorsed the Republican over the Democratic candidate.
4. **What Constitutes Bias?**
   a) Biases have been measured in many ways.
   b) Some have tabulated positive or negative references to issues or political leaders and candidates, others use more sophisticated concepts of bias.

VI. **PREVAILING THEMES IN POLITICAL NEWS (pp. 166-168)**
A. **Nationalism**
1. Most coverage of foreign affairs is framed in a pro-American, patriotic fashion.
2. It is also ethnocentric, to the degree that it reports on symbols of patriotism such as the valor of American troops or hostages.
   a) Much less is covered concerning the massacres in foreign lands such as East Timor, Bosnia, Rwanda, Nigeria, Cambodia, and Indonesia.
   b) The news generally harmonizes well with U.S. foreign policy and the media usually accept the government's view of U.S. allies and enemies.

   c) When the U.S. was assisting Iraq in its war against Iran, Saddem Hussein was depicted in a positive light: with the coming of the Gulf War, media characterizations of him changed dramatically.

B. **Approval of the American economic system**
1. News coverage concerning free markets, free international trade, and minimal regulation tends to be favorable.
2. U.S. capitalism wins approval, while social democracies with comprehensive social welfare programs are depicted negatively; systems that reflect the U.S. System are depicted positively.

C. **Negativity and scandal**
1. In recent years, political candidates and officials have been subjected to a relentless barrage of negative coverage.
   a) Negative campaign advertisements and political scandal turn off the American public.
   b) Some of the coverage starts with negative advertisements by opponents, which are sometimes echoed in media reporting.
2. Much of the Clinton presidencies were dogged by rumors of sexual impropriety. Clinton would eventually be impeached. Sexual and financial scandals would also force other prominent political leaders out of office.

D. **Infotainment**
1. Political reporting and news presentation has become increasingly more entertainment oriented.
   a) Cable television, the Internet and the multiplication of media outlets have all contributed to the entertainment slant of journalism.
   b) The punditry of network programs such as *The Washington Gang, Politically Incorrect,* and *Hard Ball* all indicate the drive by media executives to recapture audiences that they have lost to cable programming and the Internet.
   c) The bitter conflicts between the various political elements in society are perfect grist for the "infotainment" mill.
2. If the constitutionally arranged conflict between the president and Congress is especially exploited by the media when it can be personalized, as it was in the years when House Speaker Newt Gingrich was doing battle with President Bill Clinton.

E. **Limited, fragmented, and incoherent political information**
1. Corporate ownership, prevailing technology, organization of the news and the profit motive all influence the absence of substantive news coverage in the modern era.
2. Structural characteristics of the media result in the news that tends to be episodic, fragmented, personalized, and dramatic rather than sustained, analytical, or dispassionate.
3. Popular sovereignty and democracy suffer because the public's capacity to form intelligent opinions is limited.

VII. EFFECTS OF THE MEDIA ON POLITICS (pp. 168-172)

A. The media powerfully affect public opinion and policymaking in a number of ways, including setting the agenda for public debate and framing how issues are understood.

B. **Agenda setting**
 1. News coverage often reflects the issues that people are most concerned with in the country.
 2. This is not just based on public interest, it is also an effect of media influence. People tend to be concerned with the social problems that they come into contact with through media coverage.
 3. Publicity about crime may reflect editors' fears or a few dramatic incidents rather than a rising crime rate.
 4. One scholarly study shows that in the foreign policy area, media choices about coverage shape to what presidents pay attention.

C. **Framing and effects on policy preferences**
 1. The media's framing or interpretations of stories influence how society thinks about political problems.
 2. Whether citizens ascribe poverty to the individual poor person or to the economic system depends partly on whether the media run stories about poor individuals or about overall economic trends like wage stagnation and unemployment. Peoples' policy preferences are also impacted by media coverage.

D. **Impact on policymaking**
 1. The media impact public policy *indirectly* by influencing what citizens think about issues and the government in turn, gauges public opinion.
 2. The media also affect who is elected to office by framing ideas about who would make a good leader.
 3. The media also have a *direct* impact on policymaking as they provide information about political competitors' activities.

E. **Cynicism**
 1. "**Attack journalism**" has had a tremendous impact on the general cynicism that many citizens have expressed concerning politics and political leaders over the past twenty years.
 2. Personal behavior and the private lives of political leaders have become increasingly fair game. As well, coverage of money and special interest maneuvering has contributed to an increasing disenchantment with government and politics in the United States.

VIII. GOVERNMENT REGULATION OF THE MEDIA (pp. 172-176)

A. The U.S. Constitution protects freedom of press and although the U.S. government has less legal control over the mass media, it does have the authority to regulate the electronic media.

B. **Print media**
1. Violation of the Alien and Sedition Acts of 1798 resulted in the arrests and imprisonment of several Anti-Federalist newspaper editors.
2. Since then however, the First Amendment has been interpreted to allow broad publication rights as long as they do not infringe on national security.
3. **Prior restraint**-The Constitution prohibits government's use of pre-publication censorship or restraining techniques against material to which it objects.
   a) When president Nixon sought to use prior restraint tactics against the *New York Times* and *Washington Post* which planned on publishing secret Defense Department *Pentagon Papers* concerning U.S. involvement in Vietnam, the Supreme Court rejected the president's arguments.
   b) **Wartime controls**-Nixon's attempts might have been more successful had there been an active war at the time of the lawsuit. The government has exercised broad restraint powers in war times especially if news coverage threatens the lives of U.S. soldiers or national security.

C. **The electronic media**
1. The government has greater regulatory powers over electronic media than print media.
2. **Government licensing of the airwaves**-Ever since the passage of the Radio Act of 1927 and the Communications Act of 1934—which established the FCC—the government has had the power to license radio and television stations and set the rules for licenses renewals.
   a) The FCC dictates the frequencies of television and radio stations. The Telecommunications Act of 1996 revolutionized the industry by allowing telephone companies, cable companies, and broadcasters to control, free of charge, public airwaves.
   b) The massive mergers that are discussed above in this chapter were made possible through the 1996 Act.
3. **Public service broadcasting**-Broadcasters, under the direction of the FCC are required to provide a minimal number of hours of news and "public service" programming. The FCC, which once imposed public service programming under the threat of license renewals, no longer enforces the public service requirement to any serious degree.
4. **Fairness**-The fairness doctrine (1949), which once required that licensees present contrasting viewpoints on controversial issues of public importance, is not enforced today.
5. **Equal time**-The 1934 Communications Act stipulated that news outlets grant air time, equally, to candidates in pursuit of political office. The 1960 Nixon versus Kennedy debate effectively suspended the equal time provision which has since become irrelevant in political coverage and debates. The provision was changed in 1983 to permit broadcasters to show debates among candidates of their choosing.

6. **Rate Regulation**-Federal and local regulations which imposed rate controls through the 1996 Act, have not yet had the intended effect of lowering prices through increased competition. Taken as a whole, government regulation of the media is no longer significant; the trend has been toward a free market system with little government interference.

D. **The Internet**
1. The Internet has been much more difficult for the federal government to regulate than radio and television.
2. Congress's and the executive branch's attempts to ban obscenity on the Internet have been ruled unconstitutional so far.

E. **Judging the media**
1. The evolution of the American media from the serious political debates of the eighteenth century to the contemporary phase of "attack journalism," and "infotainment," news does not bode well for democracy if it hinges on extensive public deliberation and discussion.
2. A crucial question that emerges from this discussion whether political competition is vigorous enough to provide diverse, reliable cues to the public.

IX. SUMMARY (pp. 176-178)

A. *Structural factors* have greatly determined the organization of the mass media in the United States.
1. The many technological developments, changes in both the population and economy, and the development of privately owned corporate-dominated media have shaped the ways in which the American media do business.
2. The profit motive should not be underestimated when evaluating the operations and organization of the American mass media.
   a) The profit motive leads the major media to appeal to large audiences by limiting the quantity and depth of political news, by appealing to patriotism and other mainstream political values.
   b) Newsgathering for the nation is centered mainly in New York City and Washington, D.C. Whether the media have a ideological bias is an ongoing debate.
      (1) The noted liberality of news journalists is offset by the conservatism of official news sources and share-holding owners and editors. The media have a tremendous impact on public opinion and public policy.
      (2) The American government does not have as much control over the mass media as do governments in other countries, but censorship is permissible in war times and domestic crises.
   c) The Internet remains relatively free from government regulation. The mass media are essential to the workings of democracy in a large modern nation. The development of mass media in the United States has undoubtedly helped

democracy, but it has also created real causes for concern.

Terms for Review

Use this list to review essential principles, functions, and concepts from this chapter. Refer to your textbook for help in identifying and defining terms on this list. When you study, do not merely memorize terms; ask questions about the material you are reviewing, and look for the importance or significance of each item.

agenda setting

approval ratings

attack journalism

beat

bias

equal time provision

fairness doctrine

framing

infotainment

media landscape

nationalism

newsworthy

objective news

prior restraint

think tanks

watchdog

yellow journalism

Research Topics: Applying What You Have Learned

You will derive more benefit from your reading if you try to apply what you have learned. Some of the suggested research topics can be answered exclusively from your text, while others require you to conduct some basic research on your own. The references suggested under **Internet Sources** *will help you in your search..*

- Divide a sheet of paper in half vertically. Your assignment will be to draft a balanced debate on the advantages and disadvantages of the mass media for a democratic society. On one side, list the ways in which the mass media can be detrimental to democracy and the public interest. On the other side, respond to each charge by listing the ways in which the *same factors* could actually enhance democracy and the public interest.

- The roles of the media have changed since the eighteenth century. Have the media abandoned their role as "watchdog" over the government? Create a list of the ways that the media have developed both adversarial and "cozy" relationships with governmental leaders.

- How might the profit motive of the mass media influence democracy in America? Is democracy likely to be strengthened or hindered by the business aspect of media coverage? Are the media likely to cover issues or subjects that might negatively impact sales or their corporate advertisers? Provide short answer responses to these questions.

Internet Sources

A number of sites on the World Wide Web serve as "gateways" to vast collections of material on American government and politics. The following Internet resources are recommended for students who would like to do some additional research in the areas covered by this chapter. These references would also be helpful in expanding on the questions suggested under Research Topics.

Almost every television news organization has a Web site on the Internet:

ABC News http://www.abc.com
CBS News http://www.cbs.com
CNN Interactive http://www.cnn.com/
NBC News http://www.nbc.com

The same is true of the major national newspapers:

Chicago Tribune http://www.chicago.tribune.com
Los Angeles Times http://www.latimes.com
New York Times http://www.nytimes.com
San Jose Mercury News http://www.sjmercury.com
USA Today http://www.usatoday.com
Washington Post http://www.washingtonpost.com

Other sources for studies on media trends and effect on society include:

The Center for Media and Public Affairs www.cmpa.com
Studies, commentaries and forums on media and public affairs.

The Pew Research Center for the People and the Press www.people-press.org/
The most complete public opinion survey on citizen evaluations of the quality of media coverage of public affairs.

Self-Evaluation

Circle the correct answer for each question. Questions are listed in the same order in which the information appears in the text. Use the Answer Key in the back of the Study Guide *to check your responses.*

1. The First Amendment to the U.S. Constitution provides for
   a. Equal protection.
   b. Protection against unreasonable searches and seizures.
   c. Freedom of the press.
   d. Government regulation of the mass media.

2. Yellow journalism is
   a. The color of the newspapers that were used by the eighteenth century printing presses.
   b. Official government news information.
   c. Pornographic material.
   d. Sensational; newspaper stories with large headlines and, in some cases, color cartoons.

3. Which of the following newspapers influenced the government's actions in the 1898 Spanish-   American War?
   a. *The New York Times.*
   b. *New York Journal.*
   c. *Reader's Digest.*
   d. *New York World.*

4. Which national newspaper claims to print "all the news that is fit to print"?
   a. *The New York Journal.*
   b. *The Chicago Tribune.*
   c. *The New York Times.*
   d. *The Los Angeles Times.*

5. The federal government has greater regulatory authority over
   a. National newspapers.
   b. Local newspapers.
   c. News magazines.
   d. Electronic media.

6. Commercial radio stations were established in
   a. The 1910s.
   b. The 1920s.
   c. The 1930s.
   d. The 1940s.

7. Which of the following American wars was the first to be fully covered by television?
   a. The Civil War.

b. World War I.

c. World War II.

d. The Vietnam War.

8. Prior Restraint occurs when
   a. The media regulate themselves.
   b. When newspapers recall stories that are printed.
   c. Government authorities attempt to prevent the publication of material to which it objects.
   d. Media professionals interpret the public's views of favorable and unfavorable stories.

9. All but which of the following corporations dominate the magazine business?
   a. Time Warner.
   b. News Corp.
   c. Gannett.
   d. General Electric.

10. All but which of the following corporations dominate the television industry?
    a. General Electric.
    b. Westinghouse.
    c. Disney.
    d. Gannett.

11. Viacom/CBS own all but which of the following media companies?
    a. Nickelodeon.
    b. Showtime.
    c. Paramount Pictures.
    d. Time Warner

12. Infotainment is
    a. Another name for yellow journalism.
    b. The merging of hard news and entertainment in news presentations.
    c. The merging of soft news and entertainment in news presentations.
    d Political newsmaking

13. (T/F) Nearly all media in the United States are family owned businesses.

14. (T/F) Corporate ownership of the mass media has declined since the early 1990s.

15. (T/F) Government regulation of the media is greatest during wars.

16. (T/F) Beat reporters and government officials tend to have adversarial relationships.

17. (T/F)   The mass media have only minimal effects on politics in the United States.

18. (T/F)   The FCC regulates print media.

Chapter 7
INTEREST GROUPS and CORPORATIONS

Key Concepts and Objectives

The Key Concepts and Objectives provide a look at the fundamental goals and ideas of this chapter. This section serves as a guide to a basic understanding of the objectives of your textbook.

After reading this chapter, you should be able to:

- Explain what James Madison meant by the mischief of factions.
- Describe what interest groups are, what role they play in American politics, and how they try to shape public policy.
- Identify the various types of interest groups, and determine what we can learn by looking at the organizational form or type of interest.
- Describe how interest groups lobby Congress, the executive branch, and the courts.
- Assess the extent of corporate political power and the privileged place of the corporation in policymaking.
- Contrast the position of the corporation with that of public interest groups in the American political culture.
- Understand why your authors say the interest group system in its present form makes political equality less likely and thus helps to diminish democracy in the United States.
- Identify the "insiders" and "outsiders" in the American political system.
- Identify key terms and concepts used in Chapter 7.

Chapter Overview

This section provides a brief overview of the chapter contents. Read this section as a preview before reading your textbook. Then use this material as a review to help you retain information from your reading.

→ **LOBBYING FOR CHINA**

Chapter 7 raises questions concerning the role that *interest groups* play in American politics, how interest groups fit into a democratic society, and whether biases exist in the interest group system. It also deals with the growth and proliferation of interest groups and the manner in which interest groups lobby in all three branches of government. The goal of this chapter is to better understand the relationship between interest groups and democracy. It is important to understand whether **popular sovereignty, political equality, and political liberty** are enriched or diminished by the activities of interest groups and businesses. To answer these questions, we must first understand how **structural, political linkage, and governmental factors** shape interest groups and what they do. The opening vignette highlights the important role played by interest groups and businesses in American politics and the many tools of influence they use.

Under U.S. law, certain nations must seek **most favored nation (MFN) status** to avoid extremely high tariffs and other restrictions on their products. Only communist countries and so-called rogue states that are not members of the World Trade Organization must seek MFN status. The president makes a decision each year about the MFN status of a particular nation, which Congress can override by a two-thirds vote. Although presidential determination about China's trade status has prevailed for the past 16 years, the debate in Congress has intensified. The repression of the pro-democracy movement in Beijing's Tiananmen Square in 1989 reinforced opposition to China's MFN status. The political coalition that developed in 1997 to oppose granting MFN to China was made up of a surprising assortment of private and public interest groups and human rights organizations. Despite an impressive array of opponents, there were not enough votes in Congress to override President Clinton's granting of MFN to China for another year.

There was also an impressive array of American corporations which lobbied the White House and Congress in support of granting China MFN. Boeing and Airbus, TRW, General Electric, the major auto companies, were among the many companies that strengthened the hands of President Clinton and the Congressional Republican leadership that favored free trade and renewal of China's MFN status. The issue of trade with China remains the object of intense debate in the

163

United States, and the interest group and corporate alignments described in this story remain very much the same today.

→ INTEREST GROUPS IN A DEMOCRATIC SOCIETY: CONTRASTING VIEWS

Interest groups are private organizations that try to influence the behavior of political decision makers and thereby shape public policy. They are made up of people who share an interest that they are trying to protect or advance with the help of government. These groups in essence apply pressure on public officials; hence the name **pressure groups**. The term **lobby** is also commonly used to illustrate the practice of these groups talking to representatives and senators in the lobbies outside committee rooms. So it is common to hear of the "dairy lobby" or the "gun lobby."

The Evils of Factions-Interest groups have often been regarded as narrowly self-interested, out for themselves and without regard for the public good. James Madison's famous reference to the "dangers" of **factions** (his term for interest groups and narrow parties) was one of the earliest expressions of a recurring theme throughout U.S. history. In the past, "muckraking" journalists have uncovered corrupt alliances between government and huge corporate conglomerates, or trusts that exercised influence in various industries. More recently, Ross Perot's presidential campaigns (1992 and 1996) charged that special interests wield undo influence in government and politics.

Interest Group Democracy: The Pluralist Argument-Pluralists believe the interest group system contributes to democracy and the public interest because people are free to join or to organize groups that reflect their own particular interests. Some of their arguments are listed as follows.

- Free elections, while essential to a democracy, do not adequately communicate the specific wants and interests of the people to political leaders. These are more accurately, consistently and frequently conveyed to political leaders by the many groups and organizations to which people belong.
- Interest groups are easy to create: people in the United States are free to join or to organize groups that reflect their interests.
- Because of federalism, checks and balances, and the separation of powers, government power in the United States is broadly dispersed, so that governmental institutions are remarkably porous and open to the entreaties of the many and diverse groups that exist in society.
- Because of the ease of group formation and the accessibility of government, all legitimate interests in society can have their views taken into account by some public official. Thus the system is highly democratic.

Pluralists see the interest group system as an aid to democratic representation in a manner similar to instruments like public opinion and elections.

→ INTEREST GROUP FORMATION: STRUCTURAL, POLITICAL LINKAGE, AND GOVERNMENTAL FACTORS

The number of interest groups began to escalate in the late 1960s and has continued to grow steadily. In 1996, more than 17,500 lobbyists worked in Washington, D.C., up from 4,000 in 1977. The increase is partly the result of the growing number of interest or citizens groups organized around a cause or idea, rather than an economic or occupational interest, the traditional basis for forming interest groups. These include environmental, consumer protection, anti-abortion, family values, good government, civil rights, pro-life, and women's organizations. Business, producer, and occupational groups dominate. During the Reagan years, the number of interests representing corporations increased dramatically, while the number of citizens groups declined. Your authors provide a list of reasons why so many interest groups exist in the United States:

Diverse Interests-There are various racial, religious, ethnic and occupational groups in the United States, representing their interests. These interests usually take organizational forms. The computer revolution demonstrates how interests emerge around an industry and how associations are formed to guard them.

Rules of the Game-The constitution encourages the formation of interest groups. The First Amendment guarantees citizens free speech, free assembly, and the right to petition the government, all of which are essential to citizens' ability to form interest group organizations. The system of federalism, with its separation of powers and checks and balances also reinforces interest group activity because there is no single center of decision making in the country. The result is relatively easy access to public officials in the United States.

Growth in Government-As government's responsibilities increase, people, groups, and organizations are increasingly affected by the actions of government. Consequently, these entities are likely to protect and advance their interests through lobbying.

Disturbances-Disturbance theory contends that interest groups form when individuals' interests are threatened, usually by some change in the social and economic environment or in government policy.

Incentives-Even if people are disturbed by some policy or act of government, they may not form or join groups unless there is some material benefit to them. These benefits are not accessible to nonmembers. The **freerider** problem emerges when individuals can reap the benefits of group membership without joining the group. All women are likely to benefit from the efforts of the

National Organization of Women (NOW) whether they belong to the organization or not. This problem suggests how difficult it is to form interests groups. The proliferation of groups in the 1960s and 1970s suggest that groups form not only around selective, material incentives but also around "purposive" (ideological, issue-oriented) incentives and around "solidaristic" (in the sense of being part of something that one values) ones. People join groups because they believe in their cause or because they enjoy belonging to them.

→ WHAT INTERESTS ARE REPRESENTED

Interest groups can be examined by organizational form or by the type of interest represented. American interest groups come in a wide variety of forms, ranging from very small organizations to associations made up of combinations of other organizations. Interest groups may also be classified by the type of interest they represent; in this way, political scientist **E. E. Schattschneider** has distinguished between **private interests** and **public interests.** Public interests are interests that are connected in one way or another to the general welfare of the community, whereas private interests are associated with economic benefits for some fraction of the community.

Private Interest Groups-Many different kinds of private interest groups are active in American politics.

Producers-Agricultural businesses represent one type of interest designed to protect those corporations that produce some good or service. Producer groups wield significant power because of the vital role they play in the nation's economy. The American Dairy Association, the American Wheat Growers Association, the Business Roundtable, and Microsoft are listed among the producer interests in society.

Professionals-Doctors, lawyers, and dentists all have powerful lobbies in the various states and Washington, D.C. The American Medical Association (AMA) and the American Dental Association (ADA) were instrumental in defeating the Clinton health plan in the early 1990s.

Unions-Labor union lobbies exist essentially to guard the interests of their members in terms of jobs, wages, and benefits. As evidenced by the failures in its opposition to NAFTA, labor's declining membership base has reduced its influence in Washington, D.C.

Public Interest Groups-Also known as *citizens groups*, public interests attempt to get government to serve the general public and public interest rather than the direct economic or occupational interests of their members. These groups surged in the 1960s. The National Association for the Advancement of Colored People (NAACP), National Organization of Women (NOW) and Gay and Lesbian Alliance Against Defamation (GLAAD), the Children's

Defense Fund and Environmental Defense Fund represent the various public interest associations that attempt to further some public or citizens cause.

→ WHAT INTEREST GROUPS DO

Interest groups are composed of people with common goals or interests who try to convey the views of some sector of society and to influence government, whether in the legislative, executive, or judicial branch, on their behalf. They are private organizations that attempt to influence the shape of public policy in a number of ways. Interest group activity includes both the inside game and the outside game.

The Inside Game-The **inside game** involves direct contact of interest group representatives and government officials. This is the older of the two strategies. It is also a function of the "old boy" network where politics are based on personal contacts. Many of the most successful lobbyists are recruited from the ranks of retired members of Congress and high-level bureaucratic officials. The insider game seems to work best when the issues are narrow and technical, do not command much media attention, public passion, or opposition by other interest groups.

Lobbying Congress-Personal relationships are key to lobbying members of Congress. Knowing the members themselves is the best chance lobbyists have of gaining an audience, but building rapport with key staff members is also helpful.

Lobbying the Executive Branch-The Environmental Protection Agency (EPA) is one of the many bureaucratic agencies in the federal government which enforces federal policies. Interest groups try to establish stable and friendly relationships with the agencies of the executive branch that are most relevant to their interests. Personal contacts and relationships are key to success in lobbying the executive branch as it is with the legislative branch.

Lobbying the Courts-The NAACP's work in the landmark *Brown v. Board of Education* (1954) case demonstrates how the federal courts can be lobbied when the executive and legislative avenues are shut. Interest groups lobby the court through *amicus curiae* ("friend of the court") briefs in cases involving other parties. These briefs make it possible for various interest groups to offer opinions supported by relevant facts as a way of persuading the Court to rule favorably in their interest. Interest groups also play some role in the appointment process of federal judges.

The Outside Game-The **outside game** is an indirect form of influence that involves interest group efforts to mobilize public opinion, voters, and important contributors in order to bring pressure on elected officials. **Grassroots** activity often gets the attention of elected officials. The outside game works most effectively when interest groups attempt to identify and mobilize popular support for its goals and to bring it to bear on elected officials.

Mobilizing Membership-Direct mail campaigns, telephone campaigns, and e-mail campaigns are ways that interest group leaders attempt to persuade policymakers.

Organizing the District-Members of Congress seek to be re-elected. Therefore, they are especially attuned to the individuals and groups in their states or districts who can affect their re-election prospects.

Shaping Public Opinion-Interest group leaders seek to "educate" the public on issues that are of importance to the interest group; this is on aspect of new style lobbying. Interest groups attempt to shape opinion in a favorable light in order to get support from political decision makers. Interest groups, in the process of framing issues of importance, use research reports, media reports, and computer technology.

Getting Involved in Campaigns and Elections-Interest groups get involved in political campaigns and elections by rating members of Congress based on their voting records. Members of interest groups engage in routine campaign activities that will assist candidates who have been endorsed by the association of the interest group. Interest groups also sponsor ballot initiatives at the state and local levels. As well, campaign fundraising is a regular activity of interest groups that seek to support or oppose a candidate or an issue.

→ POSSIBLE FLAWS OF THE PLURALIST HEAVEN

Political Scientist E.E. Schattschneider once stated that the problem with the pluralist interpretation of interest groups is that its "heavenly chorus sings with a strong upper class accent." This section of your textbook looks at possible inequalities in the interest group system and evaluates their effects—if the interest group system (or pluralism) is dominated by the upper classes, then the norm of political equality is violated and democracy is less fully developed than it might be.

Representational inequalities-There is little doubt that the interest group system favors those who are better off in society. Representational inequalities involve the question of who interest groups represent (those who are the best educated, have the highest incomes, and have the most prestigious occupations are more likely to join organizations). Corporations, business trade associations, and professional associations dominate interest groups.

Resource Inequalities-There are also **resource inequalities** because interest groups representing corporations and the professions represent a substantial resource advantage over others (these are the most economically well-off sectors of American society). Corporations, business trade associations, and professional associations dominate political action committees as well. PACs provide financial support for candidates and issues that they favor or against candidates and issues they oppose. PACs representing the least privileged sectors of American society are notable for their absence. However, "soft money" has made PACs less important in campaign financing than previously. The advantage of such **soft money** contributions is that there are no limits on allowable amounts, unlike contributions to candidates, which are limited by law. Interest groups have some expectation of a return on their investment when they contribute money to campaigns and candidates. However, some argue that there are so many interest groups that they tend to neutralize each other. This may be true on high visibility issues which involve the public and a variety of interest groups, but interest groups seem to be most influential in the small details of legislation.

Access inequality refers to inequalities of representation and resources that are accentuated by the ability of some groups to form relatively stable alliances with important government institutions and decision makers. *Subgovernments* refer to groups that are able to gain a permanent foothold within the government. **Capture** is a form of government-business relationship in which and independent regulatory agency acts in partnership with the industry it is supposed to regulate. **Interest group liberalism** is an arrangement where aspects of federal government policymaking are delegated to interest groups. The **iron triangle** refers to the association between private interest groups (usually corporation trade association), an agency in the executive branch, and committees or subcommittees in Congress. Many political scientists argue that the capture and iron triangle arrangements are no longer very common; "issue networks," have replaced them. Others believe that subgovernments are alive and well. Regardless of the whether these arrangements are more or less open to public scrutiny, the authors contend that access to government is not equal for all interests.

➔ THE SPECIAL PLACE OF BUSINESS CORPORATIONS

There is a wide range of assessments concerning the actual extent of corporate political power. Economist and political scientist **Charles Lindblom** argues that corporations *wield such disproportionate power* in American politics that they **undermine democracy**. Lindblom's book *Politics and Markets* argues, "the large private corporation fits oddly into democratic theory. Indeed, it does not fit." He came to this conclusion because the largest corporations have many more interest organizations than do their competitors, they employ a large number of lobbyists, they have many resources that they use for political purposes, they have east access to government officials, and they are able to shape public perceptions and opinions. Moreover, business holds a special place in the hearts of Americans.

However, corporate political power is not a constant; it grows and declines over a period of time. Some scholars point to issues of great importance on which business in general (or one corporation in particular) loses. The authors of your text believe that the best way to think about corporations in American politics is to see their power waxing and waning within a generally privileged position. Businesses must still mobilize and use their resources effectively. During the mid-1970s, when corporations felt themselves under attack, they responded by building broad political coalitions that proved quite effective in laying the groundwork for the deregulation that came with Republican conservatism in the 1980s and 1990s. Corporations, when united, are simply unbeatable.

→ CURING THE MISCHIEF OF FACTIONS

James Madison was thinking primarily about the tyranny of majority factions when he referred to the **mischief of factions** in Federalist #10. We now know that the **politics of faction** is usually the province of *narrow and privileged interests* rather than majorities. This **undermines political equality**—which is vital for a functioning democracy—and makes it difficult for the United States to formulate broad and coherent national policies because policies tend to be the work of agreements made between narrow factions. A number of attempts have been made to solve some of the problems of factions. **Disclosure** has been the principal tool of regulation, particularly with the **Public Utilities Act** of 1935 and the **Federal Regulation of Lobbying Act** of 1946. In 1993, Congress passed a **Clinton** administration proposal requiring that lobbyists report on virtually all of their activities. Reformers have also tried to **regulate** some of the abuses of the politics of faction. The **Ethics in Government Act** (1978) prohibits ex-officials from lobbying their former agency for one year and prohibits them from lobbying at all on any issue in which the official was substantially involved. Other efforts to alleviate some of the mischiefs of factions include attempts to **control** some of the campaign practices of political action committees (PACs). Many worry that these reforms do not get to the heart of the problem, and some political scientists have suggested that we should be focusing our efforts on strengthening *institutions of majoritarian democracy* such as the presidency, the United States' only nationally elected office.

→SUMMARY

Americans have a sense of fairness that leads them to denigrate special interests as contrary to the public good. **Pluralists** in political science see interest groups as a positive addition to the representative process in a democracy. The constitution, especially the First Amendment, encourages interest group activity. The most important private interests include business, agriculture, labor, and the professions. Public or citizens' groups try to advance some issue or ideological interest that is not connected to the direct material benefit of their own members. Still, business, trade, and professional associations dominate the interest group system, though citizen groups are also influential. Efforts to control the "mischiefs of factions" have mainly been regulatory in nature. Some reformers believe that interest groups will only cease to be a problem if the parties and presidency are strengthened.

Chapter Outline

This section gives you a comprehensive review of the chapter. Use this outline in combination with your textbook to look for key concepts and objectives, to identify essential terms and names, and to gain a basic understanding of political practices and principles from this chapter.

I. LOBBYING FOR CHINA (p. 183)

    A. The goal of this chapter is to better understand the relationship between **interest groups** and **democracy**.

        1. Are **popular sovereignty, political equality, and political liberty** enriched or diminished by the activities of interest groups and businesses?

        2. To answer this question, we must first understand how **structural, political linkage, and governmental factors** shape interest groups and what they do.

        3. The opening vignette highlights the important role played by interest groups and businesses in American politics and the many tools of influence they use.

    B. The president makes a decision each year about the **most favored nation (MFN) status** of a particular nation, which Congress can override by a two-thirds vote.

        1. Under U.S. law, certain nations must seek MFN status to avoid extremely high tariffs and other restrictions on their products.

        2. Only communist countries (China, Cuba and North Korea) and so-called rogue states (Iran, Iraq, Libya) who are not members of the World Trade Organization must seek MFN status.

    C. Although presidential determination about China's trade status has prevailed for the past 16 years, the debate in Congress has intensified.

        1. The political coalition that developed in 1997 to oppose granting MFN status to China was made up of a surprising assortment of private and public interest groups and human rights organizations.

        2. Despite an impressive array of opponents, there were not enough votes in Congress to override President Clinton's granting of MFN status to China for another year.

    D. Why President Clinton was able to prevail:

        1. Many reasonable people believe that a policy of free trade with a country such as China benefits both parties economically.

        2. Many believe the policy will eventually undermine China's autocratic government and improve human rights and the chances for democracy.

3. An imposing group of American corporations who want open trade with China lobbied intensively for a favorable decision on MFN despite the impressive opposition from organizations such as Amnesty International.
   a) Some of America's most important companies have been involved in pro-Chinese lobbying.
   b) Many large and medium-sized export-oriented firms and associations lobby through the 1000-member Business Coalition for U.S.-China Trade.
   c) There are several state-level business associations that lobby for MFN and other favorable policies toward China.
   d) This impressive coalition greatly strengthened the hands of President Clinton and the congressional Republican leadership, both of whom were favorably disposed to free trade and renewal of MFN status for China.

II. INTEREST GROUPS IN A DEMOCRATIC SOCIETY: CONTRASTING VIEWS (pp. 184-186)
A. **Interest groups**
   1. Interest groups are private organizations that try to shape public policy.
   2. Interest groups try to influence the behavior of political decision makers.
      a) Efforts to influence policymakers are often perceived as exerting pressure, so interest groups are often called **pressure groups**.
      b) The term **lobby** comes from a long history of interest groups' representatives contacting members of Congress in the lobbies, cloakrooms, and hallways of the Capitol building.
B. **The evils of factions**
   1. The American public has traditionally viewed *special interest groups* as narrowly self-interested—out for themselves, and without regard for the public good.
   2. **James Madison** warned of the dangers and divisiveness of **factions** (his term for interest groups) in *The Federalist*, No. 10.
   3. The theme of the "evils of faction" (selfish special interests) has recurred throughout American history.
      a) President **Andrew Jackson** attacked the Bank of the United States and its supporters during the presidential campaign of 1832.
      b) The purported cozy relationship between "the folks in Washington" and special interests was a strong theme in **Ross Perot's** presidential campaigns in 1992 and 1996.
C. **Interest group democracy: the pluralist argument**
   1. Many political scientists believe that interest groups actually serve as important *instruments to attain democracy* and serve the public interest.
   2. **Pluralists** believe the *interest group system is democratic* (and *not* a problem) because people are free to join or to organize groups that reflect their own interests.

a) Elections do not adequately communicate what the people want in terms of policy; the many groups and organizations to which people belong are better vehicles to convey to political leaders what the people want.

b) Groups are so easy to form that ordinary American citizens are able to create them without too much difficulty; because power is broadly dispersed, governmental institutions are open to the appeals of the broad variety of groups that exist in society.

    (1) The *interest group system is democratic* because people in the United States are free to join or to organize groups that reflect their interests.

    (2) American government is open to the influence of groups once they are formed.

c) Because of federalism, checks and balances, and the separation of powers, government power in the United States is broadly dispersed, so that government institutions are remarkably porous and open to the entreaties of the many and diverse groups that exist in society.

d) Because of the ease of forming groups and the accessibility to government, all legitimate interests in society can have their views taken into account.

III. INTEREST GROUP FORMATION: STRUCTURAL, POLITICAL LINKAGE, AND GOVERNMENTAL FACTORS (pp. 186-189)

A. The number of interest groups began to escalate in the late 1960s and has continued to grow steadily; there are now so many lobbies in Washington that they have created new lobbying organizations to protect their interests as lobbyists, known as the **American League of Lobbyists**.

B. Interest groups seem to flourish in the existence of certain **structural factors**:
1. When there are many interests
2. When the political culture supports the pursuit of private interests
3. When the rules make it easy to organize
4. When government is sufficiently active for its policies to have consequences for private parties
5. The increase in interest groups is partly the result of the growing number of interest or citizen groups organized around a cause or idea, rather than an economic or occupational interest, the traditional basis for forming interest groups.

C. **Diverse interests**
1. The United States is a diverse and complex society of many races, religions, and ethnic groups.
2. *Structural factors* such as technological development, changing occupations, and the economy contribute to the growth of interest groups

D. Rules of the political game in the United States encourage the formation of interest groups.

1. The First Amendment guarantees citizens basic rights that are essential to the ability of citizens to form organizations.
2. Government is organized in such a way that decision makers are relatively accessible to interest groups.
3. Because of federalism, checks and balances, and the separation of powers, there is no dominant center of decision making, in contrast with unitary states such as Great Britain and France; the result is that there are many more places in the United States where interest group pressure can be effective.

E. **The growth in government**
   1. As government takes on more responsibilities, it has a greater impact on facets of economic, social, and personal life.
   2. People, groups, and organizations are increasingly affected by the actions of government, so the decisions made by governmental decision makers are increasingly important.

F. **Disturbances**
   1. **Disturbance theory** of interest group formation contends that the proliferation of interests does not seem to lead to the formation of groups unless these interests are threatened in some way, usually by economic and social change.
   2. The disturbance theory is illustrated by successes of the consumer movement and the environmental protection movements during the late 1960s and the early 1970s; they played an important role in the creation of hundreds of **political action committees (PACs)** by corporations that felt threatened.

G. **Incentives**
   1. Some social scientists argue that people do not form groups when their common interests are threatened unless the group can give back some selective, material benefit to them.
   2. A **selective, material benefit** is a tangible benefit that is available to members but not to nonmembers.
      a) If someone can get the benefit without joining the group (known as a **free-rider**), then there may be no purpose in joining.
      b) The *free-rider problem* tends to occur when a group is interested in some **collective good** (as when wheat farmers do not join the National Wheat Growers Association because *all* wheat farmers—not just members—benefit from programs of governmental price support for wheat).
   3. By contrast, there has been a proliferation of public interest and ideological groups; the growth of such groups suggests purposes or incentives other than material and selective incentives.

IV. **WHAT INTERESTS ARE REPRESENTED (pp. 189-192)**
  A. Interest groups may be classified by the type of interest they represent; in this way, political scientist **E. E. Schattschneider** has distinguished between **private interests** and **public interests.**
    1. **Public interests** are interests that are connected in some way to the general welfare of the community.
    2. **Private interests** are associated with benefits for some fraction of the community.
  B. **Private interest groups**
    1. **Producers**
      a) Represent enterprises that produce goods or services, such as business or agriculture.
      b) These groups exert immense power because of the vast resources at their disposal and their strategic role in the economy.
    2. **Professionals**
      a) Represent the interests of professionals, such as doctors, lawyers, and dentists.
      b) They are very influential in the policymaking process because of their importance in local communities and because of their ability to make substantial campaign contributions.
    3. **Unions**
      a) Their primary role has been to protect the jobs of their members and work for maximum wage and benefit levels, such as pensions.
      b) Political power of unions has dramatically eroded over the past several decades, possibly due to declining membership.
  C. **Public interest groups** (sometimes called **citizens' groups**)
    1. Public interest groups try to get government to do things that will benefit the general public rather than the direct material interests of their own members.
    2. The number and influence of public interest groups has grown markedly since the late 1960s; many public interest groups were created by social movements for consumers, the environment, and women.
    3. The National Organization of Women (NOW), the National Association for the Advancement of Colored People (NAACP), the Children's Defense Fund, the Gay and Lesbian Alliance Against Defamation (GLAAD), and the Environmental Defense Fund represent various public interests.
    4. Public interest groups generally do not use material incentives.

V. **WHAT INTEREST GROUPS DO (pp. 192-197)**
  A. Interest groups are composed of people with common goals or interests who try to convey the views of some sector of society, and to influence government on their behalf; the two basic types of interest group activity are the *inside game* and the *outside game.*

175

B. The **inside game** involves *direct contact* of the interest group representative and government officials.
   1. The inside game does not involve bribery; instead, it is the politics of insiders, of the "old-boy" network, of one-on-one persuasion in which a skilled lobbyist tries to persuade a decision maker to accept the point of view of the interest group.
      a) *Access to policymakers* and a genuine understanding of the game (rules, key players, flow of the action) are critical to success.
      b) The inside game is most effective when the issues are narrow and technical, do not command much media or public attention, and do not stir up counteractivity by other interest groups.
   2. *Lobbying Congress*
      a) Committee and subcommittee staffs take on an enormous importance because the major decisions of Congress are made in the committee system.
      b) The skilled lobbyist spends a great deal of time cultivating personal contacts and relationships with the key members of committees and subcommittees and their professional staffs.
   3. *Lobbying the executive branch*
      a) Career civil servants and upper-level appointees in the executive branch have a great deal of discretionary authority.
      b) Congress tends to formulate broad policies, leaving it to bureaucratic agencies to fill in the details.
   4. *Lobbying the courts*
      a) Interest groups lobby the courts, but not in the same way as they lobby the legislative and executive branches.
      b) Groups may turn to the courts when they cannot receive satisfaction from the president or Congress, as the NAACP did with *Brown* v. *Board of Education* (1954).
      c) Lobbying is a secondary strategy for most groups because there are problems with going to court.
         (1) A group must have standing—must be a party to the case, must be able to show a direct potential injury.
         (2) Great expense—litigation is primarily an instrument of the largest and richest interest groups and corporations.
      d) How interest groups may be involved in court actions
         (1) They may file **amicus curiae** ("friend of the court") briefs in cases involving other parties, that is, the interest group brings legal arguments or facts to the attention of the court.
         (2) In this kind of brief, a person or an organization that is not party to the suit may file an argument in support of one side in hopes of swaying the views of the judge or judges; *amicus curiae* briefs are often filed in major controversies before the Supreme Court on issues such as abortion, free speech, or civil rights.

(3) They may get involved in the process of appointment and confirmation of federal judges; particularly controversial appointments have drawn interest group attention and strenuous efforts on behalf of or against the nominee.

C. The **outside game** is an *indirect* form of influence that involves **grassroots** interest group efforts to mobilize public opinion, voters, and important contributors in order to bring *pressure on elected officials* (an increasingly common form of influence).

D. Public officials are more likely to listen to lobbyists if they are convinced that the lobbyists speak for a large group of people.

  1. *Mobilizing membership*
     a) When a bill or resolution that is relevant to the interest group comes before Congress or a ruling on a regulation comes before a committee, interest groups with large membership bases will try to persuade their members to contact legislators and other officials.
     b) Typically, campaigns involving personal letters, telephone calls, telegrams, and preprinted postcards.

  2. *Organizing the district*
     a) Members of Congress are concerned with those in their state or district who can affect their chances at reelection.
     b) Interest groups will try to remain in touch with the most important campaign contributors and opinion leaders and will try to convince its own members in the state and district to put pressure on their members of Congress

  3. *Shaping public opinion*
     a) New-style lobbyists try to *"educate" the public* on issues that are important to the interest group; the idea is to shape public opinion in such a way that government officials will be favorably disposed to the views of the interest group
     b) Press conferences and mass mailing of research results are used to bolster the interest group's position.
     c) National and regional advertising campaigns try to impress their views on government decision makers; these may take the form of pressing a position on a particular issue or may involve *image advertising*, in which some company or industry conveys an image of its positive contribution to American life.
     d) Well-financed interest groups prepare materials that are of use to the mass media and may involve staged events to be covered as news items.
     e) Computerized mailing lists are used to identify specific groups to receive mailings on particular issues (**targeted mailings**).

  4. *Getting Involvement in campaigns and elections*
     a) Interest groups are associated with a wide range of electoral activities.
     b) Many interest groups *rate members of Congress*, based on their support for the interest group's position on key votes.

c) Interest groups encourage their members to *get involved* in the election campaigns of candidates who are favorable toward their interests.

d) A few interest groups (mostly public interest, or citizens' groups) will *endorse* candidates for public office; this strategy can backfire if the candidate loses and the group loses access to the winner.

e) Interest groups sometimes *sponsor ballot initiatives* at the state level, such as anti-property tax initiatives sponsored by the real estate industry in several states.

VI. **POSSIBLE FLAWS OF THE PLURALIST HEAVEN (pp. 197-203)**

A. Political Scientist E.E. Schattschneider once stated that the problem with the pluralist interpretation of interest groups is that its "heavenly chorus sings with a strong upper class accent."

B. This section of your textbook looks at possible inequalities in the interest group system and evaluates their effects—if the interest group system (or pluralism) is dominated by the upper classes, then the norm of political equality is violated and democracy is less fully developed than it might be.

C. *Representational inequalities*

1. Involves the question of *who* interest groups represent

2. Business, trade, and professional associations account for over two-thirds of all associations that have a lobbying presence in Washington, D.C. Together they dominate interest group activities.

3. The representational advantage of business and the professions is increasing, and there is evidence that business and professional groups have more permanency than others.

D. *Resource inequalities*

1. Interest groups representing corporations and the professions represent a substantial *resource advantage* over others because these are the most economically well-off sectors of American society; interest groups have some expectation of a return on their investment when they contribute money to campaigns and candidates.

2. These interest groups can afford to spend far more than other groups to hire professional lobbying firms, form their own Washington liaison offices, place advertising in the media, conduct targeted mailings, mobilize their members to contact government officials, and engage in all of the other activities of lobbying.

3. Business and the professions also dominate monetary contributions to the political parties for their campaign activities; the advantage of such **soft money** (a reference to expenditures by political parties on general public education, voter registration, and voter mobilization) contributions is that there are no limits on allowable amounts (unlike contributions to candidates, which are limited by law).

4. Corporate, trade, and professional associations dominate the world of PACs, both in numbers and in levels of spending, but PACs have become proportionately less

important in campaign financing as soft money and independent expenditures have become more important.

E. *Access inequality*—inequalities of representation and resources are accentuated by *the ability of some groups to form relatively stable alliances* with important government institutions and decision makers.

    1. **Capture**—regulatory agencies and the industries being regulated come to depend on each other for technical information, and they often trade personnel over the years; the *capture* theory notes that there is a tendency for regulatory agencies to become allies, protectors, and advocates of the industries that they were created to regulate.

    2. **Interest group liberalism**—exists in a political system where interest groups help formulate and carry out government policies; Subgovernments exist where a great deal of federal government policymaking is turned over to interest groups.

    3. **Iron triangles**—describes the alliance of private and public power in Washington, D.C.; a three-way arrangement in which an alliance is formed between a private-interest group, a bureaucratic agency, and a Congressional committee or subcommittee (as with the alliance among the Pentagon, defense contractors, and the armed forces committees of Congress); the goal of the iron triangle is to advance and protect government programs that work to the mutual benefit of its members.

    4. There is no good way of measuring the incidence of capture, clientelism, and subgovernments; and specialists today are more likely to talk about **issue networks** in which each major policy arena attracts its own broad and diverse set of actors.

F. **The special place of business corporations**

    1. There is a wide range of assessments concerning the actual extent of corporate political power.

    2. Corporations enjoy many advantages over others in the policy process; economist and political scientist **Charles Lindblom** argues that corporations *wield such disproportionate power* in American politics that they *undermine democracy*.

    3. By contrast, there are many issues of great importance on which business in general (or one corporation in particular) loses.

    4. Corporate political power is not a constant; it grows and declines over a period of time.

        a) Corporate political power was dominant during the 1920s and the Reagan 1980s, and in the 104th Congress after the 1994 elections; corporations were less able to get their way during other periods such as the early 1970s, when the power of corporations was almost matched by that of the consumer and environmental movements.

        b) During *bad economic times*, Americans want to stimulate the economy and are less interested in undertaking reforms that cut into corporate profits; during *good economic times* like the 1960s, politicians are less worried about corporate profits drying up if tax monies are expended for social purposes.

    c) Corporations are most powerful when they can build coalitions with other corporations, as occurred during the mid-1970s; broad political coalitions formed at that time became the foundation of the movement for deregulation and an important element of the conservatism that led to the election of Ronald Reagan in 1980 and a Republican Congressional majority in the 1990s.

   5. The authors of your text believe that the best way to think about corporations in American politics is to see their power waxing and waning within what Charles Lindblom called their overall privileged position; within this *generally privileged position*, corporate power may be greater at certain times and lesser at other times—but only within the boundaries of a game in which corporations enjoy advantages over other groups.

VII. CURING THE MISCHIEF OF FACTIONS (pp. 203-204)

  A. James Madison was thinking primarily about the tyranny of majority factions when he referred to the "mischief of factions."

  B. We have learned that the **politics of factions** is usually the province of *narrow and privileged interests* rather than majorities.

    1. This creates problems with respect for **democracy**:

      a) It **undermines political equality**, which is vital for a functioning democracy, and makes it *difficult for the United States to formulate broad and coherent national policies* because policies tend to be the work of agreements made among narrow factions.

      b) This creates a dilemma because the right of the people to form organizations for the purpose of petitioning the government is one of our most fundamental and cherished rights.

    2. Efforts to solve some of the problems of factions

      a) **Disclosure** has been the principal tool of regulation.

        (1) The **Public Utilities Act** (1935) required lobbyists for that industry to register with Congress, and lobbyists in all fields have been required to register since 1946.

        (2) In 1993, Congress passed a **Clinton** administration proposal requiring that lobbyists report on virtually all of their activities.

      b) Reformers have tried to **regulate** some of the most troublesome abuses of the politics of faction; the **Ethics in Government Act** (1978) prohibits former officials from lobbying their former agency for one year and prohibits them from lobbying at all on any issue in which the official was substantially involved.

      c) Other efforts to alleviate some of the "mischief of factions" include attempts to **control** some of the campaign practices of PACs.

(1) Evidence seems to suggest that PAC money in campaigns has become very important in American politics and is dominated by narrow segments of American society.

(2) Very little progress has been made in this arena.

C. Many worry that these reforms do not get to the heart of the problem, and some political scientists have suggested that we focus our efforts on strengthening institutions of **majoritarian democracy** such as political parties, the presidency, and Congress.

D. Efforts to reform the interest group system may be frustrated by the inescapable fact that highly unequal resources eventually will find their way into our political life.

VIII. SUMMARY (p. 205)

A. Americans tend to denigrate special interests as contrary to the public good.

B. Pluralists in political science see interest groups as a positive addition to the representative process of democracy.

C. The U.S. Constitution encourages interest group activity. The First Amendment protections concerning speech, assembly and association all reinforce interest associations.

D. The most influential interest associations include business, agriculture, labor, and the professions such as law and medicine.

E. Public interests, which focus on issues that are broader than the material benefits that are provided to their members, try to advance some issue or ideological interest.

F. Efforts to control the "mischiefs of factions" have mainly been regulatory in nature. Some reformers believe that interest groups will only cease to be a problem if the presidency and political parties are strengthened.

Terms for Review

Use this list to review essential principles, functions, and concepts from this chapter. Refer to your textbook for help in identifying and defining terms on this list. When you study, do not merely memorize terms; ask questions about the material you are reviewing, and look for the importance or significance of each item.

amicus curiae

capture

Civil Rights Act (1964)

civil rights movement

disturbance theory

faction

Federalist, No. 10

freerider

government regulation

grass roots

independent expenditures

inside game

interest group

interest group liberalism

iron triangles

issue networks

lobbies

lobby

majoritarian democracy

mass mobilization

most favored nations (MFN)

nongovernmental organizations (NGOs)

outside game

participation (conventional and unconventional)

pluralist

political action committees (PACs)

political equality

populist

pressure groups

producer interest groups

professional interest groups

public interest groups

Public Utilities Act (1935)

representational inequalities

scope of conflict

Seneca Falls Declaration (1848)

soft money

standing

suffrage

targeted mailings

Research Topics: Applying What You Have Learned

You will derive more benefit from your reading if you try to apply what you have learned. Some of the suggested research topics can be answered exclusively from your text, while others require you to conduct some basic research on your own. The references suggested under **Internet Sources** *will help you in your search.*

- Divide a sheet of paper in half vertically. Your assignment will be to draft a balanced debate on the advantages and disadvantages of interest groups for a democratic society. On one side, list the ways in which interest groups can be detrimental to democracy and the public interest. On the other side, respond to each charge by listing the ways in which the *same factors* could actually enhance democracy and the public interest.

- What determines whether a group is an "insider" group or an "outsider" group? List the characteristics of both and then identify specific interest groups, their causes or issues, and place them in one of the two categories.

- Write a brief essay identifying the ways that interest groups may enhance democracy. Compare your answers with the arguments that pluralists raise in favor of pluralist democracy.

Internet Sources

A number of sites on the World Wide Web serve as "gateways" to vast collections of material on American government and politics. The following Internet sources are recommended for students who would like to do additional research in areas covered by this chapter. These references would also be helpful in expanding on the questions suggested under Research Topics.

CapWeb Conservative Organizations www.capweb.net/classic/jefferson/right/orgs
A portal to conservative groups and organizations.

Center for Responsive Politics www.opensecrets.org/
Follow the money trail--who gets it? Who contributes it?--in American politics.

Justice on Campus http://joc.mit.edu/
An organization committed to the preservation of free expression and the due process rights of students on college campuses.

Labor Net www.labornet.org
Access to labor unions and information on labor issues.

National Organization of Women http://now.org
The women's organization that has long been a "player" in Washington politics.

National Rifle Association http://www.nra.org/
Home page of one of America's most politically successful interest groups.

Project VoteSmart www.vote-smart.org/
Information on interest group campaign contributions to and ratings for all members of Congress.

Rightgrrl www.rightgrrl.com/
Conservative women's issues and organizations.

Student Environmental Action Committee http://www.seac.org/
A grassroots coalition of student environmental groups.

Yahoo/Organizations and Interest Groups http://www.yahoo.com/Government/Politics/
Direct links to the home pages of scores of public and private interest groups as well as to Washington lobbying firms.

Self-Evaluation

Circle the correct answer for each question. Questions are listed in the same order in which the information appears in the text. Use the Answer Key in the back of the Study Guide to check your responses.

1. **Iron triangles** are
   a. Alliances among a private interest group, a bureaucratic agency, and a congressional committee or subcommittee.
   b. Arrangements among the Defense Department, an American embassy, and a foreign government.
   c. Agreements among three or more states to share the costs of a project that has an impact on all three states.
   d. Negotiations involving the federal government, the states, and local governments.

2. James Madison's phrase for interest groups was
   a. political parties.
   b. pressure groups.
   c. factions
   d. pluralists

185

3. Social movements
    a. Have never had a significant impact on American politics because they represent the views of small minorities.
    b. Have usually acted as political insiders within the normal channels of government and politics.
    c. Often use unconventional and disruptive tactics.
    d. Exist among groups that are basically satisfied with the *status quo*.

4. Pluralists believe that
    a. Interest groups are an important instrument for obtaining both democracy and the public interest.
    b. Interest groups occur only in societies where multiple competing interests exist, and will result in the destruction of all but the largest interests.
    c. Interest groups lead to corruption and manipulation of government institutions and, therefore, are essentially undemocratic.
    d. Interest groups damage both democracy and popular sovereignty by alienating one segment of society against another.

5. Political scientist E. E. Schattschneider
    a. Developed the theory of interest group liberalism, described as a political system in which interest groups help formulate and carry out government policies.
    b. Produced the *Harry and Louise* ads that helped defeat President Clinton's health care plan.
    c. Created the concept of the inside game and the outside game to describe interest group activity.
    d. Has distinguished between private interests and public interests.

6. Which of the following is NOT a characteristic of interest groups?
    a. Some interest groups are motivated by a desire to advance a general cause, to bring a single issue to the attention of policymakers, or to see a set of ideas form the basis of public policy.
    b. It is common for a single corporation to maintain an office in Washington in order to keep an eye on activities that might affect the company.
    c. Large-membership organizations with substantial resources can usually gain a hearing in Congress or the executive branch for their views.
    d. Most public interest groups are large-scale organizations that depend on donations from their massive list of members to finance the group's activities.

7. When an interest group files an *amicus curiae* brief, the group
    a. Requests the court to issue a restraining order to prevent interference from another person or group.

b.   Is responding to a suit for damages filed by an opposing party.
c.   Files an argument in support of one side or the other.
d.   Protests the involvement of another party in the case.

8.   The 1978 Ethics in Government Act
a.   Prohibits government officials from investing in any savings and loan institution that had previously declared bankruptcy.
b.   Forbids ex-officials from lobbying their former agency for one year after they leave office.
c.   Requires government officials to disclose any contacts they have had with constituents outside their Washington offices.
d.   Has been overturned by the U.S. Supreme Court because it constituted an invasion of personal privacy.

9.   The **inside game** of interest group activity involves
a.   Efforts to mobilize public opinion, voters, and important contributors in order to place pressure on officials.
b.   Indirect methods of bringing pressure to bear on both elected and appointed officials.
c.   The direct contact of interest group representatives and government officials.
d.   Organizing influential people in a voting district in order to turn out the vote for a particular candidate.

10. Expenditures by political parties on general public education, voter registration, and voter mobilization are known as
a.   soft money
b.   hard money
c.   campaign finance reform
d.   independent expenditures

11. Which of these structural factors is necessary for the development of a social movement?
a.   A society with members who are safe and prosperous
b.   A society with social strain and distress
c.   A society with few skills or organizational resources
d.   A society with members who believe that their actions will have no impact

12. Social movements committed to radical changes in society and the economy
a.   Usually have enough power and public support to generate a favorable response from public officials but not enough to force them to take action.
b.   Are likely to achieve a substantial number of their goals because they have many supporters and wide public sympathy.
c.   Normally result in increased respect for members of the movement and increased representation on decision-making groups.

187

   d. Rarely gain widespread popular support and almost always gain the hostility of national leaders.

13. (T/F) PACs exist in order to raise and distribute funds to candidates in political campaigns.

14. (T/F) There are no interest groups which represent people on **food stamps** in Washington, DC.

15. (T/F) The **capture** theory of regulation argues that there is a tendency for regulatory agencies to become protectors and advocates of the industries that they are supposed to regulate.

16. (T/F) Inequalities of representation and resources are accentuated by the ability of some interest groups to form relatively stable alliances with important government institutions and decision makers.

17. (T/F) An *amicus curiae* brief is also called a "friend of an interested party" brief.

18. (T/F) Public interest or citizens' groups tend to be motivated by ideological concerns or by a cause to benefit the general public.

Chapter 8
SOCIAL MOVEMENTS

Key Concepts and Objectives

The Key Concepts and Objectives provide a look at the fundamental goals and ideas of this chapter. This section serves as a guide to a basic understanding of the objectives of your textbook.

After reading this chapter, you should be able to:

- Identify the factors that are necessary for a social movement to develop and explain how new social problems often generate new social movements.
- Explain how social movements fit within the framework of a democratic society.
- Explain how social movements can convince the majority that new policies are needed.
- Understand how social movements may protect fundamental rights and encourage public awareness and participation in public affairs.
- Evaluate the impact of social movements and determine how social movements influence what government does.
- Describe the unconventional tactics of social movements.
- Show the relationship of various tactics to the success or failure of social movements, and use a specific social movement to illustrate the tactics of social movements.
- Assess the risks that are involved in participation in a social movement.
- Explain why social movements affect policymakers and help to influence what government does.
- Explain how social movements affect policymakers and help to influence what government does.
- Identify specific social movements
- Clarify the interaction between social movements and social policy.
- Identify key terms and concepts used in Chapter 8.

Chapter Overview

This section provides a brief overview of the chapter contents. Read this section as a preview before reading your textbook. Then use this material as a review to help you retain information from your reading.

➜ WOMEN WIN THE RIGHT TO VOTE

Many social movements have influenced what government does and continue to play a significant role in the struggle for democracy. The main instrument for winning the struggle to amend the Constitution admitting women to full citizenship was a powerful social movement that dared to challenge the status quo, used unconventional tactics to gain attention and sympathy, and demanded bravery and commitment from many women. By uniting around a common cause, women's organizations gained the right to vote for women. The actions of **Angelina Grimke** are used in the opening vignette to illustrate the struggle for women's rights. When she addressed the Massachusetts legislature in February 1838 and presented a petition against slavery from an estimated 20,000 women of the state, she became the first woman to speak before an American legislative body. Although she was derided as ridiculous and blasphemous by the press and clergy, her actions helped to inspire women who had entered political life through participation in the abolitionist movement also to press for women's rights.

In 1848, a group of women met at Seneca Falls, New York, and issued a declaration (modeled after the Declaration of Independence) written by **Elizabeth Cady Stanton**. The Seneca Falls Declaration stated that "All men and women are created equal" and presented a long list of violations of rights. It failed to have an immediate impact because most politically active people in the abolitionist movement believed that the first priority was to end slavery. Following the abolition of slavery, women's rights leaders like Stanton, **Susan B. Anthony**, and **Lucy Stone** pressed for equal citizenship rights for all persons, regardless of race or gender. They were bitterly disappointed when the Fourteenth Amendment declared full citizenship rights for all males born or naturalized in the United States, including those who had been slaves, but failed to include women.

In 1890, the two main women's rights organizations joined together to form the **National American Woman Suffrage Association** (NAWSA). The women's movement was now focused, mostly united, and growing more powerful every year. In 1912, NAWSA organized a march to support a constitutional amendment for suffrage, in which more than 5,000 women dressed in white paraded through the streets of Washington. Soon after the United States entered World War I in 1916 with the express purpose of "Making the world safe for democracy," women began to picket the White House, demanding full democracy be instituted in America.

After two prominent senators from New England were defeated in 1918 primarily because of the efforts of suffragists and prohibitionists, the political clout of the women's groups became apparent to elected officials. Congress passed the **Nineteenth Amendment** to the Constitution in 1919 (guaranteeing women the right to vote), and the necessary 36 states ratified it the following year.

→WHAT ARE SOCIAL MOVEMENTS?

This chapter is about **social movements**. Social movements are loosely organized collections of people and institutions who act outside established institutions to promote or resist social change. They are primarily the instruments of political outsiders who want to gain a hearing in American politics. New social problems often generate new social movements. The Christian conservative movement, for example, is a broad collection of people, churches, and other organizations that have come together to resist the **secularization** of American society and to promote religious values in American life.

Social movements are different from political parties and interest group because social movements focus on broad, society-wide issues and their tendency to act outside the normal channels of government and politics, using unconventional and often disruptive tactics. Social movement politics are often "contentious politics." The authors provide a list of characteristics of social movements:

- *Social movements are generally the political instruments of political outsiders.* Social movements often help people who are outside the mainstream gain a hearing from the public and from political decision makers. The women's suffrage movement forced the issue of for women onto the public agenda. The civil rights movement did the same for the issue of equal citizenship for African-Americans. Gays and lesbians forced the country to pay attention to issues that had long been left "in the closet." Insiders don't need social movements; they can rely instead on interest groups, political action committees (PACs), lobbyists, campaign contributions, and the like to have their voices heard.

- *Social movements are mass grassroots phenomena.* Because outsiders and excluded groups often lack the financial and political resources of insiders, they must take advantage of what that have: numbers, energy, and commitment. To gain attention, moreover, social movements often use unconventional tactics, such as demonstration and sit-ins. Officials and citizens almost always complain that social movements are ill-mannered and disruptive. For social movements, that is precisely the point.

- *Social movements are populated by individuals with a shared sense of grievance.* People would not take on the considerable risks involved in joining others in a social movement unless they felt a strong, shared sense of grievance against the status quo and a desire to bring about social change. Social movements tend to form when a significant number of people come to define their own troubles and problems not in personal terms but in more general terms (the belief that there is a common cause for all of their troubles) and when they believe that the government can be moved to take action on their behalf. Because this is a rare combination, social movements are very difficult to organize and sustain.

➔MAJOR SOCIAL MOVEMENTS IN THE UNITED STATES

This section describes some of the most important social movements that have left their mark on American political life and have shaped what government does in the United States. This chapter describes the abolitionist movement, Populist movement, women's suffrage movement, labor movement, peace ("nuclear freeze") movement, civil rights movement, anti-Vietnam War movement, women's movement, environmental movement, gay and lesbian movement, religious fundamentalist movements, pro-life (anti-abortion) movement, and more recently, an emergent anti-globalization movement.

➔SOCIAL MOVEMENTS IN A MAJORITARIAN DEMOCRACY

At first glance, social movements do not seem to fit very well with democratic theory since they usually start out as minority phenomena (whereas democracy requires majority rule) and they often use disruptive tactics. However, this section of the text looks at how social movements can help make American politics more democratic.

Encouraging Participation-Social movements may increase the level of popular involvement and interest in politics. Social movements are the instruments of outsiders. Social movements tend to increase the degree of popular involvement that is essential to a democracy (as with the women's suffrage movement that encouraged the involvement of women, as with civil rights movement that encouraged the involvement of African-Americans, and the Christian conservative movement that spurred the involvement of previously apathetic evangelicals).

Social movements also encourage popular participation by dramatizing and bringing to public attention a range of issues that have been ignored or have been dealt with behind closed doors. The ability to make politics more visible—called broadening the **scope of conflict** by political scientist E.E.Schattschneider—makes politics the province of the many rather than the few.

Overcoming Political Inequality-Social movements also allow those without substantial resources to enter the game of politics. The ability of those without resources to disrupt the status quo by mobilizing thousands to take to the streets to voice their demands—what sociologists call mass mobilization—is a powerful political tool for people on the outside looking in.

Creating New Majorities-Social movements may also help create new majorities in society. If a minority can convince enough citizens that what they want is reasonable, then the majority-rule aspect of democracy is strengthened. The labor movement, women's movement, and anti-Vietnam War movement, all began with substantial minorities that eventually won over the majority of citizens.

Overcoming Gridlock-The energy of social movements are capable of overcoming the anti-majoritarian aspects of the United States' constitutional system and get anything done. Many of the social reforms of which most Americans are most proud have been less the result of "normal" politics than of social movements started by determined and often disruptive minorities.

→FACTORS THAT ENCOURAGE THE CREATION OF SOCIAL MOVEMENTS

A combination of structural factors is apparently necessary for a social movement to develop:

The Existence of Social Distress-Those whose lives are difficult and unsafe or whose way of life or values are threatened often find social movements attractive. Social distress caused by economic, social and technological change helped create the rise of most of the major social movements in American history. In particular, the labor movement which was spurred by the **Great Depression** of the 1930s, the Christian conservative movement which was spurred by the apparent decline in religious and family values in American life; the women's movement which challenged the "glass ceiling" and obstacles to career advancement, and unequal pay, the gay and lesbian movement was spurred by the discrimination, police harassment, and violence directed at them and the AIDS epidemic are all examples of this phenomenon.

The Availability of Resources for Mobilization-Social movements occur most often when the aggrieved group has the resources (including skilled leaders) sufficient to organize those who are suffering strain and distress.

A Supportive Environment-The times must be right, in the sense that a degree of support and tolerance must exist for the movement among the public and society's leaders. More tolerant attitudes toward social movement groups in the general public help them achieve their goals.

A Sense of Efficacy Among Participants-Movement participants must believe that their actions can make a difference that other citizens and political leaders will listen and respond to their grievances. A sense of efficacy is the sense that an individual or group can make a difference.

A Spark to Set Off the Flames-Many social movements have been set off by a *catalyst* event (or series of events) that set them in motion. Rosa Parks's refusal to surrender her seat on a Montgomery, Alabama, bus in 1957 is one of the most famous catalyst events in the history of social movements in the United States.

→**TACTICS OF SOCIAL MOVEMENTS**

Social movements tend to use unconventional tactics to make themselves heard. These tactics are often dramatic and disruptive. **Sit down** strikes was a tactic of the 1930s labor movement. Sometimes violence is used by social movement groups. The civil rights movement used non-violent **civil disobedience**, student sit-ins, prayers and songs in pursuit of favorable civil rights legislation.

→**WHY SOCIAL MOVEMENTS DECLINE**

Social movements are difficult to sustain. Both external and internal factors contribute to decline.

The Unexpected Problem of Success-Success may undermine a social movement as surely as failure. Social movements, in order to survive, must find new or other issues around which to organize. Social movements often find that achieving their goals destroys their very reason for being.

Factionalism-Social movements must successfully address three different audiences: the movement's activists, the general public, and public officials. More specifically, it must maintain the enthusiasm of activists, attract more activists and support from the aggrieved group, gain sympathy from the general public, and force a positive response from public officials. The fragmentation over strategy that has characterized many social movements usually results from often contradictory goals. Movements seldom recover from these splits.

Erosion of Public Support-Social movements decline when popular support for their goals begins to erode. This may occur when the public believes that enough has been done or that the movement is asking for too much. The results of the erosion of public support usually results in fund-raising difficulties, less responsive from public officials, and greater tolerance of opposition groups. When the civil rights movement shifted its demands from ending discrimination to **affirmative action**, public support eroded dramatically.

Declining Commitment Among Movement Activists-Activists may grow weary of their struggle. Jail sentences, job loss, injury, time, and financial sacrifice together make it difficult to sustain high levels of active involvement in movements for a very long time. Only a handful of activists stay engaged in the original struggle for the long haul.

Bureaucratization-Most social movements become organized, bureaucratic interest groups with professional staffs to support, political connections to maintain, media to cultivate, and funding sources to tap. Such bureaucratic organizations tend to be conservative and cautious. The radical, dramatic, and disruptive characteristics of social movements tend to be tamed in the transition from social movement to interest groups.

The Rise of Opposition-Successful social movements almost always spark a reaction from groups that oppose their gains. The size, commitment, and resources of opposition groups may match or even exceed those of the protest movement itself. In this way, the civil rights movement sparked an anti-federal government backlash among southern whites during the 1970s and 1980s, and the successes of the environmental movement during the 1970s energized a powerful, well-funded, and well-organized counteroffensive by leading corporations and business organizations.

→**WHY SOME SOCIAL MOVEMENTS SUCCEED AND OTHERS DO NOT**

Some social movements are more successful than others for several reasons that relate to the proximity of the movement's goals to American values, its capacity to win public attention and support, and its ability to affect the political fortunes of elected leaders.

Low-Impact Social Movements-A social movement will have little impact if it has few followers or activists, has little support among the general public, and is unable to be disruptive. Powerful counterrevolutions can also limit the impact of social movements.

Repressed Social Movements-Radical social movements tend to alienate the public and they arouse the hostility of political leaders and police and military forces. The Federal Bureau of Investigation (FBI) and other federal, state, and local police agencies have historically repressed movements such as labor, and the anti-Vietnam War movements.

Partially Successful Social Movements-Movements such as the labor movement, pro-life movement, gay and lesbian movement have all had partial success in gaining public support and support from institutions of government.

Successful Social Movements-Social movements that have many supporters, win public sympathy, do not challenge the basics of the economic and social order, and wield some clout in the electoral arena are likely to achieve a substantial number of their goals. The women's suffrage movement and the civil rights movement are examples of successful movements. Movements may also be successful even if no new laws are passed. Increased respect for members of a movement, changes in underlying values, and increased representation of the group in decision-making bodies. With the Equal Rights Amendment, the women's movement enjoyed this kind of success. Though the ERA failed, women's issues came to the forefront during these years. Issues such as pay equity, family leave, sexual harassment, and attention to women's health issues are now a part of the American political agenda.

→**SUMMARY**

Social movements are an important aspect of the struggle for democracy. Social movements are mainly the instruments of political leaders who want to gain a hearing in American politics. They contribute to democracy by increasing the visibility of important issues, by encouraging wider participation in public affairs, and sometimes by providing the energy to overcome the many antimajoritarian features of the United States federal system.

Social movements try to bring about social change through grassroots collective action. A social movement's success depends upon a supportive environment, and organizational and leadership resources. The decline of particular social movements is associated with goal attainment, factional splits, the exhaustion of movement activists, and the replacement of grassroots activity by formal organization. At bottom, social movements are an important element of the American political system that add to the strength of U.S. democracy.

Chapter Outline

This section gives you a comprehensive review of the chapter. Use this outline in combination with your textbook to look for key concepts and objectives, to identify essential terms and names, and to gain a basic understanding of political practices and principles from this chapter.

I. **WOMEN WIN THE RIGHT TO VOTE (pp. 211-212)**
    A. This chapter is about social movements
        1. What they are
        2. How and why they form
        3. What tactics they use
        4. How they affect American political life and what government does
    B. The actions of **Angelina Grimke** are used in the opening vignette to illustrate the struggle for women's rights.
        1. She addressed the Massachusetts state legislature in February 1838 and presented a petition against slavery from an estimated 20,000 women of the state.
        2. She was the first woman to speak before an American legislative body, at a time when women were legally subordinate to men and shut out of civic life.
        3. She was derided as ridiculous and blasphemous by the press and clergy, but her actions helped to inspire women who had entered political life through participation through the abolitionist movement to also press for women's rights.
    C. The **Seneca Falls Declaration**

1. Meeting at Seneca Falls, New York, in 1848, a group of women issued a declaration (modeled after the Declaration of Independence) written by **Elizabeth Cady Stanton**.
2. The Seneca Falls Declaration stated that "All men and women are created equal" and presented a long list of violations of rights. It failed to have an immediate impact because most politically active people in the abolitionist movement believed that the first priority was to end slavery.
3. Following the abolition of slavery, women's rights leaders like Stanton, **Susan B. Anthony**, and **Lucy Stone** pressed for equal citizenship rights for all persons, regardless of race or gender. They were bitterly disappointed when the Fourteenth Amendment declared full citizenship rights for all males bor or naturalized in the United States, including those who had been slaves, but failed to include women.

D. Women's rights organizations were formed soon after the Civil War.
1. In 1890, the two main women's rights organizations joined together to form the **National American Woman Suffrage Association** (NAWSA). The women's movement was now focused, mostly united, and growing more powerful every year.
2. In 1912, NAWSA organized a march to support a constitutional amendment for suffrage, in which more than 5,000 women dressed in white paraded through the streets of Washington.
3. Soon after the United States entered World War I in 1916 with the express purpose of "Making the world safe for democracy," women began to picket the White House, demanding full democracy be instituted in America.
   a) As the picketing at the White House increased in numbers and intensity, the D.C. police offered the marchers no protection from antagonistic spectators who pelted the marchers with rotten fruit, vegetables, and rocks. Many women were jailed.
   b) Suffragists began hunger strikes in jail, and the authorities responded with forced feedings and isolation cells.
   c) Public outrage forced local authorities to relent and free the jailed women; public opinion had now shifted in favor of women's right to vote, the main focus of the women's rights campaign.
4. After two prominent senators from New England were defeated in 1918 primarily because of the efforts of suffragists and prohibitionists, the political clout of the women's groups became apparent to elected officials. Congress passed the **Nineteenth Amendment** to the Constitution in 1919 (guaranteeing women the right to vote), and the necessary 36 states ratified it the following year.

II. WHAT ARE SOCIAL MOVEMENTS? (pp. 213-214)

A. This chapter is about **social movements**. Social movements are loosely organized collections of people and institutions who act outside established institutions to promote or resist social change.

B. They are primarily the instruments of political outsiders who want to gain a hearing in American politics.
   a) New social problems often generate new social movements.
   b) The Christian conservative movement, for example, is a broad collection of people, churches, and other organizations that have come together to resist the **secularization** of American society and to promote religious values in American life.
C. Social movements are different from political parties and interest group because social movements focus on broad, society-wide issues and their tendency to act outside the normal channels of government and politics, using unconventional and often disruptive tactics. Social movement politics are often "contentious politics." The authors provide a list of characteristics of social movements:
   1. *Social movements are generally the political instruments of political outsiders.* Social movements often help people who are outside the mainstream gain a hearing from the public and from political decision makers.
      a) The women's suffrage movement forced the issue of for women onto the public agenda. The civil rights movement did the same for the issue of equal citizenship for African-Americans. Gays and lesbians forced the country to pay attention to issues that had long been left "in the closet."
      b) Insiders don't need social movements; they can rely instead on interest groups, political action committees (PACs), lobbyists, campaign contributions, and the like to have their voices heard.
   2. *Social movements are mass grassroots phenomena.* Because outsiders and excluded groups often lack the financial and political resources of insiders, they must take advantage of what that have: numbers, energy, and commitment.
      a) To gain attention, moreover, social movements often use unconventional tactics, such as demonstration and sit-ins.
      b) Officials and citizens almost always complain that social movements are ill-mannered and disruptive. For social movements, that is precisely the point.
   3. *Social movements are populated by individuals with a shared sense of grievance.* People would not take on the considerable risks involved in joining others in a social movement unless they felt a strong, shared sense of grievance against the status quo and a desire to bring about social change.
      a) Social movements tend to form when a significant number of people come to define their own troubles and problems not in personal terms but in more general terms (the belief that there is a common cause for all of their troubles) and when they believe that the government can be moved to take action on their behalf.
      b) Because this is a rare combination, social movements are very difficult to organize and sustain.

III.   **MAJOR SOCIAL MOVEMENTS IN THE UNITED STATES (pp. 214-216)**

A. This section describes some of the most important social movements that have left their mark on American political life and have shaped what government does in the United States.

B. This chapter describes the abolitionist movement, Populist movement, women's suffrage movement, labor movement, peace ("nuclear freeze") movement, civil rights movement, anti-Vietnam War movement, women's movement, environmental movement, gay and lesbian movement, religious fundamentalist movements, pro-life (anti-abortion) movement, and more recently, an emergent anti-globalization movement.

IV. SOCIAL MOVEMENTS IN A MAJORITARIAN DEMOCRACY (pp. 216-219)

A. At first glance, social movements do not seem to fit very well with democratic theory since they usually start out as minority phenomena (whereas democracy requires majority rule) and they often use disruptive tactics. However, this section of the text looks at how social movements can help make American politics more democratic.

B. **Encouraging participation**-Social movements may increase the level of popular involvement and interest in politics.
   1. Social movements are the instruments of outsiders.
   2. Social movements tend to increase the degree of popular involvement that is essential to a democracy (as with the women's suffrage movement that encouraged the involvement of women, as with civil rights movement that encouraged the involvement of African-Americans, and the Christian conservative movement that spurred the involvement of previously apathetic evangelicals).
   3. Social movements also encourage popular participation by dramatizing and bringing to public attention a range of issues that have been ignored or have been dealt with behind closed doors. The ability to make politics more visible—called broadening the **scope of conflict** by political scientist E.E.Schattschneider—makes politics the province of the many rather than the few.

C. **Overcoming political inequality**-Social movements also allow those without substantial resources to enter the game of politics.
   1. The ability of those without resources to disrupt the status quo by mobilizing thousands to take to the streets to voice their demands—what sociologists call **mass mobilization**—is a powerful political tool for people on the outside looking in.
   2. Social movements can convince the majority that new polices are needed.

D. **Creating new majorities**-Social movements may also help create new majorities in society.
   1. If a minority can convince enough citizens that what they want is reasonable, then the majority-rule aspect of democracy is strengthened.
   2. The labor movement, women's movement, and anti-Vietnam War movement, all began with substantial minorities that eventually won over the majority of citizens.

E. **Overcoming gridlock**-The energy of social movements are capable of overcoming the

199

anti-majoritarian aspects of the United States' constitutional system and get anything done. Many of the social reforms of which most Americans are most proud have been less the result of "normal" politics than of social movements started by determined and often disruptive minorities.

V. **FACTORS THAT ENCOURAGE THE CREATION OF SOCIAL MOVEMENTS (pp. 219-224)**

A. A combination of structural factors is apparently necessary for a social movement to develop:

1. **The existence of social distress**
    a) Those whose lives are difficult and unsafe or whose way of life or values are threatened often find social movements attractive.
    b) Social distress caused by economic, social and technological change helped create the rise of most of the major social movements in American history.

2. In particular, the labor movement which was spurred by the **Great Depression** of the 1930s, the Christian conservative movement which was spurred by the apparent decline in religious and family values in American life.

3. The women's movement which challenged the "glass ceiling" and obstacles to career advancement, and unequal pay.

4. The gay and lesbian movement was spurred by the discrimination, police harassment, and violence directed at them and the AIDS epidemic are all examples of this phenomenon.

B. **The availability of resources for mobilization**

1. Social movements occur most often when the aggrieved group has the resources (including skilled leaders) sufficient to organize those who are suffering strain and distress.

2. Resources are integral to successful social movements.

C. **A supportive environment**

1. The times must be right, in the sense that a degree of support and tolerance must exist for the movement among the public and society's leaders.

2. More tolerant attitudes toward social movement groups in the general public help them achieve their goals.

D. **A sense of efficacy among participants**

1. Movement participants must believe that their actions can make a difference that other citizens and political leaders will listen and respond to their grievances.

2. A sense of efficacy is the sense that an individual or group can make a difference.

E. **A spark to set off the flames**

1. Many social movements have been set off by a *catalyst* event (or series of events) that set them in motion.

2. Rosa Parks's refusal to surrender her seat on a Montgomery, Alabama, bus in 1957 is one of the most famous catalyst events in the history of social movements in the United States.

VI. TACTICS OF SOCIAL MOVEMENTS (pp. 224-226)

A. Social movements tend to use unconventional tactics to make themselves heard.
   1. These tactics are often dramatic and disruptive.
   2. **Sit down** strikes was a tactic of the 1930s labor movement.
   3. Sometimes violence is used by social movement groups.
B. The civil rights movement used non-violent **civil disobedience**, student sit-ins, prayers and songs in pursuit of favorable civil rights legislation.

VII. WHY SOCIAL MOVEMENTS DECLINE (pp.226-227)

A. Social movements are difficult to sustain. Both external and internal factors contribute to decline.
B. **The unexpected problem of success**
   1. Success may undermine a social movement as surely as failure. Social movements, in order to survive, must find new or other issues around which to organize.
   2. Social movements often find that achieving their goals destroys their very reason for being.
C. **Factionalism**
   1. Social movements must successfully address three different audiences: the movement's activists, the general public, and public officials.
   2. More specifically, it must maintain the enthusiasm of activists, attract more activists and support from the aggrieved group, gain sympathy from the general public, and force a positive response from public officials.
   3. The fragmentation over strategy that has characterized many social movements usually results from often contradictory goals. Movements seldom recover from these splits.
D. **Erosion of public support**
   1. Social movements decline when popular support for their goals begins to erode.
   2. This may occur when the public believes that enough has been done or that the movement is asking for too much. The results of the erosion of public support usually results in fund-raising difficulties, less responsive from public officials, and greater tolerance of opposition groups.
   3. When the civil rights movement shifted its demands from ending discrimination to **affirmative action**, public support eroded dramatically.
E. **Declining commitment among movement activists**
   1. Activists may grow weary of their struggle.
   2. Jail sentences, job loss, injury, time, and financial sacrifice together make it difficult to sustain high levels of active involvement in movements for a very long time.
   3. Only a handful of activists stay engaged in the original struggle for the long haul.
F. **Bureaucratization**
   1. Most social movements become organized, bureaucratic interest groups with

professional staffs to support, political connections to maintain, media to cultivate, and funding sources to tap.

2. Such bureaucratic organizations tend to be conservative and cautious.
3. The radical, dramatic, and disruptive characteristics of social movements tend to be tamed in the transition from social movement to interest groups.

G. **The rise of opposition**
1. Successful social movements almost always spark a reaction from groups that oppose their gains.
2. The size, commitment, and resources of opposition groups may match or even exceed those of the protest movement itself.
3. In this way, the civil rights movement sparked an anti-federal government backlash among southern whites during the 1970s and 1980s, and the successes of the environmental movement during the 1970s energized a powerful, well-funded, and well-organized counteroffensive by leading corporations and business organizations.

VIII. **WHY SOME SOCIAL MOVEMENTS SUCCEED AND OTHERS DO NOT (pp. 228-232)**
A. Some social movements are more successful than others for several reasons that relate to the proximity of the movement's goals to American values, its capacity to win public attention and support, and its ability to affect the political fortunes of elected leaders.

B. **Low-impact social movements**
1. A social movement will have little impact if it has few followers or activists, has little support among the general public, and is unable to be disruptive.
2. Powerful counterrevolutions can also limit the impact of social movements.

C. **Repressed social movements**
1. Radical social movements tend to alienate the public and they arouse the hostility of political leaders and police and military forces.
2. The Federal Bureau of Investigation (FBI) and other federal, state, and local police agencies have historically repressed movements such as labor, and the anti-Vietnam War movements.

D. **Partially successful social movements**
1. Movements such as the labor movement, pro-life movement, gay and lesbian movement have all had partial success in gaining public support and support from institutions of government.
2. Partially successful social movements do not generate enough power and public support to gain a favorable response from public officials.

E. **Successful social movements**
1. Social movements that have many supporters, win public sympathy, do not challenge the basics of the economic and social order, and wield some clout in the electoral arena are likely to achieve a substantial number of their goals.

a) The women's suffrage movement and the civil rights movement are examples of successful movements. Movements may also be successful even if no new laws are passed.

b) Increased respect for members of a movement, changes in underlying values, and increased representation of the group in decision-making bodies.

2. With the Equal Rights Amendment, the women's movement enjoyed this kind of success. Though the ERA failed, women's issues came to the forefront during these years. Issues such as pay equity, family leave, sexual harassment, and attention to women's health issues are now a part of the American political agenda.

IX. **SUMMARY (pp. 232-233)**

A. Social movements are an important aspect of the struggle for democracy. Social movements are mainly the instruments of political leaders who want to gain a hearing in American politics.

B. They contribute to democracy by increasing the visibility of important issues, by encouraging wider participation in public affairs, and sometimes by providing the energy to overcome the many antimajoritarian features of the United States federal system.

C. Social movements try to bring about social change through grassroots collective action. A social movement's success depends upon a supportive environment, and organizational and leadership resources.

D. The decline of particular social movements is associated with goal attainment, factional splits, the exhaustion of movement activists, and the replacement of grassroots activity by formal organization. At bottom, social movements are an important element of the American political system that add to the strength of U.S. democracy.

Terms for Review

Use this list to review essential principles, functions, and concepts from this chapter. Refer to your textbook for help in identifying and defining terms on this list. When you study, do not merely memorize terms; ask questions about the material you are reviewing, and look for the importance or significance of each item.

affirmative action

civil disobedience

Equal Rights Amendment (ERA)

factionalism

fundamentalist

Great Depression

integration

mass mobilization

political efficacy

populist

pro-choice

pro-life

scope of conflict

secularization

sit-down strike

suffrage

Research Topics: Applying What You Have Learned

You will derive more benefit from your reading if you try to apply what you have learned. Some of the suggested research topics can be answered exclusively from your text, while others require

*you to conduct some basic research on your own. The references suggested under **Internet Sources** will help you in your search.*

- Your textbook says that uneven participation and the role of money and activists impair political equality by giving some people more political influence than others. In what ways might social movements address this problem for less affluent Americans?

- Why do social movements decline when they realize their goals and objectives? Identify a major social movement's decline and identify the law or legislative act that brought about its decline. In this sense, are social movements self-defeating? Write a brief essay explaining the evolution of social movements from their beginnings to their declines.

- Write a brief essay describing how one movement's successes, provoked a countermovement. What was the political or social issue? What was the role of the federal government?

- What are the characteristics of social movements? Create a list that compares the characteristics of a nineteenth century, twentieth century, and twenty-first century social movement. In what ways, if any, have social movements changed over time?

A number of sites on the World Wide Web serve as "gateways" to vast collections of material on American government and politics. The following Internet sources are recommended for students who would like to do additional research in areas covered by this chapter. The references suggested under Research Resources will help you in your search.

Afronet www.afronet.com/
A Web site devoted to materials on African-American political, social, economic, and cultural life.

Christian Coalition www.cc.org/
Information and links from the nation's most influential Christian conservative organization.

Yahoo! Society and Culture www.yahoo.com/Sociaety_and_Culture/
A gateway with links to a multitude of social movements, issues, and groups.

Self-Evaluation

Circle the correct answer for each question. Questions are listed in the same order in which the information appears in the text. Use the Answer Key in the back of the Study Guide *to check your responses.*

1. Women won the right vote with the passage of
    a. The Fourteenth Amendment
    b. The Fifteenth Amendment
    c. The Seventeenth Amendment
    d. The Nineteenth Amendment

2. Social movements are generally the political instruments of
    a. The wealthy
    b. Political insiders
    c. Young people
    d. Political outsiders

3. Which of the following social movements sought to eliminate slavery?
    a. The abolitionist movement
    b. The Populist movement
    c. The Civil Rights movement
    d. Labor movement

4. Which of the following is <u>not</u> usually a characteristic of social movements?
    a. Social movements are mass grassroots phenomena
    b. Social movements are populated by individuals with a shared sense of grievance
    c. Social movements are generally the political instruments of political outsiders
    d. Social movements are generally violent

5. Which of the following has <u>not</u> been a major social movement?
    a. Abolitionist
    b. Populist
    c. Labor rights
    d. Animal rights

6. **Unconventional** political participation includes
   a. Contacting officials.
   b. Donating money.
   c. Demonstrations.
   d. Voting.

7. Which of the following movements oppose abortion?
   a. Gay and lesbian movement
   b. Pro-life
   c. Pro-choice
   d. Civil-rights

8. All but which of the following characteristics of social movements does *The Struggle for Democracy* describe?
   a. Encourages participation
   b. Overcomes political inequality
   c. Creates new majorities
   d. Eliminates conflicts

9. Which of the following factors encourage the creation of social movements?
   a. Social distress

   b. Availability of resources for mobilization
   c. A supportive environment
   d. Gender

10. Which of the following movements invented sit-down strikes?
   a. Abolitionist
   b. Civil rights
   b. Labor
   c. Women's suffrage

11. The intentional breaking of a law, and accepting the consequences as a way to publicize its unjustness, is called
   a. Sit-down strikes
   b. Civil disobedience
   c. Nonviolence
   d. Sit-ins

12. The Student Non-Violent Coordinating Committee (SNCC) was active in which of the following social movements?
   a. Civil rights

    b.   Women's suffrage
    c.   Voting rights for 18-to-20 year olds
    d.   Labor rights

13. (T/F) Success can lead to the decline of a social movement.

14. (T/F) The main goal of the women's suffrage movement was for the passage of the Equal Rights Amendment (ERA).

15. (T/F) The religious fundamentalist movement supports the right to abortion for women.

16. (T/F) The gay and lesbian movement is an example of a partially successful social movement.

17. (T/F) The civil rights movement is an example of a partially successful social movement.

18. (T/F) Public support for affirmative action has increased since the 1990s.

Chapter 9
POLITICAL PARTIES

Key Concepts and Objectives

The Key Concepts and Objectives provide a look at the fundamental goals and ideas of this chapter. This section serves as a guide to a basic understanding of the objectives of your textbook.

After reading this chapter, you should be able to:

- Trace the history of the American two-party system and explain why we have a two-party system.
- Identify structural factors that have led to periods of realignment and dealignment.
- Explain how and why American political parties are different from political parties in most other countries.
- Recognize the functions of political parties and explain why parties are important in a democracy
- Explain how the Republican and Democratic parties differ from each other, and explain why neither of the two major parties is considered to be an ideological institution
- Evaluate the effect of divided government and understand the effect of candidate-centered American politics.
- Describe the decentralized fragmented structure of party organizations in the United States.
- Identify and evaluate several of the proposals that were discussed in this chapter to make American political parties more responsible and more democrat
- Identify the role third parties play in the United States political system.
- Understand how American political parties have evolved, what they do, and how their actions affect the quality of democracy in the United States.
- Understand how parties work as political linkage institutions connecting the public with government leaders and institutions.
- Identify key terms and concepts used in Chapter 9.

This section provides a brief overview of the chapter contents. Read this section as a preview before reading your textbook. Then use this material as a review to help you retain information from your reading.

➔ THE RISE OF THE CAMPAIGN PARTY MACHINE

The status of both the Republican and Democratic parties suggests that they are healthy, vital and growing organizations. The two major parties in the United States have new offices in Washington, D.C., in-house TV and radio studios, media resources for campaigns and information dissemination. Internet service providers have become increasingly important for both parties. Each of the national committees has become a highly professionalized campaign organization, filled with highly skilled people, who provide party candidates with what they need to wage first-rate electoral campaigns.

Despite the vitality of the major parties, the public's attachment to them is increasingly weaker than in the past. This has lead some scholars to talk about the "baseless parties." One indication of this pattern is the various opinion polls showing the increasing number of independents compared to party identifiers and more "split ticket" voting; turn-out for elections is at an all time low; vital grassroots party organizations have withered and disappeared in many areas; fewer people volunteer to work in candidate campaigns; and regard for both parties has declined, as has confidence in the ability of either one to solve pressing national problems.

Parties have changed from being community-based organizations to being campaign service organizations. The public's role in this new party arrangement is limited to voting. If the description of "baseless" parties is accurate, it would mark an important change in the traditional role of political parties in the United States and have important implications for how well democracy works in the United States.

➔ THE ROLE OF POLITICAL PARTIES IN A DEMOCRACY

This chapter examines American political parties in depth. The text discusses why American political parties are the way they are and what implications this has for the workings of democracy in the United States. The text also points to structural factories such as Constitutional rules, culture, and the economy that are important in determining what kind of parties we have.

Political parties are organizations that try to win control of government by electing their people to public office. In representative democracies, parties are the principal organizations that recruit candidates for public office, run their candidates against the candidate of other political parties in competitive elections, and try to organize and coordinate the activities of government officials under party banners and programs.

Political scientist E.E. Schattschneider argues that "political parties created democracy and...modern democracy is unthinkable save in terms of parties." Parties serve an important role in organizing majorities. Parties can do a number of things to make popular sovereignty and political equality possible, such as keeping elected officials responsive and responsible, incorporating a wide range of groups into politics, heightening political interest among the public, and ensuring accountability:

Keeping Elected Officials Responsive-Competitive party elections provide a way for the people to keep elected officials responsive. Party competition enables voters to choose between alternative policy directions and to render a judgment about the past performance of a governing party and to decide whether to allow that party to continue in office. A party can also adjust its **party platform**—the party's statement of positions on the issues—to reflect the preferences of the public as a way to win elections.

Including a broad range of Groups-Political parties can enhance political equality in a democracy because they tend to include many groups. Parties must appeal to majority coalitions of many diverse groups if they are to win elections.

Stimulating Political Interest-Political parties can also stimulate interest in politics and public affairs through their efforts to win or retain power in government; they mobilize voters, bring issues to public attention, and educate on the issues that are of interest to the party. Party competition, by "expanding the scope of conflict," attracts attention and gets people involved.

Ensuring Accountability-When things go wrong or promises are not kept, the citizens can hold responsible individuals or parties accountable. Political parties can simplify the source or sources of problems on a collective basis. Citizens can pass judgment on the governing ability of a party as a whole and decide whether to retain the incumbent party or to throw it out of office in favor of the alternative party.

➔ HISTORY OF THE TWO-PARTY SYSTEM

Most nations have either a one-party or multi-party system. The United States comes closer to a pure two-party system than any other nation in the world. Most Western democracies have multiparty systems, but two parties have dominated the political scene in the United States since1836 and the Democrats and Republicans have controlled the presidency and Congress since 1860. Minor or third parties have had better success at the local level than at the national level. In 1998, the Reform Party of Ross Perot saw the election of its gubernatorial candidate of Minnesota, Jesse Ventura.

The U.S. party system has experienced a great deal of change over time. Still there have been six relatively stable periods in the history of the two-party system, each stretching over 30 or 40 years, interspersed with transitional periods also known as realignments. The most notable realignment period was between 1896 and 1932, when a party system dominated by one of the two major parties is replaced by another system dominated by the other party.

The First Party System: Federalists Versus Democratic Republicans-Alexander Hamilton formed the nation's first political party, the Federalists. Jefferson and Madison formed an opposition party called the Democratic Republicans (and later, just Republicans) who rejected the Federalists' foreign policy and domestic issues such as protective tariffs, a national bank, and federal assumption of Revolutionary War debt. The Federalist Party died out with the War of 1812 due to its identification with the British, and its image as the party of the wealthy in an increasingly democratic nation. By 1816, the first two party system evolved into a one-party system known as the **Era of Good Feelings**, where there was no party competition

The Second Party System: Democrats Versus Whigs-When presidential candidate Andrew Jackson won a plurality of the popular and electoral votes but not a majority in either, a new party system was ushered in. The House of Representatives chose John Quincy Adams. Jackson's supporters formed the Democrats and his opponents, lead by John Quincy Adams and Henry Clay, formed the Whigs. Starting in 1828, when Jackson defeated Adams for the presidency, the Democrats won six of the next eight presidential elections.

It was during the "Jacksonian Revolution" that universal white male suffrage became a reality. In the 1830s, every state except South Carolina passed laws requiring the direct election of presidential electors (who cast electoral college votes). With these changes, power in American politics gravitated to strong political parties capable of mobilizing millions of voters.

As the Civil War approached, the Whig Party died out and was replaced by *Free-Soilers* (who opposed the expansion of slavery in the territories) and anti-slavery Democrats to form the Republican Party. After running a candidate in the 1856 presidential election, its 1860 candidate Abraham Lincoln was elected president after the Democrats were divided on which candidate to put forth.

From the Civil War to 1896: Republicans and Democrats in Balance-After the Civil War and Reconstruction, the Republicans and the Democrats were equally balanced in national politics. Between 1876 and 1896, the Democrats managed to control the presidency for 8 to 20 years, the

Senate for 6 years, and the House of Representatives for 14 years. The Democrats were the party of the South, while the Grand Old Party (GOP) became the party of business, the middle class, and newly enfranchised Black African-American male voters.

The Party of System of 1896:Republican Dominance-The economic disruption at the turn of the century, spawned a number of protest movements and third parties. The Populist party, for example, garnered 8.5 percent of the total vote in the 1892 election and won four states in the electoral college on the motto "wealth belongs to him who creates it." The party formed a coalition of western and southern farmers, unions and urban industrial workers, and poor Black and white farmers in the Deep South.

In 1896, the Populist Party joined with the Democratic party to nominate William Jennings Bryan for the presidency on a campaign motto of "free coinage of silver," to help debtors with cheap currency. Amid a bitter contest, the Conservative Democrats deserted their party to join the Republicans. Populist-Democrats were considered a threat to business. The Republicans won that election and continued to dominate American politics until the Great Depression and the election of 1932. Between 1896 and 1932, the Republicans won control of both houses of Congress in 15 out of 18 elections and of the presidency in 7 out of 9.

The New Deal Party System: Democratic Party Dominance-The Great Depression, the New Deal, and the leadership of President Franklin D. Roosevelt ushered in a period of Democratic party dominance. From 1932 through 1964, the Democrats won 7 of 9 presidential elections, controlled both houses of Congress for all but four years, and dominated politics in many of the states.

During this period, the majority of people who identified with political parties, identified themselves as Democrats. The **New Deal coalition** consisted of an alliance between labor, Catholics, Jews, unionists, small and medium-sized farmers, urban dwellers, white ethnics, southerners, and African-Americans. Some multinational corporations, and major investment banks were also part of the coalition.

The Sixth Party System: Dealignment and Divided Government-By 1968, the New Deal coalition began to disintegrate; it finally collapsed in 1994. Dealignments occur when a previously no dominant party loses its preeminence but no new party takes its place as the dominant party on a long-term basis. The electoral transformations known as dealignments are not as permanent as realignments. During dealignments, the electorate becomes disenchanted with both political parties' ability to solve the nation's major problems.

➔**WHY A TWO PARTY SYSTEM?**

Why is the United States' party system so different from the many Western Democratic nation's that have multi-party systems?

Electoral Rules-The rules that organize elections are the primary determinants of what kind of party system exists.

Proportional Representation-Most democratic nations in the world use some form of proportional representation to elect their representatives. In PR systems, each party is represented in the legislature in rough proportion to the percentage of the popular vote it receives in an election. In a perfect PR system, a party that receives 40 percent of the popular vote would get 40 seats in a 100-seat legislative body. Votes for minor parties would not be wasted as they too, would receive legislative seats in proportion to votes they receive and perhaps, a place in the governing coalition. Israel and the Netherlands come close to having pure PR systems.

Winner-Take-All, Plurality Election, Single-Member Districts-In the United States, elections are organized on a winner-take-all, single-member-district basis. Under this arrangement, instead of winning a majority of votes, candidates are required to win *most* of them.

Winner-take-all electoral systems discourage minority or third party efforts because failure to come in first in the voting leaves a party with no representation at all. From the voter's point of view, winner-take-all elections means that a vote for a minor or third party is a wasted vote. At the presidential level, the nation is basically a single-district. The candidate who wins a majority of the nation's votes in the electoral college wins the presidency. In a parliamentary system, executive power is lodged in a cabinet where several parties may be represented. In winner-take-all arrangements, losing parties get no share of executive power.

Restrictions on Minor Parties-There are many legal obstacles that prevent minority parties from enjoying electoral success at the national level in the United States. In many states, minority parties and independent candidates are required to secure tens of thousands of votes in order to get on the ballot. Unlike the majority party candidates, minority party candidates must attract a minimum of 5 percent of the national votes cast in an election in order to qualify for public funding. As well, they are not reimbursed until after the election, while majority party candidates automatically receive funds *once they are nominated*. Equal time and fairness doctrine rules of the past have become obsolete in the United States except for the two major parties. Media outlets are not required to include minor party candidates in presidential debates.

Popular Attitudes-Many Americans believe that the two-party system is the only possible kind of party system that works and that each family has to choose to be either Republican or Democrat. However these ties are increasingly and steadily eroding.

Absence of A Strong Labor Movement-Unlike many European nations' where strong labor movements have contributed to the creation of Socialist and labor parties, the United States' two-party system has been less accommodating. This is partly the result of a relatively weak labor movement in the United States.

The Role of Minor Parties in the Two-Party System-Minor parties have been very weak in the United States. In its history, only the Republican Party, once a minority party, has managed to replace one of the major parties. Minor parties have come in a number of forms:

Protest parties-Minor parties often arise as part of a protest movement.

Ideological parties-Some minor parties have arisen in order to promote a coherent set of ideas, such as Socialism.

Single-Issue parties-Barely distinguishable from interest groups, some minor parties nominate candidates to run for office on a single issue such as prohibition or Free-Soil.

Splinter parties-Teddy Roosevelt's Bull Moose Party is one of the best examples of how factions from the major parties (in this case Republican) can result in the creation of minor or third parties.

➔ THE PARTIES AS ORGANIZATIONS

Political parties in most democratic nations are fairly well structured, led by party professional, and committed to a set of policies and principles. European parties also have clearly defined membership requirements, centralized control over party nominations and electoral financing, and disciplinary authority over party members holding political office.

The Ambiguous Nature of American Political Parties-While political parties were once run by "bosses" at the state and city levels, the reforms that followed ended party control over government contracts and jobs. Political machines have never existed at the national level. While there have been many influential leaders with clout, reputation, and vision, they have not been able to exercise the power of the old bosses at the local level. Many famous American presidents have had as much difficulty with their own parties as with the opposition. In the United States' two-party system, the criteria for membership is very loose.

The Organization of American Political Parties-The major parties in the United States are loose collections of local and state parties, campaign committees, candidates and officeholders, and associated interest groups that get together every four years to nominate a presidential candidate. The national parties in the United States are unable to control both the nomination of candidates running for office or the flow of money that funds electoral campaigns or the behavior of officeholders.

Party Conventions-Despite the informal qualities of American party organizations, the party conventions that are held every four years do serve to encourage coordination and cooperation among the parties. The national conventions do not dictate what happens with party candidate and party organizations at the local level. The all-white Mississippi delegation to the 1964 Democratic convention refused to endorse Lyndon Johnson, the Democratic presidential candidate.

National Party Committees-Both major American parties have a national committee which has the responsibility of conducting the business of the party during the four years between national conventions. National parties have little direct power but they provide valuable services for local and state parties and for party candidates at all levels. "Soft money" campaign finance rules have made the national committees more powerful. National committees are made up of elected committeemen and committeewomen from each of the states, a sizable staff, and a chairperson.

Congressional Campaign Committees-Congressional campaign committees aid members of Congress in their campaigns for reelection. They raise money, provide media services, conduct research, and carry out any other necessary functions. Party members in Congress control these committees

Congressional Political Action Committees (PACs)-Former Speaker of the House Newt Gingrich created GOPAC in order to assist the majority of the 53 first-term Republicans elected in the 104th Congress. Congressional (PACs) further decentralize the U.S. party structure.

State Party Organizations-Each of the states has a separate and relatively independent political party organization. State parties work with the national parties and are required to follow certain rules related to choosing delegates.

Associated Interest Groups-Though not technically part of the formal party organizations, some interest groups are so closely identified with the parties that they are almost indistinguishable. The Christian Coalition for instance, is barely distinguishable from the Republican Party. Organized labor has had a similar relationship with the Democratic Party since the Great Depression and New Deal.

The Primacy of Candidates-American politics is candidate-centered, meaning that candidates are primary in the United States political system and parties are secondary. In the past parties played the dominant role in nominating candidates in district, state, and national conventions. Today candidates are almost exclusively nominated in primaries and grassroots caucuses, where the party organizations are almost invisible.

Nomination comes to those who are best able to raise money, gain access to media, form their own electoral organizations, and win the support of powerful interest groups. Nominees are so independent they sometimes oppose party leaders and reject traditional party policies. In the

German Bundestag,(the equivalent of the House of Representatives) are less important than the political parties.

Party Goals-Parties first and foremost want to win and put their people in office. But given that there is significant fragmentation and complexity in the party organizations, each party component tends to have its own goals.

Party Activists-Party activists can be defined into two groups with different goals. *Party professionals* are the traditional party workers whose first commitment is to the party itself. They focus on winning elections by finding electable candidates. *Party amateurs* tend to be motivated by ideological or issue concerns. To them, the party is an instrument for advancing an ideological agenda or a particular issue such as civil rights or a ban on abortion. Party amateurs do want to win, but they prefer candidates who conform to their ideological or issue agenda.

Party Officeholders-Party officeholders want to retain their position or gain higher office and much of what they do is in light of that goal. This can result in parties that focus on more on elections and less on governing.

Party Voters-Party voters tend to be less ideological than other partisans. Many are loosely connected to the party organization, while others seek party victory, even if it means electing the lesser of two evils.

Party Contributors-Financial contributors give to parties for many reasons ranging from ideology and policy issues to candidate preference. Others give out of loyalty to the party.

→IDEOLOGY AND PROGRAM

The major parties in the United States are expected to be ideologically ambiguous as they must build and appeal to broad coalitions in order to win elections in the winner-take-all electoral arrangement. Many people who identify with parties are more ideologically oriented than the general public; even though parties must appeal to the public more than its loyal supporters, the parties seem to be getting more, rather than less ideological. The ideological distinctiveness of the major U.S. parties has most recently centered around issues such as abortion rights, affirmative action, and the role of government.

Public Perception of Party Ideologies-Most Americans see the Democratic Party as the liberal party and the Republican Party as the conservative party. The parties are also seen as distinct because of what constituencies support them. Americans who classify themselves as liberals overwhelmingly support the Democratic candidates; self-described conservatives overwhelmingly support Republicans.

217

Ideology in Party Platforms-The U.S. parties also write different political platforms at their party conventions. Republicans tend to talk about opportunity and freedom while the Democrats tend to talk about poverty and social welfare issues.

The Ideology of Party Activists-As in other areas, the Democratic and Republican party activists tend to reflect the same ideological preferences and values as the parties do in general, with one being conservative (Republicans) and the other being liberal (Democrats); party activists are more ideological than those who are registered as party members and the general public.

Party Ideologies In Action-Once elected, the officeholders from both parties tend to support and frame public policies in a manner that is consistent with their different ideologies.

Growing Ideological Differences Between the Parties-Newt Gingrich's 1994 Contract with America highlights the increasing differences between the major parties with the Republicans advocating free markets and less regulation, low taxes, a halt to most abortions, diminished social spending, opposition to affirmative action, and a hard line on "law and order." But not all Republicans adhere to their party's conservative mainstream on social issues. George W. Bush has attempted to articulate a new "compassionate conservatism." On the other hand, the Democrats are increasingly divided among themselves with the traditional liberals on one side and the new "centrist" wing led by the Democratic Leadership Council of Bill Clinton, on the other.

➔THE PARTIES IN GOVERNMENT AND IN THE ELECTORATE

The political party system in the United States can bridge the constitutionally designed conflict between the president and Congress when a single party controls both houses of Congress and the presidency. In parliamentary systems, there is no separation of powers between the branches of national government. The parties are the best institutions for improving the coherence and responsiveness of government in the United States when one party dominates the national government, but they are unable to command complete loyalty from their officeholding members.

➔THE PROBLEM OF DIVIDED GOVERNMENT

For the past three decades, the Republicans have controlled the White House and the Democrats have controlled Congress. After 1994, the situation was reversed. Some scholars believe that divided party control of the federal government adds to the constitutionally designed gridlock and paralysis that the Founders created. As well, each party attempts to damage the other at all costs in order to control government power in the country. Other scholars contend that unified party control did not have good results and cases in which divided control did not prevent the creation of coherent policy. There is also evidence that gridlock is not more peculiar to divided government than it is to unified government. Nevertheless, the closing of the federal government during the presidential-congressional budget battles and the intensely partisan impeachment process do not bode well for divided government.

→PARTIES IN THE ELECTORATE

In this section your authors simply reiterate the points that Americans are less inclined than in the past to identify with or to have confidence in a party, and are less willing to vote a straight party ticket. The two parties are no longer as central as they once were. Many people today have a distaste for the parties as professional campaign organizations.

→SUMMARY

The U.S. party system is unique in many ways. It has been a two party system since the 1830s and it is increasingly candidate-centered, with relatively weak national party organizations. American parties are less ideological than parties in other democracies, but the enduring and important differences between the Democrats and Republicans are becoming more evident. The rise of well-financed, professionally managed, state, national, and congressional campaign organizations which focus on television and direct-mail contact with voters, has impoverished the party grassroots. Divided government appears to further exacerbate the problems of the American political party system in the struggle for democracy.

Chapter Outline

This section gives you a comprehensive review of the chapter. Use this outline in combination with your textbook to look for key concepts and objectives, to identify essential terms and names, and to gain a basic understanding of political practices and principles from this chapter.

I. THE RISE OF THE CAMPAIGN PARTY MACHINE (p. 237)
   A. The status of both the Republican and Democratic parties suggests that they are healthy, vital and growing organizations. The two major parties in the United States have new offices in Washington, D.C., in-house TV and radio studios, media resources for campaigns and information dissemination. Internet service providers have become increasingly important for both parties.
   B. Each of the national committees has become a highly professionalized campaign

organization, filled with highly skilled people, who provide party candidates with what they need to wage first-rate electoral campaigns.

C. Despite the vitality of the major parties, the public's attachment to them is increasingly weaker than in the past. This has lead some scholars to talk about the "baseless parties."

   1. One indication of this pattern is the various opinion polls showing the increasing number of independents compared to party identifiers and more "split ticket" voting.

   2. Turn-out for elections is at an all time low; vital grassroots party organizations have withered and disappeared in many areas; fewer people volunteer to work in candidate campaigns; and regard for both parties has declined, as has confidence in the ability of either one to solve pressing national problems.

   3. Parties have changed from being community-based organizations to being campaign service organizations.

      a) The public's role in this new party arrangement is limited to voting.

      b) If the description of "baseless" parties is accurate, it would mark an important change in the traditional role of political parties in the United States and have important implications for how well democracy works in the United States.

II. THE ROLE OF POLITICAL PARTIES IN A DEMOCRACY (pp. 238-239)

A. This chapter examines American political parties in depth.

   1. The text discusses why American political parties are the way they are and what implications this has for the workings of democracy in the United States.

   2. The text also points to structural factories such as Constitutional rules, culture, and the economy that are important in determining what kind of parties we have.

      a) Political parties are organizations that try to win control of government by electing their people to public office.

      b) In representative democracies, parties are the principal organizations that recruit candidates for public office, run their candidates against the candidate of other political parties in competitive elections, and try to organize and coordinate the activities of government officials under party banners and programs.

B. Political scientist E.E. Schattschneider argues that "political parties created democracy and...modern democracy is unthinkable save in terms of parties."

C. Parties serve an important role in organizing majorities. Parties can do a number of things to make popular sovereignty and political equality possible, such as keeping elected officials responsive and responsible, incorporating a wide range of groups into politics, heightening political interest among the public, and ensuring accountability:

   1. *Keeping Elected Officials Responsive*

      a) Competitive party elections provide a way for the people to keep elected officials responsive.

      b) Party competition enables voters to choose between alternative policy directions and to render a judgment about the past performance of a governing party and to decide whether to allow that party to continue in office.

    c) A party can also adjust its **party platform**—the party's statement of positions on the issues—to reflect the preferences of the public as a way to win elections.

  2. *Including a broad range of Groups*

    a) Political parties can enhance political equality in a democracy because they tend to include many groups.

    b) Parties must appeal to majority coalitions of many diverse groups if they are to win elections.

  3. *Stimulating Political Interest*

    a) Political parties can also stimulate interest in politics and public affairs through their efforts to win or retain power in government.

    b) They mobilize voters, bring issues to public attention, and educate on the issues that are of interest to the party.

    c) Party competition, by "expanding the scope of conflict," attracts attention and gets people involved.

  4. *Ensuring Accountability*

    a) When things go wrong or promises are not kept, the citizens can hold responsible individuals or parties accountable.

    b) Political parties can simplify the source or sources of problems on a collective basis.

    c) Citizens can pass judgment on the governing ability of a party as a whole and decide whether to retain the incumbent party or to throw it out of office in favor of the alternative party.

III. HISTORY OF THE TWO-PARTY SYSTEM (pp. 239-245)

  A. Most nations have either a one-party or multi-party system.

    1. The United States comes closer to a pure two-party system than any other nation in the world.

    2. Most Western democracies have multiparty systems, but two parties have dominated the political scene in the United States since 1836 and the Democrats and Republicans have controlled the presidency and Congress since 1860.

      a) Minor or third parties have had better success at the local level than at the national level.

      b) In 1998, the Reform Party of Ross Perot saw the election of its gubernatorial candidate of Minnesota, Jesse Ventura.

  B. The U.S. party system has experienced a great deal of change over time.

    1. There have been six relatively stable periods in the history of the two-party system, each stretching over 30 or 40 years, interspersed with transitional periods also known as realignments.

    2. The most notable realignment period was between 1896 and 1932, when a party

system dominated by one of the two major parties is replaced by another system dominated by the other party.

C. **The first party system: Federalist versus Democratic Republicans**
  1. Alexander Hamilton formed the nation's first political party, the Federalists.
  2. Jefferson and Madison formed an opposition party called the Democratic Republicans (and later, just Republicans) who rejected the Federalists' foreign policy and domestic issues such as protective tariffs, a national bank, and federal assumption of Revolutionary War debt.
  3. The Federalist Party died out with the War of 1812 due to its identification with the British, and its image as the party of the wealthy in an increasingly democratic nation.
  4. By 1816, the first two party system evolved into a one-party system known as the **Era of Good Feelings**, where there was no party competition

D. **The second party system: Democrats versus Whigs**
  1. When presidential candidate Andrew Jackson won a plurality of the popular and electoral votes but not a majority in either, a new party system was ushered in.
  2. The House of Representatives chose John Quincy Adams.
     a) Jackson's supporters formed the Democrats and his opponents, lead by John Quincy Adams and Henry Clay, formed the Whigs.
     b) Starting in 1828, when Jackson defeated Adams for the presidency, the Democrats won six of the next eight presidential elections.
  3. It was during the "Jacksonian Revolution" that universal white male suffrage became a reality.
     a) In the 1830s, every state except South Carolina passed laws requiring the direct election of presidential electors (who cast electoral college votes).
     b) With these changes, power in American politics gravitated to strong political parties capable of mobilizing millions of voters.
  4. As the Civil War approached, the **Whig Party** died out and was replaced by *Free-Soilers* (who opposed the expansion of slavery in the territories) and anti-slavery Democrats to form the Republican Party.
     a) After running a candidate in the 1856 presidential election, its 1860 candidate Abraham Lincoln was elected president after the Democrats were divided on which candidate to put forth.
     b) The **Civil War** split the parties: the northern and southern wings of each party mirrored the split in the nation.

E. **From the Civil War to 1896: Republicans and Democrats** in Balance
  1. After the Civil War and **Reconstruction**, the Republicans and the Democrats were equally balanced in national politics.
     a) Between 1876 and 1896, the Democrats managed to control the presidency for 8 to 20 years, the Senate for 6 years, and the House of Representatives for 14 years.
     b) The Democrats were the party of the South, while the Grand Old Party (GOP)

became the party of business, the middle class, and newly enfranchised Black African-American male voters.

F. **The party of system of 1896:Republican dominance**
1. The economic disruption at the turn of the century spawned a number of protest movements and third parties.
2. The Populist Party, for example, garnered 8.5 percent of the total vote in the 1892 election and won four states in the electoral college on the motto "wealth belongs to him who creates it."
3. The party formed a coalition of western and southern farmers, unions and urban industrial workers, and poor Black and white farmers in the Deep South.
    a) In 1896, the Populist Party joined with the Democratic party to nominate **William Jennings Bryan** for the presidency on a campaign motto of "free coinage of silver," to help debtors with cheap currency.
    b) Amid a bitter contest, the Conservative Democrats deserted their party to join the Republicans. Populist-Democrats were considered a threat to business.
    c) The Republicans won that election and continued to dominate American politics until the Great Depression and the election of 1932.
    d) Between 1896 and 1932, the Republicans won control of both houses of Congress in 15 out of 18 elections and of the presidency in 7 out of 9.

G. **The New Deal party system**: Democratic Party dominance
1. The Great Depression, the New Deal, and the leadership of President Franklin D. Roosevelt ushered in a period of Democratic Party dominance.
2. From 1932 through 1964, the Democrats won 7 of 9 presidential elections, controlled both houses of Congress for all but four years, and dominated politics in many of the states.
    a) During this period, the majority of people who identified with political parties, identified themselves as Democrats.
    b) The **New Deal coalition** consisted of an alliance between labor, Catholics, Jews, unionists, small and medium-sized farmers, urban dwellers, white ethnics, southerners, and African-Americans. Some multinational corporations, and major investment banks were also part of the coalition.

H. **The sixth party system: Dealignment and divided government**
1. By 1968, the New Deal coalition began to disintegrate; it finally collapsed in 1994.
    a) The electoral transformations known as dealignments are not as permanent as realignments.
    b) During dealignments, the electorate becomes disenchanted with both political parties' ability to solve the nation's major problems.
2. Dealignments occur when a previously no dominant party loses its preeminence but no new party takes its place as the dominant party on a long-term basis.

IV. **WHY A TWO PARTY SYSTEM? (pp. 245-249)**

A. Why is the United States' party system so different from the many Western Democratic nations that have multi-party systems?

B. **Electoral rules**-The rules that organize elections are the primary determinants of what kind of party system exists.

C. **Proportional representation**
   1. Most democratic nations in the world use some form of proportional representation to elect their representatives.
      a) In PR systems, each party is represented in the legislature in rough proportion to the percentage of the popular vote it receives in an election.
      b) In a perfect PR system, a party that receives 40 percent of the popular vote would get 40 seats in a 100-seat legislative body. Votes for minor parties would not be wasted, as they too would receive legislative seats in proportion to the vote they receive and perhaps, a place in the governing coalition. Israel and the Netherlands come close to having pure PR systems.

D. **Winner-take-all, plurality election, single-member districts**
   1. In the United States, elections are organized on a winner-take-all, single-member-district basis.
      a) Under this arrangement, instead of winning a majority of votes, candidates are required to win *most* of them.
      b) Winner-take-all electoral systems discourage minority or third party efforts because failure to come in first in the voting leaves a party with no representation at all.
   2. From the voter's point of view, winner-take-all elections means that a vote for a minor or third party is a wasted vote.
   3. At the presidential level, the nation is basically a single-district.
      a) The candidate who wins a majority of the nation's votes in the **electoral college** wins the presidency. In a parliamentary system, executive power is lodged in a cabinet where several parties may be represented.
      b) In winner-take-all arrangements, losing parties get no share of executive power.

E. **Restrictions on minor parties**
   1. There are many legal obstacles that prevent minority parties from enjoying electoral success at the national level in the United States.
      a) In many states, minority parties and independent candidates are required to secure tens of thousands of votes in order to get on the ballot.
      b) Unlike the majority party candidates, minority party candidates must attract a minimum of 5 percent of the national votes cast in an election in order to qualify for public funding. As well, they are not reimbursed until after the election, while majority party candidates automatically receive funds *once they are nominated*.
      c) Equal time and fairness doctrine rules of the past have become obsolete in the United States except for the two major parties. Media outlets are not required to include minor party candidates in presidential debates.

F. **Popular attitudes**
   1. Many Americans believe that the two-party system is the only possible kind of party system that works and that each family has to choose to be either Republican or Democrat.
   2. However these ties are increasingly and steadily eroding.
G. **Absence of a strong labor movement**
   1. Unlike many European nations' where strong labor movements have contributed to the creation of Socialist and labor parties, the United States' two-party system has been less accommodating.
   2. This is partly the result of a relatively weak labor movement in the United States.
H. **The role of minor parties in the two-party system**
   1. Minor parties have been very weak in the United States.
   2. In its history, only the Republican Party, once a minority party, has managed to replace one of the major parties.
I. Minor parties have come in a number of forms:
   1. **Protest parties**-Minor parties often arise as part of a protest movement.
   2. **Ideological parties**-Some minor parties have arisen in order to promote a coherent set of ideas, such as Socialism.
   3. **Single-issue parties**-Barely distinguishable from interest groups, some minor parties nominate candidates to run for office on a single issue such as prohibition or Free-Soil.
   4. **Splinter parties**-Teddy Roosevelt's **Bull Moose (Progressive) Party** is one of the best examples of how factions from the major parties (in this case Republican) can result in the creation of minor or third parties.

V. **THE PARTIES AS ORGANIZATIONS (pp. 249-257)**
   A. Political parties in most democratic nations are fairly well structured, led by party professional, and committed to a set of policies and principles.
   B. European parties also have clearly defined membership requirements, centralized control over party nominations and electoral financing, and disciplinary authority over party members holding political office.
   C. **The ambiguous nature of American political parties**
      1. While political parties were once run by "bosses" at the state and city levels, the reforms that followed ended party control over government contracts and jobs.
      2. Political machines have never existed at the national level.
      3. While there have been many influential leaders with clout, reputation, and vision, they have not been able to exercise the power of the old bosses at the local level.
      4. Many famous American presidents have had as much difficulty with their own parties as with the opposition. In the United States' two-party system, the criteria for membership are very loose.
   D. **The organization of American political parties**
      1. The major parties in the United States are loose collections of local and state

parties, campaign committees, candidates and officeholders, and associated interest groups that get together every four years to nominate a presidential candidate.
2. The national parties in the United States are unable to control both the nomination of candidates running for office or the flow of money that funds electoral campaigns or the behavior of officeholders.

E. **Party conventions**
1. Despite the informal qualities of American party organizations, the party conventions that are held every four years do serve to encourage coordination and cooperation among the parties.
2. The national conventions do not dictate what happens with party candidate and party organizations at the local level. The all-white Mississippi delegation to the 1964 Democratic convention refused to endorse Lyndon Johnson, the Democratic presidential candidate.

F. **National party committees**
1. Both major American parties have a national committee which has the responsibility of conducting the business of the party during the four years between national conventions.
2. National parties have little direct power but they provide valuable services for local and state parties and for party candidates at all levels.
3. **"Soft money"** campaign finance rules have made the national committees more powerful. National committees are made up of elected committeemen and committeewomen from each of the states, a sizable staff, and a chairperson.

G. **Congressional campaign committees**
1. Congressional campaign committees aid members of Congress in their campaigns for reelection. They raise money, provide media services, conduct research, and carry out any other necessary functions.
2. Party members in Congress control these committees

H. **Congressional Political Action Committees (PACs)**
1. Former Speaker of the House Newt Gingrich created **GOPAC** in order to assist the majority of the 53 first-term Republicans elected in the 104th Congress.
2. Congressional (PACs) further decentralize the U.S. party structure.

I. **State party organizations**
1. Each of the states has a separate and relatively independent political party organization.
2. State parties work with the national parties and are required to follow certain rules related to choosing delegates.

J. **Associated interest groups**
1. Though not technically part of the formal party organizations, some interest groups are so closely identified with the parties that they are almost indistinguishable.
2. The Christian Coalition for instance, is barely distinguishable from the Republican Party. Organized labor has had a similar relationship with the Democratic Party since the Great Depression and New Deal.

K. The primacy of candidates

1. American politics is **candidate-centered**, meaning that candidates are primary in the United States political system and parties are secondary.
   a) In the past, parties played the dominant role in nominating candidates in district, state, and national conventions.
   b) Today candidates are almost exclusively nominated in primaries and grassroots caucuses, where the party organizations are almost invisible.
2. Nomination comes to those who are best able to raise money, gain access to media, form their own electoral organizations, and win the support of powerful interest groups.
3. Nominees are so independent they sometimes oppose party leaders and reject traditional party policies. In the German *Bundestag*,(the equivalent of the House of Representatives) are less important than the political parties. Political campaigns are waged between parties and their alternative programs, not between individual candidates.

L. Party goals

1. Parties first and foremost want to win and put their people in office. But given that there is significant fragmentation and complexity in the party organizations, each party component tends to have its own goals.
2. **Party activists**-Party activists can be defined into two groups with different goals.
   a) *Party professionals* are the traditional party workers whose first commitment is to the party itself. They focus on winning elections by finding electable candidates.
   b) *Party amateurs* tend to be motivated by ideological or issue concerns. To them, the party is an instrument for advancing an ideological agenda or a particular issue such as civil rights or a ban on abortion. Party amateurs do want to win, but they prefer candidates who conform to their ideological or issue agenda.
3. **Party officeholders**-Party officeholders want to retain their position or gain higher office and much of what they do is in light of that goal. This can result in parties that focus on more on elections and less on governing.
4. **Party voters**-Party voters tend to be less ideological than other partisans. Many are loosely connected to the party organization, while others seek party victory, even if it means electing the lesser of two evils.
5. **Party contributors**-Financial contributors give to parties for many reasons ranging from ideology and policy issues to candidate preference. Others give out of loyalty to the party.

M. Ideology and program

1. The major parties in the United States are expected to be ideologically **ambiguous** as they must build and appeal to **broad** coalitions in order to win elections in the winner-take-all electoral arrangement.
2. Many people who identify with parties are more ideologically oriented than the

general public; even though parties must appeal to the public more than its loyal supporters, the parties seem to be getting more, rather than less ideological.

    3. The ideological distinctiveness of the major U.S. parties has most recently centered around issues such as abortion rights, affirmative action, and the role of government.

N. **Public perception of party ideologies**

    1. Most Americans see the Democratic Party as the liberal party and the Republican Party as the conservative party.

    2. The parties are also seen as distinct because of what constituencies support them.

    3. Americans who classify themselves as liberals overwhelmingly support the Democratic candidates; self-described conservatives overwhelmingly support Republicans.

O. **Ideology in party platforms**

    1. The U.S. parties also write different political platforms at their party conventions.

    2. Republicans tend to talk about opportunity and freedom while the Democrats tend to talk about poverty and social welfare issues.

P. **The Ideology of party activists**

    1. As in other areas, the Democratic and Republican party activists tend to reflect the same ideological preferences and values as the parties do in general, with one being more **conservative** (Republicans) and the other being more **liberal** (Democrats).

    2. Party activists are more ideological than those who are registered as party members and the general public.

Q. **Party ideologies in action**

    1. Once elected, the officeholders from both parties tend to support and frame public policies in a manner that is consistent with their different ideologies.

    2. The parties differ in the *policy decisions* of their elected representatives.

R. **Growing ideological differences between the parties**

    1. Newt Gingrich's 1994 *Contract with America* highlights the increasing differences between the major parties with the Republicans advocating free markets and less regulation, low taxes, a halt to most abortions, diminished social spending, opposition to affirmative action, and a hard line on "law and order."

        a) But not all Republicans adhere to their party's conservative mainstream on social issues.

        b) Recently, George W. Bush has attempted to articulate a new "compassionate conservatism."

    2. The Democrats are increasingly divided among themselves with the traditional liberals on one side and the new "**centrist**" wing led by the Democratic Leadership Council of Bill Clinton, on the other.

VI.   **THE PARTIES IN GOVERNMENT AND IN THE ELECTORATE (pp. 257-258)**

    A. The political party system in the United States can bridge the constitutionally designed conflict between the president and Congress when a single party controls both houses of Congress and the presidency.

B. In parliamentary systems, there is no separation of powers between the branches of national government.

C. The parties are the best institutions for improving the coherence and responsiveness of government in the United States when one party dominates the national government, but they are unable to command complete loyalty from their officeholding members.

VII. THE PROBLEM OF DIVIDED GOVERNMENT (pp. 258-259)

A. For the past three decades, the Republicans have controlled the White House and the Democrats have controlled Congress. After 1994, the situation was reversed. Some scholars believe that divided party control of the federal government adds to the constitutionally designed **gridlock** and paralysis that the Founders created.

   1. As well, each party attempts to damage the other at all costs in order to control government power in the country.

   2. Other scholars contend that unified party control did not have good results and cases in which divided control did not prevent the creation of coherent policy. There is also evidence that gridlock is not more peculiar to divided government than it is to unified government.

B. Nevertheless, the closing of the federal government during the presidential-congressional budget battles and the intensely partisan impeachment process do not bode well for divided government.

VIII. PARTIES IN THE ELECTORATE (pp. 259-262)

A. In this section your authors simply reiterate the points that Americans are less inclined than in the past to identify with or to have confidence in a party, and are less willing to vote a straight party ticket.

B. The two parties are no longer as central as they once were. Many people today have a distaste for the parties as professional campaign organizations.

IX. SUMMARY (p. 262)

A. The U.S. party system is unique in many ways.

   1. It has been a two party system since the 1830s and it is increasingly candidate-centered, with relatively weak national party organizations.

   2. American parties are less ideological than parties in other democracies, but the enduring and important differences between the Democrats and Republicans are becoming more evident.

B. Although it has been comprised of the same two parties for well over a century, the two-party system has undergone a series of realignments, induced by structural changes in society and the economy.

   1. The rise of well-financed, professionally managed, state, national, and

congressional campaign organizations which focus on television and direct-mail contact with voters, has impoverished the party grassroots.

2. Divided government appears to further exacerbate the problems of the American political party system in the struggle for democracy.

Terms for Review

Use this list to review essential principles, functions, and concepts from this chapter. Refer to your textbook for help in identifying and defining terms on this list. When you study, do not merely memorize terms; ask questions about the material you are reviewing, and look for the importance or significance of each item.

Alien and Sedition Acts

Anti-federalists

Bull Moose party

congressional campaign committees

Contract with America

dealignment

Democratic party

Democratic-Republican party

direct primary

divided party government

Era of Good Feelings

Federalist party

GOPAC

gridlock

ideological parties

ideology

Libertarian party

majority

majority rule

minor parties

multiparty system

national party committees

national party conventions

New Deal coalition

nonpartisan elections

one-party system

parties in government

parties in the electorate

partisan

party chairperson

party identification

party platforms

plurality

political parties

Populist party

Progressives

proportional representation

protest parties

realignment

Republican party (GOP)

separation of powers

single-issue parties

single-member-district system

soft money

splinter parties

third parties

two-party system

Whigs

Winner-take-all-process

Research Topics: Applying What You Have Learned

You will derive more benefit from your reading if you try to apply what you have learned. Some of the suggested research topics can be answered exclusively from your text, while others require you to conduct some basic research on your own. The references suggested under **Internet Sources** *will help you in your search.*

- Why do the authors of your textbook say that political parties are important for a democratic society? What are the implications of a party system in which elected and appointed officials carrying the party label may go their own way and possibly ignore or oppose national party leaders and policy positions?

- Use the Internet to locate political party platforms for the last three presidential elections. Compare the Democratic and Republican party platforms for that period, review the major issues for each campaign year (as reflected in the platforms), and analyze the differences and similarities between the two parties. Are there any topics that appeared on the platforms in all three years? If so, were the parties consistent or inconsistent in their approaches?

- Compare and contrast political party activity in the American presidential system with those in a parliamentary system such as Great Britain.

Internet Sources

A number of sites on the World Wide Web serve as "gateways" to vast collections of material on American government and politics. The following Internet resources are recommended for students who would like to do some additional research in the areas covered by this chapter. These references would also be helpful in expanding on the questions suggested under Research Topics.

Democratic National Committee www.democrats.org/
Information about Democratic party candidates, party history, convention and national committee, state parties, stands on the issues, affiliated groups, upcoming events, and more.

National Political Index http://www.political index.com/
Links to state and local parties and affiliated organizations and interest groups.

Political Resources on the Web www.agora.stm.it/politic/
Information about political parties in all democratic countries.

Republican National Committee http://www.rnc.org/
Information about Republican party candidates, party history, convention and national committee, state parties, stands on the issues, affiliated groups, upcoming events, and more.

The Reform Party www.reformparty.org/
Learn about Reform Party candidates, proposals, and issue positions.

Self-Evaluation

Circle the correct answer for each question. Questions are listed in the same order in which the information appears in the text. Use the Answer Key in the back of the Study Guide to check your responses.

1. Political parties are
    a. Organizations that try to manipulate the public by regulating the mass media.
    b. Organizations that try to influence government by contributing large sums of money to the campaigns of candidates who support certain policies.
    c. Organizations that try to affect government procedures by exerting pressures on elected and appointed officeholders.
    d. Organizations that try to gain control over government by electing officials to public office who carry the party label.

2. In the 1994 congressional and state elections,
    a. Republicans won control of both houses of Congress for the first time in 40 years.
    b. Democrats retained control of both houses of Congress, despite charges of gridlock in the previous years.
    c. Republicans won control of the House of Representatives and the Democrats retained control on the Senate.
    d. Democrats won control of the House of Representatives and the Republicans won control of the Senate.

3. A process by which the superiority of a dominant political party diminishes without another party supplanting it is described as
    a. Alienation.
    b. Insubordination.
    c. Realignment.
    d. Dealignment.

4. It is more difficult for minor parties to win elections in the United States than in many parliamentary systems because
    a. Parliamentary systems provide funds only for minor party candidates in order to "level the field".
    b. The dominant parties in the United States have established rules that make it difficult for other parties to get on the ballot.
    c. The strong labor movement in the United States has contributed to divisiveness and a low voter turn-out.
    d. Minor parties in the United States do not nominate their candidates until close to the election, which reduces any effectiveness they might otherwise have had.

5. Most democratic nations elect their representatives on the basis of

a. Plurality, winner-take-all systems.
b. Single-member-district systems.
c. Proportional representation systems.
d. Random choice systems.

6. Which of the following statements is correct?
   a. The United States has a two-party system at the state and local levels, but it has been moving in the direction of a one-party system at the national level.
   b. In most presidential elections in the last half century, there has been a spread of at least 20 percentage points between the winning and losing candidates.
   c. Competition on the national level between the two dominant parties had been remarkably close since the end of the Civil War.
   d. Although Democrats and Republicans have controlled the presidency and Congress since 1860, minor and third parties have polled a significant percentage of popular votes in nearly one-fourth of the elections.

7. Elections that are organized on a **plurality, winner-take-all, single-member-district** basis
   a. Contribute to democracy by providing representation for third parties and minority groups.
   b. Discourage the development of minority parties because a party will have no representation at all if its candidate does not receive a plurality of the vote.
   c. Are used primarily in European nations with parliamentary forms of government.
   d. Developed in the United States in reaction to the first presidential election in 1788

8. Which of these statements concerning American political parties is **not** correct?
   a. The vagueness of party membership is a good indicator of the insubstantial nature of American parties.
   b. Parties are fairly well-constructed organizations, led by party professionals and committed to a set of policies and positions.
   c. Independent candidates can sometimes force themselves on the party through primaries or caucuses open to the public.
   d. American parties are more candidate centered than parties in most other countries.

9. Which of these statements best characterizes the position of party activists?
   a. They are generally idealists who are unwilling to compromise their principles in any way.
   b. They want, above all, to retain their position or attain higher office.
   c. They tend to take similar positions on social issues and questions involving the federal deficit.

d. They are quite different in their views than party activists and voters in the other political party.

10. The purpose of the national committees of both major parties is to
    a. Determine the ideology or political positions of the party for the next national convention.
    b. Conduct the business of the party during the four years between national conventions.
    c. Keep local parties and candidates in line with the national party during presidential election years.
    d. Recommend potential party candidates for Congress and the presidency.

11. The Framers of the U.S. Constitution
    a. Favored the development of political parties as a means to protecting liberty.
    b. Were fearful of parties and considered them to be divisive.
    c. Did not consider the effects of parties because they were not familiar with their activities.
    d. Made provisions in the Constitution for the control and regulation of political parties.

12. In which of these ways do the two major parties tend to differ?
    a. Most Americans see the Democrats as the more conservative party, in the sense of opposing government activism.
    b. Most Americans see the democrats as the more liberal party, in the sense of favoring an active federal government.
    c. Most Americans see the Republican party as the more liberal party, in the sense of opposing government activism.
    d. Most Americans see the Republican party as the more conservative party, in the sense of favoring an active federal government.

13. (T/F) The authors of your text suggest that political parties can be essential tools of popular sovereignty.

14. (T/F) *Divided party control* between Congress and the presidency helps to overcome the problems caused by the constitutional separation of powers.

15. (T/F) American political parties generally try to direct their campaigns at a specific, cohesive range of voters by running candidates from a narrow range of ethnic and racial groups.

16. (T/F) In a parliamentary system (like Great Britain's), a political party that wins a large legislative majority would have no trouble passing legislation to which its leadership was committed.

17. (T/F) One role for minor parties in a two-party system is that they sometimes articulate new ideas that may eventually be taken over by one or both of the major parties.

18. (T/F) The Alien and Sedition Acts (1798) were intended to establish controls over immigration from foreign nations.

Chapter 10
PARTICIPATION, VOTING, AND ELECTIONS

Key Concepts and Objectives

The Key Concepts and Objectives provide a look at the fundamental goals and ideas of this chapter. This section serves as a guide to a basic understanding of the objectives of your textbook.

After reading this chapter, you should be able to:

- Explain why elections are essential to the democratic process.
- Determine how the right to vote in the United States was gradually expanded over a period of time.
- Evaluate why voter turnout as a percentage of eligible voters has declined at the same time that the base of suffrage has expanded, and consider why voter turnout is lower in the United States than in most European countries.
- Understand how *structural factors* such as constitutional rules, unequal access to resources and cultural ideas help determine why some groups participate more than others.
- Evaluate how elections affect the behavior of public officials.
- Outline the process by which a viable candidate would campaign for the office of president.
- Explain what role money plays in elections, and distinguish between the effects of soft money and hard money in political campaigns.
- Assess the alternative theories of responsible party government, electoral competition, and electoral reward and punishment.
- Understand the roles of direct primaries, caucuses, and nominating conventions as integral parts of the election process.
- Identify key terms and concepts used in Chapter 10.

Chapter Overview

This section provides a brief overview of the chapter contents. Read this section as a preview before reading your textbook. Then use this material as a review to help you retain information from your reading.

→ ELECTIONS AND DEMOCRACY

Elections are fundamental to **democratic politics**. They are supposed to be the chief means by which citizens control their government does, through **popular sovereignty** and **majority rule**. Democratic theorists have suggested several processes by which **two-party elections** of representatives, like those in the United Sates, can bring about the democratic control of government. This chapter is concerned with what actually happens in American elections and whether elections really bring about democratic control.

Responsible Party Government-Democratic theorists contend that elections should present a "**real choice**". Political parties should stand for different policies, the voters should choose between them, and the winning party should carry out its mandate.

Theory-Responsible party government assumes that each of the two *political parties* is cohesive and unified; that each *takes a clear policy position that differentiates the two parties*; that citizens accurately perceive these positions and vote on the basis of them; and that the winning party will do exactly what it said it would do.

Problems-However, there is no guarantee that either party would take policy positions that actually pleases the voters, it is possible that the winning party's stand is less **unpopular** than the loser's, which may not be particularly popular at all! Also, the decisions concerning what issues and policies are presented to the public are not made by ordinary citizens, but possibly by interest groups and political leaders.

The conditions under which responsible party government is supposed to work are not ever likely to be met in the United States. By constitutional design, the parties are not very unified and cohesive. The parties **do not** always take clear stands and are sometimes deliberately ambiguous. Nor do parties always take distinct issue positions. Parties do not always keep their promises. The responsible party idea does not correspond exactly to what happens in American elections, but it comes close enough to the truth to partly describe reality.

239

Electoral competition calls for both parties to compete for votes by *taking the most popular positions* that they can. As with the responsible party theory, the two political parties each take clear, unified stands on issues, citizens vote on the basis of the issues, and the winning party does what it promises to do.

Theory-Because parties are competing for votes by taking the most popular positions, *both parties are likely to support the same policies* (those favored by the most voters); the key idea is that both parties, competing for votes, tend to take policy stands near the *median* (or midpoint) of public opinion; at the point where exactly one-half the voters are more liberal and one-half more conservative.

In theory, if all the necessary components of electoral competition are present (parties provide real choices, reflect the majority's preferences, and keep their promises, etc.,) it should not matter which party wins. Electoral competition processes hold out the promise that popular sovereignty and a perfectly democratic outcome may result from elections.

Problems-Electoral competition ensures democratic control only if the parties are unified and take clear stands, for pure and direct vote-seeking reasons; it can break down if the parties are fragmented or ambiguous, or seek contributors' dollars rather than citizens' votes. Moreover, everyone has to vote, and they must consider the issues based on the positions the parties take on them. And the parties have to keep their promises. By looking at how actual elections deviate from the theoretical ideal of electoral competition we can see specific ways in which American elections might be improved as instruments of democracy.

Electoral Reward and Punishment-A third process by which elections might bring about democratic control of government addresses the public's response to incumbent leaders and dominant parties.

Theory-Electoral reward and punishment theory assumes that voters make retrospective, backward looking judgments about how well incumbent officials have done in the *past*; they reward success with reelection and punish failure by voting incumbents out of office. Voters don't bother to form preferences about complex issues because they are merely judging how well the incumbents did in the past, whereas politicians who want to remain in office have strong incentives to solve problems that the American people want solved. Politicians' ambitions force them to anticipate what the public wants and to accomplish it.

Problems-Reward and punishment gets rid of bad political leaders only after disasters happen, without guaranteeing that the next leaders will be any better. It relies on politicians' anticipating the effects of future policies, which they do not always do successfully. Reward and punishment tends to focus on failed policies that are most visible; unpopular policies that are less visible often avoid public scrutiny. Also, politicians can manipulate the public by presenting convenient (Election Day) policy outcomes.

Imperfect Electoral Democracy-The three processes of democratic control discussed above occasionally converge and help produce an election that is enormously consequential for the direction of the United States. But none of the three processes work well enough together to guarantee perfectly democratic outcomes most of the time, indeed they often conflict: **responsible parties** and **electoral competition** tend to push in opposite directions.

To pin down politicians' responsibility, all three require more unified political parties than we actually have in the United States. The processes cannot ensure government responsiveness to all citizens unless **all** citizens have the right to vote and exercise that right; but millions of Americans cannot or do not vote. Moreover, money, organizational resources, and active campaigning may influence the stands that parties take and the outcomes of elections. The money contributors, activists, and the leaders of organized groups have more influence than ordinary citizens do; again, political equality is not realized.

→ POLITICAL PARTICIPATION

Political participation refers to *political activity by individual citizens*. It can be either **conventional** (voting, writing letters, working in campaigns) or **unconventional** (demonstrations, protests, boycotts). The most basic form of modern political participation is **voting**. In this chapter, students are asked to look at causes of low voter turnout (but relatively high participation in campaigns) in the United States, and to make comparisons with industrialized European nations. The authors look at characteristics of voters and nonvoters, and students are asked to determine if there is a relationship between the types of people who vote and the principles of popular sovereignty and political **equality**.

Expansion of the Franchise-Until passage of the Fourteenth and Fifteenth Amendments after the Civil War, it was up to each state to determine who was eligible to vote. The **franchise** (right to vote) was quite restricted in the early years of the United States, and only about 11 percent of Americans eligible to vote participated in the first presidential election (1788), or about 1 American in 40. The **expansion of the right to vote** has been one of the most important developments in the political history of the United States, and an essential part of the **struggle for democracy**.

White Male Suffrage-By 1829, property and religious requirements had been dropped in all states except North Carolina and Virginia. By contrast, European countries did not attain **universal white male suffrage** until after World War I.

Blacks, Women, and Young People-Despite the lead enjoyed by the United States, expanding the suffrage to include blacks and women was much more difficult and painful. Universal white male suffrage was often accompanied by the withdrawal of voting rights from black freedmen, even in states that did not permit slavery. The **Fifteenth Amendment** to the U.S. Constitution (1870) extended the right to all black men, but it would still require the 1965 Voting Rights Act

241

for African-Americans to be effectively enfranchised in both the North and South. In 1920, the **Nineteenth Amendment** granted women the right to vote. Residents of Washington, D.C., were permitted to vote for the president (but not Congress) after 1961. And 18-20-year olds (through the **Twenty-Sixth** Amendment) gained the franchise in 1971. Practically all citizens except convicted felons and people in mental institutions had the right to vote in the United States by the early 1970s.

Direct Partisan Elections-The Founders did not originally intend for the citizens of the United States to directly elect national government leaders. The trend toward expanding the right to vote involved the more direct election of government officials, replacing the old indirect methods that insulated officials from the public. The two-party system clarifies choices by focusing citizens' attention on just two alternatives for each office.

By 1800, most state legislatures stopped picking the presidential electors themselves. The legislatures allowed a popular vote for electors, most of whom were pledged to support the presidential candidate of one party or the other. This system, known as the **electoral college**, is still in place today. In nearly every state, there is a winner-take-all popular vote for a slate of electors, who are pledged ahead of time to support a particular candidate. The winning electors meet as the electoral college in their respective states to cast ballots to elect the president after they were selected through the popular vote. This system allows for the indirect election of the president by the citizens.

By 1840, the parties had started nominating presidential candidates in national conventions instead of congressional caucuses. The direct popular election of U.S. senators occurred in 1913 with the passage of the Seventeenth Amendment. Prior to this, state legislators chose the senators from their states to represent them in the senate.

The Vanishing Electorate-During the first century of American history, larger and larger proportions of Americans voted as suffrage expanded to more and more groups. Turnout went from about 11 percent in 1788-89 to about 57 percent in 1828 and up to 80 percent in 1840. It remained at about 80 percent until 1896. Ironically, the trend in the twentieth century has been to a lower proportion of **voter turnout**. Since 1912, between 55 and 65 percent of eligible Americans have voted in presidential elections, even fewer (40 to 50 percent) participate in non-presidential elections. In 1996, 51 percent of eligible voters did not vote in the presidential election; in **2000**____failed to vote. The United States' voting turnout rate is very low compared with other modern industrialized countries; the ideal of **political equality** is violated by low rates of voter turnout because nonvoters do not have an equal voice in political choices.

Causes of Low Turnout- Low turnout is a serious problem for democracy in the United States. Scholars have identified several possible factors:
Barriers to Voting-Barriers to voting in the United States include difficult and cumbersome voter registration procedures that require people to register *before* an election. Those who move from one community to another are required to resister to vote at their new location. In some European countries with high turnout rates, the government, and not citizens, is responsible for deciding

who is listed as eligible to vote. Belgium and Italy, for example, require citizens to vote and fine them if they don't. In most countries, elections are held on holidays. In the United States, people have to vote early or late in the day usually because of work schedules.

Same day registration, Election Day holidays, extended voting periods, more convenient absentee voting, and the 1993 federal "motor voter" law (providing for registration in motor vehicle bureaus and other government offices) are some of the ways that easier voting could increase political equality and popular sovereignty.

Lack of Attractive Choices-Countries with proportional representation or multiparty systems tend to have higher turnout rates because people have many choices from which to select. In a winner-take-all single-member district like the United States, citizens often fail to vote because of a lack of attractive candidates.

Changes in Eligibility Rules-Eligibility rules also affect turnout rates. Turnout as a proportion of eligible voters dropped just after women were enfranchised in 1920 because at first, women were less likely to vote than men. But that difference gradually disappeared as women voted at rates slightly higher than men. Turnout percentages dropped a bit after 18-year-olds won the vote in 1971 because younger people do not participate as much, because they are less firmly established in their local communities.

Alienation-Many Americans have become apathetic or alienated from politics. This alienation, which came out of the turmoil of the 1960s when national leaders were assassinated, the Vietnam War, Watergate, and the Iran-Contra scandals, has contributed to declines in turnout. Political scandals and negative campaign advertising have affected turnout negatively. Some scholars believe that negative campaigning actually increases turnout among voters.

Lack of Voter Mobilization by the Parties-The political parties have chosen not to mobilize some groups such as African-Americans, Hispanics, and the poor. The parties seem less interested in involving the "grassroots" and more interested in raising "soft money" from big donors to run highly professionalized but distant campaigns.

Campaigning Involvement and Contacting Public Officials-Despite low turnout levels, Americans are more likely than people in other countries to participate actively in campaigns, to contact public officials, and to be involved in organizations that play an important role in electoral politics.

→WHO PARTICIPATES?

Political participation in the United States varies a great deal according to people's income, education, age, and ethnicity. Those who participate have more representation and influence with elected officials than those who do not. This **unequal representation** violates the fundamental democratic norm of political equality.

Income and Education-Politically active people tend to be those with higher-than-average incomes and more formal education. They are the most likely to vote. The crucial factor in voter turnout is the level of formal education; although some evidence indicates that the more education probably vote less than the report to pollsters. Income level may be more important than education in affecting who actually votes. The poor do not significantly work for campaigns, give money, contact officials, or vote. This class bias in participation is much greater in the United States than in most other advanced countries because none of our political parties explicitly represent and try to mobilize the working and lower classes, as parties in parliamentary democracies do.

Race and Ethnicity-Blacks vote nearly as much as whites. Only levels of education and income affect the differences in voting between African-American and whites. In other words, African-Americans are at least equally likely to vote and sometimes more likely, than whites of similar education and income backgrounds. Hispanics have historically had very low turnout levels due mainly to low incomes, language problems, or suspicion of government authorities, but this has been changing, especially in heavily Hispanic populated states like California, Texas, and Florida. Asian-Americans show growing levels of participation.

Age-The very young are the least likely to vote. Those between ages 65 and 74 tend to vote at the highest levels.

Gender-There is no longer a gender gap in voting. Though men tend to be more active in other areas of participation, in 1996, women voted at slightly higher rates than men. The educational attainment of women in the United States has improved and issues such as equal pay, and abortion have become prominent in American politics.

Does It Matter Who Votes? There are many arguments that have been put forth explaining the positive and negative aspects of what groups do and what groups do not vote in the United States. Some contend that turnout rates are not as important to democracy as they might be perceived because there is not much difference in the policy preferences between those who do and those who do not vote; the results would likely be the same.

Some scholars have even claimed that low voter turnout is a positive benefit, because those with less education are uninformed on the issues anyway and their nonvoting increases the stability of the system and discourages demagoguery.

But the authors suggest that a political system which includes and mobilizes groups such as Latinos, the young, and the poor may have very different needs of government services than do more affluent citizens. When African-Americans were granted the right to vote, for instance, the number of black elected officials increased, and non-black politicians and officials paid more attention to black constituents. In any case, broader participation in U.S. elections would increase

244

popular sovereignty and political equality and would thus contribute to democracy. The limited number of Americans who vote is one major respect in which the struggle for democracy has not fully succeeded.

→ CAMPAIGNING FOR OFFICE

The kind of people who run for office, whether they take clear policy stands, whether those stands differ from each other, and whether they stand for what the average voter wants, all make a difference in what kinds of issues and alternatives are presented to voters in campaigns.

Contending for the Party Presidential Nomination-The major party candidates for president of the United States are usually chosen before the nominating conventions of the parties and the election in November every four years. The pool of presidential candidates is small; not every American has a significant chance of becoming president.

Who Has A Chance-Historically the major parties' presidential candidates have been middle-aged or elderly white men with extensive formal education, high incomes, Protestants, and experienced public figures, especially governors, senators, vice-presidents, or military heroes.

The best single stepping-stone to become president is clearly the vice-presidency, itself usually filled by former senators or governors. Since 1900, 5 of the 18 presidents have succeeded from the vice-presidency after the president's death or resignation and Nixon and Bush have been former vice-presidents elected in their own right.

Getting Started-Candidates for president start by "testing the waters," raising money, and forming campaign organizations. Names of potential candidates are mentioned in media and political circles. Potential candidates observe the polls concerning name recognition and popularity.

The ability to raise "early money" has become increasingly important in determining who drops out and who continues in the contest for the presidency. How campaigns are pitched is also important; candidates have to decide whether or not they one to present themselves as running against Washington "corruption", as a centrist, a pro-life candidate, a "compassionate conservative" or something else. Caucus and primary campaigns and victories are critical to a candidate's chances for winning office.

Primaries and Caucuses-Party nominees are chosen every four years at national party conventions, made up of state delegations from around the country. Delegates to the national nominating conventions are chosen in a series of state **primary elections** and caucuses. "**Super delegates**," usually members of Congress or local officials, supplement the Democrats' popularly elected delegates. The delegate selection process varies from state to state. Since 1952, no national party convention has taken more than one ballot count to nominate its candidate for the presidency; the preconvention front-runner has always been the nominee.

How to Win-Candidates in each party will try to establish **momentum** by winning early primaries and caucuses. The rewards include press coverage, fundraising, good standing in polls, popular support, and an advantage winning more and more contests. The early caucuses such as the Iowa Caucus and the New Hampshire Primary are critical for establishing a candidate's momentum before "Super Tuesday" on March 7th. The author list four main factors that affect candidates' success in gathering delegates:

- *General attractiveness*-Personal image conveyed by television coupled with candidate's stands on issues.
- *Viability*-The media often judge a candidate's viability according to what they read in the polls, citizens in turn support candidates who have a chance to win an election.
- *Organizational strength*-Hardworking activists can impact a candidate's chances of being elected to office.
- *Money*-A candidate's financial "war chest" is critical to success.

The Convention-Conventions have now become coronation ceremonies for presidential and vice-presidential candidates. The outcomes are always predetermined and party enthusiasts seek to present unity and the best face of the party in order to convince the media and the country that their candidate is presidential. The delegates of the Democrats and Republicans reflect the conservative, liberal, or centrist character of the two major parties.

Nomination Politics and Democracy-Party platforms—the parties' official statements of their positions on issues—attempt to appeal to party loyalists and average voters. But policy stands usually appeal to party elites and financial contributors, rather than the ordinary voter.

Incumbents-Incumbents have many important advantages over challengers. They have the machinery, party base, on the job campaigning, and ability to take credit for success and to policy failures to others such as Congress.

→THE AUTUMN CAMPAIGN

Labor Day is the traditional kick off for the Fall campaign. More recently, candidates have gotten started even earlier. For the general election, if not before, the candidates set up a campaign organization in each state. Intense fundraising continues. Candidates plan itineraries to make three or four speeches in different media markets each day, concentrating on big states and the whole country. Negative advertising and "attack" adds intensify because they have been proven effective, even if the public claims to dislike them. Parties and interest groups attempt to get potential supporters registered and to the polls.

Informing Voters-What kinds of information do voters get in presidential campaigns?

Issues-In accord with electoral competition theories, both the Republican and the Democratic candidates usually try to appeal to the average voter by taking similar, popular stands on policy, especially foreign policy. Gore and Bush both stayed close to the center in **2000**, as did Clinton and Dole in 1996. Presidential candidates usually do not say a great deal about specific policies. They tend to be vague and ambiguous in order to avoid offending voters who disagree with them. Thus, no one could object to George Bush's 1988 promise to be an "education president" and an "environmental president" or to Clinton's 1996 promise to "build a bridge to the twenty-first century."

Past Performance-Typically, candidates talk about past performances with the "outs" blaming the "ins" for problems and the "ins" boasting of successes.

Personal Characteristics-Voters are often introduced to the real or alleged personal characteristics; their competence, expertise in certain areas, strengths and/or weaknesses. Candidate personalities are not irrelevant to the democratic control of government. By the purchase of advertising and the hiring of smart consultants, money, may, in effect, overcome the popular will by distracting attention from policy positions.

Money and Elections-Private campaign contributions pose a major challenge in U.S. presidential elections, particularly because these private sources may influence government policymaking after the election is over.

The Cost of Presidential Campaigns-The 1996 presidential campaign cost $328.1 million. In **2000**, contenders have raised over $210 million before the New Hampshire Primary, the campaign season's first. **Soft money** contributions by the parties and interest group contributions have significantly impacted modern presidential campaigns. Looked at from another angle, campaign spending may not seem so big. A number of major corporations spend more per year in advertising than the total cost of the 1995-1996 presidential election. The *source* of campaign money may be more problematic for democracy than the *cost* of presidential elections. Despite reforms that required candidates to report the sources of their funds and placed limitations on individual contributions, major loopholes remain. Political equality is impaired by the limited and biased participation of citizens, and by the critical role that money and activists play in affecting election outcomes.

Where Does the Money Come From?-Public funding contributes very little to presidential campaigns. Most money comes from individuals, businesses, labor unions, and special-interest groups. The 1974 "reforms" that required candidates to report the sources of their funds and that set individual contributions at no more than $1,000 directly to a candidate, also provided for the creation of political action committees (PACs). PACs are allowed to contribute up to $5,000 per candidate, per election; individuals are allowed to contribute $5,000 to each of as many PACs as they like. Many companies set up multiple PACs for preferred candidates.

People and organizations can contribute unlimited amounts of soft money to national, state and local political parties. As well, individuals and organizations can spend unlimited amounts of money in support of any candidate so long as the ad or appeal does not specifically ask people to vote for or against a particular candidate. In short, there are many loopholes that make it possible for individuals and interests to contribute lots of money to their preferred candidates.

Does Money Talk?-Despite evidence to the contrary, many scholars contend that money does not determine the outcome of presidential elections. Where money seems to count the most is in the primary campaigns within each of the parties for the nomination. In the **general election**, one cannot safely predict the outcome based on who has spent the most money. It is widely believed, but difficult to prove, that contributors of money often get policy favors in return **after elections**. At the very least big contributors gain access to those whom they help win office.

The big contributors are wealthy individuals and corporations which have a better chance of influencing policy than ordinary citizens do, and they tend to influence it in directions different from those the general public would want. Economic power translates into political power, overcoming the legal equality embodied in the idea of **one person, one vote**.

→ ELECTION OUTCOMES

Presidential elections are held on the first Tuesday after the first Monday in each year that is divisible by four. Off-year congressional elections are held during the other even-numbered years.

How Voters Decide-The way in which people make their voting decisions affects how elections contribute to democratic control of government. Parties, candidates, and issues all have substantial effects.

Social Characteristics-Religion, socioeconomic status, religion, and ethnic backgrounds are significantly related to how citizens vote. Blacks, Jews, and lower-income citizens have tended to vote heavily for the Democrats, while white Protestants and upper-income Americans have tended to vote mostly for Republicans. The **2000** presidential election reveals that certain groups preferred Democrat Al Gore and others preferred George W. Bush.

Party Loyalties-These social patterns work through long-term attachments to, or identification with, political parties. Party loyalties are a very good predictor of how people will vote. Party loyalties are so important that some scholars speak of a **normal vote**, the proportion of the votes that each party would win if party were the only factor that affected voting decisions. The normal vote stays approximately the same from one election to another, and therefore serves as a baseline when comparing elections. Party loyalties are relatively stable and shift in large numbers only during **realignment** periods such as 1896 and 1932. However, party loyalties have been weakening, if they were not, the Democrats should have won nearly every presidential election since 1932. Most recent presidential elections have been **deviating elections**, in which the party with fewer party identifiers (the Republicans) has won.

Candidates-Even though more Americans identify with the Democrats, they have not dominated the presidency as their advantage in the party balance should allow. This is because voters pay a lot of attention to their perceptions of the personal characteristics of candidates. Candidates who have experience, appear strong and decisive and convey personal warmth have been the most successful.

Issues-Voters pay attention to issues, including issues that are not reflected in party loyalties. Decisions are sometimes based on **policy proposals** for the future, as with pledges to cut taxes or to help the poor; more often, issue voting has meant **retrospective voting** (making judgments on the basis of past performance).

Foreign Policy-Foreign policy can be important. The Democrats have been less successful than Republicans in avoiding war.

The Economy- The state of the economy usually affects the incumbent party; if times are good, it is rewarded, if times are bad, it is usually punished. The 1992 defeat of Republican George Bush is a well known example of how the economy can impact elections.

New Issues-New issues have become important to voters in recent years, including deficit spending, free trade, the role of money in politics, concern about the environment, and conflicting views about crime, pornography, and abortion.

The Electoral College-The **electoral college** system is confusing to many Americans. When American voters think they are voting for a presidential candidate, they are actually voting for a **slate of electors** who have promised to support the candidate. The outcome of presidential elections does not purely reflect the number of popular votes cast for each candidate; it depends on the votes in the electoral college.

Almost all states now have **winner-take-all** systems that select the entire slate of electors for the candidate who won the most popular votes. If no candidate receives a majority of the electoral votes (a circumstance that has not happened since 1824), the House of Representatives will select the president from among the top three candidates. For most practical purposes, the electoral college system works about the same way as if Americans chose their presidents by direct popular vote. The old idea that electors would exercise their independent judgments is no longer considered a problem, but the system does have certain other consequences.

- *It Magnifies the Popular Support of Winners*-A candidate who wins in many states, by a narrow margin in each, can win a **landslide** victory in the electoral college. It is also possible that a president could be elected who had fewer **popular votes** than an opponent if the votes produced narrow margins in many states (a situation that last occurred in 1888). Ordinarily, this magnification just

249

adds legitimacy to the democratic choice, especially when the winner has only a **plurality** of the popular vote. Many American presidents have been elected with less than 50 percent of the popular vote, including Clinton (1992 and 1996), Richard Nixon (1968), John Kennedy (1960) and Harry Truman (1948).

- *It May Let the Less Popular Candidate Win*-In theory, a president could be elected who had fewer votes than an opponent, if those votes happened to produce narrow margins in many states. This happened in 1876, when Republican Rutherford B. Hayes defeated Samuel Tilden, and in 1888, when Benjamin Harrison beat the more popular Grover Cleveland. In 1824, John Quincy Adams defeated the very popular Andrew Jackson after he was selected by the House of Representatives.
- *It Discourages Third Parties*-The electoral system discourages third parties as it can prevent a third party candidate with substantial support may get no electoral votes at all, if its support is scattered among many states (as occurred in 1992, when **Ross Perot** received 19 percent of the popular vote but zero electoral votes because he failed to win a plurality in any state).

→SUMMARY

Elections are important, not only when there is a clear choice but also when electoral reward or punishment occurs, or when electoral competition forces both parties to take similar positions to appeal to the public. In terms of the *responsible party* government theory, the fact that Republicans tend to be more conservative than Democrats on a number of economic and social issues provides voters with a measure of democratic control by enabling them to detect differences and make choices. Voters exercise control in the *electoral competition* theory by either reelecting successful incumbents or defeating unsuccessful officeholders. Elections force parties to compete by nominating centrist candidates and by taking similar popular positions, a reflection of the *electoral competition* theory. Elections in the United States help make the public's voice heard, but **political equality** is damaged by providing *more political influence to some types of people* than to others.

Chapter Outline

This section gives you a comprehensive review of the chapter. Use this outline in combination with your textbook to look for key concepts and objectives, to identify essential terms and names, and to gain a basic understanding of political practices and principles from this chapter.

I.   **ELECTIONS AND DEMOCRACY (pp. 269-274)**
     A. **The problem of democratic control**

1. **Elections** are essential for **democratic** politics: they are the principal means by which **popular sovereignty** and **majority rule** are supposed to work.
2. Can elections ensure that governments will do what the people want?
   a) In a small **participatory democracy** (like a town meeting), people vote directly on what to do.
   b) **Representative democracy** is the best that can be done in a large, complicated society; representatives are chosen to do the policymaking because it is not feasible to have everyone vote directly on policies.
B. **Responsible party government**
   1. **Theory**-Based on the idea that elections provide a real choice or alternative.
      a) Assumes that each of the two *political parties* is cohesive and unified, that each takes a *clear policy position that differentiates the two parties*, that citizens accurately perceive these positions and vote on the basis of them, and that the winning party will do exactly what it said it would do
      b) If these conditions are met, then the party the more popular policy positions will win and enact its program.
   2. **Problems**-Responsible party government *does not guarantee popular sovereignty or political equality* because crucial decisions about what the parties will stand for and what choices they will present to the voters are made by someone other than ordinary citizens (such as party leaders or interest groups).
      a) Responsible party government does not guarantee that the winning party will take policy positions that would please the voters; it can only guarantee that the winner's stand is less *un*popular than the loser's.
      b) Republican and Democratic parties are not unified or cohesive.
         (a) The parties do not always take clear stands and are sometimes deliberately ambiguous.
         (b) Voters do not vote solely on the issues.
   3. Parties do not always keep their promises after winning an election.
      a) The responsible party idea *does not correspond exactly to what happens in American elections*, but the conditions are *close enough* to the truth so that we can learn something about the reality of elections.
      b) The theory may provide some standards for judging elections, particularly with respect to the *clarity of stands on issues* and the *mobilization of voters*.
C. **Electoral competition**-both parties should compete for votes by *taking the most popular positions* that they can
   1. **Theory**-As with the responsible party theory, the two political parties each take clear, unified stands on issues, citizens vote on the basis of the issues, and the winning party does what it promises to do.
      a) Because parties are competing for votes by taking the most popular positions, *both parties are likely to support the same policies* (those favored by the most voters); the key idea is that both parties, competing for votes, tend to take policy stands near the *median* of public opinion.

251

        b) Does not promise that the parties will educate or mobilize voters

  2. **Problems**-Ensures democratic control **only** if parties are unified and take clear stands, purely for vote-seeking reasons

        a) Factors such as the need to raise campaign funds could endanger the concept of democracy.

        b) For democratic control to be perfect, everyone has to vote.

            (a) Voters must vote only on the issues and must know the positions taken by the parties, and the parties have to keep their promises.

            (b) Neither of these is likely.

        c) However, the conditions are *close enough* to the truth so that electoral competition theories can tell us something about the reality of elections.

            (a) Electoral competition is one of the reasons why government policy is influenced by public opinion.

            (b) We can see specific ways in which American elections might be improved as instruments of democracy by looking at how actual elections deviate from the theoretical ideal.

D. **Electoral reward and punishment** (also called **retrospective voting**)—a process in which people vote for the incumbents when times are good and against them when times are bad.

  1. **Theory**-In each election, voters make retrospective (backward-looking) *judgments about how well incumbent officials have done in the past.*

        a) Unified parties compete for votes by emphasizing their competence and the way they reflect the public's goals, *not* by taking specific stands on issues.

        b) Voters don't bother to form preferences about complex issues because they are merely judging how well the incumbents did in the past; politicians who want to remain in office have strong incentives to solve problems that the American people want solved.

  2. **Problems**-Has the advantage of simplicity because it requires very little of voters (just judgments of how well or how badly things have been going)

        a) Focuses only on the most crucial issues

        b) Relies on politicians' selfishness rather than their altruism; may encourage politicians to produce deceptively happy results just before elections

            (1) Allows time for deliberation and lets leaders try out experimental or temporarily unpopular policies, as long as the results work out well and please the public in time for the next election

            (2) Gets rid of bad political leaders only *after* disasters happen, without guaranteeing that the next group of leaders will be an improvement

            (3) Relies on politicians to *anticipate* the effects of future policies, which they cannot always do successfully

            (4) Reward and punishment tends to focus on failed policies that are most visible; unpopular policies that are less visible often avoid public scrutiny. Also, politicians can manipulate the public by presenting convenient (Election Day) policy outcomes.

E. **Imperfect electoral democracy**
1. Each of these three processes of democratic control works to some extent, but none of them works well enough to guarantee perfectly democratic outcomes, nor do all three acting together ensure democracy; indeed they often conflict: **responsible parties** and **electoral competition** tend to push in opposite directions.
    (1) All three require more unified political parties than we have in the United States.
    (2) These processes can bring about government responsiveness to **all** citizens only if all citizens have the right to vote and only if all citizens exercise that right..
2. **Political equality** is not achieved because the goal of total participation is not met; *nonparticipation* is a major problem for American democracy.
    a) Money, organizational resources, and activism influence the positions that parties take and the outcomes of elections (again violating the concept of political equality).
    b) Citizens' policy preferences and goals may be manipulated, so government responsiveness to them does not necessarily ensure genuine democracy.

II. **POLITICAL PARTICIPATION (pp. 274-280)**
A. Political **participation** refers to *political activity by individual citizens.*
    1. **Unconventional** participation—includes activities such as demonstrations and boycotts
    2. **Conventional** participation—includes activities such as voting, writing letters, contacting officials, giving money
B. The most basic form of modern political participation is **voting**.
    1. In this chapter, students are asked to look at causes of low voter turnout (but relatively high participation in campaigns) in the United States, and to make comparisons with industrialized European nations.
    2. The authors look at characteristics of voters and nonvoters, and students are asked to determine if there is a relationship between the types of people who vote and the principles of **popular sovereignty** and **political equality**.
C. **Expansion of the franchise**
    1. The *franchise* (right to vote) was quite *restricted* in the early years of the United States; the *expansion of the right to vote* has been one of the most important developments in the political history of the United States, and an essential part of the *struggle for democracy.*
        a) **White male suffrage** By 1829, property and religious requirements had been dropped in all states except North Carolina and Virginia. By contrast, European countries did not attain universal white male suffrage until after World War I.
        b) **Blacks, women, and young People**
            (1) The **Fifteenth Amendment** to the U.S. Constitution (1870) formally extended the right to vote to all black Americans, but most were

effectively disfranchised by **Jim Crow laws** in the South by the end of the nineteenth century and remained so until the 1960s civil rights movement and the **Voting Rights Act of 1965**.

    (2) Women won the right to vote with the **Nineteenth Amendment** (1920), following the struggle that began at the **Seneca Falls Convention** in 1848.

    (3) Residents of the District of Columbia were allowed to vote for president, but not for Congress, under provisions of the **Twenty-Third Amendment** (1961).

    (4) The **Twenty-sixth Amendment** (1971) extended the right to vote to all citizens, age 18 and over.

  c) The result of these changes at the state and national levels was an enormous *increase in the proportion of Americans who were legally eligible to vote.*

D. Direct partisan elections

1. The Founders did not originally intend for the citizens of the United States to directly elect national government leaders. The trend over our history has been toward **direct election** of more and more public officials; replacing the old indirect methods that insulated officials from the public.

  a) The development of the two-party system, together with the practice of electors pledging to vote for a particular presidential candidate, *contributed to the trend toward direct popular election* because voters could choose their president more or less directly.

  b) The two-party system clarifies choices by focusing citizens' attention on just two alternatives for each office.

2. By 1800, most state legislatures stopped picking the presidential electors themselves.

  a) The legislatures allowed a popular vote for electors, most of whom were pledged to support the presidential candidate of one party or the other. This system, known as the **electoral college**, is still in place today. In nearly every state, there is a winner-take-all popular vote for a slate of electors, who are pledged ahead of time to support a particular candidate.

  b) The winning electors meet as the electoral college in their respective states to cast ballots to elect the president after they were selected through the popular vote. This system allows for the indirect election of the president by the citizens.

3. By 1840, the parties had started nominating presidential candidates in national conventions instead of congressional caucuses.

  a) The direct popular election of U.S. senators occurred in 1913 with the passage of the Seventeenth Amendment.

  b) Prior to this, state legislators chose the senators from their states to represent them in the senate.

E. The vanishing electorate

1. Suffrage was expanded to more and more groups during the first century of American history, and larger and larger *proportions* voted.

2. Although **turnout** (the proportion of eligible people who vote) data for early elections contains inaccuracies, approximations are available.

    a) Early increases in voting participation have given way to serious decline in the twentieth century; the trend in the twentieth century has been to a *lower proportion* of voter turnout (the **vanishing electorate**).

    b) Turnout went from about 11 percent in 1788-89 to about 57 percent in 1828 and up to 80 percent in 1840. It remained at about 80 percent until 1896. Ironically, the trend in the twentieth century has been to a lower proportion of **voter turnout**.

    c) Since 1912, only about 55 to 65 percent of eligible Americans have voted in presidential elections, 40 to 50 percent in off-year (nonpresidential) congressional elections, and still lower for state and local elections, with as few as 10 to 20 percent in primaries and minor local elections.

3. In 1996, 51 percent of eligible voters did not vote in the presidential election; in **2000**____failed to vote. The United States' voting turnout rate is very low compared with other modern industrialized countries; the ideal of **political equality** is violated by low rates of voter turnout because nonvoters do not have an equal voice in political choices.

F. **Causes of low turnout**

1. Low turnout is a serious problem for democracy in the United States. Scholars have identified several possible factors.

2. *Barriers to Voting*-Barriers to voting in the United States include difficult and cumbersome voter registration procedures that require people to register *before* an election. Those who move from one community to another are required to resister to vote at their new location.

    a) In some European countries with high turnout rates, the government, and not citizens, is responsible for deciding who is listed as eligible to vote.

    b) Belgium and Italy, for example, require citizens to vote and fine them if they don't. In most countries, election days are holidays. Americans who work, must vote very early or late in the day or get special permission to leave their jobs.

    c) Same day registration, Election Day holidays, extended voting periods, more convenient absentee voting, and the **1993 federal "Motor Voter" Law** (providing for registration in motor vehicle bureaus and other government offices) are some of the ways that easier voting could increase political equality and popular sovereignty.

3. *Lack of attractive choices*-Countries with proportional representation or multiparty systems tend to have higher turnout rates because people have many choices from which to select. In a winner-take-all single-member district like the United States, citizens often fail to vote because of a lack of attractive candidate.

4. *Changes in eligibility rules*-Eligibility rules also affect turnout rates.

    a) Turnout as a proportion of eligible voters dropped just after women were enfranchised in 1920 because at first, women were less likely to vote than men.

b) But that difference gradually disappeared as women voted at rates slightly higher than men.
   (1) Turnout percentages dropped sharply after women were enfranchised (1920); the difference between male and female turnout gradually disappeared, and a slightly higher percentage of women than men voted in some recent elections (1988, 1992, and 1996, but not 1990 or 1994).
   (2) Voter turnout also dropped after 18-year-olds gained the vote; young people are not firmly established in local communities, and they do not participate as frequently.
5. The *alienation* and *apathy* about politics that many Americans felt after the 1960s (political assassinations, Vietnam War, Watergate, urban unrest) probably contributed to declines in voter turnout.
   a) Political scandals and negative campaign advertising have affected turnout negatively.
   b) Some scholars believe that negative campaigning actually increases turnout among voters.
6. *Lack of voter mobilization* by political parties and the failure of both parties to register low-income citizens—especially African-Americans and Latinos—contributed to low voter turnout in the 1980s and 1990s.

G. Campaigning involvement and contacting public officials
   a) Despite low voter turnout levels, *Americans are more likely* than people in other countries *to participate actively* in campaigns.
   b) Recent surveys show that 34 percent of Americans say they have contacted officials (most often local elected officials) in the past year.
   c) During the 1992 presidential election, approximately 18 percent of Americans gave money, 29 percent attended meetings, 8 percent attended a political rally, and 5 percent worked actively in a campaign organization.

III. **WHO PARTICIPATES?** (pp. 280-283)
A. **Income and Education**
   1. Politically active people tend to be those with higher-than-average incomes and more formal education. They are the most likely to vote.
   2. The crucial factor in voter turnout is the **level of formal education**; although some evidence indicates that the more education probably vote less than the report to pollsters.
   3. **Income level** may be more important than education in affecting who actually votes.
      a) The poor do not significantly work for campaigns, give money, contact officials, or vote.
      b) This class bias in participation is much greater in the United States than in most other advanced countries because none of our political parties explicitly represent and try to mobilize the working and lower classes, as parties in parliamentary democracies do.
B. **Race and Ethnicity**

1. Blacks vote nearly as much as whites. Only levels of education and income affect the differences in voting between African-American and whites. In other words, African-Americans are at least equally likely to vote and sometimes more likely, than whites of similar education and income backgrounds.
2. Hispanics have historically had very low turnout levels due mainly to low incomes, language problems, or suspicion of government authorities, but this has been changing, especially in heavily Hispanic populated states like California, Texas, and Florida. Asian-Americans show growing levels of participation.

C. **Age**
1. The very young are the least likely to vote. Young people tend to be less rooted in communities, less familiar with registration and voting procedures, and less clear about what stake they have in elections.
2. Those between ages 65 and 74 tend to vote at the highest levels.

D. **Gender**
1. There is no longer a gender gap in voting. Though men tend to be more active in other areas of participation, in 1996, women voted at slightly higher rates than men.
2. The educational attainment of women in the United States has improved and issues such as equal pay, and abortion have become prominent in American politics.

E. **Does it matter who votes?**
1. Some observers believe the rate of participation is unimportant because the preferences of those who vote are similar to those who do not vote; other observers say a low voter turnout rate may be a positive factor because more educated people vote.
2. In contrast to these views, the authors point out that nonvoters today are clearly different from voters; even if their expressed preferences about politics do not look very distinctive, their objective circumstances and their needs for government services differ.
3. One indication of the difference that participation can make is the great change that occurred when African-Americans began to exercise effective voting rights: the number of African-American elected officials rose sharply, and nonblack politicians and officials began to pay more attention to black constituents.
4. Broader participation would increase *popular sovereignty* and *political equality*, and thus would contribute to *democracy*.

IV. **CAMPAIGNING FOR OFFICE (pp. 283-293)**
A. The kind of people who run for office, whether they take clear policy stands, whether those stands differ from each other, and whether they stand for what the average voter wants, all make a difference in what kinds of issues and alternatives are presented to voters in campaigns.
B. **Contending for the party presidential nomination**
1. The major party candidates for president of the United States are usually chosen

before the nominating conventions of the parties and the election in November every four years.

    2. The pool of presidential candidates is small; not every American has a significant chance of becoming president.

C. **Who has a chance**

    1. Historically the major parties' presidential candidates have been middle-aged or elderly white men with extensive formal education, high incomes, Protestants, and experienced public figures, especially governors, senators, vice-presidents, or military heroes.

    2. The best single stepping-stone to become president is clearly the **vice-presidency**, itself usually filled by former senators or governors. Since 1900, 5 of the 18 presidents have succeeded from the vice-presidency after the president's death or resignation and Nixon and Bush have been former vice-presidents elected in their own right.

D. **Getting started**

    1. A person who wants to run for the presidency usually begins at least two or three years before the election by **testing the waters** (asking for support from friends and financial backers) and observing reactions.

    2. The candidate goes through several stages—national polls, informal organization, assembling advisers, formulating strategy, raising large amounts of money, and putting together organizations.

    3. **Primaries and caucuses**

        a) Since the 1970s, most of the delegates to the national **party conventions** have been chosen in state **primary elections**, with direct voting by citizens.

            (1) The Democrats' popularly elected delegates are supplemented by **superdelegates** (usually members of Congress and state and local officials), who become convention delegates by appointment.

            (2) A few states still use the **caucus** system, in which active party members and officials choose delegates to state conventions.

        b) Some primaries are open to all voters, while others are closed (reserved for those who register with the party whose primary election it is).

        c) Most successful candidates for the nomination will need to win a number of primary victories.

    4. **Momentum**

        a) It is important to establish **momentum** by winning early primaries and caucuses.

        b) Early winners tend to get press attention, financial contributions, and better standings in the polls; as a result, a number of candidates descend upon the sites of the early contests (Iowa caucuses, New Hampshire primary, Super Tuesday Southern primaries) at the beginning of each presidential election year.

    5. **How to win**

        a) Factors that affect candidates' success in gaining delegate support

b) *General attractiveness* of the candidate, including image and the candidate's positions on issues

c) The perception of *viability* (a candidate with a real chance of winning)

d) *Organizational strength*, with a large group of hardworking activists

e) *Money* to pay for television advertisements, travel, and a well-organized campaign

6. **The conventions**
   a) Characteristics of Republican and Democratic convention delegates
      (1) Delegates to both are predominately white and financially well off.
      (2) Democrats typically have many more African-American, Latino, female, and working-class delegates.
      (3) Republican delegates tend to be more conservative than the average American citizen; Democratic delegates tend to be more liberal.
   b) In most recent conventions, successful nominees have won a number of primaries and have gone on to the convention with a substantial plurality of delegates.
   c) Differences between delegates of the two parties tend to push the nominees and the positions of the parties apart, as in the *responsible party* process rather than the *electoral-competition* process.

7. **Nomination politics and democracy**
   a) The nomination process is fairly good at coming up with candidates who are personally attractive to voters and who take stands with wide popular appeal, as required by *electoral-competition* theories.
   b) Candidates of the two major parties tend to differ in certain systematic ways, in accordance with *responsible party* theories.
   c) **Party platforms** (the parties' official statements of their stands on issues) tend to include appeals to average voters, but they also have distinctive appeals to the constituencies of each party.
   d) Neither party's nominee may stand for precisely what ordinary citizens want because of the crucial role played by party activists and money givers, thereby preventing a completely democratic outcome.

E. Incumbents
   1. **Incumbent** (the current officeholder) presidents and "heir-apparent" vice-presidents may campaign in a different manner than outsiders and political challengers.
      a) Winning the *nomination* is usually easy for incumbents.
      b) Incumbent candidates campaign on the job, taking credit for policy successes while discounting failures.
   2. Incumbents also must enter and win primaries, but they have the machinery of government working for them and a unified party if times are reasonably good.

F. **The Autumn campaign**
   1. The fall campaign traditionally began on Labor Day, but now tends to start right

after the conventions or even earlier.

2. Candidates set up a campaign organization in each state; intense money raising continues, combined with a new round of **public financing**.

    a) A media blitz begins with numerous short spot commercials on television; *voter focus groups* are used to identify "hot button" emotional appeals.

    b) Candidates plan itineraries to make three or four speeches in different media markets each day, concentrating on big states and the whole country.

    c) Negative advertising and "attack" adds intensify because they have been proven effective, even if the public claims to dislike them. Parties and interest groups attempt to get potential supporters registered and to the polls.

3. Voter registration and voter turnout campaigns become important elements in campaign strategy, especially for Democrats.

G. **Informing voters**

1. What kinds of information do voters get in presidential campaigns?

2. **Issues**

    a) In accord with electoral competition theories, both the Republican and the Democratic candidates usually try to appeal to the average voter by taking similar, popular stands on policy, especially foreign policy.

    b) Gore and Bush both stayed close to the center in **2000**, as did Clinton and Dole in 1996.

        (1) Presidential candidates usually do not say a great deal about specific policies. They tend to be vague and ambiguous in order to avoid offending voters who disagree with them.

        (2) Thus, no one could object to George Bush's 1988 promise to be an "education president" and an "environmental president" or to Clinton's 1996 promise to "build a bridge to the twenty-first century."

    c) Both parties usually try to appeal to the average voter by taking similar, popular stands on policy, especially foreign policy; but they usually do differ on certain issues such as medical care, federal aid to education, social welfare, and abortion.

3. **Past performance**-Typically, candidates talk about past performances with the "outs" blaming the "ins" for problems and the "ins" boasting of successes.

4. **Personal characteristics**

    a) Candidates can give an impression of competence or incompetence; they can appear strong or weak.

    b) Democratic control of policymaking is weakened if candidates who favor unpopular policies are elected on the basis of attractive personal images.

        (1) The focus on personal image may distract attention from policy positions.

        (2) Candidates' personalities are not irrelevant to the democratic control of government, but perhaps voters can be fooled by dirty tricks or slick advertising that sells presidential candidates' personalities and tears down the opponent.

H. **Money and elections**

1. Presidential campaigns cost enormous amounts of money, and the cost has increased rapidly over time.
2. Private campaign contributions pose a major challenge in U.S. presidential elections, particularly because these private sources may influence government policymaking after the election is over.
3. **The cost of presidential campaigns**
    a) **Prenomination spending**
       (1) The 1996 presidential campaign cost $328.1 million. In **2000**, contenders have raised over $210 million before the New Hampshire Primary, the campaign season's first.
       (2) **Soft money** contributions by the parties and interest group contributions have significantly impacted modern presidential campaigns.
    b) Looked at from another angle, campaign spending may not seem so big. A number of major corporations spend more per year in advertising than the total cost of the 1995-1996 presidential election.
    c) The *source* of campaign money may be more problematic for democracy than the *cost* of presidential elections. Despite reforms that required candidates to report the sources of their funds and placed limitations on individual contributions, major loopholes remain.
    d) Political equality is impaired by the limited and biased participation of citizens, and by the critical role that money and activists play in affecting election outcomes.
4. **Where does the money come from?**
    a) Since 1971, part of the money for presidential election campaigns has been funded from **taxpayer check-offs** on income tax returns.
    b) Public funding contributes very little to presidential campaigns. Most money comes from individuals, businesses, labor unions, and special-interest groups.
       (1) The 1974 "reforms" that required candidates to report the sources of their funds and that set individual contributions at no more than $1,000 directly to a candidate, also provided for the creation of political action committees (PACs).
       (2) PACs are allowed to contribute up to $5,000 per candidate, per election; individuals are allowed to contribute $5,000 to each of as many PACs as they like. Many companies set up multiple PACs for preferred candidates. The government matches small contributions to candidates during the primaries and finances party nominees who agree to spending limits. However, public money accounted for only about 20 percent of Clinton's and Dole's expenditures in 1996.
    c) Campaign laws require candidates to report the sources of their funds and place limitations on contributions, but loopholes limit the effectiveness of the reforms.
5. **Does money talk?**

a) Despite evidence to the contrary, many scholars contend that money does not determine the outcome of presidential elections.
  (1) Where money seems to count the most is in the primary campaigns within each of the parties for the nomination. In the **general election**, one cannot safely predict the outcome based on who has spent the most money.
  (2) It is widely believed, but difficult to prove, that contributors of money often get policy favors in return **after elections**. At the very least big contributors gain access to those whom they help win office.
b) Cozy relationships (including access to policymakers) tend to develop between politicians and major contributors; contributors' money tends to increase the chances of victory for like-minded politicians (who can be counted on to do what the contributors want *without any need for pressure*).
c) The big contributors are wealthy individuals and corporations which have a better chance of influencing policy than ordinary citizens do, and they tend to influence it in directions different from those the general public would want. Economic power translates into political power, overcoming the legal equality embodied in the idea of **one person, one vote.**

V. **ELECTION OUTCOMES (pp. 293-299)**
  A. Presidential elections are held on the first Tuesday after the first Monday in November of each year that is divisible by four; off-year congressional elections are held during the other even-numbered years.
  B. **How voters decide**
    1. The *way in which people make their voting decisions affects how elections contribute to democratic control* of government.
    2. Parties, candidates, and issues all have substantial effects on how people vote.
    3. Social characteristics and party loyalties
      a) Socioeconomic status, religion, and ethnic backgrounds are significantly related to how people vote.
      b) Blacks, Jews, and lower-income citizens have tended to vote heavily for the Democrats, while white Protestants and upper-income Americans have tended to vote mostly for Republicans.
    4. The **2000** presidential election reveals that certain groups preferred Democrat Al Gore and others preferred George W. Bush.
  C. **Party loyalties**
    1. These social patterns work through long-term attachments to, or identification with, political parties. Party loyalties are a very good predictor of how people will vote.
    2. Party loyalties are so important that some scholars speak of a **normal vote**, the proportion of the votes that each party would win if party were the only factor that affected voting decisions. The normal vote stays approximately the same from one election to another, and therefore serves as a baseline when comparing elections.
    3. Party loyalties are relatively stable and shift in large numbers only during **realignment** periods such as 1896 and 1932. However, party loyalties have been

weakening, if they were not, the Democrats should have won nearly every presidential election since 1932. Most recent presidential elections have been **deviating elections**, in which the party with fewer party identifiers (the Republicans) has won.

D. **Candidates**

1. Voters' perceptions of the personal characteristics of candidates play an important role in election decisions; they vote heavily for candidates who have experience, appear strong and decisive, and seem to display personal warmth.
   a) In elections between 1952 and 1972, the contrast between Republican and Democratic candidates typically gained the Republicans 4 or 5 percentage points (just enough to overcome the Democrats' advantage in the normal vote).
   b) Even though more Americans identify with the Democrats, they have not dominated the presidency as their advantage in the party balance should allow.
2. Voters pay a lot of attention to their perceptions of the personal characteristics of candidates. Candidates who have experience, appear strong and decisive and convey personal warmth have been the most successful.

E. **Issues**
1. Voters pay attention to issues, including issues that are not reflected in party loyalties. Decisions are sometimes based on **policy proposals** for the future, as with pledges to cut taxes or to help the poor; more often, issue voting has meant **retrospective** voting (making judgments on the basis of past performance).
   a) **Foreign policy**
      (1) During nearly all of the past half-century, Republican candidates have been viewed as better at providing foreign policy strength and at keeping us out of war.
      (2) The Democrats have been less successful than Republicans in avoiding war.
   b) **The economy**
      (1) The state of the economy usually affects the incumbent party; if times are good, it is rewarded, if times are bad, it is usually punished.
      (2) The 1992 defeat of Republican George Bush is a well known example of how the economy can impact elections.
2. **New issues**
      (1) New issues have become important to voters in recent years.
      (2) Deficit spending, free trade, the role of money in politics, concern about the environment, and conflicting views about crime, pornography, and abortion are among the many new issues.

F. **The electoral college**

1. American voters may think they are voting for a presidential candidate, but they are actually voting for a slate of **electors** who have promised to support the candidate.
2. Almost all states now have **winner-take-all** systems that select the entire slate of electors for the candidate who won the most popular votes.
    a) Electors meet in their respective states and send lists of how they have voted to Washington, D.C.; the whole "college" of electors from different states never meets.
    b) If no candidate receives a majority of the electoral votes (a circumstance that has not happened since 1824), the House of Representatives will select the president from among the top three candidates.
3. For most practical purposes, the **electoral college system** works about the same way as if Americans chose their presidents by direct popular vote; the old idea that electors would exercise their independent judgments is no longer considered a problem, but the system does have certain other consequences.
4. The old idea that electors would exercise their independent judgments is no longer considered a problem, but the system does have certain other consequences.
    a) *It magnifies the support of winners*-A candidate who wins in many states, by a narrow margin in each, can win a **landslide** victory in the electoral college.
    b) It is also possible that a president could be elected who had fewer **popular votes** than an opponent if the votes produced narrow margins in many states (a situation that last occurred in 1888). Ordinarily, this magnification just adds legitimacy to the democratic choice, especially when the winner has only a **plurality** of the popular vote. Many American presidents have been elected with less than 50 percent of the popular vote, including Clinton (1992 and 1996), Richard Nixon (1968), John Kennedy (1960) and Harry Truman (1948).
    c) *It may let the less popular candidate win*-In theory, a president could be elected who had fewer votes than an opponent, if those votes happened to produce narrow margins in many states. This happened in 1876, when Republican Rutherford B. Hayes defeated Samuel Tilden, and in 1888, when Benjamin Harrison beat the more popular Grover Cleveland. In 1824, John Quincy Adams defeated the very popular Andrew Jackson after he was selected by the House of Representatives.
    d) *It discourages third parties*-The electoral system discourages third parties as it can prevent a third party candidate with substantial support may get no electoral votes at all, if its support is scattered among many states (as occurred in 1992, when **Ross Perot** received 19 percent of the popular vote but zero electoral votes because he failed to win a plurality in any state).

VI. SUMMARY (pp. 299)

A. Elections are important, not only when there is a clear choice but also when electoral reward or punishment occurs, or when electoral competition forces both parties to take similar positions to appeal to the public.

B. In terms of the *responsible party* government theory, the fact that Republicans tend to be more conservative than Democrats on a number of economic and social issues provides voters with a measure of democratic control by enabling them to detect differences and make choices.

C. Voters exercise control in the *electoral competition* theory by either reelecting successful incumbents or defeating unsuccessful officeholders. Elections force parties to compete by nominating centrist candidates and by taking similar popular positions, a reflection of the *electoral competition* theory.

D. Elections in the United States help make the public's voice heard, but **political equality** is damaged by providing *more political influence to some types of people than to others.*

Terms for Review

Use this list to review essential principles, functions, and concepts from this chapter. Refer to your textbook for help in identifying and defining terms on this list. When you study, do not merely memorize terms; ask questions about the material you are reviewing, and look for the importance or significance of each item.

caucus

convention

conventional participation

convention delegates

deviating election

disfranchisement

electoral college

electoral competition

electoral reward and punishment

electors

Federal Election Commission (FEC)

franchise

incumbent

momentum

multiparty system

normal vote

participation

participatory democracy

party caucus

party convention

party identification

platform

plurality

political action committees (PACs)

political participation

popular sovereignty

presidential electors

primary elections

proportional representation

public funding

realigning election

representative democracy

responsible party

retrospective voting

soft money

suffrage

superdelegates

taxpayer check-offs

turnout

unconventional participation

visibility

voter turnout

Voting Rights Act (1965)

winner-take-all.

Research Topics: Applying What You Have Learned

*You will derive more benefit from your reading if you try to apply what you have learned. Some of the suggested research topics can be answered exclusively from your text, while others require you to conduct some basic research on your own. The references suggested under **Internet Sources** will help you in your search.*

- Your textbook says that uneven participation and the role of money and activists impair political equality by giving some people more political influence than others. In your opinion, can this problem be solved without also violating some liberties that are important to Americans? How would you balance the two?

- Assume that you have been hired as a consultant by a major presidential contender. Your job is to outline the formal procedures and processes that must be completed. An excellent source for you to consult in completing this assignment is Stephen J. Wayne's *The Road to the White House 1996: The Politics of Presidential Elections.*

- Write a brief essay on the following question: What basic problems do you see in the system that is now used? If you were able to formulate changes in the election laws, what changes would you make in order to create more democratic control over the election process?

A number of sites on the World Wide Web serve as "gateways" to vast collections of material on American government and politics. The following resources are recommended for students who would like to do some additional research in the areas covered by this chapter. These references would also be helpful in expanding on the questions suggested under Research Topics.

Project Votesmart www.vote-smart.org/
A political portal loaded with links to information about candidates, parties, and issues.

Republican National Committee www.rnc.org/
Official site of the Republican Party with information on party positions and candidates, how to work as a volunteer or contribute money, and more.

Democratic National Convention www.democrats.org/
Official site of the Democratic Party with information on party positions and candidates, how to work as a volunteer or contribute money, and more.

The Center for Public Integrity www.publicintegrity.org
An especially good site for following the money trail, how campaign money is gathered and spent.

The National Archives Electoral College Sites www.nara.gov/fedreg/ec-hmpge.html
Everything there is to know about the law and practices of the Electoral College and the process by which it elects the president.

E-Vote www.evote.com/
Up-to-the minute news and commentary on national campaigns.

Self-Evaluation

Circle the correct answer for each question. Questions are listed in the same order in which the information appears in the text. Use the Answer Key in the back of the Study Guide *to check your responses.*

1. Because voters are clearly different from nonvoters,
   a. A political system that included and mobilized nonvoters might well produce different policies.
   b. Increased voter turnout probably would not have much effect on policies because different types of voters would cancel each other out.
   c. It really does not matter who participates because voting does not have any real influence on policymakers.
   d. Elections should be held more frequently so that nonvoters would be encouraged to participate.

2. In the **electoral college** process,
   a. The electoral winner usually is not the winner of the popular vote.
   b. The Senate will select the president if no candidate wins a majority of the electoral vote.
   c. Most states use a winner-take-all system in selecting electoral votes.
   d. A run-off election will be held if no candidate wins a majority of either the electoral or popular votes.

3. The 1996 presidential election is a classic case of
   a. Electoral punishment.
   b. Electoral reward.
   c. Electoral deviation.
   d. Electoral alienation.

4. Which of the following is NOT usually a characteristic of U.S. presidential campaigns?
   a. Candidates tend to be vague and ambiguous.
   b. Candidates emphasize symbolic matters that appeal to most people.
   c. Candidates take clear-cut positions on specific issues.
   d. Candidates try to avoid issues that would offend voters.

5. In accord with **electoral competition** theories, both the Republican and Democratic candidates usually try to
   a. Appeal to the average voter by showing that there is a clear policy distinction between the two major candidates.
   b. Appeal to the average voter by showing the candidate's party has done well when it controlled that office in the past.
   c. Appeal to the average voter by taking similar, popular stands on policy positions.
   d. Appeal to the average voter by showing that the candidate will support the party's position on key issues.

6. **Unconventional** political participation includes
   a. Contacting officials.
   b. Donating money.
   c. Demonstrations.
   d. Voting.

7. Since the 1970s, most of the delegates to both the Democratic and Republican national conventions have been chosen by
   a. Direct primaries.
   b. State conventions.
   c. Caucuses.
   d. Petition.

8. In most recent national conventions,
   a. The party nominee has been the candidate who was favored by big business and corporate officers.
   b. The party nominee has been the candidate who was most popular with rank-and-file party identifiers in the nation as a whole.
   c. The party nominee has been the candidate who received the most endorsements from newspapers and was given the most favorable attention by television commentators.
   d. There has been no discernable pattern concerning characteristics of the party nominees.

9. The clearest predictor of who will vote is
   a. Level of education.
   b. Party membership.
   c. Ideology.
   d. Gender.

10. At the beginning of each presidential election year, a number of candidates descend upon the sites of early contests because
    a. A certain proportion of campaign money must be expended in each state in order to be eligible for federal matching funds.
    b. The national committees of the two major parties require all candidates to participate in at least two-thirds of the state primaries.
    c. Candidates' names will be dropped from later primaries if they do not receive a minimum of 10 percent of the vote in each state.
    d. It is important for a candidate to establish momentum by winning early primaries and caucuses.

11. The **responsible party** theory assumes that
    a. Citizens will vote on the basis of candidate style rather than issues.
    b. Parties should compete for votes by taking the most popular positions that they can.
    c. Each of the two major parties is cohesive and unified.

    d.   The winning party will compromise with the losing party on major decisions.

12. The first barriers to fall in the process of expanding the right to vote were those concerning
    a.   Gender.
    b.   Race.
    c.   Property and religion.
    d.   Age and literacy.

13. (T/F) According to your text, the Motor Voter law of 1993 caused a decrease in voter registration because the requirements make it more difficult and time-consuming for many people to register and vote.

14. (T/F) When viewed as a proportion of the eligible population, more people participate in politics in the United States today than participated during most of the nineteenth century.

15. (T/F) **Superdelegates** at the national conventions are people with special political knowledge and skills who were elected by the general public on statewide ballots.

16. (T/F) A **normal vote** refers to the proportion of the votes that each party would win if party were the only factor that affected voting decisions.

17. (T/F) One way to see the effects of **electoral reward and punishment** is to look at the number of votes for members of Congress that the incumbent party wins in off-year elections.

18. (T/F) Despite the low voter turnout levels in the United States, Americans are more likely than people in other countries to participate actively in campaigns.

Chapter 11
CONGRESS

The Key Concepts and Objectives provide a look at the fundamental goals and ideas of this chapter. This section serves as a guide to a basic understanding of the objectives of your textbook.

After reading this chapter, you should be able to:

- Describe how Congress has changed since the Constitution was written.
- Discuss how Congress is shaped by the U.S. Constitution.
- Explain what is meant by the institutionalization of Congress, and show how that has affected congressional procedures.
- Describe how members of Congress are elected, and explain how congressional elections affect the quality of representation in the United States.
- Explain the advantage of incumbency, and assess the role of money and interest groups in congressional elections.
- Clarify how Congress is guided by both formal rules and informal norms.
- Identify the four main types of legislation, and show how a bill becomes a law.
- Review the differences between the House of Representatives and the Senate.
- Explain why the committee system is central to an understanding of the legislative process.
- Describe the functions of legislative leaders and political parties in Congress.
- Establish why the authors of your textbook refer to the organization of Congress as fragmented and decentralized.
- Describe structural changes that have shaped Congress and the decision-making process.
- Decide whether Congress carries out the representative responsibility in a way that can be considered democratic.
- Identify key terms and concepts used in Chapter 11.

This section provides a brief overview of the chapter contents. Read this section as a preview before reading your textbook. Then use this material as a review to help you retain information from your reading.

→ INTRODUCTION TO PART FOUR: GOVERNMENT AND GOVERNING

The chapters in **Part Four** of the text examine how federal *government* institutions operate and how and why public officials, both elected and appointed, behave as they do in office (*governing*). The chapters in this part assume that government institutions and public officials can only be understood in their structural and political contexts. What government does is influenced strongly by *structural factors* such as the constitutional rules, the economy, the political culture, society, and the nation's place in the world. What government does is also shaped by *political linkage* institutions such as elections, parties, interest groups, public opinion, and social movements that transmit the preference of individuals and groups to public officials.

Chapter 11 examines the factors that affect the ability of Congress to be both effective and responsive to the American people. *Democracy* is the evaluative thread that runs through each chapter; each chapter examines the nature of these barriers and evaluates some proposed reforms to make government more democratic.

→ THE 2000 CONGRESSIONAL ELECTIONS

This chapter examines how Congress works as a representative and a governing institution. The text focuses on how the ability and willingness of the members of Congress to meet their complex responsibilities is affected by a variety of actors and institutions. The authors address the question of the democratic character of Congress and how the struggle for democracy has affected its development.

Republicans are in a position to exercise considerable power on a number of fronts, including investigations of President Clinton and his judicial and executive branch appointments. They have maintained a majority of the seats in both chambers of Congress since the 1992 elections.

→ STRUCTURAL FOUNDATIONS OF THE MODERN CONGRESS

A number of structural factors have strongly shaped how the modern Congress works. The most important of these factors are reviewed in this section.

Constitutional Design-We can see the ambivalence of the Founders toward **democracy** in their design of the legislative branch. The framers of the Constitution were ambivalent about democracy and concerned about the possibility of government tyranny, but they also wanted an energetic government capable of accomplishing its assigned tasks. These multiple objectives and concerns are reflected in the constitutional design of Congress.

Empowering Congress-The constitutional rules they established significantly affect what Congress is like today. The Framers intended for the legislative branch to be the center of policymaking. **Article I, Section I,** of the Constitution, gave Congress the power to make the laws: "All legislative power herein granted shall be vested in a Congress of the United States." For the Framers, Congress was the to be the main bearer of federal government powers. In listing its powers and responsibilities in *Article I Section 8*—the **enumerated powers**—they were largely defining the powers of the federal government itself. The Framers enhanced the enumerated powers of Congress by adding the **elastic clause**, granting broad power to Congress to pass whatever legislation was necessary to carry out its enumerated powers.

Constraining Congress-Congress's power was also limited by the Framers. First, they made Congress a **bicameral** body—divided into two chambers—so that legislation could occur only after patient deliberations. Single-house legislative bodies were assumed less deliberative. In **Article I, Section 9** prohibits **bills of attainder, ex post facto laws**, the granting of nobility status, and the suspension of the right of **habeas corpus**. The **Bill of Rights** was also directed at limiting Congress's legislative powers. Moreover, the Framers provided civil liberty protections in the statement "Congress shall make no law..."

They created separate legislative, executive, and judicial branches (**separation of powers**) and gave each of them some role to play in the activities of the others (**checks and balances**) (see *The Federalist, No.51*, in the Appendix); though Congress would be the center of government, it would be surrounded by competing centers of government power. This fragmentation of governmental power affects how Congress works and also makes it difficult to fashion coherent and effective public policies.

Bicameralism and Representation-Congress is organized into two legislative chambers with different principles of representation as well as different constitutional responsibilities. With the Great Compromise, the Framers created two "virtually autonomous chambers," the House of Representatives which was apportioned on the basis of population and the Senate on the basis of equal representation of the states. In the House, terms of office for members was set at two years. In the Senate, terms of office for members was set at six years, with only one-third of the seats up for election in each two-year election cycle.

Originally, the Constitution provided for the election of senators by state legislatures, not by the people. This was changed by the passage of the **Seventeenth Amendment** (1913). The Constitution also assigns particular responsibilities to each of the legislative chambers such as the House's power to bring charges of impeachment against the president for "high crimes and misdemeanors," which it did in the case of Bill Clinton; the Senate has the power to conduct the trial of the president and remove him from office, if the impeachment charges are proved to its satisfaction.

Federalism-Moreover, some powers and responsibilities are granted to the national government, some are shared, and some are reserved for the states in our **federal system**. It is inevitable that conflicts will occur between state governments and the national government, and federalism infuses localism into congressional affairs. Such conflicts sometimes reach the Supreme Court for resolution as it did in *United States v. Lopez (1995)*, where the Court ruled that Congress had gone too far in the use of its commerce clause powers when it passed a law banning firearms in and around public schools. The Court felt that this was a state, not federal issue. Because members of Congress come to Washington as the representatives of states and districts, they also consider local concerns when making national policies.

→ REPRESENTATION AND DEMOCRACY

This section of the text asks whether members of Congress carry out their *representative* responsibility in a way that can be considered *democratic*.

Styles of Representation-English politician and philosopher Edmund Burke distinguished between two principal styles of representation; delegates and trustees. As a **delegate**, the representative tries to mirror perfectly the views of his or her constituents. As a **trustee**, the representative acts independently, trusting his or her own judgment of how to best serve the public interest. Burke believed in the trustee style and Abraham Lincoln advocated the delegate style. Members of Congress choose between these two styles depending upon whether or not they have "safe seats". Senators with Six-year terms are more inclined to use the trustee style because they face the electorate less frequently.

Members of Congress: Race, Gender and Occupation-One way to represent is to be similar to that which is being represented, to reflect the basic characteristics of the constituency such as race, gender, ethnicity, occupation, religion, age, and so forth. In this sense, the U.S. Congress is highly *unrepresentative*.

Gender and Race-Nearly all members of Congress have been white males; women and racial minorities are significantly underrepresented, especially in the Senate. Black representation in Congress peaked during the post-Reconstruction period, when African-Americans played an important role in several southern states. Blacks disappeared from Congress after the reimposition of white supremacy in the South at the end of the nineteenth century.

Even though there were examples of African-American congressmen in New York City and Chicago, their numbers only began to increase in the 1960s. Between the 104th and 106th Congresses, their numbers increased from 26 to 37 representatives; this number is still well below the proportion of blacks in the American population. All but four twentieth-century African-American representatives were Democrats; in the 106th Congress, only one black member of Congress was Republican.

Though Hispanics are even more poorly represented than African-Americans relative to their proportion of the population, the increase in their number in recent years has given the Hispanic caucus more influence than in the past. Only six served in the 106th Congress. Only one Native American holds a seat in the U.S. Senate.

The first woman to sit in Congress was Jeannette Rankin of Montana, a suffragist and pacifist, in 1916. In 1992, considered by many to be the **"year of the woman,"** 48 women were elected to the House of Representatives and 7 to the Senate. In 1992, Carol Moseley Braun (D-Ill) became the first African-American woman to be elected to the Senate (she lost her seat in the 1998 election). Women are grossly underrepresented in Congress compared to their slim majority status among American citizens. Leadership on important committees continue to elude women in Congress.

Occupation-Members of Congress also tend to come from wealthy families. They are better educated than the remainder of the population and come from relatively few occupational backgrounds, particularly from legal, business and banking industries. Individuals with blue-collar backgrounds are noticeably absent. Some question whether it matters that Congress is demographically unrepresentative. Some observers suggest that the need to face the electorate forces lawmakers to be attentive to all significant groups in their **constituencies**, regardless of their own backgrounds. However, many who are not represented (such as women, racial minorities, and the poor) believe that their interests would get a better hearing if their numbers were substantially increased in Congress. The demographic disparity suggests a violation of the norm of **political equality**, an important element of **democracy**.

The Electoral Connection-The election is the principal instrument in a democracy for linking citizens to government officials. Let's see how congressional elections affect the quality of representation in the United States.

Electoral Districts-Each state is entitled to two senators. Equal representation in the Senate gives extraordinary power in the legislative process to small states. This arrangement can substantially distort popular sentiment, and in this way can diminish democracy.

Reapportionment-Representation in the House of Representatives is based on population, with **reapportionment** based on the national census every 10 years. State legislatures draw the boundary lines, and the party that controls the state legislature will usually try to draw district lines in a way that will help them win elections. After the **census** some states keep the same number of seats; others gain or lose them. The Supreme Court ruled in *Wesberry v. Sanders* (1964) that the principle of **one person, one vote** applies to how congressional districts are drawn. **Gerrymandering** occurs when boundary lines are drawn to ensure the election of a particular party, group, or person (the term dates to the 1811 redistricting process when Governor **Elbridge Gerry** of Massachusetts signed a bill that created a district that looked like a salamander to editorial cartoonists).

Congressional districts are now approximately the same size in terms of population, but state legislatures are still relatively free to draw district lines *where* they choose. The party that controls the state legislature usually tries to draw district lines in a way that will help them win elections, and the resulting districts are often odd-looking and convoluted (rather than compact and contiguous). The Supreme Court has tried to prevent the most flagrant abuses, especially when some identifiable group of voters (like racial minorities) is disadvantaged, but it is a practice that is difficult to regulate. The 1982 amendments to the **1965 Voting Rights Act**, which encouraged the states to create House districts in which racial minorities would be in the majority, resulted in the formation of 24 new **majority-minority districts** (districts drawn purposely so that a racial minority is the majority). The Supreme Court first encouraged the creation of majority-minority districts, then appeared to have second thoughts about districts that are highly irregular in form, noncontiguous, and unconnected to traditional political jurisdictions (*Shaw v. Reno*, 1993), or that are drawn solely to aid one race (*Miller v. Johnson*, 1995).

Money and Congressional Elections-This chapter also looks at the relationship between money and congressional elections. Running for a congressional seat is very expensive, and keeps getting more expensive. Although the candidate who spends the most money does not always win, the amount of money spent is related to the probability of winning. *Incumbents* (who need the funds the least) have the easiest time raising money and they spend the most in races for both houses.

Open-seat election races in which no incumbent is involved, also attract and use lots of money. Money to support congressional campaigns comes from four main sources: individuals, parties, the candidates, and **political action committees (PACs)**. Contributions from PACs go primarily to incumbents. The largest share comes from individual contributors, PACs are the next largest contributor. This is the fastest growing part of the campaign financing system; PACs are free to spend without limit on general-issue campaigns that are often thinly veiled efforts to help a particular candidate or party (sometimes referred to as *parallel campaigns*). Many people believe that the increased role of PACs also increases the influence of interest groups and business interests. There are no legal limits on donations to the parties for general education, registration, and get-out-the-vote campaigns. There are also no limits on how much of this *soft money* parties can spend, even though the spending obviously benefits individual candidates.

Republicans filibustered the 1997 *McCain-Feingold* campaign finance reform bill. But Democrats have been no more committed to serious reform either. Being the minority party in Congress, they had the luxury of allowing the Republicans to take the heat for blocking reform. The McCain-Feingold bill failed again in 1999.

The Incumbency Factor-Incumbents—current officeholders—win at much higher rates in the House today than ever before. The ability of House incumbents to get reelected improved especially from the late 1940s into the 1990s, allowing the Democratic Party to maintain control over the House of Representatives for four decades (from 1955 to 1994), even as Republicans like Dwight Eisenhower, Richard Nixon, Ronald Reagan, and George Bush were winning presidential elections. Incumbents are almost always successful in being re-elected.

Why Incumbents Have the Advantage-The textbook points to a number of advantages that incumbents enjoy over challengers. PACs and interest groups want access to key decision makers, and the flow of money is particularly heavy for those who sit on key committees or hold important leadership posts. Incumbents use congressional resources to advertise their accomplishments and keep their names before the public (although there are some restrictions designed to limit abuse). The **franking privilege** allows members to mail newsletters, legislative updates, surveys, and other self-promoting literature free of charge. Travel budgets permit lawmakers to make frequent visits back to their state or district. Incumbents also use their offices to **service the district**. In this way, **casework** involves helping constituents solve red-tape problems with the federal bureaucracy, and **pork** (derived from the expression "bringing home the bacon") is used to provide federal dollars in the form of contracts, facilities, and subsidies.

How Representative? Members of Congress may be doing a relatively good job of representing their constituents: research shows that members vote in conformity with majority opinion in their districts about two-thirds of the time. Congress produces laws that are consistent with national public opinion at about the same rate. Congress however, ignored public opinion on the impeachment of Bill Clinton. In many cases, Congress does **not** follow public opinion. Nevertheless, the **incumbency factor** should not be exaggerated: *turnover in Congress is significant* due to voluntary retirements, redistricting changes, and some electoral defeats.

➜ HOW CONGRESS WORKS

Congress plays an important part in making policy; it remains the most powerful legislature among Western democratic nations. In this section, the text focuses on how Congress is organized and functions as a working legislative body.

The Congressional Agenda-Congress exists in a rich structural, political, and governmental environment that helps determine its priorities. The judicial and executive branches of government are constant influences on the congressional agenda, and the agenda is also shaped by various groups and individuals, including interest groups, voters, constituents, the media, and social movements.

The congressional agenda is also a product of its constitutional responsibilities. For example, Congress is obligated to create the nation's budget which it does in a highly complex authorization and appropriation process. Much of what Congress does by way of lawmaking is in response to the legislative program of the president, usually presented in conjunction with the annual **State of the Union**, economic, and budget messages. Pressure groups and influential individuals also impact Congress's workload. The media are continuous players in shaping what issues are attended to in the legislative branch. Social movements also try to impose their own priorities on Congress. Finally, structural change mobilizes political and governmental institutions, groups, and individuals. Economic dislocations caused by the process of globalization often trigger demands for congressional action.

Political Parties in Congress-At the start of each new Congress, each party caucus meets to select party committees and leaders. The majority party in Congress selects the Speaker of the House of Representatives, while the majority party in the Senate selects the president pro tempore (usually its most senior member) and the majority leader. The majority party in each house also selects the chairs of the committees and subcommittees and determined the party ratios for each.

The Party Composition of Congress-The Democratic Party dominated the modern Congress until the 1994 elections. It was the majority party in the House of Representatives for all but four years between 1933 and 1994. In the Senate, Republicans were in the majority for only ten years during this same period. The Republicans have dominated both chambers since 1994.

Party Voting in Congress- Congress is *fragmented and decentralized* by the electoral needs of lawmakers and the organization of Congress along committee lines. At the opening of each new Congress, the two houses organize their legislative business along party lines. Party labels are important **cues** for members of Congress as they decide how to vote. *Party affiliation is the best predictor* of the voting behavior of members of Congress. Both houses of Congress are becoming more *partisan*. It is not entirely clear whether party voting differences are caused directly by party affiliation or indirectly by the character of the constituencies. Ideology, (Republican conservatism versus Democratic liberalism and centrism) strengthens the glue of party unity and increases partisanship.

Congressional Leadership-The political parties also work through the leadership structure of Congress because the leaders of the majority political party are also the leaders of the House and Senate.

Leadership in the House-The **Speaker of the House of Representatives** is treated as the spokesperson for the House and also for the majority party. This position is constitutionally recognized for succession to the presidency, immediately after the vice-president. Other powers of the Speaker include referral of bills to committee, control of the House agenda, appointment of select committees, and direction of floor debate. There have been many powerful individual speakers, but the position was weakened until about 1974 when the Democratic Caucus staged a revolt against committee chairs and restored some of the powers of the Speaker, especially in making committee assignments. Newt Gingrich was one of the most powerful Speakers of the House in recent history. He led the conservative Republican agenda with the Contract With America that ushered in a Republican congressional majority in 1994. By 1998 however, Gingrich resigned from his position amid protests against him after Republicans lost some of their numerical advantage in Congress after the election that year.

The majority party in the House also selects a **majority floor leader** to help the Speaker plan strategy and manage the legislative business of the House. The minority party elects a **minority floor leader**, who serves as the chief spokesperson and legislative strategist for the opposition. Each party has **party whips** who act as liaisons between the leaders and the rank and file, count heads on important bills, explain leadership positions, try to persuade members to vote with the party, gather legislative intelligence, and ensure that supporters get to the floor to cast their votes. The minority party elects a **minority floor leader**, who is assisted by a **minority whip**.

Leadership in the Senate-Senate Leadership is less visible than in the House, and those with formal leadership titles exercise little influence. The Vice-President of the United States serves as the presiding officer (**President of the Senate**). The office is designated by the U.S. Constitution, *not* elected by the House as are the other leadership positions. The President of the Senate is seldom in attendance because this is essentially a ceremonial office with no power other than the right to vote to break a tie. The **president *pro tempore*** is the temporary presiding officer. This is also a ceremonial office, and the incumbent rarely acts as presiding officer. The **Senate majority leader** is the dominant figure in the Senate but has less substantial powers than those of Speaker of the House. The majority leader has influence in committee assignments, assignment of office space, control of access to the floor of the Senate, and scheduling of Senate business. The power of the position is personal and not institutional: the degree of actual influence is based less on formal powers than on skills such as personal persuasion. The **minority leader** exercises less power than the Majority Leader, but a skilled politician can use the position to articulate the minority legislative program and force concessions from the majority.

Congressional Committees-Most of the work of Congress takes place in its **committees** and **subcommittees**. Committees are where many of the details of legislation are hammered out and where much of the details of legislation are hammered out and where much of the overnight of executive branch agencies takes place. Congressional Committees in the United States are more important in policymaking than other democratic nations such as Great Britain.

Why Congress Has Committees-They serve as *screening* devices, allowing only a small percentage of bills to take up the time of the parent legislative bodies, and thereby allow Congress to rationally process the huge flow of business that comes before it. They permit *specialization* because members of staff develop expertise to handle complex issues and to face executive branch experts on equal terms. They are useful to members of Congress who use their committee positions to *enhance their chances for reelection*; a legislator usually tries to secure committee assignments that will permit efficient servicing of his or her constituency. The principle of **seniority** generally prevails in the appointment of committee chairs. Getting on the right committee is important for reelection and for achieving the policy goals of members of Congress.

Types of Committees in Congress-There are several kinds of committees, each of which serves a special function in the legislative process.

Standing Committees-These are **permanent committees** organized to be first stop for potential new laws. The size of the standing committees and their subject-matter jurisdiction in today's Congress were set in the Legislative Reorganization Act of 1946. The ratio of Democrats to Republicans on each committee is set through negotiations between the majority and minority leaders.

Because of Congress's workload, negotiations, **hearings**, and **markup** (rewriting a bill in committee) concerning bills take place in subcommittees. Congressional committees were decentralized in the 1970s as they grew in number, but during the 1990s, this pattern of committee expansion was reversed as leadership agreed that congressional effectiveness was being undermined by radical decentralization.

Select Committees-These committees are temporary committees created to conduct studies or investigations. They have no power to send bills to the House or Senate floor. They exist to resolve matters that standing committees cannot or do not wish to handle. Select committees investigated the Watergate scandal, the Iran-Contra affair, and other issues and events.

Joint Committees-These are committees consisting of members from both houses that are organized to facilitate the flow of legislation. Before a bill can go to the president for signature, it must pass in identical form in each chamber. The committee that irons out the differences between the House and the Senate versions is called a **conference committee**, and one is created anew for each piece of major legislation. Some political observers call conference committees the "third house of Congress." Much of the power of conference committees comes from the fact that bills reported by them to the House and Senate must be voted up or down; no new amendments are allowed.

How Congress Members Get on Committees-Being on the right committee is important for reelection and for achieving policy goals. Committee assignments are determined by the political parties, guided by the members' **seniority** and preferences. Democrats use a Steering Committee, chaired by their floor leader, to make committee assignments. House Republicans use a Steering Committee on which the Speaker has control of one-fourth of the votes, to make assignments. In the Senate, both parties use small steering committees made up of party veterans and leaders to make assignments. The seniority principle usually prevails in the appointment of committee and subcommittee chairs. **Ranking minority** members are the most senior members of the minority party on a committee.

The Role of Committee Chairs-Committee chairs have periodically held a great deal of influence in Congress. From 1910 to 1970, committee chairs held substantial power (at the expense of the Speaker of the House). During the early to mid 1990s, a more assertive Speaker of the House weakened committee chair positions. Committee chairs remain the most influential and active members of their committees. They cannot command obedience, but they are at the center of all of the lines of communication, retain the power to schedule meetings and control the agenda, control the committee staff, manage committee funds, appoint members to conference committees, to whom some deference is owed.

Rules and Norms in the House and Senate-Congress is guided by both formal rules and informal norms of behavior. **Norms** are generally accepted expectations about how people ought to behave and how business ought to proceed, while **rules** specify how things should be done and what is not allowed. The norm of **reciprocity** (mutual deference) is particularly important in the House of Representatives. Members of the House are expected to become specialists in some area or areas of policy, and members are expected to defer to the judgment of specialists on most bills. It would be unusual for a member of the House to introduce major bills during his or her first term in office. The norm of reciprocity is much less evident in the Senate; a senator has more prestige and power than a representative, and senators are generally unwilling to wait their turn for a term or two. The House is much more **rule-bound** than the Senate because of its large size. The House tends to be more organized and hierarchical, and debate on the floor is limited. Leaders have more power, procedures are more structured, and individual members have a harder time making a name for themselves. The atmosphere in the Senate is more relaxed and informal than in the House; each senator is more independent than House counterparts. Senate rules provide for unrestricted floor debate unless it is shortened by **unanimous consent** (which means that business can be blocked by a single dissenter) or ended by **cloture**. Senators may try to talk a bill to death through the **filibuster**.

282

→ LEGISLATIVE RESPONSIBILITIES: HOW A BILL BECOMES A LAW

It is relatively easy to block bills from becoming laws. At each step along the way, a "no" decision can stop the passage of a bill in its tracks. Only about six percent of all bills that are introduced in Congress are enacted into law.

Introducing a Bill-Although bills can be introduced only by a member of Congress, they are often written in the executive branch or even by interest groups. In the House, a member introduces a bill by putting it into the **hopper** (a box watched over by one of the House clerks). In the Senate, a member must announce a bill to the body after being recognized by the presiding officer. The bill is then assigned a number, with the prefix *H.R.* in the House *S.* in the Senate. The lawmaker who introduces the bill or resolution is known as the sponsor.

Committee Action on a Bill-The presiding officer in the Senate and the Speaker of the House *refer the bill* to the appropriate *standing committee*. Committee chairs will normally pass the bill to the appropriate *subcommittee*. Most bills die at this stage, when either the subcommittee or the full committee declines to consider it further. Only bills that receive a *favorable* report from the committee are likely to be heard by the parent body. Only a small percentage will be favorably reported back to the floor. A **discharge petition** signed by a majority of House members can force a committee to relinquish control over a bill, but this procedure is rarely successful. If a bill is accepted for consideration, the subcommittee generally holds hearings, taking testimony from people for and against it. The bill is debated and negotiated and possibly rewritten. The subcommittee then may submit the bill to the full committee, under the directions of the chair, the committee may simply **rubber-stamp** the bill and move it along for floor action.

Floor Action on a Bill-Congressional leaders schedule a bill for **floor debate** if it is favorably reported from committee. In the House of Representatives, a bill will normally go to the **Rules Committee** for a *rule* (the terms under which the bill will be considered), such as the time for debate and the number—if any—of amendments allowed). The Rules Committee may choose not to issue a rule, to drag its feet, or to grant a **closed rule** that does not permit amendments. Floor debate is more important in the Senate where committees are less influential than in the House. By contrast, rules in the Senate do not limit debate. After the floor debate, the entire membership of the chamber votes on a bill, either as reported by the committee or (more often), after amendments have been added. If the bill receives a favorable vote, it then goes through the same obstacle course in the other chamber or awaits action by the other house if the bill was introduced there at the same time.

Conference Committee-Conflicting versions of a bill must be rewritten by a *conference committee* so that a single bill gains the approval of both houses before it is sent to the president. A bill from a conference committee must be voted yes or no on the floor of both chambers. If both houses approve it, the bill is forwarded to the president for consideration.

Presidential Action-The president (or his aides) is aware of the bill and its status throughout the legislative process. He can sign the bill into law, he can take no action and allow it to become law within tens days, or he can **veto** it and return it to Congress. A president can also kill a bill at the end of a congressional session if he **pocket vetoes** it by taking no action and Congress adjourns before ten days pass.

Legislative Oversight of the Executive Branch-Oversight is another important responsibility of Congress. Oversight is keeping an eye on how the executive branch carries out the provisions of the laws that Congress has passed and on possible abuses of power by executive branch officials, including the president.

The subcommitees and committees are chiefly responsible for oversight. Also, hearings are an important part of the oversight process. Congress also spends an increasing amount of time on oversight. Congress usually pays attention to matters brought to them by others, mainly by constituents, the media, and interest groups. Finally, Congress's most powerful instrument of oversight of the Executive Branch is impeachment.

Congress and the American People-The way Congress is organized and operates greatly influences the kinds of public policies we have, how people feel about government, and the quality of democracy.

Congress as a Policymaker- Some argue that Congress is so parochial and fragmented that it cannot fashion coherent public policy. First, Congress is filled with members who are concerned with constituent approval and reelection. Lawmakers worry more about themselves than about the standing and effectiveness of their institution or its collective national policymaking responsibilities. Second, because lawmakers are responsive to organized interests, serve the constituency as their first order of business, and try to avoid difficult decisions that might put their reelection at risk, Congress would rather practice "distributive" politics in which benefits are parceled out to a wide range of constituency and interest groups claimants. Your authors contend that the evidence concerning these arguments is mixed. Congress has functioned best as a policymaker when the president, supported by the existence of a national majority in favor of a particular course of action, is able to provide strong leadership.

Congress and the American People-Americans tend to approve of the representatives of their own states, but not of Congress in general; they have low regard for Congress as an institution. Scholars offer various views to explain this. Among them is the view that it indicates rising partisanship, grid-lock between Congress and the president, and the apparent influence in Congress of special interests. Others suggest that the American people are turned off by the messy process of politics and prefer that the job be done quietly and efficiently.

→ SUMMARY

The Framers of the Constitution wanted to fashion a legislative branch that was both energetic and limited. They granted Congress legislative power, gave it an existence independent of the executive branch, and enumerated many powers. They also provided for a system of checks and balances and separation of powers, created a bicameral body, and strictly denied certain powers to Congress. There have been many influences on how Congress does its business. It has become more institutionalizes and professional than the Framers probably intended.

The authors contend that Congress is a representative institution. Its members are constantly balancing the preferences of constituents, contributors, and interest groups. Elections dominate the time and energy of lawmakers and shape how Congress organizes itself and goes about its business. Congress does its work through subcommittees and committees. Other tools help the members coordinate and expedite legislative business.

This section gives you a comprehensive review of the chapter. Use this outline in combination with your textbook to look for key concepts and objectives, to identify essential terms and names, and to gain a basic understanding of political practices and principles from this chapter.

I. **INTRODUCTION TO PART FOUR: GOVERNMENT AND GOVERNING (p. 303)**
   A. The chapters in Part Four examine how government institutions operate and how and why public officials behave as they do while in office.
   B. The chapters in this part assume that government institutions and public officials can only be *understood in their structural and political contexts*.
      1. What government does is influenced strongly by structural factors (such as constitutional rules, the economy, the political culture, the nature of the population, and the nation's place in the world).
      2. The actions of government are also shaped by political linkage institutions (such as elections, parties, interest groups, public opinion, and social movements), which transmit the preferences of individuals and groups to public officials.
   C. Democracy is the evaluative thread that runs through each chapter.
      1. The text asks about the degree to which federal government institutions and public officials advance or retard the practice of democracy.

2. The authors of your textbook conclude that democratic practices have gradually improved over the years, but that significant barriers to the full realization of democracy still exist.

II. THE 2000 CONGRESSIONAL ELECTIONS (HERE) (pp. 305-306)

A. This chapter examines how Congress works as a representative and a governing institution.

1. The text focuses on how the ability and willingness of the members of Congress to meet their complex responsibilities is affected by a variety of actors and institutions.

2. The authors address the question of the democratic character of Congress and how the struggle for democracy has affected its development.

B. Republicans are in a position to exercise considerable power on a number of fronts, including investigations of President Clinton and his judicial and executive branch appointments. They have maintained a majority of the seats in both chambers of Congress since the 1992 elections.

III. STRUCTURAL FOUNDATIONS OF THE MODERN CONGRESS (pp. 307-311)

A. A number of structural factors have strongly shaped how the modern Congress works. The most important of these factors are reviewed in this section.

B. **Constitutional design**

1. The framers of the Constitution were ambivalent about democracy and concerned about the possibility of government tyranny, but they also wanted an energetic government capable of accomplishing its assigned tasks. These multiple objectives and concerns are reflected in the constitutional design of Congress.

2. **Empowering Congress**

a) The constitutional rules they established significantly affect what Congress is like today. The Framers intended for the legislative branch to be the center of policymaking.

b) **Article I, Section I,** of the Constitution, gave Congress the power to make the laws: "All legislative power herein granted shall be vested in a Congress of the United States." For the Framers, Congress was the to be the main bearer of federal government powers.

c) In listing its powers and responsibilities in *Article I Section 8*—the **enumerated powers**—they were largely defining the powers of the federal government itself. The Framers enhanced the enumerated powers of Congress by adding the **elastic clause**, granting broad power to Congress to pass whatever legislation was necessary to carry out its enumerated powers.

d) Defines responsibilities of the House of Representatives and the Senate that are specific to only one chamber

(1) House of Representatives—originates revenue bills; power to bring *impeachment* charges
(2) Senate—power of *advice and consent* over appointments and treaties; power to try impeachment charges.

3. **Constraining Congress**
   a) Although the framers wanted to create an energetic government with a strong legislative branch, they also wanted to limit congressional power in order to prevent tyranny.
   b) Congress is divided into *two houses* (**bicameralism**), following the precedent set by the British Parliament; this was consistent with the **republican** idea that laws should be made only after thoughtful deliberation.
   c) Prohibitions in **Article I, Section 9**
      (1) **Bills of attainder**—a legislative act that declares a person guilty of a crime and imposes punishment without a judicial trial
      (2) *Ex post facto* **laws**—retroactive criminal legislation
      (3) Right to a writ of *habeas corpus* may be suspended only in times of rebellion or invasion—a court order demanding that a prisoner be brought to court, where cause must be shown for his or her detention
      (4) Granting titles of nobility
   d) The **Bill of Rights** added other prohibitions; the **First Amendment** (perhaps the most important constitutional stipulation protecting political liberty) begins with the words "Congress shall make no law."
4. Although the framers saw the legislative branch as the vital center of a vigorous national government, they made sure that Congress was surrounded by *competing centers of government power*.
   a) They created separate legislative, executive, and judicial branches (**separation of powers**) and gave each of them some role to play in the activities of the others (**checks and balances**) (see *The Federalist, No.51*, in the Appendix); designed to prevent *tyranny*.
   b) This *fragmentation of governmental power* affects how Congress works and makes it difficult to fashion coherent and effective public policies.
5. **Bicameralism and representation**
   a) Congress is organized into two legislative chambers with different principles of representation as well as different constitutional responsibilities.
   b) With the Great Compromise, the Framers created two "**virtually autonomous chambers**," the **House of Representatives** which was apportioned on the basis of population and the **Senate** on the basis of equal representation of the states. In the House, terms of office for members was set at two years. In the Senate, terms of office for members was set at six years, with only one-third of the seats up for election in each two-year election cycle.
C. **Representation in Congress**

1. **Apportionment** was established through the **Great Compromise,** based on population in the House of Representatives and on equal representation of the states in the Senate (which enhanced the power of states with small populations).
2. Originally, the Constitution provided for the election of senators by state legislatures, not by the people. This was changed by the passage of the **Seventeenth Amendment** (1913).
   a) The Constitution also assigns particular responsibilities to each of the legislative chambers such as the House's power to bring charges of impeachment against the president for "high crimes and misdemeanors," which it did in the case of Bill Clinton.
   b) The Senate has the power to conduct the trial of the president and remove him from office, if the impeachment charges are proved to its satisfaction.

D. **Federalism**
   1. In our **federal system**, some powers and responsibilities are granted to the national government, some are shared, and some are reserved for the states.
   2. It is inevitable that conflicts will occur between state governments and the national government.
   3. Such conflicts sometimes reach the Supreme Court for resolution as it did in *United States v. Lopez (1995),* where the Court ruled that Congress had gone too far in the use of its commerce clause powers when it passed a law banning firearms in and around public schools. The Court felt that this was a state, not federal issue.

   4. Federalism also infuses localism into congressional affairs: because members of Congress come to Washington as the representatives of states and districts, they inevitably consider local concerns when making national policies.

IV. **REPRESENTATION AND DEMOCRACY (pp. 311-322)**
   A. This section of your text asks whether members of Congress carry out the *representative* responsibility in a way that can be considered *democratic.*
   B. **Styles of Representation**
   1. English parliamentarian and philosopher **Edmund Burke** described two principal styles of representation in 1774.
      a) **Delegate** theory—the representative tries to reflect the views of his or her constituents
      b) **Trustee** theory—the representative acts independently and uses his or her best judgment of the issues
   2. In the U.S. Congress, senators and representatives without real electoral competition can afford to choose the trustee style, and senators (who have six-year terms) usually have more latitude than representatives (with two-year terms) to assume this style.

3. Burke believed in the trustee style and **Abraham Lincoln** advocated the delegate style.

C. **Members of Congress: race, gender and occupation**

1. **Gender and Race**-One way to represent is to be similar to that which is being represented, to reflect the basic characteristics of the constituency such as race, gender, ethnicity, occupation, religion, age, and so forth. In this sense, the U.S. Congress is highly *unrepresentative.*

    a) Even though there were examples of African-American congressmen in New York City and Chicago, their numbers only began to increase in the 1960s.

    b) Between the 104th and 106th Congresses, their numbers increased from 26 to 37 representatives; this number is still well below the proportion of blacks in the American population.

    c) All but four twentieth-century African-American representatives were Democrats; in the 106th Congress, only one black member of Congress was Republican.

2. Though **Hispanics** are even more poorly represented than African-Americans relative to their proportion of the population, the increase in their number in recent years has given the Hispanic caucus more influence than in the past. Only six served in the 106th Congress. Only one **Native American** holds a seat in the U.S. Senate.

3. The first woman to sit in Congress was Jeannette Rankin of Montana, a suffragist and pacifist, in 1916. In 1992, considered by many to be the "**year of the woman**," 48 women were elected to the House of Representatives and 7 to the Senate.

    a) In 1992, Carol Moseley Braun (D-Ill) became the first African-American woman to be elected to the Senate (she lost her seat in the 1998 election).

    b) Women are grossly underrepresented in Congress compared to their slim majority status among American citizens. Leadership on important committees continue to elude women in Congress.

4. **Occupation**

    a) Members of Congress also tend to come from wealthy families. They are better educated than the remainder of the population and come from relatively few occupational backgrounds, particularly from legal, business and banking industries.

    b) Individuals with blue-collar backgrounds are noticeably absent. Some question whether it matters that Congress is demographically unrepresentative.

    c) Some observers suggest that the need to face the electorate forces lawmakers to be attentive to all significant groups in their **constituencies**, regardless of their own backgrounds.

        (1) However, many who are not represented (such as women, racial minorities, and the poor) believe that their interests would get a better hearing if their numbers were substantially increased in Congress.

        (2) The demographic disparity suggests a violation of the norm of **political equality**, an important element of **democracy**.

D. **The Electoral connection**
1. The election is the principal instrument in a democracy for linking citizens to government officials.
2. Congressional elections affect the quality of representation in the United States.
3. **Electoral districts**
   a) Each state is entitled to two senators.
   b) Equal representation in the Senate gives extraordinary power in the legislative process to small states. This arrangement can substantially distort popular sentiment, and in this way can diminish democracy.
4. **Reapportionment**
   a) Representation in the House of Representatives is based on population, with **reapportionment** based on the national **census** every 10 years. State legislatures draw the boundary lines, and the party that controls the state legislature will usually try to draw district lines in a way that will help them win elections.
   b) After the census some states keep the same number of seats; others gain or lose them. The Supreme Court ruled in *Wesberry v. Sanders* (1964) that the principle of **one person, one vote** applies to how congressional districts are drawn.
   c) **Gerrymandering** occurs when boundary lines are drawn to ensure the election of a particular party, group, or person (the term dates to the 1811 redistricting process when Governor **Elbridge Gerry** of Massachusetts signed a bill that created a district that looked like a salamander to editorial cartoonists).
   d) The 1982 amendments to the **1965 Voting Rights Act**, which encouraged the states to create House districts in which racial minorities would be in the majority, resulted in the formation of 24 new **majority-minority districts** (districts drawn purposely so that a racial minority is the majority); the Supreme Court first encouraged the creation of majority-minority districts, then appeared to have second thoughts about districts that are highly irregular in form, noncontiguous, and unconnected to traditional political jurisdictions (*Shaw v. Reno*, 1993), or that are drawn solely to aid one race (*Miller v. Johnson*, 1955).

E. **Money and congressional elections**
1. This chapter also looks at the relationship between money and congressional elections. Running for a congressional seat is very expensive, and keeps getting more expensive.
   a) Although the candidate who spends the most money does not always win, the amount of money spent is related to the probability of winning.
   b) *Incumbents* (who need the funds the least) have the easiest time raising money

and they spend the most in races for both houses. **Open-seat** election races in which no incumbent is involved, also attract and use lots of money.

    (1) Money to support congressional campaigns comes from four main sources: individuals, parties, the candidates, and **political action committees (PACs)**.

    (2) Contributions from PACs go primarily to incumbents. The largest share comes from individual contributors, PACs are the next largest contributor. This is the fastest growing part of the campaign financing system; PACs are free to spend without limit on general-issue campaigns that are often thinly veiled efforts to help a particular candidate or party (sometimes referred to as *parallel campaigns*).

2. Many people believe that the increased role of PACs also increases the influence of interest groups and business interests.

    (1) There are no legal limits on donations to the parties for general education, registration, and get-out-the-vote campaigns.

    (2) There are also no limits on how much of this *soft money* parties can spend, even though the spending obviously benefits individual candidates.

3. Republicans filibustered the 1997 *McCain-Feingold* campaign finance reform bill. But Democrats have been no more committed to serious reform either. Being the minority party in Congress, they had the luxury of allowing the Republicans to take the heat for blocking reform. The McCain-Feingold bill failed again in 1999.

F. **The incumbency factor**

1. **Incumbents**—current officeholders—win at much higher rates in the House today than ever before.

    a) The ability of House incumbents to get reelected improved especially from the late 1940s into the 1990s, allowing the Democratic Party to maintain control over the House of Representatives for four decades (from 1955 to 1994), even as Republicans like Dwight Eisenhower, Richard Nixon, Ronald Reagan, and George Bush were winning presidential elections.

    b) Incumbents are almost always successful in being re-elected.

2. **Why incumbents have the advantage**

    a) Incumbents attract contributions; PACs and interest groups want access to key decision makers; the flow of money is particularly heavy for those who sit on key committees or hold important leadership posts.

    b) Incumbents use congressional resources to advertise their accomplishments and keep their names before the public (although there are some restrictions designed to limit abuse).

        (1) The **franking privilege** allows members to mail newsletters, legislative updates, surveys, and other self-promoting literature free of charge.

        (2) Travel budgets permit lawmakers to make frequent visits back to their state or district.

(3) Incumbents use their offices to **service the district**.
  (a) **Casework**—helping constituents solve red-tape problems with the federal bureaucracy
  (b) **Pork** (derived from the expression "bringing home the bacon")—providing federal dollars in the form of contracts, facilities, and subsidies

3. **How representative**?
  a) Members of Congress may be doing a relatively good job of representing their constituents: research shows that members vote in conformity with majority opinion in their districts about two-thirds of the time.
  b) Congress produces laws that are consistent with national public opinion at about the same rate. Congress however, ignored public opinion on the impeachment of Bill Clinton.
  c) In many cases, Congress does **not** follow public opinion. Nevertheless, the **incumbency factor** should not be exaggerated: *turnover in Congress is significant* due to voluntary retirements, redistricting changes, and some electoral defeats.

V. **HOW CONGRESS WORKS (pp. 322-334)**
  A. Congress plays an important part in making policy; it remains the most powerful legislature among Western democratic nations. In this section, the text focuses on how Congress is organized and functions as a working legislative body.
  B. **The congressional agenda**
    1. The other branches of government are a constant influence on the congressional agenda.
      a) Congress exists in a rich structural, political, and governmental environment that helps determine its priorities.
      b) Federal courts may rule on the constitutionality of laws passed by Congress; if laws are overturned, they may be followed by legislative reaction.
      c) The president and the executive branch are important in shaping the legislative agenda; many bills originate in the executive branch, and much of what Congress does is in response to the legislative program of the president.
      d) Congress monitors how the president and the federal bureaucracy administer the laws.
      e) The Senate is responsible for approving or disapproving presidential appointments and treaties.
    2. The congressional agenda is also shaped by various groups and individuals, including interest groups, voters, constituents, the media, and social movements.
    3. Political and governmental institutions, groups, and individuals are mobilized by **structural change** such as economic dislocations, population change, and changes in the U.S. military position.
    4. The congressional agenda is also a product of its constitutional responsibilities.

a) For example, Congress is obligated to create the nation's budget which it does in a highly complex authorization and appropriation process.

b) Much of what Congress does by way of lawmaking is in response to the legislative program of the president, usually presented in conjunction with the annual **State of the Union**, economic, and budget messages.

   (1) Pressure groups and influential individuals also impact Congress's workload.

   (2) The media are continuous players in shaping what issues are attended to in the legislative branch.

c) Social movements also try to impose their own priorities on Congress. Finally, structural change mobilizes political and governmental institutions, groups, and individuals. Economic dislocations caused by the process of globalization often trigger demands for congressional action.

C. **Political parties in Congress**

1. At the start of each new Congress, each party caucus meets to select party committees and leaders.

   a) The majority party in Congress selects the Speaker of the House of Representatives, while the majority party in the Senate selects the president pro tempore (usually its most senior member) and the majority leader.

   b) The majority party in each house also selects the chairs of the committees and subcommittees and determined the party ratios for each.

2. **The party composition of Congress**

   a) The Democratic Party dominated the modern Congress until the 1994 elections. It was the majority party in the House of Representatives for all but four years between 1933 and 1994.

   b) In the Senate, Republicans were in the majority for only ten years during this same period. The Republicans have dominated both chambers since 1994.

3. **Party voting in Congress**

   a) Congress is *fragmented and decentralized* by the electoral needs of lawmakers and the organization of Congress along committee lines.

   b) At the opening of each new Congress, the two houses organize their legislative business along party lines. Party labels are important **cues** for members of Congress as they decide how to vote.

   c) *Party affiliation is the best predictor* of the voting behavior of members of Congress.

      (1) Both houses of Congress are becoming more *partisan.* It is not entirely clear whether party voting differences are caused directly by party affiliation or indirectly by the character of the constituencies.

      (2) Ideology, (Republican conservatism versus Democratic liberalism and centrism) strengthens the glue of party unity and increases partisanship.

D. **Congressional leadership**-The political parties also work through the leadership structure of Congress because the leaders of the majority political party are also the leaders of the House and Senate.

1. **Leadership in the House**
    a) **Speaker of the House**—leader of the House of Representatives; the Speaker is treated as the spokesperson on policymaking for the House and also for the majority party.
    b) He is in the line of succession to the presidency, following the vice-president.
        (1) Other powers of the Speaker include referral of bills to committee, control of the House agenda, appointment of select committees, and direction of floor debate.
        (2) There have been many powerful individual speakers, but the position was weakened until about 1974 when the Democratic Caucus staged a revolt against committee chairs and restored some of the powers of the Speaker, especially in making committee assignments.
        (3) **Newt Gingrich** was one of the most powerful Speakers of the House in recent history. He led the conservative Republican agenda with the **Contract with America** that ushered in a Republican congressional majority in 1994. By 1998 however, Gingrich resigned from his position amid protests against him after Republicans lost some of their numerical advantage in Congress after the election that year.
    c) Neither House nor party rules spell out the responsibilities of the office; the nature of the job depends very much on what the Speaker wants and on the current office holder's talents and energy.
2. The majority party in the House also selects a **majority floor leader** to help the Speaker plan strategy and manage the legislative business of the House.
    a) The minority party elects a **minority floor leader**, who serves as the chief spokesperson and legislative strategist for the opposition.
    b) The minority whip tries to mobilize the party and also seeks out members of the majority party who might be won over against the House leadership on key issues.
        (1) Each party has **party whips** who act as liaisons between the leaders and the rank and file, count heads on important bills, explain leadership positions, try to persuade members to vote with the party, gather legislative intelligence, and ensure that supporters get to the floor to cast their votes.
        (2) The 1998 elections brought changes in Republican party leadership positions.
3. **Leadership in the Senate**
    a) Senate Leadership is less visible than in the House, and those with formal leadership titles exercise little influence. The Vice-President of the United States serves as the presiding officer (**President of the Senate**). The office is designated by the U.S. Constitution, *not* elected by the House as are the other

leadership positions. The President of the Senate is seldom in attendance because this is essentially a ceremonial office with no power other than the right to vote to break a tie.

   b) The **president** *pro tempore* is the temporary presiding officer. This is also a ceremonial office, and the incumbent rarely acts as presiding officer.
   c) The **Senate majority leader** is the dominant figure in the Senate but has less substantial powers than those of Speaker of the House. The majority leader has influence in committee assignments, assignment of office space, control of access to the floor of the Senate, and scheduling of Senate business. The power of the position is personal and not institutional: the degree of actual influence is based less on formal powers than on skills such as personal persuasion.
   d) The **minority leader** exercises less power than the Majority Leader, but a skilled politician can use the position to articulate the minority legislative program and force concessions from the majority.

E. **Congressional committees**
   1. Most of the work of Congress takes place in its **committees** and **subcommittees**.
      a) Committees are where many of the details of legislation are hammered out and where much of the details of legislation are hammered out and where much of the overnight of executive branch agencies takes place.
      b) Congressional Committees in the United States are more important in policymaking than other democratic nations such as Great Britain.
   2. **Why Congress has committees**
      a) They serve as *screening* devices—allowing only a small percentage of bills to take up the time of the parent legislative bodies—and thereby allow Congress to rationally process the huge flow of business that comes before it.
      b) They permit *specialization*—members of staff develop expertise to handle complex issues and to face executive branch experts on equal terms.
      c) They are useful to members of Congress who use their committee positions to *enhance their chances for reelection*; legislators usually try to secure committee assignments that will permit efficient servicing of their constituencies.
   3. **Types of congressional committees**
      a) **Standing Committees**—relatively permanent committees that remain in existence from one congress to another, organized with *subject-matter* jurisdiction
         (1) House and Senate bills are normally referred first to one of the standing committees.
         (2) The *ratio* of Democrats to Republicans is set for each house through a process of negotiation between majority and minority party leaders; the majority party has a majority on each of the committees and controls the

chair, and it usually demands an extra-heavy majority on the most important committees.

    (3) Because of Congress's workload, negotiations, **hearings**, and **markup** (rewriting a bill in committee) concerning bills take place in subcommittees. Congressional committees were decentralized in the 1970s as they grew in number, but during the 1990s, this pattern of committee expansion was reversed as leadership agreed that congressional effectiveness was being undermined by radical decentralization.

  b) **Select committees**

    (1) These committees are temporary committees created to conduct studies or investigations. They have no power to send bills to the House or Senate floor. They exist to resolve matters that standing committees cannot or do not wish to handle.

    (2) Select committees investigated the Watergate scandal, the Iran-Contra affair, and other issues and events.

  c) **Joint committees**—comprised of members from both houses

    (1) Organized to expedite business and facilitate the flow of legislation

    (2) Before a bill can go to the president for signature, it must pass in identical form in each chamber. The committee that irons out the differences between the House and the Senate versions is called a **conference committee**, and one is created anew for each piece of major legislation.

    (3) Some political observers call conference committees the "third house of Congress." Much of the power of conference committees comes from the fact that bills reported by them to the House and Senate must be voted up or down; no new amendments are allowed.

    (4) House Republicans gave then-Speaker Newt Gingrich greatly broadened powers to create **ad hoc task forces** to handle legislative business closely associated with the Contract with America and other matters central to the Republican agenda, such as Medicare reform; Gingrich created over 30 such task forces in the 104th and 105th Congresses.

 4. **How Congress members get on committees**

  a) Being on the right committee is important for reelection and for achieving policy goals.

    (1) Committee assignments are determined by the political parties, guided by the members' **seniority** and preferences.

    (2) Democrats use a Steering Committee, chaired by their floor leader, to make committee assignments. House Republicans use a Steering Committee on which the Speaker has control of one-fourth of the votes, to make assignments.

  b) In the Senate, both parties use small steering committees made up of party veterans and leaders to make assignments. The seniority principle usually prevails in the appointment of committee and subcommittee chairs. **Ranking minority** members are the most senior members of the minority party on a committee.

5. **The role of committee chairs**
   a) Committee chairs have periodically held a great deal of influence in Congress. From 1910 to 1970, committee chairs held substantial power (at the expense of the Speaker of the House). During the early to mid 1990s, a more assertive Speaker of the House weakened committee chair positions.
   b) Committee chairs remain the most influential and active members of their committees. They cannot command obedience, but they are at the center of all of the lines of communication, retain the power to schedule meetings and control the agenda, control the committee staff, manage committee funds, appoint members to conference committees, to whom some deference is owed.

6. **Rules and norms in the House and Senate**
   a) Congress is guided by both formal rules and informal norms of behavior. **Norms** are generally accepted expectations about how people ought to behave and how business ought to proceed, while **rules** specify how things should be done and what is not allowed.
      (1) The norm of **reciprocity** (mutual deference) is particularly important in the House of Representatives. Members of the House are expected to become specialists in some area or areas of policy, and members are expected to defer to the judgment of specialists on most bills. It would be unusual for a member of the House to introduce major bills during his or her first term in office.
      (2) The norm of reciprocity is much less evident in the Senate; a senator has more prestige and power than a representative, and senators are generally unwilling to wait their turn for a term or two.
   b) The House is much more **rule-bound** than the Senate because of its large size. The House tends to be more organized and hierarchical, and debate on the floor is limited. Leaders have more power, procedures are more structured, and individual members have a harder time making a name for themselves.
   c) The atmosphere in the Senate is more relaxed and informal than in the House; each senator is more independent than House counterparts. Senate rules provide for unrestricted floor debate unless it is shortened by **unanimous consent** (which means that business can be blocked by a single dissenter) or ended by **cloture**. Senators may try to talk a bill to death through the **filibuster**.

VI. LEGISLATIVE RESPONSIBILITIES: HOW A BILL BECOMES A LAW (pp. 334-339)

A. It is relatively easy to block bills from becoming laws. At each step along the way, a "no" decision can stop the passage of a bill in its tracks. Only about six percent of all bills that are introduced in Congress are enacted into law.

B. Introducing a bill
1. Although bills can be introduced only by a member of Congress, they are often written in the executive branch or even by interest groups.
   a) In the House, a member introduces a bill by putting it into the **hopper** (a box watched over by one of the House clerks).
   b) In the Senate, a member must announce a bill to the body after being recognized by the presiding officer. The bill is then assigned a number, with the prefix *H.R.* in the House *S.* in the Senate.
2. The lawmaker who introduces the bill or resolution is known as the sponsor.

C. Committee action on a bill
1. The presiding officer in the Senate and the Speaker of the House *refer the bill* to the appropriate *standing committee*. Committee chairs will normally pass the bill to the appropriate *subcommittee*.
   a) Most bills die at this stage, when either the subcommittee or the full committee declines to consider it further. Only bills that receive a *favorable* report from the committee are likely to be heard by the parent body. Only a small percentage will be favorably reported back to the floor.
   b) A **discharge petition** signed by a majority of House members can force a committee to relinquish control over a bill, but this procedure is rarely successful. If a bill is accepted for consideration, the subcommittee generally holds hearings, taking testimony from people for and against it.
2. The bill is debated and negotiated and possibly rewritten. The subcommittee then may submit the bill to the full committee, under the directions of the chair, the committee may simply **rubber-stamp** the bill and move it along for floor action.

D. Floor action on a bill
1. Congressional leaders schedule a bill for **floor debate** if it is favorably reported from committee.
   a) In the House of Representatives, a bill will normally go to the **Rules Committee** for a *rule* (the terms under which the bill will be considered), such as the time for debate and the number—if any—of amendments allowed).
   b) The Rules Committee may choose not to issue a rule, to drag its feet, or to grant a **closed rule** that does not permit amendments. Floor debate is more important in the Senate where committees are less influential than in the House.
   c) By contrast, rules in the Senate do not limit debate. After the floor debate, the entire membership of the chamber votes on a bill, either as reported by the committee or (more often), after amendments have been added.
2. If the bill receives a favorable vote, it then goes through the same obstacle course in the other chamber or awaits action by the other house if the bill was introduced there at the same time.

E. **Conference committee**
   1. Conflicting versions of a bill must be rewritten by a *conference committee* so that a single bill gains the approval of both houses before it is sent to the president. A bill from a conference committee must be voted **yes or no** on the floor of both chambers.
   2. If both houses approve it, the bill is forwarded to the president for consideration.
F. **Presidential action**
   1. The president (or his aides) is aware of the bill and its status throughout the legislative process. He can sign the bill into law, he can take no action and allow it to become law within tens days, or he can **veto** it and return it to Congress.
   2. A president can also kill a bill at the end of a congressional session if he **pocket vetoes** it by taking no action and Congress adjourns before ten days pass.
G. **Legislative oversight of the executive branch**
   1. Oversight is another important responsibility of Congress. Oversight is keeping an eye on how the executive branch carries out the provisions of the laws that Congress has passed and on possible abuses of power by executive branch officials, including the president.
   2. The subcommittees and committees are chiefly responsible for oversight. Also, hearings are an important part of the oversight process. Congress also spends an increasing amount of time on oversight. Congress usually pays attention to matters brought to them by others, mainly by constituents, the media, and interest groups. Finally, Congress's most powerful instrument of oversight of the Executive Branch is impeachment.

VII. **CONGRESS, PUBLIC POLICY AND THE AMERICAN PEOPLE (pp. 339-340)**
   A. The way Congress is organized and operates greatly influences the kinds of public policies we have, how people feel about government, and the quality of democracy.
   B. **Congress as a Policymaker**
      1. Some argue that Congress is so parochial and fragmented that it cannot fashion coherent public policy.
         a) First, Congress is filled with members who are concerned with constituent approval and reelection. Lawmakers worry more about themselves than about the standing and effectiveness of their institution or its collective national policymaking responsibilities.
         b) Second, because lawmakers are responsive to organized interests, serve the constituency as their first order of business, and try to avoid difficult decisions that might put their reelection at risk, Congress would rather practice "distributive" politics in which benefits are parceled out to a wide range of constituency and interest groups claimants.
      2. Your authors contend that the evidence concerning these arguments is mixed. Congress has functioned best as a policymaker when the president, supported by

the existence of a national majority in favor of a particular course of action, is able to provide strong leadership.

C. **Congress and the American people**
   1. Americans tend to approve of the representatives of their own states, but not of Congress in general; they have low regard for Congress as an institution.
   2. Scholars offer various views to explain this. Among them is the view that it indicates rising partisanship, grid-lock between Congress and the president, and the apparent influence in Congress of special interests.

D. Others suggest that the American people are turned off by the messy process of politics and prefer that the job be done quietly and efficiently

VIII. SUMMARY (p. 341)
   A. The Framers of the Constitution wanted to fashion a legislative branch that was both energetic and limited.
   B. They granted Congress legislative power, gave it an existence independent of the executive branch, and enumerated many powers.
   C. They also provided for a system of checks and balances and separation of powers, created a bicameral body, and strictly denied certain powers to Congress. There have been many influences on how Congress does its business. It has become more institutionalizes and professional than the Framers probably intended.

Terms for Review

Use this list to review essential principles, functions, and concepts from this chapter. Refer to your textbook for help in identifying and defining terms on this list. When you study, do not merely memorize terms; ask questions about the material you are reviewing, and look for the importance or significance of each item.

ad hoc task force

advise and consent

bicameralism

bill

bills of attainder

casework

caucus

checks and balances

closed rule

cloture

committee of the whole

committee system

concurrent resolution

conference committees

congressional staff

conservative coalition

constituency

constituent

Contract with America

delegate

discharge petition

elastic clause

enumerated powers

ex post facto

filibuster

floor debate

franking privilege

gerrymander

habeas corpus

hearings

hopper

impeachment

implied powers

incumbent

joint committees

joint resolution

majority and minority floor leaders

majority-minority districts

markup

norms and rules

open seat election

oversight

party caucus

partisan

pocket veto

political action committees (PACs)

"pork"

President of the Senate

private bill

public bill

ranking minority member

reapportionment

reciprocity

resolution

Rules Committee

screening

select committee

seniority

separation of powers

soft money

Speaker of the House

standing committees

Steering and Policy Committee

subcommittees

trustee

unanimous consent

veto

voting cues

whip

Research Topics: Applying What You Have Learned

You will derive more benefit from your reading if you try to apply what you have learned. Some of the suggested research topics can be answered exclusively from your text, while others require

*you to conduct some basic research on your own. The references suggested **under Internet Sources** will help you in your search.*

- Identify which members of your state's delegation hold leadership positions in Congress. You should establish characteristics such as age, gender, religion, race, and previous occupation. How closely do these characteristics correspond with national averages given in the textbook? You may want to refer first to *Politics in America* (published by Congressional Quarterly Press) and *The Almanac of American Politics* (published by National Journal Press) as sources for leadership positions. The Internet is an excellent tool for this purpose.

- Prepare a brief evaluation of your own member of the U.S. House of Representatives. How often does he or she visit the home district? What committees does your legislator serve on? How accessible is your legislator? Are you aware of your representative's policy positions? If not, is it because your congressperson has not taken clear stands, or is it due to your own lack of awareness? (You may want to review your legislator's roll call votes in the *Congressional Quarterly Weekly Report*.)

- The following quotation is from Alexander Hamilton in *The Federalist* No. 51: "In republican government, the legislative authority naturally predominates. The remedy for this inconvenience is to divide the legislature into different branches...." Given the many structural and political changes that have occurred since the Constitution was written, how would you evaluate Hamilton's statement *from a current perspective*?

Internet Sources

A number of sites on the World Wide Web serve as "gateways" to vast collections of material on American government and politics. The following Internet resources are recommended for students who would like to do some additional research in the areas covered by this chapter. These references would also be helpful in expanding on the questions suggested under Research Topics.

Capweb www.capweb.net
An extremely rich site for information on Congress. Features include commentary on the issues before Congress, access to information on pending legislation, legislative schedules and ways to contact members of Congress, caucuses, committees, rules, histories of the House and Senate,

and much more. Links, as well, to Congressional Quarterly *(journal) and* The Hill *(weekly newspaper), the House and Senate, and the other two federal branches.*

Federal Election Commission http://www.fec.gov/
Information on campaign finance for presidential and congressional elections.

Thomas http://thomas.loc.gov/
Expansive repository of information on the House of Representatives, including the full text and progress of bills, the Congressional Record, legislative procedures and rules, committee actions, and more.

U.S. House of Representatives Home Page http://www.house.gov/
House schedule, House organization and procedures, links to House committees, information on contacting representatives, and historical documents on the House of Representatives.

U.S. Senate Home Page http://www.senate.gov/
Similar to the House of Representatives Home Page, focused on the Senate. One exciting new feature is a virtual tour of the Capitol.

Circle the correct answer for each question. Questions are listed in the same order in which the information appears in the text. Use the Answer Key in the back of the Study Guide *to check your responses.*

1. Conference committees
   a. Are among the important standing committees of Congress.
   b. Handle hearings on bills that are too technical for the select committees.
   c. Are elected by vote of the House and Senate.
   d. Reconcile conflicting versions of a bill in the House and Senate.

2. The original Constitution called for
   a. Direct election of senators by the people.
   b. Indirect election of senators through an electoral college.
   c. Election of senators by state legislatures.
   d. Appointment of senators by the president.

3. Which statement correctly describes the composition of Congress following the 1996 elections?
    a. Control of Congress has alternated equally between the two major parties for the past half-century.
    b. The Republican party gained control of both houses of Congress for the first time in more than 40 years.
    c. The Republican party lost several seats in the House of Representatives but maintained its majority position in both the House and Senate.
    d. The president's party has won control of Congress in every presidential election year since the Eisenhower era.

4. Congressional **casework** includes
    a. Filing legal briefs on behalf of public interest groups.
    b. Helping constituents solve red-tape problems with the federal bureaucracy.
    c. Intervening with police when constituents are held without reasonable bail.
    d. Introducing legislation that would regulate the judicial branch.

5. Legislative **oversight** involves
    a. Maintaining control over expenditures by congressional staff.
    b. Keeping an eye on how the executive branch carries out the provisions of congressional statutes.
    c. Regulating the activities of lobbyists and political action committees.
    d. Establishing procedures for implementation of congressional codes of conduct.

6. The demographic make-up of Congress
    a. Is basically representative of the demographic balance of the U.S. population.
    b. Has remained virtually unchanged for 200 years.
    c. Overrepresents women and ethnic minorities.
    d. Suggests some violation of the norm of political equality.

7. The framers of the Constitution wanted the legislative branch to be
    a. The center of policymaking for the federal government.
    b. Unlimited in power over the federal government.
    c. Subordinate to the executive branch.
    d. Combined with the executive, similar to the British system.

8. What is the single best predictor we have concerning the voting behavior of members of Congress?
    a. Tradition
    b. Political party
    c. Ideology

d. Presidential leadership

9. Which of these statements is correct?
   a. Candidates from both major parties spend such enormous amounts of money on campaigns that the amount spent by either candidate has little relationship to the final outcome.
   b. Incumbents are reelected in such high numbers that they are able to spend relatively limited funds, and are usually outspent by their opponents.
   c. Federal campaign law now strictly limit the amounts of money that can be spent campaigning for Congress.
   d. Although the candidate who spends the most money does not always win, the amount of money spent is related to the probability of winning.

10. The **trustee theory** of representation calls on representatives to
    a. Reflect the views of his or her constituents.
    b. Use his or her own best judgment of the issues.
    c. Represent the views of his or her political party.
    d. Concentrate on the needs of organized interest groups.

11. Which of these conclusions was reached by the authors of your textbook concerning the relationship between Congress and democracy?
    a. Congress is frequently an effective instrument of democracy.
    b. Congress is primarily an undemocratic institution.
    c. Congress is sometimes democratic but it is less democratic than European parliaments.
    d. Congress is democratic because members are popularly elected, but it is not effective in governing.

12. Which of these is NOT one of the purposes of congressional committees?
    a. They consolidate bills and resolutions so that some parts of most proposals are eventually voted on by the House and Senate.
    b. They become areas of specialization whose members and staff develop expertise to handle complex issues.
    c. They are useful to members of Congress who use their committee positions to generate benefits for their districts or states.
    d. They serve as screening devices, allowing only a small percentage of bills to take up the time of the parent legislative bodies.

13. (T/F) As Congress grew in size and considered more complex issues, it became less institutionalized and professionalized.

14. (T/F) Congressional **rules** specify how things should be done and what is not allowed.

15. (T/F) Fragmentation of governmental power in the United States makes it difficult for Congress to fashion coherent and effective public policies.

16. (T/F) Republicans are in a position to exercise considerable power on a number of fronts in the 106th Congress (1999-2001), including continued investigations of President Clinton and his judicial and executive branch appointments and policies.

17. (T/F) The **advantage of incumbency** means than incumbents can only be removed from office by impeachment or resignation.

18. (T/F) The evidence presented by the authors of your textbook suggests that Congress is generally unresponsive even when the public is aware of issues and expresses its opinion.

Chapter 12
THE PRESIDENT

Key Concepts and Objectives

The Key Concepts and Objectives provide a look at the fundamental goals and ideas of this chapter. This section serves as a guide to a basic understanding of the objectives of your textbook.

After reading this chapter, you should be able to:

- Explain how and why the presidency has expanded into a more powerful office than the one envisioned by the framers of the Constitution.
- Determine how individual presidents have been important in expanding the scope of the office of president.
- Identify the key aides who are the president's closest and most trusted advisers, and describe their basic functions.
- Explain why different presidents with differing parties or philosophies often seem to pursue similar policies.
- Understand why the president is not able to maintain a firm control over the bureaucracy and the executive branch of government.
- Identify the many "hats" that a president must wear, as suggested by Clinton Rossiter.
- Explain why presidents are often at odds with Congress, and determine what factors tend to make a president successful in relations with Congress.
- Understand why different types of presidents often pursue very similar policies.
- Explain how presidents both react to and manipulate public opinion.
- Determine whether presidents listen to the public and respond to public preferences.
- Identify changes that have led to the democratizing of the presidency, and evaluate how democratic the presidency is today.
- Identify key terms and concepts used in Chapter 12

This section provides a brief overview of the chapter contents. Read this section as a preview before reading your textbook. Then use this material as a review to help you retain information from your reading.

→THE REAGAN REVOLUTION

The opening vignette illustrates the effects of the "Reagan Revolution." When Ronald Reagan took office in 1981, he interpreted his landslide victory as a *mandate* to pursue sweeping changes—he promised sweeping cuts in taxes, federal programs, and regulations as a way "to get government off the backs of the people," and a rapid buildup of U.S. armed forces as a way to regain respect and influence in the world. Tax and budget proposals were given top priority in what Reagan announced as his Program for Economic Recovery. Reagan got most of what he wanted in domestic budget cuts and the defense buildup. Politicians were impressed by the scale of Reagan's electoral victory and by the height of his popularity. The "Reagan Revolution" had profound effects, not all of them positive—although some economic growth occurred, the legacies of the 1980s included a massive increase in the national debt (which *tripled* in the Reagan years), deterioration in the international trade position of the United States, and dramatic increases in the scale of income and wealth inequality. Social programs, though not cut as drastically as Reagan wanted, remained under severe pressure in later years because less tax revenue was available. Nevertheless, the Reagan Revolution was a huge political success, and played a role in the resurgence of the Republican Party and its eventual capture of Congress in 1994. To understand the Reagan Revolution, we need to consider not only the personality, style, will, and effectiveness of Reagan as president but also the governmental, political, and structural contexts within which he operated (just as with other presidents).

Chapter 12 shows how the president works within a framework determined by constitutional design and the evolution of the office, a particular governmental and political environment, and a larger context of economic, social, cultural, and international **structure**. The decisions and choices made by the president profoundly affect the nature of our political life, but presidents themselves are constrained in what they can do by other institutions, including Congress, and even by the executive branch itself. Moreover, the kinds of presidents we get are largely determined by such political-level factors as public opinion, interest groups, and political parties. This chapter focuses on the interplay among individual presidents, the office of the presidency, and the spheres of government, political linkage, and structure.

→THE EXPANDING PRESIDENCY

The American presidency has grown considerably since the beginnings of the United States. There has been an obvious increase in presidential responsibilities, burdens, power, and impact since the nation's founding.

The Washington and Bush/Gore Presidencies Compared; (HERE)

When **Bush/Gore** was sworn into office in January, 2001, he presided over a federal budget with over $1.8 trillion in annual expenditures and a federal establishment with nearly 2.4 million civilian employees. He was commander in chief of about 1.4 million men and women in uniform; bases at home and scattered throughout the world; and nearly 20,000 deliverable nuclear warheads, enough to obliterate every medium-sized or large city in the world many times over

The United States in 2001 had a population of almost **278 million** diverse people, living in cities, suburbs, and countryside and working in many industries; a gross domestic product (GDP) of over $9.5 trillion; and a land area of some 3.8 million square miles, stretching from Alaska to Florida and from Hawaii to Maine.

When **George Washington** took office as the first president, he had a total budget of $4 million between 1789 and 1791. Washington had few employees to oversee. His cabinet consisted of just five officials; the secretaries of state, war, and the treasury, a postmaster general, and an attorney general (who acted as the president's personal attorney, rather than as head of a full-fledged Justice Department. The entire Department of State consisted of just one secretary; one chief clerk, and one messenger. In 1790, there were about 700 Americans in uniform. The entire United States consisted of the 13 original eastern and southeastern states, with a population of **4 million** people living on 864,746 square miles of mostly farm land.

The Founders' Conception of the Presidency-The Founders' conception of the office of president was much more limited than what we see in the modern presidency, but the vague language of the Constitution has been flexible enough to include the great expansion of the presidency that has occurred. **Article II of the Constitution** provided for a single executive who would be strong, compared to his role under the Congress-dominated **Articles of Confederation**.

The Dormant Presidency-Until the end of the nineteenth century, the presidency conformed basically to the designs and intentions of the Founders. Policymaking at the federal level tended to be located in Congress, and the presidency did not dominate the political life of the nation. Presidents saw their responsibility as primarily involving the execution of policies that were decided by Congress.

Structural Factors-It was not until the late nineteenth century that the American economy was transformed from a simple, free market economy of farmers and small firms to a corporate-dominated economy, with units so large that their actions had social consequences. This eventually led to demands for more government supervision of the American economic system. As this role of government grew, so did the roles of the president. Only in the twentieth century did the United States become a world power involved in military, diplomatic, and economic activities around the globe. The power and responsibility of the presidency has developed along with these structural changes. Events and actions of several presidents during the late eighteenth and nineteenth centuries formed expectations and established precedents.

Important Early Presidents-George Washington was an important American president because he was its first. As well, he solidified the prestige of the presidency at a time when executive power was mistrusted. He also affirmed the primacy of the president in foreign affairs and set a precedent for fashioning a domestic legislative agenda. **Thomas Jefferson's** purchase of the Louisiana Territory form France (the Louisiana Purchase) doubled the size of the United States and opened the continent of the Americas all the way to the Pacific Ocean. **Andrew Jackson** helped transform the presidency into a popular institution, as symbolized by his vigorous opposition to the Bank of the United States (which was viewed as a tool of the wealthy).

James Polk, though not widely regarded as a "great" president, energetically exercised presidential war powers in the war with Mexico, which resulted in the annexation of large tracts of southwestern land including California. **Abraham Lincoln's** leadership in the American Civil War is legendary. In order to win the war, he invoked emergency powers based on a broad interpretation of the Constitution as he suspended the right of habeas corpus and allowed citizens to be tried in military courts; he signed the Emancipation Proclamation which effectively ended slavery in the South.

The Twentieth-Century Transformation-More enduring changes in the presidency came only in the twentieth century, when new structural conditions made an expanded presidency both possible and necessary.

Theodore Roosevelt-The assassination of president William McKinley in 1901 led to Theodore Roosevelt's "stewardship" theory of the presidency when he took office. Roosevelt especially expanded the war powers and diplomatic role of the presidency. Against Congress's wishes he sent the "Great White Fleet" of navy steamships around the world to demonstrate American power; he intervened in Central America to establish the Panama Canal Zone and to protect American political and economic interests; and he successfully mediated disputes between Japan and Russia, for which he won the Nobel Peace Prize. Domestically, Roosevelt pushed for regulation of corporations or "**trusts**", and he established many national parks.

Woodrow Wilson-Wilson's "**New Freedom**" domestic program built on the Progressive Era measures of Teddy Roosevelt, including further regulation of the economy through the Federal Reserve Board (1913) and the Federal Trade Commission (1914). Under Wilson, **World War I** emerged as a major world military and economic power; the federal government and the presidency never returned to their earlier modest scale.

Franklin Roosevelt presided over the most significant expansion of presidential functions and activities in American history. Most observers consider Roosevelt's presidency to be the **beginning of the modern presidency**, reflecting Roosevelt's response to the Great Depression and World War II.

The Impact of the New Deal-At the beginning of 1933, more than one-third of non-farm workers were unemployed, many companies went bankrupt, and many farmers list their land. In the first 100 days of the Roosevelt administration (with a Democratic congressional majority) pushed into law a series of economic, work relief measures. By the end of the 1930s, a whole new structure was in place to coordinate government agencies, and the **Executive Office of the President** was established in 1939 to help the president oversee the federal bureaucracy.

The Impact of World War II-The biggest changes resulted from World War II when government mobilized the entire population and the economy for the war effort. The aftermath of World War II established the United States as a *military superpower*, and all U.S. presidents since the time of Roosevelt have administered a huge national state with large standing armed forces, nuclear weapons, and military bases all around the world.

John F. Kennedy-JFK was the first president to use television as both a campaign tool and as an instrument for influencing the public and political actors in Washington, D.C., the states, and other countries as he sought support for Civil Rights, the Cuban missile crisis, and other issues.

How Important Are Individual Presidents? Individual presidents have played important roles in expanding the office of the president to its present form. It is unlikely that every American president would have purchased the Louisiana Territory, as did Jefferson or responded to the Great Depression and World War II, as did FDR. Yet presidents are also products of the times in which they live; they step into situations that have deep historical roots and dynamics of their own. The great upsurges in presidential power and activity were, at least in part, a result of forces at the structural level, the result of developments in the economy, American society, and the international system. There is an important mix between **presidential personality and character** and deeper structural factors such as the existence of military, foreign policy or economic crises, that determines which presidents leave a positive historical mark and transform their office.

➔ THE MANY ROLES OF THE PRESIDENT

Since Franklin Roosevelt's day, the American presidency has involved powers and duties—unimaginable to the Founders—that touch the daily lives of everyone in the United States. Political Scientist Clinton Rossiter's symbolism of the many "hats" worn by the president is used in this chapter to illustrate the powers and duties of the office, such as **chief of state, commander in chief, legislator, manager of the economy, chief diplomat**, and **party leader**. Scholars sometimes question whether the job of the president is too much to handle: each presidential function is demanding. Together they are overwhelming, but presidents have gradually acquired many aides and advisers to assist them.

Chief of State-The president is a symbol of national authority and unity. It is the president who performs many ceremonial duties that are carried out by members of royal families in other nations, such as funerals, proclaiming official days, honoring heroes, and celebrating anniversaries.

Commander in Chief-The president's "war powers" have grown enormously. Various presidents have exercised war powers regardless of Congress's objections. The Constitution explicitly grants the American president command over the armed forces.

Legislator-While the constitutional responsibility for the nation's legislative agenda rests on Congress, the office of the president has become increasingly involved in directing the nation's legislative course. It is primarily during the annual **State of the Union** address to Congress and the American people, that the president presents budgetary and legislative proposals. During the twentieth century, many American presidents have labeled their legislative programs with catchy and idealistic names such as Wilson's **New Freedom**, FDR's **New Deal**, Truman's **Fair Deal**, Kennedy's **New Frontier**, and Johnson's **Great Society**. The president now directs both domestic and international policies on trade, health care, crime, taxes and so forth.

Manager of the Economy-The president is now expected to "do something" about the economy when things are going badly. The Great Depression established that the federal government has a role to play in fighting economic downturns. Conservative presidents often feel compelled to involve the federal government in the prevention of bank failures, the stimulation of economic growth, and the promotion of exports abroad. In the new global economy, presidents have become increasingly engaged in the effort to open world markets on equitable terms to American goods and services.

Chief Diplomat-The constitutional power to make treaties and to appoint and receive ambassadors, assigns the main diplomatic responsibility of the United States to the presidency. This is a very visible role as the president travels abroad, meeting with foreign leaders, and negotiating and signing treaties.

Head of the Political Party-In addition to other responsibilities, the president is the formal leader of his party while in office. The roles of leader of all the people and leader of narrower

314

party interests may appear contradictory except for the fact that presidents often believe that the public good is best served by the party's agenda on military, economic, and other policy matters.

→ THE PRESIDENT'S STAFF AND CABINET

Chapter 12 analyzes the president's staff and cabinet and summarizes their functions. Each of the president's functions is too demanding for one individual to manage alone. The number and responsibilities of the many presidential advisors and helpers have become so extensive, that they have come to form what some call the **"institutional presidency."**

The White House Staff-The White House staff includes a number of key aides who are the president's closest and most trusted advisers, but the exact shape of the White House staff changes from one presidency to another and is used by different presidents in a variety of ways. Members of the White House staff generally have access to the president and the key offices.

Chief of Staff-Most presidents designate the chief of staff as their top advisor because of the many responsibilities, individuals, and activities he or she organizes on behalf of the president. Different presidents have managed access to themselves by using various systems; FDR used a *competitive* system in which his closest advisors had equal but limited power and access. Dwight Eisenhower, used to *the hierarchical* military staff system, gave overall responsibility to his chief of staff. Under Reagan, the chief of staff shared power *collegially* with an Assistant to the President and Counselor to the President.

National Security Advisor-The national security advisor generally meets with the president on a daily basis to brief him on the latest events and to offer advice on what to do. Several national security advisors have been strong foreign policy managers and active, world-hopping diplomats who sometimes clashed with the secretaries of state and defense.

Other Advisors-The president also utilizes the services of many other advisors who brief and make political and policy recommendations. Some hold official positions, some do not. Prominent in every administration is the press secretary, who holds press conferences, briefs the media, and serves as the voice of the administration. Nearly all presidents have a **legal counsel** and **special assistants** to act as a liaison with Congress, deal with interest groups, handle political matters, and oversee intergovernmental relations. Several presidents' wives–including **Eleanor Roosevelt**, **Rosalyn Carter**, **Nancy Reagan**, and **Hillary Rodham Clinton** have served as informal but influential advisers on a wide range of affairs.

Power and Accountability-The president consults with the White House staff members every day'; they are the ones who do their best to see to it that he gets his way. A call from a staff member is treated with great deference throughout Washington and the nation. Staff members are expected to speak accurately for the president. They must do what the president wants, or what they think he would want if he knew the details. The ideal staffer knows exactly what the president wants and does it. It is helpful for a president, in times of scandal, to be able to create the *impression* that staff members have acted on their own.

The **Executive Office of the President (EOP)** is a group of permanent presidential staff organizations that perform specialized functions. The EOP has a measure of independence, but employees are generally loyal and responsive to the president. The exact composition of the EOP changes from one administration to another. The **Office of Management and Budget (OMB)** advises the president on how much the administration should propose to spend for each government program and where the money will come from. It exercises **legislative clearance** by examining the budgetary implications of proposed legislation for cost and consistency with the president's philosophy and goals. The **Council of Economic Advisers (CEA)** consists of a small group of economists who advise the president on economic policy. In some administrations, the head of the CEA exercises great influence because of his relationship to the president. The **National Security Council (NSC)** is a body of leading officials for the **Department of State**, **Department of Defense**, the **Central Intelligence Agency (CIA)**, the military, and other agencies who advise the president on foreign affairs. The NSC, headed by the president's **national security adviser**, is charged with various analytical and coordinating tasks. The NSC has been particularly active in crisis situations and covert operations.

The Vice-Presidency-The vice president has no constitutional powers or duties except to serve as *president of the Senate* (a ceremonial function with no real power). The primary responsibility of the vice-president is to serve in the capacity that historians once referred to as "a heartbeat away from the presidency." Theodore Roosevelt, Calvin Coolidge, Harry Truman, Lyndon Johnson and Gerald Ford each stepped up from the vice-presidency after the resignation or death of the president. Two others, namely Nixon and George Bush, were elected to the presidency on their own after serving as vice president..

A Once-Insignificant Office-Any function other than presiding over the Senate is at the discretion of the president, and vice-presidents often spend their time running minor errands of state or carrying out limited diplomatic missions. One former vice-president to FDR once said, that the office was "not worth a pitcher of warm piss." Many vice-presidents have been virtually frozen out of the policymaking process. For example, Harry S. Truman had no idea that the **Manhattan Project**, which built the atomic bomb that he would order used once he came president, even existed.

Increasing Importance of the Vice Presidency- Recent presidents have begun to make more use of their vice-presidents and to see the office as potential training ground for those who may take over the presidency. Presidents usually want their vice-presidents to succeed them.

Presidential Succession-In 1804, the **Twelfth Amendment** fixed the flaw in the original Constitution to the United States under which Aaron Burr, Thomas Jefferson's running-mate in 1800, had tied Jefferson in electoral votes and tried, in the House of Representatives, to grab the presidency for himself. Since then, vice-presidents have been elected specifically to that office on a party ticket with their president. The **Twenty-Fifth Amendment** (ratified in 1967) provides for presidential succession in the event of the temporary or permanent inability of a president to discharge his office. It also states that if the vice-presidency becomes vacant, the president can nominate a new vice-president, who takes office on confirmation by both houses of Congress. This is how **Gerald Ford** became president in 1973, when vice-president Spiro Agnew was forced to resign his office amid tax evasion charges, and how Nelson Rockerfeller became vice-president in 1974, when Ford replaced Richard Nixon as president.

The Cabinet-The presidential cabinet is not mentioned in the Constitution, but all presidents have had one. George Washington established the practice of meeting with his top executive officials as a group to discuss policy matters. Later presidents continued the practice; some held frequent meetings, whereas others had only occasional meetings. In recent times, the cabinet has consisted of the heads of the major executive departments plus the vice-president, the director of the CIA, and other officials that the president designates.

Limited Role-Presidents have rarely relied on the cabinet as a decision-making body. Most recent presidents have only infrequently convened the cabinet as a collective body and have seldom done serious business with it. Presidents realize that they alone will be held responsible for decisions, so they tend to reserve that power to themselves.

Why the Weak Cabinet? A major reason for the weakness of the cabinet is that the government has grown large and specialized. Most department heads are experts in their own areas, with little to contribute elsewhere. As well, cabinet members have constituencies to satisfy, including permanent civil servants in their departments and the organized interests that their departments serve. They may have substantial political stature of their own, somewhat independent of the president's. Presidents often reward loyal parts of their electoral coalitions with appointments of individuals from particular interest groups. For example, the secretary of commerce usually has strong ties to the business community. Cabinet appointments can be symbols of diversity as well.

Close Confidants-Most presidents include close personal friends and political allies to their cabinets. For example, John F. Kennedy appointed his brother Robert F. Kennedy as attorney general. At bottom, cabinet members acquire importance from their own talents and characteristics and from their relationships with the president or with their own departments and constituencies, not from their membership in the cabinet as a collective body.

➔THE PRESIDENT AND THE BUREAUCRACY

Presidents have significant controls with regard to the **bureaucracy**, but the president's *ability to give orders* and to gain bureaucratic acquiescence is limited. The bureaucracy is itself a partly independent governmental actor, and it is subject to influences from the political linkage factors (especially from public opinion and organized interests, often working through Congress).

Giving Orders-Many people erroneously assume that the president has firm control over the executive branch of government. Presidents can issue orders, as the case of Truman versus General Douglas MacArthrur demonstrates, but a drastic use of presidential powers can be coslty and makes sense only as a last resort, after all other methods have failed.

However, direct command is seldom feasible in the day-to-day operation of government. Presidents cannot keep personal track of each of the millions of government officials and employees, but can only issue general guidelines (sometimes in the form of executive orders) and pass them down the chain of subordinates. Moreover, lower-level officials, protected by civil service from being fired, may have their own interests.

Persuasion-To a large extent, presidents must persuade other executive branch officials to take certain actions—political scientist **Richard Neustadt** said that *"presidential power is the power to persuade,"* compromise, and bargain with others and convince them that what he wants is in the country's best interest and in their own. Presidents can also appoint officials who share his goals; put White House observers in second-level department positions, reshuffle, reorganize, or even-with the consent of Congress-abolish agencies that are not responsive; influence agency budgets and programs through OMB review, and stimulate pressure of departments by Congress and the public.

→THE PRESIDENT AND CONGRESS: PERPETUAL TUG-OF-WAR

Your text notes that the president and Congress are in a perpetual tug-of-war. Our constitutional structure means that presidents are limited and affected in what they can do by Congress. The president and Congress are frequently in an adversarial relationship. This is a *structural* fact of American politics.

Conflict by Constitutional Design-It was intended by the Founders when they created a system of **checks and balances** in the Constitution, setting **"ambition to counter ambition"** in order to prevent tyranny. Since virtually all constitutional powers are shared, there is a potential for conflict over virtually all aspects of government policy.

Shared Powers-The president is authorized by the Constitution to propose legislation and to sign or veto bills passed by Congress, but both houses of Congress must pass any laws and can override presidential vetoes. The Senate must approve presidential appointments of ambassadors and high officials, and treaties with foreign countries. Presidents can nominate federal judges, including Supreme Court judges, but the Senate must approve them. Presidents administer the executive branch, but Congress appropriates funds for it to operate.

Presidents cannot always count on the members of Congress—even members of his own party— to agree with him. When there is **divided government**-when different parties control the executive and legislative branches-the conflict between the president and Congress over national goals can be especially difficult to overcome.

Separate Elections-In many parliamentary systems, the national legislatures (Congress) choose the chief executive so that unified party control is ensured. In the United States, there are separate elections for the president and members of Congress. In presidential election years, two-thirds of the senators do not have to face election and are therefore insulated from new political forces that may affect the choice of a president. In off-year elections (nonpresidential) all members of the House of Representatives and only one-third of the senators face election.

Outcomes-In all these ways, the constitutional structure of the United States ensures that what the president can do is limited and influenced by Congress, which in turn reflects the various political forces that may differ from those that affect the president. Some say this leads to "gridlock." The recent federal government shutdowns, investigations, impeachment and trial, treaty and appointment conflicts suggest that gridlock is a reality in divided governments.

Cycles of Dominance-The uneven expansion of the presidency has meant that there has been a shifting ascendancy of one branch over another, with different branches dominant from time to time. Presidents tend to dominate during times of national crisis. When the crisis is over, there is often a reaction against crisis management, a reduction in federal government activity, and a return to a more relaxed system of congressional government. Most scholars agree that the twentieth-century presidency has probably been more dominant than Congress. The uneven expansion of the presidency throughout American history can be interpreted in terms of its shifting relationship with Congress.

What makes a president successful with Congress?-There are many reasons why individual presidents have been successful in their dealings with Congress and why others have failed. Some of these reasons are structural, while others tend to be political.

Party and Ideology-The most important factor has to do with the number of people in Congress who agree with the president in ideology and party affiliation. When the same party controls both the executive and legislative branches, presidents are more likely to get their way than they do in divided governments. Party members tend to be like-minded; they tend to vote together because they share the same values, and for the same reason, they tend to go along with a president of their own party.

Foreign Policy Issues-Presidents tend to better on foreign policy issues than on domestic ones. Political scientist **Aaron Wildavsky** argued that there are **"two presidencies,"** domestic and foreign, with the latter president much more dominant. Congress and the president tend to get along better on military-related foreign policy matters in order to present a unified face to the world and potentially hostile countries. **Vietnam**, however, has changed this dichotomy to some degree. When foreign policy concerns trade and other global economic issues, Congress tends to be more assertive.

Vetoes-The president usually wins when he threatens or actually vetoes legislation. The percentage of veto success may be misleadingly high, because presidents like to preserve an image of invulnerability; they generally avoid casting vetoes that might be overridden by Congress.

Popularity-Most political scientists agree that presidential effectiveness with Congress is significantly affected by how popular a president is with the American people. Members of Congress fear opposing a highly visible proposal of a popular president because of the potential for electoral punishment.

Legislative Skills-Presidential skills matter. Many presidents have nurtured legislative relationships. They carefully organize their liaison staffs, conduct head counts of voting intentions, and pass out favors and compromises in order to win.

→THE PRESIDENT AND THE PEOPLE: AN EVOLVING RELATIONSHIP

In addition to constitutional rules, **political forces** such as public opinion, the political parties, and organized interests, significantly impact the relationships between the president and Congress. A very special relationship has evolved over time between the American president and American people.

Getting Closer to the People-The Founders thought of the president as an elite leader, relatively distant from the people. Their view was that the president would interact frequently with Congress but only rarely with the people. Most nineteenth-century presidents and presidential candidates believed and practiced this ideal, but the system quickly evolved into a more democratic one, in which the people played a more direct role. The Founders did not envision a close relationship between the president and the citizenry; he was not to be a direct agent of the people.

More Democratic Elections-The Founders sough to insulate the president from potential popular whims that could lead to tyranny. But the system of government in the United States quickly evolved and with it, the presidency became the most popular office in the country. The two-party system developed, with parties nominating candidates and running pledged electors and the states legislatures allowing ordinary citizens to vote on the electors. Voting rights were also broadened so that property and religious qualifications and race, gender, and age restrictions were eliminated.

Going Public-By the beginning of the twentieth century, the presidency had undergone a basic transformation. **Theodore Roosevelt** gave a series of speech-making tours in order to win passage of legislation to regulate the railroads, and **Woodrow Wilson** created an entirely new constitutional theory advocating close connections between the president and the public. He argued that presidents are unique because only they are chosen by the entire nation.

Using the Media-Television has made it possible for modern presidents to speak directly to the public, unlike their predecessors who had to hope that the print media would present their cases accurately to the public. Presidents use the media to present certain desired images and to appear *presidential*; as an effective head of state, especially on foreign soil.

Leading Public Opinion-A determined president can use his office as a "bully pulpit," to accomplish goals. At the same time, presidents have occasionally misled the public and have manipulated public opinion; sometimes they ignore public opinion or defy it. Consistent with the general theme of the text, the authors of your textbook question whether **democracy** is *advanced or retarded* by developments within the presidency.

The text notes that the *power to lead* the public also implies a *power to manipulate* public opinion, particularly in foreign affairs where presidents can most easily control information. Some *safeguards* can be found in the capacity of the public to judge character and the ability of other national leaders to counteract a deceitful president.

Responding to the Public-The relationship between the president and the public is reciprocal. Presidents are close to the public; they both lead public opinion and respond to it. The public elects presidents whose views and values are consistent with its own; a candidate whose goals are far out of line with what the public favors does not usually win office in the first place. Electoral competition produces presidents who tend to share the public's policy preferences. In order to win reelection presidents try to anticipate what the public will want in order to win electoral reward and avoid electoral punishment.

Quiet Influence-What presidents *want* to do closely resembles what the public wants. In day-to-day politics, it turns out that what the president does is largely in harmony with the general public wants. When polls show that public opinion has shifted, presidents have tended to shift their policies in the same direction.

Listening to the Public-Presidents pay attention to the public. Public opinion polls have been important resources to president's and their staffs in gauging what the public mood is in a given policy area. Though such polling is often deplored, it helps presidents choose policies that the American public favors and changes or discards those that are unpopular.

The Role of Presidential Popularity-Presidential popularity is regularly measured through presidential approval ratings and other polls. Presidents are concerned with how the public approves or disapproves of "the president's handling of the job." Approval ratings also inform presidents about how the public feels at important junctures such as mid-term elections, which often reflect on how the public feels about presidential job performance. When the public is angry with the president, his party usually is punished during mid-term elections. Presidents try to figure

out what will help boost their approval ratings; time, the state of the economy, and foreign policy crises, tend to influence presidential popularity.

Time-Presidents tend to begin their administrations with about 60 percent of the nation approving of their job performance. As time proceeds, presidential approval tends to dip. Bad news hurts approval ratings, while good news often provides a boost.

The Economy-Economic bad news is the worst kind for a sitting president. When the economy sours, presidential approval ratings drop significantly. Bush suffered because of a staggered economy despite his success with the Gulf War, whereas Clinton enjoyed very high job performance ratings even while he was being investigated and eventually impeached.

War-Success in military actions usually translates into increased presidential popularity. The Korean and Vietnam Wars demonstrate how bad news on the military front can negatively affect Presidential popularity.

→INTEREST GROUPS, POLITICAL PARTIES, AND SOCIAL MOVEMENTS

Organized interest groups, political parties and social movements also influence presidents.

Interest Groups-Even though we lack solid evidence, it is clear that organized interest groups influence the president in a number of ways. Campaign contributions are one way that interest groups influence presidential policy initiatives. At the very least, presidents grant access to those interests that contribute large sums of money to their campaign and fundraising efforts.

Interest groups also have influence on the presidency because it their cooperation makes governing more manageable. Business people who supervise large corporations often influence what economic and foreign policies are carried out. Which interest groups have the most influence on policy matters depends to some extent on which party is in control of the presidency.

Political Parties-Changes in party control of the presidency produce significant changes in policy. The parties consist of activists and financiers with distinctive policy goals and of ordinary votes who differ, though less sharply, in the same sorts of ways.

Social Movements-Social movements influence the presidency by creating disruptions that are inconvenient or dangerous to ignore, forcing presidents to take actions to defuse them. Mass movements can also influence public opinion, which presidents are not inclined to ignore.

→STRUCTURAL INFLUENCES ON THE PRESIDENCY

We can speak of an **enduring presidency**, a presidency that does not merely fluctuate with the whims of whoever holds office but that reflects the goals and preferences of the people, groups, and institutions that make up American society. Even major changes from one presidency to another usually reflect the nature of party coalitions in the nation and changes in public opinion. Presidents are affected by *structural factors* such as the nature of U.S. economic and social systems and the role of the United States in the international system and the world economy. The presidency—like all other institutions of our national government—reflects influences at the political level (interest groups, political parties, and public opinion) and also structural influences (especially from the international system and the U.S. economy). Both continuities and changes in what presidents do tend to reflect structural factors that influence what kinds of problems and issues come before presidents, how people think about these problems and what they want the president to do about them, and who has the political resources and power to insist on a hearing from the president. The international system and the economy have tremendous influence on American politics and government.

The International System-Regardless of party affiliation, most all American presidents since World War II have focused on containing Soviet influence, solidifying the Western alliance, encouraging open economies in which American businesses can compete, and opposition to leftist or nationalist movements in the developing world. The reason for that continuity is that U.S. foreign policies reflected the basic features of the international system (particularly its **bipolarity**, with two superpowers), the U.S. position in that system as the dominant superpower, and the nature of U.S. economic interests in markets, raw materials, and investment opportunities. When the international system changes, presidential policies tend to reflect those changes regardless of who is in office.

The Economy-All presidents must work to help the economy grown and flourish, while keeping employment and inflation low. A healthy economy provides for popularity, tax receipts to fund government programs, and domestic peace and stability. A healthy economy requires that wealth investors have confidence in the future. This has tended to create a set of presidential policies that favor wealthy investors, regardless of party affiliation.

→SUMMARY

The American presidency has expanded significantly since the founding of the nation; only a few nineteenth-century presidents made much of a mark on the nation. These include Thomas Jefferson, James Polk, and Abraham Lincoln. During the twentieth-century, as a result of industrialization, two world wars, and the Cold War, and the Great Depression, presidential powers and resources expanded greatly. Since FDR the American presidency has expanded to its modern shape and form. Presidents must use a vast array of resources to successfully govern the United States. The personality and style of the president, his ability to persuade citizens, interests, and other government decisionmakers, significantly impact presidential success. The Founders produced a constitutionally mandated adversarial relationship between the executive and legislative branches; they engage in a perpetual tug-of-war, especially on domestic policy issues.

The presidency has become far more democratic than the Founders envisioned. Presidents listen to public opinion and respond to it, in addition to leading and sometimes manipulating the public. Interest groups, party activists, and financial contributors also influence what the president does. The modern presidency is increasingly involved in international policy matters. The president also wears many hats. A vast bureaucracy and host of presidential advisors assist the president in executing the duties of the office.

> *Chapter Outline*

This section gives you a comprehensive review of the chapter. Use this outline in combination with your textbook to look for key concepts and objectives, to identify essential terms and names, and to gain a basic understanding of political practices and principles from this chapter.

I. THE REAGAN REVOLUTION (pp. 347-348)
   A. Reagan and the modern presidency
   1. When **Ronald Reagan** took office in 1981, he interpreted his landslide victory as a *mandate* to pursue sweeping changes.
      a) Reagan promised sweeping cuts in taxes, federal social programs, and regulations as a way "to get government off the backs of the people."
      b) He also called for a rapid buildup of U.S. armed forces as a way to regain respect and influence in the world.
   2. Tax and budget proposals were given top priority in what Reagan announced as his Program for Economic Recovery:
      a) The largest tax cut in American history ($750 billion over 6 years, targeted primarily at upper-income groups and corporations)
      b) The steepest rise in defense spending in peacetime American history
      c) Major reductions in domestic social programs (eliminating some entirely, such as job training and public-service employment)

3. Democratic opposition looked formidable: Democrats controlled a large majority of seats in the House of Representatives, and the Republicans had only a slim majority in the Senate.

B. **The Reagan offensive**
   1. A skilled and shrewd deal maker
   2. He cultivated friendly relations with members of Congress from both parties, worked to build up his popularity with the general public, and exerted political pressure in conservative areas in the South with Democratic members of Congress (where a majority of voters had supported Reagan for president).
   3. He countered talk of the bill as a giveaway to the rich by insisting that it would spark economic growth and help everyone; he was an advocate of **supply-side economics** (the theory that growth created by the tax cuts would increase tax receipts).

C. **Reaction**
   1. The administration's tax bill passed easily in the Senate (72-20) and received a majority of the votes in the House of Representatives.
   2. Reagan was successful in the House mainly because of the support of Southern conservative Democrats (called **boll weevils**).
   3. Reagan got most of what he wanted in domestic budget cuts and the defense buildup.

D. **Effects**
   1. The "Reagan Revolution" had profound effects—although some economic growth occurred, the legacies of the 1980s also included a massive increase in the size of the national debt, deterioration in the international trade position of the United States, and dramatic increases in the scale of income and wealth inequality.
   2. Despite the long-term problems, the Reagan Revolution was a huge political success.

E. **Focus of the chapter**
   1. This chapter shows how the president works within a framework determined by constitutional design and the evolution of the office, a particular *governmental* and *political* environment, and a larger context of economic, social, cultural, and international *structure*.
   2. The decisions and choices made by the president—as well as his skills, personality, and character—profoundly affect the nature of our political life; but individual presidents should not be considered free agents who can do as they wish.

II. **THE EXPANDING PRESIDENCY (pp. 348-355)**
   A. Growth of the presidency: contrast with the Founders' conception of the office
      1. There has been an obvious increase in presidential responsibilities, burdens, power, and impact since the nation's founding.
      2. The Founders' conception of the office of president was much more limited than what we see in the modern presidency, but the vague language of the Constitution

has been flexible enough to include the great expansion of the presidency that has occurred (see **Article II of the Constitution**).

- a) The Constitution made the president commander in chief of the armed forces, but without any suggestion that there would be a vast standing army that presidents could commit to conflicts abroad without declarations of war.
- b) Presidents were empowered to appoint and to "require the opinion in writing" of the heads of executive departments, but without any expectation that a large federal *bureaucracy* would evolve.
- c) The Constitution provided that presidents could recommend measures to Congress, but without specifying that they would *propose legislative programs* dominating the legislative agenda.

B. **The Washington and Bush/Gore presidencies compared**
1. When **Bush/Gore** was sworn into office in January, 2001, he presided over a federal budget with over $1.8 trillion in annual expenditures and a federal establishment with nearly 2.4 million civilian employees.
   - a) He was commander in chief of about 1.4 million men and women in uniform; bases at home and scattered throughout the world; and nearly 20,000 deliverable nuclear warheads, enough to obliterate every medium-sized or large city in the world many times over
   - b) The United States in 2001 had a population of almost **278 million** diverse people, living in cities, suburbs, and countryside and working in many industries; a gross domestic product (GDP) of over $9.5 trillion; and a land area of some 3.8 million square miles, stretching from Alaska to Florida and from Hawaii to Maine.
2. When **George Washington** took office as the first president, he had a total budget of $4 million between 1789 and 1791. Washington had few employees to oversee. His cabinet consisted of just five officials; the secretaries of state, war, and the treasury, a postmaster general, and an attorney general (who acted as the president's personal attorney, rather than as head of a full-fledged Justice Department).
   - a) The entire Department of State consisted of just one secretary, one chief clerk, and one messenger. In 1790, there were about 700 Americans in uniform.
   - b) The entire United States consisted of the 13 original eastern and southeastern states, with a population of **4 million** people living on 864,746 square miles of mostly farm land.

C. **The Founders' conception of the presidency**
1. The Founders' conception of the office of president was much more limited than what we see in the modern presidency, but the vague language of the Constitution has been flexible enough to include the great expansion of the presidency that has occurred.
2. **Article II of the Constitution** provided for a single executive who would be strong, compared to his role under the Congress-dominated **Articles of**

Confederation.

D. **The dormant presidency**

   1. Until the end of the nineteenth century, the presidency conformed basically to the designs and intentions of the Founders.

      a) Policymaking at the federal level tended to be located in Congress.

      b) Presidents saw their responsibility as primarily involving the execution of policies decided by Congress.

   2. **Structural factors**

      a) It was not until the late nineteenth century that the American economy was transformed from a simple, free market economy of farmers and small firms to a corporate-dominated economy, with units so large that their actions had social consequences.

         (1) This eventually led to demands for more government supervision of the American economic system.

         (2) As this role of government grew, so did the roles of the president.

      b) Only in the twentieth century did the United States become a world power involved in military, diplomatic, and economic activities around the globe; the power and responsibility of the presidency developed along with these structural changes.

   3. Events and actions of several presidents during the late eighteenth and nineteenth centuries formed expectations and established precedents.

E. **Important early presidents**

   1. Events and actions of several presidents during the late eighteenth and nineteenth centuries formed expectations and established precedents

   2. **George Washington** (1789-1797)—solidified the prestige of the presidency; affirmed the primacy of the president in foreign affairs; set a *precedent for presidential involvement* in fashioning a domestic legislative program

   3. **Thomas Jefferson** (1801-1809)—despite his hostility to an active central government before assuming office, he took *decisive action in completing the Louisiana Purchase* from France; increased foreign policy responsibilities for the president

   4. **Andrew Jackson** (1829-1837)—helped transform the presidency into a popular institution where the needs and aspirations of the people might be met

   5. **Abraham Lincoln** (1861-1865)—invoked **emergency powers** based on a broad interpretation of the Constitution; during the Civil War, government tax revenues escalated, expenditures grew to unprecedented levels, and the number of civilian federal employees increased dramatically

F. **Twentieth-Century transformation**

   1. The more enduring changes in the presidency came in the twentieth century, when new structural conditions made an expanded presidency both possible and necessary

2. **Theodore Roosevelt** (1901-1909)—vigorously pushed the prerogatives and enhanced the powers of the presidency; he particularly emphasized his powers as commander in chief and his role as **chief diplomat**
   a) He is remembered for *interventionism* in the Caribbean and for sending the "Great White Fleet" of navy steamships around the world as a show of strength; on the domestic front, he is remembered for *trust busting*.
   b) In this administration, we see the merging of an energetic and ambitious political leader and a new set of *structural factors* in the United States, particularly its emergence as a world power and an industrialized economy.
3. **Woodrow Wilson** (1913-1921)—further expansion of the federal government and the presidency; his **New Freedom** program built upon Theodore Roosevelt's Progressive measures, including further regulation of the economy
   a) World War I brought a huge mobilization of military manpower and a large, new civilian bureaucracy.
   b) Although the temporary agencies were dismantled at the end of the war, the federal government and the presidency never returned to their earlier limited scale.
4. **Franklin Roosevelt** (1933-1945)—presided over the most significant expansion of presidential functions and activities in American history; most observers consider this to be the **beginning of the modern presidency**, reflecting Roosevelt's response to the Great Depression and World War II
5. **The impact of the New Deal**
   a) At the beginning of 1933, more than one-third of non-farm workers were unemployed, many companies went bankrupt, and many farmers list their land. In the first 100 days of the Roosevelt administration (with a Democratic congressional majority) pushed into law a series of economic, work relief measures.
   b) By the end of the 1930s, a whole new structure was in place to coordinate government agencies, and the **Executive Office of the President** was established in 1939 to help the president oversee the federal bureaucracy.
6. **The impact of World War II**
   a) The biggest changes resulted from World War II—government again mobilized the entire population and the economy for the war effort.
   b) World War II brought unprecedented governmental involvement in the economy, with temporary war agencies that set precedents for future presidential and governmental actions.
7. All U.S. presidents since the time of Franklin Roosevelt have administered a huge national state with large standing armed forces, nuclear weapons, and military bases all around the world; all have presided over a massive government apparatus that has been active in both domestic and foreign policy.
8. **John F. Kennedy**-JFK was the first president to use television as both a campaign tool and as an instrument for influencing the public and political actors in

Washington, D.C., the states, and other countries as he sought support for Civil Rights, the Cuban missile crisis, and other issues.

G. **How important are individual presidents?**

1. Individual presidents have played important roles in expanding the office of the president to its present form.

   a) It is unlikely that every American president would have purchased the Louisiana Territory, as did Jefferson or responded to the Great Depression and World War II, as did FDR.

   b) Yet presidents are also products of the times in which they live; they step into situations that have deep historical roots and dynamics of their own. The great upsurges in presidential power and activity were, at least in part, a result of forces at the **structural level**, the result of developments in the economy, American society, and the international system.

2. There is an important mix between **presidential personality and character** and deeper structural factors such as the existence of military, foreign policy or economic crises, that determines which presidents leave a positive historical mark and transform their office.

III. THE MANY ROLES OF THE PRESIDENT (pp. 355-358)

A. Since Franklin Roosevelt's day, the American presidency has involved powers and duties—unimaginable to the Founders—that touch the daily lives of everyone in the United States.

B. Political scientist **Clinton Rossiter** used the image of the *many "hats"* that presidents wear simultaneously.

C. **Chief of State**

1. The *ceremonial or symbolical role* of the president.

2. The president is the symbol of national authority and unity, in somewhat the same way that a monarch serves as chief of state in some European parliamentary nations while the prime minister serves as head of government

D. **Commander in Chief**

1. The Constitution places command over American armed forces with the presidency.

2. This vague power has grown enormously with the development of the so-called *war powers* of the president

E. **Legislator**

1. The *initiative for public policy* has shifted to the president and the executive branch, with reports such as the **State of the Union message** playing an important role; to a large extent during the twentieth century, Congress has waited for presidential actions and responded to them.

2. Congress recaptured much of the initiative after Republicans gained control of the legislature in 1994.

F. **Manager of the economy**

1. The Great Depression convinced most Americans that the federal government has a *role to play in fighting economic problems*, and the example of Franklin Roosevelt convinced most Americans of the primacy of the president in this role.
2. In the rapidly expanding global economy, presidents have become increasingly engaged in the effort to open world markets on equitable terms to American goods and services.

G. **Chief diplomat**
 1. The Constitution places primary diplomatic responsibility in the office of the president.
 2. The Constitution grants the president the power to make treaties and to appoint and receive ambassadors (which also implies the power to refuse to *recognize foreign governments*)

H. **Head of the political party**
 1. Presidents function as leader of their political party, seeking *partisan advantage* as well as the *public good*.
 2. Presidents generally see the public good and commitment to party principles as one and the same, but the public has often reacted negatively when presidents play their party leadership role too vigorously

IV. **THE PRESIDENT'S STAFF AND CABINET (pp. 358-63)**
 A. **The White House staff**
 1. The White House staff includes a number of key aides who are the president's closest and most trusted advisers.
 2. The exact shape of the White House staff changes from one presidency to another and is used by different presidents in a variety of ways
 B. **Chapter 12** analyzes the president's staff and cabinet and summarizes their functions. Each of the president's functions is too demanding for one individual to manage alone. The number and responsibilities of the many presidential advisors and helpers have become so extensive, that they have come to form what some call the **"institutional presidency."**
 C. **Chief of Staff**
 1. This official tends to serve as the president's "right hand"; specific functions are determined by the president, and people in this office have been used by different presidents in very different ways.
 2. FDR used a *competitive* system in which his closest advisors had equal but limited power and access.
 3. Dwight Eisenhower, used to *the hierarchical* military staff system, gave overall responsibility to his chief of staff.
 4. Under Reagan, the chief of staff shared power *collegially* with an Assistant to the President and Counselor to the President.
 D. **National Security Adviser**
 1. This official serves as head of the president's national security staff; generally

meets with the president on a daily basis to brief him on foreign policy matters and advise him on foreign policy decisions.

2. The national security advisor generally meets with the president on a daily basis to brief him on the latest events and to offer advice on what to do. Several national security advisors have been strong foreign policy managers and active, world-hopping diplomats who sometimes clashed with the secretaries of state and defense.

E. **Other advisors**
1. The president also utilizes the services of many other advisors who brief and make political and policy recommendations.
    a) Some hold official positions, some do not. Prominent in every administration is the press secretary, who holds press conferences, briefs the media, and serves as the voice of the administration.
    b) Nearly all presidents have a **legal counsel** and **special assistants** to act as a liaison with Congress, deal with interest groups, handle political matters, and oversee intergovernmental relations.
2. Several presidents' wives–including **Eleanor Roosevelt, Rosalyn Carter, Nancy Reagan**, and **Hillary Rodham Clinton** have served as informal but influential advisers on a wide range of affairs.

F. **Power and accountability**
1. The president consults with the White House staff members every day; they are the ones who do their best to see to it that he gets his way.
2. A call from a staff member is treated with great deference throughout Washington and the nation. Staff members are expected to speak accurately for the president.
3. They must do what the president wants, or what they think he would want if he knew the details. The ideal staffer knows exactly what the president wants and does it. It is helpful for a president, in times of scandal, to be able to create the *impression* that staff members have acted on their own.

G. **The Executive Office of the President (EOP)**
1. The EOP is a group of permanent presidential staff organizations that perform specialized functions. The EOP has a measure of independence, but employees are generally loyal and responsive to the president. The exact composition of the EOP changes from one administration to another.
2. The **Office of Management and Budget (OMB)** advises the president on how much the administration should propose to spend for each government program and where the money will come from. It exercises **legislative clearance** by examining the budgetary implications of proposed legislation for cost and consistency with the president's philosophy and goals.
3. The **Council of Economic Advisers (CEA)** consists of a small group of economists who advise the president on economic policy. In some administrations, the head of the CEA exercises great influence because of his relationship to the president.

    a) The **National Security Council (NSC)** is a body of leading officials for the **Department of State**, **Department of Defense**, the **Central Intelligence Agency (CIA)**, the military, and other agencies who advise the president on foreign affairs.

    b) The NSC, headed by the president's **national security adviser**, is charged with various analytical and coordinating tasks. The NSC has been particularly active in crisis situations and covert operations.

H. The Vice-Presidency

1. The vice president has no constitutional powers or duties except to serve as *president of the Senate* (a ceremonial function with no real power).

    a) The primary responsibility of the vice-president is to serve in the capacity that historians once referred to as "a heartbeat away from the presidency."

    b) Theodore Roosevelt, Calvin Coolidge, Harry Truman, Lyndon Johnson and Gerald Ford each stepped up from the vice-presidency after the resignation or death of the president.

2. Two others, namely Nixon and George Bush, were elected to the presidency on their own after serving as vice president.

I. A once-insignificant office

1. Any function other than presiding over the Senate is at the discretion of the president, and vice-presidents often spend their time running minor errands of state or carrying out limited diplomatic missions.

2. One former vice-president to FDR once said, that the office was "not worth a pitcher of warm piss." Many vice-presidents have been virtually frozen out of the policymaking process. For example, Harry S. Truman had no idea that the **Manhattan Project**, which built the atomic bomb that he would order used once he became president, even existed.

J. Increasing importance of the Vice Presidency

1. Recent presidents have begun to make more use of their vice-presidents and to see the office as potential training ground for those who may take over the presidency.

2. Presidents usually want their vice-presidents to succeed them.

K. Presidential succession

1. In 1804, the **Twelfth Amendment** fixed the flaw in the original Constitution to the United States under which Aaron Burr, Thomas Jefferson's running-mate in 1800, had tied Jefferson in electoral votes and tried, in the House of Representatives, to grab the presidency for himself. Since then, vice-presidents have been elected specifically to that office on a party ticket with their president.

2. The **Twenty-Fifth Amendment** (ratified in 1967) provides for presidential succession in the event of the temporary or permanent inability of a president to discharge his office. It also states that if the vice-presidency becomes vacant, the president can nominate a new vice-president, who takes office on confirmation by both houses of Congress.

3. This is how **Gerald Ford** became vice-president in 1973, when vice-president

Spiro Agnew was forced to resign his office amid tax evasion charges, and how Nelson Rockerfeller became vice-president in 1974, when Ford replaced Richard Nixon as president.

L. **The cabinet**
  1. The presidential cabinet is not mentioned in the Constitution, but all presidents have had one. George Washington established the practice of meeting with his top executive officials as a group to discuss policy matters.
  2. Later presidents continued the practice; some held frequent meetings, whereas others had only occasional meetings. In recent times, the cabinet has consisted of the heads of the major executive departments plus the vice-president, the director of the CIA, and other officials that the president designates.

M. **Limited role**
  1. Presidents have rarely relied on the cabinet as a decision-making body. Most recent presidents have only infrequently convened the cabinet as a collective body and have seldom done serious business with it.
  2. Presidents realize that they alone will be held responsible for decisions, so they tend to reserve that power to themselves.

N. **Why the weak cabinet**?
  1. A major reason for the weakness of the cabinet is that the government has grown large and specialized.
     a) Most department heads are experts in their own areas, with little to contribute elsewhere. As well, cabinet members have constituencies to satisfy, including permanent civil servants in their departments and the organized interests that their departments serve.
     b) They may have substantial political stature of their own, somewhat independent of the president's.
  2. Presidents often reward loyal parts of their electoral coalitions with appointments of individuals from particular interest groups. For example, the secretary of commerce usually has strong ties to the business community. Cabinet appointments can be symbols of diversity as well.

O. **Close confidants**
  1. Most presidents include close personal friends and political allies to their cabinets. For example, John F. Kennedy appointed his brother Robert F. Kennedy as attorney general.
  2. At bottom, cabinet members acquire importance from their own talents and characteristics and from their relationships with the president or with their own departments and constituencies, not from their membership in the cabinet as a collective body.

V. **THE PRESIDENT AND THE BUREAUCRACY (pp. 363-365)**
  A. Presidents have significant controls with regard to the **bureaucracy**, but the president's *ability* to give orders and to gain bureaucratic acquiescence is limited.

333

1. The federal bureaucracy is not merely a creature of the president.
2. The federal bureaucracy is itself a partly independent governmental actor and it is subject to influences from the political level (especially from public opinion and organized interests, often working through Congress).

B. **Giving orders**
   1. Many people erroneously assume that the president has firm control over the executive branch of government. Presidents can issue orders, as the case of Truman versus General Douglas MacArthrur demonstrates, but a drastic use of presidential powers can be costly and makes sense only as a last resort, after all other methods have failed.
   2. Direct command is seldom feasible in the day-to-day operation of government; presidents can only issue general guidelines and pass them down the chain of subordinates; lower-level officials may have their own interests.

C. **Persuasion**
   1. To a large extent, presidents must persuade other executive branch officials to take certain actions—political scientist **Richard Neustadt** said that *"presidential power is the power to persuade,"* compromise, and bargain with others and convince them that what he wants is in the country's best interest and in their own.
   2. Presidents can also appoint officials who share his goals; put White House observers in second-level department positions, reshuffle, reorganize, or even-with the consent of Congress-abolish agencies that are not responsive; influence agency budgets and programs through OMB review, and stimulate pressure of departments by Congress and the public.

VI. **THE PRESIDENT AND CONGRESS: PERPETUAL TUG-OF-WAR (pp. 365-368)**
   A. Our constitutional structure means that presidents are limited and affected by Congress in what they can do. The president and Congress are frequently in an adversarial relationship. This is a *structural* fact of American politics.
   B. **Conflict by Constitutional Design**
      1. It was intended by the Founders when they created a system of **checks and balances** in the Constitution, setting **"ambition to counter ambition"** in order to prevent tyranny.
      2. Since virtually all constitutional powers are shared, there is a potential for conflict over virtually all aspects of government policy.
   C. **Shared powers**
      1. The president is authorized by the Constitution to propose legislation and to sign or veto bills passed by Congress, but both houses of Congress must pass any laws and can override presidential vetoes.
      2. The Senate must approve presidential appointments of ambassadors and high officials, and treaties with foreign countries.
      3. Presidents can nominate federal judges, including Supreme Court judges, but the Senate must approve them. Presidents administer the executive branch, but

Congress appropriates funds for it to operate.

4. Presidents cannot always count on the members of Congress—even members of his own party—to agree with him. When there is **divided government**-when different parties control the executive and legislative branches-the conflict between the president and Congress over national goals can be especially difficult to overcome.

D. **Separate elections**
1. In many parliamentary systems, the national legislatures (Congress) choose the chief executive so that unified party control is ensured.
2. In the United States, there are separate elections for the president and members of Congress. In presidential election years, two-thirds of the senators do not have to face election and are therefore insulated from new political forces that may affect the choice of a president. In off-year elections (nonpresidential) all members of the House of Representatives and only one-third of the senators face election.

E. **Outcomes**
1. In all these ways, the constitutional structure of the United States ensures that what the president can do is limited and influenced by Congress, which in turn reflects the various political forces that may differ from those that affect the president.
2. Some say this leads to **"gridlock."** The recent federal government shutdowns, investigations, impeachment and trial, treaty and appointment conflicts suggest that gridlock is a reality in divided governments.

F. **Cycles of dominance**
1. The uneven expansion of the presidency has meant that there has been a shifting ascendancy of one branch over another, with different branches dominant from time to time.
   a) Presidents tend to dominate during times of national crisis.
   b) When the crisis is over, there is often a reaction against crisis management, a reduction in federal government activity, and a return to a more relaxed system of congressional government.
   c) Most scholars agree that the twentieth-century presidency has probably been more dominant than Congress.
2. The uneven expansion of the presidency throughout American history can be interpreted in terms of its shifting relationship with Congress.

G. **What makes a president successful with Congress?**
1. There are many reasons why individual presidents have been successful in their dealings with Congress and why others have failed. Some of these reasons are structural, while others tend to be political.
2. **Party and ideology**
   a) The most important factor has to do with the number of people in Congress who agree with the president in ideology and party affiliation.
   b) When the same party controls both the executive and legislative branches, presidents are more likely to get their way than they do in divided governments.

335

Party members tend to be like-minded; they tend to vote together because they share the same values, and for the same reason, they tend to go along with a president of their own party.

3. **Foreign policy issues**
   a) Presidents tend to do better on foreign policy issues than on domestic ones.
   b) Political scientist **Aaron Wildavsky** argued that there are **"two presidencies,"** domestic and foreign, with the latter president much more dominant.
   c) Congress and the president tend to get along better on military-related foreign policy matters in order to present a unified face to the world and potentially hostile countries.
   d) **Vietnam**, however, has changed this dichotomy to some degree. When foreign policy concerns trade and other global economic issues, Congress tends to be more assertive.

4. **Vetoes**
   a) The president usually wins when he threatens or actually vetoes legislation.
   b) The percentage of veto success may be misleadingly high, because presidents like to preserve an image of invulnerability; they generally avoid casting vetoes that might be overridden by Congress.

5. **Popularity**
   a) Most political scientists agree that presidential effectiveness with Congress is significantly affected by how popular a president is with the American people.
   b) Members of Congress fear opposing a highly visible proposal of a popular president because of the potential for electoral punishment.

6. **Legislative skills**
   a) Statistical studies reveal little or no discernible effect of a president's legislative skills; however, on crucial pieces of legislation, a president with legislative skills may have an advantage in *persuading* the legislature to adopt the president's programs
   b) Presidential skills matter. Many presidents have nurtured legislative relationships. They carefully organize their liaison staffs, conduct head counts of voting intentions, and pass out favors and compromises in order to win.

VII. **THE PRESIDENT AND THE PEOPLE: AN EVOLVING RELATIONSHIP (pp.368-374)**
   A. The complicated relationships that exist among the governmental units of the president, the executive branch as a whole, and Congress have a lot to do with various *political forces*—including the ways in which public opinion, political parties, and organized interests affect what they do differently.
   B. **Getting closer to the people**
      1. The special relationship that exists between the president and the general public is of particular importance.
      2. The Constitution envisioned a very *indirect* democracy in relationship to the

presidency; in this conception, the president was *not* to be a direct agent of the people.
   a) The Founders thought of the president as an elite leader, relatively distant from the people; their view was that the president would interact frequently with Congress but only rarely with the people.
   b) Most nineteenth-century presidents and presidential candidates believed and practiced this ideal; presidents seldom made speeches directly to the public.
   3. Presidents were not chosen directly by the voters; *state legislators chose presidential electors* who were to exercise *independent judgment* as an **electoral college**.
C. **More democratic elections**
   1. The Founders sough to insulate the president from potential popular whims that could lead to tyranny.
   2. The system quickly evolved into a more democratic one, in which the people played a more direct role.
   3. The *two-party system* evolved, with parties nominating candidates and running them under party labels; voters were provided with *clearer choices*, and electors were *pledged* in advance to support their party's candidates.
   4. Early in the nineteenth century, state legislatures began to turn the *power to choose presidential electors* over to the people through *direct election*.
   5. The *base of suffrage* broadened: by the early 1970s, the eligible electorate consisted of nearly all adults who chose to participate.
D. **Going public**
   1. By the beginning of the twentieth century, the presidency had undergone a basic transformation: presidents began to speak directly to the public.
   a) Theodore Roosevelt gave a series of speech-making tours to win passage of legislation to regulate the railroads.
   b) Woodrow Wilson created an entirely new constitutional theory advocating *close connections between the president and the public*; he argued that presidents are unique because only they are chosen by the entire nation; he also believed that presidents should both lead and respond to the public, interpreting the true desires of the citizenry, winning public support for policies in accord with those desires, and providing energetic leadership.
   2. Wilson's theory of the presidency has been followed, more and more fully, in the twentieth century: all presidents now attempt to respond to public opinion, and all try to speak directly to the people about policy.
E. **Using the media**
   1. Contemporary presidents frequently *go public* by using television to bypass Congress and the press in order to speak directly there are fewer *news* to the public about policy.
   a) Television has made it possible for modern presidents to speak directly to the public, unlike their predecessors who had to hope that the print media would

present their cases accurately to the public.

      b) Presidents use the media to present certain desired images and to appear *presidential*; as an effective head of state, especially on foreign soil..

  2. Although *conferences* with White House correspondents (where awkward questions cannot be excluded), all presidents since Hoover's administration have used radio and television to make major *addresses* to the national public each year, and there has been an increase in minor addresses to special audiences.

F. Leading public opinion

  1. Modern presidents have used television to enhance their power to **shape public opinion**. A determined president can use his office as a "bully pulpit," to accomplish goals.

      a) The *power to lead* the public also implies a *power to manipulate* public opinion, particularly in foreign affairs where presidents can most easily control information; sometimes they ignore public opinion or defy it.

      b) Some *safeguards* can be found in the capacity of the public to judge character and the ability of other national leaders to counteract a deceitful president.

  2. The most serious *threats to democracy* may come when leaders of both parties are united and no one challenges falsehoods, as sometimes occurs in cases of nationalist and apparently patriotic acts of foreign policy.

G. Responding to the public

  1. The relationship between the president and the public is reciprocal; it is a two-way street. Presidents are close to the public; they both lead public opinion and respond to it.

  2. The public elects presidents whose views and values are consistent with its own; a candidate whose goals are far out of line with what the public favors does not usually win office in the first place.

  3. Electoral competition produces presidents who tend to share the public's policy preferences. In order to win reelection presidents try to anticipate what the public will want in order to win electoral reward and avoid electoral punishment.

H. Quiet influence

  1. What presidents *want* to do closely resembles what the public wants. In day-to-day politics, it turns out that what the president does is largely in harmony with the general public wants.

  2. When polls show that public opinion has shifted, presidents have tended to shift their policies in the same direction.

I. Listening to the public

  1. Presidents pay attention to the public. Public opinion polls have been important resources to president's and their staffs in gauging what the public mood is in a given policy area.

  2. Though such polling is often deplored, it helps presidents choose policies that the American public favors and changes or discards those that are unpopular.

J. The role of presidential popularity

1. The *public's influence* works through presidential popularity or unpopularity
   a) Presidential popularity is regularly measured through presidential approval ratings and other polls. Presidents are concerned with how the public approves or disapproves of "the president's handling of the job."
   b) Presidents pay attention to these figures because they have a lot to do with how much influence the president has in Congress and with how he and his party will do in elections.
2. When the public is angry with the president, his party usually is punished during mid-term elections. Presidents try to figure out what will help boost their approval ratings; time, the state of the economy, and foreign policy crises, tend to influence presidential popularity.

K. **Time**
1. Presidents tend to begin their administrations with about 60 percent of the nation approving of their job performance.
2. As time proceeds, presidential approval tends to dip. Bad news hurts approval ratings, while good news often provides a boost.

L. **The economy**
1. Economic bad news is the worst kind for a sitting president. When the economy sours, presidential approval ratings drop significantly.
2. Bush suffered because of a staggered economy despite his success with the Gulf War, whereas Clinton enjoyed very high job performance ratings even while he was being investigated and eventually impeached.

M. **War**
1. Success in military actions usually translates into increased presidential popularity.
2. The Korean and Vietnam Wars demonstrate how bad news on the military front can negatively affect Presidential popularity.

VIII. INTEREST GROUPS, POLITICAL PARTIES, and SOCIAL MOVEMENTS (pp. 374-375)

A. Organized interest groups, political parties and social movements also influence presidents.

B. **Interest groups**
1. Even though we lack solid evidence, it is clear that organized interest groups influence the president in a number of ways.
2. Campaign contributions are one way that interest groups influence presidential policy initiatives. At the very least, presidents grant access to those interests that contribute large sums of money to their campaign and fundraising efforts.
3. Interest groups also have influence on the presidency because it their cooperation makes governing more manageable.
4. Business people who supervise large corporations often influence what economic and foreign policies are carried out. Which interest groups have the most influence on policy matters depends to some extent on **which party is in control** of the

presidency.

C. **Political parties**
   1. Changes in party control of the presidency produce significant changes in policy.
   2. The parties consist of activists and financiers with distinctive policy goals and of ordinary votes who differ, though less sharply, in the same sorts of ways.

D. **Social movements**
   1. Social movements influence the presidency by creating disruptions that are inconvenient or dangerous to ignore, forcing presidents to take actions to defuse them.
   2. Mass movements can also influence public opinion; which presidents are not inclined to ignore.

IX. **STRUCTURAL INFLUENCES ON THE PRESIDENCY (pp. 375-378)**

A. We can speak of an **enduring presidency**, a presidency that does not merely fluctuate with the whims of whoever holds office but that reflects the goals and preferences of the people, groups, and institutions that make up American society.
   1. Even major changes from one presidency to another usually reflect the nature of party coalitions in the nation and changes in public opinion.
   2. Presidents are affected by *structural factors* such as the nature of U.S. economic and social systems and the role of the United States in the international system and the world economy.
   3. The presidency—like all other institutions of our national government—reflects influences at the political level (interest groups, political parties, and public opinion) and also structural influences (especially from the international system and the U.S. economy).
   4. Both continuities and changes in what presidents do tend to reflect structural factors that influence what kinds of problems and issues come before presidents, how people think about these problems and what they want the president to do about them, and who has the political resources and power to insist on a hearing from the president.
   5. The international system and the economy have tremendous influence on American politics and government.

B. **The international system**
   1. Regardless of party affiliation, most all American presidents since World War II have focused on containing Soviet influence, solidifying the Western alliance, encouraging open economies in which American businesses can compete, and opposition to leftist or nationalist movements in the developing world.
   2. The reason for that continuity is that U.S. foreign policies reflected the basic features of the international system (particularly its **bipolarity**, with two superpowers), the U.S. position in that system as the dominant superpower, and the nature of U.S. economic interests in markets, raw materials, and investment opportunities.
   3. When the international system changes, presidential policies tend to reflect those

changes regardless of who is in office.
C. **The economy**
1. All presidents must work to help the economy grown and flourish, while keeping employment and inflation low. A healthy economy provides for popularity, tax receipts to fund government programs, and domestic peace and stability.
2. A healthy economy requires that wealth investors have confidence in the future. This has tended to create a set of presidential policies that favor wealthy investors, regardless of party affiliation.

X. **SUMMARY (p. 378)**
A. The American presidency has expanded significantly since the founding of the nation; only a few nineteenth-century presidents made much of a mark on the nation.
1. These include Thomas Jefferson, James Polk, and Abraham Lincoln. During the twentieth-century, as a result of industrialization, two world wars, and the Cold War, and the Great Depression, presidential powers and resources expanded greatly.
2. Since FDR the American presidency has expanded to its modern shape and form. Presidents must use a vast array of resources to successfully govern the United States.
3. The personality and style of the president, his ability to persuade citizens, interests, and other government decisionmakers, significantly impact presidential success.
4. The Founders produced a constitutionally mandated adversarial relationship between the executive and legislative branches; they engage in a perpetual tug-of-war, especially on domestic policy issues.
5. The presidency has become far more democratic than the Founders envisioned. Presidents listen to public opinion and respond to it, in addition to leading and sometimes manipulating the public.
   a) Interest groups, party activists, and financial contributors also influence what the president does.
   b) The modern presidency is increasingly involved in international policy matters. The president also wears many hats.
6. A vast bureaucracy and host of presidential advisors assist the president in executing the duties of the office.
7. Fluctuations in presidential popularity: presidents have strong incentives to *anticipate public reactions* and to do things that will please the public.
   a) Most presidents have begun their term of office with a fairly high favorable rating, and most have tended to lose popularity as time has passed; in general, those who lose popularity do so in response to *bad news*; *good news* increases a president's popularity.
   b) Successful military actions tend to add to presidential popularity; an unsuccessful war is bad news for a president, especially a limited war that drags on with high casualty rates (like the Korean War and the Vietnam War).

341

Terms for Review

Use this list to review essential principles, functions, and concepts from this chapter. Refer to your textbook for help in identifying and defining terms on this list. When you study, do not merely memorize terms; ask questions about the material you are reviewing, and look for the importance or significance of each item.

cabinet

checks and balances

chief diplomat

chief of staff

chief of state

commander in chief

Council of Economic Advisers (CEA)

divided government

domestic policy adviser

emergency powers

enduring presidency

executive agreement

Executive Office of the President (EOP)

habeas corpus

impoundment

international presidency

joint chief legislator

legislative clearance

line-item veto

national security adviser

National Security Council (NSC)

Office of Management and Budget (OMB)

presidential popularity

press secretary

supply-side economics

trusts

two presidencies

veto

vice-presidency

War Powers Resolution

White House Staff

Research Topics: Applying What You Have Learned

You will derive more benefit from your reading if you try to apply what you have learned. Some of the suggested research topics can be answered exclusively from your text, while others require you to conduct some basic research on your own. The references suggested under **Internet Sources** *will help you in your search.*

- Which of the allegations against President Clinton, which were made by Independent Counsel Kenneth Starr and congressional leadership, do you consider to be most serious? For example, would you place more emphasis on sexual improprieties than on charges of lying under oath, or possibly to political charges of lying to the American people? In your opinion, were the charges inflated by politics, or were they based on substance?

- The textbook notes that the most serious threats to democracy may come when leaders of both parties are united and no one challenges falsehoods, as sometimes occurs in cases of nationalist and apparently patriotic acts of foreign policy. Use this theme as the basis for a short essay in which you either support or oppose the basic premise.

- Read Article II of the Constitution, and write a brief essay in which you comment on the following statement from your textbook: "...the vague language of the Constitution proved flexible enough to encompass the great expansion of the presidency."

- Political scientists and historians have long questioned whether great presidents make great times, or whether great times and events create great presidents. What conclusion have you reached after reading this chapter?

The following resources are recommended for students who would like to do some additional research in the areas covered by this chapter. These references would also be helpful in expanding on the questions suggested under Research Topics.

Presidential Library Consortium http://metalab.unc.edu/lia/president/
Links to all existing presidential libraries and their vast repositories of information.

Roper Center http:// www.lib.uconn.edu/RoperCenter/
Reports on all major presidential performance and popularity polls.

Watergate Site www.washingtonpost.com/wp-srv/national/longterm/watergate/front.htm.
Complete information on the Watergate affair: background, congressional testimony, official statements, press coverage, speeches, court rulings, biographies of the leading players, and more.

Potus www.ipl.org/ref/POTUS
Biographies and other information about American presidents.

White House Home Page http://www.whitehouse.gov/
Information on the first family, recent presidential addresses and orders, text from news conferences, official presidential documents, and ways to contact the White House.

Self-Evaluation

Circle the correct answer for each question. Questions are listed in the same order in which the information appears in the text. Use the Answer Key in the back of the Study Guide *to check your responses.*

1. The president's cabinet
   a. Is provided for in Article II of the U.S. Constitution.
   b. Has developed primarily by custom because it is not mentioned in the Constitution.
   c. Has been designated by law as the primary advisory body in the executive branch.
   d. Meets with the president on a daily basis to devise policy strategies and implementation.

2. The most important president of the nineteenth century in terms of later development and expansion of the office was
   a. George Washington.
   b. Thomas Jefferson.
   c. Andrew Jackson.
   d. Abraham Lincoln.

3. When we look at the presidency, we find that
   a. The presidency began to dominate the political life of the nation by the time of the election of Thomas Jefferson in 1800.
   b. Although the United States became a world power in the twentieth century, the modern presidency functions essentially as the Founders expected.
   c. The growth and development of the presidency occurred primarily during isolationist periods of history when the president was the focal point of national leadership.
   d. Until the end of the nineteenth century, the presidency basically conformed to the designs and the intentions of the Founders.

4. Which president made the most frequent use of television for live press conferences?
   a. John F. Kennedy

b. Lyndon Johnson
c. Ronald Reagan
d. George Bush

5. Throughout most of our history, vice-presidents
   a. Have usually been close personal friends and political allies of the president.
   b. Have been highly regarded and effective leaders of the Senate.
   c. Have developed their own policy agendas and pursued their own political goals.
   d. Have not been personally or politically close to the president.

6. The modern presidency largely attained its shape under this president:
   a. Franklin Roosevelt.
   b. John F. Kennedy.
   c. Ronald Reagan.
   d. Bill Clinton.

7. A primary responsibility of the Office of Management and Budget (OMB) is that it
   a. Establishes the nation's monetary policy by changing the interest that is charged to member banks and lending institutions.
   b. Analyzes and conducts military operations, with particular attention paid to financial implications.
   c. Advises the president on how much the administration should propose to spend for government and where the money will come from.
   d. Analyzes the general state of the economy and advises the president on economic policy.

8. In his role as **chief of state**, the president
   a. Serves as commander in chief of the armed forces.
   b. Has assumed the leadership role in managing the nation's economy.
   c. Performs ceremonial functions and serves as the symbol of national authority and unity.
   d. Is expected to assume the initiative in forming public policy.

9. The **national security adviser** generally
   a. Holds press conferences and briefs the media on the changing role of the nation in the global arena.
   b. Organizes plans for new domestic laws and regulations and coordinates them with the nation's international agenda.
   c. Meets with the president every day in order to brief him on foreign policy matters and to advise him on foreign policy decisions.
   d. Is legally accountable for establishing and directing covert activities and foreign policy.

10. Which of the following has generally been true of presidential elections?
    a. The public has frequently failed to recognize the true goals of candidates and has often elected candidates who are out of touch with public wishes.
    b. A candidate whose goals are very far out of line with what the public favors is not likely to be elected.
    c. Once in office, presidents usually feel that public opinion is no longer important, and they can defy public opinion on major issues.
    d. Presidents normally feel that they must pay attention to public opinion only in times of great national crises.

11. Conflict between the president and Congress reflects
    a. The needs of the American public, who must be protected by the president from partisan politics in Congress.
    b. The essential nature of unitary systems, where power tends to rise to the top.
    c. A result of the conservative coalition between conservatives in the executive and legislative branches.
    d. A structural fact of American politics that was deliberately intended by the Founders.

12. Bill Clinton was elected on a platform that focused on
    a. Foreign policy and the role of multinational corporations.
    b. The need for reduction of waste and government regulation.
    c. National defense and policies to combat communism.
    d. The economy, health care, and education.

13. (T/F) Cabinet members occupy an ambiguous position in that they serve as advisers to the president but also represent their own constituencies.

14. (T/F) Most presidents receive a fairly low rating of approval at the beginning of their term, but their popularity with the public tends to improve toward the end of their term of office.

15. (T/F) Presidents tend to emerge as dominant figures during uneventful times when the president can concentrate on building his image with Congress and the public rather than during crises when the president's energies are directed elsewhere.

16. (T/F) Ronald Reagan presided over the most significant expansion of presidential functions and activities in American history.

17. (T/F) The question of which interest groups have a greater influence on policy depends partly upon which party controls the presidency.

18. (T/F) If no candidate wins a majority of electoral votes, the president will be selected by a run-off vote of the electoral college.

Chapter 13
THE FEDERAL BUREAUCRACY

Key Concepts and Objectives

The Key Concepts and Objectives provide a look at the fundamental goals and ideas of this chapter. This section serves as a guide to a basic understanding of the objectives of your textbook.

After reading this chapter, you should be able to:

- Understand the basic workings of the federal bureaucracy of the United States.
- Identify the growth of the federal bureaucracy and its relationship to the structural transformations in the U.S. economy and international system.
- Explain the differences between the federal bureaucracy of the United States and the bureaucracies of other democratic nations.
- Understand the structural influences such as the American political culture and the constitutional rules that shape the federal bureaucracy of the United States.
- Understand the influence of political linkage level actors and institutions, including voters, public opinion, and interest groups.
- Examine the responsiveness of the federal bureaucracy to the demands of the American people
- Examine the responsiveness of the federal bureaucracy to the demands of the American people.
- Understand how federal bureaucrats in specific agencies, in specific circumstances, can be relatively immune from public opinion.
- Understand the relationship of the federal bureaucracy to the struggle for democracy in America.
- Examine whether or not the federal bureaucracy enhances or diminishes democracy in America.
- Identify key terms and concepts used in Chapter 13.

Chapter Overview

This section provides a brief overview of the chapter contents. Read this section as a preview before reading your textbook. Then use this material as a review to help you retain information from your reading.

This section provides a brief overview of the chapter contents. Read this section as a preview before reading your textbook. Then use this material as a review to help you retain information from your reading.

→ THE FEDERAL BUREAUCRACY UNDER SIEGE

The April 19, 1995 bombing of the Frederick P. Murrah Federal Building in Oklahoma City, Oklahoma highlighted the animosity that some Americans felt toward the federal government of the United States. Though the bombing was the work of anti-government militia members, many people across the nation seemed to understand how anger against the federal government could trigger such a reaction.

The opening vignette underlines the fact that anti-federal government anger is a staple of American political history. This anti-federal government animus can be traced back to the Anti-Federalists' belief that that Constitution gave undue power to the central government of the United States.

In 1830, the state of South Carolina adopted the political doctrine of **nullification**, which its senator John C. Calhoun advocated as a means of disobeying federal laws that the state viewed as unconstitutional. As early as 1812, several New England states contemplated seceding from the Union of the United States in the same manner that the Confederate states actually did in 1860; prompting a bloody domestic war. During the Great Depression, even members of the Supreme Court felt that federal power had expanded too far, too fast to be constitutional. Many whites in the South grew angry with the federal government in the 1960s and 1970s because of its championing of civil rights. The CIA and FBI were the targets of the anti-war movement of the Vietnam period.

These and many other anti-federal government activities have had a profound impact on public policy in the United States. The chorus of anti-federal-government complaints has ebbed and flowed throughout history. This mood also helped focus critical attention on the federal bureaucracy, that part of the government that carries out federal policy. Americans express distrust and unhappiness with federal agencies such as the Internal Revenue Service (IRS), the Postal Service, the Bureau of Land Management, the Bureau of Alcohol, Tobacco, and Firearms (ATF), the Federal Bureau of Investigation (FBI) and the U.S. Forest Service.

➔A COMPARATIVE VIEW OF THE AMERICAN BUREAUCRACY

The American bureaucracy is different from bureaucracies in other democratic nations in ways that reflect the particular cultural influences and constitutional rules of the United States. This chapter focus on the federal bureaucracy, how it is organized, what it does, and what effects its actions have on public policies and American democracy.

Hostile Political Culture-Americans do not trust government; nor do they think it can accomplish most of the tasks assigned to it. They believe that the private sector can do a better job. As recently as 1998, most Americans reported that they **do not trust** the federal government of the United States.

The bureaucracy is influenced by this hostility in several ways. First, the American bureaucracy is surrounded by more legal restrictions and is subject to more intense legislative oversight than in other countries. Because **civil servants** have so little prestige, many of the most talented people in our society tend to stay away; they do not aspire to work in government. As well, the highest policymaking positions in the U.S. executive branch are closed to civil servants; they are reserved for presidential political appointees. This is not true in other democracies.

Incoherent Organization-The federal bureaucracy of the United States is not the standard pyramidal form as in other countries. The lines often lack control, responsibility, or accountability. Some executive branch units have no relationship at all to other agencies and departments. The bureaucracy if the United States was built piece by piece over the years in a political system without strong central government. Bureaucracies in other countries were often created at a single point in time.

Divided Control-The federal bureaucracy has two bosses: the president and Congress. These branches of government are constantly vying with one another for control. The separation of powers and checks and balances in the U.S. Constitution give each branch a role in the principal activities and responsibilities of the other branches. Most countries prefer a parliamentary system in which legislative and executive powers are combined into a single body, dominated by a cabinet and a prime minister. Civil servants in parliamentary systems are accountable to a single boss, a minister appointed by the prime minister.

Accessibility-Because of the incoherent organization, lack of a chain of command with clear lines of authority and accountability, and divided control on top, the federal bureaucracy of the United States is extremely open and porous. Individuals and groups can get a hearing and a response at various levels. This is potentially a very democratic arrangement, encouraging citizen participation in bureaucratic affairs.

→ TRANSFORMATION OF THE FEDERAL BUREAUCRACY: THE STRUCTURAL CONTEXT

Executive branch departments and officers are mentioned in the Constitution only in an indirect way. The Constitution does not go into any detail about the number or kinds of departments or agencies to be established. The Founders left this responsibility to Congress.

A brief administrative history of the United States-The most immediate causes for the transformation of the role of the federal government and the scale of the bureaucracy are political linkage sector pressures—from public opinion, voters, parties, interest groups, and social movements—on government decision makers. The more fundamental causes are changes in such structural level factors as the U.S. economy, the nation's population, and the role of the United States in the world.

Nineteenth-Century Changes-Before the Civil War the federal government had few responsibilities. The administrative apparatus of the executive branch was relatively undeveloped. The problems and opportunities created by rapid growth, westward expansion, the Industrial Revolution, and economic uncertainty in the last quarter of the nineteenth century gradually changed people's thinking about the appropriate responsibilities of government and the size of the bureaucracy.

The Corporation and the Progressives-The growth and increase in large corporations contributed to the growth and increase in the responsibilities of the federal government. Monopolies in major industries created a set of problems that mandated expanded federal responsibilities; legislation created new executive branch agencies to carry out the law.

The Great Depression-The Great Depression resulted in new programs such as work programs for the unemployed, relief for the poor, Social Security regulation of the banking and securities industries etc. Each program added new bureaucratic agencies to the executive branch.

World War II and Its Aftermath-World War II, America's new role as a superpower, and the long Cold War with the Soviet Union also brought a substantial increase in the federal government's responsibilities and the size of the executive branch. By 1950, a federal bureaucracy of substantial size and impact was firmly in place.

The Regulatory State-During the 1960s and 1970s the federal government took on responsibilities in the areas of civil rights, urban affairs, environmental and consumer protection, workplace safety, and education. Important among these initiatives was the formation of the

Department's of Health, Education and Welfare (now split into the Department of Health and Human Services, and the Department of Education). Though the Reagan Revolution slowed the growth in the federal government's responsibilities, it was unable to roll back most of the programs and agencies created since the Great Depression.

Devolution and Rollback-The 1994 Republican congressional landslide victory contributed to a decrease in the size of the federal government, the rolling back of many of its regulatory responsibilities, and a shift in the number of functions of the states. This "devolution and rollback" theme was echoed by Bill Clinton in the 1996 State of the Union address, in which he announced the "end of big government." Devolution and rollback may be related to changes in the global economy, where success seems to go to business enterprises that are "lean and mean," nimble and entrepreneurial, and to countries that allow their major companies to succeed by lowering regulatory and tax burdens. Political leaders in the United States have been paying attention recently to globalization processes and have acted to diminish the role and size of the federal government and its bureaucracy.

→HOW THE EXECUTIVE BRANCH IS ORGANIZED

The executive branch is made up of several different kinds of administrative units, which make the federal bureaucracy a very complicated entity. **Departments** are headed by cabinet-level secretaries, appointed by the president and approved by the Senate. The first three ever established were War, State, and the Treasury. Interest groups have been very influential in pressuring political decisionmakers to create new departments, such as the Departments of Agriculture and Commerce, and the Department of Education (formerly a part of the Department of Health, Education, and Welfare). Subdivisions within cabinet departments are known as **bureaus** and **agencies**. During the long reign of J. Edgar Hoover, the FBI did virtually as it pleased, even though it was (and remains) a unit within the Justice Department.

Independent Executive Agencies report directly to the president rather than to a department-or cabinet-level secretary. They are usually created to give greater control to the president in carrying out some executive function to highlight some particular public problem or issue that policymakers wish to address.

Government Corporations are agencies that operate very much like private companies. They can sell stock, retain and reinvest earnings, and borrow money, for instance. The U.S. Postal Service is such a government corporation.

Quasi-Governmental Organizations-are hybrids of public and private organizations. They allow the federal government to be involved in a particular area of activity without directly controlling it. The Corporation for Public Broadcasting fits into this category, as does the Federal Reserve Board.

Independent Regulatory Commissions-These commissions regulate sectors of public interest as "independent" departments. They stand outside the departmental structures are protected against direct presidential or congressional control. A commission is run by commissioners with long, overlapping terms, and many require a balance between Republicans and Democrats.

Foundations-These are units that are separated from the rest of government to protect them from political interference with science and the arts. Most prominent are the foundations for the Arts and for the Humanities and the National Science Foundation.

→WHAT DO BUREAUCRATS DO?

Bureaucrats engage in a wide range of activities that are relevant to the quality of democracy in the United States and affect how laws and regulations work.

Executing the Law-The term executive branch suggests the branch of the federal government that executes or carries out the law. The responsibility of executing the laws of the United States is carried out routinely as mail is delivered, troops are trained, and Social Security checks are mailed. Vague laws passed by Congress often complicate the execution of the law.

Regulating (Rule Making)-Congress often gives bureaucratic agencies the power to write specific rules. Because of the complexity of the problems that government must face, Congress tends to create agencies and to specify the job or mission that it wants done and then charges the agency with using its expertise to do the job.

Some critics believe that Congress delegates too much lawmaking to the executive branch. But Congress can change the rules written by bureaucrats if they drift too far from congressional intent or constituent desires. Others contend that there are too many rules and regulations.

Adjudicating-The National Labor Relations Board is an example of an agency with the power to conduct quasi-judicial proceedings in which disputes are resolved. Disputes may involve claims of unfair labor practices, or union related issues. Bureaucrats are unelected policymakers.

→WHO ARE THE BUREAUCRATS?

Because bureaucrats exercise substantial discretion as policymakers, we want to know who they are. How representative are they of the American people? In a democracy, one would probably want to see a pretty close correspondence between the people and bureaucrats.

The Merit Services-There are three different personnel systems in the executive branch: the career civil service, separate merit services in specific agencies, and political appointees.

The Career Civil Service-From 1828 until the late nineteenth century, the executive branch was staffed through what is commonly called the **spoils system**. It was generally accepted that the "spoils of victory" belonged to the winning party. Winners were expected to bring in their own people. This is also known as political patronage. The shortcoming of the War Department during the Civil War convinced many people that the federal personnel system needed revamping. A final catalyst for change in the system came when President James Garfield was assassinated by a person who wanted a federal job and couldn't get one in 1881.

The Civil Service Act of 1883, also known as the Pendleton Act, created a bipartisan Civil Service Commission to oversee a system of appointments to certain executive branch posts in the basis of **merit**. In 1978, Congress abolished the Civil Service Commission and replaced it with two separate agencies, the Office of Personnel Management and the Merit Systems Protection Board. The former administers the civil services laws, advertises positions, writes examinations, and acts as a clearinghouse for agencies that are looking for workers. The latter settles disputes concerning employee rights and obligations, hears employee grievances, and orders corrective action when needed.

Agency Merit Services-Congress has established separate merit systems for federal agencies that require personnel with particular kinds of training and experience appropriate to their missions. These agencies administer their own merit systems.

Declining Status of the Civil Service-The civil service in the United States suffers from a culture of antigovernment attitudes among the public and the worker preference for the private sector over the public sector. Pay and benefits for civil service workers have lagged behind the increase in the cost of living.

How Different Are Civil Servants? Civil servants share similar demographic backgrounds with the general population of the United States. Their political beliefs are also consonant with those of the general American public. They tend to favor the Democrats and to be more liberal than the general public. Woman and racial groups, together, make up a majority of civil service employees; they are overrepresented in the very lowest civil service grades and are underrepresented in the highest.

Political Appointees-The highest policymaking positions in the federal bureaucracy enter government service by way of presidential appointment. These are patronage appointments which allow the president to translate his electoral mandate into public policy by permitting him to put his people in key policymaking jobs. Presidents use patronage appointments to shore up support among electoral coalitions.

Top political appointees tend to be very unrepresentative of the American public. They tend to be much better educated and wealthier than other Americans. They also tend to be professionals, independent businesspeople, or corporate executives. High-level political appointees are subject to many influences in addition to the president, including Congress, the courts, personnel in their own departments and agencies, the press, and public opinion. On average, political appointees stay on their jobs for about 22 months before returning to private sector employment.

➜ POLITICAL AND GOVERNMENTAL INFLUENCES ON BUREAUCRATIC BEHAVIOR

Many forces such as the public, the president, Congress and the courts influence the American federal bureaucracy.

The Public-Americans focus on the content of public policies more than on the bureaucratic agencies of the bureaucrats. Americans have opinions about Social Security, but do not concern themselves with the Social Security Administration. The **IRS** is the exception.

The President-The president is the formal head of the executive branch of the federal government. Still, the president has only limited abilities to control the executive branch. Virtually every modern president has been surprised by bureaucrats who do not automatically do what the president expects.

Why Presidents Are Often Stymied by the Bureaucracy-The size and complexity of the executive branch is a main cause of presidential frustration with the federal bureaucracy. Because of civil service regulations, presidents have no say about the tenure or salary of most bureaucrats. Bureaucrats must respond to Congress and the courts as well. Finally, bureaucratic agencies are heavily insulated against presidential efforts to control them because of agency alliances with powerful interest groups.

Tools of Presidential Leadership-Presidents are capable of encouraging bureaucratic action. Presidents can use the prestige of the office to spur action. The power of appointment is also an important tool of presidential leadership. The president's power as chief budget officer of the federal government is also important. No agency of the federal bureaucracy can make its own budget request directly to Congress. The **OMB** has the statutory authority to block proposed legislation coming from any executive branch agency that it deems contrary to the president's budget or program.

Congress-Congress also exercises considerable influence over the federal bureaucracy. Legislating Agency Organization and Mission-The president shares control over the executive branch with Congress. Congress legislates the mission of bureaucratic agencies and details their organization and can change either one. Congress can also alter policy or behavior.
Confirming Presidential Appointments-The Senate has the authority to use the "advice and

consent" process in order to shape policies in bureaucratic departments and agencies. Congress can also draw out the process in a bid to gain concessions from the president and the nominee of future policies.

Controlling the Agency Budget-Congress controls the federal government's purse. It can use its control over agency budget to influence agency behavior. Congress uses the budget process to assess the performance of each agency each year, closely scrutinizing its activities before determining its next appropriation, the legal authority for the agency to spend money. Congress can cut agency budgets if it is displeased.

Oversight Hearings-Oversight hearings are an important tool which Congress uses to convey its views to bureaucrats. The IRS apologized for its aggressive tax collection methods after the Senate Finance Committee conducted hearings. But Congress is highly fragmented. This reality makes it possible for top-level bureaucrats to exploit partisan or ideological differences between congresspersons.

Interest Groups-Bureaucratic agencies often act as the supporters of interest groups against other government bodies, other interests, and the public. Interest groups are able to penetrate the federal bureaucracy and play an important role in its activities partly because of the absence of central administrative direction. Interest groups also help federal agencies that are in skirmishes with other federal agencies.

➔**COMMON CRITICISMS OF THE FEDERAL BUREAUCRACY**

Bureaucrats are often portrayed in popular culture as lazy paper shufflers or as indifferent, unresponsive, inhumane clerks denying people the benefits or services to which they are entitled. Politicians use this depiction to run as a political outsider "against Washington," promising to get the bureaucracy off the backs of citizens. The authors present four common criticisms of the federal bureaucracy and assess them:

"The Federal Bureaucracy Is Always Expanding"-Despite the early growth that occurred during the first half of the twentieth century, it remained relatively stable at about 3 million through the 1990s and dropped to less than 2.4 million since then.

"The Federal Bureaucracy Is Wasteful and Inefficient"-Because bureaucracies have discretionary control over only about 5 percent of the total federal budget, waste is kept at a minimum. Ninety-five percent is earmarked for specific purposes or it is distributed to beneficiaries by formula, or entitlements. Almost all of the federal budget goes to pay the interest on the national debt, to direct payments to individuals, and to grants-in-aid and block grants to the states and localities. As well, the federal government is compelled to provide **public goods** which the private sector tends to avoid.

"The Federal Bureaucracy Is Ineffective"-The federal bureaucracy's mixed record is exemplified by some of NASA's successes and failures. The Framers intended for the federal government to be ineffective as a means to frustrate and avoid possible tyranny in the United States.

"The Federal Bureaucracy Is Mired in Red Tape"-The authors disagree with the characterization that the federal bureaucracy is marred in red tape. They contend while there are problems with waste and inefficiency, the stereotypes greatly exaggerate the extent of the problem. They contend that many of the pathologies of the federal bureaucracy do not originate in the bureaucracy, but imposed by the Constitution.

➔REFORMING THE FEDERAL BUREAUCRACY

How one views the problems of the federal bureaucracy will dictate the reform remedies one proposes.

Scaling Back the Size of the Bureaucracy-Government can be trimmed by slimming it down and by transferring control.

"Cutting the Fat"-Political candidates often promise the citizens that they will "cut the fat" if elected. The federal bureaucracy has been reduced significantly in recent decades.

Privatizing-The process of privatization is based on two assumptions: that private business can often do things better than the government and that competitive pressure from the private sector will force government agencies to be more efficient. Many states and local communities have "contracted out" to private companies public services like trash collection, and jails and prisons management. Critics complain that private business might cur corners in order to turn a profit. As well, they contend that a private business under government contract is several steps removed from political control, and the normal instruments of democratic accountability might not be as effective as they are in controlling government agencies.

Reinventing Government-The Clinton-Gore administration promised to "reinvent government". The argument, based on influential book with the same title, proposed that to effectively transform government, cutting excess and privatizing should be coupled with the use of business principals by the federal government. Their idea is that government agencies will provide better public services if they are run like private businesses. Though Congress was unwilling to go along with this theory of government management, many changes were made in the agencies by executive order of the president.

Protecting Against Bureaucratic Abuses of Power-Many people believe that there should be greater legislative oversight of bureaucratic agencies. There are many legislative enactments that try to keep bureaucratic activity within narrow boundaries. Some reformers would like to see greater protection provided for **whistleblowers**, bureaucrats who report corruption, financial mismanagement, abuses of power, or other official deceit

Increasing Popular Participation-Citizen input is potentially an effective remedy to bureaucratic excesses and abuses. Popular sovereignty implies that administrative discretion should be narrowed as much as possible and that clear directions and unambiguous policies should be communicated by elected officials to bureaucratic agencies.

Increasing Presidential Control-Popular sovereignty requires that the elected representatives of the people closely control the bureaucracy. Popular sovereignty also implies that administrative discretion should be narrowed as much as possible and that clear directions and unambiguous policies should be communicated by elected officials to bureaucratic agencies; the president especially has an interest in seeing that the bureaucracy as a *whole* is efficient and well organized.

→ SUMMARY

The executive branch has grown in size and responsibility. The growth is a consequence of a transformation in the conception of the proper role of government because of structural changes in the economy and the society. Although bureaucracy is not a popular concept in the American political tradition, we have created a sizable one. Bureaucratic organizations have certain strengths that make them attractive for accomplishing large-scale tasks.

Bureaucrats are involved in executing the law, regulating, and adjudicating disputes. In each of these, they exercise a great deal of discretion. Because they are unelected policymakers, democratic theory demands that we be concerned about who the bureaucrats are. In the merit services, they are very much like other Americans in terms of background and attitudes. Political appointees are bureaucrats who are very different from their fellow citizens.

Several political and governmental actors and institutions affect bureaucratic behavior, including the president, Congress, the courts, interest groups, and public opinion. Those who want to make democracy more of a reality propose giving more control over the bureaucracy to the president and diminishing the role of interest groups.

Chapter Outline

Protecting Against Bureaucratic Abuses of Power-Many people believe that there should be greater legislative oversight of bureaucratic agencies. There are many legislative enactments that try to keep bureaucratic activity within narrow boundaries. Some reformers would like to see greater protection provided for **whistleblowers**, bureaucrats who report corruption, financial mismanagement, abuses of power, or other official deceit

Increasing Popular Participation-Citizen input is potentially an effective remedy to bureaucratic excesses and abuses. Popular sovereignty implies that administrative discretion should be narrowed as much as possible and that clear directions and unambiguous policies should be communicated by elected officials to bureaucratic agencies.

Increasing Presidential Control-Popular sovereignty requires that the elected representatives of the people closely control the bureaucracy. Popular sovereignty also implies that administrative discretion should be narrowed as much as possible and that clear directions and unambiguous policies should be communicated by elected officials to bureaucratic agencies; the president especially has an interest in seeing that the bureaucracy as a *whole* is efficient and well organized.

→ SUMMARY

The executive branch has grown in size and responsibility. The growth is a consequence of a transformation in the conception of the proper role of government because of structural changes in the economy and the society. Although bureaucracy is not a popular concept in the American political tradition, we have created a sizable one. Bureaucratic organizations have certain strengths that make them attractive for accomplishing large-scale tasks.

Bureaucrats are involved in executing the law, regulating, and adjudicating disputes. In each of these, they exercise a great deal of discretion. Because they are unelected policymakers, democratic theory demands that we be concerned about who the bureaucrats are. In the merit services, they are very much like other Americans in terms of background and attitudes. Political appointees are bureaucrats who are very different from their fellow citizens.

Several political and governmental actors and institutions affect bureaucratic behavior, including the president, Congress, the courts, interest groups, and public opinion. Those who want to make democracy more of a reality propose giving more control over the bureaucracy to the president and diminishing the role of interest groups.

```
Chapter
Outline
```

This section gives you a comprehensive review of the chapter. Use this outline in combination with your textbook to look for key concepts and objectives, to identify essential terms and names, and to gain a basic understanding of political practices and principles from this chapter.

I. THE FEDERAL BUREAUCRACY UNDER SIEGE (pp. 383-384)

A. The April 19, 1995 bombing of the Frederick P. Murrah Federal Building in Oklahoma City, Oklahoma highlighted the animosity that some Americans felt toward the federal government of the United States. Though the bombing was the work of anti-government militia members, many people across the nation seemed to understand how anger against the federal government could trigger such a reaction.

B. The opening vignette underlines the fact that anti-federal government anger is a staple of American political history. This anti-federal government animus can be traced back to the Anti-Federalists' belief that that Constitution gave undue power to the central government of the United States.

C. In 1830, the state of South Carolina adopted the political doctrine of **nullification**, which its senator John C. Calhoun advocated as a means of disobeying federal laws that the state viewed as unconstitutional.

   1. As early as 1812, several New England states contemplated seceding from the Union of the United States in the same manner that the Confederate states actually did in 1860; prompting a bloody domestic war.

   2. During the Great Depression, even members of the Supreme Court felt that federal power had expanded too far, too fast to be constitutional.

   3. Many whites in the South grew angry with the federal government in the 1960s and 1970s because of its championing of civil rights. The CIA and FBI were the targets of the anti-war movement of the Vietnam period.

   4. These and many other anti-federal government activities have had a profound impact on public policy in the United States.

      a) The chorus of anti-federal-government complaints has ebbed and flowed throughout history.

      b) This mood also helped focus critical attention on the federal bureaucracy, that part of the government that carries out federal policy.

   5. Americans express distrust and unhappiness with federal agencies such as the Internal Revenue Service (IRS), the Postal Service, the Bureau of Land Management, the Bureau of Alcohol, Tobacco, and Firearms (ATF), the Federal Bureau of Investigation (FBI) and the U.S. Forest Service.

II. A COMPARATIVE VIEW OF THE AMERICAN BUREAUCRACY (pp. 384-386)

A. The American bureaucracy is different from bureaucracies in other democratic nations in ways that reflect the particular cultural influences and constitutional rules of the United States.

361

B. This chapter focus on the federal bureaucracy, how it is organized, what it does, and what effects its actions have on public policies and American democracy.

C. **Hostile political culture**
   1. Americans do not trust government; nor do they think it can accomplish most of the tasks assigned to it. They believe that the private sector can do a better job.
   2. As recently as 1998, most Americans reported that they **do not trust** the federal government of the United States.

D. The bureaucracy is influenced by this hostility in several ways.
   1. First, the American bureaucracy is surrounded by more legal restrictions and is subject to more intense legislative oversight than in other countries.
   2. Because **civil servants** have so little prestige, many of the most talented people in our society tend to stay away; they do not aspire to work in government.
   3. As well, the highest policymaking positions in the U.S. executive branch are closed to civil servants; they are reserved for presidential political appointees. This is not true in other democracies.

E. **Incoherent organization**
   1. The federal bureaucracy of the United States is not the standard pyramidal form as in other countries.
      a) The lines often lack control, responsibility, or accountability.
      b) Some executive branch units have no relationship at all to other agencies and departments.
   2. The bureaucracy if the United States was built piece by piece over the years in a political system without strong central government. Bureaucracies in other countries were often created at a single point in time.

F. **Divided control**
   1. The federal bureaucracy has two bosses: the president and Congress.
      a) These branches of government are constantly vying with one another for control. The separation of powers and checks and balances in the U.S. Constitution give each branch a role in the principal activities and responsibilities of the other branches.
      b) Most countries prefer a parliamentary system in which legislative and executive powers are combined into a single body, dominated by a cabinet and a prime minister.
   2. Civil servants in parliamentary systems are accountable to a single boss, a minister appointed by the prime minister.

G. **Accessibility**
   1. Because of the incoherent organization, lack of a chain of command with clear lines of authority and accountability, and divided control on top, the federal bureaucracy of the United States is extremely open and porous.
   2. Individuals and groups can get a hearing and a response at various levels. This is potentially a very democratic arrangement, encouraging citizen participation in

bureaucratic affairs.

III. TRANSFORMING THE FEDERAL BUREAUCRACY: THE STRUCTURAL CONTEXT (pp. 386-390)

A. Executive branch departments and officers are mentioned in the Constitution only in an indirect way.

B. The Constitution does not go into any detail about the number or kinds of departments or agencies to be established. The Founders left this responsibility to Congress.

C. **A brief administrative history of the United States**

1. The most immediate causes for the transformation of the role of the federal government and the scale of the bureaucracy are political linkage sector pressures—from public opinion, voters, parties, interest groups, and social movements—on government decision makers.

2. The more fundamental causes are changes in such structural level factors as the U.S. economy, the nation's population, and the role of the United States in the world.

D. **Nineteenth-Century changes**

1. Before the Civil War the federal government had few responsibilities.
   a) The administrative apparatus of the executive branch was relatively undeveloped.
   b) The problems and opportunities created by rapid growth, westward expansion.

2. The Industrial Revolution, and economic uncertainty in the last quarter of the nineteenth century gradually changed people's thinking about the appropriate responsibilities of government and the size of the bureaucracy.

E. **The corporation and the Progressives**

1. The growth and increase in large corporations contributed to the growth and increase in the responsibilities of the federal government.

2. Monopolies in major industries created a set of problems that mandated expanded federal responsibilities; legislation created new executive branch agencies to carry out the law.

F. **The Great Depression**

1. The Great Depression resulted in new programs such as work programs for the unemployed, relief for the poor, Social Security regulation of the banking and securities industries etc.

2. Each program added new bureaucratic agencies to the executive branch.

G. **World War II and its aftermath**

1. World War II, America's new role as a superpower, and the long Cold War with the Soviet Union also brought a substantial increase in the federal government's responsibilities and the size of the executive branch.

2. By 1950, a federal bureaucracy of substantial size and impact was firmly in place.

H. **The regulatory state**

1. During the 1960s and 1970s the federal government took on responsibilities in the areas of civil rights, urban affairs, environmental and consumer protection,

workplace safety, and education. Important among these initiatives was the
formation of the Department's of Health, Education and Welfare (now split into
the Department of Health and Human Services, and the Department of Education).

2. Though the Reagan Revolution slowed the growth in the federal government's
responsibilities, it was unable to roll back most of the programs and agencies
created since the Great Depression.

I. **Devolution and rollback**
1. The 1994 Republican congressional landslide victory contributed to a decrease in
the size of the federal government, the rolling back of many of its regulatory
responsibilities, and a shift in the number of functions of the states.
2. This "devolution and rollback" theme was echoed by Bill Clinton in the 1996 State
of the Union address, in which he announced the "end of big government."
3. Devolution and rollback may be related to changes in the global economy, where
success seems to go to business enterprises that are "lean and mean," nimble and
entrepreneurial, and to countries that allow their major companies to succeed by
lowering regulatory and tax burdens.
4. Political leaders in the United States have been paying attention recently to
globalization processes and have acted to diminish the role and size of the federal
government and its bureaucracy.

IV. **HOW THE EXECUTIVE BRANCH IS ORGANIZED (pp. 390-392)**
A. The executive branch is made up of several different kinds of administrative units,
which make the federal bureaucracy a very complicated entity.
1. *Departments* are headed by cabinet-level secretaries, appointed by the president
and approved by the Senate.
   a) The first three ever established were War, State, and the Treasury.
   b) Interest groups have been very influential in pressuring political
   decisionmakers to create new departments, such as the Departments of
   Agriculture and Commerce, and the Department of Education (formerly a part
   of the Department of Health, Education, and Welfare).
   c) Subdivisions within cabinet departments are known as *bureaus* and *agencies*.
2. During the long reign of J. Edgar Hoover, the FBI did virtually as it pleased, even
though it was (and remains) a unit within the Justice Department. *Independent
executive agencies* report directly to the president rather than to a department-or
cabinet-level secretary.
3. They are usually created to give greater control to the president in carrying out
some executive function to highlight some particular public problem or issue that
policymakers wish to address.
   a) *Government corporations* are agencies that operate very much like private
   companies. They can sell stock, retain and reinvest earnings, and borrow
   money, for instance. The U.S. Postal Service is such a government corporation.
   b) *Quasi-governmental organizations*-are hybrids of public and private

organizations. They allow the federal government to be involved in a particular area of activity without directly controlling it. The Corporation for Public Broadcasting fits into this category, as does the Federal Reserve Board.

    c) *Independent regulatory commissions*-These commissions regulate sectors of public interest as "independent" departments. They stand outside the departmental structures are protected against direct presidential or congressional control. A commission is run by commissioners with long, overlapping terms, and many require a balance between Republicans and Democrats.

    d) *Foundations*-These are units that are separated from the rest of government to protect them from political interference with science and the arts. Most prominent are the foundations for the Arts and for the Humanities and the National Science Foundation.

V. WHAT DO BUREAUCRATS DO? (pp. 392-393)

  A. Bureaucrats engage in a wide range of activities that are relevant to the quality of democracy in the United States and affect how laws and regulations work.

  B. **Executing the law**
1. The term executive branch suggests the branch of the federal government that executes or carries out the law.
2. The responsibility of executing the laws of the United States is carried out routinely as mail is delivered, troops are trained, and Social Security checks are mailed.
3. Vague laws passed by Congress often complicate the execution of the law.

  C. **Regulating (rule making)**
1. Congress often gives bureaucratic agencies the power to write specific rules.
    a) Because of the complexity of the problems that government must face, Congress tends to create agencies and to specify the job or mission that it wants done and then charges the agency with using its expertise to do the job.
    b) Some critics believe that Congress delegates too much lawmaking to the executive branch. But Congress can change the rules written by bureaucrats if they drift too far from congressional intent or constituent desires.
2. Others contend that there are too many rules and regulations.

  D. **Adjudicating**
1. The National Labor Relations Board is an example of an agency with the power to conduct quasi-judicial proceedings in which disputes are resolved.
2. Disputes may involve claims of unfair labor practices, or union related issues. Bureaucrats are un-elected policymakers.

VI. WHO ARE THE BUREAUCRATS? (pp. 393-398)

  A. Because bureaucrats exercise substantial discretion as policymakers, we want to know who they are. How representative are they of the American people?

B. In a democracy, one would probably want to see a pretty close correspondence between the people and bureaucrats.

C. **The merit services**
   1. There are three different personnel systems in the executive branch: the career civil service, separate merit services in specific agencies, and political appointees.
      a) **The career civil service**-From 1828 until the late nineteenth century, the executive branch was staffed through what is commonly called the **spoils system**.
         (1) It was generally accepted that the "spoils of victory" belonged to the winning party.
         (2) Winners were expected to bring in their own people. This is also known as political *patronage*.
         (3) The shortcoming of the War Department during the Civil War convinced many people that the federal personnel system needed revamping.
         (4) A final catalyst for change in the system came when President James Garfield was assassinated by a person who wanted a federal job and couldn't get one in 1881.
      b) **The Civil Service Act of 1883**, also known as the Pendleton Act, created a bipartisan Civil Service Commission to oversee a system of appointments to certain executive branch posts in the basis of **merit**.
         (1) In 1978, Congress abolished the Civil Service Commission and replaced it with two separate agencies, the Office of Personnel Management and the Merit Systems Protection Board.
         (2) The former administers the civil services laws, advertises positions, writes examinations, and acts as a clearinghouse for agencies that are looking for workers. The latter settles disputes concerning employee rights and obligations, hears employee grievances, and orders corrective action when needed.
      c) **Agency merit services**-Congress has established separate merit systems for federal agencies that require personnel with particular kinds of training and experience appropriate to their missions. These agencies administer their own merit systems.
   2. **Declining status of the civil service**-The civil service in the United States suffers from a culture of antigovernment attitudes among the public and the worker preference for the private sector over the public sector. Pay and benefits for civil service workers have lagged behind the increase in the cost of living.

D. **How different are civil servants?**
   1. Civil servants share similar demographic backgrounds with the general population of the United States. Their political beliefs are also consonant with those of the general American public.

2. They tend to favor the Democrats and to be more liberal than the general public. Woman and racial groups, together, make up a majority of civil service employees; they are overrepresented in the very lowest civil service grades and are underrepresented in the highest.

E. **Political appointees**
   1. The highest policymaking positions in the federal bureaucracy enter government service by way of presidential appointment.
      a) These are patronage appointments which allow the president to translate his electoral mandate into public policy by permitting him to put his people in key policymaking jobs.
      b) Presidents use patronage appointments to shore up support among electoral coalitions.
   2. Top political appointees tend to be very unrepresentative of the American public.
      a) They tend to be much better educated and wealthier than other Americans.
      b) They also tend to be professionals, independent businesspeople, or corporate executives.
   3. High-level political appointees are subject to many influences in addition to the president, including Congress, the courts, personnel in their own departments and agencies, the press, and public opinion. On average, political appointees stay on their jobs for about 22 months before returning to private sector employment.

VII. **POLITICAL AND GOVERNMENTAL INFLUENCES ON BUREAUCRATIC BEHAVIOR (pp. 398-402)**
   A. Many forces such as the public, the president, Congress and the courts influence the American federal bureaucracy.
   B. **The public**
      1. Americans focus on the content of public policies more than on the bureaucratic agencies of the bureaucrats.
      2. Americans have opinions about Social Security, but do not concern themselves with the Social Security Administration. The **IRS** is the exception.
   C. **The president**
      1. The president is the formal head of the executive branch of the federal government.
      2. Still, the president has only limited abilities to control the executive branch.
      3. Virtually every modern president has been surprised by bureaucrats who do not automatically do what the president expects.
   D. *Why presidents are often stymied by the bureaucracy*
      1. The size and complexity of the executive branch is a main cause of presidential frustration with the federal bureaucracy.
         a) Because of civil service regulations, presidents have no say about the tenure or salary of most bureaucrats.
         b) Bureaucrats must respond to Congress and the courts as well.

2. Finally, bureaucratic agencies are heavily insulated against presidential efforts to control them because of agency alliances with powerful interest groups.

E. *Tools of presidential leadership*
   1. Presidents are capable of encouraging bureaucratic action.
      a) Presidents can use the prestige of the office to spur action.
      b) The power of appointment is also an important tool of presidential leadership.
      c) The president's power as chief budget officer of the federal government is also important.
   2. No agency of the federal bureaucracy can make its own budget request directly to Congress. The **OMB** has the statutory authority to block proposed legislation coming from any executive branch agency that it deems contrary to the president's budget or program.

F. **Congress**
   1. Congress also exercises considerable influence over the federal bureaucracy.
   2. **Legislating agency organization and mission**
      a) The president shares control over the executive branch with Congress.
      b) Congress legislates the mission of bureaucratic agencies and details their organization and can change either one. Congress can also alter policy or behavior.
   3. *Confirming presidential appointments*
      a) The Senate has the authority to use the "advice and consent" process in order to shape policies in bureaucratic departments and agencies.
      b) Congress can also draw out the process in a bid to gain concessions from the president and the nominee of future policies.
   4. *Controlling the agency budget*
      a) Congress controls the federal government's purse. It can use its control over agency budget to influence agency behavior.
      b) Congress uses the budget process to assess the performance of each agency each year, closely scrutinizing its activities before determining its next appropriation, the legal authority for the agency to spend money. Congress can cut agency budgets if it is displeased.
   5. **Oversight hearings**
      a) Oversight hearings are an important tool which Congress uses to convey its views to bureaucrats. The IRS apologized for its aggressive tax collection methods after the Senate Finance Committee conducted hearings.
      b) But Congress is highly fragmented. This reality makes it possible for top-level bureaucrats to exploit partisan or ideological differences between congresspersons.

G. **Interest groups**
   1. Bureaucratic agencies often act as the supporters of interest groups against other government bodies, other interests, and the public.
   2. Interest groups are able to penetrate the federal bureaucracy and play an important

role in its activities partly because of the absence of central administrative direction.

3. Interest groups also help federal agencies that are in skirmishes with other federal agencies.

VIII. COMMON CRITICISMS OF THE FEDERAL BUREAUCRACY (pp. 402-404)

A. Bureaucrats are often portrayed in popular culture as lazy paper shufflers or as indifferent, unresponsive, inhumane clerks denying people the benefits or services to which they are entitled.

B. Politicians use this depiction to run as a political outsider "against Washington," promising to get the bureaucracy off the backs of citizens. The authors present four common criticisms of the federal bureaucracy and assess them:

1. **"The federal bureaucracy is always expanding"**-Despite the early growth that occurred during the first half of the twentieth century, it remained relatively stable at about 3 million through the 1990s and dropped to less than 2.4 million since then.

2. **"The federal bureaucracy is ineffective"**-The federal bureaucracy's mixed record is exemplified by some of NASA's successes and failures. The Framers intended for the federal government to be ineffective as a means to frustrate and avoid possible tyranny in the United States.

3. **"The federal bureaucracy is wasteful and inefficient"**-Because bureaucracies have discretionary control over only about 5 percent of the total federal budget, waste is kept at a minimum. Ninety-five percent is earmarked for specific purposes or it is distributed to beneficiaries by formula, or entitlements. Almost all of the federal budget goes to pay the interest on the national debt, to direct payments to individuals, and to grants-in-aid and block grants to the states and localities. As well, the federal government is compelled to provide **public goods** which the private sector tends to avoid.

4. **"The federal bureaucracy is mired in red tape"**-The authors disagree with the characterization that the federal bureaucracy is marred in red tape. They contend while there are problems with waste and inefficiency, the stereotypes greatly exaggerate the extent of the problem. They contend that many of the pathologies of the federal bureaucracy do not originate in the bureaucracy, but imposed by the Constitution.

IX. REFORMING THE FEDERAL BUREAUCRACY (PP. 404-408)

A. How one views the problems of the federal bureaucracy will dictate the reform remedies one proposes.

B. **Scaling back the size of the bureaucracy**-Government can be trimmed by slimming it down and by transferring control.

C. "Cutting the fat"

1. Political candidates often promise the citizens that they will "cut the fat" if elected.

369

2. The federal bureaucracy has been reduced significantly in recent decades.

D. **Privatizing**

1. The process of privatization is based on two assumptions: that private business can often do things better than the government and that competitive pressure from the private sector will force government agencies to be more efficient.

   a) Many states and local communities have "contracted out" to private companies public services like trash collection, and jails and prisons management.

   b) Critics complain that private business might cur corners in order to turn a profit.

   c) As well, they contend that a private business under government contract is several steps removed from political control, and the normal instruments of democratic accountability might not be as effective as they are in controlling government agencies.

2. **Reinventing government**

   a) The Clinton-Gore administration promised to "reinvent government".

      (1) The argument, based on   influential book with the same title, proposed that in order to effectively transform government, cutting excess and privatizing should be coupled with the use of business principals by the federal government.

      (2) Their idea is that government agencies will provide better public services if they are run like private businesses.

   b) Though Congress was unwilling to go along with this theory of government management, many changes were made in the agencies by executive order of the president.

3. **Protecting against bureaucratic abuses of power**

   a) Many people believe that there should be greater legislative oversight of bureaucratic agencies.

   b) There are many legislative enactments that try to keep bureaucratic activity within narrow boundaries.

   c) Some reformers would like to see greater protection provided for **whistleblowers**, bureaucrats who report corruption, financial mismanagement, abuses of power, or other official deceit.

4. **Increasing popular participation**

   a) Citizen input is potentially an effective remedy to bureaucratic excesses and abuses.

   b) Popular sovereignty implies that administrative discretion should be narrowed as much as possible and that clear directions and unambiguous policies should be communicated by elected officials to bureaucratic agencies.

5. **Increasing presidential control**

E. Popular sovereignty requires that the elected representatives of the people closely control the bureaucracy.

F. Popular sovereignty also implies that administrative discretion should be narrowed as much as possible and that clear directions and unambiguous policies should be communicated by elected officials to bureaucratic agencies; the president especially has an interest in seeing that the bureaucracy as a *whole* is efficient and well organized.

X. SUMMARY (pp. 408-409)

A. The executive branch has grown in size and responsibility. The growth is a consequence of a transformation in the conception of the proper role of government because of structural changes in the economy and the society.

B. Although bureaucracy is not a popular concept in the American political tradition, we have created a sizable one. Bureaucratic organizations have certain strengths that make them attractive for accomplishing large-scale tasks.

C. Bureaucrats are involved in executing the law, regulating, and adjudicating disputes. In each of these, they exercise a great deal of discretion.
　1. Because they are unelected policymakers, democratic theory demands that we be concerned about who the bureaucrats are.
　2. In the merit services, they are very much like other Americans in terms of background and attitudes.
　3. Political appointees are bureaucrats who are very different from their fellow citizens.

D. Several political and governmental actors and institutions affect bureaucratic behavior, including the president, Congress, the courts, interest groups, and public opinion.

E. Those who want to make democracy more of a reality propose giving more control over the bureaucracy to the president and diminishing the role of interest groups.

Use this list to review essential principles, functions, and concepts from this chapter. Refer to your textbook for help in identifying and defining terms on this list. When you study, do not merely memorize terms; ask questions about the material you are reviewing, and look for the importance or significance of each item.

appropriation

civil servants

civil service

cost-benefit analysis

devolution

entitlements

patronage

public goods

red tape

regulatory

spoils system

whistle-blowers

Research Topics: Applying What You Have Learned

*You will derive more benefit from your reading if you try to apply what you have learned. Some of the suggested research topics can be answered exclusively from your text, while others require you to conduct some basic research on your own. The references suggested under **Internet Sources** will help you in your search.*

- Think about the various ways in which the bureaucracy of the federal government directly impacts your life as a citizen of the United States. List the ways in which bureaucracy improves the quality of life for the citizens of the United States and some of the ways that bureaucracy may diminish it.

- Compare the American civil service to that of another developed nation from the West. Is the United States' bureaucracy any more or less efficient? Outline the areas where the American civil service system is more or less efficient than the nation to which it is compared.

- In a short essay, compare the federal bureaucracy to the three major branches of government. Based on your reading of this chapter explain how the federal bureaucracy may be more or less democratic than each of the others.

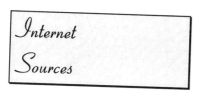

The following resources are recommended for students who would like to do some additional research in the areas covered by this chapter. These references would also be helpful in expanding on the questions suggested under Research Topics.

Fedworld *http://www.fedworld.gov/*

The gateway to the federal government's numerous Web sites and Gophers; connections to virtually every federal department, bureau, commission, and foundation, as well as access to government statistics and reports.

Yahoo: Executive Branch *http://yahoo.com/Government/Executive_Branch/*

Similar to Fedworld; which to use depends on personal taste.

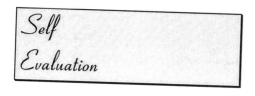

Circle the correct answer for each question. Questions are listed in the same order in which the information appears in the text. Use the Answer Key in the back of the Study Guide to check your responses.

1. In all but which of the following decades did a very strong anti-federal-government mood emerge?
   a. 1790s
   b. 1830s
   c. 1940s
   d. 1970s
   e. 1990s

2. Americans tend to _____ the federal bureaucracy
   a. trust

    b. distrust

3. The federal bureaucracy has_____ boss(es) according to your text?

    a. one
    b. two
    c. three
    d. many
    e. zero

4. Which of the following events "forever changed how Americans thought about the U.S. government"?

    a. The Great Depression
    b. World War I
    c. World War II
    d. The Cold War

5. Which of the following is NOT one of the administrative units of the federal bureaucracy ?

    a. departments
    b. agencies
    c. foundations
    d. congressional committees

6. Which of the two major political parties has been committed to paring down the size of the federal government?

    a. Democrats
    b. Republicans

7. Which of the following federal departments was not part of the administration of George Washington?

    a. Department of War
    b. Department of State
    c. Department of Treasury
    d. The Department of Housing and Urban development

8. Which of the following acts is also known as the Pendelton Act?

    a. The OMB
    b. The Civil Service Act (1883)
    c. The Sherman Antitrust Act (1890)
    d. The Pure Food and Drug Act (1906)
    e. The Federal Trade and Commissions Act (1914)

9. From the 1820s to the 1890s, the "spoils system" benefited

    a. Election winners

    b. Election losers

10. Women and racial groups are _____ in the very lowest civil service grades and are
_____ in the highest.
    a. Overrepresented and underrepresented
    b. Underrepresented and overrepresented
    c. None of the above

11. Which of the following presidents appointed the highest number of women and racial groups
to the executive branch?
    a. Bush
    b. Carter
    c. Clinton
    d. Ford
    e. Reagan

12. Which of the following presidents, out of frustration, thought of the federal bureaucracy as an
"alien institution"?
    a. Bush
    b. Carter
    c. Clinton
    d. Nixon
    e. Reagan

13. (T/F) Appropriation is the legal authority for a state government agency to spend money
from the U.S. Treasury.

14. (T/F) Congress has no oversight responsibilities over the federal bureaucracy.

15. (T/F) Privatization is the process of turning over certain government functions to the private

sector.

16. (T/F) The 1995 bombing of the Frederick P. Murrah Building in Oklahoma City was aimed
mainly at the state government in Oklahoma.

17. (T/F) The idea of "ending big government" is the opposite to the idea of "devolution and
rollback."

18. (T/F) The president controls agency budgets in order to influence agency behavior.

Chapter 14
THE COURTS

Key Concepts and Objectives

The Key Concepts and Objectives provide a look at the fundamental goals and ideas of this chapter. This section serves as a guide to a basic understanding of the objectives of your textbook.

After reading this chapter, you should be able to:

- Describe how the judicial system operates.
- Trace the origin and development of judicial review.
- Explain how appointments are made to the federal courts, and identify factors that are important in the selection and confirmation processes.
- Outline the organization and jurisdiction of the federal court system.
- Identify the screening mechanisms of the U.S. Supreme Court.
- Explain how the Supreme Court functions and makes decisions.
- Identify key personnel involved in the federal court system, and summarize their responsibilities.
- Discuss the continuing debates on judicial activism and original intent.
- Explain how and why judicial interpretations of the Constitution have changed over the course of U.S. history.
- Trace the three major periods in the history of constitutional law in the United States.
- Summarize governmental, political linkage, and structural influences on the federal court system.
- Analyze the role of the Supreme Court as a national policymaker, and assess its role in a democratic society.
- Identify key terms and concepts used in Chapter 14.

This section provides a brief overview of the chapter contents. Read this section as a preview before reading your textbook. Then use this material as a review to help you retain information from your reading.

➔ **THE COURT CHANGES COURSE ON *ROE* V. *WADE***

Chapter 14 reflects on the ways in which the Court makes decisions that have important consequences for the American people. The Court is embedded in a governmental, political linkage, and structural environment that shapes its behavior. Courts must coexist with other governmental bodies (such as Congress, the president, and executive branch departments and agencies) that have their own powers, interests, constituencies, and conceptions of the public good. Political linkage influences are exerted by interest groups, social movements, and public opinion. Changes in constitutional law and judicial interpretation have been influenced by structural factors such as population growth, industrialization, and economic change.

The Court does not initiate or pass new laws, but it *interprets* the meaning of law and the Constitution. In this sense, it makes law and is a national policymaker. The authors use the Supreme Court decisions in the abortion cases of *Roe* v. *Wade* (1973) and *Webster* v. *Reproductive Health Services* (1989) to illustrate how the Court makes decisions that have important consequences for the American people. The language of the U.S. Constitution did not change in the time that elapsed between *Roe* and *Webster*, but the interpretation of the constitutional standing of privacy and the right of the states to regulate abortions had changed significantly. However, the *Roe* decision was also a catalyst for the growth of the pro-life movement, which is committed to ending legal abortion in the United States. This movement would become an important part of the conservative Republican coalition that dominated American politics in the 1980s. The conservative movement, with the antiabortion issue at its core, managed to break away significant numbers of Catholics and southern white Protestants from the New Deal coalition, which dominated American politics for so long, and helped refashion the public agenda in the nation.

A string of retirements from the Supreme Court gave President Reagan the opportunity to refashion the Court in his own conservative image. Though Reagan failed in his attempt to appoint ultraconservative Robert Bork to the Court, he was able to appoint conservatives Sandra

Day O'Connor, Antonin Scalia, and Anthony Kennedy; he elevated Justice William Rhenquist to the position of chief justice.

→ THE STRUCTURAL CONTEXT OF COURT BEHAVIOR

The U.S. Constitution reserves all judicial power of the United States in a single Supreme Court and lower courts which Congress created. Chief Justice Charles Evans Hughes (1907) once stated that even though the United States is governed by a Constitution, the Constitution is what the judges say it is, and that the judiciary is the safeguard of liberty and property under the Constitution.

Constitutional Powers-The Constitution addresses the Supreme Court in **Article III**, a considerably shorter and less specific article than Articles I and II which address Congress and the presidency, respectively. The document says little about the powers of the judicial branch in relationship to the other federal branches or about its responsibilities in the area of constitutional interpretation. Article III creates a federal judicial branch; it created the office of "chief justice of the United States"; it states that judges shall serve life terms; it specifies the categories of cases the Court may or must hear; and it grants Congress the power to create additional federal courts as needed. Article III of the Constitution is virtually devoid of detail.

The Concept of Judicial Review-Judicial review, the power of the Supreme Court to declare state and federal laws and actions null and void when they were unconstitutional, continues to be at the center of debate over whether the Framers intended for the Court to have that power. In sharp contrast to the views of James Madison and Thomas Jefferson, Alexander Hamilton believed that the power of judicial review was inherent in the separation of powers and was essential to balanced government. In Federalist, No. 78, Hamilton argued that the very purpose of constitutions is to place limitations on the powers of government, and it is only the Court that can ensure such limits in the United States. Hamilton's position was probably the prevailing one among the Framers, who believed in the idea that there was **a higher law** to which governments and nations must conform.

Marbury v. Madison-Chief Justice **John Marshall** claimed the power of judicial review for the Supreme Court in *Marbury v. Madison* (1803), the so-called *midnight judges* case. The Court ruled that Marbury (one of the "midnight appointments") was entitled to his commission and that Madison had broken the law in failing to deliver it. However, the Court could not compel Madison to comply with the law because the provision of the **Judiciary Act of 1789**, which granted the Court the power to issue *writs of mandamus* (a court order compelling an official to act) in such cases, was itself unconstitutional. It was unconstitutional because it sought to expand the *original jurisdiction* of the Supreme Court as defined in Article III. Thus, by "limiting" the court, judicial review was established as belonging to the judicial branch alone.

The Court has been much less reluctant to overrule the laws of the states and localities; it has done so over 1,000 times.

Judicial Review and Democracy-Judicial review raises questions about democracy. It involves the right of unelected federal judges, with life tenures, to set aside the actions of elected officials. Some observers believe that this is the only way to guarantee certain protections against majority tyranny and government tyranny. Others believe that judicial review has no place in a democratic society.

→ **THE U.S. COURT SYSTEM: ORGANIZATION AND JURISDICTION**

The court system of the United States is a federal court system. There is one system for the national government and another in each of the states. Each state has its own system of courts, which adjudicate cases on the basis of its own constitution, statutes, and administrative rules.

Constitutional Provisions-The organization and jurisdiction of the court system are examined in considerable detail in this chapter. The Supreme Court is the only court specifically mentioned in Article III of the Constitution. The organization of the federal court system is determined by Congress, which has established a three-tiered system of District Courts, Courts of Appeal, and the Supreme Court. Based on a pyramidal system, the bottom consists of 94 U.S. federal district courts, with at least one district in each state, at the center, 13 courts of appeal, and at the top of the pyramid is the Supreme Court. These courts are known as the **constitutional courts**. **Legislative courts** which focus on taxes and maritime law, were established under Article I.

Article III is vague in terms of addressing the Court's responsibilities, but it does require that federal judges serve "during good behavior," and that Congress cannot reduce the salaries of the judges once they are in office. Article III also specifies the kinds of cases that are solely the province of the federal courts: The *Constitution, federal statutes* and *treaties, admiralty* and *maritime issues, controversies in which the U.S. government is a party, disputes between the states, disputes between a state and a citizen of another state,* and *disputes between a state (or citizen of a state) and foreign states or citizens.*

Federal District Courts are **trial courts** of **original jurisdiction** (the first courts to hear a case). Most cases (criminal and civil) in the federal court system are first heard in one of the 94 district courts, and most of the business of the federal courts takes place at this level. This is the only level of federal court that uses juries and witnesses. Some District Court cases are heard by **petit** (trial) **juries,** or **grand juries** (which bring indictments), whereas others are heard by a judge.

U.S. Courts of Appeal are intermediate-level courts of **appellate jurisdiction**. Courts of appeal do not hear new cases, hence the name **appellate court,** and new factual evidence cannot be introduced; appeals are based on legal issues rather than questions of factual material that are submitted in the form of **briefs** that set out the legal issues at stake. Judges usually convene as *panels of three* or more to hear **oral arguments** from the lawyers on each side of the case and to cross-examine them on points of law. The panel issues a **decision**, often weeks or even months after the oral arguments. The United States is divided into **12 geographical circuits** to hear appeals from the district courts. There is a **thirteenth appeals court** called the U.S Court of Appeals for the Federal Circuit which hears cases on patents and government contracts.

Once appellate decisions are published, they become **precedents** which guide the decisions of other judges in the same circuit. The doctrine of closely following precedents as the basis for legal reasoning is known as **stare decisis**.

The Supreme Court-The **U.S. Supreme Court** is a court of **both original jurisdiction and appellate jurisdiction**. Original jurisdiction of the Supreme Court is established by the Constitution and can only be changed by amendment. Because of original jurisdiction, some cases must first be heard in the Supreme Court. Appellate jurisdiction, which accounts for the great bulk of its caseload, is set by congressional statute. The Supreme Court is the highest appellate court in the federal court system. Appellate jurisdiction is *discretionary*; that is, the Supreme Court decides for itself whether to accept the case.

➔APPOINTMENT TO THE FEDERAL BENCH

Because federal judges are appointed for life and make important decisions, it matters in a democratic society who they are and how representative of they are of the public.

Who Are the Appointees?- Appointees to the federal bench do, by custom, have to be lawyers. Nearly half of the Supreme Court judges of the twentieth century have had no prior experience as judges. Supreme Court justices tend to come from backgrounds that are more privileged than most Americans, and from the most elite parts of the legal profession. In the entire history of the Supreme Court, there have been only two black justices, two women, six Jews, and seven Catholics. Judicial appointments at other levels also significantly underrepresent parts of the American population, although circuit and district courts are more representative than the Supreme Court.

The Appointment Process-All federal judges are appointed by the president with the **advice and consent** of the Senate. The Constitution does not establish any qualifications or criteria for the judicial branch, but custom dictates that they must be lawyers. Presidents look at many factors besides merit in making appointments and usually nominate people for the Court who agree with them on ideological and policy grounds. Presidents delegate the responsibility of judicial nominee selection with influential senators, party luminaries, state and local bar associations, legal scholars, and leaders of influential interest groups,. The FBI conducts background checks of the leading candidates, and the **American Bar Association** is asked to evaluate them. The president then consults members of the **Senate Judiciary Committee** before the nomination is forwarded. **Senatorial Courtesy** is given to the senior senator from the home state for district court appointments, but it has no standing before circuit courts or the Supreme Court, whose district is the entire nation. The past political and ideological positions of federal court nominees are a fairly reliable guide to their later behavior on the bench.

➔THE SUPREME COURT IN ACTION

The Supreme Court meets from the First Monday in October until late June or early July, depending on the press of business.

Norms of Operation-A set of unwritten but clearly understood rules of behavior—called *norms*—shapes how the Court does things. One norm is *secrecy*, which keeps court deliberations and discussions out of public view. The media are kept at a distance from the judges and Court proceedings. *Courtesy* is another norm. Justices show one another a great deal of respect regardless of their personal feelings. *Seniority* is another norm. Seniority determines the assignment of office space, the seating arrangements in open court (the most junior at the ends, and the order of speaking in conference (the chief justice, then the most senior, and so on down the line). Justices are also expected t o stick closely to *precedent* when they decide cases. When the Court departs from precedent, it is essentially exercising judicial review of past decisions.

Controlling the Agenda-Court has a number of **screening mechanisms**, sometimes established on a case-by-case basis, to control its **docket** (agenda of cases to be heard) and to focus its attention on cases that involve important federal or constitutional questions. Major screening mechanisms include requirements that cases must be **real and adverse** (must involve a real dispute between two parties), parties in a case must have **standing** (must have a real and direct interest in the issues), and cases must be **ripe** (must be ready for a decision). The most important tool that the Court has for controlling its agenda is the power to grant (or not to grant) a **writ of certiorari** ("cert"), an order from an appellate court to lower courts demanding that they *send up a complete record of the case*. Under the **rule of four**, petitions are granted cert if at least four justices vote in favor. A grant of cert indicates a decision by the Court that an appellate case raises an important federal or constitutional issue that it is prepared to consider. If cert is denied, the *decision of the lower court stands*.

Deciding Cases-Cases that are granted cert will be scheduled for **oral argument**. Briefs are welcomed from other parties who may be interested in the disputes. They submit "friend of the court," or *amicus curiae* briefs. After reading the briefs and hearing **oral arguments**, the justices meet in **conference** to deliberate and reach a decision. The custom is for each justice to state his or her position, starting with the chief justice and moving through the ranks in order of seniority. The *vote is not final* until it has been publicly announced by the Court. Justices have an opportunity to change their votes in response to the written opinions.

Appellate cases involve considerable study, writing, and discussion among the judges before the decision is released. In important cases, the decision may be accompanied by written **opinions** that *explain the reasoning* of the court. Decisions establish **precedents** that guide other judges. The **majority opinion** (the **opinion of the Court**) is a statement of the legal reasoning that supports *the decision of the Court*. The **concurring opinion** is the opinion of a justice or justices who support the majority decision, but who have different legal reasons for doing so. The **dissenting opinion** is the reasoning of the minority. Dissenting opinions often involve reasoning that becomes the basis for future Court majorities.

Law Clerks-Law clerks are typically young lawyers from prominent academic institutions. The clerk's main role is to assist the justices to whom they are assigned in the preparation of cases.

➔THE SUPREME COURT AS A NATIONAL POLICYMAKER

People often say that the Court should not *make policy* but should only *settle disputes*. However, **the Court can't help but make public policy** because the disputes it settles involve contentious public issues and fundamental questions about the meaning of our constitutional rules. The modern Court sees itself as the "**highest judicial tribunal for settling policy conflicts**." At the same time, there are certain restrictions on the Court's power to make policy: it must wait for cases to reach it, it must stay close to precedent, and the Court must worry about the problem of compliance because the judiciary does not have enforcement powers.

Structural change and Constitutional Interpretation -Scholars generally identify three periods in the history of constitutional interpretation by the Supreme Court in the United States, one stretching from the founding to the Civil War, the next from the need of the Civil War to the Great Depression, and the last from World War II to the present.

Period 1: National Power and Property Rights- In the first period, the Court helped settle the question of the nature of the federal Union. The United States experienced significant growth and change during the first 75 years of its existence. This growth was accompanied by changes in constitutional law. Chief Justice John Marshall, who presided over the Supreme Court from 1801 to 1835, was the key judicial figure during this important period. Marshall was a Federalist, and the major decisions of the Court during his tenure reflect the influence of Alexander Hamilton. Marshall interpreted the Constitution to mean "maximum protection to property rights and maximum support for the idea of nationalism. This view was evident in the *Fletcher v. Peck* (1810), *Dartmouth College v. Woodward* (1819), and *Gibbons v. Ogden* (1824), cases.

Period 2: Government and the Economy-in the second, it helped define the role of the government in a free enterprise economy. The Framers created a system of centralized federalism, and a number of decisions by the Marshall Court enhanced national power by placing *emphasis on a strong central government*. In the second period, the Civil War and the Industrial

Revolution triggered the development of an *industrial, mass production economy* that was *dominated by the business corporation.* The reading of **laissez-faire** economic theory into constitutional law made the Supreme Court the principal ally of business in the late nineteenth and early twentieth centuries. Although the **Fourteenth Amendment** was intended to guarantee the citizenship rights of former slaves, Section 1 was gradually translated by the Court to mean protection of corporations and other forms of business from state regulation. The alliance between business and the Supreme Court continued until the **Great Depression** of the 1930s. The **New Deal** reflected a new national consensus about the need for a greatly expanded federal government with new responsibilities, formed in reaction to the Great Depression. By the end of the 1930s, the Court came to defer to the political branches of government and abandoned its effort to prevent the government from playing a central role in the management of the economy and the regulation of business.

Period 3:Individual Rights and Liberties-in the third, it focused on issues of civil liberties and civil rights. Three fundamental issues of American constitutional law—the relationship of the states to the nation, the nature of private property, and the national economy, and the role of government in the management of the economy—were essentially settled by the World War II broke out. Since World War II (the third period), the Court has turned its attention to the relationship between government and individuals. It has made significant strides in expanding the realm of **individual freedom.** Particularly during the tenure of Chief Justice **Earl Warren**, the Court rendered a series of decisions that expanded protections for rights of free expression and association, religious expression, fair trials, and civil rights for minorities.

The Debate Over Judicial Activism-Scholars continue to examine the role of **judicial activism** (policymaking by judges, as contrasted with **judicial self-restraint,** which calls for judges to engage in narrow and limited interpretation of the law). Has the Court become too involved in national policymaking?

Judicial Review-The Court claimed the right of judicial review in *Marbury v. Madison* (1803). Modern Courts have been more inclined to exercise this power than previous Courts.

Reversing the Decisions of Past Supreme Courts-A respect for precedence is an important norm that guides the Court's decisionmaking. The Warren, Burger, and Rehnquist Courts have not been reluctant to overturn previous Court decisions. The most dramatic case being the reversal of *Plessy* by *Brown* and the *Roe-to-Webster* changes, as well as the relatively rapid overturns of precedents involving the rights of criminal defendants.

Deciding "Political" Issues-Critics claim that the Court is taking on too many matters that would be better left to the elected branches of government. The drawing of congressional districts is another "political" issue that the Court continues to visit. With *Baker v. Carr* (1962) **(One Person, One Vote),** the Court ruled that the federal courts could hear challenges to legislative malapportionment under the equal protection clause of the Fourteenth Amendment. Malapportionment means drawing legislative district lines in such a way that the resulting districts vary substantially in population. The Court had long avoided apportionment issues prior to the 1960 census, which revealed major changes in the populations of the states and localities. The Court had previously defined these types of issues as "political." The doctrine distinguishing "political" matters from "judicial" matters was first articulated by Chief Justice John Marshall in *Marbury v. Madison* (1803) and refined by Chief Justice Roger Taney in *Luther v. Borden* (1849). It was applied to the legislative apportionment issue in *Colegrove v. Green* (1946), in which Justice Felix Frankfurter wrote that "the Court ought not to enter this political thicket."

Remedies-The most criticized aspect of judicial activism is the tendency for federal judges to impose broad remedies on states and localities. A **remedy** is what a court determines must be done to rectify a wrong.

Original Intention-Advocates of **original intention** and its twin **strict construction** believe that the Court must be guided by the original intentions of the framers and the words found in the Constitution. They believe that the expansion of rights that has occurred since the mid-1960s (such as the right to privacy that formed the basis for *Roe* v. *Wade*) has no foundation in the framers' intentions or the text of the Constitution. Advocates of **loose construction** believe that the intentions of the Founders are impossible to determine and would be unreasonably constricting in the twentieth century. They believe that judges must try to reconcile the fundamental principles of the Constitution with changing conditions. The modern Court is clearly more activist than it was in the past. Most justices today hold a more expansive view of the role of the Court in framing national policy than had their predecessors. Both liberals and conservatives have been activist, depending on the issues involved.

The debate between "originalists" and more liberal views of constitutional interpretation continues. Opponents of original intention believe that the intentions of the Founders are not only impossible to determine but also unduly constricting. In this view, jurists must try to reconcile the fundamental principles of the Constitution with changing conditions in the United States. The Court today is more activist than it was in the past; most justices today hold more expansive view of the role of the Court in forging national policy than their predecessors did.

→OUTSIDE INFLUENCES ON THE COURT

The courts make public policy and will continue to do so. Yet many other governmental and political linkage actors and institutions influence what they do. Structural factors continue to influence how the Court operates and what the Court does.

Governmental Factors-The Supreme Court must coexist with other governmental bodies that have their own powers, interests, constituencies, and visions of the public good. Being without "purse or sword," the Court cannot forces others to obey its decisions. It can only hope that respect for the law and the Court will cause government officials to do what it has mandated in a decision.

Presidential Influence-The Court must rely on the president to enforce its rulings. After the 1954 *Brown* decision, president Eisenhower was reluctant to enforce it. The president also influences the Court through the appointment process. He can also file suits through the Justice Department, try to move public opinion against the Court, and threaten to introduce legislation to alter the Court's organization or jurisdiction.

Congressional Influences-Congress retains the power to change the size, organization, and appellate jurisdiction of the federal courts. In 1802 for example, Thomas Jefferson postponed a session of the Supreme Court so that the Court would not be able to hear a suit that challenged the repeal by Congress of the Federal Judiciary Act of 1801. During the Civil War, Congress removed the Court's jurisdiction over *habeas corpus* cases so that civilians could be tried in military courts. Congress controls the salaries of federal judges and the Congress must confirm nominees before appointments. Congress can also change statutes or pass new laws that specifically challenge Supreme Court decisions.

Political Linkage Factors-The Supreme Court is influenced by political linkage factors, such as social movements, interest groups, and elections.

Groups and Movements-Interest groups, social movements, and the public directly influence the Court. An important political tactic of interest groups and social movements is the **test case**. A test case is an action brought by a group that is designed to challenge the constitutionality of a law or an action by government. *Brown v. Board of Education* is probably the most notable test case in recent history. Many test cases take the form of **class action suits**. These are suits brought by an individual on behalf of a group or class of people who are in a similar situation.

Leaders-Social and economic leaders influence the Court. They have substantial influence through the media, the interest group system, party politics, and elections at all levels. The Court is also influenced by developments on issues and doctrines within the legal profession as they are expressed by bar associations, law journals, and law schools.

Public Opinion-There is evidence that the Court pays attention to public opinion. Some research suggests that the Court conforms to public opinion about as much as the president and Congress do (about three-fifths of the time). Justices read the same papers and watch television as do other citizens.

→SUMMARY

Article III of the Constitution is vague about the powers and responsibilities of the U.S. Supreme Court. The Constitution is silent on the matter of judicial review. Still the Court has fashioned a powerful position for itself in American politics, coequal with the executive and legislative branches. The federal court system is made up of three parts which include 94 federal district courts, in which most cases originate; 13 appeals courts; and the Supreme Court which has both appellate and original jurisdiction.

The court operates on the basis of certain norms: secrecy, courtesy, seniority, and adherence to precedent. The court controls its agenda by granting or not granting certiorari. The Supreme Court is a national policymaker that is presided with unelected, life-tenured justices. But the judges are influenced by many political linkage and governmental factors.

Constitutional interpretation by the Supreme Court has progressed through three stages. The decisions of the Court are influenced by structural, political linkage, and governmental factors. The president and Congress are especially important in terms of their influence on the Court. Judicial activism and judicial restraint are issues that are based on how Courts approach precedence and the doctrine of original intent. The authors contend that the appropriate role of the Court is to encourage the play of popular sovereignty, political equality, and liberty in American politics. We have learned at various places in this book that the Court does not always live up to these standards. Some scholars believe that the Court can play a role in enriching democracy by raising the most fundamental issues of our political life to public attention.

Chapter Outline

This section gives you a comprehensive review of the chapter. Use this outline in combination with your textbook to look for key concepts and objectives, to identify essential terms and names, and to gain a basic understanding of political practices and principles from this chapter.

I. THE COURT CHANGES COURSE ON *ROE* V. *WADE* (p. 413)
    A. Context of the chapter
        1. This chapter considers the ambiguous relationship between the Court and democracy.
        2. The opening vignette illustrates how the Court makes decisions that have important consequences for the American people, which raises fundamental issues about democracy (the central theme of this book).
        3. By interpreting the law, *the Court is a national policymaker.*

B. In the 1973 case of *Roe* v. *Wade* (7-2 decision with Justice **Harry Blackmun** writing the opinion), the U.S. Supreme Court ruled that a state's interest in regulating abortion to protect the life of a fetus can only override a woman's fundamental right to privacy when the fetus becomes *viable* (able to live on its own).

C. The *Roe* decision was a catalyst for the formation of the pro-life movement, which became an important part of the conservative Republican coalition that dominated American politics in the 1980s.

D. Sixteen years later, in the case of *Webster* v. *Reproductive Health Services* (5-4 decision with Chief Justice **William Rehnquist** writing the opinion), the Court diminished a woman's right to have an abortion by upholding a Missouri law that barred the use of public monies and facilities to perform abortions and required physicians to test for fetal viability at 20 weeks; several states soon began to legislate various limits on abortions.

E. The language of the U.S. Constitution had not changed in the time that elapsed between *Roe* and *Webster*, but the *interpretation* of the *constitutional standing of privacy* and the *right of the states* to regulate abortions had changed significantly; *Webster* was decided by a much more conservative court with several Reagan appointees.

F. However, the *Roe* decision was also a catalyst for the growth of the pro-life movement, which is committed to ending legal abortion in the United States.
   1. This movement would become an important part of the conservative Republican coalition that dominated American politics in the 1980s.
   2. The conservative movement, with the antiabortion issue at its core, managed to break away significant numbers of Catholics and southern white Protestants from the New Deal coalition, which dominated American politics for so long, and helped refashion the public agenda in the nation.

G. A string of retirements from the Supreme Court gave President Reagan the opportunity to refashion the Court in his own conservative image. Though Reagan failed in his attempt to appoint ultraconservative Robert Bork to the Court, he was able to appoint conservatives Sandra Day O'Connor, Antonin Scalia, and Anthony Kennedy; he elevated Justice William Rhenquist to the position of chief justice.

II. **THE STRUCTURAL CONTEXT OF COURT BEHAVIOR (pp. 414-417)**
   A. **Article III** of the U.S. Constitution (the Judicial Article) provides very little detail about the organization and operations of the judicial branch.
   B. It does not provide much guidance about what the judicial branch is supposed to do or how it is supposed to go about its job.
   C. **Constitutional powers**
      1. The Constitution addresses the Supreme in **Article III**, a considerably shorter and less specific article than Articles I and II which address Congress and the presidency, respectively.

2. The document says little about the powers of the judicial branch in relationship to the other federal branches or about its responsibilities in the area of constitutional **interpretation**.

3. Article III creates a federal judicial branch; it created the office of "chief justice of the United States"; it states that judges shall serve life terms; it specifies the categories of cases the Court may or must hear; and it grants Congress the power to create additional federal courts as needed. Article III of the Constitution is virtually devoid of detail.

D. **The concept of judicial review**

1. There is no explicit reference in the Constitution to **judicial review** (the power of the Court to rule on the constitutionality of state and federal laws and executive actions).

2. The framers believed that the Constitution ought to prevail when other laws were in conflict with it, but the question arose over *who* should make the determination of constitutionality; in general, the attitudes of the time supported the idea that judges (who were free from popular pressures and familiar with the legal tradition) were best able to decide when statutory and administrative law were in conflict with the fundamental law.

E. *Marbury v. Madison*

1. Chief Justice **John Marshall** claimed the power of judicial review for the Supreme Court in *Marbury v. Madison* (1803), the so-called *midnight judges* case.

   a) The Court ruled that Marbury (one of the "midnight appointments") was entitled to his commission and that Madison had broken the law in failing to deliver it.

   b) However, the Court could not compel Madison to comply with the law because the provision of the **Judiciary Act of 1789**, which granted the Court the power to issue **writs of *mandamus*** (a court order compelling an official to act) in such cases, was itself unconstitutional. It was unconstitutional because it sought to expand the *original jurisdiction* of the Supreme Court as defined in Article III. Thus, by "limiting" the court, judicial review was established as belonging to the judicial branch alone; in Marshall's words, "it is emphatically the province and duty of the judicial department to say what the law is."

2. The Court has shown considerable *restraint in its exercise of judicial review*.

   a) It was not used for another 54 years after *Marbury*, and has been used to declare acts of Congress unconstitutional only about 100 times in our history.

   b) State and local laws have been overruled with greater frequency (more than 1,000 times).

   c) The Court has been much less reluctant to overrule the laws of the states and localities; it has done so over 1,000.

3. Additional judicial positions were created by the Federalist Congress and filled by the outgoing Federalist president (**John Adams**) in the final days of his

389

administration, after **Thomas Jefferson** and the Republicans gained control of the presidency and the legislature; the apparent intention of these **midnight appointments** was to ensure Federalist dominance of the judiciary.

    a) **William Marbury's** commission was signed and sealed, but it was not delivered to him before the new administration took office; Jefferson's Secretary of State **James Madison** refused to deliver the commission.

    b) Marbury (one of the "midnight appointments") claimed that the secretary of state was obligated to deliver the commission; he sued Madison, and asked the Supreme Court to issue a **writ of *mandamus*** (a court order compelling a public official to act).

4. **The Court's dilemma**

    a) If the Court decided in favor of Marbury, Madison would almost surely refuse to obey, opening the Court to ridicule; because Marshall was a prominent Federalist, the Jeffersonians might even be provoked to take more extreme measures against the Court.

    b) If the Court ruled in favor of Madison, it would suggest that an executive official could defy the clear provisions of the law without incurring any penalty.

5. **Judicial review and democracy**

    a) The authors of your textbook note that judicial review raises **questions about democracy**: it involves the right of a body *shielded from direct accountability* to set aside the actions of governmental bodies whose members are elected.

    b) There are conflicting views on the issue: some observers believe that this is the only way to protect the rights of minorities and to preserve the rules of the democratic process; others believe that it has no place in a democratic society.

III. THE U.S. COURT SYSTEM: ORGANIZATION AND JURISDICTION (pp. 417-422)

A. The court system of the United States is a federal court system. There is one system for the national government and another in each of the states (known as the **dual court system**). Each state has its own system of courts, which adjudicate cases on the basis of its own constitution, statutes, and administrative rules.

1. Most laws, legal disputes, and court decisions are located in the states, but the most important *political* and *constitutional* issues eventually reach the federal courts.

2. Although they share a **common law** tradition, each of the states has created a slightly different body of legal precedents, especially in the area of private law.

B. **Constitutional provisions**

1. The only court *specifically mentioned* in **Article III** of the Constitution is the **Supreme Court**; Congress was given the task of establishing "such inferior courts as the Congress may from time to time ordain and establish."

a) Beginning with the Judiciary Act of 1789, Congress has on several occasions reorganized the federal court system.
b) Today, the **constitutional courts** (federal courts created by Congress under the authority of Article III) are organized in a three-tier pyramidal system: 94 federal district courts, with at least one district in each state, 13 courts of appeal, and 1 supreme court.
c) Congress has also created a number of **legislative courts** (created by Congress under the authority of Article I) to adjudicate cases in highly specialized areas such as taxes and maritime law.

2. **Article III guidelines**
   a) Federal judges serve "during good behavior" (in practice, this means for life); **impeachment** by Congress is the only way to remove a federal judge.
   b) Congress cannot reduce the salaries of judges once they are in office; this provision was designed to maintain the independence of the judiciary.
3. Article III specifies the **jurisdiction** (authority to hear cases) of the federal courts:
   a) Cases involving the Constitution, federal statutes, and treaties
   b) Admiralty and maritime issues
   c) Controversies in which the U.S. government is a party
   d) Disputes between the states
   e) Disputes between a state and a citizen of another state
   f) Disputes between a state or citizen of a state and foreign states or citizens

C. **Federal District Courts**
1. **Trial courts** of **original jurisdiction** (the first courts to hear a case)
2. Most cases in the federal court system are first heard in one of the 94 district courts, and most of the business of the federal courts takes place at this level.
3. **Grand juries** are used to **indict** (bring charges against) a defendant in criminal cases.
4. This is the only level of federal court that uses juries and witnesses; some cases are heard by **petit** (trial) **juries** while some are heard by a judge (**bench trial**).

D. **U.S. Courts of Appeal**
1. Intermediate-level courts of **appellate jurisdiction**
2. Courts of appeal do not hear new cases; they hear only cases on appeal.
3. The United States is divided into eleven geographic regions (**circuits**) to hear appeals from the district courts; two additional circuit courts of appeal (the D.C. Circuit Court and the Court of Appeals for the Federal Circuit) are located in Washington, D.C.
4. Procedure
   a) Judges usually convene as *panels* of three or more to hear **oral arguments** from the lawyers on each side of the case and to cross-examine them on points of law.

        (1) Lawyers for each side make their case for the judges by submitting **briefs** that set out the legal issues and by giving short oral presentations.

        (2) New factual evidence cannot be introduced; appeals are based on legal issues rather than questions of factual material, and no witnesses are called or cross-examined.

        (3) The panel issues a **decision**, often weeks or even months after the oral arguments.

    b) Decisions establish **precedents** that guide other judges

        (1) *Stare decisis* is the doctrine of closely following precedent as the basis for legal reasoning; past decisions serve as the basis for current similar decisions.

        (2) Judges will sometimes depart from precedent, but it is an important legal principle that has great influence.

  E. **The Supreme Court**

    1. A court of both original jurisdiction and appellate jurisdiction

    2. The size of the Court is determined by Congress; the number has been set at nine since 1869 (eight associate justices and one chief justice).

    3. *Congress* determines the *appellate* jurisdiction of the Supreme Court.

      a) The Supreme Court serves as an appellate court for the federal appeals courts and for the highest courts of the states.

      b) Appellate jurisdiction is *discretionary*; the Supreme Court decides for itself whether to accept the case.

    4. The *Constitution* establishes the *original* jurisdiction of the Supreme Court:

      a) Disputes involving ambassadors and other diplomatic personnel

      b) Cases in which two or more states are parties to the dispute

      c) Disputes between the federal government and a state

      d) Disputes between a state and a citizen from another state

    5. As the highest appellate court in the federal court system, the decisions and opinions of the Supreme Court become the most important sources of precedent on federal and constitutional questions for courts *at all levels* of jurisdiction.

IV. **APPOINTMENT TO THE FEDERAL BENCH (pp. 422-425)**

  A. **Who are the appointees?**

    1. The Constitution does not establish any qualifications or criteria for the judicial branch; *by custom*, judges and justices must be lawyers.

    2. Almost one-half of all Supreme Court justices during this century have had *no prior experience as judges* (including some of the most prominent and influential justices such as John Marshall, Louis Brandeis, Harlan Stone, Charles Evans Hughes, Felix Frankfurter, Earl Warren, and William Rehnquist).

    3. Supreme Court justices tend to come from backgrounds that are more privileged than most Americans, and from the most elite parts of the legal profession; judicial

appointments at other levels also significantly underrepresent parts of the American population, although circuit and district courts are more representative than the Supreme Court.

B. **The appointment process**
1. All federal judges are nominated by the president and confirmed (approved) by the Senate.
2. Presidents pay special attention to judicial appointments because they are a way for presidents to affect public policy long after they leave office.
3. After defining the kind of person he wants in general terms, the president delegates the task of identifying judicial candidates to one or more senior White House staff members and the attorney general.
   a) Lists of potential candidates are drawn up after wide consultation with influential senators, party leaders, state and local bar associations, legal scholars, and leaders of important interest groups.
   b) The FBI conducts background checks of the leading candidates, and the American Bar Association is asked to evaluate them.
   c) The president and his advisers consult with key senators (especially those on the Judiciary Committee, which will conduct advise and consent hearings) before nominations are forwarded to the Senate.
   d) By custom, nominations for district court judgeships are subject to **senatorial courtesy** (the right of the senior senator from the president's party in the state where the district court is located to approve the nominee).
   e) Presidents usually nominate people for the Court who agree with them on ideological and policy grounds
4. **Advise and consent**
   a) The Senate's power to confirm or reject presidential nominations
   b) Of the 143 nominees for the Supreme Court in our history, the Senate has refused to approve only 28 nominees; only 5 rejections to the Supreme Court have occurred in this century (but there have also been several near-defeats).
   c) Rejection of nominees has usually occurred when the president was politically weak and vulnerable or when the opposing party was in control of the Senate, especially when the president was trying to make **lame-duck** appointments (nominations made by the incumbent after a successor has been already been elected).
C. Past political and ideological positions of federal court nominees are generally a good guide to their later behavior on the bench; however, presidents are sometimes surprised (and disappointed) with their nominees—liberal presidents may find that their nominees are more conservative than expected, while conservative presidents may find that their nominees are more liberal than expected.

V.   **THE SUPREME COURT IN ACTION (pp. 425-430)**

A. The Supreme Court is in session from the first Monday in October (set by statute) until late June or early July.

B. **Norms of operation**
1. The Court is a tradition-bound institution defined by many **rituals** (such as entering the courtroom in order of seniority) and long-standing **norms** (which are unwritten but clearly understood ways of behaving)
2. Secrecy—when meeting in conference to argue and decide cases, the justices meet alone, without secretaries or clerks; this keeps conflicts between justices out of the public eye and elevates the stature of the Court, but also means that we know less about the inner workings of the Court than about either of the other branches of government
3. Courtesy—in public, justices treat each other with great formality and respect; differences of opinion are usually respected
4. Seniority—an important norm used to determine the assignment of office space, the seating arrangements in open court, the order of speaking in conference, and the order of voting
5. Precedent—when the Court departs from precedent, it is essentially overruling its own past actions; in most cases, departure from precedent comes only in very small steps over many years, although change can come more quickly if there is a significant ideological turnover on the Court

C. **Controlling the agenda**
1. The Court has a number of **screening mechanisms** (sometimes established on a case-by-case basis) to control its **docket** (agenda of cases to be heard) and to focus its attention on cases that involve *important* federal or constitutional questions.
2. Cases must be **real and adverse**—they must involve a real dispute between two parties.
3. Parties in a case must have **standing**—they must have a real and direct interest in the issues that are raised.
4. Cases must be **ripe**—the case must be ready for a decision because all other avenues of appeal have been exhausted *before* coming to court, and the injury has already taken place; the Court will not accept hypothetical cases.
5. Appeals must be filed within a specified time limit, paperwork must be proper and complete, and a filing fee of $200 must be paid; requirements may be waived if a petitioner is indigent and files an affidavit *in forma pauperis* ("in the manner of a pauper"), such as the landmark case of *Gideon* v. *Wainwright* (1963), which established the right to counsel in criminal cases.
6. The most important tool that the Court has for controlling its agenda is the power to grant—or not to grant—a **writ of *certiorari*** ("cert")—an order from an appellate court to lower courts demanding that they send up a *complete record of the case.*
   a) A grant of cert is a decision of the Court that an appellate case raises an important federal or constitutional issue that it is prepared to consider.

b) Under the **rule of four**, petitions are granted cert if at least four justices vote in favor.
c) Few petitions survive all of these hurdles.
  (1) Of the almost 8,000 cases that are filed each session, the Court grants cert for only about 100.
  (2) The *decision of the lower court stands* in cases where cert is denied.

D. **Deciding cases**
  1. Cases that are granted cert will be scheduled for **oral argument**.
    a) Lawyers on each side are alerted to the key issues that the justices wish to consider, and *new briefs* are invited; in particularly important cases, *amicus curiae* ("friend of the court") briefs may be submitted by parties who have a concern in the dispute but who are not immediate parties to the case, including individuals, interest groups, or some agency of the federal government (such as the Justice Department or even the president).
    b) Cases are usually argued for one hour, with one-half hour given to each side in the dispute.
      (1) Oral argument is not so much a presentation of arguments as it is a give and take between the lawyers and the justices (and among the justices themselves); justices may question the lawyers during oral argument.
      (2) When the federal government is a party to the case, the **solicitor general** or one of his deputies presents the oral arguments.
  2. After reading the briefs and hearing oral arguments, the justices meet in **conference** to deliberate and reach a **decision**.
    a) The custom is for each justice to state his or her position, starting with the chief justice and moving through the ranks in order of seniority.
    b) The statement of each justice makes it clear in most cases how the court is divided on the issues, so votes are usually not necessary.
    c) The vote taken in conference *is not final until the decision has been publicly released*; thus, the justices have an opportunity to change their votes as the written opinions are developed.
  3. **Written opinion**—a statement of the legal reasoning that supports *the decision of the Court*
    a) **Majority opinion** (the **opinion of the Court**)—by tradition, the Chief Justice assigns the majority opinion if he voted with the majority in conference (and sometimes assigns it to himself); if the Chief Justice votes with the minority (dissenters), the senior member of the majority assigns the opinion (this is one of the norms referred to previously)
    b) **Concurring opinion**—the opinion of a justice or justices who support the majority decision but have different legal reasons for doing so
    c) **Dissenting opinion**—the reasoning of the minority; dissenting opinions often involve reasoning that becomes the basis for future Court majorities

4. **Law clerks**
    a) Recruited from among recent top-ranking graduates of the most prestigious law schools.
    b) They assist the justice to whom they are assigned in the preparation of cases

VI. **THE SUPREME COURT AS A NATIONAL POLICYMAKER (pp. 430-436)**
A. Policymaking
    1. People often say that the Court should not *make policy* but should only *settle disputes*; however, **the Court can't help but make public policy** because the disputes it settles involve contentious public issues and fundamental questions about the meaning of our constitutional rules. The Court sees itself as the "highest judicial tribunal for settling policy conflicts."
    2. There are certain restrictions on the Court's power to make policy: it must wait for cases to reach it, it must stay close to precedent, and the Court must worry about the problem of compliance because the judiciary does not have enforcement powers.
B. **Structural change and constitutional interpretation**
    1. The text lists three periods in the history of U.S. constitutional law
    2. This section of your text looks at how changes in constitutional law have been influenced by **structural factors**, especially by economic change.
    3. **Period 1: National power and property rights**
        a) Significant growth and change during the first 75 years of the nation's existence was accompanied by changes in constitutional law (see Chapter 4).
        b) Chief Justice **John Marshall** (1801-1835) was a follower of the doctrines of Alexander Hamilton, who advocated a strong national government, an alliance between government and business in which industry was encouraged, and a national free market economy without regulatory restraints from state and local governments.
    4. **Period 2: Government and the economy**
        a) The Civil War and the Industrial Revolution triggered the development of an industrial, mass production economy that was *dominated by corporations*.
        b) The Supreme Court became the principal ally of business in the late nineteenth and early twentieth centuries; although the **Fourteenth Amendment** was *intended to guarantee the citizenship rights of former slaves*, Section 1 was gradually *translated by the Court to mean protection of corporations* (which had been interpreted as **"persons"** under the law in the *Dartmouth College* case) and other forms of business from state regulation.
        c) The New Deal era
            (1) The alliance between business and the Supreme Court continued until the **Great Depression** of the 1930s.

(2) The **New Deal** reflected a new national consensus about the need for a greatly expanded federal government with new responsibilities, formed in reaction to the Great Depression.

    (a) The Supreme Court (with justices born in the nineteenth century and committed to the concept of a link between the Constitution and *laissez-faire* economic doctrine) overturned major New Deal legislation in 1935 and 1936.

    (b) The Court overturned the Agricultural Adjustment Act, the National Industrial Recovery Act, the Bituminous Coal Act (which regulated wages and working conditions in the mining industry), and a New York minimum wage law.

    (c) Faced with Roosevelt's landslide election in 1936, increasing public hostility toward the Court, and Roosevelt's plan to **pack the court**, the Court reversed itself in 1937 by accepting the Social Security Act, the Labor Relations Act, and state minimum wage laws (a change that has been referred to as the *"switch in time that saved nine,"* in the sense that the reversal may have saved the prestige of the Court).

  d) By the end of the 1930s, the Court came to defer to the political branches of government and abandoned its effort to prevent the government from playing a central role in the management of the economy and the regulation of business.

5. **Period 3: Individual rights and liberties**
  a) Three fundamental issues of American constitutional law–the relationship of the states to the nation, the nature of private property and the national economy, and the role of government in the management of the economy–were essentially settled before World War II broke out.
  b) Since World War II, the Court has turned its attention to the relationship between government and individuals; it has made significant strides in expanding the realm of **individual freedom**; particularly during the tenure of Chief Justice **Earl Warren**, the Court rendered a series of decisions that expanded protections for rights of free expression and association, religious expression, fair trials, and civil rights for minorities.
  c) Constitutional law and the Court are responsive in the long run to changes in the world around them; a new conservative majority has moved the Court to reconsider many of its earlier decisions on rights and liberties and on the relationship between the national and state governments.

C. **The debate over judicial activism**
  1. Judicial activism is policymaking by judges, as contrasted with **judicial self-restraint**, which calls for judges to engage in narrow and limited interpretation of the law)
  2. **Judicial review**
    a) The power was claimed in the 1803 case of *Marbury* v. *Madison* but was not

exercised to any great extent until the late nineteenth century.

    b) The Court has become more willing in modern times to monitor the activities of other governmental entities, especially at the state level

3. **Reversing the decisions of past Supreme Courts**
   a) Although *adherence to precedent* is one of the *traditional norms* that guides judicial decision making, the Warren, Burger, and Rehnquist Courts (particularly the last) have not hesitated to overturn previous Court decisions
   b) The most dramatic instance was the reversal of *Plessy* v. *Ferguson* by *Brown* v. *Board of Education of Topeka*; others include the *Roe* to *Webster* change reviewed in the opening story of this chapter and the rapid overturns of precedents involving the rights of criminal defendants.
   c) Critics claim that this creates instability and uncertainty about the meaning of the law, and an inappropriate assertion of power.
   d) Others claim that the Court must be able to fit the law with the times and changing circumstances.

4. **Deciding political issues**
   a) The Court has traditionally refused to accept cases involving "political" issues (questions that should be handled by the executive and legislative branches). Critics claim that the Court is increasingly taking on matters that are political, but others argue that the Court is obligated to protect rights when basic constitutional rights such as equality of citizenship are at risk. With *Baker v. Carr* (1962) **(one person, one vote)** the Court ruled that the federal courts could hear challenges to legislative malapportionment under the equal protection clause of the Fourteenth Amendment.

5. **Remedies** (what a court decides must be done to correct a wrong)—with the tremendous increase in the number of **class action suits** (brought on behalf of an entire class of people, such as all people affected by an incident of environmental damage) since the 1960s, the Court has shown a greater willingness to impose **remedies** that require governmental bodies to take action; such remedies often require that governments spend public funds

6. Advocates of **loose construction** believe that the intentions of the Founders are impossible to determine and would be unreasonably constricting in the twentieth century.
   a) They believe that the intentions of the Founders are not only impossible to determine, but unduly constricting.
   b) In this view, jurists must try to reconcile the fundamental principles of the Constitution with changing conditions in the United States.

7. Advocates of **original intention** (and its twin **strict construction**) believe that the Court must be guided by the original intentions of the framers and the words found in the Constitution.

8. The modern Court is more activist than it was in the past.

a) Most justices today hold a more expansive view of the role of the Court in framing national policy than had their predecessors.

b) Both *liberals and conservatives have been activist*, depending on the issues.

9. **Malapportionment** means drawing legislative district lines in such a way that the resulting districts vary substantially in population.

a) The Court had long avoided apportionment issues prior to the 1960 census, which revealed major changes in the populations of the states and localities.

b) The Court had previously defined these types of issues as "political." The doctrine distinguishing "political" matters from "judicial" matters was first articulated by Chief Justice John Marshall in *Marbury v. Madison* (1803) and refined by Chief Justice Roger Taney in *Luther v. Borden* (1849).

c) It was applied to the legislative apportionment issue in *Colegrove v. Green* (1946), in which Justice Felix Frankfurter wrote that "the Court ought not to enter this political thicket."

10. The debate between "originalists" and more liberal views of constitutional interpretation continues.

a) Opponents of original intention believe that the intentions of the Founders are not only impossible to determine but also unduly constricting.

b) In this view, jurists must try to reconcile the fundamental principles of the Constitution with changing conditions in the United States.

11. The Court today is more activist than it was in the past; most justices today hold more expansive view of the role of the Court in forging national policy than their predecessors did.

VII. OUTSIDE INFLUENCES ON THE COURT (pp. 436-440)

A. The courts make public policy and will continue to do so. Yet many other governmental and political linkage actors and institutions influence what they do.

B. Structural factors continue to influence how the Court operates and what the Court does.

1. **Governmental factors**

a) The Supreme Court must coexist with other governmental bodies that have their own powers, interests, constituencies, and visions of the public good.

b) Being without "purse or sword," the Court cannot forces others to obey its decisions.

2. It can only hope that respect for the law and the Court will cause government officials to do what it has mandated in a decision.

C. **Presidential influence**

1. The Court must rely on the president to enforce its rulings. After the 1954 *Brown* decision, president Eisenhower was reluctant to enforce it.

2. The president also influences the Court through the appointment process. He can also file suits through the Justice Department, try to move public opinion against the Court, and threaten to introduce legislation to alter the Court's organization or

jurisdiction.
D. **Congressional influences**
   1. Congress retains the power to change the size, organization, and appellate jurisdiction of the federal courts.
      a) In 1802 for example, Thomas Jefferson postponed a session of the Supreme Court so that the Court would not be able to hear a suit that challenged the repeal by Congress of the Federal Judiciary Act of 1801.
      b) During the Civil War, Congress removed the Court's jurisdiction over *habeas corpus* cases so that civilians could be tried in military courts.
   2. Congress controls the salaries of federal judges and the Congress must confirm nominees before appointments.
   3. Congress can also change statutes or pass new laws that specifically challenge Supreme Court decisions.
E. **Political linkage factors**-The Supreme Court is influenced by political linkage factors, such as social movements, interest groups, and elections.
F. **Groups and movements**
   1. Interest groups, social movements, and the public directly influence the Court.
      a) An important political tactic of interest groups and social movements is the **test case**.
      b) A test case is an action brought by a group that is designed to challenge the constitutionality of a law or an action by government.
      c) *Brown v. Board of Education* is probably the most notable test case in recent history.
   2. Many test cases take the form of **class action suits**. These are suits brought by an individual on behalf of a group or class of people who are in a similar situation.
G. **Leaders**
   1. Social and economic leaders influence the Court.
   2. They have substantial influence through the media, the interest group system, party politics, and elections at all levels.
   3. The Court is also influenced by developments on issues and doctrines within the legal profession as they are expressed by bar associations, law journals, and law schools.
H. **Public opinion**
   1. There is evidence that the Court pays attention to public opinion.
   2. Some research suggests that the Court conforms to public opinion about as much as the president and Congress do (about three-fifths of the time).
   3. Justices read the same papers and watch television as do other citizens.

VIII. **SUMMARY (p. 440)**
   A. **Article III** of the Constitution is vague about the powers and responsibilities of the U.S. Supreme Court. The Constitution is silent on the matter of judicial review.

B. Still the Court has fashioned a powerful position for itself in American politics, coequal with the executive and legislative branches.
   1. The federal court system is made up of three parts which include 94 federal district courts, in which most cases originate; 13 appeals courts; and the Supreme Court which has both appellate and original jurisdiction.
   2. The court operates on the basis of certain norms: secrecy, courtesy, seniority, and adherence to precedent.
C. The court controls its agenda by granting or not granting certiorari. The Supreme Court is a national policymaker that is presided with unelected, life-tenured justices. But the judges are influenced by many political linkage and governmental factors.
D. Constitutional interpretation by the Supreme Court has progressed through three stages.
   1. The decisions of the Court are influenced by structural, political linkage, and governmental factors. The president and Congress are especially important in terms of their influence on the Court.
   2. Judicial activism and judicial restraint are issues that are based on how Courts approach precedence and the doctrine of original intent.
   3. The authors contend that the appropriate role of the Court is to encourage the play of popular sovereignty, political equality, and liberty in American politics.
   4. We have learned at various places in this book that the Court does not always live up to these standards. Some scholars believe that the Court can play a role in enriching democracy by raising the most fundamental issues of our political life to public attention.

Terms for Review

Use this list to review essential principles, functions, and concepts from this chapter. Refer to your textbook for help in identifying and defining terms on this list. When you study, do not merely memorize terms; ask questions about the material you are reviewing, and look for the importance or significance of each item.

advise and consent

amicus curiae

appellate jurisdiction

Chapter 14

Article III

briefs

chief justice

circuits

class action suit

concurring opinion

constitutional courts

constitutional law

courts of appeal

court packing

dissenting opinion

district courts

docket

executive privilege

grand juries

the higher law

in forma pauperis

interpretation

judicial activism

judicial restraint

judicial review

Judiciary Act of 1789

lame-duck appointments

laissez faire

law clerks

legislative courts

loose and strict construction

majority opinion (opinion of the Court)

Marbury v. *Madison* (1803)

norms and rituals

opinion

opinion of the Court

oral arguments

original jurisdiction

original intention

petit (trial) juries

plaintiff

precedents

real and adverse

remedy

right to privacy

ripeness

rule of four

screening mechanisms

senatorial courtesy

separate but equal doctrine

solicitor general

standing

stare decisis

statutes

strict constructionism

Supreme Court

test case

trial by jury

trial court

writ of *certiorari*

writ of *injunction*

writ of *mandamus*

Research Topics: Applying What You Have Learned

You will derive more benefit from your reading if you try to apply what you have learned. Some of the suggested research topics can be answered exclusively from your text, while others require you to conduct some basic research on your own. The references suggested under **Internet Sources** *will help you in your search.*

- The authors of your textbook note that the judiciary has not been representative of many groups in American society. In your opinion, should the unrepresentative nature of the federal judiciary be cause for concern? In what ways would decisions change if the courts were more representative? What criteria should be used in the nominating process.

- Visit two sessions of two different courts in your area. If possible, include a federal district court and either a state or a local court. Did you notice any differences in procedure in the different courts? How did the procedures compare with court scenes portrayed on television or in motion pictures?

- How well does the Supreme Court conform to your textbook's assessment of the criteria for democracy? What changes would need to be made to make the court more *democratic*? Would these changes have any impact on the *effectiveness* of the Court?

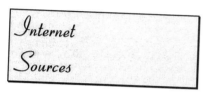

A number of sites on the World Wide Web serve as gateways to vast collections of material on American government and politics. The following Internet resources are recommended for students who would like to do some additional research in the areas covered by this chapter. These references would also be helpful in expanding on the questions suggested under Research Topics.

Federal Courts Home Page www.uscourts.gov
Information and statistics about the activities of the U.S. District Courts, Circuit Courts of Appeal, and the Supreme Court.

Legal Information Institute, Cornell University Law School http://www.law.cornell.edu
The gateway to a world of information and links to associated law and court sites on the Web. Among its sections you will find the following: the Supreme Court Calendar: Biographies and Opinions of the Justices; Directories of law firms, law schools, and legal associations; Constitutions and Codes, including U.S. statutes, regulations and judicial rules of procedure; and Court opinions, including state supreme courts.

The New York Times Supreme Court Guide www.nytimes.com/library/politics/scotus/index-scotus.html
Recently published articles about the Supreme Court and its decisions, biographies of the justices, the Court's current docket, and much more.

Circle the correct answer for each question. Questions are listed in the same order in which the information appears in the text. Use the Answer Key in the back of the Study Guide *to check your responses.*

1. What are the formal powers of the Chief Justice of the Supreme Court?
   a. He has administrative responsibilities and such additional powers as the full Supreme Court votes to authorize.
   b. He has administrative responsibilities and the power to decide which cases the Court will hear.
   c. He has substantial administrative responsibilities and has the authority to cast a tie-breaking vote when the Court cannot reach a decision.
   d. He has certain administrative responsibilities but derives most of his power from leadership abilities and the prestige of the office.

2. Supreme Court **norms** are
   a. Rules that determine which cases will be heard.
   b. Codes of judicial conduct established by Congress.
   c. Unwritten but clearly understood ways of behaving.
   d. Guidelines used by the Senate in confirming appointees.

3. Federal district courts
   a. Hear only a small portion of federal cases.
   b. Primarily exercise appellate jurisdiction.
   c. Normally use three-judge panels to hear cases.
   d. Are courts of original jurisdiction.

4. The doctrine of *stare decisis* means that
   a. A court may issue an order that compels a person to complete a legal act.
   b. A defendant must be brought before a judge or magistrate and must be informed of the charges against him or her.
   c. Judges tend to follow precedent as the basis for legal reasoning.
   d. Lower courts must send a complete record of the case to an appellate court.

5. Alexander Hamilton believed that
   a. Congress and the president should each render their own judgments in questions of judicial review.
   b. The power of judicial review was inherent in the notion of separation of powers.
   c. Judicial review was a violation of fundamental constitutional principles.

d. Authorization for judicial review should be included in a Bill of Rights.

6. Past political and ideological positions of federal court nominees
   a. Have not been analyzed to determine their effect on future behavior.
   b. Are a pretty good guide to a judge's later behavior on the bench.
   c. Do not tell us very much about positions that federal judges will take.
   d. Is considered to be privileged information and is not available to the public.

7. With reference to the federal courts of appeal,
   a. Witnesses are extensively cross-examined.
   b. Briefs cannot be introduced at this level.
   c. New factual evidence cannot be introduced.
   d. Most cases are heard by a trial jury.

8. The solicitor general
   a. Solicits funds for interest groups and private citizens who could not otherwise afford to take a case to court.
   b. Serves as the president's attorney and is the president's primary legal adviser.
   c. Serves as the representative of the U.S. government before the Supreme Court.
   d. Interprets decisions of the Supreme Court so that they may serve as precedent for state and local courts.

9. The Supreme Court opinion of *Roe* v. *Wade* (1973) was written by
   a. Justice Harry Blackmun.
   b. Chief Justice William Rehnquist.
   c. Justice Sandra Day O'Connor.
   d. Chief Justice Earl Warren.

10. The U.S. Supreme Court
    a. Is a court of original jurisdiction only.
    b. Was established by act of Congress in 1801.
    c. Has jurisdiction only over violations of state law.
    d. Has both original jurisdiction and appellate jurisdiction.

11. *Marbury* v. *Madison* (1803) established the basis for
    a. Implied powers.
    b. National supremacy.
    c. Judicial review.
    d. Advise and consent.

12. The writ of *certiorari* is

    a.   A brief submitted by individuals who a have special interest in the case but who are not parties to the dispute.

    b.   The most powerful tool that the Court has for controlling its own agenda.

    c.   One of the basic individual rights that is guaranteed by the Constitution.

    d.   A statement of the legal reasoning that supports the decision of the Court.

13. (T/F) The power of judicial review was exercised by the Court on a regular basis until the end of the nineteenth century, and then it declined in its frequency.

14. (T/F) A judicial **remedy** is what a court determines must be done to rectify a wrong.

15. (T/F) A **test case** is an action that is designed to challenge the constitutionality of a law or an action by government.

16. (T/F) Proponents of strict construction believe that the intentions of the Founders are impossible to determine and are unduly constricting.

17. (T/F) **Standing** means that the Court will not provide advisory opinions to guide the other branches.

18. (T/F) Article III of the U.S. Constitution speaks only briefly about the judicial branch and does not provide many details about judicial responsibilities.

Chapter 15
FREEDOM: THE STRUGGLE FOR CIVIL LIBERTIES

Key Concepts and Objectives

The Key Concepts and Objectives provide a look at the fundamental goals and ideas of this chapter. This section serves as a guide to a basic understanding of the objectives of your textbook.

After reading this chapter, you should be able to:

- Understand the basic meaning of civil liberties, and list specific examples that illustrate them.
- Determine how amendments to the U.S. Constitution have extended individual liberties and have made the Constitution more democratic.
- Understand why liberty and political equality are important in a democracy, and explain how rights and liberties were gradually applied to the states through the process of selective incorporation.
- Determine how the process of nationalization of the Bill of Rights grew out of structural and political developments in the United States.
- Examine the conflicts in attitudes toward protection for the rights of the accused.
- Understand the standards of strict scrutiny, intermediate scrutiny, and ordinary scrutiny, and explain how the courts use them.
- Understand the structural, political linkage, and governmental factors that influence the meaning and practice of civic freedoms.
- Identify key terms and concepts used in Chapter 15

Chapter Overview

This section provides a brief overview of the chapter contents. Read this section as a preview before reading your textbook. Then use this material as a review to help you retain information from your reading.

→ INTRODUCTION TO PART FIVE: WHAT GOVERNMENT DOES

The chapters in Part five show what government does and how effectively our political and governmental institutions operate to fulfill the needs and expectations of the American people. These chapters also address the democracy theme, asking whether public policies are the outcome of a democratic process and whether policies improve the health and vitality of democracy in the United States.

Chapters 15 and 16 look at the status of civil liberties and civil rights in the United States, with special attention paid to decisions of the Supreme Court concerning our most cherished rights and liberties. Chapter 17 examines domestic policies, with particular attention given to patterns of government spending, the tax system, regulation of the economy, and social welfare. Chapter 18 looks at American foreign and military policies.

→ CAMPUS SPEECH CODES AND FREE SPEECH

This chapter examines civil liberties in the United States. It shows that the meaning of each of our freedoms is never settled but is the subject of continuing disagreement. This chapter focuses on how structural, political linkage, and governmental factors influence the meaning and practice of our civic freedoms.

American college campuses have become an important battleground in the continuing struggle over the meaning of free speech. The opening vignette focuses on the battle over speech codes that have been instituted at many colleges and universities in an effort to prohibit speech that may offend members of minority groups.

→ CIVIL LIBERTIES IN THE CONSTITUTION

Civil liberties are constitutional provisions, laws, and practices that *protect individuals from governmental interference*. The Framers of the Constitution were particularly concerned with establishing a society in which the practice of *liberty* (or *freedom*) was paramount. As embodied in the **Bill of Rights**, civil liberties are protected by *prohibitions against government actions that threaten freedom* (such as freedom of speech and religion). Because most formal barriers to equal participation have been used to exclude *groups* of people (such as women and racial minorities), civil rights initiatives have been directed at removing group barriers and helping groups overcome disadvantages created by past patterns of discrimination.

The original Constitution protected only a few rights and liberties from the national government and almost none from state governments. Among the few protected rights were the prohibition against Congress and the states from suspending the **writ of *habeas corpus***, except when required for public safety in times of rebellion or invasion, or from passing **bills of attainder** or *ex post facto* **laws**.

Reacting to strong objections from those who wanted rights to be explicitly protected, the Federalists promised that a **bill of rights** would be added after the Constitution was ratified. The addition of the Bill of Rights made the Constitution more **democratic** by enhancing **political liberty** and by guaranteeing a setting for free political expression that makes **popular sovereignty** possible. Later amendments were added to protect rights and liberties that states or the national government had previously compromised or ignored, and twentieth-century amendments made the Constitution substantially more democratic and contributed to popular sovereignty and political equality.

→RIGHTS AND LIBERTIES IN THE NINETEENTH CENTURY

During the nineteenth century, the range of protected civil liberties in the United States was somewhat different from their range today. Especially noteworthy were the special place of property rights as a freedom to be protected and the understanding that the Bill of Rights did not apply to state governments.

Property Rights in the Early Republic-Liberty may be understood as protection against government interference in certain kinds of activities. The major liberty stated in the original Constitution was *economic,* and the *primacy of property* over other rights and liberties was reinforced by more than a century of judicial interpretation.

The Marshall Court (1801-1835)-The Court ruled in *Barron* v. *Baltimore* (1833) that the **Bill of Rights did not apply to the states**. By contrast, the **contract clause** was directly applied against state action. Under the Marshall Court, the clause became a prime defense of property against states. In Fletcher v. Peck (1810), for example, the Marshall Court upheld a sale of public land, although almost all the legislators had voted for the land sale had been bribed by the prospective purchasers. In *Dartmouth College v. Woodward* (1819), Marshall argued that New Hampshire could not modify the charter of Dartmouth College because the original charter constituted a contract that could not be changed without impairing the obligations of the original contract.

The Taney Court (1836-1864)- Under Chief Justice Taney, the Court began to make a distinction between private property used in ways that encouraged economic growth and private property used for simple enjoyment. The Taney Court often ruled in favor of the former when the two concepts of property came into conflict.

Human Property- The judicial preference for property rights was especially—and tragically—strong when it came to the rights of property with respect to human property (slavery). Until the Civil War, courts in both the North and South consistently upheld the rights of slaveholders to recapture fugitive slaves. Abolitionists and reformers found the antebellum courts to be vigilant regarding property rights but indifferent or hostile to other liberties. In *Dred Scott* v. *Sandford* (1857), Chief Justice Taney claimed that slaves were not citizens who possessed rights, but simply private property belonging to their owners. In this sense, slaves were seen as being no different from land or tools.

Property Rights After the Civil War-The Fourteenth Amendment, passed after the Civil War, was designed to guarantee the citizenship rights of the newly freed slave. It included the **Due Process Clause** which stated that no state may "deprive a person of life, liberty, or property, without due process of law." The Supreme Court subsequently interpreted this clause as a protection for businesses against regulatory efforts of the states. During the nineteenth century, *rights of property* were expanded, refined, and altered to make them consistent with an emerging industrial society. Little attention was paid to the judicial protection of civil liberties, and little progress was made in rights of women and African-Americans. The twentieth century brought new approaches to property rights and to civil liberties in general.

→ NATIONALIZATION OF THE BILL OF RIGHTS

Despite the fact that the language of the Fourteenth Amendment specifically applies to the states, liberties unrelated to property were not very much protected before the twentieth century. However, the Supreme Court gradually interpreted the due process clause to *incorporate essential liberties* in the Bill of Rights.

Selective Incorporation-The Framers were worried more about the national government intrusion on freedom than about state government intrusion. Most of the states had bills of rights of their own constitutions, and being closer to the people, state governments would be less likely to intrude on the people's freedom, or so the Framers believed. The Fourteenth Amendment included three clauses that prohibit states from violating the rights and liberties of the people living them:

-The first specifies that all persons born or naturalized in the United States are citizens of both the United States and the states in which they reside.

412

-The **privileges and immunities** clause specifies that no state "shall make or enforce any law which shall abridge the privileges and immunities of citizens of the United States.
-The **due process** clause specifies that no state shall "deprive any person of life, liberty, or property, without due process of law."

Standards for Incorporation-Instead of total incorporation, the Court has pursued a policy of selective incorporation-nationalizing or incorporating those liberties in the Bill of Rights that it deemed *fundamental* to democracy. The Court has only slowly added even traditional civil liberties to the constitutional obligations of states. **Footnote four** of the Court's opinion in *U.S. v. Carolene Products Company* (1938) spelled out the conditions in which the Supreme Court would not defer to the actions of the states or the other branches of government. The opinion of the Court, written by Justice **Harlan Fiske Stone**, suggested that most legislative enactments would be considered constitutional and subject only to **ordinary scrutiny** (presuming their constitutionality) by the courts, whereas enactments restricting liberties, limiting the democratic process, or discriminating against minorities would fall under **strict scrutiny** (presuming their unconstitutionality, placing the burden on the authors to prove otherwise). The three classes of suspect state actions that bring strict scrutiny are those that seem to

-contradict specific prohibitions in the Constitution, including those of the Bill of Rights
-restrict the democratic process
-discriminate against racial, ethnic, or religious minorities

Freedom of Speech-Congress shall make no Law....abridging the freedom of speech.

Political Speech-The **first area of incorporation** of the Bill of Rights occurred with respect to **freedom of speech**, in *Gitlow v. New York* (1925). For many years, the Court deferred to political hysteria and allowed widespread suppression of speech and publication. Though the *Gitlow* precedent proved to be an important advance for civil liberties in the United States, the Court was still willing to leave Gitlow in jail and allow the states wide latitude in controlling what they considered dangerous speech. However, freedom of speech grew in later years to such an extent that far more speech is now covered than is not. In general, government today may not regulate or interfere with the content of speech without a *compelling reason*. For a reason to be compelling, the government must show that the speech poses a **clear and present danger** that the government has a duty to prevent (the standard formulated by Justice **Oliver Wendell Holmes** in 1919 in *Schenck v. United States*).

Actions and Symbolic Speech-Speech mixed with conduct may be restricted if the restrictions are narrowly and carefully tailored to curb the conduct while leaving the speech unmolested. (Symbolic expressions include wearing armbands or picketing). The use of profanity or words that are likely to cause violence ("fighting words") may be regulated in some cases, as may symbolic actions that prevent others from carrying out legitimate activities. In *Texas v. Johnson*

(1989), a case concerning flag burning, the Rehnquist Court ruled that flag burning falls under the free expression protections of the Constitution unless imminent incitement or violence is likely. The Court has disallowed the regulation of racially motivated cross burning (in *R.A.V. v. St. Paul*, 1992). When regulations aim at hateful *actions*, the courts have approved them.

Suppression of Free Expression- A major exception to the expansion of freedom of expression has been the periodic concern about "internal security." Censorship and suppression of dissenters and radicals have been persecuted by authorities for their political speech and writings. This occurred especially during World War I and World War II (with HUAC and McCarthyism).

Freedom of the Press-Incorporation of **freedom of the press** began with the *Gitlow* case, in which the Court included freedom of the press as a freedom guaranteed by the Fourteenth Amendment. *Near v. Minnesota* (1931) marked the first case in which a *state* law was invalidated as a violation of freedom of the press. *Near* involved the question of **prior restraint,** which prevents publication *before* it has occurred.

Prior Restraint-The prohibition of prior restraints on publication remains *the core of freedom of press.* Freedom of the press and freedom of speech tend to be considered together as **freedom of expression,** so general principles applicable to free speech apply to freedom of the press as well. These principles include the ban on prior restraint and the rule that the Court will permit repression only if the state can show that the publication poses a *clear and present danger.* The Court ruled in *New York v. United States* (1971) that the U.S. government could not prevent newspapers from publishing portions of the **Pentagon Papers**, secret documents revealing the U.S. involvement in Vietnam. A major expansion of freedom of the press, enunciated in *New York Times v. Sullivan* (1964), protected newspapers against trivial or incidental errors when they were reporting on **public persons** (such as public officials). Public persons are held to a higher standard of proof than private persons when they bring libel prosecutions.

Offensive Mass Media- *Pornography* is a nonlegal term for sexual materials; the legal term is **obscenity**. Although the courts have held that obscenity is unprotected by the First Amendment, the definition of obscenity has provoked constitutional struggles for half a century; the distinction between art and obscenity can be difficult to draw. *Miller v. California* (1973) set a reasonably clear three-part test used by the courts to define obscenity:

1. The average person, applying contemporary community standards, must find that the work as a whole appeals to the prurient interest [lust].
2. The state law must specifically define what sexual conduct is obscene.
3. The work as a whole must lack serious literary, artistic, political, or scientific value.

Material is not legally obscene—and cannot be regulated under the First Amendment—if the work survives even one part of this test. Community standards, applied by juries, are used to judge whether the work appeals to lust and whether the work is clearly offensive. However, literary, artistic, political, or scientific value (called the LASP test) is only judged by the jury's assessment of the testimony of expert witnesses. If all three standards are met, then the Court allows local communities to regulate the sale of pornographic materials.

When the Clinton administration and Congress passed the **Community Decency Act** (1996), which made it a crime to transmit over the Internet or to allow the transmission of indecent materials to which minors might have access, the Court ruled unanimously that the legislation was an unconstitutional violation of the First Amendment, being overly broad and vague and violative of free speech rights of adults to send and receive information.

Free Exercise of Religion-The First Amendment includes two provisions concerning religion: it prohibits Congress from making laws that prohibit the free exercise of religion and provides that Congress shall not make laws respecting an establishment of religion. The core of the nationalized **free exercise** of religion clause is that government may not interfere with religious *beliefs*. However, religious *actions* are not absolutely protected.

Establishment of Religion-The **establishment** clause has been interpreted to require that government must take a position of *neutrality*. It must not favor one religion over another, or religious groups over the nonreligious. **Thomas Jefferson** said that this clause requires *"a wall of separation between church and state." Everson* **v.** *Board of Education* (1947) incorporated the establishment clause into the Fourteenth Amendment by sustaining a New Jersey program to reimburse parents for bus transportation to both public and parochial schools.

The *Lemon* Test- The three-pronged *Lemon* test (established in the 1971 case of *Lemon* **v.** *Kurtzman*) specifies three conditions that every law must meet to avoid establishing religion:

1. The law must have a secular *purpose*.
2. The *primary effect* of the law must be neither to advance nor to retard religion.
3. The government must not foster *excessive entanglements* between the state and religion.

School Prayer and Creation Science-Although most Americans support the use of some type of prayer in public schools, the Court has consistently ruled against such practices since it ordered that state of New York to suspend its requirement that all students in public schools recite nondenominational prayer at the start of each school day in *Engel v. Vitale* (1962). Judge Hugo Black argued that the prayer requirement was "wholly inconsistent with the establishment clause." In *Stone v. Graham* (1980), the Court ruled against posting the Ten Commandments in public school classrooms. In *Lee v. Wiesman* (1992), it ruled against allowing school-sponsored prayer at graduation ceremonies.

Unstated Rights-Besides the stated freedoms that the text addresses there are also rights that are not specifically stated. The **right to privacy** is a cherished right by most Americans that is not mentioned in the Constitution. Many scholars contend that the right to privacy is *inherent* in the Bill of Rights. The **Ninth Amendment** has been cited as proof that the Framers believed in the existence of civil liberties not specifically mentioned in the Bill of Rights: "The enumeration in the Constitution of certain rights, shall not be construed to deny or disparage others retained by the people." Also, protections against illegal searches and seizures and against quartering troops in private homes, as well as the right to free expression and conscience, support the idea of the right to privacy. The Supreme Court reinforced this view in *Griswold v. Connecticut* (1965), in which it ruled that a constitutional right to privacy exists when it struck down laws making birth control illegal.

It is unclear whether the Court supports the "**right to die**." In *Vacco v. Quill* (1997) the Court threw out two federal circuit court decisions that had overturned state laws in Washington and New York banning doctor-assisted suicide as unconstitutional. The Court ruled that there is no constitutionally protected right to die, but states could establish such a right. Jurists and scholars who take a strict constructionist position believe that only liberties specifically mentioned in the Constitution are protected liberties and that the right to privacy, has been invented out of thin air and is therefore illegitimate.

Rights of the Accused-Incorporation of **rights of the accused** involves balancing individual rights with protection of the community. Most Americans feel some ambivalence toward rights of the accused: most support constitutional rights and liberties that protect innocent persons, but most Americans also want to control crime as much as possible. Balancing those two sentiments has been a difficult task, and one that is still evolving.

Unreasonable Searches and Seizures-In *Mapp v. Ohio* (1961), the **Warren Court (1956-1968)** developed the **exclusionary rule** to prevent police and prosecutors from using evidence that had been obtained from warrantless and unreasonable searches. Until the Warren Court compelled states to abide by the **Fourth Amendment** in 1961, states frequently used **unreasonable searches and seizures** in an effort to control crime. The **Burger Court (1968-86)** allowed for a "good faith" exception to the exclusionary rule, under which prosecutors may introduce evidence obtained illegally if they can show that the police had relied on a warrant that appeared valid but later proved to be invalid. The Burger Court limited places in which *privacy* could be reasonably expected. The Court also ruled that illegally gathered evidence that would have been found without a warrant is permissible. In *Murray v. United States* (1988), the Court allowed prosecutors to use products of illegal searches if other evidence unrelated to the illegal evidence would have justified a search warrant. The combination of "good faith," "inevitable discovery," and "retroactive probable cause" has considerably narrowed the exclusionary rule.

The **Rehnquist Court** (1986-present) continued to narrow the exclusionary rule when it held in *Minnesota v. Carter* (1998) that an officer acting on a drug tip could peer through the gap in drawn Venetian blinds to observe illegal activity without violating the Fourth Amendment. In *Wyoming v. Houghton* (1999) the Court announced that police who have probable cause to search an automobile for illegal substances may also search personal possessions (such as a purse) of passengers in the car.

However, the Court also ruled that police could not search every driver or car involved in petty traffic offenses; a bag of marijuana discovered in a search incident to a speeding ticket in *Knowles v. Iowa* (1998) was excluded as the product of an illegal search.

Self-Incrimination-Concerning the **Fifth Amendment**, the **Warren Court** (1953-1969) decided that the privilege not to incriminate oneself was useless at the trial stage if police could coerce confessions before the trial took place. The Court held that, *prior to questioning*, all persons had the right to be informed of their rights to remain silent and to consult an attorney (**Miranda v. Arizona**, 1966). The Warren Court expanded due process and preferred constitutional guarantees to efficient law enforcement. The Burger Court upheld *Miranda*, but it reduced the scope and allowed exceptions. The Rehnquist Court has granted police and prosecutors more latitude in questioning suspects.

The Right to Counsel-The **Sixth Amendment's** right to counsel was nationalized-made binding on the states-in *Powell v. Alabama* (1932), the famous **Scottsboro Boys** prosecution; the Court ruled that legal counsel must be supplied to all indigent defendants accused of a capital crime any crime in which the death penalty may be imposed). *Gideon v. Wainwright* (1963) The Court ruled that defendants accused of any felony in state jurisdictions are entitled to a lawyer even if the defendant cannot afford one.

Capital Punishment-In *Furman* v. *Georgia* (1972), a split court found that death penalty laws then in existence constituted *cruel and unusual punishment* because the procedures were arbitrary and discriminatory. The federal government and many states later passed new death penalty laws, designed to meet the Court's objections. In *Gregg v. Georgia* (1976), the Court held that capital punishment was not inherently cruel or unusual, but the Court tended to create an obstacle course of standards that states had to meet.

The Rehnquist Court has tried to expedite the use of the death penalty. In *McCleskey v. Kemp* (1987) the Court chose to ignore statistical evidence that blacks who kill whites are four times as likely to be sentenced to death than whites who kill blacks. The Court ruled that individual defendants must show that racism played a role in their specific cases. In *Penry v. Lynaugh* (1989), the Court allowed the execution of a mentally retarded man convicted of murder. In *Stanford v. Kentucky,* (1989) the Court allowed the execution of a minor who had been convicted of murder. In *McClesky v. Zant* (1991) the Court made delays much less likely by eliminating many means of challenging capital convictions; the Court, in a 6-3 majority, decided to eliminate delays even though no party to the case had requested the Court do so. In *Keeney v. Tamayo-Reyes* (1992), the Court limited the right of "death row" inmates convicted in state courts to appeal the Supreme Court.

Public support for capital punishment is high; in 1999 the number of people executed by the government reached its highest level since it was reinstated in 1976. **Illinois Governor George Ryan** stopped all executions in his state system because at least 13 men on death row had been shown to have committed the crimes for which they were sentenced to death.

→ **SUMMARY**

The formal foundation of American liberties is found in the Constitution and its amendments, particularly the Bill of Rights and the Fourteenth Amendment, but their actual enjoyment depends on the actions of the courts, the behavior of government officials, and the struggle for democracy. American history has witnessed an expansion of the boundaries of liberties, especially during the twentieth century, though much remains to be done.

During the nineteenth century the Court concerned itself mainly with property rights. It nationalized the constitutional protection of civil liberties by using the Fourteenth Amendment as its main instrument. The familiar liberties of expression, association, press, and religion, as well as certain due process protections for the accused, were gradually incorporated and guaranteed throughout the nation. The expansion of rights of the accused was always hotly debated, and the conservative orientation of the present Court has resulted in the reversal of many of the due process innovations of the Warren and Burger Courts.

> *Chapter Outline*

This section gives you a comprehensive review of the chapter. Use this outline in combination with your textbook to look for key concepts and objectives, to identify essential terms and names, and to gain a basic understanding of political practices and principles from this chapter.

I. **INTRODUCTION TO PART FIVE: WHAT GOVERNMENT DOES (p. 443)**
   A. Part Five examines what government produces in terms of public policies: what government does and how effective it is in tackling the most important problems facing the United States.

B. Chapters in this part have a strong comparative aspect because evaluating how well we are doing requires that we look at what governments in other countries are doing to address similar problems.

C. These chapters also address the theme of democracy, asking whether or not public policies are the outcome of a democratic process and whether policies improve the health and vitality of democracy in the United States.

II. CAMPUS SPEECH CODES AND FREE SPEECH (p. 445)

A. This chapter examines civil liberties in the United States.

    1. **Civil liberties** are constitutional provisions, laws, and practices that *protect individuals from governmental interference*; as embodied in the **Bill of Rights**, civil liberties are *prohibitions against government actions that threaten freedom* (such as freedom of speech and religion).

    2. Chapter 15 looks at the struggle for democracy, exemplified by the efforts of many groups and individuals to protect and expand civil liberties.

    3. This chapter focuses on how *three factors–structural, political linkage, and governmental–influence the meaning and practice of our civic freedoms.*

B. American college campuses have become an important battleground in the continuing struggle over the meaning of free speech.

C. Campus speech codes have been instituted at many colleges and universities in an effort to prohibit speech that may offend members of minority groups.

    1. Many civil libertarians have fought against such codes, favoring the concept of free speech in a free society.

    2. The courts have generally sided with the civil libertarians on this issue.

III. CIVIL LIBERTIES IN THE CONSTITUTION (pp. 446-448)

A. **Civil liberties** are constitutional provisions, laws, and practices that *protect individuals from governmental interference.*

    1. The framers of the Constitution were particularly concerned with establishing a society in which the practice of *liberty* (or *freedom*) was paramount

    2. As embodied in the **Bill of Rights**, civil liberties are *prohibitions against government actions that threaten freedom* (such as freedom of speech and religion).

    3. By contrast, **civil rights** refer to governmental responsibility for *guaranteeing that all citizens are able to participate as equals* in the practice of democratic life.

B. **Constitutional liberties**

    1. The original Constitution specifically protected only a few liberties from the national government and almost none from state governments.

    2. The Framers singled out a few freedoms that were too crucial to be left unmentioned.

a) The *safeguard against tyranny* that the framers preferred was to give the national government little power with which to attack individual liberties.

b) Congress and the states were prohibited from suspending the **writ of *habeas corpus*** (a court order demanding that a prisoner be brought to court to show cause for his or her detention) except when public safety demanded it in times of rebellion or invasion, prohibited from passing **bills of attainder** (a legislative act that declares a person guilty of a crime and imposes punishment without a judicial trial), and prohibited from passing ***ex post facto* laws** (retroactive criminal legislation).

3. Objections to the absence of a more specific listing led the Federalists to promise that a **bill of rights** would be proposed as a condition for ratifying the Constitution.
    a) The Bill of Rights was passed by the 1st Congress in 1789 and was ratified by the required number of states by 1791.
    b) The Bill of Rights made the Constitution more **democratic** by *enhancing political liberty* and by *guaranteeing a context of free political expression* that makes **popular sovereignty** possible.

4. Later amendments sought to protect rights and liberties that states or the national government had previously compromised or ignored.

C. The changing impact of the Constitution
    1. Many of the freedoms we expect today are not specifically mentioned in the Constitution.
    2. Many of our rights and liberties were established in decisions by government officials and changes made by judges, political leaders, and groups.
    3. Some of our rights have evolved as the culture has changed or through partisan and ideological competition.

IV. **RIGHTS AND LIBERTIES IN THE NINETEENTH CENTURY (pp. 448-449)**
    A. **Property rights in the early republic**
        1. **Liberty** may be understood as protection against government interference in certain kinds of activities.
        2. The major liberty stated in the original Constitution was *economic*: in Article I, Section 10, the Constitution prohibited states from impairing the **obligation of contracts**.
        3. The *primacy of property* over other rights and liberties was reinforced by more than a century of judicial interpretation.
    B. The **Marshall Court** (1801-1835)
        1. The Supreme Court ruled in ***Barron* v. *Baltimore*** (1833) that the **Bill of Rights did not apply to the states.**

a) By contrast, the *contracts clause was directly applied against state action*; under the Marshall Court, the clause became a prime defense of property against interference by the states.

b) The contracts clause was used to block virtually any changes in established property relations (especially those sought by the states); in *Fletcher* v. *Peck* (1810), Chief Justice Marshall argued that even a fraudulent sale created a contract that the state could not void.

C. **Human property**
   1. The judicial preference for property rights was especially—and tragically—strong when it came to the rights of property with respect to human property (slavery).
   2. Until the Civil War, courts in both the North and South consistently upheld the rights of slaveholders to recapture fugitive slaves.
   3. In *Dred Scott* v. *Sandford* (1857), Chief Justice **Roger Taney** claimed that slaves were not citizens who possessed rights, but simply private property belonging to their owners; in this sense, slaves were seen as being no different from land or tools.

D. **Property rights after the Civil War**
   1. The Fourteenth Amendment was designed to guarantee the citizenship rights of the newly freed slaves.
      a) The **due process clause** says that no state may "deprive a person of life, liberty, or property, without due process of law."
      b) Ironically, the Supreme Court soon interpreted this clause as a protection for business against the regulatory efforts of the states.
   2. During the nineteenth century, *rights of property* were expanded, refined, and altered to make them consistent with an emerging industrial society; at the same time, little attention was paid to the judicial protection of civil liberties, and little progress was made in rights of women and African-Americans.
   3. At the same time that the Court was deleting any practical use of the Fourteenth Amendment for the protection of civil rights and liberties, it was extending its application for new protections of property (such as the use of the *due process clause to protect business* from state regulation of maximum working hours in the 1905 case of *Lochner* v. *New York*).
   4. The twentieth century brought new approaches to property rights and to civil liberties in general.

V. **NATIONALIZATION OF THE BILL OF RIGHTS (pp. 449-469)**
   A. Liberties unrelated to property were not protected very much before the twentieth century because the **Bill of Rights did not apply to state governments** (only to the national government); the **Supreme Court only gradually applied the Bill of Rights to the states through a process known as selective incorporation.**
   B. **Selective incorporation**

1. The framers were more concerned about national government intrusion on freedoms than about state government intrusion.
2. It is apparent that Congress wanted to extend the reach of the Bill of Rights when it approved the **Fourteenth Amendment** after the Civil War; three clauses specify that the *states* cannot violate rights and liberties:
    a) The amendment guarantees that all persons born or naturalized in the United States are citizens of both the United States and of the *states* in which they reside.
    b) The **privileges and immunities clause** specifies that no *state* "shall make or enforce any law which shall abridge the privileges or immunities of citizens of the United States."
    c) The **due process clause** specifies that no *state* shall "deprive any person of life, liberty, or property, without due process of law."
3. Although Congress intended to guarantee that the states would protect U.S. citizens' rights and liberties (including those found in the Bill of Rights), the Supreme Court was very slow in **nationalizing** (making rights obligatory at the state level) or **incorporating** the Bill of Rights.
    a) The Supreme Court gradually interpreted the due process clause to *incorporate essential liberties* in the Bill of Rights (that is, making constitutional protections apply against the states).
    b) Instead of total incorporation, the Court has pursued a policy of **selective incorporation**—nationalizing or incorporating those liberties in the Bill of Rights that it deemed *fundamental* to democracy.
C. **Standards for incorporation**
    1. *What standard does the Supreme Court use* in deciding whether or not to incorporate some portion of the Bill of Rights?
    2. The answer is spelled out in **footnote four** of the Court's opinion in *U.S. v. Carolene Products Company* (1938).
        a) The opinion of the Court, written by Justice **Harlan Fiske Stone**, suggested that most legislative enactments would be considered constitutional and subject only to **ordinary scrutiny** (presuming their constitutionality) by the courts, but three classes of state actions would be subject to **strict scrutiny** (presumed unconstitutional, with the burden being on the states to prove that the enactments are *compelling* and *necessary*).
        b) Three classes of *suspect state actions that bring strict scrutiny* are those that seem to:
            (1) Contradict specific prohibitions in the Constitution, including those of the Bill of Rights
            (2) Restrict the democratic process
            (3) Discriminate against racial, ethnic, or religious minorities
D. **Freedom of speech** became the **first area of incorporation**

1. **Political speech**
   a) For many, the right to speak one's mind is the first principle of a free and democratic society, yet the right to free speech was not incorporated by the Supreme Court until 1925 (***Gitlow v. New York***).
   b) Although the Court upheld the conviction of Benjamin Gitlow under the New York Criminal Anarchy Law, the majority held that the State of New York was bound by the First Amendment.
   c) Freedom of speech grew in later years to such an extent that far more speech is covered than is not.
      (1) In general, government today may not regulate or interfere with the content of speech without a *compelling reason*.
      (2) For a reason to be compelling, the government must show that the speech poses a **clear and present danger** that the government has a duty to prevent (the standard formulated by Justice **Oliver Wendell Holmes** in the 1919 case of ***Schenck v. United States***); abstract advocacy of ideas or philosophy is protected unless it meets both conditions ("clear" meaning a substantial and direct relationship, and "present" meaning immediate).
2. **Actions and symbolic speech**
   a) Speech mixed with *conduct* may be restricted under certain conditions.
      (1) **Symbolic expression** (such as wearing arm bands, burning the flag, or picketing) may receive less protection from the Court than "pure" speech.
      (2) Use of profanity or "fighting words" may be regulated in some cases.
   b) Efforts have been made to suppress *speech* that certain women and minorities find objectionable, and the courts have generally found such repression unconstitutional.
   c) By contrast, courts have approved regulations aimed at hateful *actions*; the Court has upheld state laws and municipal ordinances that keep antiabortion demonstrators some distance away from clinic entrances.
3. Suppression of free expression
   a) A major exception to the expansion of freedom of expression has resulted from concern for internal security, with periodic persecution of dissenters and radicals for their political speech and writings during the twentieth century.
   b) Censorship of dissent and protests during World War I were a precursor to abuses after the war; the anticommunist "Red scare" of the 1940s and 1950s deferred to political hysteria.
E. **Freedom of the press**
   1. Freedom of the press and freedom of speech tend to be considered together as **freedom of expression**, so general principles applicable to free speech apply to freedom of the press as well.
   2. In an aside in the *Gitlow* case, the Court included freedom of the press as a freedom guaranteed against state interference by the Fourteenth Amendment; in

Near v. *Minnesota* (1931), the Court followed up on *Gitlow* by invalidating the Minnesota Public Nuisance Law as a violation of freedom of the press.
  a) Prior restraint
    (1) *Near* involved the question of **prior restraint,** an action that prevents publication *before* it has occurred; publishers may be sued for the content of their publications after they have been published, but the state of Minnesota was trying to prevent Near and his associates from publishing in the future.
    (2) The prohibition of prior restraint of publication remains *the core of freedom of the press*; the Court places a heavy burden on the government to show justification for prior restraint.
    (3) In *New York Times Co.* v. *United States* (1971), the Court ruled that the U.S. government could not prevent newspapers from publishing portions of the *Pentagon Papers* that revealed how the United States had become involved in the Vietnam War.
  b) Freedom of the press and freedom of speech tend to be considered together as **freedom of expression**, so general principles applicable to free speech apply to freedom of the press as well.
  3. A major expansion of freedom of the press, set forth in *New York Times* v. *Sullivan* (1964), protected newspapers against trivial or incidental errors when they were reporting on **public persons** (such as public officials); public persons are held to a higher standard of proof when they bring libel prosecutions.
F. **Offensive mass media**
  1. Although the courts have held that *obscenity is not protected* by the First Amendment, the distinction between art and obscenity can be difficult to draw.
    a) **Pornography** is a *nonlegal* term for sexual materials; the *legal* term is **obscenity.**
    b) While justices admit that principled distinctions are difficult, *Miller* v. *California* (1973) set a reasonably clear three-part test used by the courts to define obscenity.
  2. Many Americans now have concerns about the availability to minors of sexually offensive material on the Internet.
    a) In 1996, Congress and President Clinton cooperated to pass the **Communications Decency Act**, which made it a crime to transmit or allow to be transmitted indecent materials over the Internet to which minors might have access.
    b) The Supreme Court decided unanimously that the legislation was an unconstitutional violation of the First Amendment, being overly broad and vague and violative of the free speech rights of adults to receive and send information (***Reno, Attorney General of the United States*** v. ***American Civil Liberties Union***, 1997).

G. **Free exercise of religion**
1. The First Amendment includes *two provisions concerning religion*:
   a) It prohibits Congress from making laws that prohibit the *free exercise* of religion.
   b) It provides that Congress shall not make laws respecting an *establishment* of religion.
2. For much of our history, the **exercise** of religion was not limited.
   a) Congress did not legislate much on the subject.
   b) The Supreme Court deferred to the states on issues of religious freedom.
   c) Because the states were not covered by the First Amendment, the free exercise of religion was protected by state constitutions or not at all.
3. The *flag salute* cases involved the constitutionality of state laws that provided for expelling public school children who refused to salute the flag and recite the Pledge of Allegiance.
   a) In *Minersville School District* **v.** *Gobitis* (1940), the Court upheld the expulsion of two children who refused to salute the flag, even though it violated their faith as Jehovah's Witnesses.
   b) In *West Virginia* **v.** *Barnette* (1943), the Court reversed *Gobitis* and firmly established free exercise of religion as protected against the states (a change brought about by a change of court personnel and the influence of public opinion; Justice **Harlan Fiske Stone's** stinging dissent in *Gobitis* was instrumental in moving liberal justices to Stone's side).
4. The *core of the nationalized free exercise clause* is that government may not interfere with religious *beliefs*; however, religious *actions* are not absolutely protected, and the Court has upheld some state laws limiting certain religious practices (such as the use of peyote in Native American religious ceremonies, a decision that was overturned in 1993 when President **Clinton** signed the Religious Freedom Restoration Act).

H. **Establishment of Religion**
1. The establishment clause has been interpreted to require that government must take a position of *neutrality*.
   a) It must not favor one religion over another, or religious groups over the nonreligious.
   b) **Thomas Jefferson** said that this clause requires *"a **wall of separation** between church and state."*
2. *Everson* **v.** *Board of Education* (1947) incorporated the establishment clause into the Fourteenth Amendment by sustaining a New Jersey program to reimburse parents for bus transportation to both public and parochial schools.
3. In *McCollum* **v.** *Board of Education* (1948), a program for teaching religion in public schools was found to be unconstitutional; but in *Zorach* **v.** *Clauson* (1952),

the Court upheld a similar program in New York because students were permitted to leave school premises early for religious instruction.

4. The establishment clause had been incorporated by this time, but the justices were having a difficult time determining what separation of church and state means in practice.

5. The **Warren** Court (1953-1969) brought together a solid church-state separationist contingent whose decisions the early **Burger** Court (1969-1973) distilled into the major doctrine of the establishment clause, the *Lemon* **test**.

   a) In *Lemon* v. *Kurtzman* (1971), Chief Justice Warren Burger specified three conditions that every law must meet to avoid establishing religion.

      (1) The law must have a *secular* (nonreligious) purpose.

      (2) The *primary effect* of the law must be neither to advance nor to retard religion (religious neutrality).

      (3) Government must never foster *excessive entanglements* between the state and religion.

   b) The *Lemon* test has erected substantial walls against mixing church and state.

6. The **Rehnquist** Court has brought a change in judicial interpretation—in *Rosenberger* v. *University of Virginia* (1995), the Court ruled that the university, which is a state-supported institution, must provide the same financial subsidy to a student religious publication that it provides to other student publications.

7. **School prayer and creation science**

   a) Although a majority of Americans support allowing a nondenominational prayer or a period of silent prayer in the schools, the Court has consistently ruled against such practices since the early 1960s.

   b) There have been some areas where the Court has ruled in favor of religious groups on related issues; for example, the Court has permitted religious groups to meet in public schools and has allowed students to pray on their own or in unofficial study groups while on public school premises.

   c) Returning prayer to the public schools is very high on the agenda of Christian conservatives.

I. **Unstated rights**

1. Unlike freedoms like speech, press, and religion, the freedom to be left alone in our private lives (generally referred to as the right to privacy) is not specifically mentioned in the Constitution.

   a) Despite its omission from the Constitution, most Americans consider the right to privacy to be one of our freedoms.

   b) Many (but not all) constitutional scholars believe that a right to privacy is **inherent** (not explicitly stated) in the Bill of Rights; they point to prohibitions against illegal searches and seizures and against quartering troops in our homes, to First Amendment rights, and to the Ninth Amendment as a reference to liberties not specifically mentioned.

c) In 1965, the Supreme Court ruled that a right to privacy exists when it struck down laws making birth control illegal (***Griswold* v. *Connecticut***).

2. Debate still continues over whether there is a constitutionally protected right to privacy.

a) Some advocates of the right to privacy see a growing danger in the ability of the new information technology to collect and make accessible a vast amount of data about all Americans.

b) The right to privacy was the constitutional basis for the ***Roe* v. *Wade*** abortion decision in 1973, but the Court has not endorsed the existence of a privacy-based "right to die" (***Vacco* v. *Quill*,** 1997).

J. **Rights of the accused**

1. Incorporation of **rights of the accused** involves balancing individual rights with protection of the community.

2. Most Americans feel some ambivalence toward rights of the accused: most support constitutional rights and liberties that protect innocent persons, but most Americans also want to control crime as much as possible.

3. Balancing those two sentiments has been a difficult task, and one that is still evolving.

K. **Unreasonable searches and seizures**

1. In *Mapp* v. *Ohio* (1961), the **Warren Court** (1956-1968) developed the **exclusionary rule** to prevent police and prosecutors from using evidence that had been obtained from warrantless and unreasonable searches.

2. Until the Warren Court compelled states to abide by the **Fourth Amendment** in 1961, states frequently used **unreasonable searches and seizures** in an effort to control crime.

3. The **Burger Court** (1968-86) allowed for a "good faith" exception to the exclusionary rule, under which prosecutors may introduce evidence obtained illegally if they can show that the police had relied on a warrant that appeared valid but later proved to be invalid.

a) The Burger Court limited places in which *privacy* could be reasonably expected.

b) The Court also ruled that illegally gathered evidence that would have been found without a warrant is permissible.

c) In *Murray* v. *United States* (1988), the Court allowed prosecutors to use products of illegal searches if other evidence unrelated to the illegal evidence would have justified a search warrant.

d) The combination of "good faith," "inevitable discovery," and "retroactive probable cause" has considerably narrowed the exclusionary rule.

4. The **Rehnquist Court** (1986-present) continued to narrow the exclusionary rule when it held in *Minnesota* v. *Carter* (1998) that an officer acting on a drug tip could peer through the gap in drawn Venetian blinds to observe illegal activity

without violating the Fourth Amendment.
   a) In *Wyoming v. Houghton* (1999) the Court announced that police who have probable cause to search an automobile for illegal substances may also search personal possessions (such as a purse) of passengers in the car.
   b) However, the Court also ruled that police could not search every driver or car involved in petty traffic offenses; a bag of marijuana discovered in a search incident to a speeding ticket in *Knowles v. Iowa* (1998) was excluded as the product of an illegal search.

5. **Self-Incrimination**
   a) Concerning the **Fifth Amendment** the **Warren Court** (1953-1969) decided that the privilege not to incriminate oneself was useless at the trial stage if police could coerce confessions before the trial took place.
   b) The Court held that, *prior to questioning*, all persons had the right to be informed of their rights to remain silent and to consult an attorney (***Miranda* v. *Arizona***, 1966).
   c) The Warren Court expanded due process and preferred constitutional guarantees to efficient law enforcement.
   d) The Burger Court upheld *Miranda*, but it reduced the scope and allowed exceptions.
   e) The Rehnquist Court has granted police and prosecutors more latitude in questioning suspects.

6. **The right to counsel**
   a) The **Sixth Amendment's** right to counsel was nationalized-made binding on the states-in *Powell v. Alabama* (1932), the famous **Scottsboro Boys** prosecution.
   b) The Court ruled that legal counsel must be supplied to all indigent defendants accused of a capital crime any crime in which the death penalty may be imposed). In *Gideon v. Wainwright* (1963) the Court ruled that defendants accused of any felony in state jurisdictions are entitled to a lawyer even if the defendant cannot afford one.

7. **Capital punishment**
   a) In *Furman* v. *Georgia* (1972), a split court found that death penalty laws then in existence constituted *cruel and unusual punishment* because the procedures were arbitrary and discriminatory.
   b) The federal government and many states later passed new death penalty laws, designed to meet the Court's objections.
   c) In *Gregg v. Georgia* (1976), the Court held that capital punishment was not inherently cruel or unusual, but the Court tended to create an obstacle course of standards that states had to meet.

8. The Rehnquist Court has tried to expedite the use of the death penalty. In *McCleskey v. Kemp* (1987) the Court chose to ignore statistical evidence that

blacks who kill whites are four times as likely to be sentenced to death than whites who kill blacks.

    a) The Court ruled that individual defendants must show that racism played a role in their specific cases.

        (1) In *Penry v. Lynaugh* (1989), the Court allowed the execution of a mentally retarded man convicted of murder.

        (2) In *Stanford v. Kentucky*, (1989) the Court allowed the execution of a minor who had been convicted of murder.

        (3) In *McClesky v. Zant* (1991) the Court made delays much less likely by eliminating many means of challenging capital convictions; the Court, in a 6-3 majority, decided to eliminate delays even though no party to the case had requested the Court do so.

        (4) In *Keeney v. Tamayo-Reyes* (1992), the Court limited the right of "death row" inmates convicted in state courts to appeal the Supreme Court.

    b) Public support for capital punishment is high; in 1999 the number of people executed by the government reached its highest level since it was reinstated in 1976. **Illinois Governor George Ryan** stopped all executions in his state system because at least 13 men on death row had been shown to have committed the crimes for which they were sentenced to death.

VI.   SUMMARY (p. 469)

    A. The formal foundation of American liberties is found in the Constitution and its amendments, particularly the Bill of Rights and the Fourteenth Amendment, but their actual enjoyment depends on the actions of the courts, the behavior of government officials, and the struggle for democracy.

    B. American history has witnessed an expansion of the boundaries of liberties, especially during the twentieth century, though much remains to be done.

    C. During the nineteenth century the Court concerned itself mainly with property rights. It nationalized the constitutional protection of civil liberties by using the Fourteenth Amendment as its main instrument.

    D. The familiar liberties of expression, association, press, and religion, as well as certain due process protections for the accused, were gradually incorporated and guaranteed throughout the nation.

    E. The expansion of rights of the accused was always hotly debated, and the conservative orientation of the present Court has resulted in the reversal of many of the due process innovations of the Warren and Burger Courts.

Terms for Review

Use this list to review essential principles, functions, and concepts from this chapter. Refer to your textbook for help in identifying and defining terms on this list. When you study, do not merely memorize terms; ask questions about the material you are reviewing, and look for the importance or significance of each item.

American Civil Liberties Union (ACLU)

bill of attainder

Bill of Rights

capital crime

civil liberties

clear and present danger

Communications Decency Act (1996)

contract clause

due process clause

equal protection clause

establishment clause

exclusionary rule

ex post facto law

free exercise clause

good faith exception

habeas corpus

incorporation

inevitable discovery

intermediate scrutiny

Lemon test

McCarthyism

nationalizing the Bill of Rights

obscenity

ordinary scrutiny

prior restraint

privileges and immunities clause

public persons and private persons

retroactive probable cause

right to privacy

selective incorporation

separate but equal doctrine

strict construction

strict scrutiny

symbolic expression

unreasonable searches and seizures

Research Topics: Applying What You Have Learned

You will derive more benefit from your reading if you try to apply what you have learned. Some of the suggested research topics can be answered exclusively from your text, while others require you to conduct some basic research on your own. The references suggested under **Internet Sources** *will help you in your search.*

- Review recent newspapers and try to identify several local issues that involve civil liberties. Write a brief essay in which you identify the problems and offer a solution.

Consider constitutional principles and probable reaction by the local community as priorities in establishing your solution.

- Flag desecration is a particularly emotional topic. Evaluate opposing viewpoints toward the question of whether flag burning should be considered as constitutionally protected symbolic expression, and review the Supreme Court's opinion in *Texas* v. *Johnson* (1989). What conclusion did you reach? How would you substantiate your opinion if your instructor were to include this as an essay question on an exam?

- We define democracy in terms of the existence of political liberty and political equality, as well as of popular sovereignty. Based on your reading of this chapter, how has nationalizing the Bill of Rights (making rights obligatory at the state level) made America more democratic? Are there any ways in which nationalizing the Bill of Rights may have made the system less democratic?

- Read the Ninth Amendment and decide what you think it means. Are people entitled to some rights that are not mentioned in the Constitution? If so, what are they? How does Jefferson's assertion of inalienable rights fit into this context?

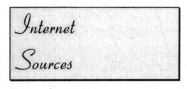

A number of sites on the World Wide Web serve as "gateways" to vast collections of material on American government and politics. The following Internet resources are recommended for students who would like to do some additional research in the areas covered by this chapter. These references would also be helpful in expanding on the questions suggested under Research Topics.

First Amendment Cyber-Tribune   http://3.trib.com//FACT/index.html
This site is so complete and well organized that it is the only one recommended in this chapter. This gateway is concerned with each of the First Amendment freedoms discussed in this chapter and provides links for each freedom to background documents, court cases, breaking news, op-ed pieces, bibliographies, First Amendment Web sites, civil liberties organizations, and even an on-line question-and-answer section.

Self-Evaluation

Circle the correct answer for each question. Questions are listed in the same order in which the information appears in the text. Use the Answer Key in the back of the Study Guide *to check your responses.*

1. The core of the **free exercise** clause is that
    a. Religious actions are protected against government interference, but religious beliefs are not absolutely protected.
    b. The free exercise of religion is protected against the federal government, but it has not been extended against the states.
    c. The clause requires a wall of separation between church and state under which government must take a position of neutrality toward religion.
    d. Government may not interfere with religious beliefs, but religious actions are not absolutely protected.

2. **Selective incorporation** is the process by which
    a. The courts presume the constitutionality of most legislative enactments.
    b. Prosecutors have been allowed to use evidence obtained from illegal searches if other evidence unrelated to the illegal evidence would have justified a search warrant.
    c. The Supreme Court has extended fundamental rights against state action.
    d. Sexual harassment was defined so that workers only had to show that the work environment was hostile or abusive.

3. **Civil liberties** refer to
    a. Constitutional provisions, laws, and practices that protect individuals from governmental interference.
    b. Governmental responsibility for guaranteeing that all citizens are able to participate as equals in the practice of democratic life.
    c. The elimination of formal barriers to equal participation by groups of people, such as minorities.
    d. Guarantees of rights that protect citizens from unfair or unjust actions by other individuals.

4. *Regents of the University of California* v. *Bakke* (1978) was based on claims of
    a. Pay equity.
    b. Suspect classification.

433

    c.   Reverse discrimination.

    d.   Sexual harassment.

5.   Which of the following statements best illustrates the immediate reaction to *Brown* v. *Board of Education* (1954)?

    a.   Despite widespread resistance, programs to desegregate the public schools were enacted almost immediately.

    b.   Little was accomplished until the president and Congress backed up the Supreme Court decision with civil rights legislation.

    c.   Violence and unrest erupted nationwide within two weeks of the Supreme Court's opinion.

    d.   The opinion was later reversed by *Plessy* v. *Ferguson* because the Court had overstepped its authority in interpreting the equal protection clause.

6.   Which of the following statements best describes a primary concern of the Framers of the U.S. Constitution?

    a.   They were especially concerned with establishing a society in which all people would eventually have an equal political voice.

    b.   They were particularly concerned with establishing a society in which the practice of liberty was paramount.

    c.   They were primarily concerned with establishing a society in which democracy would function efficiently.

    d.   They were principally concerned with establishing a society in which the costs of government would be equally shared by all people.

7.   Which of the following is permitted by the U.S. Constitution?

    a.   Congress may enact *ex post facto* law only when expressly authorized by an executive order.

    b.   Congress may pass bills of attainder only during periods of emergency such as wartime.

    c.   Congress may suspend the writ of *habeas corpus* only when public safety demands it in times of rebellion or invasion.

    d.   Congress may limit the president's commander-in-chief powers only when it appears that excessive force will be used.

8.   These programs are designed to rectify past discrimination against women and minorities.

    a.   Equitable distribution plans.

    b.   Affirmative action plans.

    c.   Massive resistance plans.

    d.   Civil disobedience plans.

9.   **Strict scrutiny** means that any use of race in law or government regulations must be based on

a. A compelling state interest for which the act in question is a necessary means.
b. Evidence that the use of race is substantially related to an important objective.
c. A presumption that the law is constitutional, which places the burden of proof on the person challenging the law to prove that it is not.
d. Conclusive evidence that the law will not have a long-range effect on the cause of minorities.

10. A government decree that a person is guilty of a crime that carries the death penalty, without benefit of a trial is called
    a. civil rights
    b. habeas corpus
    c. bills of attainder
    d. ex post facto law

11. *Schenck* v. *United States* (1919) established the doctrine of
    a. Strict scrutiny.
    b. Inevitable discovery.
    c. Clear and present danger.
    d. Retroactive probable cause.

12. *Miranda* v. *Arizona* (1966) required that
    a. An attorney must be provided for defendants in criminal cases who do not have financial resources to pay for their own attorneys.
    b. Persons detained by authorities must be informed of their right to remain silent and to consult with an attorney.
    c. Individuals have the right to remain silent when testifying before a congressional committee it the information would be incriminating.
    d. Defendants in capital punishment cases must be given wide latitude to appeal their sentences to the highest court.

13. (T/F) Footnote Four of the *Carolene Products* case spelled out the conditions under which the Supreme Court would not defer to the actions of the other branches of government or to the states.

14. (T/F) **Civil liberties** refer to constitutional provisions, laws, and practices that protect individuals from governmental interference.

15. (T/F) A **bill of attainder** is a legislative act that declares a person guilty of a crime and imposes punishment without a judicial trial.

16. (T/F) **Prior restraint** occurs if publishers are sued or punished for printing information that is hurtful or damaging to other people.

17. (T/F) The **good faith exception** permits prosecutors to introduce evidence in court that was obtained illegally if they can show that police relied on a warrant that appeared to be valid when it was used.

18. (T/F) A writ of *habeas corpus* is a legislative act that offers immunity from prosecution in exchange for a person's testimony.

Chapter 16
CIVIL RIGHTS: THE STRUGGLE FOR POLITICAL EQUALITY

Key Concepts and Objectives

The Key Concepts and Objectives provide a look at the fundamental goals and ideas of this chapter. This section serves as a guide to a basic understanding of the objectives of your textbook.

After reading this chapter, you should be able to:

- Understand the basic meaning of civil rights and list specific examples that illustrate what they are and what they do.
- Understand how civil rights have been extended to the citizenry of the United States and have made the nation more democratic.
- Understand why liberty and political equality are important in a democracy, and explain how rights were gradually applied to the states through the process of selective incorporation.
- Determine how the legal and political battles waged by the civil rights movement in the twentieth century eventually moved the courts, the president, and Congress to take the equal protection clause of the Fourteenth Amendment seriously.
- Examine the political and legal conflicts concerning issues such as affirmative action, abortion rights, and sexual harassment.
- Understand how structural, political linkage, and governmental factors, taken together, explain how civil rights has changed the course of American history.
- Understand the standards of strict scrutiny, intermediate scrutiny, and ordinary scrutiny, and explain how the courts use them.
- Identify key terms and concepts used in Chapter 16.

This section provides a brief overview of the chapter contents. Read this section as a preview before reading your textbook. Then use this material as a review to help you retain information from your reading.

→ FROM MARTIN LUTHER KING TO LOUIS FARRAKHAN

The opening vignette compares the political contexts involving the 1963 March on Washington and the 1995 "Million Man March." The differences between the two marches, their leaders, and supporting groups revealed that the racial climate in the nation had changed from one where the dominant biracial coalition that secured the landmark 1964 Civil Rights Act, and the 1965 Voting Rights Act, was displaced by one of increased racial isolation with competing visions of what civil rights policies are best for the nation's future.

The 1994 Republican congressional victory was driven by a "Contract with America," platform which did not include an agenda to bring about greater racial harmony in the nation, and was filled with promises that most observers believed would adversely affect African Americans: cuts in social programs, punitive anticrime measures, and the termination of federal entitlement programs such as Aid to Families with Dependent Children (AFDC). Affirmative action programs were eliminated in the state of California in 1995 and one year later, the president ordered a review of federal affirmative action programs after the Supreme Court relegated it to **strict scrutiny** (which presumes an act, policy, or law to be unconstitutional unless a compelling government interest could be demonstrated) in the case *Adarand Construction v. Pena* (1995). Also in 1996, California voters approved Proposition 209 which banned affirmative action in the state. Voters in Washington state followed suit in 1998.

Civil rights are government guarantees of political equality—the promise of equal treatment by government of all citizens and equal citizenship for all Americans. Civil rights became a more prominent part of the American agenda as democracy itself became more widely accepted in the United States.

→ CIVIL RIGHTS BEFORE THE TWENTIETH CENTURY

Chapter 16 looks at the development and status of civil rights in the United States. The laws that the Court interprets and the decisions that they reach in this area are products of *a complex*

438

interplay of structural, political linkage, and governmental factors. The influence of changing popular perceptions about what is required in a free and democratic society has been particularly important in the story of the changing status of rights and liberties in the United States. Concern about the civil rights protections for women and racial minorities was a comparatively late development in the United States, and most major advances were not evident until well into the twentieth century.

An Initial Absence of Civil Rights-The Constitution and Bill of Rights both neglect to mention anything about political equality beyond guaranteeing due process before the courts. The word **equality** does not appear in the Constitution, and Americans in the late eighteenth and early nineteenth centuries seemed more interested in protecting individuals against government than in guaranteeing certain political rights through government. The political inequality of African-Americans and women before the Civil War was apparent, and many African-Americans and women took an active role in fighting for their civil rights, even in that unfriendly environment. In 1857, Supreme Court Chief Justice Roger Taney stated that the Founders believed that African slaves had no rights that whites or government were bound to honor or respect in the famous *Dred Scott v. Sandford* case.

In the 1840s women such as Angelina and Sarah Grimke and Elizabeth Cady Stanton inspired many women to struggle for political equality in the United States. **The Declaration of Sentiments and Resolutions** which came out of the 1848 **Seneca Falls**, New York meeting of women stands as a landmark in the struggle for women's political equality in the United States.

The Civil War Amendments-After the Civil War, the Thirteenth Amendment to the Constitution outlawed slavery throughout the United States. The Fourteenth Amendment reversed the Dred Scott decision by guaranteeing citizenship to all who are born or naturalized in the United States. Article I of the amendment states that "no state shall make or enforce any law which shall abridge the privileges and immunities of citizens of the United States," (*the privileges and immunities clause*); "nor shall any state deprive any person of life, liberty, or property, without due process of law," (*the due process clause*): "nor deny to any person within its jurisdiction the equal protection of the laws," (*the equal protection clause*). The Fifteenth Amendment guaranteed African-American men the right to vote. ronically, the Supreme Court soon transformed the constitutional structure into a protection for property rights, but not for African-Americans or women.

Undermining the Civil War Amendments-The privileges and immunities clause of the Fourteenth Amendment was rendered virtually meaningless by *The Slaughterhouse Cases* (1873), in which the Court found that the clause protected only the rights of citizens of the United States as citizens (and not rights that were the responsibility of the states. The equal protection clause soon lost all practical meaning. In *The Civil Rights Cases* (1883), the Court ruled that the Fourteenth Amendment did not give Congress the power to prohibit discrimination unless it was practiced by state government, and even state-sponsored discrimination was found to be constitutional in *Plessy* v. *Ferguson* (1896). The Court said that the states could require separation of the races if they provided equal facilities for the races. This **separate but equal doctrine** provided the legal foundation for **Jim Crow** segregation in the South (the system of legal racial segregation that existed in the American South until the middle of the twentieth century). Moreover, the voting guarantees of the Fifteenth Amendment were rendered ineffective by a variety of devices invented to prevent African-Americans from voting in the former states of the Confederacy, such as **literacy tests, poll taxes**, and the **white primary**. With the 1876 compromise concerning the presidential election, African-Americans' rights were once again trampled when the Union Army was withdrawn from the Democratic South.

Women and the Fifteenth Amendment-Politically active women turned their attention to winning the vote for women when they were excluded from the Fifteenth Amendment's extension of the right to vote to African-Americans. Women abandoned legal challenges in court based on their inferior position after the Supreme Court decided (in *Minor* v. *Happersett*, 1874) that women's suffrage was not a right inherent in the national citizenship guarantees of the Fourteenth Amendment, and focused on exerting political pressures. Efforts of the **women's suffrage movement** finally resulted in ratification of the **Nineteenth Amendment** in 1920.

→THE CONTEMPORARY STATUS OF CIVIL RIGHTS

The Supreme Court ruled in *United States v. Carolene Products Company* (1938) that the Bill of Rights should be applied to the states based on the Fourteenth Amendment. The Court established that state action which either "restricted the democratic process" or "discriminated against racial, ethnic, or religious minorities" would trigger the **strict scrutiny** of the Court.

Civil Rights for Racial Minorities-Two basic values have dominated the story of the extension of civil rights since the mid-1960s: the ending of legal discrimination, separation, and exclusion, and the debate over actions to rectify past wrongs.

The End of "Separate but Equal"-The Constitution was long interpreted to condone slavery and segregation, but legal and political battles waged by the Civil Rights movement in the twentieth century eventually moved the courts, the president, and Congress to take the **equal protection clause** of the Fourteenth Amendment seriously. In 1944, the Supreme Court finally declared that race was a **suspect classification** that demanded strict scrutiny. However, in the case *Korematsu v. United States* (1944), the Court deferred to the **Executive Order 9066** which ordered that 100,000 Japanese-Americans be interned during World War II.

Though the Court began to weaken the "separate but equal" doctrine as early as 1944 with the *Smith v. Allwright* ruling, the great breakthrough came in *Brown* v. *Board of Education of Topeka* (1954), which overturned the **separate but equal** doctrine in public schools. The main doctrine on discrimination at the present time is clear: any use of race in law or government regulations will trigger strict scrutiny from the courts.

440

Affirmative Action-The issues are not so clear-cut in the area of government actions that favor women and racial minorities in **affirmative action** programs designed to redress past injustices. Affirmative action is central to the current state of civil rights in the United States.

Origins-Presidents Lyndon Johnson and Richard Nixon developed federal goals designed to remedy past discrimination based on gender and race. Nixon's **Philadelphia Plan** was very controversial because it was believed to be divisive as it sought to create "racial balance" in the workplace. In ***Regents of the University of California* v. *Bakke*** (1978), the Court prohibited the use of racial *quotas* by university admissions committees (*Bakke* had claimed *reverse discrimination* against white males), but apparently saw no problem with the use of *race as a factor* in hiring or admissions. More recently, the Court has said that programs that narrowly redress *specific violations* will be upheld but that broader affirmative action programs that address *societal racism* will not.

Since *Bakke*, government and higher education racial preference programs have become relatively permanent rather than temporary, affirmative action aims have shifted from redressing past discrimination to enhancing democracy.

Why Affirmative Action?-According to proponents, affirmative action is designed to accomplish the following:

- The effects of past discrimination disadvantage, to one degree or another, all members of discriminated-against groups, so simply removing barriers to advancement is insufficient. The proper remedy is to prefer members of such groups for hiring, contracts, and education until such time as they reach parity with the majority.
- In a diverse society such as the United States, tolerance and a sense of community can develop only if we work together in educational, workplace, and government institutions that are diverse.
- People from disadvantaged groups and discriminated-against groups will improve themselves only if they have experience with successful role models in important institutions.

Critics of affirmative action are not convinced by these arguments. They believe the following are true:

- Affirmative action violates one of the most basic American principles, that people be judged, rewarded, and punished as individuals, not because they are members of one group or another.
- Affirmative action benefits those within each preferred group who are already advantaged and need little help. Thus the main beneficiaries of affirmative action in higher education have been middle-class African-Americans, not the poor.
- Affirmative action seeks to remedy the effects of past discrimination by discriminating against others today simply because they belong to nonpreferred groups.

- Affirmative action increases intergroup and interracial tension by heightening the saliency of group membership. That is, social friction is increased by encouraging people to think of themselves and other members of groups and to seek group advantages in a zero-sum game in which one group's gain is another group's loss.

Public Opinion-Racial preferences in hiring, awarding of government contracts, and admission to college are very unpopular among nonpreferred groups, but they approve diversity goals. To many who support affirmative action, this is simply a reflection of the enduring racism of Americans. They believe that people who oppose affirmative action programs are hostile to racial minorities.

Some research has shown that even women, Hispanics and African-Americans believe that hiring, firing, and admission to college should be based on individual qualifications rather than on the need to serve diversity goals. It has also helped strengthen the anti-affirmative action Republican Party at all levels in the political system. Congress, the president, and the Supreme Court have all been influenced by public opposition to affirmative action.

The Supreme Court's Turnabout on Affirmative Action-The Supreme Court has been reluctant to support any law or policy which, in its view, is not colorblind. In *Wygant v. Jackson Board of Education* (1986) and *Richmond v. Croson Co.* (1989), the Court said that programs that narrowly redress specific violations will be upheld but that broader affirmative action programs that address society's racism will be struck down.

In *Adarand Constructors v. Rena* (1995) the Court ruled that the federal government must abide by the strict standards for affirmative action programs imposed on the states in the Richmond case and could not award contracts using race as the main criterion. In *Miller v. Johnson* (1995), the Court ruled that race could not be used as the basis for drawing House district lines in an effort to increase the number of racial minority members in Congress. The Court also let stand a lower court decision which eliminated race as a consideration for admission into the University of Texas Law School; it also supported California's anti-affirmative action Proposition 209.

Civil Rights for Women-The expansion of civil rights for women has taken a decidedly different path from that of racial groups.

Intermediate Scrutiny-Despite its egalitarian reputation, the Warren Court did not significantly advance the cause of women's rights. The Burger Court (1969-1986) had to decide whether to apply **ordinary scrutiny** (the presumption of constitutionality that almost all laws survive) or **strict scrutiny** (the presumption of unconstitutionality that dooms almost all laws) to sex discrimination cases. The justices felt that strict scrutiny would endanger traditional sex roles, whereas use of ordinary scrutiny would allow blatant sex discrimination to survive. Instead, the

Court applied a new standard known as **intermediate scrutiny** (government enactments that relied on gender would be constitutional if the use of gender was *substantially related* to an *important objective*). The Court has also used intermediate scrutiny in several cases to invalidate laws that discriminate against *men* (as in *Craig* v. *Boren* in 1976). The nation has not restructured civil rights for women.

Abortion Rights-When two recent University of Texas Law School graduates sought to challenge the constitutionally of a Texas statue that prohibited medical abortions except to save the life of the pregnant woman. Norma "Pixie" McCorvey, their 21-year-old client, wanted to terminate her pregnancy. McCorvey eventually had the baby, but the case went before the Court. Women's rights organizations worked to influence public opinion in favor of granting women legal abortion rights protections. The medical profession reversed its 1960 position on the issue and supported a woman's right to not complete a pregnancy. The Court linked a woman's right to abortion with the **right to privacy,** which was first established in the ***Griswold v. Connecticut*** (1965) case.

The debate continues over whether there is a constitutionally protected right to privacy. Some advocates of the right to privacy see a growing danger in the ability of the new information technology to collect and make accessible a vast amount of data about all Americans. The pro-life forces in the nation have sought to end abortion. The Supreme Court has responded to antiabortion politics by deciding two cases, *Webster v. Reproductive Health Services* (1989) and *Planned Parenthood v. Casey* (1992) that gave the states more discretion in restricting abortions.

Sexual Harassment-Citizens are protected from unwelcome sexual activity in the work place by the 1964 Civil Rights Act. The federal government has determined that creating "an intimidating, hostile, or offensive working environment" is contrary to the law. The Court has put the responsibility of maintaining a harassment-free work environment on management. The famous testimony of law professor Anita Hill at the confirmation hearings of Supreme Court nominee Clarence Thomas raised awareness of sexual harassment nationwide.

Affirmative Action-The precarious legal and political status of affirmative action guidelines and laws, reviewed in the section on racial minorities, means that affirmative action programs for women are in jeopardy across the nation. Women's organizations have fought to preserve affirmative action.

Broadening the Civil Rights Umbrella-The expansion of civil rights protections for women and racial minorities has encouraged other groups to press for expanded tights protections.

The Elderly and the Disabled-The elderly have strongly opposed age discrimination. Several federal and state laws have barred mandatory retirement. The disabled have been successful in securing civil rights protections with the passage of the Americans with Disabilities Act of 1990.

The act prohibits employment discrimination against the disabled and requires that reasonable efforts be made to make places of employment and public facilities (such as concert halls, restaurants, retail shops, schools, and government offices) accessible to them.

Gays and Lesbians-In 1986, the Supreme Court upheld a Georgia law against sodomy in *Bowers v. Hadwick* (1986), the majority opinion declared assertions of a constitutional right to homosexuality to be "facetious," meaning, witty, jesting, or playful. The executive branch, military establishment, and gay and lesbian forces struggled over the policy of "don't ask, don't tell," concerning gays in the U.S. armed forces. Gay and lesbian groups suffered major setbacks, especially concerning marital rights in the late 1990s.

Nevertheless, the Court ruled in *Romer v.Evans* (1996) that Colorado's Amendment 2, which prohibits local communities from passing gay anti-discrimination ordinances, is unconstitutional. Another positive for advocates of gay rights is the 1999 Vermont state Supreme Court ruling that its state legislature must either grant same-sex couples the same legal rights, protections and benefits as heterosexual married couples (such joint tax returns, property ownership, insurance benefits, and medical decisions involving a spouse), or legalize same-sex marriages.

→SUMMARY

Political equality is note noted in either the Constitution or Bill of Rights. The Civil War Amendments—Thirteen, Fourteen, and Fifteenth—have greatly strengthened civil rights in the United States. The "immunities and privileges" clause, "due process" clause, and "equal protection" clause of the Fourteenth Amendment, which the early Supreme Court applied to corporations instead of Blacks or other citizens, have become important staples of American democracy.

Political **equality** is one of the three pillars of democracy, equal in importance to popular sovereignty and political liberty. The advance of civil rights protections since the end of World War II has enriched American democracy because it has helped make political equality a reality in the United States. Overt discrimination against women and racial groups are no longer acceptable.
While there are still important civil rights issues that remain unsettled, the attainment of formal political equality is a reality today.

Chapter Outline

444

This section gives you a comprehensive review of the chapter. Use this outline in combination with your textbook to look for key concepts and objectives, to identify essential terms and names, and to gain a basic understanding of political practices and principles from this chapter.

I. **FROM MARTIN LUTHER KING TO LOUIS FARRAKHAN (pp. 473-474)**
    A. The opening vignette compares the political contexts involving the 1963 March on Washington and the 1995 "Million Man March."
        1. The differences between the two marches, their leaders, and supporting groups revealed that the racial climate in the nation had changed from one where the dominant biracial coalition that secured the landmark 1964 Civil Rights Act, and the 1965 Voting Rights Act, was displaced by one of increased racial isolation with competing visions of what civil rights policies are best for the nation's future.
        2. The 1994 Republican congressional victory was driven by a "Contract with America," platform which did not include an agenda to bring about greater racial harmony in the nation, and was filled with promises that most observers believed would adversely affect African Americans: cuts in social programs, punitive anticrime measures, and the termination of federal entitlement programs such as Aid to Families with Dependent Children (AFDC).
    B. Affirmative action programs were eliminated in the state of California in 1995 and one year later, the president ordered a review of federal affirmative action programs after the Supreme Court relegated it to **strict scrutiny** (which presumes an act, policy, or law to be unconstitutional unless a compelling government interest could be demonstrated) in the case *Adarand Construction v. Pena* (1995).
    C. In 1996, California voters approved Proposition 209 which banned affirmative action in the state. Voters in Washington state followed suit in 1998.

II. **CIVIL RIGHTS BEFORE THE TWENTIETH CENTURY (pp. 474-478)**
    A. **An initial absence of civil rights**
        1. The word **equality** does not appear in the Constitution, and Americans in the late eighteenth and early nineteenth centuries seemed more interested in protecting individuals against government than in guaranteeing certain political rights through government.
        2. The political inequality of African-Americans and women before the Civil War was apparent.
            a) In the South, African-Americans lived in slavery, with no rights at all; in many places outside the South, African-Americans were treated in a demeaning and inferior basis.
            b) In **Dred Scott v. Sandford** (1857), Chief Justice Taney claimed that African-Americans had no rights that whites or government were required to honor or respect.

    c) No state allowed women to vote, few allowed them to sit on juries, and some even denied them the right to own property or enter into contracts.

B. The Civil War Amendments
1. After the Civil War, Amendments 13-15 guaranteed essential political rights.
    a) **Thirteenth Amendment**—outlawed slavery throughout the United States
    b) **Fourteenth Amendment**—reversed *Dred Scott* by making all people who were born or naturalized in the United States citizens both of the United States and of states in which they resided; to secure the rights and liberties of recently freed blacks, the amendment guaranteed **due process** of law and **equal protection** of laws to **all persons**, and prohibited states from abridging the **privileges and immunities** of citizens
    c) **Fifteenth Amendment**—guaranteed black males the right to vote
2. **Undermining the effectiveness of the Civil War Amendments**
    a) Ironically, the Supreme Court soon transformed the constitutional structure into a protection for property rights, but not for African-Americans or women.
    b) The privileges and immunities clause of the Fourteenth Amendment was rendered virtually meaningless by *The Slaughterhouse Cases* (1873), in which the Court found that the clause protected only the rights of citizens of the United States as citizens (and not rights that were the responsibility of the states); in these cases, the *Court denied citizens protection against abuses by state government.*
    c) The equal protection clause soon lost all practical meaning.
        (1) In *The Civil Rights Cases* (1883), the Court ruled that the Fourteenth Amendment did not give Congress the power to prohibit discrimination unless it was practiced by state government; equal protection *did not include racial discrimination by private parties* (such as owners of restaurants and other public accommodations).
        (2) In *Plessy* v. *Ferguson* (1896), even state-sponsored discrimination was found to be constitutional.
            (a) The Court said that the states could require separation of the races if they provided equal facilities for the races.
            (b) This **separate but equal doctrine** provided the legal foundation for **Jim Crow** segregation in the South (the system of legal racial segregation that existed in the American South until the middle of the twentieth century).
3. The voting guarantees of the Fifteenth Amendment were rendered ineffective by a variety devices invented to prevent African-Americans from voting in the former states of the Confederacy.
    a) **Poll tax**—a tax to be paid as a condition of voting; kept many African-Americans away from the polls
    b) **Literacy test**—administration and evaluation of test results was up to local officials, who rarely passed blacks (including some with a college education or

even a Ph.D. degree); white voters who failed the test were permitted to vote in many states under the **grandfather clause**, which allowed anyone to vote whose grandfather had voted

    c) **White primaries**—excluded African-Americans from the process of nominating candidates through primaries, on the claim that political parties were private clubs that could define their own membership requirements

    d) Intimidation and terror—night ridings, bombings, and lynchings—were used as a deterrent to African-Americans who might try to vote; terror remained a factor until the 1960s, when the **civil rights movement** and federal intervention finally put an end to it.

4. **Women and the Fifteenth Amendment**

    a) Politically active women turned their attention to winning the vote for women when they were excluded from the Fifteenth Amendment's extension of the right to vote to African-Americans.

    b) Women abandoned legal challenges in court based on their inferior position after the Supreme Court decided (in ***Minor* v. *Happersett***, 1874) that women's suffrage was not a right inherent in the national citizenship guarantees of the Fourteenth Amendment, and turned their attention to exerting political pressure.

    c) Efforts of the **women's suffrage movement** finally resulted in ratification of the **Nineteenth Amendment** in 1920.

III. **THE CONTEMPORARY STATUS OF CIVIL RIGHTS (pp. 478-493)**
  A. **Civil rights for racial minorities**
    1. Two basic issues have dominated the story of the extension of civil rights since the mid-1960s: the ending of legal discrimination, separation, and exclusion.
    2. The debate over affirmative actions to rectify past wrongs.
  B. **The end of "Separate but Equal"**
    1. In 1944, the Supreme Court finally declared that race was a **suspect classification** that demanded strict scrutiny, which meant that any state or national enactment using racial criteria was *presumed to be unconstitutional.*
      a) In ***Smith* v. *Allwright*** (1944), the Court decided that the practice of excluding nonwhites from political-party primary elections was unconstitutional.
      b) The great breakthrough came in ***Brown* v. *Board of Education of Topeka*** (1954), which overturned the separate but equal doctrine in public schools.
    2. The main doctrine on discrimination at the present time is clear: any use of race in law or government regulations will trigger strict scrutiny from the courts.
      a) Government can defend its acts under strict scrutiny only if it can produce a *compelling* government interest for which the act in question is a *necessary* means.
      b) Almost no law survives this challenge; laws that discriminate on the basis of race do not meet the test.

C. **Affirmative action**

1. The issues are not so clear-cut in the area of *government actions that favor racial minorities* in **affirmative action** programs designed to redress past injustices.
2. Affirmative action is central to the current status of civil rights in the United States.

D. **Origins**

1. The primary goal of the civil rights movement of the 1950s and 1960s was to remove barriers to equal citizenship and opportunity for black Americans.

    a) Political leaders such as **Lyndon Johnson**, **Robert Kennedy**, and **Martin Luther King Jr.** came to believe that the advancement of black Americans would require a general societal effort to eradicate poverty by equipping the poor, both black and white, with the tools for success.

    b) **Richard Nixon** took the most important step when he required in his 1969 **Philadelphia Plan** that construction companies with federal contracts and the associated construction trade unions hire enough blacks and other minorities to achieve racial balance.

    c) In *Regents of the University of California* **v.** *Bakke* (1978), the Court prohibited the use of racial *quotas* by university admissions committees (Bakke had claimed *reverse discrimination* against white males), but apparently saw no problem with the use of *race as a factor* in hiring or admissions.

    d) More recently, the Court has said that programs that narrowly redress *specific violations* will be upheld but that broader affirmative action programs that address *societal racism* will not.

    e) The Court's direction on affirmative action seems to mirror the mood of the country: broad (and often expensive) affirmative action programs to overcome racial disadvantages by compensating an entire racial group for wrongs done to it in the past seem to many Americans to be unfair.

    f) The 1996 General Social Survey reports that over 80 percent of Americans either oppose or strongly oppose preferential hiring of blacks; when asked whether they generally support affirmative action programs, every major polling organization in 1997 and 1998 reported a majority of Americans opposed to them.

E. **Why affirmative action?**

1. According to proponents, affirmative action is designed to accomplish the following:

    a) The effects of past discrimination disadvantage, to one degree or another, all members of discriminated-against groups, so simply removing barriers to advancement is insufficient. The proper remedy is to prefer members of such groups for hiring, contracts, and education until such time as they reach parity with the majority.

    b) In a diverse society such as the United States, tolerance and a sense of community can develop only if we work together in educational, workplace,

and government institutions that are diverse.
c) People from disadvantaged groups and discriminated-against groups will improve themselves only if they have experience with successful role models in important institutions.
2. Critics of affirmative action are not convinced by these arguments. They believe the following are true:
a) Affirmative action violates one of the most basic American principles, that people be judged, rewarded, and punished as individuals, not because they are members of one group or another.
b) Affirmative action benefits those within each preferred group who are already advantaged and need little help. Thus the main beneficiaries of affirmative action in higher education have been middle-class African-Americans, not the poor.
c) Affirmative action seeks to remedy the effects of past discrimination by discriminating against others today simply because they belong to nonpreferred groups.
d) Affirmative action increases intergroup and interracial tension by heightening the saliency of group membership. That is, social friction is increased by encouraging people to think of themselves and other members of groups and to seek group advantages in a zero-sum game in which one group's gain is another group's loss.
F. **Public opinion**
1. Racial preferences in hiring, awarding of government contracts, and admission to college are very unpopular among nonpreferred groups, but they approve diversity goals.
a) To many who support affirmative action, this is simply a reflection of the enduring racism of Americans.
b) They believe that people who oppose affirmative action programs are hostile to racial minorities.
2. Some research has shown that even women, Hispanics and African-Americans believe that hiring, firing, and admission to college should be based on individual qualifications rather than on the need to serve diversity goals. It has also helped strengthen the anti-affirmative action Republican Party at all levels in the political system. Congress, the president, and the Supreme Court have all been influenced by public opposition to affirmative action.
G. **The Supreme Court's turnabout on affirmative action**
1. The Supreme Court has been reluctant to support any law or policy which, in its view, is not colorblind.
a) In *Wygant v. Jackson Board of Education* (1986) and *Richmond v. Croson Co.* (1989), the Court said that programs that narrowly redress specific violations will be upheld but that broader affirmative action programs that address society's racism will be struck down.

    b) In *Adarand Constructors v. Rena* (1995) the Court ruled that the federal government must abide by the strict standards for affirmative action programs imposed on the states in the Richmond case and could not award contracts using race as the main criterion.

    c) In *Miller v. Johnson* (1995), the Court ruled that race could not be used as the basis for drawing House district lines in an effort to increase the number of racial minority members in Congress.

  2. The Court also let stand a lower court decision which eliminated race as a consideration for admission into the University of Texas Law School; it also supported California's anti-affirmative action Proposition 209.

H. **Civil rights for women**

  1. The expansion of civil rights for women has taken a decidedly different path from that of racial groups.

  2. The nation has not restructured civil rights for women.

I. **Intermediate scrutiny**

  1. Despite its egalitarian reputation, the Warren Court did not significantly advance the cause of women's rights.

  2. The Burger Court (1969-1986) had to decide whether to apply **ordinary scrutiny** (the presumption of constitutionality that almost all laws survive) or **strict scrutiny** (the presumption of unconstitutionality that dooms almost all laws) to sex discrimination cases.

    a) The justices felt that strict scrutiny would endanger traditional sex roles, whereas use of ordinary scrutiny would allow blatant sex discrimination to survive.

    b) Instead, the Court applied a new standard known as **intermediate scrutiny** (government enactments that relied on gender would be constitutional if the use of gender was *substantially related* to an *important objective*).

    c) The Court has also used intermediate scrutiny in several cases to invalidate laws that discriminate against *men* (as in *Craig* v. *Boren* in 1976).

      (1) The Court applied a new standard known as **intermediate scrutiny** (government enactments that relied on gender would be constitutional if the use of gender was *substantially related* to an *important objective*).

      (2) The Court has also used intermediate scrutiny in several cases to invalidate laws that discriminate against *men* (such as *Craig* v. *Boren*).

  3. Women's rights have not followed the path of other rights and liberties—civil rights for women are still more a subject for the political process than for the courts.

J. **Abortion rights**

  1. *Roe* v. *Wade* (1973) transformed abortion from a legislative issue into a constitutional issue and from a matter of policy into a matter of rights.

    a) Attorneys **Sarah Weddington** and **Linda Coffee** used the case to challenge a Texas statute that prohibited physicians from performing abortions except to save the life of the pregnant woman (Weddington argued the case before the Supreme Court).

b) Disapproval of abortion decreased and discussion of abortion increased during the 1960s—the litigation over abortion reflected changes in public opinion, pressure by interest groups, and persisting inequities against women; the pro-choice team benefitted from 42 **amicus curiae** ("friend of the court") briefs.

c) Justice **Harry Blackmun**'s opinion for the majority prohibited states from interfering with a woman's decision to have an abortion in the first two trimesters of her pregnancy; Justice Blackmun based his opinion on the **right to privacy**, even though there is no mention of privacy in the Constitution (reasoning that provisions of the Ninth and Fourteenth Amendments are broad enough to encompass a woman's decision on whether or not to terminate her pregnancy).

2. Antiabortion groups mobilized after the *Roe* decision

a) *Single-issue* anti-abortion politics were important in 1976 and later elections and became an important component in the conservative Reagan movement; Reagan appointed anti-abortion judges to the federal courts.

b) The Court eventually responded to antiabortion politics by deciding two cases, *Webster* v. *Reproductive Health Services* (1989) and *Planned Parenthood* v. *Casey* (1992); the two cases gave considerable latitude to the states to restrict abortions, but (to the surprise of many observers) the majority affirmed its support for the basic principles of *Roe* in the *Planned Parenthood* opinion.

K. **Sexual harassment**

1. In 1980, the **Equal Employment Opportunity Commission (EEOC)** ruled that making sexual activity a condition of employment or promotion violates the 1964 Civil Rights Act; the Supreme Court took a major step in further defining **sexual harassment** when it ruled unanimously that workers did not have to prove that offensive actions made them unable to do their jobs or caused them psychological harm, only that the work environment was hostile or abusive (*Harris* v. *Forklift Systems, Inc.*, 1993).

2. The EEOC also ruled that creating *an intimidating, hostile, or offensive working environment* was contrary to the law.

L. **Broadening the civil rights umbrella**

1. **The elderly and the disabled**

a) Several federal and state laws now bar mandatory retirement, and the courts have begun to strike down hiring practices based on age unless a *compelling reason* can be demonstrated.

b) Disabled Americans have won some notable victories, including passage of the **Americans with Disabilities Act** of 1990, but some advocates for the disabled claim that the act depends too much on voluntary compliance rather than on mandatory penalties for noncompliance.

2. **Gays and lesbians**

a) Efforts to secure constitutional rights for gay men and lesbians illustrate political exertions in the face of governmental wavering.
   (1) When the U.S. Supreme Court upheld Georgia's law against sodomy in *Bowers* v. *Hardwick* (1986), the majority opinion declared assertions of a constitutional right to homosexuality to be facetious.
   (2) In 1996, the Supreme Court ruled that Colorado's constitutional provision—known as Amendment 2—prohibiting local communities from passing gay antidiscrimination ordinances is unconstitutional (*Romer* v. *Evans*).
b) The authors note that it is evident that the struggle for gay and lesbian rights will remain an important part of the American political agenda for a long time to come, with the eventual outcome very much in doubt.
   (1) Gay strengths include protections of privacy and sexual orientation in *state* laws—eight states and many localities ban discrimination against gays and seven other states operate under executive orders that prohibit such discrimination.
   (2) Conversely, opposition to gay rights is evident in dozens of cities that have rescinded protections for gays or refused to extend protections.
3. Another positive for advocates of gay rights is the 1999 Vermont state Supreme Court ruling that its state legislature must either grant same-sex couples the same legal rights, protections and benefits as heterosexual married couples (such joint tax returns, property ownership, insurance benefits, and medical decisions involving a spouse), or legalize same-sex marriages.

IV. **SUMMARY (p. 493)**
   A. Political equality is note noted in either the Constitution or Bill of Rights.
   B. The Civil War Amendments—Thirteenth, Fourteenth, and Fifteenth—have greatly strengthened civil rights in the United States.
      1. The "immunities and privileges" clause, "due process" clause, and "equal protection" clause of the Fourteenth Amendment, which the early Supreme Court applied to corporations instead of Blacks or other citizens, have become important staples of American democracy.
      2. Political **equality** is one of the three pillars of democracy, equal in importance to popular sovereignty and political liberty.
         a) The advance of civil rights protections since the end of World War II has enriched American democracy because it has helped make political equality a reality in the United States.
         b) Overt discrimination against women and racial groups are no longer acceptable.
      3. While there are still important civil rights issues that remain unsettled, the attainment of formal political equality is a reality today.

Terms for Review

Use this list to review essential principles, functions, and concepts from this chapter. Refer to your textbook for help in identifying and defining terms on this list. When you study, do not merely memorize terms; ask questions about the material you are reviewing, and look for the importance or significance of each item.

affirmative actions

equal protection clause

Equal Rights Amendment (ERA)

Establishment clause

free exercise clause

grandfather clause

intermediate scrutiny

Jim Crow

literacy test

poll tax

strict scrutiny

suspect classification

white primaries

Research Topics: Applying What You Have Learned

*You will derive more benefit from your reading if you try to apply what you have learned. Some of the suggested research topics can be answered exclusively from your text, while others require you to conduct some basic research on your own. The references suggested under **Internet Sources** will help you in your search.*

- Write an essay describing the evolution of women's rights. Be certain to list relevant issues such as voting rights, abortion rights, affirmative action, and sexual harassment. What are the relevant constitutional issues?

- Create a list that highlights the pros and cons of affirmative action. How does society benefit from remedial programs such as affirmative action? Does affirmative action serve its intended purpose, or is the divisiveness which it often conjures self-defeating?

- Outline all of the civil rights issues discussed in this chapter and list the relevant constitutional clauses or articles. Are people entitled to some rights that are not mentioned in the Constitution? If so, what are they?

Internet Sources

A number of sites on the World Wide Web serve as "gateways" to vast collections of material on American government and politics. The following Internet resources are recommended for students who would like to do some additional research in the areas covered by this chapter. These references would also be helpful in expanding on the questions suggested under Research Topics.

Cornel Law Library/Civil Rights http://www.law.cornell.edu
Links to the Constitution, landmark and recent Supreme Court civil rights decisions, international treaties on human rights, the Civil Rights Division of the Justice Department, and more.

Martin Luther King, Jr. Home Page http://www.seattletimes.com/mlk/
Created by the Seattle Times, *the site includes study guides on King and the civil rights movement, interactive exercises, audios of King speeches, and links to other King and civil rights Web sites.*

Yahoo/Civil Rights http://www.yahoo.com/Society_and_Culture/Civil-Rights/
Linkages to a vast compendium of information on civil rights and to organizations devoted to the protection and expansion of rights, domestic and international.

Self-Evaluation

Circle the correct answer for each question. Questions are listed in the same order in which the information appears in the text. Use the Answer Key in the back of the Study Guide *to check your responses.*

1. The word equality appears in the U.S. Constitution_____time(s).
   a. One
   b. Two
   c. Three
   d. Seven
   e. Zero

2. In which of the following Supreme Court cases did Chief Justice Roger Taney argue that African Americans had no rights that whites or government were bound to respect?
   a. *Dred Scott v. Sanford* (1857)
   b. *The Slaughterhouse Cases* (1873)
   c. *Plessy v. Ferguson* (1896)
   d. *Brown v. Board of Education, Topeka (1954)*

3. **Civil rights** refer to
   a. Constitutional provisions, laws, and practices that protect individuals from governmental interference.
   b. Governmental responsibility for guaranteeing that all citizens are able to participate as equals in the practice of democratic life.
   c. The elimination of formal barriers to equal participation by groups of people, such as minorities.
   d. Guarantees of rights that protect citizens from unfair or unjust actions by other individuals.

4. The Seneca Falls Convention focused on
   a. women's rights
   b. affirmative action

c.   abortion rights
d.   sexual harassment

5.   Which of the following cases did *Brown* v. *Board of Education* (1954) reverse?
a.   *Dred Scott v. Sandford* (1857)
b.   *The Slaughterhouse Cases* (1873)
c.   *Civil Rights Cases* (1883)
d.   *Plessy v. Ferguson* (1896)

6.   In which case did the Supreme Court rule that women's suffrage was not a right inherent in the national citizenship guarantees of the Fourteenth Amendment?
a.   *Dred Scott v. Sandford* (1857)
b.   *The Slaughterhouse Cases* (1873)
c.   *Minor v. Happersett* (1874)
d.   *Civil Rights Cases* (1883)

7.   The equal protection clause is included in the _____Amendment?
a.   2nd
b.   4th
c.   14th
d.   15th

8.   Which of the following constitutional amendments was **not** one of the Civil War Amendments?
a. 13th
b. 14th
c. 15th
d. 16th

9.   Poll taxes, grandfather clauses, literacy tests, and white primaries all concerned
a. free speech
b. women's rights
c. voting rights
d. abortion rights

10. The Supreme Court has declared that race was a **suspect classification** that demanded
a.   Strict scrutiny.
b.   Intermediate scrutiny.
b.   Moderate scrutiny.
c.   Ordinary scrutiny.

11. The *Korematsu v. United States* (1944) case concerned the civil rights of
    a. Japanese Americans
    b. African Americans
    c. Koreans
    d. Chinese

12. President Richard Nixon's "Philadelphia Plan" focused on
    a. Voting rights
    b. Affirmative action
    c. Abortion rights
    d. Sexual harassment

13. (T/F) *Regents v. Bakke* (1978) focused on voting rights.

14. (T/F) Congress is empowered by the Constitution to erect *ex post facto* laws.

15. (T/F) Women were granted the right to vote with the passage of the 17th Amendment.

16. (T/F) The Equal Rights Amendment was passed and turned into law in 1976.

17. (T/F) The United States has restructured civil rights for women, in the way it has for other groups.

18. (T/F) The Supreme Court upheld a state's law against sodomy in *Bowers v. Hardwick (1986)*.

Chapter 17
DOMESTIC POLICY: THE ECONOMY AND SOCIAL WELFARE

Key Concepts and Objectives

The Key Concepts and Objectives provide a look at the fundamental goals and ideas of this chapter. This section serves as a guide to a basic understanding of the objectives of your textbook.

After reading this chapter, you should be able to:

- Show how economic and social welfare policies are made and how they affect the well-being of American citizens.
- Explain the objectives of macroeconomic policy, and identify the tools that government uses to manage the economy.
- Examine the broad effects of government regulation and deregulation.
- Determine how economic and social welfare policies are shaped by structural, political linkage, and governmental factors.
- Explain why Social Security has a remarkably high level of support in the United States at the same time that surveys show widespread disapproval of public assistance.
- Identify the most important public assistance and social insurance programs, and explain why social insurance programs are known as entitlement programs.
- Summarize the distinction between social insurance and means-tested programs.
- Understand how national economic policy is produced by a political process that contains democratic and nondemocratic aspects.
- Identify key terms and concepts used in Chapter 17.

This section provides a brief overview of the chapter contents. Read this section as a preview before reading your textbook. Then use this material as a review to help you retain information from your reading.

➜ BUDGET CHAOS IN THE 104th CONGRESS, COMPROMISE IN THE 105th

This chapter shows how economic policies are made and how they affect the operation of the American economy and the well-being of American citizens after they are enacted. The authors focus attention on **fiscal policies** (having to do with taxing and spending), **monetary policies** (having to do with the money supply and interest rates), and **regulatory policies** (having to do with public restraints on business activities). The chapter looks at some of the major issues of contemporary American politics, including the deficit, taxes, and deregulation.

The opening story looks at the conflict between President Clinton and congressional Republicans over the issue of balancing the budget. House Republicans in the 104th Congress were eager to take on the task of reducing the size and role of the federal government. The budget bill fashioned in the House of Representatives was unprecedented. It aimed for a balanced budget over a period of seven years and included drastic cutbacks in some government services. Congressional Republicans were confident that **Bill Clinton** would waiver under threats to close down the government in the absence of a budget.

To the surprise of congressional Republicans, Clinton refused to be intimidated; he vetoed temporary measures in November and the full budget bill in December, and Republicans faced a barrage of criticism over the government shutdowns. The battle had electoral consequences in 1996. Democrats increased their numbers in the House and Bill Clinton was reelected to the presidency. Republican leadership pushed aside the budget radicals and entered into serious bipartisan negotiations with Clinton in the opening months of the 105th Congress. A landmark compromise emerged from the negotiations.

➜ WHY GOVERNMENT IS INVOLVED IN THE ECONOMY AND SOCIAL WELFARE

Governments in all modern capitalist societies play a substantial role in the management and direction of their economies.

Economic Management-Citizens have learned that the free market economy is subject to periodic bouts of **inflation** and unemployment, as well as occasional periods of unemployment and **depression**. The inclination to use the federal government to manage the national economy has been enhanced by the relative success of this endeavor since the end of World War II. The federal government also influences the economy as the largest customer in the United States.

Social Welfare-A **welfare state** is a society with a set of government programs that protect the minimum standards of living. Although the details of their programs differ, all rich democracies have social welfare states. Though market economies have produced unprecedented levels of wealth and improved living standards in the rich democracies over the past century, they have also produced disruptions and hardships: recessions and depressions; technological joblessness; and regional economic transformations, as industries come and go. The extended family is less common as economic change brings pressure on people to move to where jobs are located, to extend the period of education and training, and to have two wage earners in each household. Families in rich democracies today are not only smaller but also less likely to stay intact—the divorce rate is high in these countries.

→ ECONOMIC POLICY

Serious disagreements exist among political leaders, economic scholars, and the public about which policies are likely to achieve the desired goals. Economic policies have consequences for the American people.

The Goals of Economic Policy-Political leaders seek to produce positive economic results when they set economic policies. Economic policy goals sometimes are in conflict, and important trade-offs are involved whenever economic policies are selected.

Economic Growth-Sustained economic growth (defined by the authors as an annual increase in the **gross domestic product**, or **GDP**) is sought by economic policymakers. Americans want an economy that brings more jobs, more products, and higher incomes. Economic growth also produces increased profits, so business tends to support this goal. For politicians a thriving economy that grows, translates into votes and popularity. Economic growth is also a remedy for social problems such as poverty.

Low Unemployment-Low unemployment has historically been associated with economic growth, while economic **recessions** bring slower job growth and rising unemployment rates. High unemployment often breeds unrest and political instability.

Stable Prices-Political leaders seek policies that dampen inflation and provide stable prices. Depressions bring a collapse of the job market. Setting economic policy is a delicate balancing act because such policies often require slower economic growth, with its lower wages and higher levels of unemployment.

A Positive Balance of Payments-The **balance of payments** is the difference between the value of a nation's imports and the value of its exports, including both manufactured goods and services such as insurance and banking.

Minimizing Externalities-The negative side effects that come with economic growth, such as air and water pollution, toxic wastes, and workplace injuries and health hazards. These side effects of economic activity--called **negative externalities**--have generated enormous public pressure for compensatory government action; government must be careful to avoid regulating too much.

Supporting Key Economic Sectors-Government must ensure the economic wealth of the nation even when the private sector does not. All European countries and the United States subsidize farmers. The United States government encourages business activity in the public and especially, private sectors.

The Tools of Macroeconomic Policy-Government has influence in the economy by way of the rate of inflation, the level of unemployment, and the growth of income and output in the national economy. Since World War II, government leaders, economists, and citizens have expected government to use whatever means it has available to ensure good economic outcomes. **Macroeconomic** policy looks at the performance of the economy as a whole or broad areas of the economy such as employment. The objective is to achieve full employment, steady economic growth, and stable prices. Government officials try to meet this goal by using fiscal and monetary tools. **Fiscal policy** involves altering government finances by raising or lowering government spending, raising or lowering taxes, and raising or lowering government borrowing (depending on the needs of the economy at a particular point in time).

Monetary policy-Government policy to influence interest rates and control the supply of money in circulation, is carried out primarily through the operations of the **Federal Reserve Board** (the **Fed,** created in 1913). As the nation's **central bank,** the Fed oversees the banking system and sets the nation's monetary policy. Actions by the Fed affect how much money is available to businesses and individuals in banks, savings and loans, and credit unions. It influences interest rates and the money supply.

The Debate About the Proper Role of Government- Debates about the role that government should play in managing the economy greatly influences national policy.

Keynesians-Kenynesianism traces its roots to English economist **John Maynard Keynes**, who wrote in 1936 that capitalist economies do not consistently operate at a level that fully employs a nation's workers or keeps its factories operating at full levels of productivity.

Monetarism-Monetarism includes economists like **Milton Friedman** who argue that the key to a healthy economy is the proper management of the *supply of money and credit* by *central banks* (the Federal Reserve Board).

The Supply-siders-Those who believe that drastic cuts in taxes and federal regulation will drive entrepreneurship are known as supply-side economists. This was the economic philosophy that was dominant during the Reagan years. The outcome of this economic philosophy was a drastically large budget deficit. Industrial policy advocates believe that government should play a role in building and funding the infrastructure that will make the United States more competitive in global markets.

→ THE FEDERAL BUDGET AND FISCAL POLICY

Decisions by the president and Congress on spending and taxes in the federal budget constitute America's fiscal policy.

Government Spending-The federal government spent a little more than $1.8 trillion in 1999; a fourfold increase since 1960. Federal **outlays** have expanded significantly. Wars produce dramatic increases in federal government spending. From the 1930s to the 1980s, the relative spending level of the federal government steadily increased. From the early 1980s to the present, the relative scale of federal spending first leveled off and then declined. This decrease has been partly caused by a substantial decrease in the relative size of the national defense budget in the post-Cold War environment, and some cuts in domestic programs instituted by presidents Reagan and Bush.

Spending Priorities-The percent of federal government expenditures for national defense declined by seven percent (from twenty-three to sixteen) between 1980 and 1999. In 1960 it was over fifty percent. Outlays for *human resources* (Welfare, health, veteran's benefits, education and training) have increased considerably, constituting about sixty-one percent of federal spending. Outlays for *physical resources* (transportation, energy, and the environment have declined since 1980. Other federal non-defense outlays, which support programs ranging from housing to agriculture, national parks, science and technology, international affairs, and the administration of justice, attract six cents of every federal dollar spent.

Taxes-The U.S. tax system is different from other countries in the kinds of taxes we impose. Although the American system of taxation shares some features with other countries, it is unique in a number of ways.

Size of the Tax Bite-The level of taxes levied by all governments in the United States as a proportion of GDP is 34 percent; a low number compared to other rich democracies. Americans' share of taxes as a percentage of their incomes has stayed about the same for the past 25 years.

Forms of Taxation-The national government depends primarily on personal and corporate income taxes and on payroll taxes, while states derive most of their revenues from sales taxes, and local governments rely most heavily on property taxes. Since 1960 the share of tax revenues from corporations has decreased and the share from payroll taxes for Social Security and Medicare has increased dramatically.

Complexity of Our Tax System-The U.S. tax code is a very complex document with many exceptions to the rules for individuals , companies, and communities. *Tax expenditures* amounted to about $500 billion in 1999. By contrast, other nations depend more on sales and consumption taxes (mostly value-added taxes).

The Deficit and the National Debt-The **budget deficit** is the *annual shortfall* between what the government spends and what it takes in. The government must borrow the money to cover the shortfall and must pay interest on the borrowed money. Government borrowing takes the form of Treasury bonds, bills, notes to American citizens and institutions or to foreign individuals and institutions, and even to the government itself (through units like the Social Security Trust Fund). The **national debt** refers to the *total of what the government owes*. Interest on the national debt is an important component of annual federal outlays.

Size of the Debt and the Deficit-Most of the national debt *prior to the 1980s* was accumulated during major wars; after each war, the debt relative to the GDP declined. The pattern changed dramatically in the 1980s when the size of annual deficits, the rate of growth in the national debt, and the interest paid on the national debt reached unprecedented levels.

The Deficit and Surplus Issues in American Politics- Enough voters, politicians, and business leaders have worried recently about deficits and the national debt to make them hot issues today. With the federal budget now in surplus and the debt gradually becoming smaller, budget politics in Washington has shifted to the problem of what to do with the extra dollars.

Subsidizing Business-All governments in the rich democracies support a variety of economic activities considered important to society, but which are unlikely to occur at optimum levels without taxpayer help. In Western Europe, **public ownership** of essential economic activities is common, while in the United States, government support for business enterprises is more likely to take the form of **tax incentives**. Programs that pay direct **subsidies** to private businesses are an important part of the economic policy environment at all levels of American government.

Regulation-Government regulation is an important part of what the federal government does. Federal agencies issue rules that private businesses must follow.

What Government Regulates-Government regulation of private business increased during the twentieth century. Scholars disagree on why this has happened.

Democratic Explanation-Many observers believe that **government regulation of business** is the result of pressures placed by the public on policymakers (such as demands for solutions to pollution, monopolistic prices, unsafe products, and risky financial practices); in a democracy, politicians must respond to popular pressures or face the prospect of being voted out of office.

The Business Power Explanation-Conversely, *the economic theory of regulation* holds that regulation is caused by the political efforts of powerful business firms that turn to government for protection against competitors. Regulation allows firms to restrict overall output, to deny entry to business competitors, and to maintain above-market prices.

A History of American Regulation- The history of regulation in the United States illustrates how the interaction of democratic and nondemocratic factors has produced the regulatory agencies and policies that we have today.

Progressive Era Regulation- Between 1900 and World War I, laws were passed to regulate some of the activities of powerful new corporations. Labor, Populists, and middle-class Americans anxious about the conditions reported by the muckrakers, journalists, and novelists such as Upton Sinclair (*The Jungle*), Frank Norris (*The Octopus*) and Ida Tarbell (A History of the Standard Oil *Company)* who exposed current dangerous, monopolistic and unethical business practices. Landmark regulatory measures included the **Federal Trade Commission Act**, the **Meat Inspection Act, the Pure Food and Drug Act, and the Federal Reserve Act**. But Business often benefited from the many regulatory enactments of the period.

New Deal Regulation-The next wave of regulatory reform occurred during the New Deal in the 1930s. The regulatory innovations of this period aimed squarely at speculative and unsafe practices in the banking and securities industries that had contributed to the onset of the Great Depression.

The Sixties and Seventies-The success of the consumer, environmental and civil rights movements from the late Sixties to the late Seventies resulted in a substantial increase in the federal government's regulation of business. Agencies such as the EPA and FDA issued numerous rules that affected business operations and decisions. This was one of the only times in U.S. history when business was on the defensive, unable to halt the imposition of laws and regulations to which it was strongly opposed.

Deregulation- By the end of the 1970s, the mood of opinion leaders had turned against regulation. The change in climate was first apparent in the **deregulation** of the airline, banking, railroad, and trucking industries under President Jimmy Carter; it reached its maturity under President Ronald Reagan's program of regulatory relief. This program slowed the regulatory writing process and reduced investigatory and research capabilities of regulatory agencies.

President Reagan appointed heads of regulatory units who wanted to reduce the functions of their agencies. The deregulation offensive was continued by George Bush, who appointed Vice-President **Dan Quayle** to head the Competitive Council. President **Bill Clinton** reversed many Reagan-Bush era policies, especially those related to the environment. At the same time, Clinton continued to use antiregulatory rhetoric much of the time.

The Future of Regulation-The authors of your textbook believe that the regulatory state is likely to expand in the future owing to factors that include problems created by deregulation—such as the collapse of the savings and loan industry—and the introduction of new products that will probably stimulate public demands for government intervention. There was little permanent deregulation achieved during the 1980s. Most regulatory policies are supported by the public. Even at the height of Reagan's popularity, polls continued to show overwhelming support for most regulatory programs. The ready availability of pornography on the Internet ahs triggered efforts by Christian conservatives and others to regulate its content. The rise in cigarette use by teenagers has led to calls for increased regulation of the tobacco industry.

Making Economic Policy: The Main Players-There are many influences that shape American economic policies on taxing, spending, regulation, and business subsidies. They have a great deal to do with the kinds of economic policies that are put in place.

Political Linkage Factors- *Interest groups*, especially those representing business, take interest in economic policy. Business interest groups are attentive especially to the regulatory activities of the federal government. Changes in the regulatory climate may have profound effects on the viability and profitability of business enterprises, so their lobbyists stay in touch with executive and congressional actors.

Voters and Public Opinion-The public also has influence on economic policies. The public is particularly concerned with unemployment, inflation, and growth. Elected officials attempt to keep these factors under control in order to gain electoral rewards.

Political Parties-Each party has its own electoral and financial constituency, made up of groups with identifiable economic interests. Labor, racial groups, and lower-income Americans have traditionally supported the Democrats. Business and upper-income Americans have traditionally supported the Republicans. Inequality decreases slightly when Democrats control the presidency and increases slightly when Republicans control it.

Governmental Factors-The president, Congress, and the Federal Reserve Board are particularly important in fashioning economic policies.

The President-The president is instrumental in setting economic policy. The **Employment Act of 1946** requires the president to report on the state of the economy and recommend action to ensure full employment and economic stability. The legislative program of most modern presidents contains proposals for spending, taxing, and regulation that usually have broad macroeconomic effects. Successful presidents build good relations with Congress, and they must be skillful at affecting the behavior of the Federal Reserve Board if they want it to regulate the money supply and interest rates in a way that is consistent with the presidential program. The president is advised on economic matters by the **Council of Economic Advisors (CEA)**, the director of the **Office of Management and Budget (OMB)**, and the secretary of the **Treasury**.

Congress-Actions of **Congress** also have macroeconomic effects. The overall balance of expenditures and revenues acts as a *fiscal* instrument, either stimulating or retarding the economy. Congress is helped in its economic policymaking activities by the **Congressional Budget Office (CBO)**. Congress' *oversight* role is important in economic policymaking.

The Federal Reserve Board-The Federal Reserve Board makes monetary policy for the nation. The role of the Fed has changed since 1913 when it was used to provide funds for member banks that found themselves short of cash. In the 1950s, it took on broad macroeconomic responsibilities in an effort to control interest rates and the money supply. The Fed is made up of seven members (called governors) who serve overlapping 14-year terms and a chair who serves a renewable 4-year term. The president appoints each. Federal Reserve Chairman Alan Greenspan has been credited, correctly or incorrectly, as the guiding monetary hand behind the economic boom and low inflation of the 1990s.

→ SOCIAL WELFARE

Another important domain of domestic policy in the United States is social welfare, a broad range of programs that protects the minimum standards of living of families and individuals against unemployment, income loss and poverty, physical and mental illness and disability, family disintegration, and old age. Such programs account for the largest share of the annual federal budget.

Outline of the American Welfare State-A **social welfare state** is a society with a set of government programs that protect minimum standards of living. Social welfare in the United States is provided by a complex mix of programs.

Types of Programs-Distinctions can be made among social welfare progress *based on methods of dispensing benefits*, including **social insurance** programs in which individuals contribute to an insurance fund through payroll taxes and receive benefits based on their contributions (such as Social Security) and **means-tested** programs in which benefits are distributed on the basis of need (such as Medicaid and food stamps). Means-tested programs are the programs that the public generally refers to as *welfare*. Distinctions can also be drawn between social welfare programs that *pay people directly* and those that *provide a service*. **Cash transfer** programs are social welfare programs that pay people directly, such as unemployment insurance; programs that **provide a service** include Medicare, which pays hospitals on behalf of recipients. Finally, distinctions may be *based on administration* of social welfare programs. Some of these programs are administered directly from Washington, D.C. (such as Social Security), while others are jointly administered by federal and state governments (such as Medicaid); these programs reflect wide variation in benefits in various states. A substantial amount of money is spent on what the U.S. budget calls social welfare. Social insurance programs are termed **entitlement** programs because benefits are received as a *matter of right* based on contributions.

Cost of the Social Welfare State-The federal, state, and local governments of the United States spend a great deal of money supporting the welfare state; in 1999, it spent $787 billion on Social Security, Medicare, Medicaid, and means-tested entitlement programs, almost 48 percent of the federal budget. Of this total, social insurance programs account for the lion's share, a bit more than one-third of federal government expenditures in 1999.

Most of the benefits of the American welfare state do not go to the poor. Those who were fully employed during their work lives, had the highest incomes, and paid the maximum level of Social Security taxes are the main beneficiaries. The poverty rate for children in the United States is increasingly high. Almost one child in five now lives below **the poverty line**.

Social Security and Other Social Insurance Programs-Social insurance programs that guard against loss of income due to old age, disability, and illness are the largest, most popular, and fastest-growing parts of the American welfare state.

Old Age, Survivors, and Disability Insurance-OASDI, usually referred to as Social Security, is the largest social insurance program. Social Security was created in 1935 to assist the elderly and later, survivors ("widows and orphans program"). Coverage of the disabled was added in 1956. OASDI is funded by a payroll tax on employees under the Federal Insurance Contributions Act (FICA on individuals' pay stubs). The Self-employed pay into a similar trust fund. Unlike private insurance, premiums paid into the fund are not sufficient to pay for the level of benefits actually received. For the most part, Social Security is funded by payroll taxes levied on *currently employed* Americans. However, the great popularity of the Social Security program means that political leaders are unlikely to allow it to go bankrupt.

Medicare-This type of social insurance has grown into one of the largest federal programs in terms of total dollar expenditures. It pays for a substantial portion of the hospital, doctor, and drug costs of retirees and the disabled. Rapidly rising health care costs since Medicare was established in 1965 have pushed outlays to such high levels that efforts to control its costs have become a staple of American politics. It is funded by a payroll tax on employees and employers, assisted by federal subsidies.

Unemployment insurance-This type of social insurance is administered by the states underfederal guidelines, with the level of benefits set by the states (which show wide variations). It is financed by federal and state taxes on employers. The level of benefits is set by the states, and there are wide variations among them.

Do Social Insurance Programs Work?- In an era when it is fashionable to deride the ability of government to do anything well, it is important to know about the relative success of America's social insurance programs. There have been both successes and problems with American social insurance programs.

Successes-Among successes, the authors of your textbook note that benefits provide an income floor for the retired and pay for costly medical services that would otherwise impoverish many who have serious illnesses and long hospital stays. Improvement in the standard of living of the elderly is evident in the decline of the official poverty rate for them.

Problems-By contrast, problems include the *regressive* overall effect of social insurance programs (that is, the well-off receive more benefits than those with more limited resources). Moreover, financial stability of Social Security and Medicare has been achieved only because Congress has steadily raised payroll taxes—FICA (Social Security) and Medicare taxes now take a larger amount of paychecks for a majority of Americans than the personal income tax. Political tension seems to be building between the elderly who receive benefits and those who are still working and paying FICA taxes to support the programs.

Means-Tested Programs (Welfare)-Welfare only accounts for a small part of the annual federal budget. Yet it has attracted more opposition than virtually anything else government does. Increasing numbers of people are convinced that public assistance doesn't work. The authors analyze evidence that supports both sides of the argument concerning the viability of public assistance. In particular, opponents believe that welfare undermines the work ethic, encourages family disintegration, and creates a permanent dependent class. However, available research does not support many of the criticisms. Many social scientists blame slow growth in the American economy and job migration from central cities (rather than welfare) as the main causes of dependency and family breakup.

Food Stamps-This program is available to Americans below a certain income level. Benefit levels are set by the states under general federal guidelines, with substantial variation among the states. Stamps can be used only for food, they cannot be used for alcohol, cigarettes, or gambling. The program has made a significant dent in malnutrition in the United States.

Medicaid-The federal government provides *matching funds* to the states so that they can provide medical assistance for indigent citizens under the **Medicaid** program. The states formulate their own eligibility requirements and set their own benefit levels. The problem of noninclusion is a serious one. Eligibility rules are complex and tend to exclude those who are not extremely poor, blind, disabled, or children with out-of-work parents. At the same time, the inability to restrain Medicaid costs is one of the primary reasons for the fiscal difficulties of the states.

Supplemental Security Income-Also known as **SSI**, this program was created in 1974 in order to provide benefits to the elderly, blind, and disabled poor whom social insurance programs are insufficient to elevate above the poverty line. The 1996 welfare reform bill denied SSI to legal immigrants, but the provision was rescinded in 199t for legal immigrants already resident in the United States.

Head Start-This is by far the most popular means-tested social welfare program. It reaches about 300,000 children per year in an effort to prepare poor preschool children for entrance into public schools.

Welfare Block Grants-The president and Congress agreed to "change welfare as we know it." President Clinton reluctantly signed the Temporary Assistance to Needy Families Act (TANF), which created a new system of public assistance. The new welfare system is complex and in its early stages. It includes the following features:

- The status of welfare assistance as a federal entitlement has been ended. The families of poor children are no longer guaranteed assistance by the federal government.
- The design and administration of welfare programs have been turned over to the individual states. In the end, the United States will have 50 different welfare systems.
- States receive block grants from the federal government to help them finance the welfare systems they devise. States can use up to 30 percent of the grants on non-cash benefit programs for the poor (such as childcare, training, transportation, and the like).
- The head of every of every family receiving welfare is required to work within two years of receiving benefits and is limited to a total of five years of benefits. States are allowed to impose even more stringent time requirements. States are allowed to use their own funds, not federal block grant money, to extend the two-year and five-year limits.
- Unmarried teenage parents can receive welfare benefits only if they stay in school and live with an adult.
- Future legal immigrants are ineligible for benefits during their first five years in the United States.
- States must provide Medicaid to all who qualify under current law.
- The eligibility of poor who are not raising children to receive food stamps is severely restricted.

Proponents of the legislation suggest that the new welfare system will end welfare dependence, reestablish the primacy of the family, improve the income situation of the poor as they enter the job market, and help balance the federal budget. Opponents of the legislation say that the new system will lead to more poverty, homelessness, and hunger, especially among children once recipients use up their time limits.

The Earned Income Tax Credit-The working poor benefit greatly from a provision in the tax code that allows low-income individuals with at least one child to claim a credit against taxes owed or, for some, to receive a direct cash transfer from the IRS. This provision of the tax code benefits over 50 million low-income Americans without much bureaucratic fuss.

→ HOW THE AMERICAN WELFARE STATE COMPARES TO OTHERS

Social welfare states vary from country to country. There are *minimal or liberal* states and there are *developed or social democratic* welfare states. The United States is very close to the minimal end of the spectrum.

How the United States Differs-The United States is different from other welfare states.

- *The U.S. welfare state developed later than others.* National health insurance was introduced in Germany in the late nineteenth century; it was available in almost all Western European nations by 1950. Medicare for the elderly and Medicaid for the indigent didn't happen in the United States until the 1960s.
- *The American welfare state is smaller than most.* Despite complaints about size and cost, the United States has one of the smallest of the social welfare states. Among the rich democracies, only Japan and Australia spend less than the United States on welfare.
- *The American welfare state covers fewer people than other welfare states.* Many nations cover their entire populations with social welfare. Family allowances in such places as Austria, the Netherlands, Norway, and Sweden go to all citizens who have children. Medical coverage is universal in most of the OECD nations. In the United States, over 40 million Americans have no health insurance coverage.
- *The elderly do considerably better than the young in the American welfare state.* Medicare and Social Security outstrip the rate of growth of programs that benefit the nonelderly poor, especially children. In most other welfare states, family allowances and universal medical coverage make benefit distributions more balanced.
- *The American welfare state is less redistributive.* The degree of income equality in the OECD nations (with the exception of Japan) is a function of the amount of money they spend on social welfare programs and the degree to which program coverage is universal. The United States ranks very low on both, so our social welfare state does not make much of a dent in the degree of income and wealth inequality in comparison with those of other nations.

- *The American welfare state is less of private employers.* All Western welfare states require that employers help employees with their parenting obligations. All require employers to offer maternity and parenting leaves with pay. In the United States, the Family and Medical Leave Act requires all companies with 50 or more employees to grant maternity and parenting leaves; payment is not guaranteed by law.
- The American welfare state does not include universal health care. The OECD countries either provide health services directly, offer universal health insurance coverage, or use some combination of the two.

Are the Western European Welfare States Becoming More Like Us?-Competitive pressures in the global economy are forcing major companies in every country to become more "lean and mean." Similar pressures are forcing even very rich nations to become more concerned about the high taxes and budget deficits that seem to be associated with highly developed welfare states. These conditions adversely affect the international competitiveness of countries and their business enterprise. Other countries are resorting to measures such as cutting welfare rolls and increasing the retirement age. Still Western European political leaders have not been able to do much more than chip away at the edges of the welfare state.

Why the American Welfare State Is Different-Structural and political linkage factors influence the kind of social welfare state that the United States has.

Constitutional Rules-Federalism is one of the reasons why social welfare programs were introduced in the United States at such a late date. Federalism also accounts for the *administrative complexity* of our social welfare state: divided and shared authority characterizes many programs, with joint funding and administration. Federalism has brought great unevenness in program coverage, with great variation from state to state in benefits, eligibility requirements, and rules. The only programs that are uniform across the United States are Social Security and Medicare.

Racial and Ethnic Diversity-Racial and ethnic tensions have influenced the shape of the American welfare state—some of the hostility toward public assistance is probably related to the fact that African-Americans make up a disproportionately large share of welfare recipients (even though they are a minority of all recipients). In homogenous societies, like many in Europe, voters are more willing to support generous welfare programs because recipients are felt to be very much like them. Recipients are considered to be one of "us" rather than one of "them".

Political Culture-Almost every aspect of the American political culture works against a generous and comprehensive welfare state, including a belief in **individualism** that emphasizes independence, responsibility, and autonomy. Interest groups overrepresent business, the well-to-do, and the professions; these are not groups that generally push for the expansion of the welfare state. However, the elderly are probably more influential in American politics than the elderly in

471

other countries (where strong political parties diminish the power of interest groups). Moreover, our political culture supports more voluntary efforts in welfare matters than other nations do (leaving government with less responsibility). Generous and comprehensive welfare states—such as those in Europe—are almost always large and centralized states supported by high taxes.

Business Power-Business plays a particularly important role in American politics; almost without exception, the business community has opposed the creation of a welfare state along European lines. Doctors, hospital corporations, insurance companies, and nursing home owners are major players in the Americans system of interest group politics, and they continuously press politicians to maintain the United States' system of mixed government-private enterprise medical care.

Weak Labor Unions-American labor unions have never been very strong or influential when compared with labor unions in other Western capitalist countries. Countries where the working class is organized and exercises significant political power have extensive welfare states; countries where the working class is not well organized and fails to exercise significant political power have minimal welfare states. The proportion of American workers who join labor unions has always been lower in the United States than in other capitalist countries and is steadily declining.

→ SUMMARY

The federal government plays an important role in national economic affairs and in providing social welfare for its citizens. Both arises from the problems created by a dynamic free enterprise market economy and the demand by people in a democratic society that government lend a helping hand. The **effects of economic and social welfare policies on democracy** in the United States are mixed. Social insurance has strengthened the health and well-being of the elderly and has contributed to more **equality** for the elderly; in this sense, social insurance has been an important factor in enhancing **popular sovereignty** and **political equality**. By contrast, those on public assistance have not had the same benefits. Most important, welfare does not appear to leave much room for the development of dignity, independence, and self-confidence among recipients that is so essential for democratic citizenship.

With respect to macroeconomic policy, the government uses both fiscal and monetary tools to try to encourage economic growth and low inflation. The annual budget fashioned by the president and Congress is the main too of fiscal policy; decisions by the Federal Reserve Board that affect the supply of money in the economy serve as the main tool of monetary policy. Monetary Policy has become increasingly important as problems in controlling the budget deficit have made fiscal policy less effective and less attractive.

The federal government also subsidizes essential infrastructure that would otherwise not be made available by private enterprise and plays and important regulatory role. The origins of the government's role may be found in market failures and diseconomies that triggered popular and business pressures on government.

In terms of domestic policy outcomes, there seems to be a fairly close fit between what the majority of Americans want and what the federal government does. Although Americans say they think government is too big and spends too much, they generally support those programs that make it so big. Economic policies are formulated by presidents and members of Congress who are sensitive to the wishes of the electorate. By contrast, monetary policy is fashioned by a Federal Reserve Board that is largely insulated from the pressures of democratic politics.

Democratic politics played an important role in the formation of the American social welfare state. The primary components of social welfare in the United States (Social Security and public assistance) were only enacted because of pressure from the public on political and economic leaders.

Chapter Outline

This section gives you a comprehensive review of the chapter. Use this outline in combination with your textbook to look for key concepts and objectives, to identify essential terms and names, and to gain a basic understanding of political practices and principles from this chapter.

I. BUDGET CHAOS IN THE 104th CONGRESS, COMPROMISE IN THE 105th (pp. 497-498)

A. The annual decision about the budget is one of the most important things that the president and Congress do.
   1. It is important because it determines in broad outline what activities and programs will be carried out by the federal government and how the government will go about paying for them.
   2. This chapter looks at a broad range of these federal government activities and programs and the impact that they have on the American people.
B. In the 104th Congress, House Republicans were eager to take on the task of cutting back on the size and role of the federal government; the budget bill they fashioned was unprecedented.
   1. It aimed for a balanced budget over a period of seven years.
   2. It included many provisions about specific federal programs normally left to the congressional committees, including drastic cutbacks in the regulatory responsibilities of the federal government, a slowdown in Medicare funding, a tax

cut, and the transformation of welfare and Medicaid into block grants run by the states.

C. Senate Republicans forced some changes in the bill, including a smaller tax cut and less stringent cutbacks in environmental regulation, but they went along with most of what the House Republicans were trying to achieve.

D. Congressional Republicans were confident that **Bill Clinton** would waiver under threats to close down the government in the absence of a budget.
1. To their surprise, Clinton refused to be intimidated; he vetoed temporary measures in November and the full budget bill in December.
2. After each veto, the federal government shut down, with only "essential" services permitted to operate under temporary funding measures.

E. Republican leaders were unprepared for the firestorm of criticism.
1. They—and not the president—received most of the public blame.
2. The president produced a balanced budget, but one that would not be damaging to the environment, education, or the elderly.
3. Realizing that their most conservative members would never agree to the Clinton plan and sensing the rising public anger at the government shutdown, congressional leaders abandoned their effort to pass a radical budget bill.

F. The battle had electoral consequences in 1996.
1. Democrats increased their numbers in the House, and Bill Clinton was reelected to the presidency.
2. Republican leadership pushed aside the budget radicals and entered into serious bipartisan negotiations with Clinton in the opening months of the 105th Congress; a landmark compromise emerged from the negotiations.

II. **WHY GOVERNMENT IS INVOLVED IN THE ECONOMY AND SOCIAL WELFARE (pp. 498-500)**

A. **Economic management**
1. Governments in all modern capitalist societies play a substantial role in the management and direction of their economies; the willingness to use government (primarily through fiscal and monetary policy) in order to *manage the economy* has been enhanced by its relative success since the end of World War II.
2. Government also plays a role because its purchases are so substantial that its actions inevitably have an impact on the economy.
3. Citizens have learned that the free market economy is subject to periodic bouts of **inflation** and unemployment, as well as occasional periods of unemployment and **depression**.
4. The inclination to use the federal government to manage the national economy has been enhanced by the relative success of this endeavor since the end of World War II. The federal government also influences the economy as the largest customer in the United States.

B. **Social welfare**
   1. A **welfare state** is a society with a set of government programs that protect the minimum standards of living of families and individuals; although the details of their programs differ, all rich democracies have social welfare states.
   2. Protection is provided against loss of income due to economic instability, old age, illness and disability, and family disintegration.
   3. Although the details of their programs differ, all rich democracies have social welfare states.
      a) Though market economies have produced unprecedented levels of wealth and improved living standards in the rich democracies over the past century, they have also produced disruptions and hardships: recessions and depressions; technological joblessness; and regional economic transformations, as industries come and go.
      b) The extended family is less common as economic change brings pressure on people to move to where jobs are located, to extend the period of education and training, and to have two wage earners in each household.
   4. Families in rich democracies today are not only smaller but also less likely to stay intact—the divorce rate is high in these countries.

III. **ECONOMIC POLICY (pp. 500-504)**
   A. **The goals of economic policy**
      1. Political leaders seek to produce positive economic results when they set economic policies.
         a) Economic policy goals sometimes are in conflict, and important trade-offs are involved whenever economic policies are selected.
         b) Serious disagreements exist among political leaders, economic scholars, and the public about which policies are likely to achieve the desired goals.
      2. Economic growth (defined by the authors as an annual increase in the **gross domestic product**, or **GDP**) is sought by economic policymakers. Economic policies have consequences for the American people.
   B. **Economic growth**
      1. Sustained economic growth (defined by the authors as an annual increase in the **gross domestic product**, or **GDP**) is sought by economic policymakers.
         a) Americans want an economy that brings more jobs, more products, and higher incomes.
         b) Economic growth also produces increased profits, so business tends to support this goal.
      2. For politicians a thriving economy that grows, translates into votes and popularity. Economic growth is also a remedy for social problems such as poverty.
   C. **Low unemployment**
      1. Low unemployment has historically been associated with economic growth, while

economic **recessions** bring slower job growth and rising unemployment rates.
2. High unemployment often breeds unrest and political instability.

D. **Stable prices**
1. Political leaders seek policies that dampen inflation and provide stable prices. Depressions bring a collapse of the job market.
2. Setting economic policy is a delicate balancing act because such policies often require slower economic growth, with its lower wages and higher levels of unemployment.

E. **A positive balance of payments**
1. The **balance of payments** is the difference between the value of a nation's imports and the value of its exports, including both manufactured goods and services such as insurance and banking.
2. The U.S. trade deficit has been in the red for many years, despite several attempts at correction by presidents and Congresses.

F. **Minimizing externalities**
1. The negative side effects that come with economic growth, such as air and water pollution, toxic wastes, and workplace injuries and health hazards.
2. These side effects of economic activity--called **negative externalities**--have generated enormous public pressure for compensatory government action; government must be careful to avoid regulating too much.

G. **Supporting key economic sectors**
1. Government must ensure the economic wealth of the nation even when the private sector does not. For example, all European countries and the United States subsidize farmers.
2. The United States government encourages business activity in the public and especially, private sectors.

H. **The tools of macroeconomic policy**
1. Government has influence in the economy by way of the rate of inflation, the level of unemployment, and the growth of income and output in the national economy.
2. Since World War II, government leaders, economists, and citizens have expected government to use whatever means it has available to ensure good economic outcomes.
3. **Macroeconomic** policy looks at the performance of the economy as a whole or broad areas of the economy such as employment.
   a) The objective is to achieve full employment, steady economic growth, and stable prices.
   b) Government officials try to meet this goal by using fiscal and monetary tools.
4. **Fiscal policy** involves altering government finances by raising or lowering government spending, raising or lowering taxes, and raising or lowering government borrowing (depending on the needs of the economy at a particular point in time).

I. **Monetary policy**
1. Government policy to influence interest rates and control the supply of money in circulation, is carried out primarily through the operations of the **Federal Reserve Board** (the **Fed,** created in 1913).
2. As the nation's **central bank,** the Fed oversees the banking system and sets the nation's monetary policy.
3. Actions by the Fed affect how much money is available to businesses and individuals in banks, savings and loans, and credit unions. It influences interest rates and the money supply.

J. **The debate about the proper role of government**
1. People generally agree that government has a role to play in the management of the economy.
2. Debates about the role that government should play in managing the economy greatly influence national policy.

K. **Keynesian**s
1. Kenynesianism traces its roots to English economist **John Maynard Keynes**, who wrote in 1936 that capitalist economies do not consistently operate at a level that fully employs a nation's workers or keeps its factories operating at full levels of productivity.
2. Most Keynesians have come down on the spending side of the equation and are associated with an activist conception of the role of government most favored by liberal Democrats.

L. **Monetarism**
1. Monetarism includes economists like **Milton Friedman** who argue that the key to a healthy economy is the proper management of the *supply of money and credit* by *central banks* (the Federal Reserve Board).
2. Monetarists believe that federal balanced budgets are essential because unbalanced budgets make it difficult for central banks to control the money supply properly.
3. Moneterism is the economic policy of those who believe in a minimal federal government and the virtues of the free market most associated with conservatives and Republicans.

M. **The supply-siders**
1. Those who believe that drastic cuts in taxes and federal regulation will drive entrepreneurship are known as supply-side economists.
   a) This was the economic philosophy that was dominant during the Reagan years.
   b) The outcome of this economic philosophy was a drastically large budget deficit.
2. Industrial policy advocates believe that government should play a role in building and funding the infrastructure that will make the United States more competitive in global markets.

IV. **THE FEDERAL BUDGET AND FISCAL POLICY**

A. Decisions by the president and Congress on spending and taxes in the federal budget constitute America's fiscal policy. Fiscal policy influences the American economy at every level.

B. **Government spending**
   1. The federal government spent a little more than $1.8 trillion in 1999; a fourfold increase since 1960.
      a) Federal **outlays** have expanded significantly.
      b) Wars produce dramatic increases in federal government spending.
   2. From the 1930s to the 1980s, the relative spending level of the federal government steadily increased.
   3. From the early 1980s to the present, the relative scale of federal spending first leveled off and then declined. This decrease has been partly caused by a substantial decrease in the relative size of the national defense budget in the post-Cold War environment, and some cuts in domestic programs instituted by presidents Reagan and Bush.

C. **Spending priorities**
   1. The percent of federal government expenditures for national defense declined by seven percent (from twenty-three to sixteen) between 1980 and 1999. In 1960 it was over fifty percent.
   2. Outlays for *human resources* (Welfare, health, veteran's benefits, education and training) have increased considerably, constituting about sixty-one percent of federal spending.
   3. Outlays for *physical resources* (transportation, energy, and the environment have declined since 1980.
   4. Other federal non-defense outlays, which support programs ranging from housing to agriculture, national parks, science and technology, international affairs, and the administration of justice, attract six cents of every federal dollar spent.

D. **Taxes**
   1. The U.S. tax system is different from other countries in the kinds of taxes we impose.
   2. Although the American system of taxation shares some features with other countries, it is unique in a number of ways.
   3. Size of the tax bite
   4. The level of taxes levied by all governments in the United States as a proportion of GDP is 34 percent; a low number compared to other rich democracies.
   5. Americans' share of taxes as a percentage of their incomes has stayed about the same for the past 25 years.

E. **Forms of taxation**
   1. The national government depends primarily on personal and corporate income taxes and on payroll taxes, while states derive most of their revenues from sales taxes, and local governments rely most heavily on property taxes.
   2. Since 1960 the share of tax revenues from corporations has decreased and the share

478

from payroll taxes for Social Security and Medicare has increased dramatically.

F. **Complexity of our tax system**
   1. The U.S. tax code is a very complex document with many exceptions to the rules for individuals , companies, and communities.
   2. *Tax expenditures* amounted to about $500 billion in 1999. By contrast, other nations depend more on sales and consumption taxes (mostly value-added taxes).

G. **The deficit and the national debt**
   1. The **budget deficit** is the *annual shortfall* between what the government spends and what it takes in.
      a) The government must borrow the money to cover the shortfall and must pay interest on the borrowed money.
      b) Government borrowing takes the form of Treasury bonds, bills, notes to American citizens and institutions or to foreign individuals and institutions, and even to the government itself (through units like the Social Security Trust Fund).
   2. The **national debt** refers to the *total of what the government owes*. Interest on the national debt is an important component of annual federal outlays.

H. **Size of the debt and the deficit**
   1. Most of the national debt *prior to the 1980s* was accumulated during major wars; after each war, the debt relative to the GDP declined.
   2. The pattern changed dramatically in the 1980s when the size of annual deficits, the rate of growth in the national debt, and the interest paid on the national debt reached unprecedented levels.

I. **The deficit and surplus issues in American politics**
   1. Enough voters, politicians, and business leaders have worried recently about deficits and the national debt to make them hot issues today.
   2. With the federal budget now in surplus and the debt gradually becoming smaller, budget politics in Washington has shifted to the problem of what to do with the extra dollars.

J. **Subsidizing business**
   1. All governments in the rich democracies support a variety of economic activities considered important to society, but which are unlikely to occur at optimum levels without taxpayer help.
   2. In Western Europe, **public ownership** of essential economic activities is common, while in the United States, government support for business enterprises is more likely to take the form of **tax incentives**.
   3. Programs that pay direct **subsidies** to private businesses are an important part of the economic policy environment at all levels of American government.

K. **Regulation**
   1. Government regulation is an important part of what the federal government does.
   2. Federal agencies issue rules that private businesses must follow.

L. **What government regulates**
  1. Government regulation of private business increased during the twentieth century.
  2. Scholars disagree on why this has happened.

M. **Democratic explanation**
  1. Many observers believe that **government regulation of business** is the result of pressures placed by the public on policymakers (such as demands for solutions to pollution, monopolistic prices, unsafe products, and risky financial practices).
  2. In a democracy, politicians must respond to popular pressures or face the prospect of being voted out of office.

N. **The business power explanation**
  1. Conversely, *the economic theory of regulation* holds that regulation is caused by the political efforts of powerful business firms that turn to government for protection against competitors.
  2. Regulation allows firms to restrict overall output, to deny entry to business competitors, and to maintain above-market prices.

O. **A history of American regulation**
  1. The history of regulation in the United States illustrates how the interaction of democratic and nondemocratic factors has produced the regulatory agencies and policies that we have today.
  2. There is a long history of regulation in the United States.

P. **Progressive Era regulation**
  1. Between 1900 and World War I, laws were passed to regulate some of the activities of powerful new corporations.
  2. Labor, Populists, and middle-class Americans anxious about the conditions reported by the muckrakers, journalists, and novelists such as Upton Sinclair (*The Jungle*), Frank Norris (*The Octopus*) and Ida Tarbell (A History of the Standard Oil *Company)* who exposed current dangerous, monopolistic and unethical business practices.
  3. Landmark regulatory measures included the **Federal Trade Commission Act**, the **Meat Inspection Act, the Pure Food and Drug Act, and the Federal Reserve Act**. But Business often benefited from the many regulatory enactments of the period.

Q. **New Deal regulation**
  1. The next wave of regulatory reform occurred during the New Deal in the 1930s.
  2. The regulatory innovations of this period aimed squarely at speculative and unsafe practices in the banking and securities industries that had contributed to the onset of the Great Depression.

R. **The Sixties and Seventies**
  1. The success of the consumer, environmental and civil rights movements from the late Sixties to the late Seventies resulted in a substantial increase in the federal government's regulation of business.

2. Agencies such as the EPA and FDA issued numerous rules that affected business operations and decisions.

3. This was one of the only times in U.S. history when business was on the defensive, unable to halt the imposition of laws and regulations to which it was strongly opposed.

S. **Deregulation**

1. By the end of the 1970s, the mood of opinion leaders had turned against regulation. The change in climate was first apparent in the **deregulation** of the airline, banking, railroad, and trucking industries under President Jimmy Carter; it reached its maturity under President Ronald Reagan's program of regulatory relief.

2. This program slowed the regulatory writing process and reduced investigatory and research capabilities of regulatory agencies.

   a) President Reagan appointed heads of regulatory units who wanted to reduce the functions of their agencies.

   b) The deregulation offensive was continued by George Bush, who appointed Vice-President **Dan Quayle** to head the Competitive Council.

3. President **Bill Clinton** reversed many Reagan-Bush era policies, especially those related to the environment. At the same time, Clinton continued to use antiregulatory rhetoric much of the time.

T. **The future of regulation**

1. The authors of your textbook believe that the regulatory state is likely to expand in the future owing to factors that include problems created by deregulation—such as the collapse of the savings and loan industry—and the introduction of new products that will probably stimulate public demands for government intervention.

2. There was little permanent deregulation achieved during the 1980s.
   a) Most regulatory policies are supported by the public.
   b) Even at the height of Reagan's popularity, polls continued to show overwhelming support for most regulatory programs.

3. The ready availability of pornography on the Internet ahs triggered efforts by Christian conservatives and others to regulate its content. The rise in cigarette use by teenagers has led to calls for increased regulation of the tobacco industry.

U. **Making economic policy: The main players**

1. There are many influences that shape American economic policies on taxing, spending, regulation, and business subsidies.

2. They have a great deal to do with the kinds of economic policies that are put in place.

V. **Political linkage factors**

1. *Interest groups*, especially those representing business, take interest in economic policy. Business interest groups are attentive especially to the regulatory activities of the federal government.

2. Changes in the regulatory climate may have profound effects on the viability and

profitability of business enterprises, so their lobbyists stay in touch with executive and congressional actors.

   3. *Voters and public opinion*
   a) The public also has influence on economic policies.
   b) The public is particularly concerned with unemployment, inflation, and growth. Elected officials attempt to keep these factors under control in order to gain electoral rewards.

   4. *Political parties*
   a) Each party has its own electoral and financial constituency, made up of groups with identifiable economic interests.
   b) Labor, racial groups, and lower-income Americans have traditionally supported the Democrats.
   c) Business and upper-income Americans have traditionally supported the Republicans.

   5. Inequality decreases slightly when Democrats control the presidency and increases slightly when Republicans control it.

W. **Governmental factors**
   1. The president, Congress, and the Federal Reserve Board are particularly important in fashioning economic policies.
   2. Political leaders in a democracy have an interest in a strong and growing economy.

X. **The president**
   1. The president is instrumental in setting economic policy.
   a) The **Employment Act of 1946** requires the president to report on the state of the economy and recommend action to ensure full employment and economic stability.
   b) The legislative program of most modern presidents contains proposals for spending, taxing, and regulation that usually have broad macroeconomic effects.
   c) Successful presidents build good relations with Congress, and they must be skillful at affecting the behavior of the Federal Reserve Board if they want it to regulate the money supply and interest rates in a way that is consistent with the presidential program.
   2. The president is advised on economic matters by the **Council of Economic Advisors (CEA)**, the director of the **Office of Management and Budget (OMB)**, and the secretary of the **Treasury**.

Y. **Congress**
   1. Actions of **Congress** also have macroeconomic effects. The overall balance of expenditures and revenues acts as a *fiscal* instrument, either stimulating or retarding the economy.
   2. Congress is helped in its economic policymaking activities by the **Congressional Budget Office (CBO)**. Congress' *oversight* role is important in economic

policymaking.

Z. **The Federal Reserve Board**
  1. The Federal Reserve Board makes monetary policy for the nation.
     a) The role of the Fed has changed since 1913 when it was used to provide funds for member banks that found themselves short of cash.
     b) In the 1950s, it took on broad macroeconomic responsibilities in an effort to control interest rates and the money supply.
     c) The Fed is made up of seven members (called governors) who serve overlapping 14-year terms and a chair who serves a renewable 4-year term. The president appoints each.
  2. Federal Reserve Chairman **Alan Greenspan** has been credited, correctly or incorrectly, as the guiding monetary hand behind the economic boom and low inflation of the 1990s.

V. **SOCIAL WELFARE (pp. 514-525)**
  A. Another important domain of domestic policy in the United States is social welfare, a broad range of programs that protects the minimum standards of living of families and individuals against unemployment, income loss and poverty, physical and mental illness and disability, family disintegration, and old age.
  B. Such programs account for the largest share of the annual federal budget.
  C. **Outline of the American welfare state**
  1. A **social welfare state** is a society with a set of government programs that protect minimum standards of living.
  2. Social welfare in the United States is provided by a complex mix of programs.
  D. **Types of programs**
  1. Distinctions can be made among social welfare progress *based on methods of dispensing benefits*, including **social insurance** programs in which individuals contribute to an insurance fund through payroll taxes and receive benefits based on their contributions (such as Social Security) and **means-tested** programs in which benefits are distributed on the basis of need (such as Medicaid and food stamps).
     a) Means-tested programs are the programs that the public generally refers to as *welfare*.
     b) Distinctions can also be drawn between social welfare programs that *pay people directly* and those that *provide a service.*
     c) **Cash transfer** programs are social welfare programs that pay people directly, such as unemployment insurance; programs that **provide a service** include Medicare, which pays hospitals on behalf of recipients.
  2. Distinctions may be *based on administration* of social welfare programs. Some of these programs are administered directly from Washington, D.C. (such as Social Security), while others are jointly administered by federal and state governments (such as Medicaid); these programs reflect wide variation in benefits in various

states. A substantial amount of money is spent on what the U.S. budget calls social welfare. Social insurance programs are termed **entitlement** programs because benefits are received as a *matter of right* based on contributions.

E. **Cost of the social welfare State**
   1. The federal, state, and local governments of the United States spend a great deal of money supporting the welfare state; in 1999, it spent $787 billion on Social Security, Medicare, Medicaid, and means-tested entitlement programs, almost 48 percent of the federal budget. Of this total, social insurance programs account for the lion's share, a bit more than one-third of federal government expenditures in 1999.
   2. Most of the benefits of the American welfare state do not go to the poor. Those who were fully employed during their work lives, had the highest incomes, and paid the maximum level of Social Security taxes are the main beneficiaries. The poverty rate for children in the United States is increasingly high. Almost one child in five now lives below **the poverty line**.

F. Social Security and Other Social Insurance Programs
   1. Social insurance programs that guard against loss of income due to old age, disability, and illness are the largest, most popular, and fastest-growing parts of the American welfare state.
   2. Social insurance programs are termed entitlement programs because benefits are received as a matter of right based on contributions.
   3. There are a number of social insurance programs that are designed to meet different contingencies.
   4. Social insurance programs that guard against loss of income due to old age, disability, and illness are the largest, most popular, and fastest-growing parts of the American welfare state.

G. *Old Age, Survivors, and Disability Insurance*
   1. OASDI, usually referred to as Social Security, is the largest social insurance program. Social Security was created in 1935 to assist the elderly and later, survivors ("widows and orphans program").
   2. Coverage of the disabled was added in 1956.
      a) OASDI is funded by a payroll tax on employees under the Federal Insurance Contributions Act (FICA on individuals' pay stubs).
      b) The Self-employed pay into a similar trust fund. Unlike private insurance, premiums paid into the fund are not sufficient to pay for the level of benefits actually received.
   3. For the most part, Social Security is funded by payroll taxes levied on *currently employed* Americans. However, the great popularity of the Social Security program means that political leaders are unlikely to allow it to go bankrupt.
   4. *Medicare*
      a) This type of social insurance has grown into one of the largest federal programs in terms of total dollar expenditures.

b) It pays for a substantial portion of the hospital, doctor, and drug costs of retirees and the disabled.

5. Rapidly rising health care costs since Medicare was established in 1965 have pushed outlays to such high levels that efforts to control its costs have become a staple of American politics. It is funded by a payroll tax on employees and employers, assisted by federal subsidies.

H. **Unemployment insurance**
1. This type of social insurance is administered by the states under federal guidelines, with the level of benefits set by the states (which show wide variations). It is financed by federal and state taxes on employers.
2. The level of benefits is set by the states, and there are wide variations among them.

I. **Do social insurance programs work?**
1. In an era when it is fashionable to deride the ability of government to do anything well, it is important to know about the relative success of America's social insurance programs.
2. There have been both successes and problems with American social insurance programs.

J. **Successes**
1. Among successes, the authors of your textbook note that benefits provide an income floor for the retired and pay for costly medical services that would otherwise impoverish many who have serious illnesses and long hospital stays.
2. Improvement in the standard of living of the elderly is evident in the decline of the official poverty rate for them.

K. **Problems**
1. By contrast, problems include the *regressive* overall effect of social insurance programs (that is, the well-off receive more benefits than those with more limited resources).
2. Moreover, financial stability of Social Security and Medicare has been achieved only because Congress has steadily raised payroll taxes—FICA (Social Security) and Medicare taxes now take a larger amount of paychecks for a majority of Americans than the personal income tax.
3. Political tension seems to be building between the elderly who receive benefits and those who are still working and paying FICA taxes to support the programs.

L. **Means-tested programs (Welfare)**
1. Welfare only accounts for a small part of the annual federal budget.
   a) Yet it has attracted more opposition than virtually anything else government does.
   b) Increasing numbers of people are convinced that public assistance doesn't work.
   c) The authors analyze evidence that supports both sides of the argument concerning the viability of public assistance.
      (1) In particular, opponents believe that welfare undermines the work ethic,

                 encourages family disintegration, and creates a permanent dependent class.

        (2) However, available research does not support many of the criticisms.

  2. Many social scientists blame slow growth in the American economy and job migration from central cities (rather than welfare) as the main causes of dependency and family breakup.

M. Food stamps

1. This program is available to Americans below a certain income level.
2. Benefit levels are set by the states under general federal guidelines, with substantial variation among the states.
3. Stamps can be used only for food, they cannot be used for alcohol, cigarettes, or gambling.
4. The program has made a significant dent in malnutrition in the United States.

N. Medicaid

1. The federal government provides *matching funds* to the states so that they can provide medical assistance for indigent citizens under the **Medicaid** program.
2. The states formulate their own eligibility requirements and set their own benefit levels.
3. The problem of noninclusion is a serious one.
4. Eligibility rules are complex and tend to exclude those who are not extremely poor, blind, disabled, or children with out-of-work parents. At the same time, the inability to restrain Medicaid costs is one of the primary reasons for the fiscal difficulties of the states.

O. Supplemental security income

1. Also known as **SSI**, this program was created in 1974 in order to provide benefits to the elderly, blind, and disabled poor whom social insurance programs are insufficient to elevate above the poverty line.
2. The 1996 welfare reform bill denied SSI to legal immigrants, but the provision was rescinded in 199t for legal immigrants already resident in the United States.

P. Head Start

1. This is by far the most popular means-tested social welfare program.
2. It reaches about 300,000 children per year in an effort to prepare poor preschool children for entrance into public schools.

Q. Welfare block grants

1. The president and Congress agreed to "change welfare as we know it."
2. President Clinton reluctantly signed the Temporary Assistance to Needy Families Act (TANF), which created a new system of public assistance.
3. The new welfare system is complex and in its early stages. It includes the following features:
   a) The status of welfare assistance as a federal entitlement has been ended. The families of poor children are no longer guaranteed assistance by the federal government.

    b) The design and administration of welfare programs have been turned over to the individual states. In the end, the United States will have 50 different welfare systems.

    c) States receive block grants from the federal government to help them finance the welfare systems they devise. States can use up to 30 percent of the grants on non-cash benefit programs for the poor (such as childcare, training, transportation, and the like).

  4. The head of every of every family receiving welfare is required to work within two years of receiving benefits and is limited to a total of five years of benefits. States are allowed to impose even more stringent time requirements. States are allowed to use their own funds, not federal block grant money, to extend the two-year and five-year limits.

    a) Unmarried teenage parents can receive welfare benefits only if they stay in school and live with an adult.

    b) Future legal immigrants are ineligible for benefits during their first five years in the United States.

    c) States must provide Medicaid to all who qualify under current law.

    d) The eligibility of poor who are not raising children to receive food stamps is severely restricted.

  5. Proponents of the legislation suggest that the new welfare system will end welfare dependence, reestablish the primacy of the family, improve the income situation of the poor as they enter the job market, and help balance the federal budget.

  6. Opponents of the legislation say that the new system will lead to more poverty, homelessness, and hunger, especially among children once recipients use up their time limits.

  7. *The earned income tax credit*

    a) The working poor benefit greatly from a provision in the tax code that allows low-income individuals with at least one child to claim a credit against taxes owed or, for some, to receive a direct cash transfer from the IRS.

    b) This provision of the tax code benefits over 50 million low-income Americans without much bureaucratic fuss.

R. **How the American welfare state compares to others**

  1. Social welfare states vary from country to country. There are *minimal or liberal* states and there are *developed or social democratic* welfare states.

  2. The United States is very close to the minimal end of the spectrum.

S. **How the United States differs**

  1. The United States is different from other welfare states.

  2. *The U.S. welfare state developed later than others.* National health insurance was introduced in Germany in the late nineteenth century; it was available in almost all Western European nations by 1950. Medicare for the elderly and Medicaid for the indigent didn't happen in the United States until the 1960s.

3. *The American welfare state is smaller than most.* Despite complaints about size and cost, the United States has one of the smallest of the social welfare states. Among the rich democracies, only Japan and Australia spend less than the United States on welfare

4. *The American welfare state covers fewer people than other welfare states.* Many nations cover their entire populations with social welfare. Family allowances in such places as Austria, the Netherlands, Norway, and Sweden go to all citizens who have children. Medical coverage is universal in most of the OECD nations. In the United States, over 40 million Americans have no health insurance coverage.

5. *The elderly do considerably better than the young in the American welfare state.* Medicare and Social Security outstrip the rate of growth of programs that benefit the nonelderly poor, especially children. In most other welfare states, family allowances and universal medical coverage make benefit distributions more balanced.

6. *The American welfare state is less redistributive.* The degree of income equality in the OECD nations (with the exception of Japan) is a function of the amount of money they spend on social welfare programs and the degree to which program coverage is universal. The United States ranks very low on both, so our social welfare state does not make much of a dent in the degree of income and wealth inequality in comparison with those of other nations.

7. *The American welfare state is less of private employers.* All Western welfare states require that employers help employees with their parenting obligations. All require employers to offer maternity and parenting leaves with pay. In the United States, the Family and Medical Leave Act requires all companies with 50 or more employees to grant maternity and parenting leaves; payment is not guaranteed by law.

8. The American welfare state does not include universal health care. The OECD countries either provide health services directly, offer universal health insurance coverage, or use some combination of the two.

T. **Are the Western European welfare states becoming more like us?**
    1. Competitive pressures in the global economy are forcing major companies in every country to become more "lean and mean."
    2. Similar pressures are forcing even very rich nations to become more concerned about the high taxes and budget deficits that seem to be associated with highly developed welfare states.
        a) These conditions adversely affect the international competitiveness of countries and their business enterprise.
        b) Other countries are resorting to measures such as cutting welfare rolls and increasing the retirement age.
    3. Still Western European political leaders have not been able to do much more than chip away at the edges of the welfare state.

U. **Why the American welfare state is different**

1. Structural and political linkage factors influence the kind of social welfare state that the United States has.
2. All modern capitalist countries have social welfare states.
3. The United States is very close to being at the minimum end of the spectrum; ours is one of the smallest of the welfare states (but generates many complaints about its size and cost).
4. Comparison of the United States to social welfare states in the **Organization of Economic Cooperation and Development (OECD)**—Western Europe, Japan, Australia, and New Zealand.

V. **Constitutional rules**
   1. **Federalism** is one of the reasons why social welfare programs were introduced in the United States at such a late date.
   2. Federalism also accounts for the *administrative complexity* of our social welfare state: divided and shared authority characterizes many programs, with joint funding and administration.
   3. Federalism has brought great unevenness in program coverage, with great variation from state to state in benefits, eligibility requirements, and rules. The only programs that are uniform across the United States are Social Security and Medicare.

W. **Racial and ethnic diversity**
   1. Racial and ethnic tensions have influenced the shape of the American welfare state—some of the hostility toward public assistance is probably related to the fact that African-Americans make up a disproportionately large share of welfare recipients (even though they are a minority of all recipients).
   2. In homogenous societies, like many in Europe, voters are more willing to support generous welfare programs because recipients are felt to be very much like them. Recipients are considered to be one of "us" rather than one of "them".

X. **Political culture**
   1. Almost every aspect of the American political culture works against a generous and comprehensive welfare state, including a belief in **individualism** that emphasizes independence, responsibility, and autonomy.
   2. Interest groups overrepresent business, the well-to-do, and the professions; these are not groups that generally push for the expansion of the welfare state.
   3. However, the elderly are probably more influential in American politics than the elderly in other countries (where strong political parties diminish the power of interest groups).
   4. Moreover, our political culture supports more voluntary efforts in welfare matters than other nations do (leaving government with less responsibility). Generous and comprehensive welfare states—such as those in Europe—are almost always large and centralized states supported by high taxes.

Y. **Business power**

    1. Business plays a particularly important role in American politics; almost without exception, the business community has opposed the creation of a welfare state along European lines.

    2. Doctors, hospital corporations, insurance companies, and nursing home owners are major players in the Americans system of interest group politics, and they continuously press politicians to maintain the United States' system of mixed government-private enterprise medical care.

Z. **Weak labor unions**

    1. American labor unions have never been very strong or influential when compared with labor unions in other Western capitalist countries.

    2. Countries where the working class is organized and exercises significant political power have extensive welfare states; countries where the working class is not well organized and fails to exercise significant political power have minimal welfare states.

    3. The proportion of American workers who join labor unions has always been lower in the United States than in other capitalist countries and is steadily declining.

VI. **SUMMARY (pp. 525-527)**

A. The federal government plays an important role in national economic affairs and in providing social welfare for its citizens.

    1. Both arises from the problems created by a dynamic free enterprise market economy and the demand by people in a democratic society that government lend a helping hand.

    2. The **effects of economic and social welfare policies on democracy** in the United States are mixed. Social insurance has strengthened the health and well-being of the elderly and has contributed to more **equality** for the elderly; in this sense, social insurance has been an important factor in enhancing **popular sovereignty** and **political equality**.

    3. By contrast, those on public assistance have not had the same benefits.

    4. Most important, welfare does not appear to leave much room for the development of dignity, independence, and self-confidence among recipients that is so essential for democratic citizenship.

    5. With respect to macroeconomic policy, the government uses both fiscal and monetary tools to try to encourage economic growth and low inflation.

    6. The annual budget fashioned by the president and Congress is the main too of fiscal policy; decisions by the Federal Reserve Board that affect the supply of money in the economy serve as the main tool of monetary policy.

    7. Monetary Policy has become increasingly important as problems in controlling the budget deficit have made fiscal policy less effective and less attractive.

    8. The federal government also subsidizes essential infrastructure that would otherwise not be made available by private enterprise and plays and important

regulatory role. The origins of the government's role may be found in market failures and discconomies that triggered popular and business pressures on government.

9. In terms of domestic policy outcomes, there seems to be a fairly close fit between what the majority of Americans want and what the federal government does. Although Americans say they think government is too big and spends too much, they generally support those programs that make it so big. Economic policies are formulated by presidents and members of Congress who are sensitive to the wishes of the electorate. By contrast, monetary policy is fashioned by a Federal Reserve Board that is largely insulated from the pressures of democratic politics.

10. Democratic politics played an important role in the formation of the American social welfare state. The primary components of social welfare in the United States (Social Security and public assistance) were only enacted because of pressure from the public on political and economic leaders.

Terms for Review

Use this list to review essential principles, functions, and concepts from this chapter. Refer to your textbook for help in identifying and defining terms on this list. When you study, do not merely memorize terms; ask questions about the material you are reviewing, and look for the importance or significance of each item.

balance of payments

budget deficit

depression

discount rate

entitlements

fiscal policy

gross domestic product

inflation

Keynesians

macroeconomic policy

means-tested

monetarists

monetary policy

national debt

negative externalities

poverty line

recession

regulations

social insurance

welfare state

Research Topics: Applying What You Have Learned

You will derive more benefit from your reading if you try to apply what you have learned. Some of the suggested research topics can be answered exclusively from your text, while others require you to conduct some basic research on your own. The references suggested under Internet Sources will help you in your search.

- Look at the U.S. National Debt Clock on the Internet (located at http://www.brillig.com/debt_clock/). Check the same site a few days later. How much change has occurred?

- There are several interesting simulations on the Internet, including some that permit you to play "what if" scenarios. Select one and see what happens as you change various parts of the budget. Be sure to notice the effect that your changes may have on other parts of the budget. A budget simulation is located at this Internet site: http://garnet.berkeley.edu:3333/budget/budget.html.

- Your authors note that the Fed is an undemocratic institution in that its members are not elected by the people, it meets in secret to make important decisions, and it is not obligated to give reasons for its actions. Are there any ways by which the Federal Reserve Board could be made more democratic? Would these changes have any effects on the Fed's effectiveness?

- On some occasions, the nation's monetary policy has appeared to be moving in a different direction than fiscal policy. What do you think would account for differences in approach? (*Hint*: Think about the fact that monetary policy is primarily in the hands of appointed officials, whereas fiscal policy is primarily set by elected officeholders.)

- The share of national income going to the bottom 20 percent of the population in the United States is considerably lower than in other industrialized countries. Do you think this inequality is a natural outcome of a free market system, or do you believe that this is an unjust outcome that should be corrected? Write a short essay in which you analyze both sides of this proposition.

Internet Sources

A number of sites on the World Wide Web serve as "gateways" to vast collections of material on American government and politics. The following Internet resources are recommended for students who would like to do some additional research in the areas covered by this chapter. These references would also be helpful in expanding on the questions suggested under Research Topics.

American Enterprise Institute http://www.aei.org/
A prominent conservative think tank with information about social policy.

Budget of the United States http://www.acess.gpo.gov/usbudget/
The budget of the United States, with numbers, documentation, and analyses.

Electronic Policy Network www.epn.org/
Reports from liberal think tanks on social welfare issues.

Fedstats http://www.fedstats.gov
Links to statistics and data from a broad range of federal government agencies, including those most relevant for economic and social welfare policy in the United States. These include the Federal Reserve Board, the Bureau of Labor Statistics, the Social Security Administration, the Bureau of Census, the Bureau of Economic Analysis, and Administration for Children and Families.

Public Agenda Online www.publicagenda.org/
A nonpartisan site with comprehensive information about government policies, alternative proposals to solve societal problems, and what the public thinks about existing and alternative policies.

Self-Evaluation

Circle the correct answer for each question. Questions are listed in the same order in which the information appears in the text. Use the Answer Key in the back of the Study Guide *to check your responses.*

1. Inflation is
   a. A severe drop in economic activity
   b. A condition of lowering prices
   c. A condition of rising prices
   d. Gaining control of the business cycle

2. The federal government spends most of its money on
   a. Social insurance
   b. Means tested programs
   c. Medicare
   d. Entitlement programs

3. The federal **budget deficit** is
   a. The total of what government owes to individuals and institutions.

    b.   The annual shortfall between what the government spends and what it takes in.

    c.   The rate of interest that government must pay on short-term financial obligations.

    d.   The measure of efficiency and fairness that is built into the tax code.

4.   Unemployment insurance
    a.   Pays for a substantial portion of the hospital, doctor, and drug costs of retirees and the disabled.
    b.   Is the largest of the social insurance programs, accounting for a large share of the federal deficit.
    c.   Includes an automatic cost of living adjustment (COLA) that is set by Congress.
    d.   Is administered by the states under federal guidelines, with the level of benefits set by the states.

5.   Economist John Maynard Keynes called on government to
    a.   Engage in national strategic planning to guide investment to high-technology sectors and away from outmoded industries.
    b.   Increase the supply of goods and services in the economy by removing barriers to individual investment and entrepreneurship.
    c.   Use the central bank to set and enforce long-range targets for growth in the money supply that matches the rate of growth in productivity.
    d.   Increase government spending or cut taxes during economic downturns to stimulate productivity and increase money in circulation.

6.   The objective of **macroeconomic** policy is to
    a.   Achieve full employment, steady economic growth, and stable prices.
    b.   Study the activities of a single sector of the economy.
    c.   Integrate the functions of the executive and legislative branches of government in setting economic policy.
    d.   Analyze the relationship between the poverty rate and the decline of family values.

7.   Decisions of the Federal Reserve Board play an important role in setting the nation's
    a.   Fiscal policy.
    b.   Monetary policy.
    c.   Supply-side policy.
    d.   Social welfare policy.

8.   Which of the following is a **means-tested** program?
    a.   Unemployment insurance
    b.   Medicare
    c.   Social Security
    d.   Medicaid

9. The passage of the Social Security Act in 1935
   a. Marked the first time any industrialized nation guaranteed a minimum income to its residents.
   b. Was the first step that the United States took toward building a social insurance safety net.
   c. Established the basis for the federal government's means-tested programs.
   d. Was originally intended to provide assistance only for children and the disabled.

10. Concerning social welfare programs, the American form of federalism has resulted in
    a. Relative uniformity in state laws, which produce only modest variation in eligibility requirements and benefits among the states.
    b. Great unevenness among the states in program coverage, with variation in benefits, eligibility requirements, and rules.
    c. Enactment of federal laws that cover most social welfare programs, so state rules and regulations have little or no impact on benefits and eligibility.
    d. Joint funding and administration of all social welfare programs, with costs and regulations evenly shared between the federal government and the states.

11. **A social welfare state** is
    a. A society with a set of government programs that protect the minimum standards of living.
    b. Strongly based on the benefits of the free market and individualism.
    c. Used primarily in underdeveloped nations with relatively young populations.
    d. One of the fundamental freedoms that is protected in the Bill of Rights.

12. The balance of payments is
    a. When people with high incomes pay a higher percentage of their income in taxes than do low wage earners.
    b. When all income earners pay the same percentage of their income in taxes.
    c. When taxes are based on factors other than income, such as tax breaks for the elderly.
    d. The annual difference between payments and recipients between a country and its trading partners.

13. (T/F) Although the details of their programs differ, all rich democracies provide social welfare benefits for their citizens.

14. (T/F) A **recession** refers to a period of increase in overall economic activity.

15. (T/F) **Entitlement** programs payments are made automatically to people who meet certain eligibility requirements.

16. (T/F) Most benefits of the American welfare state go to those with incomes below the official poverty line.

17. (T/F) The national government defends primarily on income taxes.

18. (T/F) **Means-tested** programs are plans in which contracts are awarded to small businesses with adequate resources to administer the program.

Chapter 18
FOREIGN POLICY AND NATIONAL DEFENSE

Key Concepts and Objectives

The Key Concepts and Objectives provide a look at the fundamental goals and ideas of this chapter. This section serves as a guide to a basic understanding of the objectives of your textbook.

After reading this chapter, you should be able to:

- Trace the major policies pursued by the United States during the era of the Cold War.
- Identify the major policymakers involved in making and carrying out U.S. foreign policy.
- Explain why presidents and others at the governmental level of analysis often play a more formative role in shaping foreign policy than in determining domestic policy.
- Evaluate the role of corporations and interest groups in making American foreign policy.
- Consider the question of whether covert operations necessarily conflict with the idea of democracy.
- Investigate the role that the American public plays in making foreign policy.
- Explain why democratic control is more difficult and less complete in foreign policymaking than in domestic policymaking.
- Understand what structural level factors are responsible for U.S. superpower status.
- Understand how the democratic process affects foreign and defense policies.
- Understand the causes of the Cold War, and explain how and why the United States emerged from the Cold War as the only remaining superpower.
- Identify key terms and concepts used in Chapter 18.

Chapter Overview

This section provides a brief overview of the chapter contents. Read this section as a preview before reading your textbook. Then use this material as a review to help you retain information from your reading.

➔ THE SENATE DEFEATS THE NUCLEAR TEST BAN TREATY

This chapter discusses American foreign and military policies; how they are made, and how they affect Americans and others. American foreign and military policies are the product of the interaction of structural factors (such as American economic and military power, the collapse of the Soviet Union, and "globalization"), political linkage level factors (such as the choices the media make about foreign news coverage, public opinion about what the US role in the world ought to be, and what various interest groups want the government to do), and governmental factors (such as the objectives and actions of presidents, members of Congress, and important executive branch agencies like the Central Intelligence Agency and the Joint Chiefs of Staff).

The foreign policy and national defense issues that American policymakers face today in the post-Colld War world are different from those they faced in the past. The U.S. Senate's refusal to ratify the **Nuclear Test Ban Treaty** that President Clinton had signed in 1996, surprised people in many circles. The treaty was designed to slow the spread of nuclear weapons, but it was soundly defeated in the Senate. Some contended that with the defeat of the treaty, the United States had lost its moral authority and any leverage it might have in trying to persuade India, Pakistan and North Korea to sign the treaty and China, Russia, Egypt and Israel (all of whom have signed the treaty) to ratify it.

Relatively speaking, the Senate's consideration of the Test Ban treaty was very brief. As well, the treaty was brought to a vote on the floor of the Senate even after 52 senators (a majority) signed a plea to Majority Leader Trent Lott to postpone the vote. In addition, the debate was conducted in an atmosphere of bitter partisanship, with both Democrats and Republicans as another tool with which to score points against their opponents.

The treaty may have been defeated because it was fatally flawed, with the effect of diminishing U.S. sovereignty and threatening the usefulness of nuclear arsenal, without doing much about the proliferation of nuclear weapons. It may also have been the case that President Clinton and Senate Democrats made important tactical mistakes, such as not including Republicans in the original treaty negotiations, not acting in a bi-partisan manner in the Senate process, and insisting on Senate consideration of the treaty when the Republicans were the majority. It is also possible that Senate Republicans wanted to embarrass Bill Clinton and further damage his historical legacy. Finally, the treaty may have been a reflection of the fact that, without the Cold War or the serious threat of a large-scale shooting war, the office of president has lost some power and prestige in foreign and military affairs and Congress has become increasingly willing and anxious to flex its muscles in these areas, as it has always done in domestic affairs. There may also be some confusion about how America should behave in its role as the sole global superpower.

→ FOREIGN POLICY AND DEMOCRACY: A CONTRADICTION IN TERMS?

Foreign policy—especially policy concerning wars or crises—has traditionally been different from domestic policy. Presidents and the executive branch have often played a much more important part than they do domestically, and they have had an unusual degree of autonomy in foreign policy. The ordinary **political factors** (such as public opinion and interest groups) have often been set aside in favor of considerations of the **national interest**, as defined by a small number of national security advisers. Much of foreign policy is also influenced by **structural factors**, including the power and resources of the United States, its economic interests abroad, and the nature and behavior of other nations. The superpower status of the United States is a crucial structural fact for understanding international relations and American foreign policy. American power and resources have been important in a whole series of U.S. actions abroad since World War II. The public does have some influence of foreign policy, especially in the areas of trade, immigration, and corporate global behavior and less at strictly military affairs. The struggle over ratification of the North American Free Trade Agreement (**NAFTA**) is a good example.

→ THE UNITED STATES AS A SUPERPOWER: HISTORY AND STRUCTURE

This chapter looks at the structure and history of the United States as a **superpower**. The ability to send massive numbers of troops, warplanes, and aircraft carriers to the Persian Gulf region in 1990 reflected the status of the United States as a superpower. Enormous economic power enables the United States to field the most powerful armed forces in the world. For decades, the Soviet Union squeezed its smaller economy in order to produce a military establishment that looked roughly equal to that of the United States. After the 1991 collapse of the Soviet Union, a large part of its forces reverted to Russia. Their economy fell into disarray, and Russia's capability to use force abroad is very much in doubt, except on its immediate periphery.

By the middle at the 1990s, the United States was the *only* superpower. No other nation had the rapid deployment capabilities, bases, and weapons systems that could project force anywhere in the world. The superpower status of the United States is *a crucial structural fact* for understanding international relations and American foreign policy. American power and resources have been important in a whole series of U.S. actions abroad since World War II. This superpower status may largely account for the exertion of U.S. influence around the world.

The Cold War-After World War II, the United States and the Soviet Union were engaged in a series of confrontations—a **Cold War** that lasted for more than 40 years. Theories such as George Kennan's **containment doctrine** played an influential role in the development of U.S. foreign policy during that period of history. The **Truman Doctrine** (the idea that the United States would help "free peoples" resist "armed minorities or outside pressures") and the **Marshall Plan** provided massive amounts of economic aid to devastated European economies while pursuing U.S. policies to resist communist expansion. **NATO** (the North American Treaty Organization) was created as an anti-Soviet military alliance after World War II and the Russians responded by creating the **Warsaw Pact**. The Korean War—in which the United States and South Africa fought North Korea and China—divided

Combined the Soviet Union and the United States spent nearly $12 trillion during the Cold War. Both the United States and the Soviet Union built large numbers of strategic bombers that could drop nuclear warheads on the other country, and both began ballistic missile programs. **Mutually assured destruction (MAD)** deterred either side from launching a nuclear attack and was instrumental in the negotiation of trade and arms control agreements, including the **Strategic Arms Limitation Treaty (SALT I).**

The **Vietnam War**—ostensibly fought in an effort to prevent a takeover of South Vietnam by the **Viet Cong**, or National Liberation Front—was a major setback for American foreign policy. The war's costs in money, casualties, and social disruption discouraged intervention abroad for a period of time. The **Nixon** administration pursued a policy of *rapprochement* (closer relations) with China and *détente* (relaxation of tensions) with the Soviet Union.

The End of the Cold War-Beginning in 1989, a series of dramatic world events completely transformed international affairs. In 1985 Soviet leader Mikhail Gorbachev introduced an economic program known as *perestroika* (restructuring), and more political freedom through *glasnost* (openness). There was a failed coup against Gorbachev in 1991. The Soviet Union eventually fell apart as the Baltic republics (Estonia, Latvia, and Lithuania) became completely independent, and virtually all the other 12 republics, including the Ukraine and Russia insisted on independence. In 1997, NATO extended eastward when former Soviet bloc members Poland, Hungary, and the Czech Republic formally applied to join the anti-Soviet alliance. The collapse of the Soviet empire left the United States as the only true superpower, but with some major problems unresolved (including questions concerning the thousands of nuclear weapons still in the hands of republics from the former Soviet Union).

The Structural Bases of American Superpower Status-Events and the strategies of political actors are important in shaping world affairs, but a nation's place in the international system is largely determined by its relative economic, military and cultural power. At the beginning of the century, the United States is particularly advantaged in all three areas.

Economic Power-The United States has the world's largest economy, with an annual gross domestic product of more than $8.5 trillion. The GDP of the United States is larger than that of China, Japan, Germany, India, Great Britain, and Russia.

By all indications the relative strength of the American economy is increasing. The U.S. economy has boomed as its companies have established their dominance in the economic sectors that matter most in the new global economy: telecommunications, mass entertainment, biotechnology, software, finance, e-commerce, business services, transportation, and computer chips. The United States' economic preeminence is likely to continue for some time.

Military Power-The United States has the most powerful armed forces in the world. The United States spent nearly $275 billion in 1999 on its armed forces and has almost 1.4 million men and women on active military duty. The air force has 550 **intercontinental ballistic missiles (ICBMs)** and 191 bombers, each carrying multiple nuclear warheads. The navy has 12 aircraft carriers, 17 nuclear missile submarines (armed with 432 multiple-warhead missiles) and many warships. The army is organized into ten divisions, backed by large numbers of tanks, artillery, and tactical missiles with nuclear warheads. No other country in the world comes close to matching the power of the U.S. armed forces. The United States has military bases throughout the world; over 100,000 troops stationed in Europe and another 100,000 stationed in Asia.

"Soft Power"-Multinational corporations, which originated in the United States such as McDonald's, Kentucky Fried Chicken, and Disney, as well as Hollywood entertainment, contribute to American "soft power." Soft power is the power to influence through culture, ideology, and language and it enhances the U.S.'s harder economic and military powers.

➔ PROBLEMS OF THE POST-COLD WAR WORLD

There are several views concerning what America's role should be as the world's sole superpower. The Cold War is gone and with it have gone the clarity and coherence that the bi-polar conflict lent to policymaking. Isolationists, unilateralists, and multilateralists, have all articulated their positions on the new American role in the world.

Isolationists-The isolationists would have the United States arm itself in self-defense, avoid "entangling alliances", and let other countries solve their own problems.

Unilateralists-The unilateralists would have the United States actively engage in the world, based on the belief that what goes on elsewhere around the world affects American interests, without regard for alliances, treaties or what other nations want.

Multilateralists-The multilateralists would support American interests in the world on the bases of cooperation and collaboration with other countries. This theme in U.S. foreign policy can be seen in its participation in NATO operations in Kosovo and in its participation in the international agreements that created the World Trade Organization (WTO).

New Security Issues-The United States faced a completely changed world in the 1990s, but many questions about national security and international relations remained. With the threat of a nuclear Armageddon between the superpowers gone, a number of new security issues developed.

Russia and the Former Soviet Union-The collapse of the centralized communist regime threw into the question the fate of the vast Soviet armed forces, with their millions of troops and stockpiles of nuclear weapons, some of which have shown up on international underground markets; causing concern of the dangers of **nuclear proliferation**. Questions emerged concerning how the United States could help the newly freed countries of Eastern Europe, which are likely to continue to experience ethnic strife. Particularly since democracy and free enterprise have not worked effectively there.

The Balkans-Bitter ethnic conflicts between the Serbs, Croats, and Muslims of the former Yugoslavia continue to challenge American policy makers. Some feel that the problems of the Balkans should be addressed and solved by Europeans, while others feel that the United States should play a principal role.

Japan, China, and the Pacific-With the end of the Cold War, questions have emerged concerning how much reduction can or should there be in the vast U.S. naval forces in the Pacific Ocean or in troops stationed in South Korea and elsewhere; debates continued over whether economic and political relations should be normalized with China's still authoritarian regime which governs over a huge population, fast-growing economy and modernizing military. Some observers have warned of a great "clash of civilizations" between the West and "Confucian" China.

The Developing World-Observers have asked if regional conflicts in the Middle East and elsewhere could be solved, and whether the United States would need to periodically send troops as a "policeman of the world." Conflicts between the Israelis and the Palestinians, Iraq and Iran, or drug trafficking from places like Colombia, Peru, and Mexico continue to press American leaders on whether to intervene or not intervene.

Economic and Social Dilemmas-It is apparent that America's exalted status as the world's only military superpower and its preeminent economic power has not made U.S. foreign policy problems go away. In fact, national security has taken on new and broader meanings and encompasses new problems.

International Trade-At the height of its world economic power after World War II, international economic communities were characterized by **free trade** (trade without government restraints) and a system in which many countries negotiated lower tariff barriers through the **General Agreement on Tariffs and Trade (GATT)**. By the late 1960s, the rebuilt economies of Germany and Japan began to challenge American goods both abroad and in the United States; competition also came from newly industrialized countries (NICs) such as South Korea, Taiwan, Singapore, and Hong Kong, as well as from the increasingly integrated European Economic Community (EEC). By the mid-1980s, Americans were importing many more goods than we were exporting (creating a *multibillion-dollar trade deficit*). The trade deficit meant that many goods were cheaper in the U.S. but it also meant that many goods—formerly produced in America by American workers—were now being produced elsewhere. Under this competitive pressure, the United States began to exert *unilateral pressures* on other nations to lower hidden barriers and reduce subsidies that hurt American exports. We also began to press for voluntary quotas and other policies to control imports to the United States. Policymakers in the United States negotiated the **North American Free Trade Agreement (NAFTA)** with Canada and Mexico, which was implemented after a vote in Congress in 1993, and the Clinton administration concluded a comprehensive free trade agreement with 116 countries under the Uruguay Round of the GATT. The agreement, which was signed in 1994, set up a **World Trade Organization (WTO)** for enforcement.

Foreign Aid-The world is divided into rich nations and poor nations. As a percentage of the U.S. budget, *spending on foreign aid is very low* and has been declining (amounting to about 0.1 percent of the U.S. GDP in 1999). This is much lower, proportionately, than the aid given by countries such as Denmark, Norway, Sweden, and France. Most U.S. foreign aid is devoted to military and security purposes (not to food, education, or related areas). The U.S. has provided funds for development, population programs, and the environment to the World Bank, United Nations, and other international agencies to assist poorer countries.

Arms Sales-The United States has been one of the world's largest *sellers of weapons* to other countries. With the demise of the Soviet Union, the United States is by far the biggest arms exporter in the world, with $31.8 billion in sales in 1999.

The Global Environment-Americans realize that environmental problems cross national borders. The United States and Canada have agreed to reduce acid rain, for example. Many nations have attempted to negotiate agreement on oil spills, ozone layer protection, and the prevention of global warming. Environmentalists express particular concern about the rapid cutting and burning of tropical rain forests, which removes oxygen-producing trees and at the same time pours smoke and carbon dioxide into the atmosphere.

The Drug Trade-Illegal drugs from southern border nations such as Mexico, Haiti, Colombia, Bolivia, and Peru complicate U.S. relations with them. Part of the problem of eliminating the drug trade is that demand for drugs is very high in the rich countries, including the United States.

Immigration-People tend to follow jobs. And developments in transportation have made it possible for more people to migrate in pursuit of a better way of life for themselves and their families. Especially noteworthy is the migration from poor Third World countries to the rich countries of the West.

➔ WHO MAKES FOREIGN POLICY?

The president and the executive branch are the primary *governmental* decision makers concerning most foreign policy issues, but Congress is often involved in decisions concerning foreign trade and aid, military bases and contracts, and other matters that directly impact their constituents' local interests. People and institutions in the *political* sphere (such as public opinion, the mass media, and interest groups) affect what both Congress and the executive branch do. Certain aspects of *structure* (such as population size and economic and military strength) affect and limit what actors in the political and governmental spheres do.

Different types of foreign policy are made in very different ways: **crisis decision making** (involving sudden threats and requiring quick action) and **covert operations** (secret or semisecret operations) belong almost entirely to the executive branch; the executive branch also takes the lead on broader issues of **defense policy**; but there is much more involvement by Congress, the general public, interest groups, and others; **foreign trade** and international economic policy sometimes provoke substantial political conflict.

The Executive Branch-Because the Constitution gives the principal diplomatic and war power to the president, the president is the top decision maker on foreign policy and military issues. The president has help from many people and government units.

National Security Council-Established in 1947, the **National Security Council (NSC)** is the primary formal body for *coordinating the various civilian and military agencies involved in foreign policy*. In times of crisis, the NSC's Situation Room becomes a *command center* for the president, in close touch with the departments of state and defense, as well as with embassies and military units around the world.

The Department of State-The president's chief arm for carrying out diplomatic activity is the State Department. The **Department of State** is organized along both *functional* (such as economic affairs, human rights, narcotics, terrorism) and *geographic* lines (with bureaus for Europe and Canada, Africa, East Asia and the Pacific, Inter-American Affairs, and the Near East and South Asia).

505

Department of Commerce and U.S. Trade Representative-Issues of trade, U.S. corporate investment in other countries, and protection of intellectual property rights (patents and copyrights) have become more important with the global economy. The Department of Commerce and the Office of the U.S. Trade Representative have become increasingly important.

Embassies Abroad-270 American embassies and missions in more than 170 countries report to the Department of State. U.S. embassies help American citizens traveling abroad and business people cultivate good relations with host countries. Most ambassadors (about two out of three) are career foreign service officers. The rest are political appointees.

Department of Defense-The top levels of the Department of Defense (DOD) are housed in the Pentagon in Arlington, Virginia. The Pentagon is a five-sided complex holding more than 23,000 employees. The **organization of the Department of Defense (DOD)** is complex: it is designed to ensure a clear, *hierarchical* military command structure, with the civilian **secretary of defense** who has authority over the entire department and reports directly to the president; the organization must reflect *civilian control* of the military; and it is designed to make the different *services* (Army, Navy, Marine Corps, and Air Force) work together while also maintaining their separate identities. The uniformed chiefs of each branch serve together in the **Joint Chiefs of Staff (JCS).**

Interservice Rivalry-The organization of the Defense Department represents a series of shifting compromises. There are inevitable tensions between civilian control, military hierarchy and between the unity and the independence of the services. Interservice rivalry can be fierce.

Intelligence Agencies-The U.S. intelligence forces increased during the Reagan administrations. Most estimates put its size at around 150,000 to 160,000 employees and its budget around $10 t0 $13 billion. The intelligence budget apparently rose to about $28 billion in the mid-1990s, and it shows no signs of declining.

Spy Technology-The most expensive U.S. intelligence agencies are located in the DOD. They are technologically oriented and provide most of the raw intelligence information. These include the **National Security Agency (NSA)**, responsible for intercepting and monitoring electronic messages from around the world, and the **National Reconnaissance Office (NRO)**, which is responsible for satellite reconnaissance.

Military Intelligence-Each of the armed services has a separate tactical intelligence unit. The **Defense Intelligence Agency (DIA)** was established in 1961 to consolidate the armed service intelligence units.

The Central Intelligence Agency- The CIA was established in 1947 to advise the National Security Council, to coordinate all U.S. intelligence agencies, to gather and evaluate intelligence information, and to carry out such additional functions as the NSC directed. The additional functions came to include covert operations, which made the agency much more important than originally envisioned. Covert operations, designed to influence or overthrow governments abroad, were the most visible trademark of the CIA. Covert operations are supposed to be secret, or at least officially "deniable."

Direct supervision of covert operations is confined to small groups of executive branch officials; neither Congress nor the public is much involved. Critics have objected that these operations infringe on the independence of foreign countries (especially when popular or freely elected governments are overthrown) and that covert operations sometimes contaminate the CIA's intelligence gathering. Most important in terms of the democracy theme is that the very idea of **covert operations seems to conflict with the idea of democracy**; questions are raised as to *how the public can control government actions* if it does not know about them. *Congress generally plays a less active role in foreign policy than in domestic policy.*

Congress-Congress has traditionally played a less active role in foreign than in domestic policy. The executive branch, with its vast intelligence and national security apparatus, has far more information, expertise, and control of events. Nevertheless, Congress has become more assertive since the end of the Cold War. With the elimination of the Soviet threat, Congress no longer feels as compelled as before to defer to the president in many foreign policy areas.

Constitutional Powers-The Constitution grants Congress certain powers relative to foreign policy, but those powers have become less important with the transformation of executive authority. The power to *declare war* becomes less important when most armed conflicts have been initiated by the executive branch without asking for a declaration of war. The Senate's control over spending, treaty ratification, and the appointment of ambassadors are all power that make a difference. At times, Congress has used its treaty or spending powers to challenge the president on important issues: trying to force an end to the Vietnam War, creating difficulties over the Panama Canal treaty and the SALT II arms control treaty, defeating the Nuclear Test Ban Treaty, resisting the Reagan administration's aid to the Nicaraguan Contras, and barely acquiescing to military and peacekeeping operations in Bosnia and Kosovo.

Congressional Acquiescence-The Senate's power to *ratify treaties* means less when the executive branch relies heavily on *executive agreements* that do not require Senate approval. When congressional authorization *has* been needed, Congress went along with most executive initiatives on nearly all major issues of the Cold War; Congress has also acquiesced with most covert operations.

Despite earlier historical assessments to the contrary, it is now clear that public opinion does have substantial effects on policymaking; studies of issues such as arms control show that policymakers often have considered public opinion in making their decisions. At the same time, the executive branch has considerable leeway—public opinion seldom demands that particular actions be taken in setting foreign policy. The executive branch can often shape public opinion to its own ends by putting its own interpretation on world events and by creating or encouraging events that will alter the public's thinking. Moreover, the mass media have tended to convey the government's point of view to the public in the arena of foreign policy.

Appropriating Money for Defense and Foreign Policy-Spending is the one area where Congress has exerted its greatest influence on foreign policy matters. Military bases and contracts are a special focus of attention. Despite defense downsizing after the end of the Cold War, expensive weapon systems like the *Seawolf* submarine and the *B-2* bomber kept surviving, with energetic backing by members of Congress in the states where they are built. Under congressional pressure, the commission on base closings and the Clinton administration decided to keep open some bases that the military said it did not need.

Trade and Immigration-Congress has pushed for retaliatory trade policies toward countries such as Japan, China, and other competitors. Disputes over restricting legal immigration into the United States have also become very contentious, though curbs on illegal immigration have been popular with both parties and the public.

Public Opinion and the Mass Media-Public Opinion has some influence on foreign policy. Public Opinion is sometimes ignored and may sometimes be manipulated.

Responsiveness to the Public-It was once thought that public opinion on foreign policy was so uninformed, unstable, and weak that it could not have much effect of foreign policymaking. It is now clear that public opinion does, in fact, have substantial influence.

Lawmaking for Policymakers-The executive branch has considerable leeway. Seldom does public opinion demand that particular actions be taken abroad. More often, the public tends to go along with what the president does during the early stages of an action. **Electoral reward and punishment** creates incentives for presidents to do things that will please the public in the long run.

Shaping Opinion- The executive branch often shapes public opinion by putting its own interpretation on world events and especially by creating or encouraging events that will alter the public's thinking. According to political scientists V.O. Key Jr., public opinion mainly sets up "dikes" that confine policy to certain broad channels. The president and the executive branch largely determine the flow. But the mass media have played an increasingly important role in placing issues on the agenda and framing the debate about them.

Corporations, Interest groups and Social Movements-There is considerable disagreement over the *role of corporations and interest groups* in establishing American foreign policy. Some observers maintain that executive branch officials are motivated entirely by a concern for the **national interest**, but others say that conceptions of national interest are largely determined by the narrow interests of wealthy and well-organized individuals and corporations.

The Stakes for Business-American corporations are among the most active players in the global economy, producing, marketing, and selling goods and services around the world. Many American-based multinational firms seek free trade policies and diplomatic or military protection abroad. Other firms, especially those relying on U.S. markets but threatened by foreign competition (e.g., in automobiles, steel, clothing, and consumer electronics), have sought government subsidies, tariffs, or quotas against foreign goods.

Ethnic Groups-Certain ethnic groups sometimes affect U.S. foreign policy. This is true in the case of U.S. policy toward Israel, in which, widespread public sympathy toward that country is reinforced by the efforts of the American-Israel Public Affairs Committee (AIPAC) and by various organized groups representing Jewish Americans. African-Americans were influential in U.S. policy toward apartheid in South Africa and military rule in Haiti. Cuban-American groups have had an important impact on U.S. policy toward Fidel Castro's Cuba.

Interest Groups and Social Movements-Interest groups have become increasingly drawn into the politics of foreign policymaking. Labor unions have become very involved with trade agreement issues, pushing for wage guarantees, and work safety provisions in trade agreements so that jobs at home are not lost to cheap labor markets abroad. Farm organizations have pressed trade negotiators to include environmental and health provisions in trade agreements so that cheap agricultural products do not put American framers out of business. Religious groups have also exerted influence.

➔ SUMMARY

The United States has become the world's only military superpower, with a much larger economy and much more powerful armed forces than any other nation. It grew into this role during the roughly 200 years of westward expansion and settlement, industrialization, and the active involvement in World War I and World War II. For nearly forty years, the U.S. and the Soviet Union were engaged in an often tense Cold War, competing for influence in Europe, fighting Soviet allies in Korea and Vietnam, and skirmishing over the Third World. When the Soviet Union collapsed in 1989, attention turned to other issues, including regional and ethnic conflicts, international economic competition, efforts at transition to democracy and free markets in Russia and Eastern Europe, problems of world poverty, and the global environment.

The executive branch has recently seen its foreign policy prerogatives challenged by Congress. Congress has asserted itself chiefly on matters of foreign trade and aid, military bases, and procurement contracts.

Some of the most important factors that affect U.S. foreign policy are **structural factors**. *Economic and military strength* makes it possible to produce war planes, ships, and ground forces that gives the United States the capability to intervene where it chooses. The size of the U.S. economy and its deep involvement in world trade and investment have created U.S. interests around the world.

┌─────────────────────────────┐
│ *Chapter Outline* │
└─────────────────────────────┘

This section gives you a comprehensive review of the chapter. Use this outline in combination with your textbook to look for key concepts and objectives, to identify essential terms and names, and to gain a basic understanding of political practices and principles from this chapter.

I.   **THE SENATE DEFEATS THE NUCLEAR TEST BAN TREATY (p. 533)**

    A. This chapter discusses American foreign and military policies; how they are made, and how they affect Americans and others.

    B. American foreign and military policies are the product of the interaction of structural factors (such as American economic and military power, the collapse of the Soviet Union, and "globalization"), political linkage level factors (such as the choices the media make about foreign news coverage, public opinion about what the U.S. role in the world ought to be, and what various interest groups want the government to do), and governmental factors (such as the objectives and actions of presidents, members of Congress, and important executive branch agencies like the Central Intelligence Agency and the Joint Chiefs of Staff).

    C. The foreign policy and national defense issues that American policymakers face today in the post-Colld War world are different from those they faced in the past.

       1. The U.S. Senate's refusal to ratify the **Nuclear Test Ban Treaty** that President Clinton had signed in 1996, surprised people in many circles.

       2. The treaty was designed to slow the spread of nuclear weapons, but it was soundly defeated in the Senate.

       3. Some contended that with the defeat of the treaty, the United States had lost its moral authority and any leverage it might have in trying to persuade India, Pakistan and North Korea to sign the treaty and China, Russia, Egypt and Israel (all of whom have signed the treaty) to ratify it.

    D. Relatively speaking, the Senate's consideration of the Test Ban Treaty was very brief. As well, the treaty was brought to a vote on the floor of the Senate even after 52 senators (a majority) signed a plea to Majority Leader Trent Lott to postpone the vote.

1. In addition, the debate was conducted in an atmosphere of bitter partisanship, with both Democrats and Republicans as another tool with which to score points against their opponents.
2. The treaty may have been defeated because it was fatally flawed, with the effect of diminishing U.S. sovereignty and threatening the usefulness of nuclear arsenal, without doing much about the proliferation of nuclear weapons.
3. It may also have been the case that President Clinton and Senate Democrats made important tactical mistakes, such as not including Republicans in the original treaty negotiations, not acting in a bi-partisan manner in the Senate process, and insisting on Senate consideration of the treaty when the Republicans were the majority.
4. It is also possible that Senate Republicans wanted to embarrass Bill Clinton and further damage his historical legacy.
5. The treaty may have been a reflection of the fact that, without the Cold War or the serious threat of a large-scale shooting war, the office of president has lost some power and prestige in foreign and military affairs and Congress has become increasingly willing and anxious to flex its muscles in these areas, as it has always done in domestic affairs. There may also be some confusion about how America should behave in its role as the sole global superpower.

II. FOREIGN POLICY AND DEMOCRACY: A CONTRADICTION IN TERMS? (534-535)

A. **Foreign policy**—especially policy concerning wars or crises—has traditionally been different from domestic policy.
   1. Presidents and the executive branch have often played a much more important part than they do domestically, and they have had an unusual degree of autonomy in foreign policy.
   2. The ordinary **political factors** (such as public opinion and interest groups) have often been set aside in favor of considerations of **national interest**, as defined by a small number of national security advisers.
      a) Public opinion has not been irrelevant, but at times it has been reshaped or ignored.
      b) In crisis situations, the public has often accepted the president's actions in a "rally 'round the flag" practice, at least as long as the results seemed good and there was little disagreement among the elite.
   3. Much of foreign policy is influenced by **structural factors**, including the power and resources of the United States, its economic interests abroad, and the nature and behavior of other nations.
B. Several **features of foreign affairs tend to limit the role of public opinion** in policymaking.
   1. Complexity of international matters

2. Remoteness of international matters from day-to-day life
3. Unpredictability of other countries' actions
4. The need for speed, unity, and secrecy—together with the concentration of authority in the executive branch—mean that the public can easily be excluded.
5. Government policy can sometimes shape public opinion rather than be shaped by it.

C. Despite these factors, the American public plays a larger role in the making of foreign policy than is often apparent, and its influence appears to be increasing.

III. **THE UNITED STATES AS A SUPERPOWER: HISTORY AND STRUCTURE (535-542)**

A. This chapter looks at the structure and history of the United States as a **superpower**.
B. The ability to send massive numbers of troops, warplanes, and aircraft carriers to the Persian Gulf region in 1990 reflected the status of the United States as a superpower.
   1. Enormous economic power enables the United States to field the most powerful armed forces in the world.
   2. For decades, the Soviet Union squeezed its smaller economy in order to produce a military establishment that looked roughly equal to that of the United States.
C. After the 1991 collapse of the Soviet Union, a large part of its forces reverted to Russia. Its economy fell into disarray, and Russia's capability to use force abroad is very much in doubt, except on its immediate periphery.
D. By the middle at the 1990s, the United States was the *only* superpower. No other nation had the rapid deployment capabilities, bases, and weapons systems that could project force anywhere in the world.
   1. The superpower status of the United States is *a crucial structural fact* for understanding international relations and American foreign policy. American power and resources have been important in a whole series of U.S. actions abroad since World War II.
   2. This superpower status may largely account for the exertion of U.S. influence around the world.
   3. The United States emerged with its economy and population essentially intact.
   4. Only the Soviet Union was in a position to rival the United States as a world power.
E. **The Cold War**
   1. After World War II, the United States and the Soviet Union were engaged in a series of confrontations—a **Cold War** that lasted for more than 40 years.
   2. Beginnings of the Cold War
      a) When World War II left the Soviet army occupying many countries of Eastern and Central Europe, American policymakers formulated a doctrine of **containment**: diplomatic, economic, and military means should be used to prevent the Soviet Union from extending its influence further.

512

b) In March 1947, President **Truman** enunciated the **Truman Doctrine**, in which the United States should help "free peoples" resist "armed minorities or outside pressures."

c) Beginning in 1947, the United States provided billions of dollars in aid under the **Marshall Plan** (formally titled the *European Recovery Program*) to rebuild the devastated economies of its European allies.

3. The **Federal Republic of Germany** (usually referred to as West Germany) was established, and various communist-dominated regimes were set up in Eastern Europe.

4. Multilateral military *alliances* were formed on both sides.

a) The **North Atlantic Treaty Organization (NATO)** was established in 1949 as an anti-Soviet alliance, and the **Warsaw Pact** was signed by the Soviet bloc in 1955 (formalizing a system that was already in existence).

b) Sharply divided boundaries divided Eastern from Western Europe.

5. Both the United States and the Soviets had *nuclear capability* (A-bombs and H-bombs).

F. The **Korean War**

1. The first big armed struggle of the Cold War broke out in Korea.

a) The Korean War pitted the United States and South Korea—fighting under terms of a UN resolution—against North Korea and later China.

b) A bitter and unpopular war, the fighting eventually bogged down around the original border between North and South Korea.

c) The war ended in 1953.

2. **Consequences of the Korean War**

a) It led to a massive U.S. military buildup that became a permanent fixture of American policy until the early 1990s.

b) The Korean War expanded the Cold War from Europe to the entire periphery of the Soviet Union and communist China.

c) The United States took on many new commitments around the world; historians have found that some of these moves were worked out before the Korean War began as part of a general plan for intensified anti-communist policies embodied in a National Security Council document.

G. **Stalemate**

1. We can now see that the Cold War in Europe essentially ended (or stabilized) in the early 1950s after the Korean War, with most of the world divided into two opposing camps that had fairly fixed boundaries and a reasonably stable balance of power.

a) Combined the Soviet Union and the United States spent nearly $12 trillion during the Cold War.

b) Both sides amassed large numbers of strategic bombers and nuclear warheads.

2. Both sides attained a sort of *nuclear parity*; **mutually assured destruction (MAD)**—a *situation of nuclear stalemate* in which both sides could retaliate with nuclear weapons to destroy an attacking nation—was eventually seen as a source of stability and a basis for arms control agreements; including the **Strategic Arms Limitation Treaty (SALT I).**

3. **The Vietnam War**
   a) The Vietnam war was ostensibly fought in an effort to prevent a takeover of South Vietnam by the **Viet Cong,** or National Liberation Front—was a major setback for American foreign policy.
   b) The war's costs in money, casualties, and social disruption discouraged intervention abroad for a period of time.
   c) The **Nixon** administration pursued a policy of *rapprochement* (closer relations) with China and *détente* (relaxation of tensions) with the Soviet Union.

4. **The end of the Cold War**
   a) Beginning in 1989, a series of dramatic world events completely transformed international affairs.
      (1) In 1985 Soviet leader Mikhail Gorbachev introduced an economic program known as *perestroika* (restructuring), and more political freedom through *glasnost* (openness).
      (2) There was a failed coup against Gorbachev in 1991.
      (3) The Soviet Union eventually fell apart as the Baltic republics (Estonia, Latvia, and Lithuania) became completely independent, and virtually all the other 12 republics, including the Ukraine and Russia insisted on independence.
   b) In 1997, NATO extended eastward when former Soviet bloc members Poland, Hungary, and the Czech Republic formally applied to join the anti-Soviet alliance.

H. **The structural bases of American superpower status**
   1. Events and the strategies of political actors are important in shaping world affairs, but a nation's place in the international system is largely determined by its relative economic, military and cultural power.
   2. At the beginning of the century, the United States is particularly advantaged in all three areas.

I. **Economic power**
   1. The United States has the world's largest economy, with an annual gross domestic product of more than $8.5 trillion.
   2. The GDP of the United States is larger than that of China, Japan, Germany, India, Great Britain, and Russia.
   3. By all indications the relative strength of the American economy is increasing. The U.S. economy has boomed as its companies have established their dominance in the economic sectors that matter most in the new global economy:

telecommunications, mass entertainment, biotechnology, software, finance, e-commerce, business services, transportation, and computer chips. The United States' economic preeminence is likely to continue for some time.

J. **Military power**
1. The United States has the most powerful armed forces in the world.
2. The United States spent nearly $275 billion in 1999 on its armed forces and has almost 1.4 million men and women on active military duty.
   a) The air force has 550 **intercontinental ballistic missiles (ICBMs)** and 191 bombers, each carrying multiple nuclear warheads.
   b) The navy has 12 aircraft carriers, 17 nuclear missile submarines (armed with 432 multiple-warhead missiles) and many warships.
   c) The army is organized into ten divisions, backed by large numbers of tanks, artillery, and tactical missiles with nuclear warheads.
3. No other country in the world comes close to matching the power of the U.S. armed forces. The United States has military bases throughout the world; over 100,000 troops stationed in Europe and another 100,000 stationed in Asia.

K. **"Soft power"**
1. Multinational corporations, which originated in the United States such as McDonald's, Kentucky Fried Chicken, and Disney, as well as Hollywood entertainment, contribute to American "soft power."
2. Soft power is the power to influence through culture, ideology, and language and it enhances the U.S.'s harder economic and military powers.

IV. **PROBLEMS OF THE POST-COLD WAR WORLD (pp. 542-550)**
A. There are several views concerning what America's role should be as the world's sole superpower.
B. The Cold War is gone and with it have gone the clarity and coherence that the bi-polar conflict lent to policymaking. Isolationists, unilateralists, and multilateralists, have all articulated their positions on the new American role in the world.

C. **Isolationists**
1. The isolationists would have the United States arm itself in self-defense, avoid "entangling alliances", and let other countries solve their own problems.
2. The yearning for a "fortress America" may have been the desire of the members of Congress who voted against the Nuclear Test Ban Treaty.

D. **Unilateralists**
1. The unilateralists would have the United States actively engage in the world, based on the belief that what goes on elsewhere around the world affects American interests, without regard for alliances, treaties or what other nations want.
2. The existence of such a theme in American foreign policy may better explain the defeat of the Nuclear Test Ban Treaty.

E. **Multilateralists**
1. The multilateralists would support American interests in the world on the bases of

cooperation and collaboration with other countries.

2. This theme in U.S. foreign policy can be seen in its participation in NATO operations in Kosovo and in its participation in the international agreements that created the World Trade Organization (WTO).

F. **New security issues**
1. The United States faced a completely changed world in the 1990s, but many questions about national security and international relations remained.
2. With the threat of a nuclear Armageddon between the superpowers gone, a number of new security issues developed.

G. **Russia and the former Soviet Union**
1. The collapse of the centralized communist regime threw into the question the fate of the vast Soviet armed forces, with their millions of troops and stockpiles of nuclear weapons, some of which have shown up on international underground markets; causing concern of the dangers of **nuclear proliferation**.
2. Questions emerged concerning how the United States could help the newly freed countries of Eastern Europe, which are likely to continue to experience ethnic strife. Particularly since democracy and free enterprise have not worked effectively there.

H. **The Balkans**
1. Bitter ethnic conflicts between the Serbs, Croats, and Muslims of the former Yugoslavia continue to challenge American policy makers.
2. Some feel that the problems of the Balkans should be addressed and solved by Europeans, while others feel that the United States should play a principal role.

I. **Japan, China, and the Pacific**
1. With the end of the Cold War, questions have emerged concerning how much reduction can or should there be in the vast U.S. naval forces in the Pacific Ocean or in troops stationed in South Korea and elsewhere.
2. Debates continued over whether economic and political relations should be normalized with China's still authoritarian regime which governs over a huge population, fast-growing economy and modernizing military.
3. Some observers have warned of a great "clash of civilizations" between the West and "Confucian" China.

J. **The developing world**
1. Observers have asked if regional conflicts in the Middle East and elsewhere could be solved, and whether the United States would need to periodically send troops as a "policeman of the world."
2. Conflicts between the Israelis and the Palestinians, Iraq and Iran, or drug trafficking from places like Colombia, Peru, and Mexico continue to press American leaders on whether to intervene or not intervene.

K. **Economic and social dilemmas**
1. It is apparent that America's exalted status as the world's only military superpower and its preeminent economic power has not made U.S. foreign policy problems go

516

away.

2. In fact, national security has taken on new and broader meanings and encompasses new problems.

L. **International trade**
1. At the height of its world economic power after World War II, international economic communities were characterized by **free trade** (trade without government restraints) and a system in which many countries negotiated lower tariff barriers through the **General Agreement on Tariffs and Trade (GATT)**.
2. By the late 1960s, the rebuilt economies of Germany and Japan began to challenge American goods both abroad and in the United States; competition also came from newly industrialized countries (NICs) such as South Korea, Taiwan, Singapore, and Hong Kong, as well as from the increasingly integrated Economic Community of Europe (EC).
3. By the mid-1980s, Americans were importing many more goods than we were exporting (creating a *multibillion-dollar trade deficit*).
   a) The trade deficit meant that many goods were cheaper in the U.S. but it also meant that many goods—formerly produced in America by American workers—were now being produced elsewhere.
   b) Under this competitive pressure, the United States began to exert *unilateral pressures* on other nations to lower hidden barriers and reduce subsidies that hurt American exports.
   c) We also began to press for voluntary quotas and other policies to control imports to the United States. Policymakers in the United States negotiated the **North American Free Trade Agreement (NAFTA)** with Canada and Mexico, which was implemented after a vote in Congress in 1993, and the Clinton administration concluded a comprehensive free trade agreement with 116 countries under the Uruguay Round of the GATT.
4. The agreement, which was signed in 1994, set up a **World Trade Organization (WTO)** for enforcement.

M. **Foreign aid**
1. The world is divided into rich nations and poor nations.
2. As a percentage of the U.S. budget, *spending on foreign aid is very low* and has been declining (amounting to about 0.1 percent of the U.S. GDP in 1999).
   a) This is much lower, proportionately, than the aid given by countries such as Denmark, Norway, Sweden, and France.
   b) Most U.S. foreign aid is devoted to military and security purposes (not to food, education, or related areas).
3. The U.S. has provided funds for development, population programs, and the environment to the World Bank, United Nations, and other international agencies to assist poorer countries.

N. *Arms sales*

1. The United States has been one of the world's largest *sellers of weapons* to other countries.
2. With the demise of the Soviet Union, the United States is by far the biggest arms exporter in the world, with $31.8 billion in sales in 1999.

O. **The global environment**
   1. Americans realize that environmental problems cross national borders.
      a) The United States and Canada have agreed to reduce acid rain, for example.
      b) Many nations have attempted to negotiate agreement on oil spills, ozone layer protection, and the prevention of global warming.
   2. Environmentalists express particular concern about the rapid cutting and burning of tropical rain forests, which removes oxygen-producing trees and at the same time pours smoke and carbon dioxide into the atmosphere.

P. **The drug trade**
   1. Illegal drugs from southern border nations such as Mexico, Haiti, Colombia, Bolivia, and Peru complicate U.S. relations with them.
   2. Part of the problem of eliminating the drug trade is that demand for drugs is very high in the rich countries, including the United States.

Q. **Immigration**
   1. People tend to follow jobs.
   2. Developments in transportation have made it possible for more people to migrate in pursuit of a better way of life for themselves and their families.
   3. Especially noteworthy is the migration from poor Third World countries to the rich countries of the West.

V. **WHO MAKES FOREIGN POLICY? (pp. 550-556)**
   A. The president and the executive branch are the primary *governmental* decision makers concerning most foreign policy issues, but Congress is often involved in decisions concerning foreign trade and aid, military bases and contracts, and other matters that directly impact their constituents' local interests.
   B. People and institutions in the *political* sphere (such as public opinion, the mass media, and interest groups) affect what both Congress and the executive branch do.
   C. Certain aspects of *structure* (such as population size and economic and military strength) affect and limit what actors in the political and governmental spheres do.
   D. Different types of foreign policy are made in very different ways: **crisis decision making** (involving sudden threats and requiring quick action) and **covert operations** (secret or semisecret operations) belong almost entirely to the executive branch; the executive branch also takes the lead on broader issues of **defense policy**; but there is much more involvement by Congress, the general public, interest groups, and others; **foreign trade** and international economic policy sometimes provoke substantial political conflict.
   E. **The executive branch**

1. Because the Constitution gives the principal diplomatic and war power to the president, the president is the top decision maker on foreign policy and military issues.
2. The president has help from many people and government units.

F. **National Security Council**
   1. Established in 1947, the **National Security Council (NSC)** is the primary formal body for *coordinating the various civilian and military agencies involved in foreign policy.*
   2. In times of crisis, the NSC's Situation Room becomes a *command center* for the president, in close touch with the departments of state and defense, as well as with embassies and military units around the world.

G. **The Department of State**
   1. The president's chief arm for carrying out diplomatic activity is the State Department.
   2. The **Department of State** is organized along both *functional* (such as economic affairs, human rights, narcotics, terrorism) and *geographic* lines (with bureaus for Europe and Canada, Africa, East Asia and the Pacific, Inter-American Affairs, and the Near East and South Asia).

H. **Department of Commerce and U.S. Trade Representative**
   1. Issues of trade, U.S. corporate investment in other countries, and protection of intellectual property rights (patents and copyrights) have become more important with the global economy.
   2. The Department of Commerce and the Office of the U.S. Trade Representative have become increasingly important.

I. **Embassies abroad**
   1. 270 American embassies and missions in more than 170 countries report to the Department of State. U.S. embassies help American citizens traveling abroad and business people cultivate good relations with host countries.
   2. Most ambassadors (about two out of three) are career foreign service officers. The rest are political appointees.

J. **Department of Defense**
   1. The top levels of the Department of Defense (DOD) are housed in the Pentagon in Arlington, Virginia. The Pentagon is a five-sided complex holding more than 23,000 employees.
   2. The **organization of the Department of Defense (DOD)** is complex: it is designed to ensure a clear, *hierarchical* military command structure, with the civilian **secretary of defense** who has authority over the entire department and reports directly to the president; the organization must reflect *civilian control* of the military; and it is designed to make the different *services* (Army, Navy, Marine Corps, and Air Force) work together while also maintaining their separate identities.

519

    3. The uniformed chiefs of each branch serve together in the **Joint Chiefs of Staff (JCS)**.

    4. *Interservice rivalry*

      a) The organization of the Defense Department represents a series of shifting compromises.

      b) There are inevitable tensions between civilian control, military hierarchy and between the unity and the independence of the services.

      c) Interservice rivalry can be fierce.

K. Intelligence agencies

    1. The U.S. intelligence forces increased during the Reagan administrations.

    2. Most estimates put its size at around 150,000 to 160,000 employees and its budget around $10 t0 $13 billion.

    3. The intelligence budget apparently rose to about $28 billion in the mid-1990s, and it shows no signs of declining.

    4. *Spy Technology*

      a) The most expensive U.S. intelligence agencies are located in the DOD.

      b) They are technologically oriented and provide most of the raw intelligence information.

      c) These include the **National Security Agency (NSA)**, responsible for intercepting and monitoring electronic messages from around the world, and the **National Reconnaissance Office (NRO)**, which is responsible for satellite reconnaissance.

    5. *Military intelligence*

      a) Each of the armed services has a separate tactical intelligence unit.

      b) The **Defense Intelligence Agency (DIA)** was established in 1961 to consolidate the armed service intelligence units.

    6. *The Central Intelligence Agency*

      a) The CIA was established in 1947 to advise the National Security Council, to coordinate all U.S. intelligence agencies, to gather and evaluate intelligence information, and to carry out such additional functions as the NSC directed.

      b) The additional functions came to include covert operations, which made the agency much more important than originally envisioned.

      c) Covert operations, designed to influence or overthrow governments abroad, were the most visible trademark of the CIA. Covert operations are supposed to be secret, or at least officially "deniable."

    7. Direct supervision of covert operations is confined to small groups of executive branch officials; neither Congress nor the public is much involved.

      a) Critics have objected that these operations infringe on the independence of foreign countries (especially when popular or freely elected governments are overthrown) and that covert operations sometimes contaminate the CIA's intelligence gathering.

b) Most important in terms of the democracy theme is that the very idea of **covert operations seems to conflict with the idea of democracy**; questions are raised as to *how the public can control government actions* if it does not know about them.

c) *Congress generally plays a less active role in foreign policy than in domestic policy.*

L. **Congress**

1. Congress has traditionally played a less active role in foreign than in domestic policy.

   a) The executive branch, with its vast intelligence and national security apparatus, has far more information, expertise, and control of events.

   b) Nevertheless, Congress has become more assertive since the end of the Cold War.

2. With the elimination of the Soviet threat, Congress no longer feels as compelled as before to defer to the president in many foreign policy areas.

M. **Constitutional Powers**

1. The Constitution grants Congress certain powers relative to foreign policy, but those powers have become less important with the transformation of executive authority.

   a) The power to *declare war* becomes less important when most armed conflicts have been initiated by the executive branch without asking for a declaration of war.

   b) The Senate's control over spending, treaty ratification, and the appointment of ambassadors are all power that make a difference.

2. At times, Congress has used its treaty or spending powers to challenge the president on important issues: trying to force an end to the Vietnam War, creating difficulties over the Panama Canal treaty and the SALT II arms control treaty, defeating the Nuclear Test Ban Treaty, resisting the Reagan administration's aid to the Nicaraguan Contras, and barely acquiescing to military and peacekeeping operations in Bosnia and Kosovo.

N. **Congressional acquiescence**

1. The Senate's power to *ratify treaties* means less when the executive branch relies heavily on *executive agreements* that do not require Senate approval.

2. When congressional authorization *has* been needed, Congress went along with most executive initiatives on nearly all major issues of the Cold War; Congress has also acquiesced with most covert operations.

3. Despite earlier historical assessments to the contrary, it is now clear that public opinion does have substantial effects on policymaking; studies of issues such as arms control show that policymakers often have considered public opinion in making their decisions.

   a) At the same time, the executive branch has considerable leeway—public opinion seldom demands that particular actions be taken in setting foreign policy.

    b) The executive branch can often shape public opinion to its own ends by putting its own interpretation on world events and by creating or encouraging events that will alter the public's thinking.

  4. Moreover, the mass media have tended to convey the government's point of view to the public in the arena of foreign policy.

O. **Appropriating money for defense and foreign policy**

  1. Spending is the one area where Congress has exerted its greatest influence on foreign policy matters.

  2. Military bases and contracts are a special focus of attention. Despite defense downsizing after the end of the Cold War, expensive weapon systems like the *Seawolf* submarine and the *B-2* bomber kept surviving, with energetic backing by members of Congress in the states where they are built.

  3. Under congressional pressure, the commission on base closings and the Clinton administration decided to keep open some bases that the military said it did not need.

P. **Trade and immigration**

  1. Congress has pushed for retaliatory trade policies toward countries such as Japan, China, and other competitors.

  2. Disputes over restricting legal immigration into the United States have also become very contentious, though curbs on illegal immigration have been popular with both parties and the public.

Q. Public opinion and the mass media

  1. Despite earlier historical assessments to the contrary, it is now clear that public opinion does have substantial effects on policymaking.

  2. Studies of issues such as arms control show that policymakers often have considered public opinion in making their decisions.

  3. **Responsiveness to the public**

    a) It was once thought that public opinion on foreign policy was so uninformed, unstable, and weak that it could not have much effect of foreign policymaking.

    b) It is now clear that public opinion does, in fact, have substantial influence.

  4. **Lawmaking for policymakers**

    a) The executive branch has considerable leeway.

      (1) Seldom does public opinion demand that particular actions be taken abroad.

      (2) More often, the public tends to go along with what the president does during the early stages of an action.

    b) **Electoral reward and punishment** creates incentives for presidents to do things that will please the public in the long run.

  5. **Shaping opinion**

    a) The executive branch often shapes public opinion by putting its own interpretation on world events and especially by creating or encouraging events that will alter the public's thinking.

    b) According to political scientists V.O. Key Jr., public opinion mainly sets up "dikes" that confine policy to certain broad channels.

    c) The president and the executive branch largely determine the flow. But the mass media have played an increasingly important role in placing issues on the agenda and framing the debate about them.

  R. Corporations, interest groups, and social movements

    1. There is considerable disagreement over the *role of corporations and interest groups* in establishing American foreign policy.

    2. Some observers maintain that executive branch officials are motivated entirely by a concern for the **national interest**, but others say that conceptions of national interest are largely determined by the narrow interests of wealthy and well-organized individuals and corporations.

  S. **The stakes for business**

    1. American corporations are among the most active players in the global economy, producing, marketing, and selling goods and services around the world.

    2. Many American-based multinational firms seek free trade policies and diplomatic or military protection abroad.

    3. Other firms, especially those relying on U.S. markets but threatened by foreign competition (e.g., in automobiles, steel, clothing, and consumer electronics), have sought government subsidies, tariffs, or quotas against foreign goods.

  T. **Ethnic groups**

    1. Certain ethnic groups sometimes affect U.S. foreign policy.

    a) This is true in the case of U.S. policy toward Israel, in which, widespread public sympathy toward that country is reinforced by the efforts of the American-Israel Public Affairs Committee (AIPAC) and by various organized groups representing Jewish Americans.

    b) African-Americans were influential in U.S. policy toward apartheid in South Africa and military rule in Haiti.

    c) Cuban-American groups have had an important impact on U.S. policy toward Fidel Castro's Cuba.

VI. **SUMMARY (p. 557)**

  A. The United States has become the world's only military superpower, with a much larger economy and much more powerful armed forces than any other nation.

    1. It grew into this role during the roughly 200 years of westward expansion and settlement, industrialization, and the active involvement in World War I and World War II.

    2. For nearly forty years, the U.S. and the Soviet Union were engaged in an often tense Cold War, competing for influence in Europe, fighting Soviet allies in Korea and Vietnam, and skirmishing over the Third World.

3. When the Soviet Union collapsed in 1989, attention turned to other issues, including regional and ethnic conflicts, international economic competition, efforts at transition to democracy and free markets in Russia and Eastern Europe, problems of world poverty, and the global environment.

   a) The executive branch has recently seen its foreign policy prerogatives challenged by Congress.

   b) Congress has asserted itself chiefly on matters of foreign trade and aid, military bases, and procurement contracts.

4. Some of the most important factors that affect U.S. foreign policy are **structural factors**. *Economic and military strength* makes it possible to produce war planes, ships, and ground forces that gives the United States the capability to intervene where it chooses. The size of the U.S. economy and its deep involvement in world trade and investment have created U.S. interests around the world.

B. Although democratic control may be increasing, the authors of your textbook conclude that **democratic control over foreign policy is incomplete**; the *struggle for democracy* is a continuing theme in the area of foreign policy.

C. The American political system tends to fall short of the ideals of **popular sovereignty** and **political equality**.

1. Although public opinion is often taken into account, the centralization of decisions in the executive branch means that *popular participation* is limited.

2. Secrecy means that the public often does not know what the government is doing and, therefore, cannot hold it *accountable*.

3. Government control of information means that the public can sometimes be manipulated.

D. The domestic impacts of foreign policy are becoming stronger and more obvious; democratic control of foreign policy may increase as more and more Americans become aware of international affairs, insist on knowing what their government is doing, and demand government responsiveness to the popular will.

Terms for Review

Use this list to review essential principles, functions, and concepts from this chapter. Refer to your textbook for help in identifying and defining terms on this list. When you study, do not merely memorize terms; ask questions about the material you are reviewing, and look for the importance or significance of each item.

Central Intelligence Agency (CIA)

electoral reward and punishment

cold war

containments

covert operations

Department of Defense (DOD)

Department of State

European Union (EU)

General Agreement on Tariffs and Trade (GATT)

intercontinental ballistic missiles (ICBMs)

isolationists

Joint Chiefs of Staff (JCS)

Korean War

Marshall Plan

multilateralist

mutually assured destruction (MAD)

national interest

National Reconnaissance Organization (NRO)

national security adviser

National Security Agency (NSA)

National Security Council (NSC)

North American Free Trade Agreement (NAFTA)

North Atlantic Treaty Organization (NATO)

Pentagon

secretary of defense

smart bombs

Strategic Arms Control Agreements (SALT)

Strategic Arms Reduction Talks (START)

superpower

trade deficit

Truman Doctrine

unilateralists

Vietnam War

Warsaw Pact

World Trade Organization (WTO)

Research Topics: Applying What You Have Learned

You will derive more benefit from your reading if you try to apply what you have learned. Some of the suggested research topics can be answered exclusively from your text, while others require you to conduct some basic research on your own. The references suggested under **Internet Sources** *will help you in your search.*

- Look up the web site for *USA Today* (http://www.usatoday.com). Click on the *USA Today* index of topics, and select several that deal with foreign affairs. Is the emphasis in these articles on presidential or on congressional influence on foreign policy decision making? Does partisanship (political party) seem to play a strong role in decision making, or are other factors more important?

- Critics claim that Americans usually do not have a great deal of knowledge of (or interest in) foreign policy. Do you agree or disagree with this statement? If it is true, what are the political implications?

- With reference to covert activities, the authors of your textbook pose the following question: How can the public control government actions it does not know about? At this point in your reading, what is your assessment of this question, in terms of your textbook's *democracy* theme? Do covert activities conflict with the idea of democracy?

Internet Sources

A number of sites on the World Wide Web serve as "gateways" to vast collections of material on American government and politics. The following Internet resources are recommended for students who would like to do some additional research in the areas covered by this chapter. These references would also be helpful in expanding on the questions suggested under Research Topics.

Amnesty International http://www.amnesty.org
Reports and documents from the international human rights organization.

Defense Link www.defenselink.mil/
The home page of the Department of Defense.

Freeworld http://www.fedworld.gov
Links to the home pages of all federal departments and agencies involved in foreign affairs and national defense, including the State Department, the Central Intelligence Agency, the Commerce Department, and the Defense Department.

International Herald Tribune Online http://www.iht.com/
Complete international news with a much broader perspective than that found in most U.S. newspapers and other media outlets.

National Security Website www.nationalsecurity.org/spons.html
Essays and news about foreign and military policy, sponsored by the Heritage Foundation, from a conservative point of view.

Chapter 15

Peacenet http://www.peacenet.apc.org/peacenet/
A Web site devoted to peace, social and economic justice, and human rights; information on all of these subjects as well as links to organizations working in these fields.

Statistical Resources on the Web: Military and Defense
www.lib.umich.edu/Webhome/Documents.center/stats.html
A vast statistical and information compendium on military and national security issues; covers the United States and other countries.

United Nations http://www.un.org/
Home page of the United Nations; links to a wealth of statistics, documents and reports, UN departments and conferences and information on reaching UN Officials.

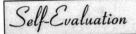

Circle the correct answer for each question. Questions are listed in the same order in which the information appears in the text. Use the Answer Key in the back of the Study Guide *to check your responses.*

1. **Ethnic cleansing** is associated with the policies of the Serbs in
    a. Bosnia.
    b. Israel.
    c. Iraq.
    d. Poland.

2. The doctrine of **containment** was based on the assumption that
    a. The Eastern bloc nations were seeking peaceful solutions.
    b. The United States was an imperialist nation.
    c. The Soviet Union was an expansionist state.
    d. The West must take action to destroy the Berlin Wall.

3. Which of the following former Soviet bloc nations did not join NATO in 1997?
    a. Poland
    b. Hungary
    c. Yugoslavia
    d. The Czech Republic

4. The spread of a country's values, ideology, and way of life to other nations is known as
   a. hard power
   b. soft power
   c. superpower
   d. multilateralism

5. Those who believe that the United States should vigorously use its military and diplomatic power to pursue American national interests in the world on a "go it alone" basis are known as
   a. hawks
   b. doves
   c. unilateralists
   d. multilateralists
   e. isolationists

6. Which of the following is a common market formed in order to allow free trade and free population movement among its nations
   a. NAFTA
   b. GATT
   c. WTO
   d. EU

7. The final line of control over the Department of Defense is under
   a. Civilian control.
   b. Military control.
   c. Economic control.
   d. Foreign control.

8. The North American Free Trade Agreement (NAFTA) was an agreement between all but which of the following nations?
   a. Japan
   b. United States
   c. Canada
   d. Mexico

9. Under the Uruguay Round of the **General Agreement on Tariffs and Trade** (GATT), the Clinton administration signed an agreement that
   a. Allocated additional aid to allies in the Middle East and around the periphery of the former Soviet Union.
   b. Exerted pressures on European nations to lower hidden barriers to trade and reduce subsidies that hurt American exports.

c. Eventually opened the door for creating a North American Free Trade Agreement (NAFTA).
d. Cut tariffs by one-third and for the first time reduced restrictions on trade in agricultural products and financial services.

10. Which of these statements is correct?
   a. The constitutional authority to declare war in an emergency situation belongs to the president.
   b. Only Congress can declare war.
   c. Congress and the president must act together to enact a declaration of war.
   d. The U.S. Supreme Court rules on the legality of a declaration of war.

11. The **North Atlantic Treaty Organization** (NATO) was a
   a. Multilateral military alliance formed as an anti-Soviet association.
   b. Unilateral arrangement developed by the United States in the face of increasing Soviet threats.
   c. Multilateral pact formed by the Soviet bloc to combat the Western nations.
   d. Unilateral arrangement for peace under United Nations auspices.

12. The program under which the United States provided billions of dollars in aid to rebuild the economies of its European allies was known as the
   a. Berlin Airlift.
   b. Truman Doctrine.
   c. Warsaw Pact.
   d. Marshall Plan.

13. (T/F) The nuclear balance between the USA and USSR was threatened during the Cuban Missile Crisis in 1962.

14. (T/F) Glasnost was a policy of the Soviet Union focusing on restructuring economic affairs in that country.

15. (T/F) The U.S. **intelligence community** is very small and limited in scope.

16. (T/F) The strategy of **mutually assured destruction** (MAD) was designed to create a situation of nuclear stalemate.

17. (T/F) The Warsaw pact was created to oppose NATO.

18. (T/F) Covert operations are secret or semisecret operations.

ANSWER KEY

CHAPTER 1: DEMOCRACY AND AMERICAN POLITICS

1. a	7. b	13. T
2. a	8. d	14. T
3. c	9. d	15. T
4. c	10. c	16. F
5. d	11. b	17. T
6. a	12. c	18. F

CHAPTER 2: THE CONSTITUTION

1. d	7. c	13. F
2. b	8. d	14. F
3. c	9. c	15. T
4. d	10. b	16. T
5. a	11. c	17. T
6. d	12. c	18. F

CHAPTER 3: FEDERALISM; STATES AND NATION

1. d	7. d	13. F
2. c	8. a	14. T
3. c	9. d	15. F
4. d	10. c	16. F
5. a	11. T	17. T
6. b	12. T	18. F

CHAPTER 4: THE STRUCTURAL FOUNDATIONS OF AMERICAN GOVERNMENT AND POLITICS

1. d	7. d	13. F
2. b	8. d	14. T
3. a	9. c	15. F
4. d	10. a	16. F
5. c	11. a	17. T
6. c	12. T	18. F

CHAPTER 5: PUBLIC OPINION

1. b	7. c	13. F
2. c	8. d	14. T
3. c	9. a	15. T
4. c	10. d	16. T
5. d	11. b	17. F
6. d	12. a	18. T

CHAPTER 6: MASS MEDIA

1. c	7. d	13. F
2. d	8. c	14. F
3. b	9. d	15. T
4. a	10. d	16. F
5. d	11. d	17. F
6. b	12. b	18. F

CHAPTER 7: INTEREST GROUPS AND CORPORATIONS

1. a	7. c	13. T
2. c	8. b	14. T
3. c	9. c	15. T
4. a	10. a	16. T
5. d	11. b	17. F
6. a	12. d	18. T

CHAPTER 8: SOCIAL MOVEMENTS

1. d	7. b	13. T
2. d	8. d	14. F
3. a	9. d	15. F
4. d	10. b	16. T
5. d	11. b	17. F
6. c	12. a	18. F

CHAPTER 9: POLITICAL PARTIES

1. d	7. b	13. T
2. a	8. b	14. F
3. d	9. d	15. F
4. b	10. b	16. T
5. c	11. b	17. T
6. c	12. b	18. F

CHAPTER 10: PARTICIPATION, VOTING AND ELECTIONS

1. a	7. a	13. F
2. c	8. b	14. F
3. b	9. a	15. F
4. c	10. d	16. T
5. c	11. c	17. T
6. c	12. c	18. T

CHAPTER 11: CONGRESS

1. d	7. a	13. F
2. c	8. b	14. F
3. c	9. d	15. T
4. b	10. b	16. T
5. b	11. a	17. F
6. d	12. a	18. F

CHAPTER 12: THE PRESIDENT

1. b	7. c	13. T
2. d	8. c	14. F
3. d	9. c	15. F
4. a	10. b	16. F
5. d	11. d	17. T
6. a	12. d	18. F

CHAPTER 13: THE FEDERAL BUREAUCRACY

1. c	7. d	13. F
2. b	8. b	14. F
3. b	9. a	15. T
4. a	10. a	16. F
5. d	11. c	17. F
6. b	12. d	18. T

CHAPTER 14: THE COURTS

1. d	7. c	13. T
2. c	8. c	14. T
3. d	9. a	15. T
4. c	10. d	16. F

5. b   11. c   17. F
6. b   12. b   18. T

CHAPTER 15: FREEDOM: THE STRUGGLE FOR CIVIL LIBERTIES

1. c	7. d	13. F
2. b	8. b	14. F
3. b	9. a	15. T
4. a	10. a	16. F
5. d	11. c	17. F
6. b	12. d	18. T

CHAPTER 16: CIVIL RIGHTS: THE STRUGGLE FOR POLITICAL EQUALITY

1. e	7. c	13. F
2. a	8. d	14. F
3. b	9. c	15. F
4. a	10. a	16. F
5. d	11. a	17. F
6. c	12. b	18. T

CHAPTER 17: DOMESTIC POLICY: THE ECONOMY AND SOCIAL WELFARE

1. c	7. b	13. T
2. a	8. d	14. F
3. b	9. b	15. T
4. d	10. b	16. F
5. d	11. a	17. T
6. a	12. d	18. F

CHAPTER 18: FOREIGN POLICY AND NATIONAL DEFENSE

1. a	7. a	13. T
2. c	8. a	14. F
3. c	9. d	15. F
4. b	10. b	16. T
5. c	11. a	17. T
6. d	12. d	18. T